Digital Video and HDTV
Algorithms and Interfaces

The Morgan Kaufmann Series in Computer Graphics and Geometric Modeling
Series Editor: Brian A. Barsky, University of California, Berkeley

Digital Video and HDTV Algorithms and Interfaces
Charles Poynton

Texturing & Modeling: A Procedural Approach, Third Edition
David S. Ebert, F. Kenton Musgrave, Darwyn Peachey, Ken Perlin, and Steven Worley

Geometric Tools for Computer Graphics
Philip Schneider and David Eberly

Understanding Virtual Reality: Interface, Application, and Design
William Sherman and Alan Craig

Jim Blinn's Corner: Notation, Notation, Notation
Jim Blinn

Level of Detail for 3D Graphics
David Luebke, Martin Reddy, Jonathan D. Cohen, Amitabh Varshney, Benjamin Watson, and Robert Huebner

Pyramid Algorithms: A Dynamic Programming Approach to Curves and Surfaces for Geometric Modeling
Ron Goldman

Non-Photorealistic Computer Graphics: Modeling, Rendering, and Animation
Thomas Strothotte and Stefan Schlechtweg

Curves and Surfaces for CAGD: A Practical Guide, Fifth Edition
Gerald Farin

Subdivision Methods for Geometric Design: A Constructive Approach
Joe Warren and Henrik Weimer

Computer Animation: Algorithms and Techniques
Rick Parent

The Computer Animator's Technical Handbook
Lynn Pocock and Judson Rosebush

Advanced RenderMan: Creating CGI for Motion Pictures
Anthony A. Apodaca and Larry Gritz

Curves and Surfaces in Geometric Modeling: Theory and Algorithms
Jean Gallier

Andrew Glassner's Notebook: Recreational Computer Graphics
Andrew S. Glassner

Warping and Morphing of Graphical Objects
Jonas Gomes, Lucia Darsa, Bruno Costa, and Luiz Velho

Jim Blinn's Corner: Dirty Pixels
Jim Blinn

Rendering with Radiance: The Art and Science of Lighting Visualization
Greg Ward Larson and Rob Shakespeare

Introduction to Implicit Surfaces
Edited by Jules Bloomenthal

Jim Blinn's Corner: A Trip Down the Graphics Pipeline
Jim Blinn

Interactive Curves and Surfaces: A Multimedia Tutorial on CAGD
Alyn Rockwood and Peter Chambers

Wavelets for Computer Graphics: Theory and Applications
Eric J. Stollnitz, Tony D. DeRose, and David H. Salesin

Principles of Digital Image Synthesis
Andrew S. Glassner

Radiosity & Global Illumination
François X. Sillion and Claude Puech

Knotty: A B-Spline Visualization Program
Jonathan Yen

User Interface Management Systems: Models and Algorithms
Dan R. Olsen, Jr.

Making Them Move: Mechanics, Control, and Animation of Articulated Figures
Edited by Norman I. Badler, Brian A. Barsky, and David Zeltzer

Geometric and Solid Modeling: An Introduction
Christoph M. Hoffmann

An Introduction to Splines for Use in Computer Graphics and Geometric Modeling
Richard H. Bartels, John C. Beatty, and Brian A. Barsky

Digital Video and HDTV Algorithms and Interfaces

Charles Poynton

Publishing Director: Diane Cerra

Publishing Services Manager: Edward Wade

Production Editor: Howard Severson

Design, illustration, and composition: Charles Poynton

Editorial Coordinator: Mona Buehler

Cover Design: Frances Baca

Copyeditor: Robert Fiske

Proofreader: Sarah Burgundy

Printer: The Maple-Vail Book Manufacturing Group

Cover images: Close-up of woman/Eyewire; Circuit connection/Artville; Medical prespectives/Picture Quest

Morgan Kaufmann Publishers
An imprint of Elsevier Science
340 Pine Street, Sixth Floor
San Francisco, CA 94104-3205
www.mkp.com

Printed in the United States of America

2007 2006 2005 2004 2003 5 4 3 2 1

Library of Congress Control Number: 2002115312
ISBN: 1-55860-792-7

This book is printed on acid-free paper.

In memory of my mother,

Marjorie Johnston

1926 – 2002

and

to Quinn and Georgia,

and the new family tree

A foreword by Jim Blinn

One of the most exciting technological achievements of our time is the impending convergence – though some would say collision – between Television and Computer Imaging. An outside observer might find this statement puzzling. Television and computer graphics seem to have so much in common that they should already be converged. Both deal with images that are displayed on electronic displays. Both break an image down into scan lines and pixels. Both express pixels with three components. Both refresh the image continually to keep the picture visible. But in fact there are a host of subtle differences that have made combining the two much more difficult than would seem necessary. TV and computers use different standards for timing, different voltages, different pixel counts, different intensity coding, and different color spaces. These differences are all similar enough to seduce the unwary into thinking they are the same, but they are different enough to cause very annoying problems.

Someone coming from a computer graphics background might even think that the people designing video standards were being deliberately perverse. Refresh rates of 29.97 frames per second, image heights of 486 lines (Or is it 483 lines? Er, maybe it's 480 lines!), sampling every other scan line at different times (i.e., interlacing), doing matrix arithmetic on nonlinearly encoded color signals – who comes up with this stuff?

In fact, the decisions that form the basis of video standards were the results of constraints of the technology at the time it was developed, often decades ago. These included limitations on available signal bandwidth (necessitating some form of image compression) and limitations on the processing operations available inexpensively using purely analog circuitry. (Think how difficult it would be to perform a DCT in analog circuitry.) Given these limitations, the choices made sense and were even very clever. But just digitizing these analog signals does not change their timing, or interlacing requirements, or the color space selection necessary to conform to the standard.

Moving into the digital domain does, however, present new processing options, and new devices to display the results on: namely, computers. Most relatively modern computers have display hardware that can display grids of 1600×1200 pixels and higher, and (as part of the digital TV convergence) many have optional display modes that exactly match the high definition television standards of 1280×720 and 1920×1080. This raises the intriguing notion that the most common HDTV display device will be an existing computer monitor rather than a newly purchased home TV set.

And once you get the signals into a computer and know how to interpret them (by reading this book) there is no end to the fun you can have. A very capable computer system for manipulation of standard definition television is now ridiculously cheap. Given Moore's law of computer improvement, a factor of 2 every 18 months, systems equally facile for the six-times-as-many pixels of HDTV will be here before you know it. In fact, computers are getting faster and computer storage is getting bigger so quickly that, in the collision with TV, which of the two is bowling over the other is fairly apparent.

We are all looking forward to the benefits that will result from the convergence/collision between Digital Television and Computers. This book is an invaluable reference in how digital video is done, both for TV people and for Computer Graphics people, and it will go a long way toward accelerating the convergence and in minimizing the damage it may cause to either party.

— Jim Blinn, Microsoft Research

A foreword by Mark Schubin

Y. In the abbreviation for the predicted computer catastrophe that was to occur just after midnight of 1/1/2000, Y2K, *Y* stood for *year.* In many responses to computer-asked questions, *Y* stands for yes.

In video, *Y* has traditionally stood for the signal carrying non-color-related level and detail information, as in *YIQ*, *YUV*, *YC*, *Y/B–Y/R–Y*, etc. But does it really? And, even if it does, should it be called *Y*, or something else?

Like many other aspects of modern life, electronic pictures have been around long enough to pick up many traditions. Scientists discussed image scanning in the early part of the 19th century. British patent 9745, issued in 1843, included scanning lines; it was for a fax machine. German patent 30105, issued in 1885, included both scanning lines and sequential frames; it was for a video system.

History (as we currently know it) records October 25th, 1925 as the first time a live recognizable image of a human face was carried from a video camera to a video display. Within a few years, the term *high-definition television* appeared. After all, if early images had just eight scanning lines, then 60 were surely enough for high definition. In 1935, the British government defined HDTV as having at least 240 lines.

When 441-line television was demonstrated at the New York World's Fair in 1939, it was hailed as the advent of HDTV in the United States. Today, video engineers call thousand-line images *HDTV* even as they demonstrate 2000-line systems.

At every stage of the development of video imaging, there was a great deal of research into how to make the systems work best. Was the research done on the mechanical-scanning (spinning-disk) systems of the 1920s and 1930s applicable to later tube-based systems? Is the research associated with tube-based imaging applicable to modern solid-state systems?

Is gamma still important in the digital age? What about uneven-bandwidth color axes? Is it necessary to deal with subcarrier-to-horizontal-sync phase?

Y, in the shorthand of electronic messaging, is also a question. It's not one of the traditional questions of journalism: who, what, when, where, and how. It's not a question normally answered in reference books and textbooks. Fortunately, it's a question Charles Poynton asks. In researching this book, applicable to current and future imaging systems, he studied papers dating back to the days of mechanical television. He discovered which traditions had a solid basis and which didn't and, therefore, could (and should) be ignored or changed.

I was present at a standardization meeting where Charles explained why there was no good reason to drag 1035-active-line analog HDTV, and nonsquare sampling, into the digital era. He offered 1080 lines and square sampling instead. Many of the others in the room were outraged at his iconoclastic suggestion. Today, 1080 active lines is the globally accepted common image format for HDTV.

Readers of this book will learn not just the what and how of digital video but also the why (and the *Y* and *Y'*). It's the "Gamma Sutra" – a guide to the pleasures of understanding electronic pictures. It's like having the world's best teacher giving you a private seminar on whatever you need to know. Enjoy!

— Mark Schubin, Television Engineer and Writer

Contents

Figures

Tables

Preface

When I completed my previous book, *A Technical Introduction to Digital Video*, published by Wiley in 1996, I realized that two major topics were missing: video compression technology, and high-definition television (HDTV). With this book, I remedy those omissions.

Video technology continues to advance, though, and I'm already aware of topics that need further discussion. Obviously, we can predict further "convergence" – Jim Blinn might say collision – between video and computer graphics. We can expect developments in personal video recorders (PVRs); metadata; hard disk recording; transport of video using TCP/IP network protocols; and perhaps deployment of MPEGs 4, 7, and 21. This book provides a solid description of the theory and practice of video, and I believe that it will provide a good foundation for understanding these developments.

Layout and typography

I designed this book with wide margins. I write notes here, and I encourage you to do the same!

When Quinn Morris was proofreading a draft chapter of this book, she circled, in red, two lines at the top of a page that were followed by a new section. She drew an arrow indicating that the two lines should be moved to the bottom of the previous page. She didn't immediately realize that the lines had wrapped to the top of the page because there was no room for them earlier. She marked them nonetheless, and explained to me that they needed to be moved because that section should start at the top of the page. Quinn understood the awkward page break – and she was only twelve years old! I have spent a lot of time executing the

Bringhurst, Robert, *The Elements of Typographic Style*, version 2.4, (Vancouver, B.C.: Hartley & Marks, 2001).

Tschichold, Jan, *The Form of the Book* (London: Lund Humphries, 1991). [Originally published in German in 1975.]

Tufte, Edward R., *Envisioning Information* (Cheshire, Conn.: Graphic Press, 1990).

illustration, layout, and typesetting for this book, based upon my belief that this story is told not only through the words but also through pictures and layout.

In designing and typesetting this book, I was inspired by the work of Robert Bringhurst, Jan Tschichold, and Edward R. Tufte; their books are cited in the margin.

Formulas

It is said that every formula in a book cuts the potential readership in half. I hope readers of this book can compute that after a mere ten formulas my readership would drop to 2^{-10}! I decided to retain formulas, but they are not generally necessary to achieve an understanding of the concepts. If you are intimidated by a formula, just skip it and come back later if you wish. I hope that you will treat the mathematics the way that Bringhurst recommends that you treat his mathematical description of the principles of page composition. In Chapter 8 of his classic book, *Elements of Typographic Style*, Bringhurst says,

> "The mathematics are not here to impose drudgery upon anyone. On the contrary, they are here entirely for pleasure. They are here for the pleasure of those who like to examine what they are doing, or what they might do or have already done, perhaps in the hope of doing it still better. Those who prefer to act directly at all times, and leave the analysis to others, may be content in this chapter to study the pictures and skim the text."

www.poynton.ca/DVAI/

I tried carefully to avoid errors while preparing this book. Nonetheless, despite my efforts and the efforts of my reviewers, I expect that a few errors have crept in. As in my previous book, I will compile errata for this book and make the corrections available at the URL indicated in the margin. Please report any error that you discover, and I will endeavor to repair it!

Charles Poynton
Toronto, 2002-11-04

Acknowledgments

My introduction to digital video was writing microcode for hardware conceived by John Lowry and engineered by Richard Kupnicki. John Ross, founder of Ross Video, continued my education in video. I thank all three.

I spent many hours at CJOH-TV in Ottawa, Canada, testing my theories at the invitation of CJOH's Vice-President of Engineering, Austin Reeve. I thank him for his confidence, good humor, and patience. I also thank Bryn Matthews for his confidence in this venture.

Much of the material in this book originated from my courses, seminars, and tutorials. In 1995, Linda Young of DuArt Film & Video organized the seminar *Pixels, Pictures, and Perception* in New York, and invited Thor Olson, John Watkinson, Mark Schubin, and me to participate. Mark suggested the title for that seminar. That title became the working title for this book. I am also grateful for the contributions of people who have attended and contributed to my many SIGGRAPH courses.

I'd like to acknowledge three influential high school teachers: Mr. Davidson, Mr. Harrison, and Mr. Moher. They left a lasting influence.

Thanks to my colleagues LeRoy DeMarsh, Junji Kumada, Ed Giorgianni, and Bill Cowan, each of whom spent many hours teaching me about color.

Thanks to several colleagues and mentors at Sun Microsystems: Andreas Bechtolsheim, Paul Borrill, John Gage,

Barry Medoff, and Bill Joy. These people contributed to the creation of a remarkable software and hardware engineering culture at Sun, and I am proud to be a practitioner of their style of engineering.

I thank the colleagues who encouraged me in this project, many of whom reviewed the manuscript at various stages: David Bancroft, Jody Booth, Phil Cannata, Joseph Goldstone, Mitchell Golner, Bill Herz, Norm Hurst, Michael Isnardi, George Joblove, Mike Keyes, Dave LeHoty, Tad Marburg, Bill Miller, Cam Morrison, Don Nelson, Neil Neubert, Glenn Reitmeier, Alan Roberts, John Ross, Johann Safar, Roderick Snell, Peter Symes, Michele Van Dyke-Lewis, John Watkinson, and Sophie Wilson. Many of you will find some of your ideas – and even some of your words and phrases! – among these pages. Thanks to Carl Girod at SMPTE for helping me with many questions related to standards.

I owe a debt of gratitude to four people who have been not only colleagues but close personal friends for nearly two decades: C.R. Caillouet, Pierre DeGuire, Charlie Pantuso, and Mark Schubin. All four have contributed greatly to my understanding of video.

Diane Cerra is my patient and thoughtful editor, for my first book and for this one. Her ideas and hard work shaped both books. Thanks also to Howard Severson, my diligent and sensitive production editor.

Thanks to Georgia and Quinn Morris, who changed me. Quinn carefully checked Table 21.1 and discovered an arithmetic error; she also corrected several spelling mistakes and suggested several improvements in layout.

Thanks to my family, for their love and encouragement: Peg, Al, Kim, Brenna, Alana, Dad, and Jean. Thanks also to my new family members Jeri, Corot, Ben, and Paige.

Thanks to Barbara, the love of my life. Without her, this book would have been completed several years earlier – but I would have enjoyed life much less!

Part 1

Introduction

Raster images 1

This chapter introduces the basic features of the pixel array. I explain how the pixel array is digitized from the image plane, how pixel values are related to brightness and color, and why most imaging systems use pixel values that are nonlinearly related to light intensity.

Imaging

In human vision, the three-dimensional world is imaged by the lens of the eye onto the retina, which is populated with photoreceptor cells that respond to light having wavelengths ranging from about 400 nm to 700 nm. In video and in film, we build a camera having a lens and a photosensitive device, to mimic how the world is perceived by vision. Although the shape of the retina is roughly a section of a sphere, it is topologically two dimensional. In a camera, for practical reasons, we employ a flat *image plane,* sketched in Figure 1.1 below, instead of a section of a sphere. Image science concerns analyzing the continuous distribution of optical power that is incident on the image plane.

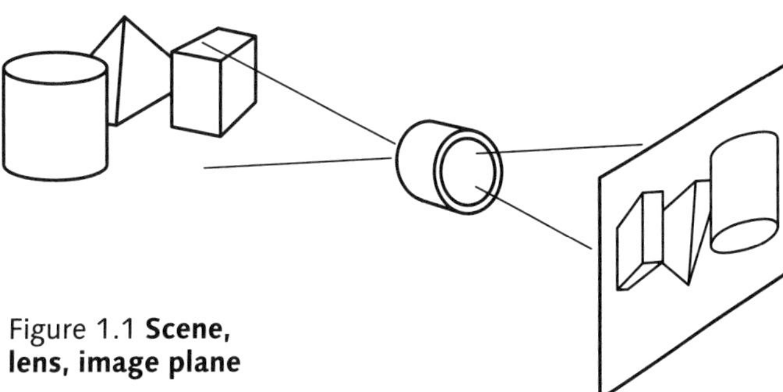

Figure 1.1 **Scene, lens, image plane**

Video image

Video
4:3
1.33:1

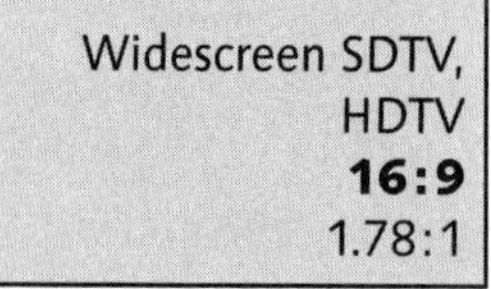

Figure 1.2 **Aspect ratio** of video, HDTV, and film are compared. Aspect ratio is properly written width:height (not height:width).

Film image

35 mm still film
3:2
1.5:1

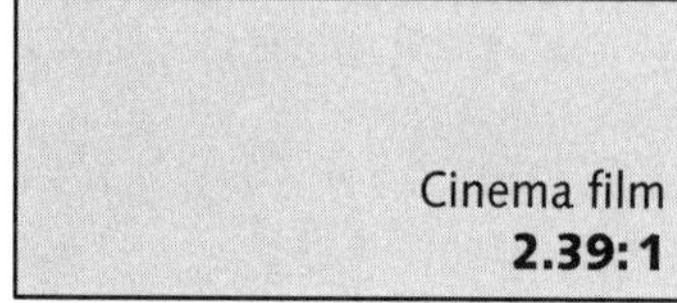

Aspect ratio

Schubin, Mark, "Searching for the Perfect Aspect Ratio," in *SMPTE Journal* 105 (8): 460–478 (Aug. 1996). The 1.85:1 aspect ratio is achieved with a spherical lens (as opposed to the aspherical lens used for anamorphic images).

Aspect ratio is simply the ratio of an image's width to its height. Standard aspect ratios for film and video are sketched, to scale, in Figure 1.2 above. Conventional *standard-definition television* (SDTV) has an aspect ratio of 4:3. *Widescreen* refers to an aspect ratio wider than 4:3. Widescreen television and *high-definition television* (HDTV) have an aspect ratio of 16:9. Cinema film commonly uses 1.85:1 ("flat," or "spherical"). In Europe and Asia, 1.66:1 is usually used.

The 2.39:1 ratio for cinema film is recent; formerly, 2.35:1 was used. The term *anamorphic* in video usually refers to a 16:9 widescreen variant of a base video standard, where the horizontal dimension of the 16:9 image is transmitted in the same time interval as the 4:3 aspect ratio standard. See page 99.

To obtain 2.39:1 aspect ratio ("Cinemascope," or colloquially, "scope"), film is typically shot with an aspherical lens that squeezes the horizontal dimension of the image by a factor of two. The projector is equipped with a similar lens, to restore the horizontal dimension of the projected image. The lens and the technique are called *anamorphic.* In principle, an anamorphic lens can have any ratio; in practice, a ratio of two is ubiquitous.

Film can be transferred to 4:3 video by cropping the sides of the frame, at the expense of losing some picture content. *Pan-and-scan*, sketched in Figure 1.3 opposite, refers to choosing, on a scene-by-scene basis during film transfer, the 4:3 region to be maintained.

Many directors and producers prefer their films not to be altered by cropping, so many movies on VHS and DVD are released in *letterbox* format, sketched in Figure 1.4 opposite. In letterbox format, the entire film image is maintained, and the top and bottom of the 4:3 frame are unused. (Either gray or black is displayed.)

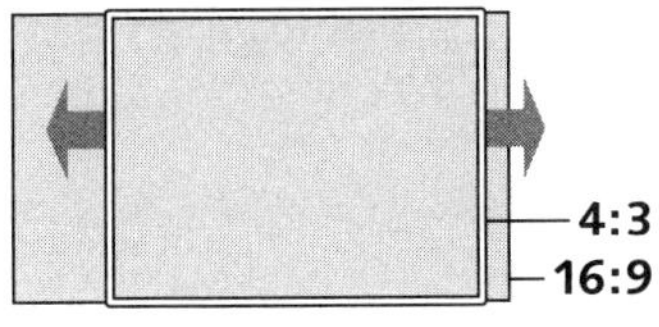

Figure 1.3 **Pan-and-scan** crops the width of widescreen material – here, 16:9 – for a 4:3 aspect ratio display.

Figure 1.4 **Letterbox format** fits widescreen material – here, 16:9 – to the width of a 4:3 display.

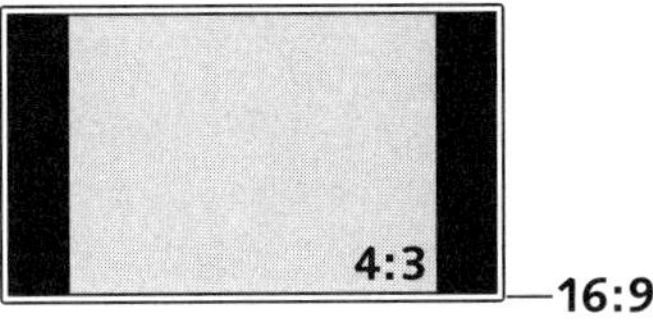

Figure 1.5 **Pillarbox format** (sometimes called *sidebar*) fits narrow-aspect-ratio material to the height of a 16:9 display.

With the advent of widescreen consumer television receivers, it is becoming common to see 4:3 material displayed on widescreen displays in *pillarbox* format, in Figure 1.5. The full height of the display is used, and the left and right of the widescreen frame are blanked.

Digitization

Signals captured from the physical world are translated into digital form by *digitization*, which involves two processes, sketched in Figure 1.6 overleaf. A signal is digitized by subjecting it to both *sampling* (in time or space) and *quantization* (in amplitude). The operations may take place in either order, though sampling usually precedes quantization. Quantization assigns an integer to signal amplitude at an instant of time or a point in space, as I will explain in *Quantization,* on page 17.

1-D sampling

A continuous one-dimensional function of time, such as sound pressure of an audio signal, is sampled through forming a series of discrete values, each of which is a function of the distribution of intensity across a small interval of time. *Uniform sampling,* where the time intervals are of equal duration, is nearly always used. Details will be presented in *Filtering and sampling,* on page 141.

2-D sampling

A continuous two-dimensional function of space is sampled by assigning, to each element of a sampling grid (or lattice), a value that is a function of the distribution of intensity over a small region of space. In digital video and in conventional image processing, the samples lie on a regular, rectangular grid.

Figure 1.6 **Digitization** comprises *sampling* and *quantization*, in either order. Sampling density, expressed in units such as pixels per inch (ppi), relates to resolution. Quantization relates to the number of bits per pixel (bpp). Total data rate or data capacity depends upon the product of these two factors.

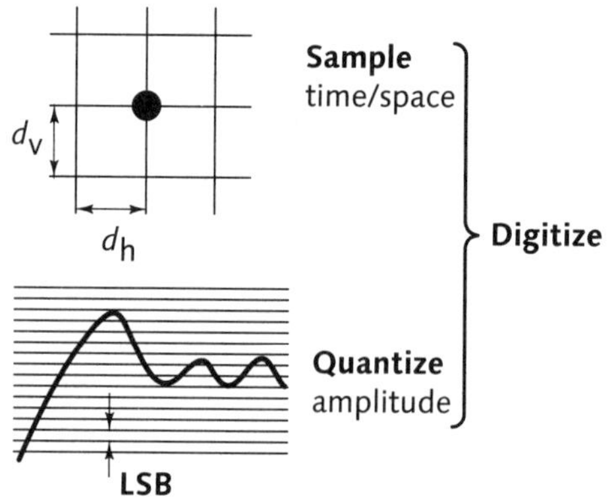

Samples need not be digital: a *charge-coupled device* (CCD) camera is inherently sampled, but it is not inherently quantized. Analog video is not sampled horizontally but is sampled vertically by scanning and sampled temporally at the frame rate.

Pixel array

In video and computing, a pixel comprises the set of *all* components necessary to represent color. Exceptionally, in the terminology of digital still camera imaging devices, a pixel is *any* component individually.

A digital image is represented by a rectangular array (matrix) of *picture elements* (*pels*, or *pixels*). In a grayscale system, each pixel comprises a single component whose value is related to what is loosely called brightness. In a color system, each pixel comprises several components – usually three – whose values are closely related to human color perception.

In *multispectral* imaging, each pixel has two or more components, representing power from different wavelength bands. Such a system may be described as having color, but multispectral systems are usually designed for purposes of science, not vision: A set of pixel component values in a multispectral system usually has no close relationship to color perception.

Each component of a pixel has a value that depends upon the brightness and color in a small region surrounding the corresponding point in the sampling lattice. Each component is usually quantized to an integer value occupying between 1 and 16 bits – often 8 bits – of digital storage.

Figure 1.7 **Pixel arrays** of several imaging standards are shown, with their counts of image columns and rows. 480*i*29.97 SDTV, indicated here as 720×480, and SIF, have nonsquare sampling. Analog SDTV broadcast may contain a few more than 480 picture lines; see *Picture lines,* on page 324. For explanations of QCIF and SIF, see *Glossary of video signal terms, on page 609.*

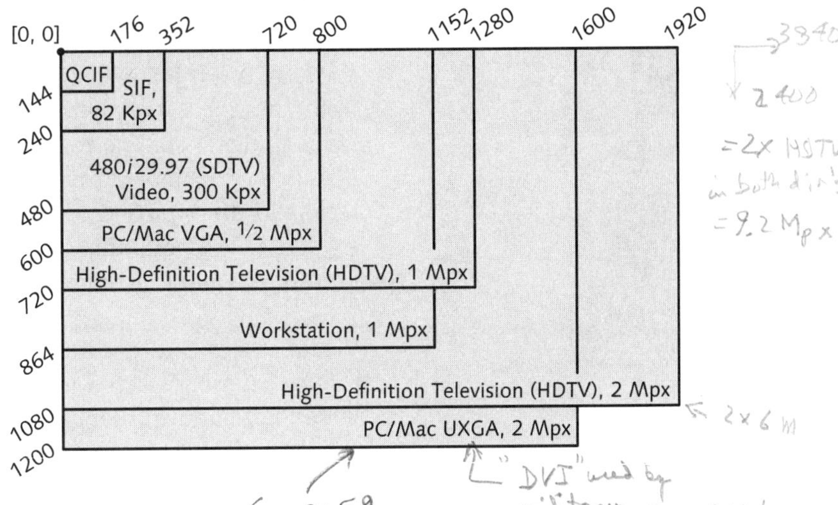

The pixel array is stored in digital memory. In video, the memory containing a single image is called *a framestore*. In computing, it's called *a framebuffer*.

A typical video camera or digital still camera has, in the image plane, one or more CCD image sensors, each containing hundreds of thousands – or perhaps a small number of millions – of photosites in a lattice. The total number of pixels in an image is simply the product of the number of image columns (technically, *samples per active line*, S_{AL}) and the number of image rows (*active lines*, L_A). The total pixel count is often expressed in kilopixels (Kpx) or megapixels (Mpx). Pixel arrays of several image standards are sketched in Figure 1.7. Scan order is conventionally left to right, then top to bottom, numbering rows and columns from [0, 0] at the top left.

I prefer the term *density* to *pitch:* It isn't clear whether the latter refers to the dimension of an element, or to the number of elements per unit distance.

A system that has equal horizontal and vertical sample density is said to have *square sampling*. In a system with square sampling, the number of samples across the picture width is the product of the aspect ratio and the number of picture lines. (The term *square* refers to the sample density; *square* does not mean that image information associated with each pixel is distributed uniformly throughout a square region.)

ITU-T Group 4 fax is standardized with about 195.9 ppi horizontally and 204.1 ppi vertically, but that is now academic since computer fax systems assume square sampling with exactly 200 pixels/inch.

In computing, it is standard to use square sampling. Some imaging and video systems use sampling lattices where the horizontal and vertical sample pitch are unequal: *nonsquare sampling.* This situation is sometimes misleadingly referred to as "rectangular sampling," but a square is also a rectangle!

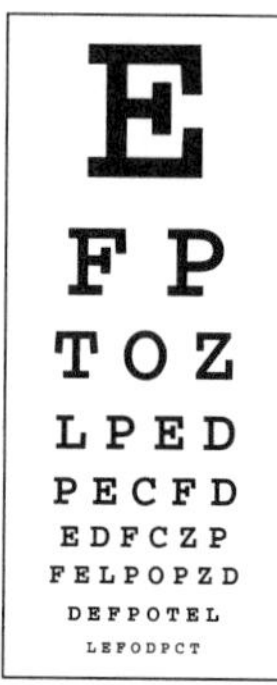

Figure 1.8 **Snellen chart**

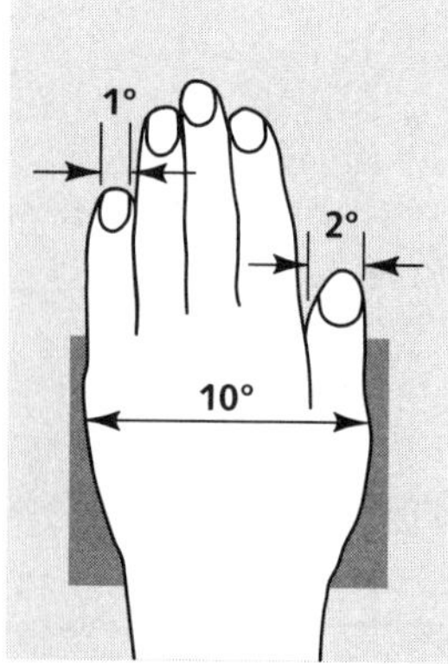

Figure 1.9 **Astronomers' rule of thumb**

Visual acuity

When an optometrist measures your visual acuity, he or she may use the Snellen chart, represented in Figure 1.8 in the margin. The results of this test depend upon viewing distance. The test is standardized for a viewing distance of 20 feet. At that distance, the strokes of the letters in the 20/20 row subtend one sixtieth of a degree ($\frac{1}{60}°$, one minute of arc). This is roughly the limit of angular discrimination of normal vision.

Visual angles can be estimated using the astronomers' rule of thumb depicted in Figure 1.9 in the margin: When held at arm's length, the joint of the thumb subtends about two degrees. The full palm subtends about ten degrees, and the nail of the little finger subtends about one degree. (The angular subtense of the full moon is about half a degree.)

Viewing distance and angle

If you display a white flatfield on a CRT with typical spot size, scan line structure is likely to be visible if the viewer is located closer than the distance where adjacent image rows (scan lines) at the display surface subtend an angle of one minute of arc ($\frac{1}{60}°$) or more.

To achieve viewing where scan-line pitch subtends $\frac{1}{60}°$, viewing distance should be about 3400 times the distance d between scan lines – that is, 3400 divided by the scan line density (e.g., in pixels per inch, ppi):

$$distance \approx 3400 \cdot d \approx \frac{3400}{ppi}; \quad 3400 \approx \frac{1}{\sin\left(\frac{1}{60}\right)^{\circ}} \qquad \text{Eq 1.1}$$

At that distance, there are about 60 pixels per degree. Viewing distance expressed numerically as a multiple of picture height should be approximately 3400 divided by the number of image rows (L_A):

$$distance \approx \frac{3400}{L_A} \times PH \qquad \text{Eq 1.2}$$

SDTV has about 480 image rows (picture lines). The scan-line pitch subtends $\frac{1}{60}°$ at a distance of about seven times picture height (PH), as sketched in Figure 1.10 opposite, giving roughly 600 pixels across

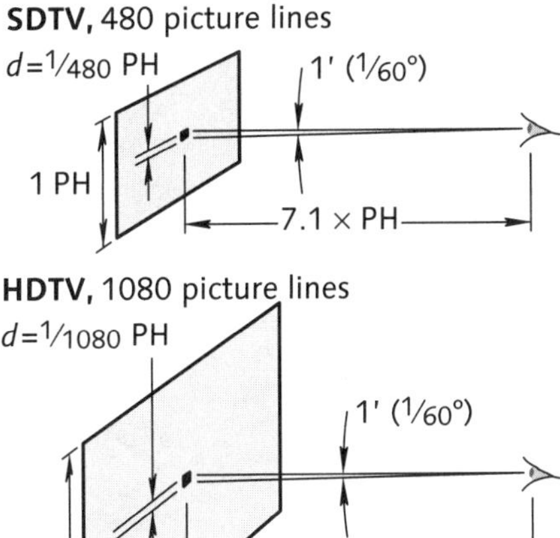

Figure 1.10 **Viewing distance** where scan lines become invisible occurs approximately where the scan-line pitch subtends an angle of about one minute of arc (1⁄60°) at the display surface. This is roughly the limit of angular discrimination for normal vision.

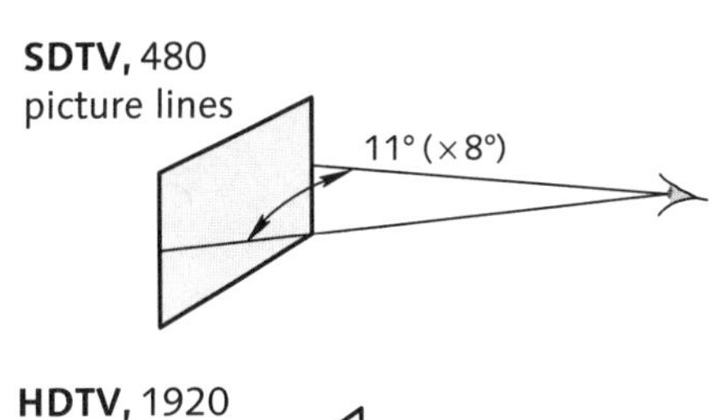

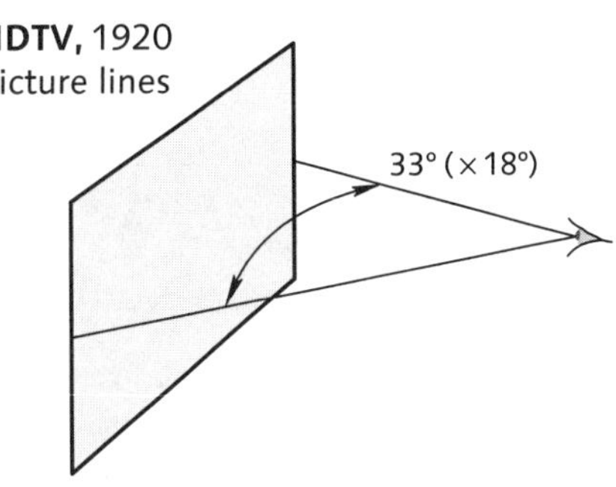

Figure 1.11 **Picture angle** of SDTV, sketched at the top, is about 11° horizontally and 8° vertically, where scan lines are invisible. In 1920×1080 HDTV, horizontal angle can increase to about 33°, and vertical angle to about 18°, preserving the scan-line subtense.

the picture width. Picture angle is about 11°, as shown in Figure 1.11. With your hand held at arm's length, your palm ought to just cover the width of the picture. This distance is about 4.25 times the display diagonal, as sketched in Figure 1.12 in the margin. For HDTV with 1080 image rows, the viewing distance that yields the 1⁄60° scan-line subtense is about 3.1 PH (see the bottom of Figure 1.10), about 1.5 times the display diagonal.

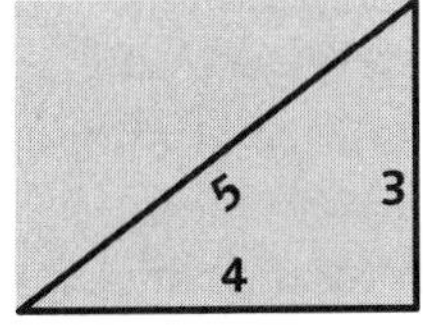

Figure 1.12 **Picture height** at an aspect ratio of 4:3 is 3⁄5 of the diagonal; optimum viewing distance for conventional video is 4.25 times the diagonal. Picture height at 16:9 is about half the diagonal; optimum viewing distance for 2 Mpx HDTV is 1.5 times the diagonal.

For SDTV, the total horizontal picture angle at that viewing distance is about 11°. Viewers tend to choose a viewing distance that renders scan lines invisible; angular subtense of a scan line (or pixel) is thereby preserved. Thus, the main effect of higher pixel count is to enable viewing at a wide picture angle. For 1920×1080 HDTV, horizontal viewing angle is tripled to 33°, as sketched in Figure 1.11. The "high definition" of HDTV does not squeeze six times the number of pixels into the same visual angle! Instead, the entire image can potentially occupy a much larger area of the viewer's visual field.

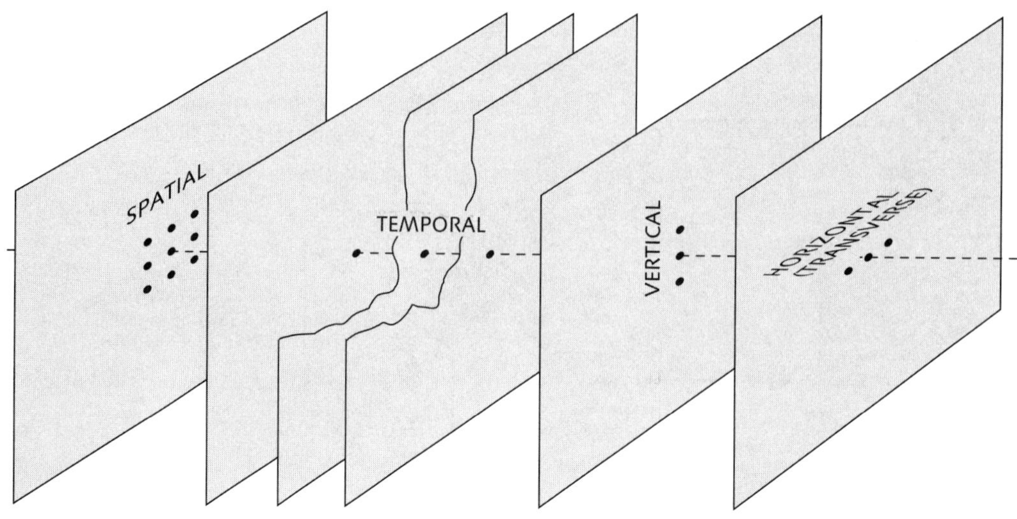

Figure 1.13 **Spatio-temporal domains**

Spatiotemporal domains

A sequence of still pictures captured and displayed at a sufficiently high rate – typically between 24 and 60 pictures per second – can create the illusion of motion, as I will describe on page 51. Sampling in time, in combination with 2-D (spatial) sampling, causes digital video to be sampled in three axes – horizontal, vertical, and temporal – as sketched in Figure 1.13 above. One-dimensional sampling theory, to be detailed in *Filtering and sampling*, on page 141, applies along each axis.

At the left of Figure 1.13 is a sketch of a two-dimensional *spatial* domain of a single image. Some image processing operations, such as certain kinds of filtering, can be performed separately on the horizontal and vertical axes, and have an effect in the spatial domain – these operations are called *separable*. Other processing operations cannot be separated into horizontal and vertical facets, and must be performed directly on a two-dimensional sample array. Two-dimensional sampling will be detailed in *Image digitization and reconstruction*, on page 187.

Lightness terminology

In a grayscale image, each pixel value represents what is loosely called *brightness*. However, brightness is defined formally as *the attribute of a visual sensation according to which an area appears to emit more or less light*. This definition is obviously subjective, so *brightness* is an inappropriate metric for image data.

See Appendix B, *Introduction to radiometry and photometry,* on page 601.

Intensity is radiant power in a particular direction; *radiance* is intensity per unit projected area. These terms disregard wavelength composition. But in color imaging, wavelength is important! Neither of these quantities is a suitable metric for color image data.

The term *luminance* is often carelessly and incorrectly used to refer to *luma;* see below. In image reproduction, we are usually concerned not with (absolute) luminance, but with *relative luminance*, to be detailed on page 206.

Luminance is radiance weighted by the spectral sensitivity associated with the brightness sensation of vision. Luminance is proportional to intensity. Imaging systems rarely use pixel values proportional to luminance; values nonlinearly related to luminance are usually used.

Illuminance is luminance integrated over a half-sphere.

Lightness – formally, CIE L^* – is the standard approximation to the perceptual response to luminance. It is computed by subjecting luminance to a nonlinear transfer function that mimics vision. A few grayscale imaging systems have pixel values proportional to L^*.

Regrettably, many practitioners of computer graphics, and of digital image processing, have a cavalier attitude toward these terms. In the *HSB*, *HSI*, *HSL*, and *HSV* systems, *B* allegedly stands for brightness, *I* for intensity, *L* for lightness, and *V* for value. None of these systems computes brightness, intensity, luminance, or value according to any definition that is recognized in color science!

Value refers to measures of lightness apart from CIE L^*. In image science, *value* is rarely – if ever – used in any sense consistent with accurate color. (Several different value scales are graphed in Figure 20.2 on page 208.)

Color images are sensed and reproduced based upon *tristimulus values,* whose amplitudes are proportional to intensity but whose spectral compositions are carefully chosen according to the principles of color science. As their name implies, tristimulus values come in sets of 3.

The image sensor of a digital camera produces values, proportional to radiance, that approximate red, green, and blue (*RGB*) tristimulus values. (I call these values *linear-light*.) However, in most imaging systems, *RGB* tristimulus values are subject to a nonlinear transfer function – *gamma correction* – that mimics the perceptual response. Most imaging systems use *RGB* values that are *not* proportional to intensity. The notation *R'G'B'* denotes the nonlinearity.

See Appendix A, *YUV and luminance considered harmful,* on page 595.

Luma (*Y'*) is formed as a suitably weighted sum of *R'G'B'*; it is the basis of luma/color difference coding. Luma is comparable to lightness; it is often carelessly and incorrectly called *luminance* by video engineers.

Nonlinear image coding

Figure 1.14 **Contrast sensitivity test pattern** reveals that a *just-noticeable difference* (JND) occurs when the step between luminance levels is 1% of *Y*.

Vision cannot distinguish two luminance levels if the ratio between them is less than about 1.01 – in other words, the visual threshold for luminance difference is about 1%. This *contrast sensitivity* threshold is established by experiments using the test pattern such as the one sketched in Figure 1.14 in the margin; details will be presented in *Contrast sensitivity,* on page 198.

Consider pixel values proportional to luminance, where code zero represents black, and the maximum code value of 255 represents white, as in Figure 1.15. Code 100 lies at the point on the scale where the ratio between adjacent luminance values is 1%: The boundary between a region of code 100 samples and a region of code 101 samples is likely to be visible.

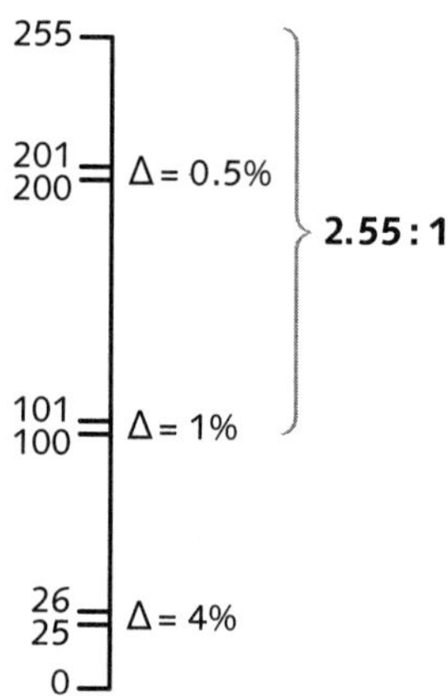

Figure 1.15 **The "code 100" problem** with linear-light coding is that at code levels below 100, the steps between code values have ratios larger than the visual threshold: The steps are liable to be visible.

As the pixel value decreases below 100, the difference in luminance between adjacent codes becomes increasingly perceptible: At code 25, the ratio between adjacent luminance values is 4%. In a large area of smoothly varying shades of gray, these luminance differences are likely to be visible or even objectionable. Visible jumps in luminance produce artifacts known as *contouring* or *banding*.

Linear-light codes above 100 suffer no banding artifacts. However, as code value increases toward white, the codes have decreasing perceptual utility: At code 200, the luminance ratio between adjacent codes is just 0.5%, near the threshold of visibility. Codes 200 and 201 are visually indistinguishable; code 201 could be discarded without its absence being noticed.

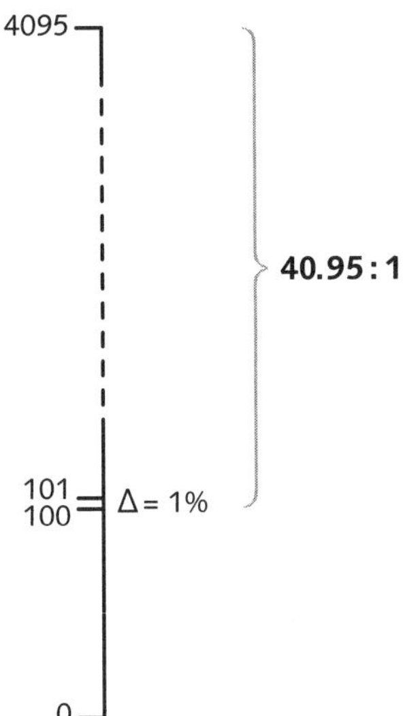

Figure 1.16 **The "code 100" problem is mitigated** by using more than 8 bits to represent luminance. Here, 12 bits are used, placing the top end of the scale at 4095. However, the majority of these 4096 codes cannot be distinguished visually.

High-quality image reproduction requires a ratio of at least 30 to 1 between the luminance of white and the luminance of black, as I will explain in *Contrast ratio,* on page 197. In 8-bit linear-light coding, the ratio between the brightest luminance (code 255) and the darkest luminance that can be reproduced without banding (code 100) is only 2.55:1. Linear-light coding in 8 bits is unsuitable for high-quality images.

This "code 100" problem can be mitigated by placing the top end of the scale at a code value higher than 100, as sketched in Figure 1.16 in the margin. If luminance is represented in 12 bits, white is at code 4095; the luminance ratio between code 100 and white reaches 40.95:1. However, the vast majority of those 4096 code values cannot be distinguished visually; for example, codes 4001 through 4040 are visually indistinguishable. Rather than coding luminance linearly with a large number of bits, we can use many fewer code values assigned nonlinearly on a perceptual scale.

$$\frac{\lg 100}{\lg 1.01} \approx 463; \quad 1.01^{463} \approx 100$$

If the threshold of vision behaved strictly according to the 1% relationship across the whole tone scale, then luminance could be coded logarithmically. For a contrast ratio of 100:1, about 463 code values would be required, corresponding to about 9 bits. In video, for reasons to be explained in *Luminance and lightness,* on page 203, instead of modeling the lightness sensitivity of vision as a logarithmic function, we model it as a power function with an exponent of about 0.4.

Conversely, monitor *R'G'B'* values are proportional to reproduced luminance raised to approximately the 0.4-power.

The luminance of the red, green, or blue primary light produced by a monitor is proportional to voltage (or code value) raised to approximately the 2.5-power. This will be detailed in Chapter 23, *Gamma,* on page 257.

The *cathode ray tube* (CRT) is the dominant display device for television receivers and for desktop computers.

Amazingly, a CRT's transfer function is nearly the inverse of vision's lightness sensitivity! The nonlinear lightness response of vision and the power function intrinsic to a CRT combine to cause monitor voltage, or code value, to exhibit perceptual uniformity, as demonstrated in Figures 1.17 and 1.18 overleaf.

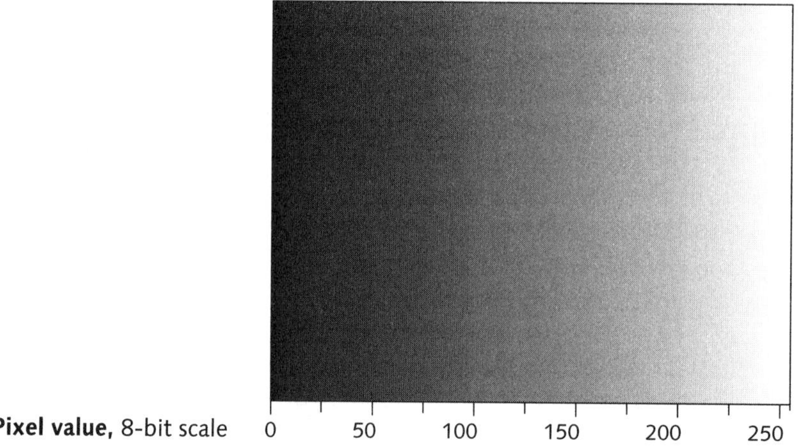

Figure 1.17 **Grayscale ramp** on a CRT display is generated by writing successive integer values 0 through 255 into the columns of a framebuffer. When processed by a digital-to-analog converter (DAC), and presented to a CRT display, a perceptually uniform sweep of lightness results. A naive experimenter might conclude – mistakenly! – that code values are proportional to intensity.

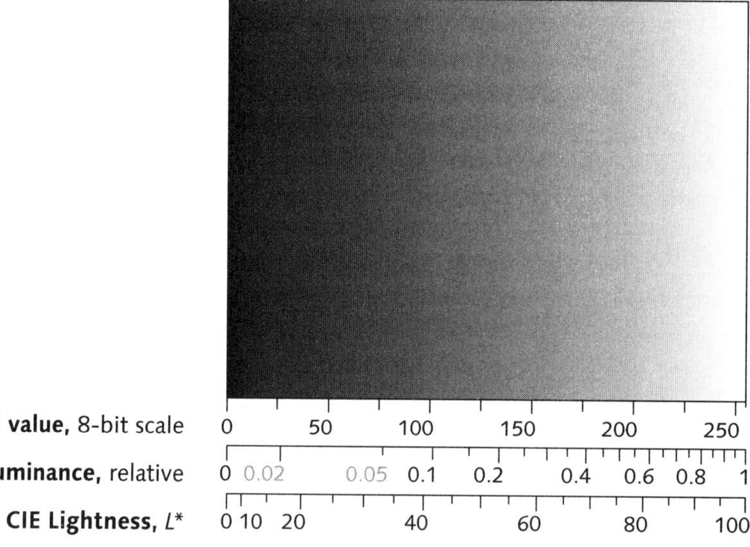

Figure 1.18 **Grayscale ramp augmented** with CIE lightness (L^*, on the middle scale), and CIE relative luminance (*Y*, proportional to intensity, on the bottom scale). The point midway across the screen has lightness value midway between black and white. There is a near-linear relationship between code value and lightness. However, luminance at the midway point is only about 18% of white! Luminance produced by a CRT is approximately proportional to the 2.5-power of code value. Lightness is roughly proportional to the 0.4-power of luminance. Amazingly, these relationships are near inverses. Their near-perfect cancellation has led many workers in video, computer graphics, and digital image processing to misinterpret the term *intensity*, and to underestimate the importance of nonlinear transfer functions.

In video, this perceptually uniform relationship is exploited by *gamma correction* circuitry incorporated into every video camera. The *R'G'B'* values that result from gamma correction – the values that are processed, recorded, and transmitted in video – are roughly proportional to the square root of scene intensity: *R'G'B'* values are nearly perceptually uniform. Perceptual uniformity allows as few as 8 bits to be used for each *R'G'B'* component. Without perceptual uniformity, each component would need 11 bits or more. Digital still cameras adopt a similar approach.

See *Bit depth requirements,* on page 269.

Linear and nonlinear

Image sensors generally convert photons to electrons: They produce signals whose amplitude is proportional to physical intensity. Video signals are usually processed through analog circuits that have linear response to voltage, or digital systems that are linear with respect to the arithmetic performed on the codewords. Video systems are often said to be linear.

However, linearity in one domain cannot be carried across to another domain if a nonlinear function separates the two. In video, scene luminance is in a linear optical domain, and the video signal is in a linear electrical domain. However, the nonlinear gamma correction imposed between the domains means that luminance and signal amplitude are *not* linearly related. When you ask a video engineer if his system is linear, he will say, "Of course!" – referring to linear voltage. When you ask an optical engineer if her system is linear, she will say, "Of course!" – referring to intensity, radiance, or luminance. However, if a nonlinear transform lies between the two systems, a linear operation performed in one domain is not linear in the other.

If your computation involves perception, nonlinear representation may be required. If you perform a discrete cosine transform (DCT) on image data as part of image compression, as in JPEG, you should use nonlinear coding that exhibits perceptual uniformity, because you wish to minimize the perceptibility of the errors that will be introduced by the coding process.

Luma and color difference components

Some digital video equipment uses *R'G'B'* components directly. However, human vision has considerably less ability to sense detail in color information than in lightness. Provided lightness detail is maintained, color detail can be reduced by *subsampling*, which is a form of filtering (or averaging).

A color scientist might implement subsampling by forming relative luminance as a weighted sum of linear *RGB* tristimulus values, then imposing a nonlinear transfer function approximating CIE lightness (L^*). In video, we depart from the theory of color science, and implement an engineering approximation to be introduced in *Constant luminance,* on page 75. Component video systems convey image data as a luma component, Y', approximating lightness, and two color difference components – C_B and C_R in the digital domain, or P_B and P_R in analog – that represent color disregarding lightness. The color difference components are subsampled to reduce their data rate. I will explain $Y'C_BC_R$ and $Y'P_BP_R$ components in *Introduction to luma and chroma,* on page 87.

SDTV/HDTV

Until recently, it was safe to use the term *television,* but the emergence of widescreen television, high-definition television, and other new systems introduces ambiguity into that unqualified word. Surprisingly, there is no broad agreement on definitions of standard-definition television (SDTV) and high-definition television (HDTV). I classify as SDTV any video system whose image totals fewer than ¾ million pixels. I classify as HDTV any video system with a native aspect ratio of 16:9 whose image totals ¾ million pixels or more. *Digital television* (DTV) encompasses digital SDTV and digital HDTV. Some people and organizations consider SDTV to imply component digital operation – that is, NTSC, PAL, and component analog systems are excluded.

Quantization 2

A signal whose amplitude takes a range of continuous values is *quantized* by assigning to each of several (or several hundred or several thousand) intervals of amplitude a discrete, numbered level. In *uniform quantization*, the *steps* between levels have equal amplitude. Quantization discards signal information lying between quantizer levels. Quantizer performance is characterized by the extent of this loss. Figure 2.1 below shows, at the left, the transfer function of a uniform quantizer.

Resolution properly refers to spatial phenomena; see page 65. It is a mistake to refer to a sample as having 8-bit resolution: Say *quantization* or *precision* instead.

A truecolor image in computing is usually represented in *R'G'B'* components of 8 bits each, as I will explain on page 36. Each component ranges from 0 through 255, as sketched at the right of Figure 2.1: Black is at zero, and white is at 255. Grayscale and truecolor data in computing is usually coded so as to exhibit approximate perceptual uniformity, as I described on page 13: The steps are not proportional to intensity, but are instead uniformly spaced perceptually. The number of steps required depends upon properties of perception.

To make a 100-foot-long fence with fence posts every 10 feet, you need 11 posts, not ten! Take care to distinguish *levels* (in the left-hand portion of Figure 2.1, eleven) from *steps* or *risers* (here, ten).

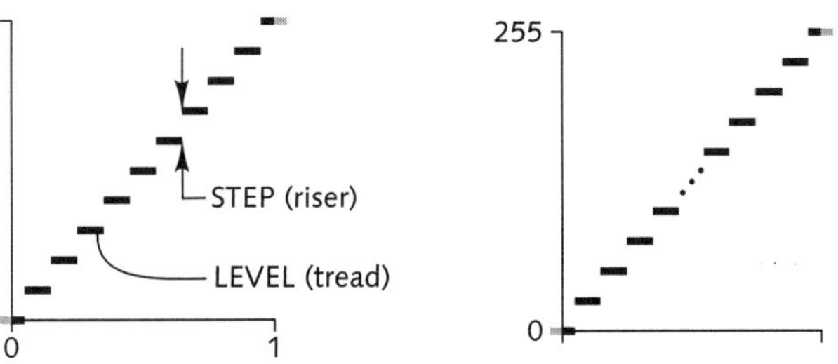

Figure 2.1 **Quantizer transfer function** is shown at the left. The usual 0 to 255 range of quantized *R'G'B'* components in computing is sketched at the right.

Decibels

In following sections, I will describe signal amplitude, noise amplitude, and the ratio between these – the *signal to noise ratio* (SNR). In engineering, ratios such as SNR are usually expressed in logarithmic units. A power ratio of 10:1 is defined as a *bel* (B), in honor of Alexander Graham Bell. A more practical measure is one-tenth of a bel – a *decibel* (dB). This is a power ratio of $10^{0.1}$, or about 1.259. The ratio of a power P_1 to a power P_2, expressed in decibels, is given by Equation 2.1, where the symbol lg represents base-10 logarithm. Often, signal power is given with respect to a reference power P_{REF}, which must either be specified (often as a letter following dB), or be implied by the context. Reference values of 1 W (dBW) and 1 mW (dBm) are common. This situation is expressed in Equation 2.2. A doubling of power represents an increase of about 3.01 dB (usually written 3 dB). If power is multiplied by ten, the change is +10 dB; if reduced to a tenth, the change is –10 dB.

Eq 2.1 Power ratio, in decibels:

$$m = 10 \lg \frac{P_1}{P_2} \quad \text{(dB)}$$

Eq 2.2 Power ratio, with respect to a reference power:

$$m = 10 \lg \frac{P}{P_{REF}} \quad \text{(dB)}$$

Consider a cable conveying a 100 MHz radio frequency signal. After 100 m of cable, power has diminished to some fraction, perhaps $1/8$, of its original value. After another 100 m, power will be reduced by the same fraction again. Rather than expressing this cable attenuation as a unitless fraction 0.125 per 100 m, we express it as 9 dB per 100 m; power at the end of 1 km of cable is -90 dB referenced to the source power.

Eq 2.3 Power ratio, in decibels, as a function of voltage:

$$m = 20 \lg \frac{V_1}{V_2} \quad \text{(dB)}$$

The decibel is defined as a power ratio. If a voltage source is applied to a constant impedance, and the voltage is doubled, current doubles as well, so power increases by a factor of four. More generally, if voltage (or current) into a constant impedance changes by a ratio r, power changes by the ratio r^2. (The log of r^2 is 2 log r.) To compute decibels from a voltage ratio, use Equation 2.3. In digital signal processing (DSP), digital code levels are treated equivalently to voltage; the decibel in DSP is based upon voltage ratios.

Voltage ratio	*Decibels*
10	20 dB
2	6 dB
1.112	1 dB
1.0116	0.1 dB
1	0 dB
0.5	-6 dB
0.1	-20 dB
0.01	-40 dB
0.001	-60 dB

Table 2.1 **Decibel examples**

Table 2.1 in the margin gives numerical examples of decibels used for voltage ratios.

The *oct* in *octave* refers to the eight whole tones in music, *do, re, me, fa, sol, la, ti, do,* that cover a 2:1 range of frequency.

A *stop* in photography is a 2:1 ratio of illuminance.

A 2:1 ratio of frequencies is an *octave*. When voltage halves with each doubling in frequency, an electronics engineer refers to this as a loss of *6 dB per octave*. If voltage halves with each doubling, then it is reduced to one-tenth at ten times the frequency; a 10:1 ratio of quantities is a *decade*, so 6 dB/octave is equivalent to 20 dB/decade. (The base-2 log of 10 is very nearly $^{20}/_{6}$.)

Noise, signal, sensitivity

Analog electronic systems are inevitably subject to noise introduced from thermal and other sources. Thermal noise is unrelated to the signal being processed. A system may also be subject to external sources of interference. As signal amplitude decreases, noise and interference make a larger relative contribution.

Processing, recording, and transmission may introduce noise that is uncorrelated to the signal. In addition, *distortion* that is correlated to the signal may be introduced. As it pertains to objective measurement of the performance of a system, distortion is treated like noise; however, a given amount of distortion may be more or less perceptible than the same amount of noise. Distortion that can be attributed to a particular process is known as an *artifact*, particularly if it has a distinctive perceptual effect.

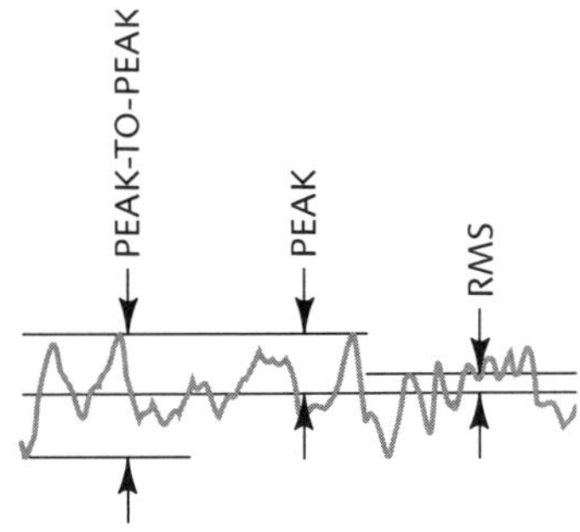

Figure 2.2 **Peak-to-peak, peak, and RMS values** are measured as the total excursion, half the total excursion, and the square root of the average of squared values, respectively. Here, a noise component is shown.

In video, *signal-to-noise ratio* (SNR) is the ratio of the peak-to-peak amplitude of a specified signal, often the reference amplitude or the largest amplitude that can be carried by a system, to the root mean square (RMS) magnitude of undesired components including noise and distortion. (It is sometimes called PSNR, to emphasize *peak* signal; see Figure 2.2 in the margin.) SNR is expressed in units of decibels. In many fields, such as audio, SNR is specified or measured in a physical (intensity) domain. In video, SNR usually applies to gamma-corrected components *R', G', B'*, or *Y'* that are in the perceptual domain; so, SNR correlates with perceptual performance.

Sensitivity refers to the minimum source power that achieves acceptable (or specified) SNR performance.

Quantization error

Eq 2.4 Theoretical SNR limit for a *k*-step quantizer:

$$20 \lg \left(k \sqrt{12} \right)$$

The factor of root-12, about 11 dB, accounts for the ratio between peak-to-peak and RMS; for details, see Schreiber (cited below).

A quantized signal takes only discrete, predetermined levels: Compared to the original continuous signal, *quantization error* has been introduced. This error is correlated with the signal, and is properly called *distortion*. However, classical signal theory deals with the addition of noise to signals. Providing each quantizer step is small compared to signal amplitude, we can consider the loss of signal in a quantizer as addition of an equivalent amount of noise instead: Quantization diminishes signal-to-noise ratio. The theoretical SNR limit of a *k*-step quantizer is given by Equation 2.4. Eight-bit quantization, common in video, has a theoretical SNR limit (peak-to-peak signal to RMS noise) of about 56 dB.

Some people use the word *dither* to refer to this technique; other people use the term for schemes that involve spatial distribution of the noise. The technique was first described by Roberts, L.G., "Picture coding using pseudo-random noise," in *IRE Trans.* IT-8 (2): 145–154 (1962). It is nicely summarized in Schreiber, William F., *Fundamentals of Electronic Imaging Systems,* Third Edition (Berlin: Springer-Verlag, 1993).

If an analog signal has very little noise, then its quantized value can be nearly exact when near a step, but can exhibit an error of nearly ±½ a step when the analog signal is midway between quantized levels. In video, this situation can cause the reproduced image to exhibit *noise modulation*. It is beneficial to introduce, prior to quantization, roughly ±½ of a quantizer step's worth of high-frequency random or pseudorandom noise to avoid this effect. This introduces a little noise into the picture, but this noise is less visible than low-frequency "patterning" of the quantization that would be liable to result without it. SNR is slightly degraded, but subjective picture quality is improved. Historically, video digitizers implicitly assumed that the input signal itself arrived with sufficient analog noise to perform this function; nowadays, analog noise levels are lower, and the noise should be added explicitly at the digitizer.

The degree to which noise in a video signal is visible – or objectionable – depends upon the properties of vision. To minimize noise visibility, we digitize a signal that is a carefully chosen nonlinear function of luminance (or tristimulus values). The function is chosen so that a given amount of noise is approximately equally perceptible across the whole tone scale from black to white. This concept was outlined in *Nonlinear image coding,* on page 12; in the sections to follow, linearity and perceptual uniformity are elaborated.

Linearity

Electronic systems are often expected to satisfy the *principle of superposition;* in other words, they are expected to exhibit *linearity.* A system g is linear *if and only if* (iff) it satisfies both of these conditions:

$$g(a \cdot x) \equiv a \cdot g(x) \qquad \text{[for scalar } a\text{]} \qquad \text{Eq 2.5}$$

$$g(x + y) \equiv g(x) + g(y)$$

The function g can encompass an entire system: A system is linear iff the sum of the individual responses of the system to any two signals is identical to its response to the sum of the two. Linearity can pertain to steady-state response, or to the system's temporal response to a changing signal.

Linearity is a very important property in mathematics, signal processing, and video. Many electronic systems operate in the linear intensity domain, and use signals that directly represent physical quantities. One example is compact audio disc (CD) coding: *Sound pressure level* (SPL), proportional to physical intensity, is quantized linearly into 16-bit samples.

Human perception, though, is nonlinear. Image signals that are captured, recorded, processed, or transmitted are often coded in a nonlinear, perceptually uniform manner that optimizes perceptual performance.

Perceptual uniformity

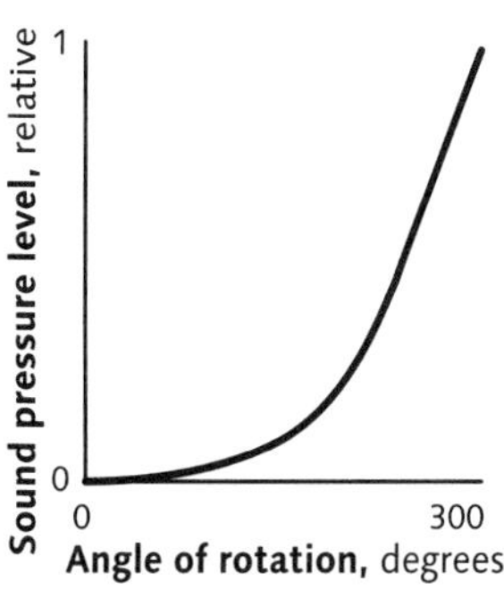

Figure 2.3 **Audio taper**

A coding system is *perceptually uniform* if a small perturbation to the coded value is approximately equally perceptible across the range of that value. If the volume control on your radio were physically linear, the logarithmic nature of loudness perception would place all of the perceptual "action" of the control at the bottom of its range. Instead, the control is designed to be perceptually uniform. Figure 2.3, in the margin, shows the transfer function of a potentiometer with standard *audio taper:* Rotating the knob 10 degrees produces a similar perceptual increment in volume throughout the range of the control. This is one of many examples of perceptual considerations embedded into the engineering of an electronic system.

Bellamy, John C., *Digital Telephony*, Second Edition (New York: Wiley, 1991), 98–111 and 472–476.

As I have mentioned, CD audio is coded linearly, with 16 bits per sample. Audio for digital telephony usually has just 8 bits per sample; this necessitates nonlinear coding. Two coding laws are in use, A-law and µ-law; both of these involve decoder transfer functions that are comparable to bipolar versions of Figure 2.3.

In video (including motion-JPEG and MPEG), and in digital photography (including JPEG/JFIF), *R'G'B'* components are coded in a perceptually uniform manner. Noise visibility is minimized by applying a nonlinear transfer function – *gamma correction* – to each tristimulus value sensed from the scene. The transfer function standardized for studio video is detailed in *Rec. 709 transfer function,* on page 263. In digital still cameras, a transfer function resembling that of sRGB is used; it is detailed in *sRGB transfer function,* on page 267. Identical nonlinear transfer functions are applied to the red, green, and blue components; in video, the nonlinearity is subsequently incorporated into the luma and chroma ($Y'C_BC_R$) components. The approximate inverse transfer function is imposed at the display device: A CRT has a nonlinear transfer function from voltage (or code value) to luminance; that function is comparable to Figure 2.3 on page 21. Nonlinear coding is the central topic of Chapter 23, *Gamma,* on page 257.

For engineering purposes, we consider *R'*, *G'*, and *B'* to be encoded with identical transfer functions. In practice, encoding gain differs owing to white balance. Also, the encoding transfer functions may be adjusted differently for artistic purposes during image capture or postproduction.

Headroom and footroom

Excursion in analog 480*i* systems is often expressed in *IRE units*, which I will introduce on page 327.

Excursion (or colloquially, *swing*) refers to the range of a signal – the difference between its maximum and minimum levels. In video, reference excursion is the range between standardized *reference white* and *reference black* levels.

In high-quality video, it is necessary to preserve transient signal undershoots below black, and overshoots above white, that are liable to result from processing by digital and analog filters. Studio video standards provide footroom below reference black, and headroom above reference white. Headroom allows code values that exceed reference white; therefore, you should distinguish between *reference* white and *peak* white.

Figure 2.4 **Footroom and headroom** are provided in digital video standards to accommodate filter undershoot and overshoot. For processing, black is assigned to code 0; in an 8-bit system, *R'*, *G'*, *B'*, or luma (*Y'*) range 0 through 219. At an 8-bit interface according to Rec. 601, an offset of +16 is added (indicated in italics). Interface codes 0 and 255 are reserved for synchronization; those codes are prohibited in video data.

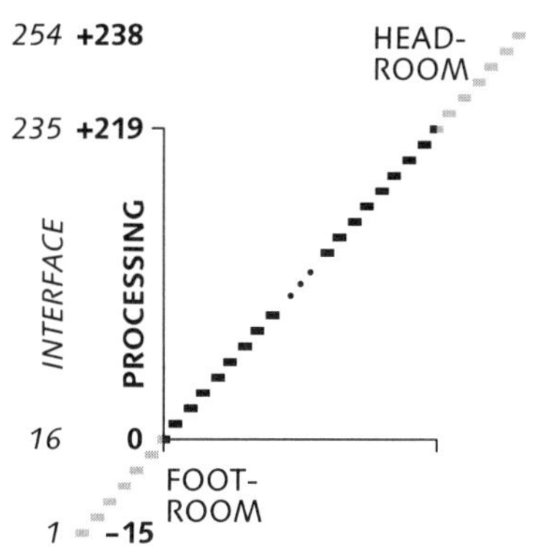

I represent video signals on an abstract scale where reference black has zero value independent of coding range. I assign white to an appropriate value, often 1, but sometimes other values such as 160, 219, 255, 640, or 876. A sample is ordinarily represented in hardware as a fixed-point integer with a limited number of bits (often 8 or 10). In computing, *R'G'B'* components of 8 bits each typically range from 0 through 255; the right-hand sketch of Figure 2.1 on page 17 shows a suitable quantizer.

Eight-bit studio standards have 219 steps between reference black and reference white. Footroom of 15 codes, and headroom of 19 codes, is available. For no good reason, studio standards specify asymmetrical footroom and headroom. Figure 2.4 above shows the standard coding range for *R'*, *G'*, or *B'*, or luma.

At the hardware level, an 8-bit interface is considered to convey values 0 through 255. At an 8-bit digital video interface, an offset of +16 is added to the code values shown in Figure 2.4: Reference black is placed at code 16, and white at 235. I consider the offset to be added or removed at the interface, because a signed representation is necessary for many processing operations (such as changing gain). However, hardware designers often consider digital video to have black at code 16 and white at 235; this makes interface design easy, but makes signal arithmetic design more difficult.

Figure 2.5 **Mid-tread quantizer for C_B and C_R** bipolar signals allows zero chroma to be represented exactly. (*Mid-riser* quantizers are rarely used in video.) For processing, C_B and C_R abstract values range ±112. At an 8-bit studio video interface according to Rec. 601, an offset of +128 is added, indicated by the values in italics. Interface codes 0 and 255 are reserved for synchronization, as they are for luma.

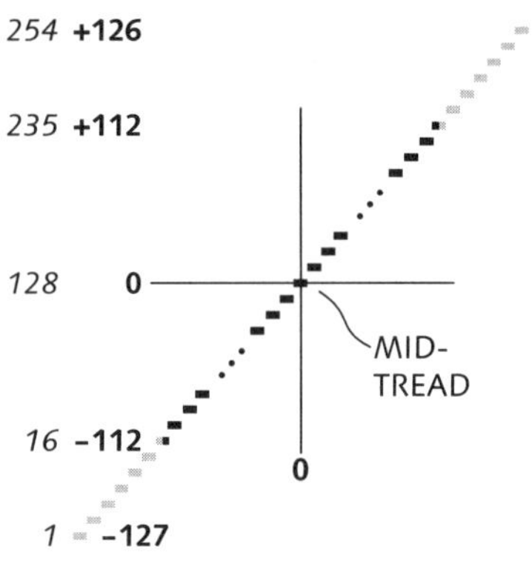

Figure 2.4 showed a quantizer for a unipolar signal such as luma. C_B and C_R are bipolar signals, ranging positive and negative. For C_B and C_R it is standard to use a *mid-tread* quantizer, such as the one in Figure 2.5 above, so that zero chroma has an exact reprtesentation. For processing, a signed representation is necessary; at a studio video interface, it is standard to scale 8-bit color difference components to an excursion of 224, and add an offset of +128. Unfortunately, the reference excursion of 224 for C_B or C_R is different from the reference excursion of 219 for Y'.

$R'G'B'$ or $Y'C_BC_R$ components of 8 bits each suffice for broadcast quality distribution. However, if a video signal must be processed many times, say for inclusion in a multiple-layer composited image, then roundoff errors are liable to accumulate. To avoid roundoff error, recording equipment, and interfaces between equipment, should carry 10 bits each of $Y'C_BC_R$. Ten-bit studio interfaces have the reference levels of Figures 2.4 and 2.5 multiplied by 4; the extra two bits are appended as least-significant bits to provide increased precision. Intermediate results within equipment may need to be maintained to 12, 14, or even 16 bits.

BRIGHTNESS and CONTRAST controls 3

This chapter introduces the BRIGHTNESS and CONTRAST controls of video. Beware: Their names are sources of confusion! These operations are normally effected in the nonlinear domain – that is, on gamma-corrected signals. These operations are normally applied to each of the red, green, and blue components simultaneously.

The CONTRAST control applies a scale factor – in electrical terms, a gain adjustment – to *R'G'B'* components. (On processing equipment, it is called VIDEO LEVEL; on some television receivers, it is called PICTURE.) Figure 3.1 below sketches the effect of the CONTRAST control, relating video signal input to light output at the display. The CONTRAST control affects the luminance that is reproduced for the reference white input signal; it affects lower signal levels proportionally, ideally having no effect on zero signal (reference black). Here I show contrast altering the *y*-axis (luminance) scaling; however, owing to the properties of the display's 2.5-power function, suitable scaling of the *x*-axis – the video signal – would have an equivalent effect.

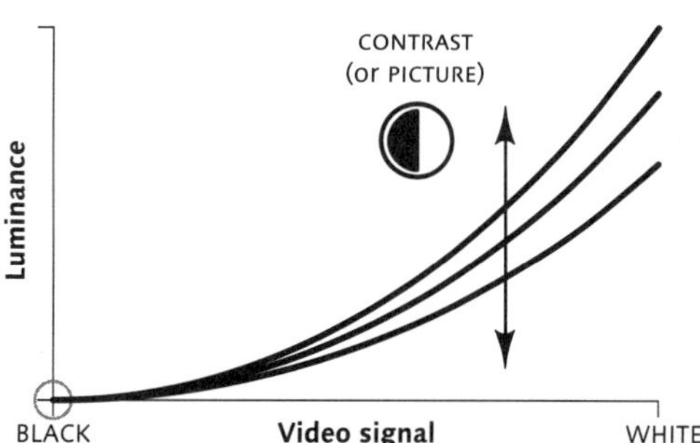

Figure 3.1 **CONTRAST control** determines the luminance (proportional to intensity) produced for white, with intermediate values toward black being scaled appropriately. In a well-designed monitor, adjusting CONTRAST maintains the correct black setting – ideally, zero input signal produces zero luminance at any CONTRAST setting.

Figure 3.2 BRIGHTNESS **control** has the effect of sliding the black-to-white video signal scale left and right along the 2.5-power function of the display. Here, BRIGHTNESS is set too high; a significant amount of luminance is produced at zero video signal level. No video signal can cause true black to be displayed, and the picture content rides on an overall pedestal of gray. Contrast ratio is degraded.

Figure 3.3 BRIGHTNESS **control is set correctly** when the reference black video signal level is placed precisely at the point of minimum perceptible light output at the display. In a perfectly dark viewing environment, the black signal would produce zero luminance; in practice, however, the setting is dependent upon the amount of ambient light in the viewing environment.

Figure 3.4 BRIGHTNESS **control set too low** causes a range of input signal levels near black to be reproduced "crushed" or "swallowed," reproduced indistinguishably from black. A cinematographer might describe this situation as "lack of details in the shadows," however, *all* information in the shadows is lost, not just the details.

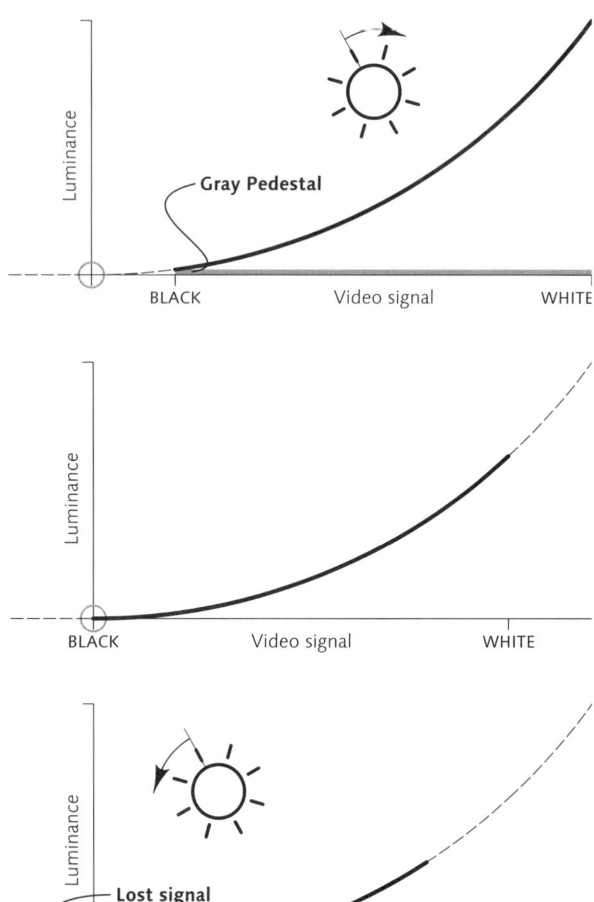

When BRIGHTNESS is set as high as indicated in Figure 3.2, the effective power law exponent is lowered from 2.5 to about 2.3; when set as low as in Figure 3.4, it is raised to about 2.7. For the implications of this fact, see page 84.

The BRIGHTNESS control – more sensibly called BLACK LEVEL – effectively slides the black-to-white range of the video signal along the power function of the display. It is implemented by introducing an offset – in electrical terms, a *bias* – into the video signal. Figure 3.3 (middle) sketches the situation when the BRIGHTNESS control is properly adjusted: Reference black signal level produces zero luminance. Misadjustment of BRIGHTNESS is a common cause of poor displayed-image quality. If BRIGHTNESS is set too high, as depicted in Figure 3.2 (top), contrast ratio suffers. If BRIGHTNESS is set too low, as depicted in Figure 3.4 (bottom), picture information near black is lost.

To set BRIGHTNESS (or BLACK LEVEL), first display a picture that is predominantly or entirely black. Set the control to its minimum, then increase its level until the display just begins to show a hint of dark gray. The setting is somewhat dependent upon ambient light. Modern display equipment is sufficiently stable that frequent adjustment is unnecessary.

SMPTE RP 71, *Setting Chromaticity and Luminance of White for Color Television Monitors Using Shadow-Mask Picture Tubes.*

Once BRIGHTNESS is set correctly, CONTRAST can be set to whatever level is appropriate for comfortable viewing, provided that clipping and blooming are avoided. In the studio, the CONTRAST control can be used to achieve the standard luminance of white, typically 103 $cd \cdot m^{-2}$.

In addition to having user controls that affect *R'G'B'* components equally, computer monitors, video monitors, and television receivers have separate red, green, and blue internal adjustments of gain (called DRIVE) and offset (called SCREEN, or sometimes CUTOFF). In a display, BRIGHTNESS (or BLACK LEVEL) is normally used to compensate for the display, not the input signal, and thus should be implemented following gain control.

In processing equipment, it is sometimes necessary to correct errors in black level in an input signal while maintaining unity gain: The BLACK LEVEL control should be implemented prior to the application of gain, and should not be called BRIGHTNESS. Figures 3.5 and 3.6 overleaf plot the transfer functions of CONTRAST and BRIGHTNESS controls in the video signal path, disregarding the typical 2.5-power function of the display.

LCD: liquid crystal display

LCD displays have controls labeled BRIGHTNESS and CONTRAST, but these controls have different functions than the like-named controls of a CRT display. In an LCD, the BRIGHTNESS control, or the control with that icon, typically alters the backlight luminance.

BRIGHTNESS and CONTRAST controls in desktop graphics

Adobe's Photoshop software established the de facto effect of BRIGHTNESS and CONTRAST controls in desktop graphics. Photoshop's BRIGHTNESS control is similar to the BRIGHTNESS control of video; however, Photoshop's CONTRAST differs dramatically from that of video.

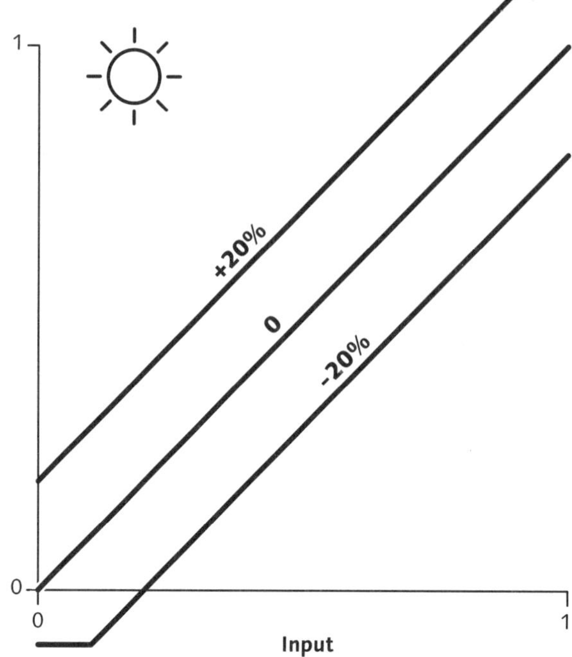

Figure 3.5 **Brightness (or black level) control in video** applies an offset, roughly ±20% of full scale, to *R'G'B'* components. Though this function is evidently a straight line, the input and output video signals are normally in the gamma-corrected (perceptual) domain; the values are *not* proportional to intensity. At the minimum and maximum settings, I show clipping to the Rec. 601 footroom of $-^{15}/_{219}$ and headroom of $^{238}/_{219}$. (Light power cannot go negative, but electrical and digital signals can.)

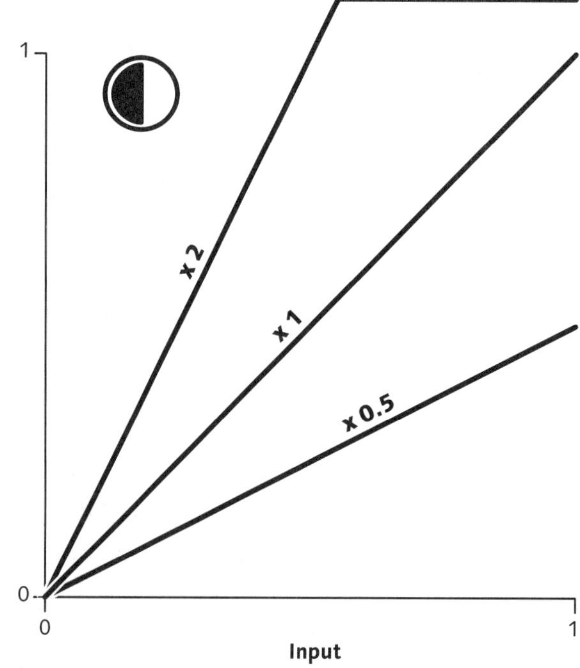

Figure 3.6 **Contrast (or video level) control in video** applies a gain factor between roughly 0.5 and 2.0 to *R'G'B'* components. The output signal clips if the result would fall outside the range allowed for the coding in use. Here I show clipping to the Rec. 601 headroom limit.

Figure 3.7 BRIGHTNESS **control in Photoshop** applies an offset of –100 to +100 to *R'G'B'* components ranging from 0 to 255. If a result falls outside the range 0 to 255, it saturates; headroom and footroom are absent. The function is evidently linear, but depending upon the image coding standard in use, the input and output values are generally nonlinearly related to luminance (or tristimulus values).

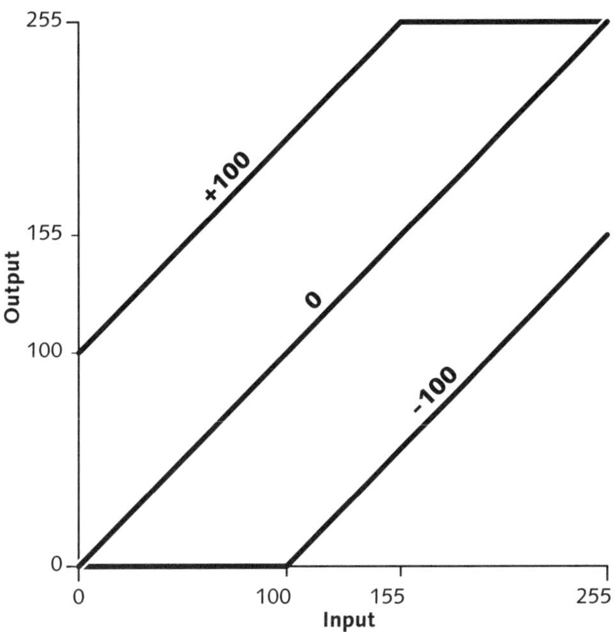

Figure 3.8 CONTRAST **control in Photoshop** subtracts 127.5 from the input, applies a gain factor between zero (for CONTRAST setting of –100) and infinity (for CONTRAST setting of +100), then adds 127.5, saturating if the result falls outside the range 0 to 255. This operation is very different from the action of the CONTRAST control in video.

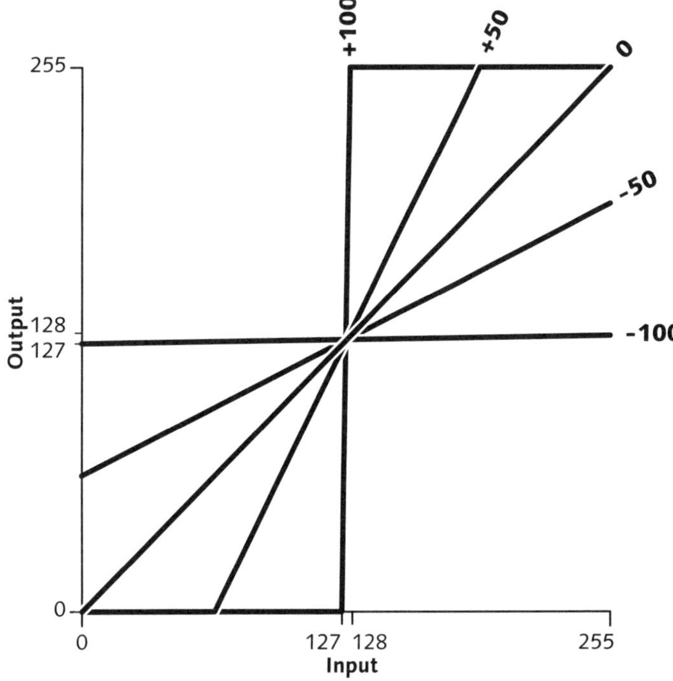

The transfer functions of Photoshop's controls are sketched in Figures 3.7 and 3.8. R', G', and B' component values in Photoshop are presented to the user as values between 0 and 255. BRIGHTNESS and CONTRAST controls have sliders ranging ±100.

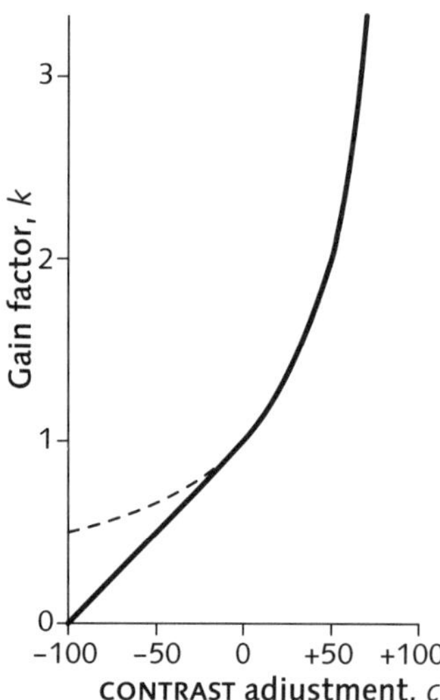

Figure 3.9 **Photoshop CONTRAST control's gain factor** depends upon CONTRAST setting according to this function.

Eq 3.1

$$k = \begin{cases} 1 + \dfrac{c}{100}, & -100 \le c < 0 \\ \dfrac{1}{1 - \dfrac{c}{100}}, & 0 \le c < 100 \end{cases}$$

BRIGHTNESS effects an offset between -100 and +100 on the R', G', and B' components. Any result outside the range 0 to 255 clips to the nearest extreme value, 0 or 255. Photoshop's BRIGHTNESS control is comparable to that of video, but its range (roughly ±40% of full scale) is greater than the typical video range (of about ±20%).

Photoshop's CONTRAST control follows the application of BRIGHTNESS; it applies a gain factor. Instead of leaving reference black (code zero) fixed, as a video CONTRAST control does, Photoshop "pivots" the gain adjustment around the midscale code. The transfer function for various settings of the control is graphed in Figure 3.8.

The gain available from Photoshop's CONTRAST control ranges from zero to infinity, far wider than video's typical range of 0.5 to 2. The function that relates Photoshop's CONTRAST to gain is graphed in Figure 3.9 in the margin. From the -100 setting to the 0 setting, gain ranges linearly from zero through unity. From the 0 setting to the +100 setting, gain ranges nonlinearly from unity to infinity, following a reciprocal curve; the curve is described by Equation 3.1.

The power function that relates Macintosh QuickDraw $R'G'B'$ components to intensity is explained on page 273.

$$0.58 = \frac{1.45}{2.5}$$

In desktop graphics applications such as Photoshop, image data is usually coded in a perceptually uniform manner, comparable to video $R'G'B'$. On a PC, $R'G'B'$ components are by default proportional to the 0.4-power of reproduced luminance (or tristimulus) values. On Macintosh computers, QuickDraw $R'G'B'$ components are by default proportional to the 0.58-power of displayed luminance (or tristimulus). However, on both PC and Macintosh computers, the user, system software, or application software can set the transfer function to nonstandard functions – perhaps even linear-light coding – as I will describe in *Gamma*, on page 257.

Raster images in computing 4

This chapter places video into the context of computing. Images in computing are represented in three forms, depicted schematically in the three rows of Figure 4.1 overleaf: *symbolic image description, raster image,* and *compressed image*.

- **A symbolic image description** does not directly contain an image, but contains a high-level 2-D or 3-D geometric description of an image, such as its objects and their properties. A two-dimensional image in this form is sometimes called a *vector graphic*, though its primitive objects are usually much more complex than the straight-line segments suggested by the word *vector*.

- **A raster image** enumerates the grayscale or color content of each pixel directly, in scan-line order. There are four fundamental types of raster image: *bilevel, pseudocolor, grayscale,* and *truecolor*. A fifth type, *hicolor*, is best considered as a variant of truecolor. In Figure 4.1, the five types are arranged in columns, from low quality at the left to high quality at the right.

- **A compressed image** originates with raster image data, but the data has been processed to reduce storage and/or transmission requirements. The bottom row of Figure 4.1 indicates several compression methods. At the left are lossless (data) compression methods, generally applicable to bilevel and pseudocolor image data; at the right are lossy (image) compression methods, generally applicable to grayscale and truecolor.

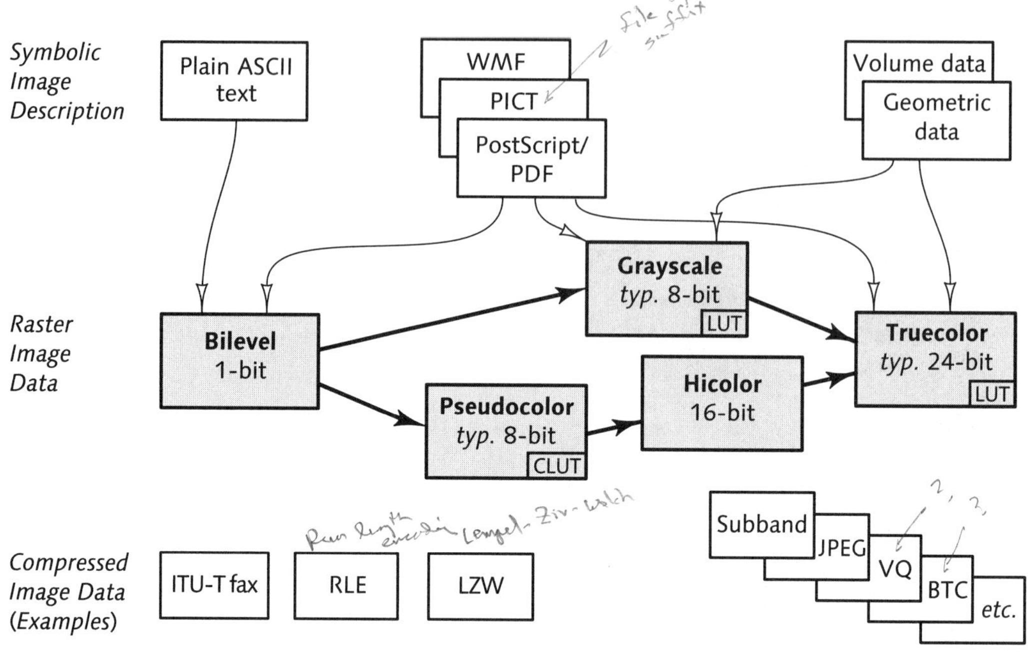

Figure 4.1 **Raster image data** may be captured directly, or may be rendered from symbolic image data. Traversal from left to right corresponds to conversions that can be accomplished without loss. Some raster image formats are associated with a lookup table (LUT) or color lookup table (CLUT).

The grayscale, pseudocolor, and truecolor systems used in computing involve lookup tables (LUTs) that map pixel values into monitor *R'G'B'* values. Most computing systems use perceptually uniform image coding; however, some systems use linear-light coding, and some systems use other techniques. For a system to operate in a perceptually uniform manner, similar to or compatible with video, its LUTs need to be loaded with suitable transfer functions. If the LUTs are loaded with transfer functions that cause code values to be proportional to intensity, then the advantages of perceptual uniformity will be diminished or lost.

Murray, James D., and William vanRyper, *Encyclopedia of Graphics File Formats,* Second Edition (Sebastopol, Calif.: O'Reilly & Associates, 1996).

Many different file formats are in use for each of these representations. Discussion of file formats is outside the scope of this book. To convey photographic-quality color images, a file format must accommodate *at least* 24 bits per pixel. To make maximum perceptual use of a limited number of bits per component, nonlinear coding should be used, as I outlined on page 12.

Symbolic image description

Many methods are used to describe the content of a picture at a level of abstraction higher than directly enumerating the value of each pixel. Symbolic image data is converted to a raster image by the process of *rasterizing*. Images are *rasterized* (or *imaged* or *rendered*) by interpreting symbolic data and producing raster image data. In Figure 4.1, this operation passes information from the top row to the middle row.

Geometric data describes the position, size, orientation, and other attributes of objects; 3-D geometric data may be interpreted to produce an image from a particular viewpoint. Rasterizing from geometric data is called *rendering;* truecolor images are usually produced.

Adobe's PostScript system is widely used to represent 2-D illustrations, typographic elements, and publications. PostScript is essentially a programming language specialized for imaging operations. When a PostScript file is executed by a PostScript interpreter, the image is rendered. (In PostScript, the rasterizing operation is often called raster image processing, or *RIPping*.)

Once rasterized, raster image data generally cannot be transformed back into a symbolic description: A raster image – in the middle row of Figure 4.1 – generally cannot be returned to its description in the top row. If your application involves rendered images, you may find it useful to retain the symbolic data even after rendering, in case the need arises to rerender the image, at a different size, perhaps, or to perform a modification such as removing an object.

Images from a fax machine, a video camera, or a grayscale or color scanner originate in raster image form: No symbolic description is available. Optical character recognition (OCR) and raster-to-vector techniques make brave but generally unsatisfying attempts to extract text or geometric data from raster images.

Raster images

There are four distinct types of raster image data:

- *Bilevel*, by definition 1 bit per pixel
- *Grayscale*, typically 8 bits per pixel
- *Truecolor*, typically 24 bits per pixel
- *Pseudocolor*, typically 8 bits per pixel

Hicolor, with 16 bits per pixel, is a variant of truecolor.

Grayscale and truecolor systems are capable of representing continuous tone. Video systems use only truecolor (and perhaps grayscale as a special case).

In the following sections, I will explain bilevel, grayscale, hicolor, truecolor, and pseudocolor in turn. Each description is accompanied by a block diagram that represents the hardware at the back end of the framebuffer or graphics card (including the *digital-to-analog converter*, DAC). Alternatively, you can consider each block diagram to represent an algorithm that converts image data to monitor R', G', and B' components.

Bilevel

Each pixel of a bilevel (or two-level) image comprises one bit, which represents either black or white – but nothing in between. In computing this is often called *monochrome*. (That term ought to denote shades of a single hue; however, in common usage – and particularly in video – *monochrome* denotes the black-and-white, or grayscale, component of an image.)

Since the invention of data communications, binary zero (0) has been known as *space*, and binary one (1) has been known as *mark*. A "mark" on a CRT emits light, so in video and in computer graphics a binary one (or the maximum code value) conventionally represents white. In printing, a "mark" deposits ink on the page, so in printing a binary one (or in grayscale, the maximum pixel value) conventionally represents black.

Grayscale

A grayscale image represents an effectively continuous range of tones, from black, through intermediate shades of gray, to white. A grayscale system with a sufficient number of bits per pixel, 8 bits or more, can represent a black-and-white photograph. A grayscale system may or may not have a lookup table (LUT); it may or may not be perceptually uniform.

In printing, a grayscale image is said to have *continuous tone*, or *contone* (distinguished from *line art* or *type*). When a contone image is printed, *halftoning* is ordinarily used.

Hicolor

Hicolor graphics systems store 16-bit pixels, partitioned into *R'*, *G'*, and *B'* components. Two schemes are in use. In the *5-5-5* scheme, sketched in Figure 4.2 below, each pixel comprises 5 bits for each of red, green, and blue. (One bit remains unused, or is used as a one-bit transparency mask – a crude "alpha" component. See page 334.) In the *5-6-5* scheme, sketched in Figure 4.3 below, each pixel comprises 5 bits of red, 6 bits of green, and 5 bits of blue.

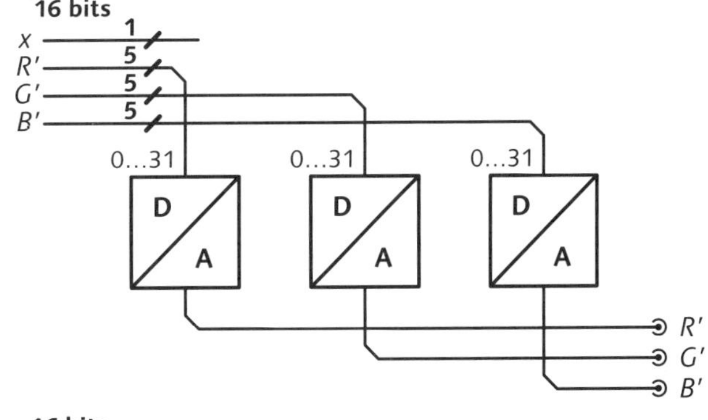

Figure 4.2 **Hicolor (16-bit, 5-5-5) graphics** provides 2^{15}, or 32768 colors ("thousands of colors"). Note the absence of LUTs: Image data is perceptually coded, relying upon the implicit 2.5-power function of the monitor. D/A signifies digital-to-analog conversion.

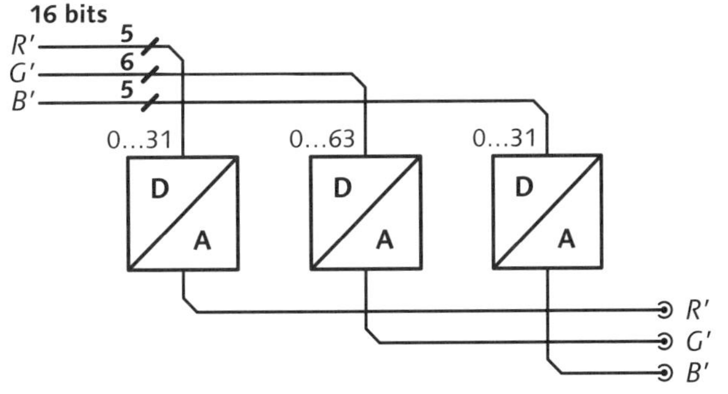

Figure 4.3 **Hicolor (16-bit, 5-6-5) graphics** provides 2^{16}, or 65536 colors. Like the 5-5-5 scheme, image data is perceptually coded. An extra bit is assigned to the green channel.

R′G′B′ codes in hicolor systems are directly applied to the DACs, and are linearly translated into monitor voltage with no intervening LUT. The response of the monitor produces luminance proportional to the 2.5-power of voltage. So, hicolor image coding is perceptually uniform, comparable to video *R′G′B′* coding. However, 32 (or even 64) gradations of each component are insufficient for photographic-quality images.

Truecolor

A truecolor system has separate red, green, and blue components for each pixel. In most truecolor systems, each component is represented by a *byte* of 8 bits: Each pixel has 24 bits of color information, so this mode is often called "24-bit color" (or "millions of colors"). The *RGB* values of each pixel can represent 2^{24}, or about 16.7 million, distinct codes. In computing, a truecolor framebuffer usually has three *lookup tables* (LUTs), one for each component. The LUTs and DACs of a 24-bit truecolor system are sketched in Figure 4.4 below.

Most truecolor systems have LUTs as by-products of their capability to handle pseudocolor, where like-sized CLUTs are necessary.

The mapping from image code value to monitor voltage is determined by the content of the LUTs. Owing to the perceptually uniform nature of the monitor, the best perceptual use is generally made of truecolor pixel values when each LUT contains an identity function ("ramp") that maps input to output, unchanged.

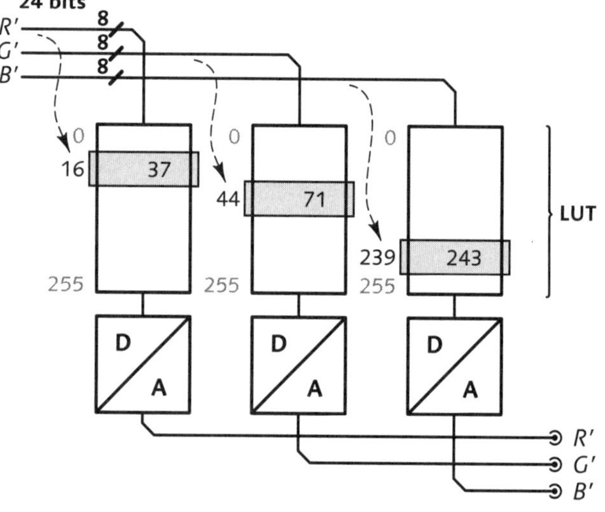

Figure 4.4 **Truecolor (24-bit) graphics** usually involves three programmable lookup tables (LUTs). The numerical values shown here are from the default Macintosh LUT. In video, *R′G′B′* values are transmitted to the DACs with no intervening lookup table. To make a truecolor computer system display video properly, the LUTs must be loaded with ramps that map input to output unchanged.

In computing, the LUTs can be set to implement an arbitrary mapping from code value to tristimulus value (and so, to intensity). The total number of pixel values that represent distinguishable colors depends upon the transfer function used. If the LUT implements a power function to impose gamma correction on linear-light data, then the code-100 problem will be at its worst. With 24-bit color and a properly chosen transfer function, photographic quality images can be displayed and geometric objects can be rendered smoothly shaded with sufficiently high quality for many applications. But if the LUTs are set for linear-light representation with 8 bits per component, contouring will be evident in many images, as I mentioned on page 12. Having 24-bit truecolor is *not* a guarantee of good image quality. If a scanner claims to have 30 bits (or 36 bits) per pixel, obviously each component has 10 bits (or 12 bits). However, it makes a great deal of difference whether these values are coded physically (as linear- light luminance, loosely "intensity"), or coded perceptually (as a quantity comparable to lightness).

Poynton, Charles, "The rehabilitation of *gamma*," in Rogowitz, B.E., and T.N. Pappas, eds., *Human Vision and Electronic Imaging III*, Proc. SPIE/IS&T Conf. 3299 (Bellingham, Wash.: SPIE, 1998).

In video, either the LUTs are absent, or each is set to the identity function. Studio video systems are effectively permanently wired in truecolor mode with perceptually uniform coding: Code values are presented directly to the DACs, without intervening lookup tables.

It is easiest to design a framebuffer memory system where each pixel has a number of bytes that is a power of two; so, a truecolor framebuffer often has four bytes per pixel – "32-bit color." Three bytes comprise the red, green, and blue color components; the fourth byte is used for purposes other than representing color. The fourth byte may contain overlay information. Alternatively, it may store an *alpha* component (α) representing opacity from zero (fully transparent) to unity (fully opaque). In computer graphics, the alpha component conventionally multiplies components that are coded in the linear-light domain. In video, the corresponding component is called *linear key*, but the key signal is not typically proportional to tristimulus value (linear light) – instead, *linear* refers to code level, which is nonlinearly related to intensity.

Concerning alpha, see page 334.

Figure 4.5 **Pseudocolor (8-bit) graphics** systems use a limited number of integers, usually 0 through 255, to represent colors. Each pixel value is processed through a *color lookup table* (CLUT) to obtain red, green, and blue output values to be delivered to the monitor.

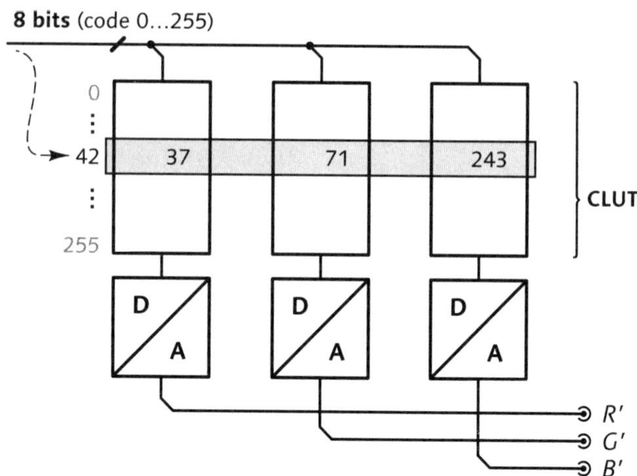

Pseudocolor

In a *pseudocolor* (or *indexed color*, or *colormapped*) system, several bits – usually 8 – comprise each pixel in an image or framebuffer. This provides a moderate number of unique codes – usually 256 – for each pixel. Pseudocolor involves "painting by numbers," where the number of colors is rather small. In an 8-bit pseudocolor system, any particular image, or the content of the framebuffer at any instant in time, is limited to a selection of just 2^8 (or 256) colors from the universe of available colors.

I reserve the term *CLUT* for pseudocolor. In grayscale and truecolor systems, the LUTs store transfer functions, not colors. In Macintosh, pseudocolor CLUT values are roughly, but not optimally, perceptually coded.

Each code value is used as an index into a *color lookup table* (CLUT, *colormap*, or *palette*) that retrieves *R'G'B'* components; the DAC translates these linearly into voltage levels that are applied to the monitor. (Macintosh is an exception: Image data read from the CLUT is in effect passed through a second LUT.) Pseudocolor CLUT values are effectively perceptually coded.

The CLUT and DACs of an 8-bit pseudocolor system are sketched in Figure 4.5 above. A typical lookup table retrieves 8-bit values for each of red, green, and blue, so each of the 256 different colors can be chosen from a universe of 2^{24}, or 16777216, colors. (The CLUT may return 4, 6, or more than 8 bits for each component.)

Pseudocolor image data is always accompanied by the associated colormap (or *palette*). The colormap may be fixed, independent of the image, or it may be specific to the particular image (*adaptive* or *optimized*).

The browser-safe palette forms a radix-6 number system with *RGB* digits valued 0 through 5.

$216 = 6^3$

A popular choice for a fixed CLUT is the *browser safe* palette comprising the 216 colors formed by combinations of 8-bit *R'*, *G'*, and *B'* values chosen from the set {0, 51, 102, 153, 204, 255}. This set of 216 colors fits nicely within an 8-bit pseudocolor CLUT; the colors are perceptually distributed throughout the *R'G'B'* cube.

Pseudocolor is appropriate for images such as maps, schematic diagrams, or cartoons, where each color or combination is either completely present or completely absent at any point in the image. In a typical CLUT, adjacent pseudocolor codes are generally completely unrelated; for example, the color assigned to code 42 has no necessary relationship to the color assigned to code 43.

Conversion among types

In Figure 4.1, traversal from left to right corresponds to conversions that can be accomplished without loss.

Disregarding pseudocolor for the moment, data in any of the other four schemes of Figure 4.1 can be "widened" to any scheme to the right simply by assigning the codes appropriately. For example, a grayscale image can be widened to truecolor by assigning codes from black to white. Widening adds bits but not information.

A pseudocolor image can be converted to hicolor or truecolor through software application of the CLUT. Conversion to hicolor is subject to the limited number of colors available in hicolor mode. Conversion to truecolor can be accomplished without loss, provided that the truecolor LUTs are sensible.

Concerning conversions in the reverse direction, an image can be "narrowed" without loss only if it contains only the colors or shades available in the mode to its left in Figure 4.1; otherwise, the conversion will involve loss of shades and/or loss of colors.

Ashdown, Ian, *Color Quantization Bibliography*, Internet, <ftp://ftp.ledalite.com/pub/cquant97.bib>

A truecolor or hicolor image can be approximated in pseudocolor through software application of a fixed colormap. Alternatively, a *colormap quantization* algorithm can be used to examine a particular image (or sequence of images), and compute a colormap that is optimized or adapted for that image or sequence.

Display modes

Figure 4.6
Display modes

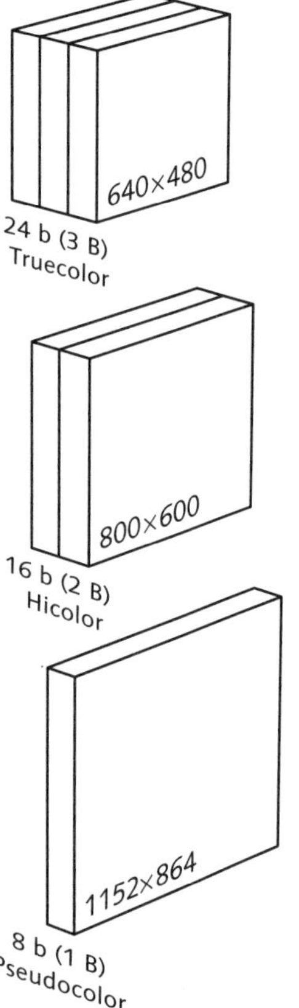

A high data rate is necessary to refresh a PC or workstation display from graphics memory. Consequently, graphics memory has traditionally been implemented with specialized "video RAM" (VRAM) devices. A low-cost graphics adapter generally has a limited amount of this specialized memory, perhaps just one or two megabytes. Recently, it has become practical for graphics adapters to refresh from main memory (DRAM); this relaxes the graphics memory capacity constraint.

Modern PC graphics subsystems are programmable among pseudocolor, hicolor, and truecolor modes. (Bilevel and grayscale have generally fallen into disuse.) The modes available in a typical system are restricted by the amount of graphics memory available. Figure 4.6 sketches the three usual modes available in a system having one megabyte (1 MB) of VRAM.

The top sketch illustrates truecolor (24 bits per pixel) operation. With just 1 MB of VRAM the pixel count will be limited to ⅓ megapixel, 640×480 ("VGA"). The advantage is that this mode gives access to millions of colors simultaneously.

To increase pixel count to half a megapixel with just 1 MB of VRAM, the number of bits per pixel must be reduced from 24. The middle sketch shows hicolor (16 bit per pixel) mode, which increases the pixel count to ½ megapixel, 800×600. However, the display is now limited to just 65536 colors at any instant.

To obtain a one-megapixel display, say 1152×864, pixel depth is limited by 1 MB of VRAM to just 8 bits. This forces the use of pseudocolor mode, and limits the number of possible colors at any instant to just 256.

In addition to constraining the relationship between pixel count and pixel depth, a display system may constrain the maximum pixel rate. A pixel rate constraint – 100 megapixels per second, for example – may limit the refresh rate at high pixel counts.

A computer specialist might refer to display pixel count, such as 640×480, 800×600, or 1152×864, as "resolution." An image scientist gives *resolution* a much more specific meaning; see *Resolution,* on page 65.

Image files

Images in bilevel, grayscale, pseudocolor, or truecolor formats can be stored in files. A general-purpose image file format stores, in its header information, the count of columns and rows of pixels in the image.

Image width is the product of so-called resolution and the count of image columns; height is computed similarly from the count of image rows.

Many file formats – such as TIFF and EPS – store information about the intended size of the image. The intended image width and height can be directly stored, in absolute units such as inches or millimeters. Alternatively, the file can store sample density in units of *pixels per inch* (ppi), or less clearly, *dots per inch* (dpi). Sample density is often confusingly called "resolution."

A *point* is a unit of distance equal to 1⁄72 inch. The width of the stem of this bold letter **I** is one point, about 0.353 mm (that is, 353 μm).

In some software packages, such as Adobe Illustrator, the intended image size coded in a file is respected. In other software, such as Adobe Photoshop, viewing at 100% implies a 1:1 relationship between file pixels and display device pixels, disregarding the number of pixels per inch in the file and of the display. Image files without size information are often treated as having 72 pixels per inch; application software unaware of image size information often uses a default of 72 ppi.

"Resolution" in computer graphics

In computer graphics, a pixel is often associated with an intensity distribution uniformly covering a small square area of the screen. In liquid crystal displays (LCDs), plasma display panels (PDPs), and digital micromirror displays (DMDs), discrete pixels such as these are constructed on the display device. When such a display is driven digitally at native pixel count, there is a one-to-one relationship between framebuffer pixels and device pixels. However, a graphic subsystem may resample by primitive means when faced with a mismatch between framebuffer pixel count and display device pixel count. If framebuffer count is higher, pixels are dropped; if lower, pixels are replicated. In both instances, image quality suffers.

CRT displays typically have a Gaussian distribution of light from each pixel, as I will discuss in the next chapter. The typical spot size is such that there is some overlap in the distributions of light from adjacent pixels. You might think that overlap between the distributions of light produced by neighboring display elements, as in a CRT, is undesirable. However, image display requires a certain degree of overlap in order to minimize the visibility of pixel structure or scan-line structure. I will discuss this issue in *Image structure,* on page 43.

Two disparate measures are referred to as *resolution* in computing:

- The count of image columns and image rows – that is, columns and rows of pixels – in a framebuffer

- The number of pixels per inch (ppi) intended for image data (often misleadingly denoted dots per inch, dpi)

An image scientist considers *resolution* to be delivered to the viewer; resolution is properly estimated from information displayed at the display surface (or screen) itself. The two measures above all limit resolution, but neither of them quantifies resolution directly. In *Resolution,* on page 65, I will describe how the term is used in image science and video.

Image structure 5

A naive approach to digital imaging treats the image as a matrix of independent pixels, disregarding the spatial distribution of light intensity across each pixel. You might think that optimum image quality is obtained when there is no overlap between the distributions of neighboring pixels; many computer engineers hold this view. However, continuous-tone images are best reproduced if there is a certain degree of overlap; sharpness is reduced slightly, but pixel structure is made less visible and image quality is improved.

Don't confuse PSF with *progressive segmented-frame* (PsF), described on page 62.

The distribution of intensity across a displayed pixel is referred to as its *point spread function* (PSF). A one-dimensional slice through the center of a PSF is colloquially called a *spot profile.* A display's PSF influences the nature of the images it reproduces. The effects of a PSF can be analyzed using filter theory, which I will discuss for one dimension in the chapter *Filtering and sampling,* on page 141, and for two dimensions in *Image digitization and reconstruction,* on page 187. A pixel whose intensity distribution uniformly covers a small square area of the screen has a point spread function referred to as a "box." PSFs used in continuous-tone imaging systems usually peak at the center of the pixel, fall off over a small distance, and overlap neighboring pixels to some extent.

Figure 5.1 **"Box" reconstruction** of a bitmapped graphic image is shown.

Image reconstruction

Figure 5.1 reproduces a portion of a bitmapped (bilevel) graphic image, part of a computer's desktop display. Each sample is either black or white. The element with horizontal "stripes" is part of a window's titlebar; the checkerboard background is intended to integrate to gray. Figure 5.1 shows reconstruction of the image with a "box" distribution. Each pixel is uniformly shaded across its extent; there is no overlap between pixels. This typifies an image as displayed on an LCD.

Figure 5.2 **Gaussian reconstruction** is shown for the same bitmapped image as Figure 5.1. I will detail the one-dimensional *Gaussian function* on page 150.

A CRT's electron gun produces an electron beam that illuminates a spot on the phosphor screen. The beam is deflected to form a raster pattern of scan lines that traces the entire screen, as I will describe in the following chapter. The beam is not perfectly focused when it is emitted from the CRT's electron gun, and is dispersed further in transit to the phosphor screen. Intensity produced for each pixel at the face of the screen has a "bell-shaped" distribution resembling a two-dimensional Gaussian function. With a typical amount of spot overlap, the checkerboard area of this example will display as a nearly uniform gray as depicted in Figure 5.2 in the margin. You might think that the blur caused by overlap between pixels would diminish image quality. However, for continuous-tone ("contone") images, some degree of overlap is not only desirable but necessary, as you will see from the following examples.

Figure 5.3 at the top of the facing page shows a 16×20-pixel image of a dark line, slightly more than one pixel wide, at an angle 7.2° off-vertical. At the left, the image data is reconstructed using a box distribution. The jagged and "ropey" nature of the reproduction is evident. At the right, the image data is reconstructed using a Gaussian. It is blurry, but less jagged.

Figure 5.4 in the middle of the facing page shows two ways to reconstruct the same 16×20 pixels (320 bytes) of continuous-tone grayscale image data. The left-hand image is reconstructed using a box function, and the right-hand image with a Gaussian. I constructed this example so that each image is 4 cm (1.6 inches) wide. At typical reading distance of 40 cm (16 inches), a pixel subtends 0.4°, where visual acuity is near its maximum. At this distance, when reconstructed with a box function, the pixel structure of each image is highly visible;

I introduced visual acuity on page 8. For details, see *Contrast sensitivity function (CSF)*, on page 201.

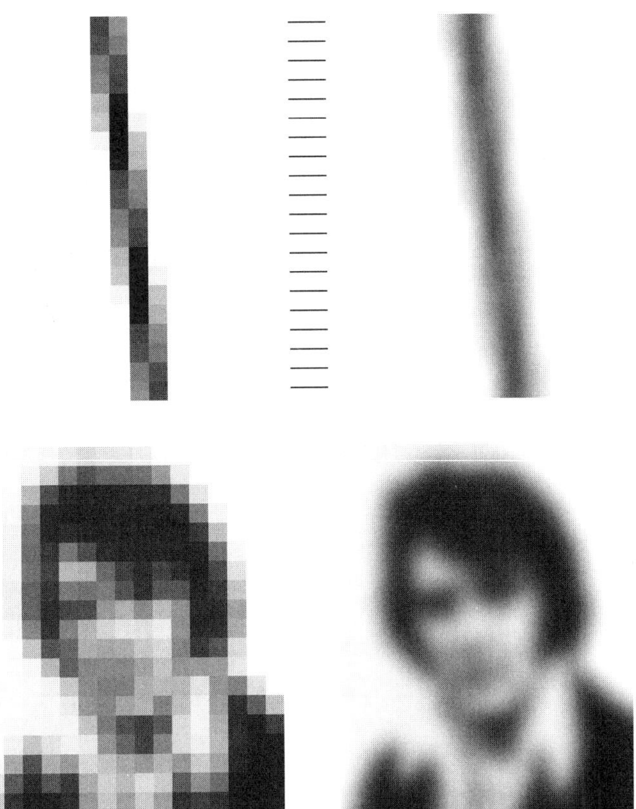

Figure 5.3 **Diagonal line reconstruction.** At the left is a near-vertical line slightly more than 1 pixel wide, rendered as an array 20 pixels high that has been reconstructed using a box distribution. At the right, the line is reconstructed using a Gaussian distribution. Between the images I have placed a set of markers to indicate the vertical centers of the image rows.

Figure 5.4 **Contone image reconstruction.** At the left is a continuous-tone image of 16×20 pixels that has been reconstructed using a box distribution. The pictured individual cannot be recognized. At the right is exactly the same image data, but reconstructed by a Gaussian function. The reconstructed image is very blurry but recognizable. Which reconstruction function do you think is best for continuous-tone imaging?

visibility of the pixel structure overwhelms the perception of the image itself. The bottom right image is reconstructed using a Gaussian distribution. It is blurry, but easily recognizable as an American cultural icon. This example shows that sharpness is not always good, and blurriness is not always bad!

Figure 5.5 **One frame of an animated sequence**

Figure 5.5 in the margin shows a 16×20-pixel image comprising 20 copies of the top row of Figure 5.3 (left). Consider a sequence of 20 animated frames, where each frame is formed from successive image rows of Figure 5.3. The animation would depict a narrow vertical line drifting rightward across the screen at a rate of 1 pixel every 8 frames. If image rows of Figure 5.3 (left) were used, the width of the moving line would appear to jitter frame-to-frame, and the minimum lightness would vary. With Gaussian reconstruction, as in Figure 5.3 (right), motion portrayal is much smoother.

Sampling aperture

In a practical image sensor, each element acquires information from a finite region of the image plane; the value of each pixel is a function of the distribution of intensity over that region. The distribution of sensitivity across a pixel of an image capture device is referred to as its *sampling aperture,* sort of a PSF in reverse – you could call it a point "collection" function. The sampling aperture influences the nature of the image signal originated by a sensor. Sampling apertures used in continuous-tone imaging systems usually peak at the center of each pixel, fall off over a small distance, and overlap neighboring pixels to some extent.

In 1915, Harry Nyquist published a landmark paper stating that a sampled analog signal cannot be reconstructed accurately unless all of its frequency components are contained strictly within half the sampling frequency. This condition subsequently became known as the *Nyquist criterion;* half the sampling rate became known as the *Nyquist rate.* Nyquist developed his theorem for one-dimensional signals, but it has been extended to two dimensions. In a digital system, it takes at least two elements – two pixels or two scanning lines – to represent a cycle. A *cycle* is equivalent to a *line pair* of film, or two "TV lines" (TVL).

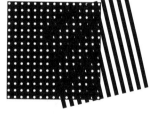

Figure 5.6 **Moiré pattern** a form of aliasing in two dimensions, results when a sampling pattern (here the perforated square) has a sampling density that is too low for the image content (here the dozen bars, 14° off-vertical). This figure is adapted from Fig. 3.12 of Wandell's *Foundations of Vision* (cited on page 195).

In Figure 5.6 in the margin, the black square punctured by a regular array of holes represents a grid of small sampling apertures. Behind the sampling grid is a set of a dozen black bars, tilted 14° off the vertical, representing image information. In the region where the image is sampled, you can see three wide dark bars tilted at 45°. Those bars represent spatial *aliases* that arise because the number of bars per inch (or mm) in the image is greater than half the number of apertures per inch (or mm) in the sampling lattice. Aliasing can be prevented – or at least minimized – by imposing a spatial filter in front of the sampling process, as I will describe for one-dimensional signals in *Filtering and sampling,* on page 141, and for two dimensions in *Image presampling filters,* on page 192.

Nyquist explained that an arbitrary signal can be reconstructed accurately only if more than two samples are taken of the highest-frequency component of the signal. Applied to an image, there must be at least twice as many samples per unit distance as there are image elements. The checkerboard pattern in Figure 5.1 (on page 43) doesn't meet this criterion in either the vertical or horizontal dimensions. Furthermore, the titlebar element doesn't meet the criterion vertically. Such elements can be represented in a bilevel image only when they are in precise registration – "locked" – to the imaging system's sampling grid. However, images captured from reality almost never have their elements precisely aligned with the grid!

Figure 5.7 **Bitmapped graphic image, rotated**

Point sampling refers to capture with an infinitesimal sampling aperture. This is undesirable in continuous-tone imaging. Figure 5.7 in the margin shows what would happen if a physical scene like that in Figure 5.1 were rotated 14°, captured with a point-sampled camera, and displayed with a box distribution. The alternating on-off elements are rendered with aliasing in both the checkerboard portion and the titlebar. (Aliasing would be evident even if this image were to be reconstructed with a Gaussian.) This example emphasizes that in digital imaging, we must represent arbitrary scenes, not just scenes whose elements have an intimate relationship with the sampling grid.

A suitable presampling filter would prevent (or at least minimize) the Moiré artifact of Figure 5.6, and prevent or minimize the aliasing of Figure 5.7. When image content such as the example titlebar and the desktop pattern of Figure 5.2 is presented to a presampling filter, blurring will occur. Considering only bitmapped images such as Figure 5.1, you might think the blurring to be detrimental, but to avoid spatial aliasing in capturing high-quality continuous-tone imagery, some overlap is necessary in the distribution of sensitivity across neighboring sensor elements.

Having introduced the aliasing artifact that results from poor capture PSFs, we can now return to the display and discuss reconstruction PSFs (spot profiles).

Spot profile

The designer of a display system for continuous-tone images seeks to make a display that allows viewing at a wide picture angle, with minimal intrusion of artifacts such as aliasing or visible scan-line or pixel structure. Picture size, viewing distance, spot profile, and scan-line or pixel visibility all interact. The display system designer cannot exert direct control over viewing distance; spot profile is the parameter available for optimization.

On page 45, I demonstrated the difference between a box profile and a Gaussian profile. Figures 5.3 and 5.4 showed that some overlap between neighboring distributions is desirable, even though blur is evident when the reproduced image is viewed closely.

When the images of Figure 5.3 or 5.4 are viewed from a distance of 10 m (33 feet), a pixel subtends a minute of arc ($1/60°$). At this distance, owing to the limited acuity of human vision, both pairs of images are apparently identical. Imagine placing beside these images an emissive display having an infinitesimal spot, producing the same total flux for a perfectly white pixel. At 10 m, the pixel structure of the emissive display would be somewhat visible. At a great viewing distance – say at a pixel or scan-line subtense of less than $1/180°$, corresponding to SDTV viewed at three times normal distance – the limited acuity of the human visual system causes all three displays to appear identical. As the viewer moves closer, different effects become apparent, depending upon spot profile. I'll discuss two cases: Box distribution and Gaussian distribution.

Box distribution

A typical digital projector – such as an LCD or a DMD – has a spot profile resembling a box distribution covering nearly the entire width and nearly the entire height corresponding to the pixel pitch. There is no significant gap between image rows or image columns. Each pixel has three color components, but the optics of the projection device are arranged to cause the distribution of light from these components to be overlaid. From a great distance, pixel structure will not be visible. However, as viewing distance decreases, aliasing ("the jaggies") will intrude. Limited performance of projection lenses mitigates aliasing somewhat; however, aliasing can be quite noticeable, as in the examples of Figures 5.3 and 5.4 on page 45.

In a typical direct-view digital display, such as an LCD or a PDP, each pixel comprises three color components that occupy distinct regions of the area corresponding to each pixel. Ordinarily, these components are side-by-side. There is no significant gap between image rows. However, if one component (say green) is turned on and the others are off, there is a gap between columns. These systems rely upon the limited acuity of the viewer to integrate the components into a single colored area. At a close viewing distance, the gap can be visible, and this can induce aliasing.

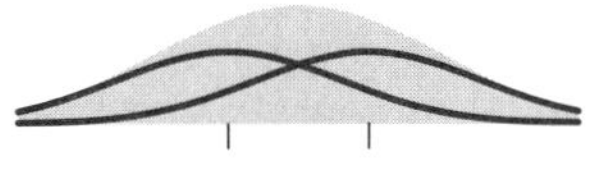

The viewing distance of a display using a box distribution, such as a direct-view LCD or PDP, is limited by the intrusion of aliasing.

Gaussian distribution

As I have mentioned, a CRT display has a spot profile resembling a Gaussian. The CRT designer's choice of spot size involves a compromise illustrated by Figure 5.8.

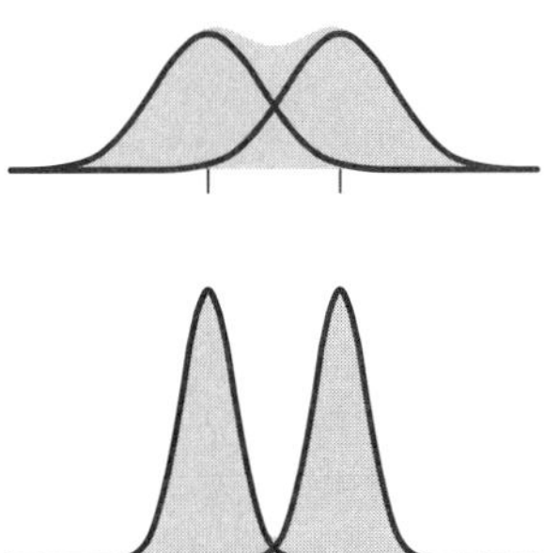

Figure 5.8 **Gaussian spot size.** Solid lines graph Gaussian distributions of intensity across two adjacent image rows, for three values of spot size. The areas under each curve are identical. The shaded areas indicate their sums. In progressive scanning, adjacent image rows correspond to consecutive scan lines. In interlaced scanning, to be described in the following chapter, the situation is more complex.

- For a Gaussian distribution with a very small spot, say a spot width less than $1/2$ the scan-line pitch, line structure will become evident even at a fairly large viewing distance.

- For a Gaussian distribution with medium-sized spot, say a spot width approximately equal to the scan-line pitch, the onset of scan-line visibility will occur at a closer distance than with a small spot.

- As spot size is increased beyond about twice the scan-line pitch, eventually the spot becomes so large that no further improvement in line-structure visibility is achieved by making it larger. However, there is a serious disadvantage to making the spot larger than necessary: Sharpness is reduced.

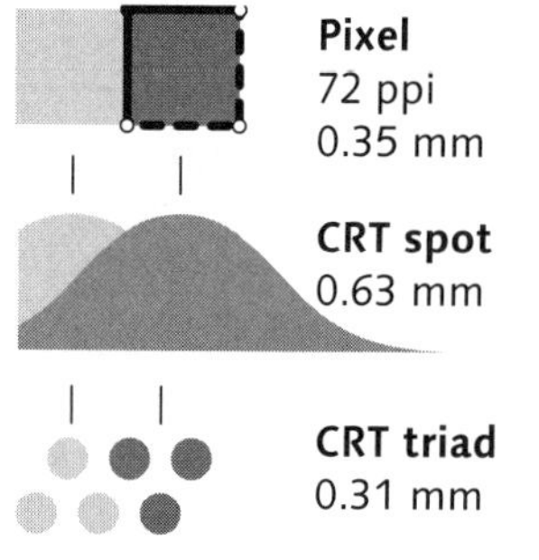

Figure 5.9 **Pixel/spot/triad.** *Triad* refers to the smallest complete set of red-producing, green-producing, and blue-producing elements of a display. CRT triads have no direct relationship to pixels; what is usually called *dot pitch* is properly called *triad pitch*.

A direct-view color CRT display has several hundred thousand, or perhaps a million or more, *triads* of red, green, and blue phosphor dots deposited onto the back of the display panel. (A Sony Trinitron CRT has a thousand or more vertical stripes of red, green, and blue phosphor.) *Triad pitch* is the shortest distance between like-colored triads (or stripes), ordinarily expressed in millimeters. There is not a one-to-one relationship between pixels and triads (or stripes). A typical CRT has a Gaussian spot whose width exceeds both the distance between pixels and the distance between triads. Ideally, there are many more triads (or stripes) across the image width than there are pixels – 1.2 times as many, or more.

You saw at the beginning of this chapter that in order to avoid visible pixel structure in image display some overlap is necessary in the distributions of light produced by neighboring display elements. Such overlap reduces sharpness, but by how much? How much overlap is necessary? I will discuss these issues in the Chapter *Resolution*, on page 65. First, though, I introduce the fundamentals of raster scanning.

Raster scanning 6

I introduced the pixel array on page 6. In video, the samples of the pixel array are sequenced uniformly in time to form scan lines, which are in turn sequenced in time throughout each frame interval. This chapter outlines the basics of this process of *raster scanning.* In Chapter 11, *Introduction to component SDTV,* on page 95, I will present details on scanning in conventional "525-line" and "625-line" video. In *Introduction to composite NTSC and PAL,* on page 103, I will introduce the color coding used in these systems. In Chapter 13, *Introduction to HDTV,* on page 111, I will introduce scanning in high-definition television.

Flicker, refresh rate, and frame rate

A sequence of still pictures, captured and displayed at a sufficiently high rate, can create the illusion of motion.

Flicker is sometimes redundantly called *large-area flicker*. Take care to distinguish *flicker*, described here, from *twitter*, to be described on page 57. See Fukuda, Tadahiko, "Some Characteristics of Peripheral Vision," *NHK Tech. Monograph No.* 36 (Tokyo: NHK Science and Technical Research Laboratories, Jan. 1987).

Many displays for moving images emit light for just a fraction of the frame time: The display is black for a certain duty cycle. If the flash rate – or *refresh* rate – is too low, flicker is perceived. The flicker sensitivity of vision is dependent upon the viewing environment: The brighter the environment, and the larger the angle subtended by the picture, the higher the flash rate must be to avoid flicker. Because picture angle influences flicker, flicker depends upon viewing distance.

The brightness of the reproduced image itself influences the flicker threshold to some extent, so the brighter the image, the higher the refresh rate must be. In a totally dark environment, such as the cinema,

Viewing environment	*Ambient illumination*	*Refresh (flash) rate, Hz*	*Frame rate, Hz*
Cinema	Dark	48	24
Television	Dim	50	25
	Dim	≈60	≈30
Office	Bright	various, e.g., 66, 72, 76, 85	same as refresh rate

Table 6.1 **Refresh rate** refers to the shortest interval over which the whole picture is displayed – the flash rate.

The fovea has a diameter of about 1.5 mm, and subtends a visual angle of about 5°.

flicker sensitivity is completely determined by the luminance of the image itself. Peripheral vision has higher temporal sensitivity than central (foveal) vision, so the flicker threshold increases to some extent with wider viewing angles. Table 6.1 summarizes refresh rates used in film, video, and computing:

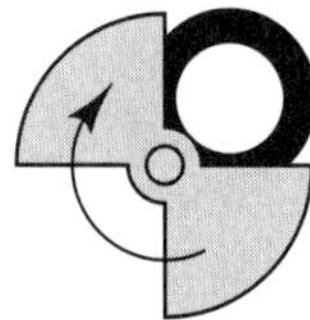

Figure 6.1 **Dual-bladed shutter** in a film projector flashes each frame twice. Rarely, 3-bladed shutters are used; they flash each frame thrice.

In the darkness of a cinema, a flash rate of 48 Hz is sufficient to overcome flicker. In the early days of motion pictures, a frame rate of 48 Hz was thought to involve excessive expenditure for film stock, and 24 frames per second were found to be sufficient for good motion portrayal. So, a conventional film projector uses a dual-bladed shutter, depicted in Figure 6.1, to flash each frame twice. Higher realism can be obtained with single-bladed shutters at 60 frames per second or higher.

Television refresh rates were originally chosen to match the local AC power line frequency. See *Frame, field, line, and sample rates,* on page 371.

In the dim viewing environment typical of television, such as a living room, a flash rate of 60 Hz suffices. The interlace technique, to be described on page 56, provides for video a function comparable to the dual-bladed shutter of a film projector: Each frame is flashed as two fields. Refresh is established by the field rate (twice the frame rate). For a given data rate, interlace doubles the apparent flash rate, and provides improved motion portrayal by doubling the temporal sampling rate. Scanning without interlace is called *progressive*.

Farrell, Joyce E., et al., "Predicting Flicker Thresholds for Video Display Terminals," in Proc. Society for Information Display 28 (4): 449–453 (1987).

A computer display used in a bright environment such as an office may require a refresh rate above 70 Hz to overcome flicker. (See Farrell.)

Introduction to scanning

In *Flicker, refresh rate, and frame rate,* on page 51, I outlined how refresh rate is chosen so as to avoid flicker. In *Viewing distance and angle,* on page 8, I will outline how spatial sampling determines the number of pixels in the pixel array. Video scanning represents pixels in sequential order, so as to acquire, convey, process, or display every pixel during the fixed time interval associated with each frame.

In analog video, information in the image plane is scanned left to right at a uniform rate during a fixed, short interval of time – the *active line time*. Scanning establishes a fixed relationship between a position in the image and a time instant in the signal. Successive lines are scanned at a uniform rate from the top to the bottom of the image, so there is also a fixed relationship between vertical position and time.

The word *raster* is derived from the Greek word *rustum* (rake), owing to the resemblance of a raster to the pattern left on newly raked sand.

The stationary pattern of parallel scanning lines disposed across the image is the *raster*. Digital video conveys samples of the image matrix in the same order that information would be conveyed in analog video: first the top line (left to right), then successive lines.

Line is a heavily overloaded term. *Lines* may refer to the total number of raster lines: Figure 6.2 shows "525-line" video, which has 525 total lines. *Line* may refer to a line containing picture, or to the total number of lines containing picture – in this example, 480. *Line* may denote the AC power line, whose frequency is very closely related to vertical scanning. Finally, *lines* is a measure of resolution, to be described in *Resolution,* on page 65.

In cameras and displays, a certain time interval is consumed in advancing the scanning operation – in *retracing* – from one line to the next. Several line times are consumed by vertical retrace, from the bottom of one scan to the top of the next. A CRT's electron gun must be switched off (blanked) during these intervals, so they are called *blanking intervals*. The *horizontal blanking interval* occurs between scan lines; the *vertical blanking interval* (VBI) occurs between frames (or fields). Figure 6.2 overleaf shows the blanking intervals of "525-line" video. The horizontal and vertical blanking intervals required for a CRT are large fractions of the line time and frame time: Vertical blanking consumes roughly 8% of each frame period.

In an analog video interface, synchronization information (*sync*) is conveyed during the blanking intervals. In principle, a digital video interface could omit blanking intervals and use an interface clock corresponding just

Figure 6.2 **Blanking intervals** for "525-line" video are indicated here by a dark region surrounding a light-shaded rectangle that represents the picture. The *vertical blanking interval* (VBI) consumes about 8% of each field time; horizontal blanking consumes about 15% of each line time.

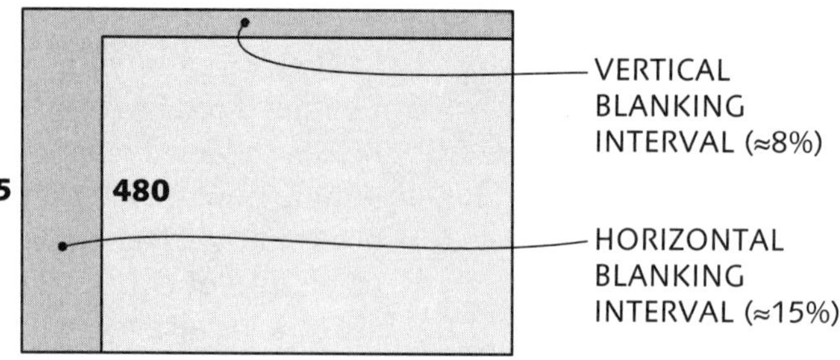

The count of 480 picture lines in Figure 6.2 is a recent standard; some people would say 483 or 487. See *Picture lines*, on page 324.

to the active pixels. However, this would be impractical, because it would lead to two clock domains in equipment that required blanking intervals, and this would cause unnecessary complexity in logic design. Instead, digital video interfaces use clock frequencies chosen to match the large blanking intervals of typical display equipment. What would otherwise be excess data capacity is put to good use conveying audio signals, captions, test signals, error detection or correction information, or other data or metadata.

Scanning parameters

In *progressive scanning*, all of the lines of the image are scanned in order, from top to bottom, at a picture rate sufficient to portray motion. Figure 6.3 at the top of the facing page indicates four basic scanning parameters:

- *Total lines* (L_T) comprises all of the scan lines, that is, both the vertical blanking interval and the picture lines.
- *Active lines* (L_A) contain the picture.
- *Samples per total line* (S_{TL}) comprises the samples in the total line, including horizontal blanking.
- *Samples per active line* (S_{AL}) counts samples that are permitted to take values different from blanking level.

The *production aperture*, sketched in Figure 6.3, comprises the array S_{AL} columns by L_A rows. The samples in the production aperture comprise the pixel array; they are *active*. All other sample intervals comprise blanking; they are *inactive* (or *blanked*), though they may convey vertical interval information

Figure 6.3 **Production aperture** comprises the array S_{AL} columns by L_A rows. Blanking intervals lie outside the production aperture; here, blanking intervals are darkly shaded. The product of S_{AL} and L_A yields the active pixel count per frame. Sampling rate (f_S) is the product of S_{TL}, L_T, and frame rate.

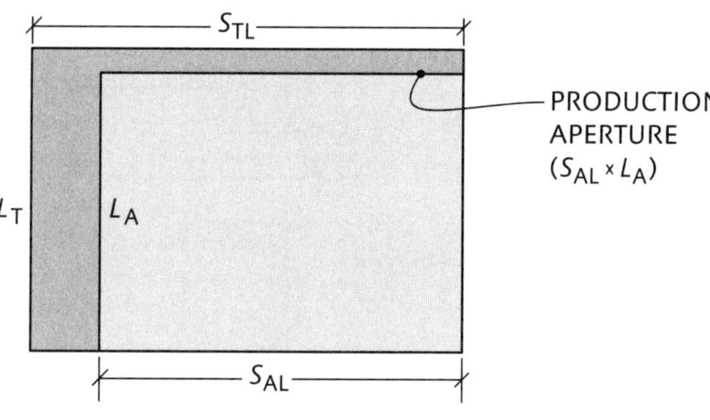

Figure 6.4 **Clean aperture** should remain subjectively free from artifacts arising from filtering. The clean aperture excludes blanking transition samples, indicated here by black bands outside the left and right edges of the picture width, defined by the count of samples per picture width (S_{PW}).

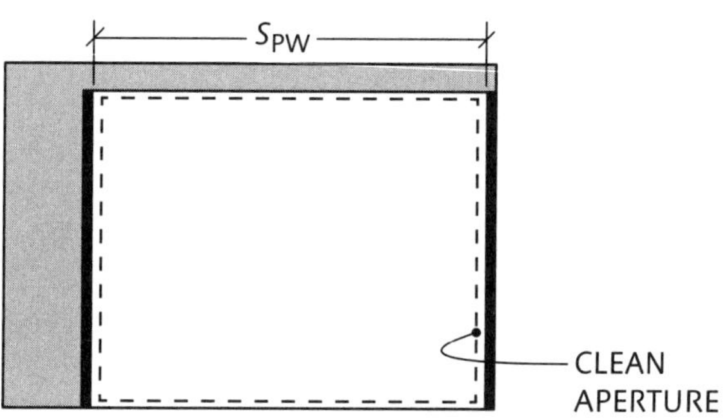

such as VITS, VITC, or closed captions. Consumer display equipment must blank these lines, or place them offscreen.

The horizontal center of the picture lies midway between the central two luma samples, and the vertical center of the picture lies vertically midway between two image rows.

At the left-hand edge of picture information on a scan line, if the video signal immediately assumes a value greatly different from blanking, an artifact called *ringing* is liable to result when that transition is processed through an analog or digital filter. A similar circumstance arises at the right-hand picture edge. In studio video, the signal builds to full amplitude, or decays to blanking level, over several *transition* samples ideally forming a raised cosine shape.

See *Transition samples*, on page 323.

Active samples encompass not only the picture, but also the transition samples; see Figure 6.4 above. Studio equipment should maintain the widest picture possible within the production aperture, subject to appropriate blanking transitions.

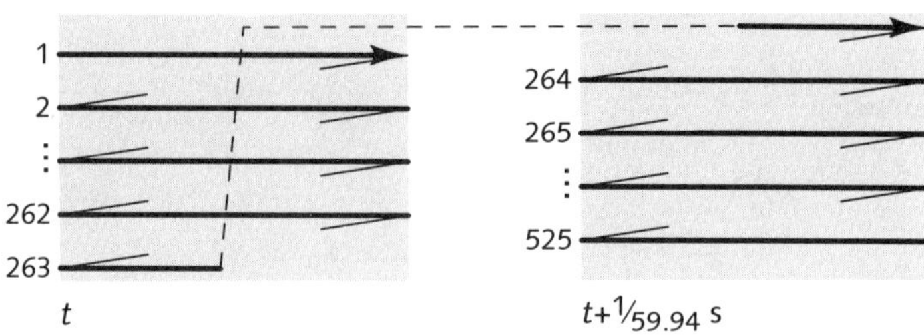

Figure 6.5 **Interlaced scanning** forms a complete picture – the *frame* – from two *fields*, each comprising half of the total number of scanning lines. The second field is delayed by half the frame time from the first. This example shows 525 lines.

Interlaced scanning

I have treated the image array as a matrix of S_{AL} by L_A pixels, without regard for the spatial distribution of light intensity across each pixel – the *spot profile*. If spot profile is such that there is a significant gap between the intensity distributions of adjacent image rows (scan lines), then scan-line structure will be visible to viewers closer than a certain distance. The gap between scan lines is a function of scan-line pitch and spot profile. *Spot size* can be characterized by spot diameter at 50% intensity. For a given scan-line pitch, a smaller spot size will force viewers to be more distant from the display if scan lines are to be rendered invisible.

I detailed spot profile in *Image structure*, on page 43.

Interlacing is a scheme by which we can reduce spot size without being thwarted by scan-line visibility. The full height of the image is scanned with a narrow spot, leaving gaps in the vertical direction. Then, $1/50$ or $1/60$ s later, the full image height is scanned again, but offset vertically so as to fill in the gaps. A frame now comprises two *fields*, denoted *first* and *second*. The scanning mechanism is depicted in Figure 6.5 above. For a given level of scan-line visibility, this technique enables closer viewing distance than would be possible for progressive display. Historically, the same raster standard was used across an entire television system, so interlace was used not only for display but also for acquisition, recording, and transmission.

It is confusing to refer to fields as *odd* and *even*. Use *first field* and *second field* instead.

Noninterlaced (*progressive* or *sequential*) scanning is universal in desktop computers and in computing. Progressive scanning has been introduced for digital television and HDTV. However, the interlace technique remains ubiquitous in conventional broadcast television, and is dominant in HDTV.

RCA trademarked the word *Proscan*, but RCA – now Thomson – confusingly uses that word to describe both progressive and interlaced television receivers!

Twitter

The flicker susceptibility of vision stems from a wide-area effect: As long as the complete height of the picture is scanned sufficiently rapidly to overcome flicker, small-scale picture detail, such as that in the alternate lines, can be transmitted at a lower rate. With progressive scanning, scan-line visibility limits the reduction of spot size. With interlaced scanning, this constraint is relaxed by a factor of two. However, interlace introduces a new constraint, that of *twitter.*

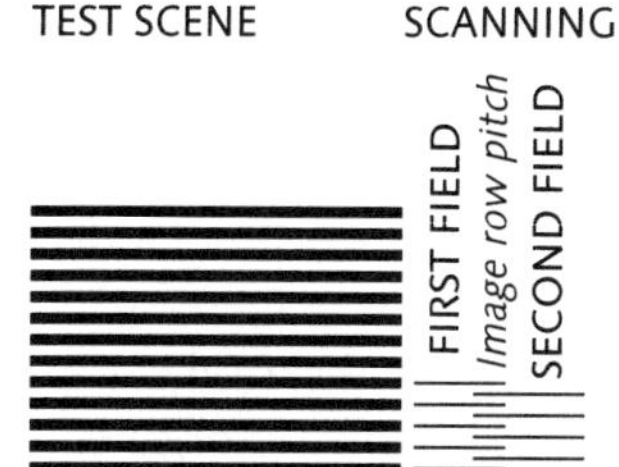

Figure 6.6 **Twitter** would result if this scene were scanned at the indicated line pitch by a camera without vertical filtering, then displayed using interlace.

If an image has vertical detail at a scale comparable to the scanning line pitch – for example, if the fine pattern of horizontal line pairs in Figure 6.6 is scanned – then interlaced display causes the content of the first and the second fields to differ markedly. At practical field rates – 50 or 60 Hz – this causes twitter, a small-scale phenomenon that is perceived as a scintillation, or an extremely rapid up-and-down motion. If such image information occupies a large area, then flicker is perceived instead of twitter. Twitter is sometimes called *interline flicker,* but that is a bad term because flicker is by definition a wide-area effect.

Twitter is produced not only from degenerate images such as the fine black-and-white lines of Figure 6.6, but also from high-contrast vertical detail in ordinary images. High-quality video cameras include optical spatial lowpass filters to attenuate vertical detail that would otherwise be liable to produce twitter. When computer-generated imagery (CGI) is interlaced, vertical detail must be filtered in order to avoid flicker. A circuit to accomplish this is called a *twitter filter.*

Interlace in analog systems

Interlace is achieved in analog devices by scanning vertically at a constant rate between 50 and 60 Hz, and scanning horizontally at an odd multiple of half that rate. In SDTV in North America and Japan, the field rate is 59.94 Hz; line rate (f_H) is $^{525}/_{2}$ ($262\frac{1}{2}$) times that rate. In Asia, Australia, and Europe, the field rate is 50 Hz; the line rate is $^{625}/_{2}$ ($312\frac{1}{2}$) times the field rate.

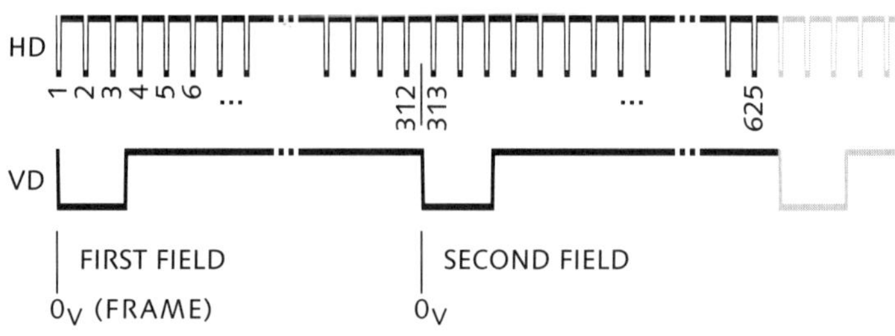

Figure 6.7 **Horizontal and vertical drive** pulses effect interlace in analog scanning. 0_V denotes the start of each field. The halfline offset of the second 0_V causes interlace. Here, 576*i* scanning is shown.

Figure 6.7 above shows the *horizontal drive* (HD) and *vertical drive* (VD) pulse signals that were once distributed in the studio to cause interlaced scanning in analog equipment. These signals have been superseded by a combined *sync* (or *composite sync*) signal; vertical scanning is triggered by *broad pulses* having total duration of 2½ or 3 lines. Sync is usually imposed onto the video signal, to avoid separate distribution circuits. Analog sync is coded at a level "blacker than black."

Details will be presented in *Analog SDTV sync, genlock, and interface* on page 399.

Interlace and progressive

For a given viewing distance, sharpness is improved as spot size becomes smaller. However, if spot size is reduced beyond a certain point, depending upon the spot profile of the display, either scan lines or pixels will become visible, or aliasing will intrude. In principle, improvements in bandwidth or spot profile reduce potential viewing distance, enabling a wider picture angle. However, because consumers form expectations about viewing distance, we assume a constant viewing distance and say that *resolution* is improved instead.

A rough conceptual comparison of progressive and interlaced scanning is presented in Figure 6.8 opposite. At first glance, an interlaced system offers twice the number of pixels – loosely, twice the spatial resolution – as a progressive system with the same data capacity and the same frame rate. Owing to twitter, spatial resolution in a practical interlaced system is not double that of a progressive system at the same data rate. Historically, cameras have been designed to avoid producing so much vertical detail that twitter would be objectionable. However, resolution is increased by a factor large enough that interlace has historically been

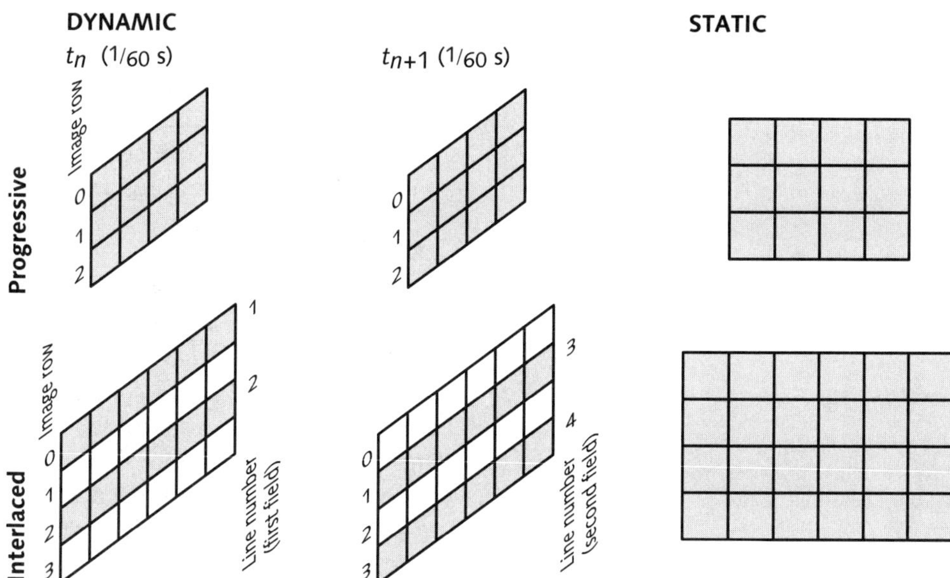

Figure 6.8 **Progressive and interlaced scanning** are compared. The top left sketch depicts an image of 4×3 pixels transmitted during an interval of $\frac{1}{60}$ s. The top center sketch shows image data from the same 12 locations transmitted in the following $\frac{1}{60}$ s interval. The top right sketch shows the spatial arrangement of the 4×3 image, totalling 12 pixels; the data rate is 12 pixels per $\frac{1}{60}$ s. At the bottom left, 12 pixels comprising image rows 0 and 2 of a 6×4 image array are transmitted in $\frac{1}{60}$ s. At the bottom center, the 12 pixels of image rows 1 and 3 are transmitted in the following $\frac{1}{60}$ s interval. At the bottom right, the spatial arrangement of the 6×4 image is shown: The 24 pixel image is transmitted in $\frac{1}{30}$ s. Interlaced scanning has the same data rate as progressive, but at first glance has twice the number of pixels, and potentially twice the resolution.

considered worthwhile. The improvement comes at the expense of introducing some aliasing and some vertical motion artifacts. Also, interlace makes it difficult to process motion sequences, as I will explain on page 61.

Notation	*Pixel array*
VGA	640×480
SVGA	800×600
XGA	1024×768
SXGA	1280×1024
UXGA	1600×1200
QXGA	2048×1365

Table 6.2 **Scanning in computing** has no standardized notation, but these notations are widely used.

Scanning notation

In computing, display format may be denoted by a pair of numbers: the count of pixels across the width of the image, and the number of picture lines. Alternatively, display format may be denoted symbolically – VGA, SVGA, XGA, etc., as in Table 6.2. Square sampling is implicit. This notation does not indicate refresh rate.

Traditionally, video scanning was denoted by the total number of lines per *frame* (picture lines plus sync and vertical blanking overhead), a slash, and the *field* rate in hertz. (Interlace is implicit unless a slash and *1:1* is appended to indicate progressive scanning; a slash and *2:1* makes interlace explicit.) 525/59.94/2:1 scanning is used in North America and Japan; 625/50/2:1 prevails in Europe, Asia, and Australia. Until very recently, these were the only scanning systems used for broadcasting.

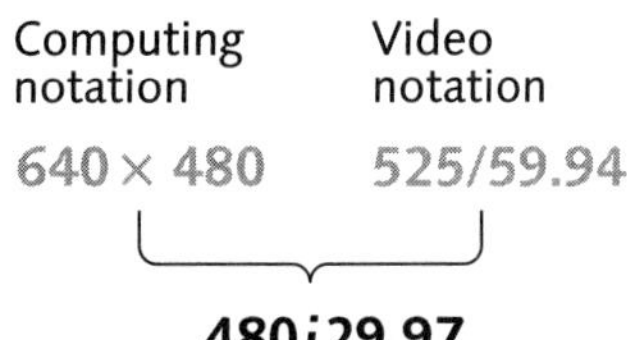

Figure 6.9 **My scanning notation** gives the count of active (picture) lines, *p* for progressive or *i* for interlace, then the frame rate. Because some people write 480*p*60 when they mean 480*p*59.94, the notation *60.00* should be used to emphasize a rate of exactly 60 Hz.

Recently, digital technology has enabled several new scanning standards. Conventional scanning notation cannot adequately describe the new scanning systems, and a new notation is emerging, depicted in Figure 6.9: Scanning is denoted by the count of active (picture) lines, followed by *p* for progressive or *i* for interlace, followed by the frame rate. I write the letter *i* in lowercase, and in italics, to avoid potential confusion with the digit 1. For consistency, I also write the letter *p* in lowercase italics. Traditional video notation (such as 625/50) is inconsistent, juxtaposing lines per *frame* with *fields* per second. Some people seem intent upon carrying this confusion into the future, by denoting the old 525/59.94 as 480*i*59.94. In my notation, I use frame rate.

Since all 480*i* systems have a frame rate of 29.97 Hz, I use 480*i* as shorthand for 480*i*29.97. Similarly, I use 576*i* as shorthand for 576*i*25.

In my notation, conventional 525/59.94/2:1 video is denoted 480*i*29.97; conventional 625/50/2:1 video is denoted 576*i*25. HDTV systems include 720*p*60 and 1080*i*30. Film-friendly versions of HDTV are denoted 720*p*24 and 1080*p*24. Aspect ratio is not explicit in the new notation: 720*p*, 1080*i*, and 1080*p* are implicitly 16:9 since there are no 4:3 standards for these systems, but 480*i*30.00 or 480*p*60.00 could potentially have either conventional 4:3 or widescreen 16:9 aspect ratio.

Interlace artifacts

An interlaced camera captures 60 (or 50) unique fields per second. If a scene contains an object in motion with respect to the camera, each field carries half the object's spatial information, but information in the second field will be displaced according to the object's motion.

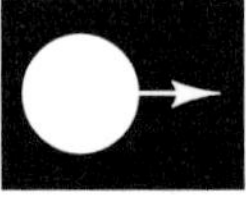

Figure 6.10 **Test scene**

Consider the test scene sketched in Figure 6.10, comprising a black background partially occluded by a white disk that is in motion with respect to the

Figure 6.11 **Interlaced capture** samples the position of a football at about 60 times per second, even though frames occur at half that rate. (A soccer ball takes 50 positions per second.)

camera. The first and second fields imaged from this scene are illustrated in Figure 6.11. (The example neglects capture blur owing to motion during the exposure; it resembles capture by a CCD camera set for a very short exposure time.) The image in the second field is delayed with respect to the first by half the frame time (that is, by $1/60$ s or $1/50$ s); by the time the second field is imaged, the object has moved.

Upon interlaced display, the time sequence of interlaced fields is maintained: No temporal or spatial artifacts are introduced. However, reconstruction of progressive frames is necessary for high-quality resizing, repositioning, upconversion, downconversion, or standards conversion. You can think of an interlaced signal as having its lines rearranged (permuted) compared to a progressive signal; however, in the presence of motion, simply stitching two fields into a single frame produces spatial artifacts such as that sketched in Figure 6.12. Techniques to avoid such artifacts will be discussed in *Deinterlacing,* on page 437.

Figure 6.12 **Static lattice** approach to stitching two fields into a frame produces the "mouse's teeth" or "field tearing" artifact on moving objects.

Examine the interlaced (bottom) portion of Figure 6.8, on page 59, and imagine an image element moving slowly down the picture at a rate of one row of the pixel array every field time – in a 480*i*29.97 system, $1/480$ of the picture height in $1/60$ s, or one picture height in 8 seconds. Owing to interlace, half of that image's vertical information will be lost! At other rates, some portion of the vertical detail in the image will be lost. With interlaced scanning, vertical motion can cause serious motion artifacts.

Motion portrayal

In *Flicker, refresh rate, and frame rate,* on page 51, I outlined the perceptual considerations in choosing refresh rate. In order to avoid objectionable flicker, it is necessary to flash an image at a rate higher than the rate necessary to portray its motion. Different applications have adopted different refresh rates, depending on the image quality requirements and viewing conditions. Refresh rate is generally engineered into a video system; once chosen, it cannot easily be changed.

Flicker is minimized by any display device that produces steady, unflashing light for the duration of the frame time. You might regard a nonflashing display to be more suitable than a device that flashes; many modern devices do not flash. However, if the viewer's gaze tracks an element that moves across the image, a display with a pixel duty cycle near 100% – that is, an *on-time* approaching the frame time – will exhibit smearing of that element. This problem becomes more severe as eye tracking velocities increase, such as with the wide viewing angle of HDTV.

Poynton, Charles, "Motion portrayal, eye tracking, and emerging display technology," in Proc. 30th SMPTE Advanced Motion Imaging Conference (New York: SMPTE, 1996), 192–202.

Film at 24 frames per second is transferred to interlaced video at 60 fields per second by *2-3 pulldown*. The first film frame is transferred to two video fields, then the second film frame is transferred to three video fields; the cycle repeats. The 2-3 pulldown is normally used to produce video at 59.94 Hz, not 60 Hz; the film is run 0.1% slower than 24 frames per second. I will detail the scheme in *2-3 pulldown*, on page 429. The 2-3 technique can be applied to transfer to progressive video at 59.94 or 60 frames per second. Film is transferred to 576*i* video using *2-2 pulldown:* Each film frame is scanned into two video fields (or frames); the film is run 4% fast.

Historically, this was called *3-2 pulldown*, but with the adoption of SMPTE RP 197, it is now more accurately called *2-3 pulldown*. See page 430.

Segmented frame (24PsF)

A scheme called *progressive segmented-frame* has been adopted to adapt HDTV equipment to handle images at 24 frames per second. The scheme, denoted *24PsF*, samples in progressive fashion: Both fields represent the same instant in time, and vertical filtering to reduce twitter is both unnecessary and undesirable. However, lines are rearranged to interlaced order for studio distribution and recording. Proponents of the scheme claim compatibility with interlaced processing and recording equipment, a dubious objective in my view.

The *progressive segmented-frame* (PsF) technique is known in consumer SDTV systems as *quasi-interlace*. PsF is not to be confused with *point spread function*, PSF.

Video system taxonomy

Insufficient channel capacity was available at the outset of television broadcasting to transmit three separate color components. The NTSC and PAL techniques were devised to combine (*encode*) the three color components into a single *composite* signal. Composite video

Table 6.3 **Video systems are classified** as analog or digital, and component or composite (or S-video). SDTV may be represented in component, hybrid (S-video), or composite forms. HDTV is always in component form. (Certain degenerate forms of analog NTSC and PAL are itemized in Table 49.1, on page 581.)

		Analog	*Digital*
HDTV	*Component*	$R'G'B'$, ${}^{709}Y'P_BP_R$	4:2:2 ${}^{709}Y'C_BC_R$
SDTV	*Component*	$R'G'B'$, ${}^{601}Y'P_BP_R$	4:2:2 ${}^{601}Y'C_BC_R$
	Hybrid	S-video	
	Composite	NTSC, PAL	$4f_{SC}$

The $4f_{SC}$ notation will be introduced on page 108.

remains in use for analog broadcast and in consumers' premises; much composite digital ($4f_{SC}$) equipment is still in use by broadcasters in North America. However, virtually all new video equipment – including all consumer digital video equipment, and all HDTV equipment – uses component video, either $Y'P_BP_R$ analog components or $Y'C_BC_R$ digital components.

A video system can be classified as component HDTV, component SDTV, or composite SDTV. Independently, a system can be classified as analog or digital. Table 6.3 above indicates the six classifications, with the associated color encoding schemes. Composite NTSC and PAL video encoding is used only in 480*i* and 576*i* systems; HDTV systems use only component video. S-video is a hybrid of component analog video and composite analog NTSC or PAL; in Table 6.3, S-video is classified in its own seventh (hybrid) category.

Conversion among systems

By NTSC, I do not mean 525/59.94 or 480*i*; by PAL, I do not mean 625/50 or 576*i*! See *Introduction to composite NTSC and PAL*, on page 103. Although SECAM is a composite technique in that luma and chroma are combined, it has little in common with NTSC and PAL. SECAM is obsolete for video production; see page 576.

In video, *encoding* traditionally referred to converting a set of $R'G'B'$ components into an NTSC or PAL composite signal. Encoding may start with $R'G'B'$, $Y'C_BC_R$, or $Y'P_BP_R$ components, or may involve matrixing from $R'G'B'$ to form luma (Y') and intermediate [U, V] or [I, Q] components. Quadrature modulation then forms modulated chroma (C); luma and chroma are then summed. *Decoding* historically referred to converting an NTSC or PAL composite signal to $R'G'B'$. Decoding involves luma/chroma separation, quadrature demodulation to recover [U, V] or [I, Q], then scaling to recover [C_B, C_R] or [P_B, P_R], or matrixing of luma and chroma to recover $R'G'B'$. *Encoding* and *decoding* are now general terms; they may refer to JPEG, M-JPEG, MPEG, or other encoding or decoding processes.

Transcoding refers to the technical aspects of conversion; signal modifications for creative purposes are not encompassed by the term.

Transcoding traditionally referred to conversion among different color encoding methods having the same scanning standard. Transcoding of component video involves chroma interpolation, matrixing, and chroma subsampling. Transcoding of composite video involves decoding, then reencoding to the other standard. With the emergence of compressed storage and digital distribution, the term *transcoding* is now applied toward various methods of recoding compressed bitstreams, or decompressing then recompressing.

Scan conversion refers to conversion among scanning standards having different spatial structures, without the use of temporal processing. If the input and output frame rates differ, motion portrayal is liable to be impaired. (In desktop video, and low-end video, this operation is sometimes called *scaling*.)

In radio frequency (RF) technology, *upconversion* refers to conversion of a signal to a higher carrier frequency; *downconversion* refers to conversion of a signal to a lower carrier frequency.

Historically, *upconversion* referred to conversion from SDTV to HDTV; *downconversion* referred to conversion from HDTV to SDTV. Historically, these terms referred to conversion of a signal at the same frame rate as the input; nowadays, frame rate conversion might be involved. High-quality upconversion and downconversion require spatial interpolation. That, in turn, is best performed in a progressive format: If the source is interlaced, intermediate deinterlacing is required, even if the target format is interlaced.

Watkinson, John, *The Engineer's Guide to Standards Conversion* (Petersfield, Hampshire, England: Snell & Wilcox, 1994).

Standards conversion denotes conversion among scanning standards having different frame rates. Historically, the term implied similar pixel count (such as conversion between 480*i* and 576*i*), but nowadays a standards converter might incorporate upconversion or downconversion. Standards conversion requires a fieldstore or framestore; to achieve high quality, it requires several fieldstores and motion-compensated interpolation. The complexity of standards conversion between 480*i* and 576*i* is the reason that it has been difficult for broadcasters and consumers to convert European material for use in North America or Japan, or vice versa.

Resolution 7

To avoid visible pixel structure in image display, some overlap is necessary in the distributions of light produced by neighboring display elements, as I explained in *Image structure*, on page 43. Also, to avoid spatial aliasing in image capture, some overlap is necessary in the distribution of sensitivity across neighboring sensor elements. Such overlap reduces sharpness. In this chapter, I will explain *resolution*, which is closely related to sharpness. Before introducing resolution, I must introduce the concepts of *magnitude frequency response* and *bandwidth*.

Magnitude frequency response and bandwidth

Rather than analyzing a spot of certain dimensions, we analyze a group of closely spaced identical elements, characterizing the spacing between the elements. This allows mathematical analysis using *transforms*, particularly the Fourier transform and the *z*-transform.

The top graph in Figure 7.1 overleaf shows a one-dimensional sine wave test signal "sweeping" from zero frequency up to a high frequency. (This could be a one-dimensional function of time such as an audio waveform, or the waveform of luma from one scan line of an image.) A typical optical or electronic imaging system involves temporal or spatial dispersion, which causes the response of the system to diminish at high frequency, as shown in the middle graph. The envelope of that waveform – the system's *magnitude frequency response* – is shown at the bottom.

An electrical engineer may call this simply *frequency response*. The qualifier *magnitude* distinguishes it from other functions of frequency such as phase frequency response.

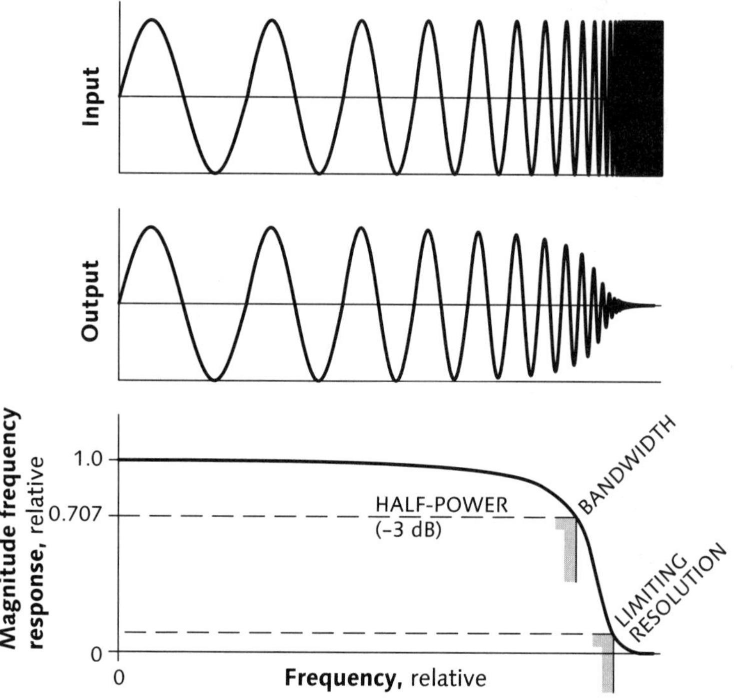

Figure 7.1 **Magnitude frequency response** of an electronic or optical system typically falls as frequency increases. Bandwidth is measured at the half-power point (-3 dB), where response has fallen to 0.707 of its value at a reference frequency (often zero frequency, or *DC*). Useful visible detail is obtained from signal power beyond the half-power bandwidth, that is, at depths of modulation less than 70.7%. I show *limiting resolution,* which might occur at about 10% response.

There are other definitions of bandwidth, but this is the definition that I recommend. In *magnitude squared response,* the half-power point is at 0.5 on a linear scale.

Bandwidth characterizes the range of frequencies that a system can capture, record, process, or transmit. *Half-power bandwidth* (also known as *3 dB bandwidth*) is specified or measured where signal magnitude has fallen 3 dB – that is, to the fraction 0.707 – from its value at a reference frequency (often zero frequency, or *DC*). Useful visual information is typically available at frequencies higher than the bandwidth. In image science, *limiting resolution* is determined visually.

The maximum rate at which an analog or digital electronic signal can change state – in an imaging system, between black and white – is limited by frequency response, and is therefore characterized by bandwidth.

Figure 7.1 shows abstract input and output signals. When bandwidth of an optical system is discussed, it is implicit that the quantities are proportional to intensity. When bandwidth of video signals is discussed, it is implicit that the input and output electrical signals are gamma-corrected.

When digital information is processed or transmitted through analog channels, bits are coded into *symbols* that ideally remain independent. Dispersion in this context is called *intersymbol interference* (*ISI*).

Many digital technologists use the term *bandwidth* to refer to *data rate;* however, the terms properly refer to different concepts. *Bandwidth* refers to the frequency of signal content in an analog or digital signal. *Data rate* refers to digital transmission capacity, independent of any potential signal content. A typical studio SDTV signal has 5.5 MHz signal bandwidth and 13.5 MB/s data rate – the terms are obviously not interchangeable.

Kell effect

Television systems in the 1930s failed to deliver the maximum resolution that was to be expected from Nyquist's work (which I introduced on page 46). In 1934, Kell published a paper quantifying the fraction of the maximum theoretical resolution achieved by RCA's experimental television system. He called this fraction *k;* later, it became known as the *Kell factor* (less desirably denoted *K*). Kell's first paper gives a factor of 0.64, but fails to give a complete description of his experimental method. A subsequent paper (in 1940) described the method, and gives a factor of 0.8, under somewhat different conditions.

k for *Kell factor* is unrelated to *K rating,* sometimes called *K factor,* which I will describe on page 542.

Kell, R.D., A.V. Bedford, and G.L. Fredendall, "A Determination of the Optimum Number of Lines in a Television System," in *RCA Review* 5: 8–30 (July 1940).

Kell's *k* factor was determined by subjective, not objective, criteria. If the system under test had a wide, gentle spot profile resembling a Gaussian, closely spaced lines on a test chart would cease to be resolved as their spacing diminished beyond a certain value. If a camera under test had an unusually small spot size, or a display had a sharp distribution (such as a box), then Kell's *k* factor was determined by the intrusion of objectionable artifacts as the spacing reduced – also a subjective criterion.

Hsu, Stephen C.,"The Kell Factor: Past and Present," in *SMPTE Journal* 95 (2): 206–214 (Feb. 1986).

Kell and other authors published various theoretical derivations that justify various numerical factors; Stephen Hsu provides a comprehensive review. In my opinion, such numerical measures are so poorly defined and so unreliable that they are now useless. Hsu says:

Kell factor is defined so ambiguously that individual researchers have justifiably used different theoretical and experimental techniques to derive widely varying values of *k*.

Today I consider it poor science to quantify a Kell *factor.* However, Kell made an important contribution to television science, and I think it entirely fitting that we honor him with the Kell *effect:*

In a video system – including sensor, signal processing, and display – Kell effect refers to the loss of resolution, compared to the Nyquist limit, caused by the spatial dispersion of light power. Some dispersion is necessary to avoid aliasing upon capture, and to avoid objectionable scan line (or pixel) structure at display.

I introduced twitter on page 57.

Kell's 1934 paper concerned only progressive scanning. With the emergence of interlaced systems, it became clear that twitter resulted from excessive vertical detail. To reduce twitter to tolerable levels, it was necessary to reduce vertical resolution to substantially below that of a well-designed progressive system having the same spot size – for a progressive system with a given *k*, an interlaced system having the same spot size had to have lower *k*. Many people have lumped this consideration into "Kell factor," but researchers such as Mitsuhashi identify this reduction separately as an *interlace factor* or *interlace coefficient.*

Mitsuhashi, Tetsuo, "Scanning Specifications and Picture Quality," in Fujio, T., et al., *High Definition television*, NHK Science and Technical Research Laboratories Technical Monograph 32 (June 1982).

Resolution

SDTV (at roughly 720×480), HDTV at 1280×720, and HDTV at 1920×1080 all have different pixel counts. Image quality delivered by a particular number of pixels depends upon the nature of the image data (e.g., whether the data is raster-locked or Nyquist-filtered), and upon the nature of the display device (e.g., whether it has box or Gaussian reconstruction).

In computing, unfortunately, the term *resolution* has come to refer simply to the count of vertical and hori-

Resolution properly refers to spatial phenomena. It is confusing to refer to a sample as having 8-bit "resolution"; use *precision* or *quantization*.

zontal pixels in the pixel array, without regard for any overlap at capture, or overlap at display, that may have reduced the amount of detail in the image. A system may be described as having "resolution" of 1152×864 – this system has a total of about one million pixels (one megapixel, or 1 Mpx). Interpreted this way, "resolution" doesn't depend upon whether individual pixels can be discerned ("resolved") on the face of the display.

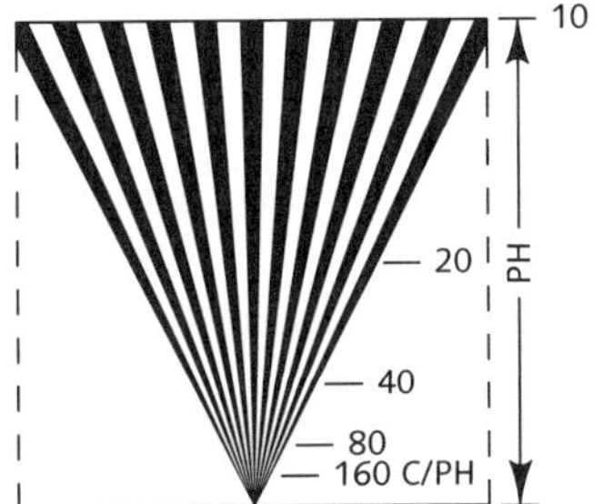

Figure 7.2 **Resolution wedge** pattern sweeps various horizontal frequencies through an imaging system. This pattern is calibrated in terms of cycles per picture *height* (here signified PH); however, with the pattern in the orientation shown, *horizontal* resolution is measured.

Resolution in a digital image system is bounded by the count of pixels across the image width and height. However, as picture detail increases in frequency, electronic and optical effects cause response to diminish even within the bounds imposed by sampling. In video, we are concerned with resolution that is delivered to the viewer; we are also interested in limitations of bandwidth in capture, recording, processing, and display. In video, resolution concerns the maximum number of line pairs (or cycles) that can be resolved on the display screen. This is a subjective criterion! Resolution is related to perceived sharpness.

Resolution is usually expressed in terms of spatial frequency, whose units are cycles per picture width (C/PW) horizontally, and cycles per picture height (C/PH) vertically, or units closely related to these. Figure 7.2 depicts a resolution test chart. In the orientation presented, it sweeps across horizontal frequencies, and can be used to estimate horizontal resolution. Turned 90°, it can be used to sweep through vertical frequencies, and thereby estimate vertical resolution.

Resolution in video

Spatial phenomena at an image sensor or at a display device may limit both vertical and horizontal resolution. However, analog processing, recording, and transmission in video limits bandwidth, and thereby affects only horizontal resolution. *Resolution* in consumer electronics refers to horizontal resolution. Vertical resampling is now common in consumer equipment, and this potentially affects vertical resolution. In transform-based compression (such as JPEG, DV, and MPEG), dispersion comparable to overlap between pixels occurs; this affects horizontal and vertical resolution.

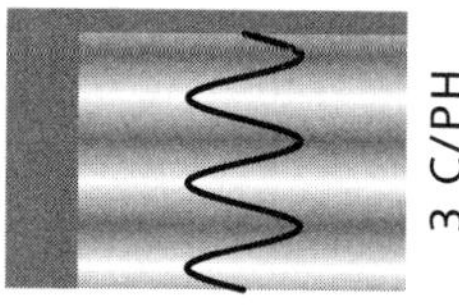

Figure 7.3 **Vertical resolution** concerns vertical frequency. This sketch shows image data whose power is concentrated at a vertical frequency of 3 cycles per picture height (C/PH).

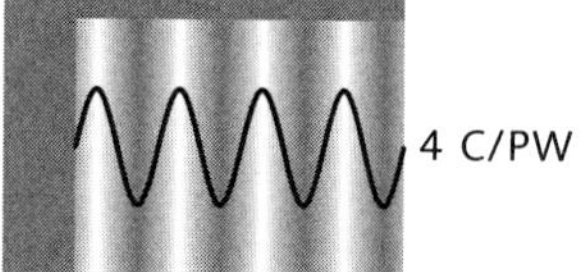

Figure 7.4 **Horizontal resolution** concerns horizontal frequency. This sketch shows a horizontal frequency of 4 cycles per picture width (C/PW); at 4:3 aspect ratio, this is equivalent to 3 C/PH.

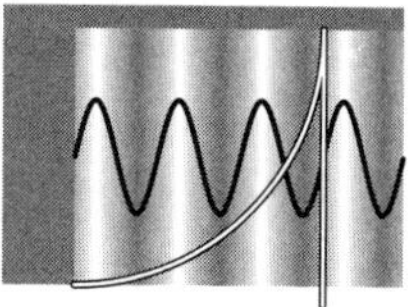

Figure 7.5 **Resolution in consumer television** refers to horizontal resolution, expressed with reference to picture height (not width), and in units of vertical samples (scan lines, or pixels, not cycles). The resulting unit is *TV lines per picture height* – that is, TVL/PH, or "TV lines."

Figure 7.3 illustrates how vertical resolution is defined; Figures 7.4 and 7.5 show horizontal resolution. Confusingly, horizontal resolution is often expressed in units of "TV lines per picture *height*." Once the number of resolvable lines is estimated, it must be corrected for the aspect ratio of the picture. In summary:

Resolution in TVL/PH – colloquially, "TV lines" – is twice the horizontal resolution in cycles per picture width, divided by the aspect ratio of the picture.

This definition enables the same test pattern calibration scale to be used both vertically and horizontally.

In analog video, the signal along each scan line is continuous; bandwidth places an upper bound on horizontal resolution. However, even in analog video, raster scanning samples the image in the vertical direction. The count of picture lines is fixed by a raster standard; the associated vertical sampling places an upper bound on vertical resolution.

Vertical detail in an interlaced system is affected by both the Kell effect and an interlace effect. Historically, a Kell factor of about 0.7 and an interlace factor of about 0.7 applied, producing an overall factor of 0.5.

Figure 7.6 **Vertical resolution in 480*i* systems** can't quite reach the Nyquist limit of 240 cycles (line pairs), owing to Kell and interlace factors. Vertical resolution is diminished, typically to $\frac{7}{10}$ of 240 – that is, to 166 C/PH.

Equivalent horizontal resolution to 166 C/PH is obtained by multiplying by the 4:3 aspect ratio, obtaining 221 C/PW.

Picture content consumes about 85% of the total line time. Dividing 221 C/PW by 0.85 yields 260 cycles per total line. Line rate is 15.734 kHz; 260 cycles during one complete line period corresponds to a video frequency of about 4.2 MHz, the design point of NTSC. There are 79 "TV lines" per megahertz of bandwidth.

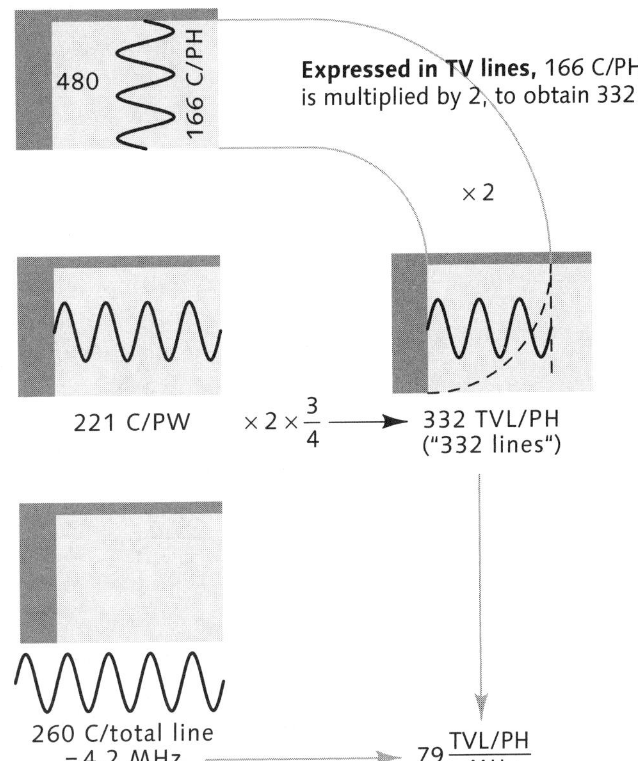

As a consequence, early interlaced systems showed no advantage in resolution over progressive systems of the same bandwidth. However, scan lines were much less visible in the interlaced systems.

$$\frac{221}{1 - 0.15} = 260$$

Figure 7.6 above summarizes how vertical and horizontal spatial frequency and bandwidth are related for 480*i* television. The image height is covered by 480 picture lines. Sampling theory limits vertical image content to below 240 C/PH if aliasing is to be avoided. Reduced by Kell and interlace factors combining to a value of 0.7, about 166 C/PH of vertical resolution can be conveyed. At 4:3 aspect ratio, equivalent horizontal resolution corresponds to $\frac{4}{3}$ times 166, or about 221 C/PW. For a horizontal blanking overhead of 15%, that corresponds to about 260 cycles per total line time. At a line rate of 15.734 kHz, the video circuits should have a bandwidth of about 4.2 MHz. Repeating this calculation for 576*i* yields 4.7 MHz.

The NTSC, in 1941, was well aware of the Kell factor, and took it into account when setting the monochrome television standard with 525 total lines and about 480 picture lines. The numbers that I have quoted work out perfectly to achieve matched vertical and horizontal resolution, but there is no evidence that the NTSC performed quite this calculation.

The relationship between bandwidth (measured in engineering units, MHz) and horizontal resolution (measured in consumer units, TVL/PH) depends upon blanking overhead and aspect ratio. For 480*i* systems:

$$\begin{aligned} & \frac{1\,\mathrm{MHz}}{f_{\mathrm{H}}} \cdot 2 \cdot \frac{1}{\mathrm{AR}} \cdot \frac{S_{\mathrm{PW}}}{S_{\mathrm{TL}}} \\ = & \frac{1\,\mathrm{MHz}}{15.734\,\mathrm{kHz}} \cdot 2 \cdot \frac{3}{4} \cdot \frac{711}{858} \\ = & \, 79 \, \frac{\mathrm{TVL/PH}}{\mathrm{MHz}} \end{aligned} \qquad \text{Eq 7.1}$$

Studio SDTV has 720 S_{AL}; resolution higher than 540 TVL/PH is pointless.

In 480*i* video, there are 79 TVL/PH per megahertz of bandwidth. NTSC broadcast is limited to 4.2 MHz, so horizontal resolution is limited to 332 "TV lines." In 576*i* systems, there are 78 TVL/PH per megahertz of video. Most 625-line PAL broadcast systems have bandwidth roughly 20% higher than that of NTSC, so have correspondingly higher potential resolution.

Viewing distance

Pixel count in SDTV and HDTV is fixed by the corresponding scanning standards. In *Viewing distance and angle*, on page 8, I described how optimum viewing distance is where the scan-line pitch subtends an angle of about $1/60°$. If a sampled image is viewed closer than that distance, scan lines or pixels are liable to be visible. With typical displays, SDTV is suitable for viewing at about 7·PH; 1080*i* HDTV is suitable for viewing at a much closer distance of about 3·PH.

A computer user tends to position himself or herself where scan-line pitch subtends an angle greater than $1/60°$ – perhaps at half that distance. However, at such a close distance, individual pixels are likely to be discernible, perhaps even objectionable, and the quality of continuous-tone images will almost certainly suffer.

Pixel count places a constraint on the closest viewing distance; however, visibility of pixel or scan-line structure in an image depends upon many other factors such as sensor MTF, spot profile (PSF), and bandwidth. In principle, if any of these factors reduces the amount of detail in the image, the optimum viewing distance is pushed more distant. However, consumers have formed an expectation that SDTV is best viewed at about 7·PH; when people become familiar with HDTV they will form an expectation that it is best viewed at about 3·PH.

Bernie Lechner found, in unpublished research, that North American viewers tend to view SDTV receivers at about 9 ft. In similar experiments at Philips Labs in England, Jackson found a preference for 3 m. This viewing distance is sometimes called the *Lechner distance* – or in Europe, the *Jackson distance*! These numbers are consistent with Equation 1.2, on page 8, applied to a 27-inch (70 cm) diagonal display.

Rather than saying that improvements in bandwidth or spot profile enable decreased viewing distance, and therefore wider picture angle, we assume that viewing distance is fixed, and say that resolution is improved.

Interlace revisited

We can now revisit the parameters of interlaced scanning. At luminance and ambient illumination typical of television receivers, a vertical scan rate of 50 or 60 Hz is sufficient to overcome flicker. As I mentioned on page 56, at practical vertical scan rates, it is possible to flash alternate image rows in alternate vertical scans without causing flicker. This is *interlace.* The scheme is possible owing to the fact that temporal sensitivity of the visual system decreases at high spatial frequencies.

Twitter is introduced, however, by vertical detail whose scale approaches the scan-line pitch. Twitter can be reduced to tolerable levels by reducing the vertical detail somewhat, to perhaps 0.7 times. On its own, this reduction in vertical detail would push the viewing distance back to 1.4 times that of progressive scanning.

However, to maintain the same sharpness as a progressive system at a given data capacity, all else being equal, in interlaced scanning only half the picture data needs to be transmitted in each vertical scan period (field). For a given frame rate, this reduction in data per scan enables pixel count per frame to be doubled.

The pixels gained could be exploited in one of three ways: By doubling the row count, by doubling the column count, or by distributing the additional pixels proportionally to image columns and rows. Taking the third approach, doubling the pixel count would increase column count by 1.4 and row count by 1.4, enabling a reduction of viewing distance to 0.7 of progressive scan. This would win back the lost viewing distance associated with twitter, and would yield equivalent performance to progressive scan.

Twitter and scan-line visibility are inversely proportional to the count of image rows, a one-dimensional quantity. However, sharpness is proportional to pixel count, a two-dimensional (areal) quantity. To overcome twitter at the same picture angle, 1.4 times as many image rows are required; however, 1.2 times as many rows and 1.2 times as many columns are still available to improve picture angle.

Ideally, though, the additional pixels owing to interlaced scan should not be distributed proportionally to picture width and height. Instead, the count of image columns should be increased by about 1.7 (1.4×1.2), and the count of image rows by about 1.2. The 1.4 increase in the row count alleviates twitter; the factor of 1.2 increase in both row and column count yields a small improvement in viewing distance – and therefore picture angle – over a progressive system.

Interlaced scanning was chosen over progressive in the early days of television, half a century ago. All other things being equal – such as data rate, frame rate, spot size, and viewing distance – various advantages have been claimed for interlace scanning.

- If you neglect the introduction of twitter, and consider just the static pixel array, interlace offers twice the static resolution for a given bandwidth and frame rate.

- If you consider an interlaced image of the same size as a progressive image and viewed at the same distance – that is, preserving the picture angle – then there is a decrease in scan-line visibility.

Constant luminance 8

Video systems convey color image data using one component to represent lightness, and two other components to represent color, absent lightness. In *Color science for video,* on page 233, I will detail how luminance can be formed as a weighted sum of linear *RGB* values that are proportional to optical power. Transmitting relative luminance – preferably after imposition of a nonlinear transfer function – is called the *Principle of Constant Luminance*.

Video systems depart from this principle and implement an engineering approximation. A weighted sum of linear *RGB* is not computed. Instead, a nonlinear transfer function is applied to each linear *RGB* component, then a weighted sum of the nonlinear *gamma-corrected R'G'B'* components forms what I call *luma.* (Many video engineers carelessly call this *luminance*.) As far as a color scientist is concerned, a video system uses the theoretical matrix coefficients of color science but uses them in the wrong block diagram: In video, gamma correction is applied *before* the matrix, instead of the color scientist's preference, after.

The term *luminance* is widely misused in video. See *Relative luminance,* on page 206, and Appendix A, *YUV and luminance considered harmful,* on page 595.

In this chapter, I will explain why and how all video systems depart from the principle. If you are willing to accept this departure from theory as a fact, then you may safely skip this chapter, and proceed to *Introduction to luma and chroma,* on page 87, where I will introduce how the luma and color difference signals are formed and subsampled.

Applebaum, Sidney, "Gamma Correction in Constant Luminance Color Television Systems," in Proc. IRE, 40 (11): 1185–1195 (Oct. 1952).

The principle of constant luminance

Ideally, the lightness component in color video would mimic a monochrome system: Relative luminance would be computed as a properly weighted sum of (linear-light) *R*, *G*, and *B* tristimulus values, according to the principles of color science that I will explain in *Transformations between RGB and CIE XYZ*, on page 251. At the decoder, the inverse matrix would reconstruct the linear *R*, *G*, and *B* tristimulus values:

Figure 8.1 **Formation of relative luminance**

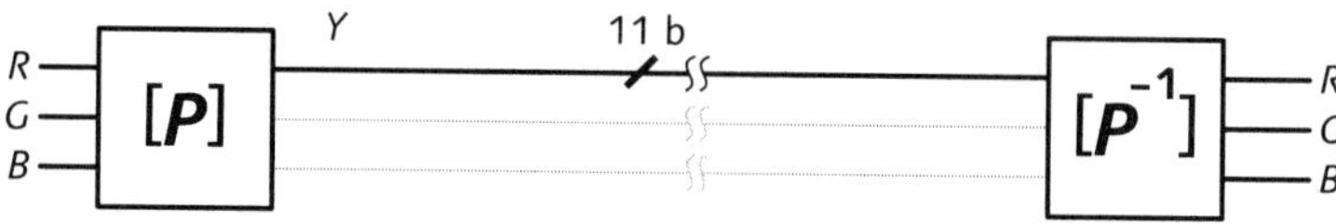

Two color difference (chroma) components would be computed, to enable chroma subsampling; these would be conveyed to the decoder through separate channels:

Figure 8.2 **Chroma components (linear)**

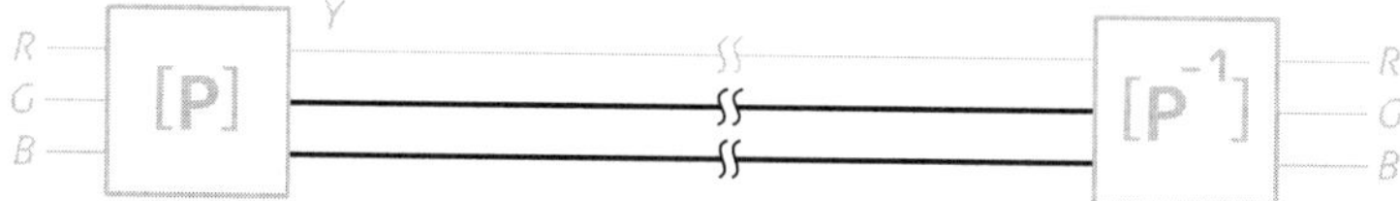

Set aside the chroma components for now: No matter how they are handled, all of the relative luminance is recoverable from the luminance channel.

If relative luminance were conveyed directly, 11 bits or more would be necessary. Eight bits barely suffice if we use *Nonlinear image coding*, introduced on page 12, to impose perceptual uniformity: We could subject relative luminance to a nonlinear transfer function that mimics vision's lightness sensitivity. Lightness can be approximated as CIE *L** (to be detailed on page 208); *L** is roughly the 0.4-power of relative luminance.

Figure 8.3 **Nonlinearly coded relative luminance**

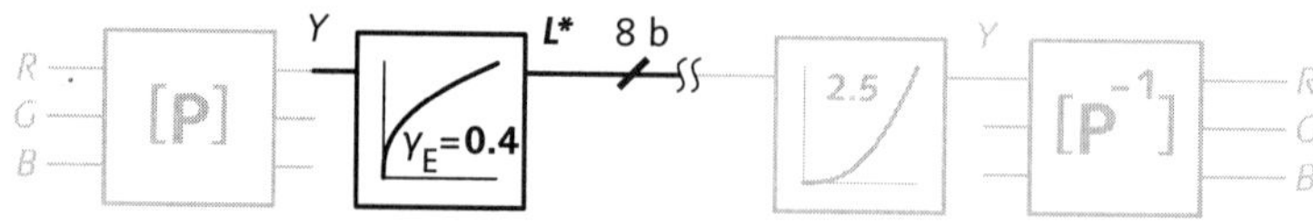

The inverse transfer function would be applied at decoding:

Figure 8.4 **Nonlinearly coded relative luminance**

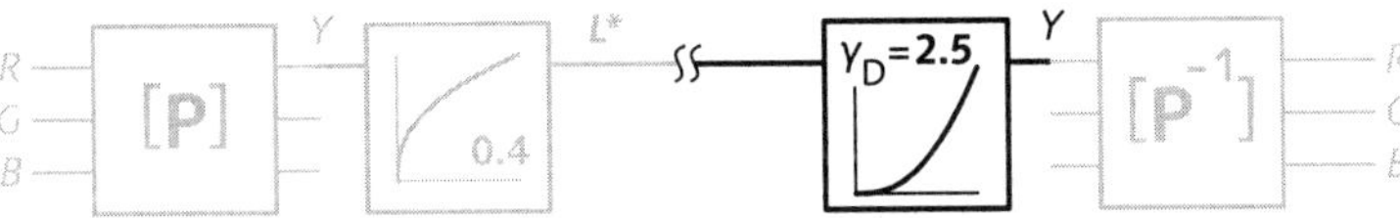

If a video system were to operate in this manner, it would exhibit the *Principle of Constant Luminance:* All of the relative luminance would be present in, and recoverable from, a single component.

Compensating the CRT

Unfortunately for the theoretical block diagram – but fortunately for video, as you will see in a moment – the electron gun of a CRT monitor introduces a power function having an exponent of approximately 2.5:

Figure 8.5 **CRT transfer function**

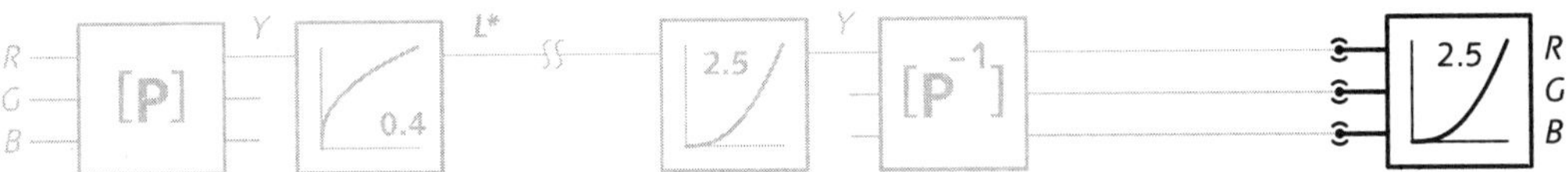

In a constant luminance system, the decoder would have to invert the monitor's power function. This would require insertion of a compensating transfer function – roughly a $1/2.5$-power function – in front of the CRT:

Figure 8.6 **Compensating the CRT transfer**

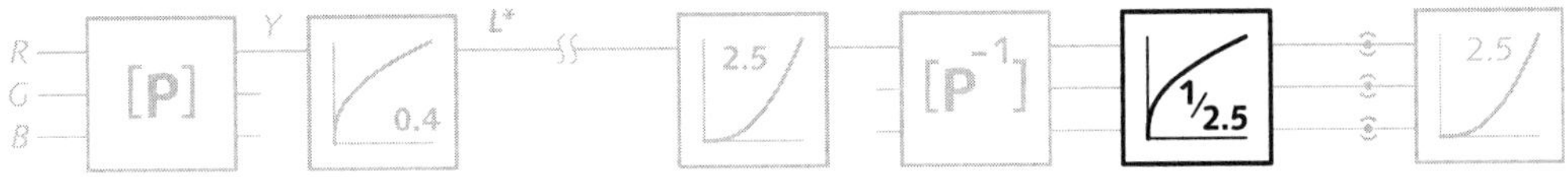

The decoder would now include two power functions: An inverse *L** function with an exponent close to 2.5 to undo the perceptually uniform coding, and a power function with an exponent of $1/2.5$ to compensate the CRT. Having two nonlinear transfer functions at every decoder would be expensive and impractical. Notice that the exponents of the power functions are 2.5 and $1/2.5$ – the functions are inverses!

Departure from constant luminance

To avoid the complexity of incorporating two power functions into a decoder's electronics, we begin by rearranging the block diagram, to interchange the "order of operations" of the matrix and the CRT compensation:

Figure 8.7 **Rearranged decoder**

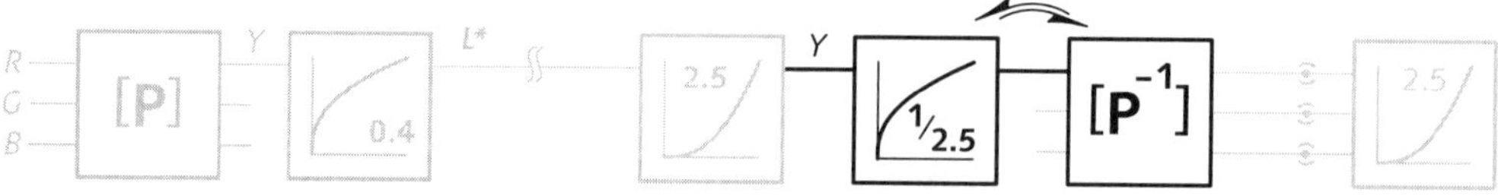

Upon rearrangement, the two power functions are adjacent. Since the functions are effectively inverses, the combination of the two has no effect. Both functions can be dropped from the decoder:

Figure 8.8 **Simplified decoder**

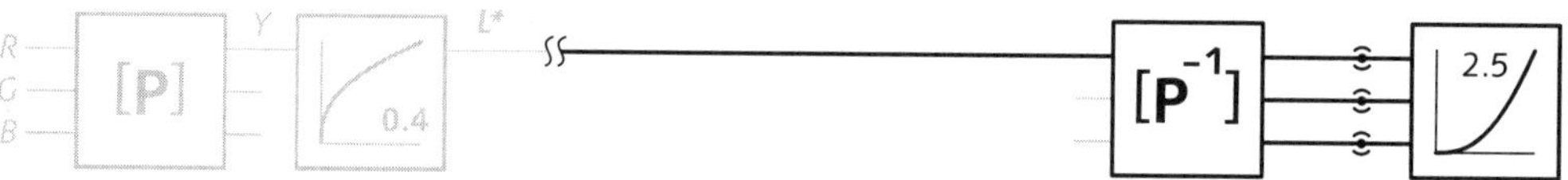

The decoder now comprises simply the inverse of the encoder matrix, followed by the 2.5-power function that is intrinsic to the CRT. Rearranging the decoder requires that the encoder also be rearranged, so as to mirror the decoder and achieve correct end-to-end reproduction of the original *RGB* tristimulus values:

Figure 8.9 **Rearranged encoder**

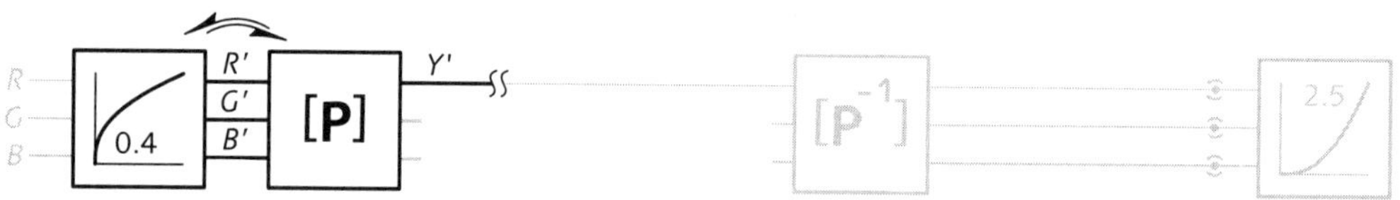

Television engineers who are uneducated in color science often mistakenly call luma (*Y'*) by the name *luminance* and denote it by the unprimed symbol *Y*. This leads to great confusion, as I explain in Appendix A, on page 595.

The rearranged flow diagram of Figure 8.9 is *not* mathematically equivalent to the arrangement of Figures 8.1 through 8.4! The encoder's matrix no longer operates on (linear) tristimulus signals, and relative luminance is no longer computed. Instead, a nonlinear quantity *Y'*, denoted *luma*, is computed and transmitted. Luma involves an engineering approximation: The system no longer adheres strictly to the *Principle of Constant Luminance* (though it is often mistakenly claimed to do so).

Tristimulus values are correctly reproduced by the arrangement of Figure 8.9, and it is highly practical. Figure 8.9 encapsulates the basic signal flow for all video systems; it will be elaborated in later chapters.

In the rearranged encoder, we no longer use CIE L^* to optimize for perceptual uniformity. Instead, we use the inverse of the transfer function inherent in the CRT. A 0.4-power function accomplishes approximately perceptually uniform coding, and reproduces tristimulus values proportional to those in the original scene.

You will learn in the following chapter, *Rendering intent*, that the 0.4 value must be altered to about 0.5 to accommodate a perceptual effect. This alteration depends upon viewing environment; display systems should have adjustments for rendering intent, but they don't! Before discussing the alteration, I will outline the repercussions of the nonideal block diagram.

"Leakage" of luminance into chroma

Until now, we have neglected the color difference components. In the rearranged block diagram of Figure 8.9 at the bottom of the facing page, color differences components are "matrixed" from *nonlinear* (gamma-corrected) $R'G'B'$:

Figure 8.10 **Chroma components**

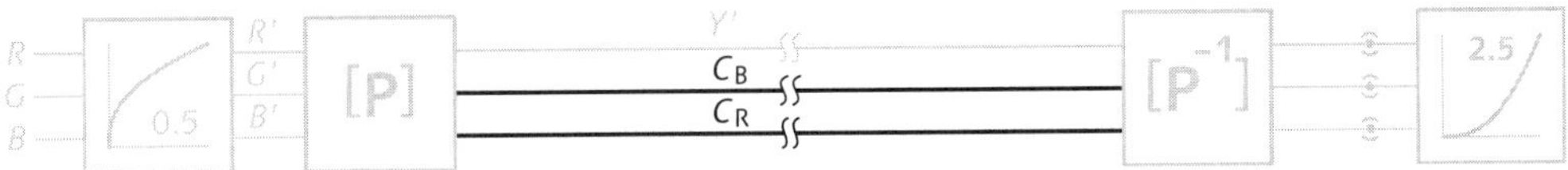

In a true constant luminance system, no matter how the color difference signals are handled, all of the relative luminance is carried by the luminance channel. In the rearranged system, most of the relative luminance is conveyed through the Y' channel; however, some relative luminance can be thought of as "leaking" into the color difference components. If the color difference components were not subsampled, this would present no problem. However, the color difference components are formed to enable subsampling! So, we now turn our attention to that.

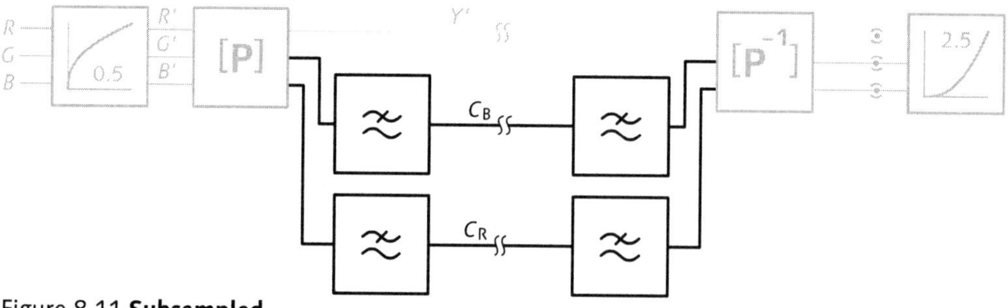

Figure 8.11 **Subsampled chroma components**

In Figure 8.11 above, I show the practical block diagram of Figure 8.10, augmented with subsampling filters in the chroma paths. With nonconstant luminance coding, some of the relative luminance traverses the chroma pathways. Subsampling not only removes detail from the color components, it also removes detail from the "leaked" relative luminance. Consequently, relative luminance is incorrectly reproduced: In areas where luminance detail is present in saturated colors, relative luminance is reproduced too dark, and saturation is reduced. This is the penalty that must be paid for lack of strict adherence to the Principle of Constant Luminance. These errors are perceptible by experts, but they are very rarely noticeable – let alone objectionable – in normal scenes. The departure from theory is apparent in the dark band appearing between the green and magenta color bars of the standard video test pattern, depicted in Figure 8.12 in the margin.

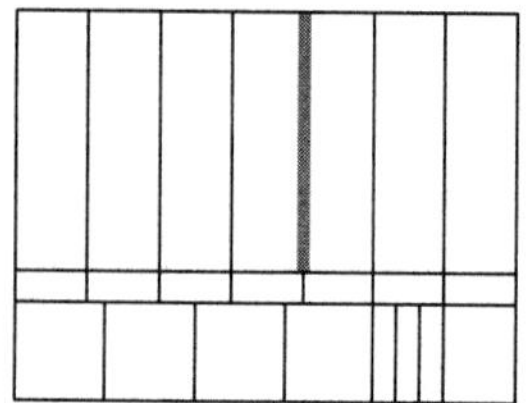

Figure 8.12 **Failure to adhere to constant luminance** is evident in the dark band in the green-magenta transition of the colorbar test signal.

To summarize signal encoding in video systems: First, a nonlinear transfer function, *gamma correction*, comparable to a square root, is applied to each of the linear *R*, *G*, and *B* tristimulus values to form *R'*, *G'*, and *B'*. Then, a suitably weighted sum of the nonlinear components is computed to form the luma signal (*Y'*). Luma approximates the lightness response of vision. Color difference components *blue minus luma* (*B'*–*Y'*) and *red minus luma* (*R'*–*Y'*) are formed. (Luma, *B'*–*Y'*, and *R'*–*Y'* can be computed from *R'*, *G'*, and *B'* simultaneously, through a 3×3 matrix.) The color difference components are then subsampled (filtered), using one of several schemes – including 4:2:2, 4:1:1, and 4:2:0 – to be described starting on page 87.

The notation *4:2:2* has come to denote not just chroma subsampling, but a whole set of SDTV interface parameters.

Rendering intent 9

Examine the flowers in a garden at noon on a bright, sunny day. Look at the same garden half an hour after sunset. Physically, the spectra of the flowers have not changed, except by scaling to lower luminance levels. However, the flowers are markedly less colorful after sunset: Colorfulness decreases as luminance decreases.

Reproduced images are usually viewed at a small fraction, perhaps $1/100$ or $1/1000$, of the luminance at which they were captured. If reproduced luminance were made proportional to scene luminance, the reproduced image would appear less colorful, and lower in contrast, than the original scene.

Giorgianni, Edward J., and T.E. Madden, *Digital Color Management: Encoding Solutions* (Reading, Mass.: Addison-Wesley, 1998).

To reproduce contrast and colorfulness comparable to the original scene, we *must* alter the characteristics of the image. An engineer or physicist might strive to achieve mathematical linearity in an imaging system; however, the required alterations cause reproduced luminance to depart from linearity. The dilemma is this: We can achieve mathematical linearity, or we can achieve correct appearance, but we cannot simultaneously do both! Successful commercial imaging systems sacrifice mathematics to achieve the correct perceptual result.

I use the term *white* to refer to diffuse white, which I will explain on page 83.

If "white" in the viewing environment is markedly darker than "white" in the environment in which it was captured, the tone scale of an image must be altered. An additional reason for correction is the surround effect, which I will now explain.

Figure 9.1 **Surround effect.** The three squares surrounded by light gray are identical to the three squares surrounded by black; however, each of the black-surround squares is apparently lighter than its counterpart. Also, the contrast of the black-surround series appears lower than that of the white-surround series.

DeMarsh, LeRoy E., and Edward J. Giorgianni, "Color Science for Imaging Systems," in *Physics Today*, Sept. 1989 , 44–52.

Surround effect

Human vision adapts to an extremely wide range of viewing conditions, as I will detail in *Adaptation,* on page 196. One of the mechanisms involved in adaptation increases our sensitivity to small brightness variations when the area of interest is surrounded by bright elements. Intuitively, light from a bright surround can be thought of as spilling or scattering into all areas of our vision, including the area of interest, reducing its apparent contrast. Loosely speaking, the visual system compensates for this effect by "stretching" its contrast range to increase the visibility of dark elements in the presence of a bright *surround*. Conversely, when the region of interest is surrounded by relative darkness, the contrast range of the vision system decreases: Our ability to discern dark elements in the scene decreases. The effect is demonstrated in Figure 9.1 above, from DeMarsh and Giorgianni. The surround effect stems from the perceptual phenomenon called the *simultaneous contrast effect*, also known as *lateral inhibition*.

Image-related scattered light is called *flare.*

Simultaneous contrast has another meaning, where it is a contraction of *simultaneous contrast ratio* (distinguished from *sequential contrast ratio*). See *Contrast ratio,* on page 197.

The surround effect has implications for the display of images in dark areas, such as projection of movies in a cinema, projection of 35 mm slides, or viewing of television in your living room. If an image were reproduced with the correct relative luminance, then when viewed in a dark or dim surround, it would appear lacking in contrast.

Image reproduction is not simply concerned with physics, mathematics, chemistry, and electronics: Perceptual considerations play an essential role.

Tone scale alteration

Tone scale alteration is necessary mainly for the two reasons that I have described: The luminance of a reproduction is typically dramatically lower than the luminance of the original scene, and the surround of a reproduced image is rarely comparable to the surround of the original scene. Two additional reasons contribute to the requirement for tone scale alteration: limitation of contrast ratio, and specular highlights.

Simultaneous contrast ratio is the ratio of luminances of the lightest and darkest elements of a scene (or an image). For details, see *Contrast ratio*, on page 197.

An original scene typically has a ratio of luminance levels – a *simultaneous contrast ratio* – of 1000:1 or more. However, contrast ratio in the captured image is limited by optical flare in the camera. Contrast ratio at the display is likely to be limited even further – by physical factors, and by display flare – to perhaps 100:1.

Diffuse white refers to the luminance of a diffusely reflecting white surface in a scene. Paper reflects diffusely, and white paper reflects about 90% of incident light, so a white card approximates diffuse white. However, most scenes contain shiny objects that reflect directionally. When viewed in certain directions, these objects reflect specular highlights having luminances perhaps ten times that of diffuse white. At the reproduction device, we can seldom afford to reproduce diffuse white at merely 10% of the maximum luminance of the display, solely to exactly reproduce the luminance levels of the highlights! Nor is there any need to reproduce highlights exactly: A convincing image can be formed with highlight luminance greatly reduced from its true value. To make effective use of luminance ranges that are typically available in image display systems, highlights must be compressed.

Incorporation of rendering intent

The correction that I have mentioned is achieved by subjecting luminance – or, in the case of a color system, tristimulus values – to an end-to-end power function having an exponent between about 1.1 and 1.6. The exponent depends primarily upon the ratio of scene luminance to reproduction luminance. The exponent depends to some degree upon the display physics and the viewing environment. Nearly all image reproduction systems require some tone scale alteration.

In *Constant luminance*, on page 75, I outlined considerations of nonlinear coding in video. Continuing the sequence of sketches from Figure 8.9, on page 78, Figure 9.2 shows that correction for typical television viewing could be effected by including, in the decoder, a power function having an exponent of about 1.25:

Figure 9.2 **Imposition of rendering at decoder**

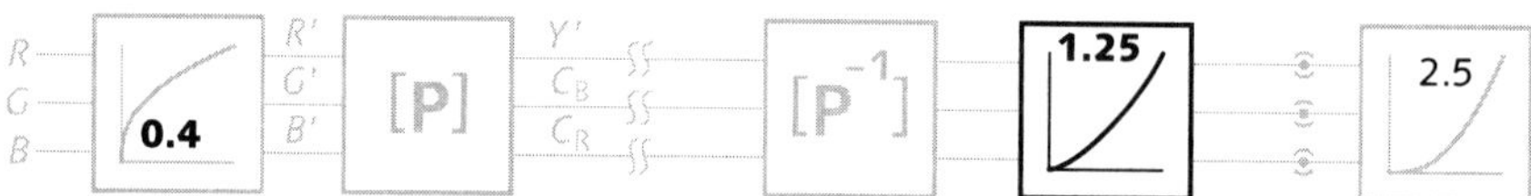

Observe that a power function is already a necessary part of the encoder. Instead of altering the decoder, we modify the encoder's power function to approximate a 0.5-power, instead of the physically correct 0.4-power:

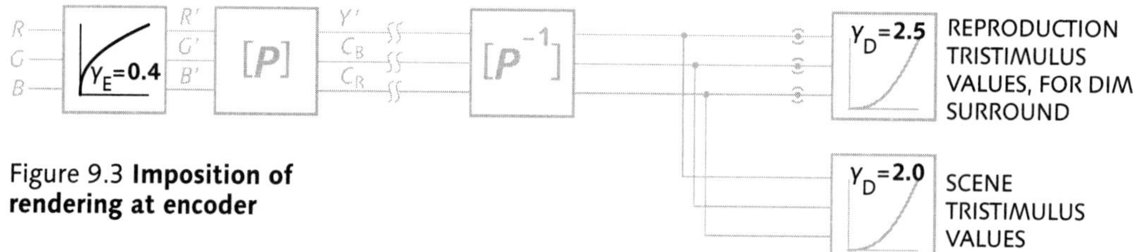

Figure 9.3 **Imposition of rendering at encoder**

Concatenating the 0.5-power at encoding and the 2.5-power at decoding produces the end-to-end 1.25-power required for television display in a dim surround. To recover scene tristimulus values, the encoding transfer function should simply be inverted; the decoding function then approximates a 2.0-power function, as sketched at the bottom right of Figure 9.3.

As I mentioned in the marginal note on page 26, depending upon the setting of the BRIGHTNESS control, the effective power function exponent at a CRT varies from its nominal 2.5 value. In a dark viewing environment – such as a home theater – the display's BRIGHTNESS setting will be reduced; the decoder's effective exponent will rise to about 2.7, and the end-to-end

Imaging system	Encoding exponent	"Advertised" exponent	Decoding exponent	Typ. Surround	End-to-end exponent
Cinema	0.6	0.6	2.5	Dark	1.5
Television (Rec. 709, see page 263)	0.5	0.45	2.5	Dim	1.25
Office (sRGB, see page 267)	0.45	0.42	2.5	Light	1.125

Table 9.1 **End-to-end power functions** for several imaging systems. The encoding exponent achieves approximately perceptual coding. (The "advertised" exponent neglects the scaling and offset associated with the straight-line segment of encoding.) The decoding exponent acts at the display to approximately invert the perceptual encoding. The product of the two exponents sets the end-to-end power function that imposes the rendering intent.

power will rise to about 1.5. In a bright surround – such as a computer in a desktop environment – BRIGHTNESS will be increased; this will reduce the effective exponent to about 2.3, and thereby reduce the end-to-end exponent to about 1.125.

The encoding exponent, decoding exponent, and end-to-end power function for cinema, television, and office CRT viewing are shown in Table 9.1 above.

Fairchild, Mark D., *Color Appearance Models* (Reading, Mass.: Addison-Wesley, 1998).

James, T.H., ed., *The Theory of the Photographic Process*, Fourth Edition (Rochester, N.Y.: Eastman Kodak, 1977). See Ch. 19 (p. 537), *Preferred Tone Reproduction*.

In film systems, the necessary correction is designed into the transfer function of the film (or films). Color reversal (slide) film is intended for viewing in a dark surround; it is designed to have a gamma considerably greater than unity – about 1.5 – so that the contrast range of the scene is expanded upon display. In cinema film, the correction is achieved through a combination of the transfer function ("gamma" of about 0.6) built into camera negative film and the overall transfer function ("gamma" of about 2.5) built into print film.

Some people suggest that NTSC should be gamma-corrected with power of $1/2.2$, and PAL with $1/2.8$. I disagree with both interpretations; see page 268.

I have described video systems as if they use a pure 0.5-power law encoding function. Practical considerations necessitate modification of the pure power function by the insertion of a linear segment near black, as I will explain in *Gamma*, on page 257. The exponent in the Rec. 709 standard is written ("advertised") as 0.45; however, the insertion of the linear segment, and the offsetting and scaling of the pure power function segment of the curve, cause an exponent of about 0.51 to best describe the overall curve. (To describe gamma as 0.45 in this situation is misleading.)

Rendering intent in desktop computing

In the desktop computer environment, the ambient condition is considerably brighter, and the surround is brighter, than is typical of television viewing. An end-to-end exponent lower than the 1.25 of video is called for; a value around 1.125 is generally suitable. However, desktop computers are used in a variety of different viewing conditions. It is not practical to originate every image in several forms, optimized for several potential viewing conditions! A specific encoding function needs to be chosen. Achieving optimum reproduction in diverse viewing conditions requires selecting a suitable correction at display time. Technically, this is easy to achieve: Modern computer display subsystems have hardware lookup tables (LUTs) that can be loaded dynamically with appropriate curves. However, it is a challenge to train users to make a suitable choice.

In the sRGB standard, the exponent is written ("advertised") as $1/2.4$ (about 0.417). However, the insertion of the linear segment, and the offsetting and scaling of the pure power function segment of the curve, cause an exponent of about 0.45 to best describe the overall curve. See *sRGB transfer function,* on page 267.

In the development of the sRGB standard for desktop computing, the inevitability of local, viewing-dependent correction was not appreciated. That standard promulgates an encoding standard with an effective exponent of about 0.45, different from that of video. We are now saddled with image data encoded with two standards having comparable perceptual uniformity but different rendering intents. Today, sRGB and video (Rec. 709) coding are distinguished by the applications: sRGB is used for still images, and Rec. 709 coding is used for motion video images. But image data types are converging, and this dichotomy in rendering intent is bound to become a nuisance.

Video cameras, film cameras, motion picture cameras, and digital still cameras all capture images from the real world. When an image of an original scene or object is captured, it is important to introduce rendering intent. However, scanners used in desktop computing rarely scan original objects; they usually scan reproductions such as photographic prints or offset-printed images. When a reproduction is scanned, rendering intent has already been imposed by the first imaging process. It may be sensible to adjust the original rendering intent, but it is not sensible to introduce rendering intent that would be suitable for scanning a real scene or object.

Introduction to luma and chroma 10

Video systems convey image data in the form of one component that represents lightness, and two components that represent color, disregarding lightness. This scheme exploits the reduced color acuity of vision compared to luminance acuity: As long as lightness is conveyed with full detail, detail in the color components can be reduced by subsampling (filtering, or averaging). This chapter introduces the concepts of luma and chroma encoding; details will be presented in *Luma and color differences*, on page 281.

Luma

A certain amount of noise is inevitable in any image digitizing system. As explained in *Nonlinear image coding*, on page 12, we arrange things so that noise has a perceptually similar effect across the entire tone scale from black to white. The lightness component is conveyed in a perceptually uniform manner that minimizes the amount of noise (or quantization error) introduced in processing, recording, and transmission.

Ideally, noise would be minimized by forming a signal proportional to CIE luminance, as a suitably weighted sum of linear R, G, and B tristimulus signals. Then, this signal would be subjected to a transfer function that imposes perceptual uniformity, such as the CIE L^* function of color science that will be detailed on page 208. As explained in *Constant luminance*, on page 75, there are practical reasons in video to perform these operations in the opposite order. First, a nonlinear transfer function – *gamma correction* – is applied to each of the linear R, G, and B tristimulus signals: We impose the Rec. 709 transfer function, very similar to a square root, and roughly comparable to the CIE lightness (L^*) function. Then a weighted sum of the resulting nonlinear R', G', and B' components is computed to form a *luma* signal (Y') representative of lightness. SDTV uses coefficients that are standardized in Rec. 601 (see page 97):

The prime symbols here, and in following equations, denote nonlinear components.

$$^{601}Y' = 0.299\,R' + 0.587\,G' + 0.114\,B' \qquad \text{Eq 10.1}$$

Unfortunately, luma for HDTV is coded differently from luma in SDTV! Rec. 709 specifies these coefficients:

Luma is coded differently in large (HDTV) pictures than in small (SDTV) pictures!

$$^{709}Y' = 0.2126\,R' + 0.7152\,G' + 0.0722\,B' \qquad \text{Eq 10.2}$$

Sloppy use of the term *luminance*

CIE: Commission Internationale de l'Éclairage

The term *luminance* and the symbol Y were established by the CIE, the standards body for color science. Unfortunately, in video, the term *luminance* has come to mean *the video signal representative of luminance* even though the components of the video signal have been subjected to a nonlinear transfer function. At the dawn of video, the nonlinear signal was denoted Y', where the prime symbol indicated the nonlinear treatment. But over the last 40 years the prime has not appeared consistently; now, both the term *luminance* and the symbol Y conflict with their CIE definitions, making them ambiguous! This has led to great confusion, such as the incorrect statement commonly found in computer graphics textbooks and digital image-processing textbooks that in the YIQ or YUV color spaces, the Y component is identical to CIE luminance!

See Appendix A, *YUV and luminance considered harmful*, on page 595.

I use the term *luminance* according to its CIE definition; I use the term *luma* to refer to the video signal; and I am careful to designate nonlinear quantities with a prime. However, many video engineers, computer graphics practitioners, and image-processing specialists use these terms carelessly. You must be careful to determine whether a linear or nonlinear interpretation is being applied to the word and the symbol.

Color difference coding (chroma)

Luma and color differences can be computed from R', G', and B' through a 3×3 matrix multiplication.

In component video, three components necessary to convey color information are transmitted separately. Rather than conveying $R'G'B'$ directly, the relatively poor color acuity of vision is exploited to reduce data capacity accorded to the color information, while maintaining full luma detail. First, luma is formed according to Marginal note (or for HDTV, Marginal note). Then, two *color difference* signals based upon gamma-corrected *B′ minus luma* and *R′ minus luma,* B'–Y' and R'–Y', are formed by "matrixing." Finally, subsampling (filtering) reduces detail in the color difference (or *chroma*) components, as I will outline on page 93. Subsampling incurs no loss in sharpness at any reasonable viewing distance.

$Y'P_BP_R$

In component analog video, B'–Y' and R'–Y' are scaled to form color difference signals denoted P_B and P_R, which are then analog lowpass filtered (horizontally) to about half the luma bandwidth.

$Y'C_BC_R$

In component digital video, M-JPEG, and MPEG, B'–Y' and R'–Y' are scaled to form C_B and C_R components, which can then be subsampled by a scheme such as 4:2:2 or 4:2:0, which I will describe in a moment.

$Y'UV$

In composite NTSC or PAL video, B'–Y' and R'–Y' are scaled to form U and V components. Subsequently, U and V are lowpass filtered, then combined into a modulated chroma component, C. Luma is then summed with modulated chroma to produce the composite NTSC or PAL signal. Scaling of U and V is arranged so that the excursion of the composite signal (Y'+C) is constrained to the range $-1/3$ to $+4/3$ of the unity excursion of luma. U and V components have no place in component analog or component digital video.

$Y'IQ$

Composite NTSC video was standardized in 1953 based upon I and Q components that were essentially U and V components rotated 33° and axis-exchanged. It was intended that excess detail would be removed from the Q component so as to improve color quality. The scheme never achieved significant deployment in receivers, and I and Q components are now obsolete.

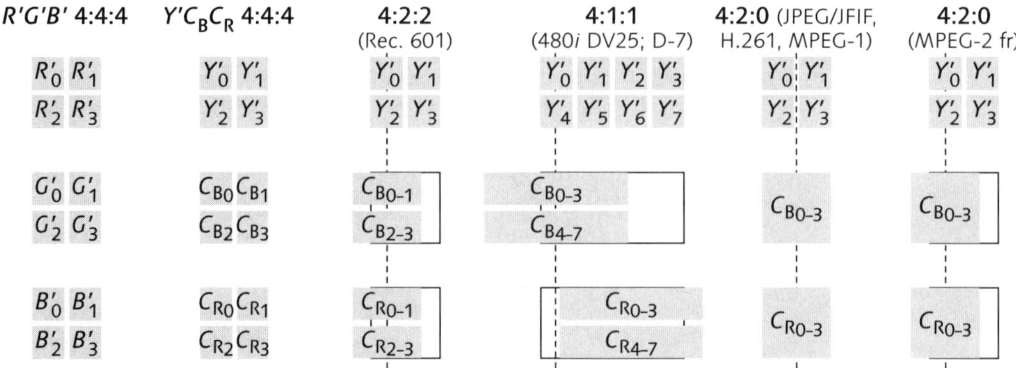

Figure 10.1 **Chroma subsampling.** A 2×2 array of *R'G'B'* pixels is matrixed into a luma component Y' and two color difference components C_B and C_R. Color detail is reduced by subsampling C_B and C_R; providing full luma detail is maintained, no degradation is perceptible. In this sketch, samples are shaded to indicate their spatial position and extent. In 4:2:2, in 4:1:1, and in 4:2:0 used in MPEG-2, C_B and C_R are cosited (positioned horizontally coincident with a luma sample). In 4:2:0 used in JPEG/JFIF, H.261, and MPEG-1, C_B and C_R are sited interstitially (midway between luma samples).

Chroma subsampling

4:4:4

In Figure 10.1 above, the left-hand column sketches a 2×2 array of *R'G'B'* pixels. Prior to subsampling, this is denoted 4:4:4 *R'G'B'*. With 8 bits per sample, this 2×2 array of *R'G'B'* would occupy a total of 12 bytes. Each *R'G'B'* triplet (pixel) can be transformed ("matrixed") into $Y'C_BC_R$, as shown in the second column; this is denoted 4:4:4 $Y'C_BC_R$.

In component digital video, data capacity is reduced by subsampling C_B and C_R using one of three schemes.

4:2:2

$Y'C_BC_R$ studio digital video according to Rec. 601 uses 4:2:2 sampling: C_B and C_R components are each subsampled by a factor of 2 horizontally. C_B and C_R are sampled together, coincident (*cosited*) with even-numbered luma samples. The 12 bytes of *R'G'B'* are reduced to 8, effecting 1.5:1 lossy compression.

4:1:1

Certain digital video systems, such as 480*i*29.97 DV25, use 4:1:1 sampling, whereby C_B and C_R components are each subsampled by a factor of 4 horizontally, and cosited with every fourth luma sample. The 12 bytes of *R'G'B'* are reduced to 6, effecting 2:1 compression.

4:2:0

This scheme is used in JPEG/JFIF, H.261, MPEG-1, MPEG-2, and consumer 576*i*25 DVC. C_B and C_R are each subsampled by a factor of 2 horizontally and a factor of 2 vertically. The 12 bytes of $R'G'B'$ are reduced to 6. C_B and C_R are effectively centered vertically halfway between image rows. There are two variants of 4:2:0, having different horizontal siting. In MPEG-2, C_B and C_R are cosited horizontally. In JPEG/JFIF, H.261, and MPEG-1, C_B and C_R are sited interstitially, halfway between alternate luma samples.

ITU-T Rec. H.261, known casually as *p*×64 ("p times 64"), is a videoconferencing standard.

Figure 10.2 overleaf summarizes the various schemes.

Subsampling effects 1.5:1 or 2:1 lossy compression. However, in studio terminology, subsampled video is referred to as *uncompressed:* The word *compression* is reserved for JPEG, M-JPEG, MPEG, or other techniques.

Chroma subsampling notation

At the outset of digital video, subsampling notation was logical; unfortunately, technology outgrew the notation. In Figure 10.3 below, I strive to clarify today's nomenclature. The first digit originally specified luma sample rate relative to 3⅜ MHz. HDTV was once supposed to be described as 22:11:11! The leading digit has, thankfully, come to be relative to the sample rate in use. Until recently, the initial digit was always 4, since all chroma ratios have been powers of two – 4, 2, or 1. However, 3:1:1 subsampling has recently been commercialized in an HDTV production system (Sony's HDCAM), and in the SDL mode of consumer DV (see page 468), so *3* may now appear as the leading digit.

The use of *4* as the numerical basis for subsampling notation is a historical reference to sampling at roughly four times the NTSC color subcarrier frequency. The $4f_{SC}$ rate was already in use for composite digital video.

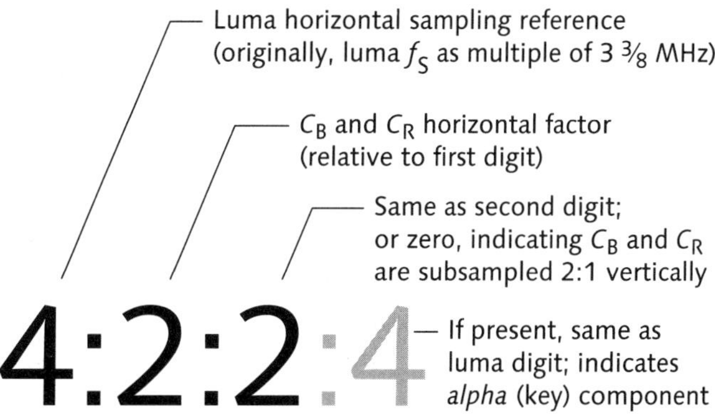

Figure 10.3 **Chroma subsampling notation** indicates, in the first digit, the luma horizontal sampling reference. The second digit specifies the horizontal subsampling of C_B and C_R with respect to luma. The third digit originally specified the horizontal subsampling of C_R. The notation developed without anticipating vertical subsampling; a third digit of zero now denotes 2:1 vertical subsampling of both C_B and C_R.

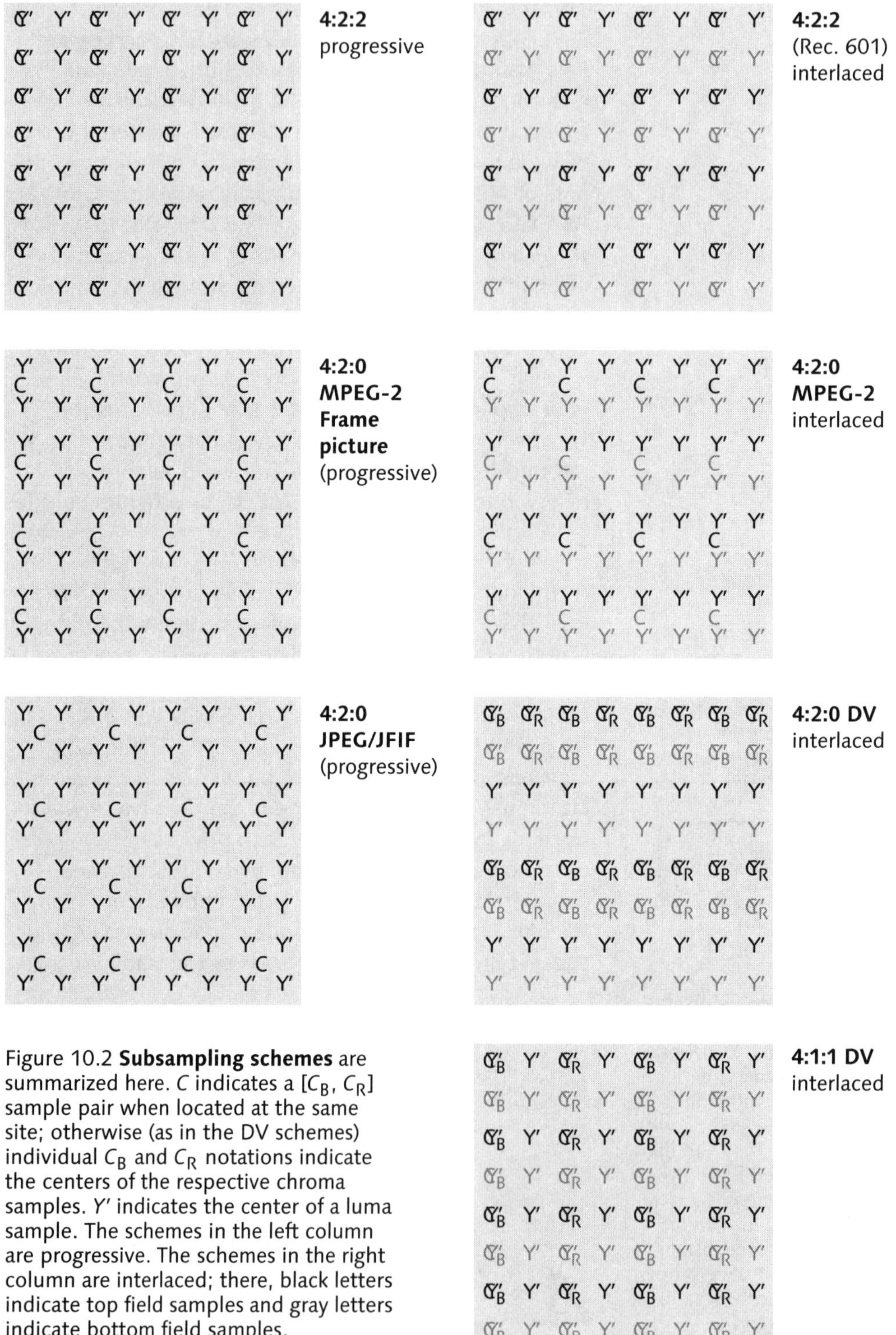

Figure 10.2 **Subsampling schemes** are summarized here. *C* indicates a [C_B, C_R] sample pair when located at the same site; otherwise (as in the DV schemes) individual C_B and C_R notations indicate the centers of the respective chroma samples. *Y'* indicates the center of a luma sample. The schemes in the left column are progressive. The schemes in the right column are interlaced; there, black letters indicate top field samples and gray letters indicate bottom field samples.

Chroma subsampling filters

In chroma subsampling, the encoder discards selected color difference samples after filtering. A decoder approximates the missing samples by interpolation.

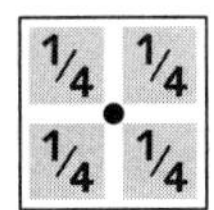

Figure 10.4 **Interstitial chroma filter for JPEG/JFIF** averages samples over a 2×2 block. Shading represents the spatial extent of luma samples. The black dot indicates the effective subsampled chroma position, equidistant from the four luma samples. The outline represents the spatial extent of the result.

To perform 4:2:0 subsampling with minimum computation, some systems simply average C_B over a 2×2 block, and average C_R over the same 2×2 block, as sketched in Figure 10.4 in the margin. To interpolate the missing chroma samples prior to conversion back to *R'G'B'*, low-end systems simply replicate the subsampled C_B and C_R values throughout the 2×2 quad. This technique is ubiquitous in JPEG/JFIF stillframes in computing, and is used in M-JPEG, H.261, and MPEG-1. This simple averaging process causes subsampled chroma to take an effective horizontal position halfway between two luma samples, what I call *interstitial* siting, not the cosited position standardized for studio video.

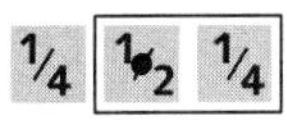

Figure 10.5 **Cosited chroma filter for Rec. 601, 4:2:2** causes each filtered chroma sample to be positioned coincident – *cosited* – with an even-numbered luma sample.

A simple way to perform 4:2:2 subsampling with horizontal cositing as required by Rec. 601 is to use weights of [$1/4$, $1/2$, $1/4$], as sketched in Figure 10.5. 4:2:2 subsampling has the advantage of no interaction with interlaced scanning.

A cosited horizontal filter can be combined with [$1/2$, $1/2$] vertical averaging, as sketched in Figure 10.6, to implement 4:2:0 as used in MPEG-2.

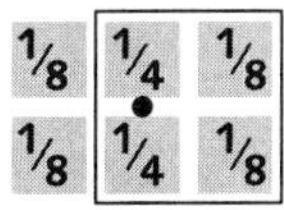

Figure 10.6 **Cosited chroma filter for MPEG-2, 4:2:0** produces a filtered result sample that is cosited horizontally, but sited interstitially in the vertical dimension.

Simple averaging filters like those of Figures 10.4, 10.5, and 10.6 have acceptable performance for stillframes, where any alias components that are generated remain stationary, or for desktop-quality video. However, in a moving image, an alias component introduced by poor filtering is liable to move at a rate different from the associated scene elements, and thereby produce a highly objectionable artifact. High-end digital video equipment uses sophisticated subsampling filters, where the subsampled C_B and C_R of a 2×1 pair in 4:2:2 (or of a 2×2 quad in 4:2:0) take contributions from several surrounding samples. The relationship of filter weights, frequency response, and filter performance will be detailed in *Filtering and sampling*, on page 141.

Chroma in composite NTSC and PAL

The video literature often calls these quantities *chrominance*. That term has a specific meaning in color science, so in video I prefer the term *modulated chroma*.

I introduced the color difference components P_BP_R and C_BC_R, often called *chroma components*. They accompany luma in a component video system. I also introduced *UV* and *IQ* components; these are intermediate quantities in the formation of *modulated chroma*.

See *Introduction to composite NTSC and PAL*, on page 103. Concerning SECAM, see page 576.

Historically, insufficient channel capacity was available to transmit three color components separately. The NTSC technique was devised to combine the three color components into a single *composite* signal; the PAL technique is both a refinement of NTSC and an adaptation of NTSC to 576*i* scanning. (In SECAM, the three color components are also combined into one signal. SECAM is a form of composite video, but the technique has little in common with NTSC and PAL, and it is of little commercial importance today.)

Encoders traditionally started with *R'G'B'* components. Modern analog encoders usually start with $Y'P_BP_R$ components; digital encoders (sometimes called a 4:2:2 to $4f_{SC}$ converters) usually start with $Y'C_BC_R$ components. NTSC or PAL encoding involves these steps:

- Component signals are matrixed and conditioned to form color difference signals *U* and *V* (or *I* and *Q*).
- *U* and *V* (or *I* and *Q*) are lowpass-filtered, then *quadrature modulation* imposes the two color difference signals onto an unmodulated color subcarrier, to produce a *modulated chroma* signal, *C*.
- Luma and chroma are summed. In studio video, summation exploits the *frequency-interleaving* principle.

Composite NTSC and PAL signals were historically analog; nowadays, they can be digital ($4f_{SC}$), though as I mentioned in *Video system taxonomy*, on page 62, composite video is being rapidly supplanted by component video in the studio, in consumers' premises, and in industrial applications. For further information, see *Introduction to composite NTSC and PAL*, on page 103.

Introduction to component SDTV 11

In *Raster scanning,* on page 51, I introduced the concepts of raster scanning; in *Introduction to luma and chroma,* on page 87, I introduced the concepts of color coding in video. This chapter combines the concepts of raster scanning and color coding to form the basic technical parameters of 480*i* and 576*i* systems. This chapter concerns modern systems that use component color – $Y'C_BC_R$ (Rec. 601), or $Y'P_BP_R$. In *Introduction to composite NTSC and PAL,* on page 103, I will describe NTSC and PAL composite video encoding.

Scanning standards

Two scanning standards are in use for conventional analog television broadcasting in different parts of the world. The 480*i*29.97 system is used primarily in North America and Japan, and today accounts for roughly ¼ of all television receivers. The 576*i*25 system is used primarily in Europe, Asia, Australia, Korea, and Central America, and accounts for roughly ¾ of all television receivers. 480*i*29.97 (or 525/59.94/2:1) is colloquially referred to as *NTSC,* and 576*i*25 (or 625/50/2:1) as *PAL*; however, the terms NTSC and PAL properly apply to color encoding and not to scanning standards. It is obvious from the scanning nomenclature that the line counts and field rates differ between the two systems: In 480*i*29.97 video, the field rate is exactly $^{60}/_{1.001}$ Hz; in 576*i*25, the field rate is exactly 50 Hz.

The notation *CCIR* is often wrongly used to denote 576*i*25 scanning. The former CCIR (now ITU-R) standardized many scanning systems, not just 576*i*25.

Several different standards for 480*i*29.97 and 576*i*25 digital video are sketched in Figure 11.1 overleaf.

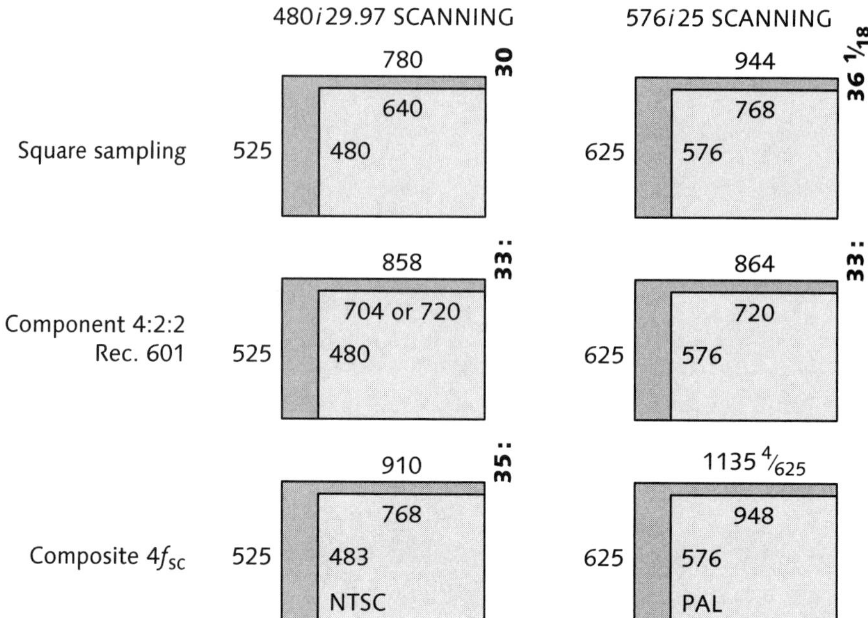

Figure 11.1 **SDTV digital video rasters** for 4:3 aspect ratio. 480*i*29.97 scanning is at the left, 576*i*25 at the right. The top row shows square sampling ("square pixels"). The middle row shows sampling at the Rec. 601 standard sampling frequency of 13.5 MHz. The bottom row shows sampling at four times the color subcarrier frequency ($4f_{SC}$). Above each diagram is its count of samples per total line (S_{TL}); ratios among S_{TL} values are written vertically in bold numerals.

Monochrome systems having 405/50 and 819/50 scanning were once used in Britain and France, respectively, but transmitters for these systems have now been decommissioned.

Analog broadcast of 480*i* usually uses NTSC color coding with a color subcarrier of about 3.58 MHz; analog broadcast of 576*i* usually uses PAL color coding with a color subcarrier of about 4.43 MHz. It is important to use a notation that distinguishes scanning from color, because other combinations of scanning and color coding are in use in large and important regions of the world. Brazil uses PAL-M, which has 480*i* scanning and PAL color coding. Argentina uses PAL-N, which has 576*i* scanning and a 3.58 MHz color subcarrier nearly identical to NTSC's subcarrier. In France, Russia, and other countries, SECAM is used. Production equipment is no longer manufactured for any of these obscure standards: Production in these countries is done using 480*i* or 576*i* studio equipment, either in the component domain or in 480*i* NTSC or 576*i* PAL. These studio signals are then *transcoded* prior to broadcast: The color encoding is altered – for example, from PAL to SECAM – without altering scanning.

See *PAL-M, PAL-N* on page 575, and *SECAM* on page 576. Consumer frustration with a diversity of functionally equivalent standards has led to proliferation of multistandard TVs and VCRs in countries using these standards.

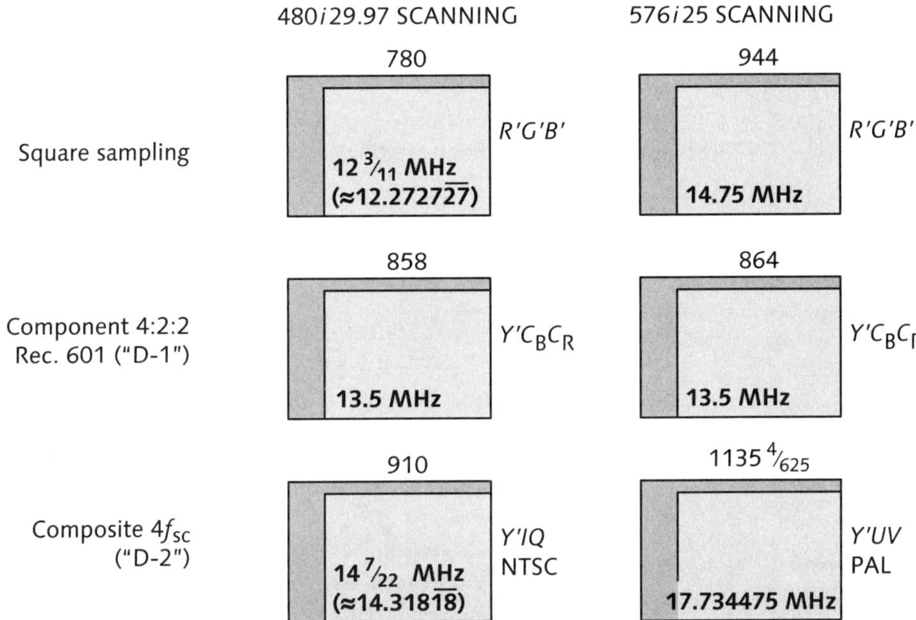

Figure 11.2 **SDTV sample rates** are shown for six different 4:3 standards, along with the usual color coding for each standard. There is no realtime studio interface standard for square-sampled SDTV. The *D-1* and *D-2* designations properly apply to videotape formats.

Figure 11.1 indicates S_{TL} and S_{AL} for each standard. The S_{AL} values are the result of some complicated issues to be discussed in *Choice of S_{AL} and S_{PW} parameters* on page 325. For details concerning my reference to 483 active lines (L_A) in 480*i* systems, see *Picture lines,* on page 324.

ITU-R Rec. BT.601-5, *Studio encoding parameters of digital television for standard 4:3 and wide-screen 16:9 aspect ratios.*

Figure 11.2 above shows the standard 480*i*29.97 and 576*i*25 digital video sampling rates, and the color coding usually associated with each of these standards. The 4:2:2, $Y'C_BC_R$ system for SDTV is standardized in *Recommendation BT. 601* of the ITU Radiocommunication Sector (formerly CCIR). I call it *Rec. 601*.

With one exception, all of the sampling systems in Figure 11.2 have a whole number of samples per total line; these systems are *line-locked*. The exception is composite $4f_{SC}$ PAL sampling, which has a noninteger number ($1135\,^4\!/_{625}$) of samples per total line; this creates a huge nuisance for the system designer.

System	480*i*29.97	576*i*25
Picture:sync ratio	10:4†	7:3
Setup, percent	7.5‡	0
Count of equalization, broad pulses	6	5
Line number 1, and 0_V, defined at:	First equalization pulse of field	First broad pulse of frame
Bottom picture line in:	First field	Second field

Table 11.1 **Gratuitous differences** between 480*i* and 576*i*

† The EBU N10 component analog interface for $Y'P_BP_R$, occasionally used for 480*i*, has 7:3 picture-to-sync ratio.

‡ 480*i* video in Japan, and the EBU N10 component analog interface, have zero setup. See page 327.

480*i* and 576*i* have gratuitous differences in many technical parameters, as summarized in Table 11.1 above.

Different treatment of interlace between 480*i* and 576*i* imposes different structure onto the picture data. The differences cause headaches in systems such as MPEG that are designed to accommodate both 480*i* and 576*i* images. In Figures 11.3 and 11.4 below, I show how field order, interlace nomenclature, and image structure are related. Figure 11.5 at the bottom of this page shows how MPEG-2 identifies each field as either *top* or *bottom*. In 480*i* video, the bottom field is the first field of the frame; in 576*i*, the top field is first.

Figures 11.3, 11.4, and 11.5 depict just the image array (i.e., the active samples), without vertical blanking lines. MPEG makes no provision for halflines.

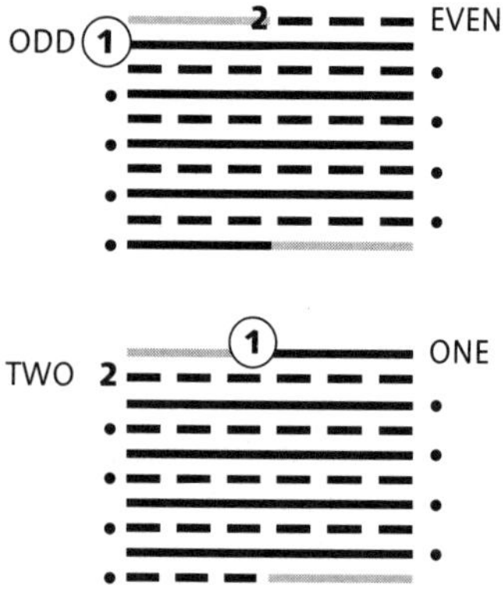

Figure 11.3 **Interlacing in 480*i*.** The first field (historically called *odd*, here denoted **1**) starts with a full picture line, and ends with a left-hand halfline containing the bottom of the picture. The second field (here dashed, historically called *even*), transmitted about 1⁄60 s later, starts with a right-hand halfline containing the top of the picture; it ends with a full picture line.

Figure 11.4 **Interlacing in 576*i*.** The first field includes a right-hand halfline containing the top line of the picture, and ends with a full picture line. The second field, transmitted 1⁄50 s later, starts with a full line, and ends with a left-hand halfline that contains the bottom of the picture. (In 576*i* terminology, the terms *odd* and *even* are rarely used, and are best avoided.)

BOTTOM TOP

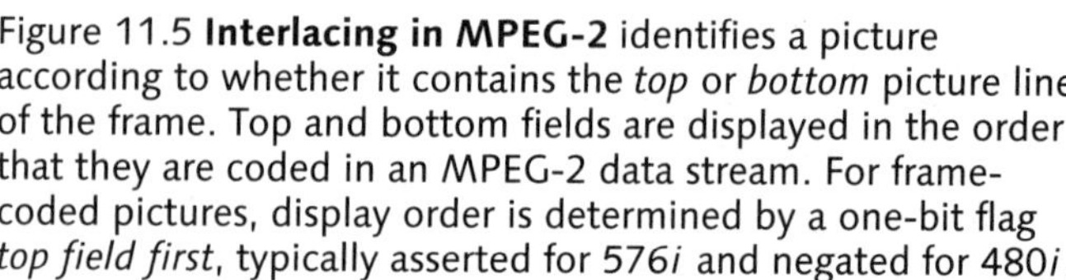

Figure 11.5 **Interlacing in MPEG-2** identifies a picture according to whether it contains the *top* or *bottom* picture line of the frame. Top and bottom fields are displayed in the order that they are coded in an MPEG-2 data stream. For frame-coded pictures, display order is determined by a one-bit flag *top field first*, typically asserted for 576*i* and negated for 480*i*.

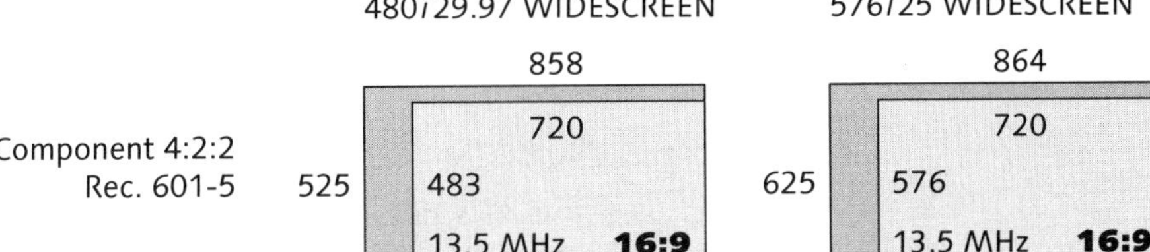

Figure 11.6 **Widescreen SDTV sampling** uses the standard 13.5 MHz sampling rate, effectively stretching samples horizontally by $4/3$ compared to the 4:3 aspect ratio base standard.

Widescreen (16:9) SDTV

Television programming has historically been produced in 4:3 aspect ratio. However, wide aspect ratio programming – originated on film, HDTV, or widescreen SDTV – is now economically important. Also, there is increasing consumer interest in widescreen programming. Consumers dislike the blank areas of the display that result from letterboxing. Consequently, SDTV standards are being adapted to handle 16:9 aspect ratio. Techniques to accomplish this are known as *widescreen SDTV*. That term is misleading, though: Because there is no increase in pixel count, a so-called widescreen SDTV picture cannot be viewed with a picture angle substantially wider than regular (4:3) SDTV. (See page 43.) So widescreen SDTV does not deliver HDTV's major promise – that of dramatically wider viewing angle – and a more accurate term would be *wide aspect ratio SDTV*.

The technique of Figure 11.6 is used on many widescreen DVDs. A DVD player can be configured to subsample vertically by a factor of $3/4$, to letterbox such a recorded image for 4:3 display. (Some DVDs are recorded letterboxed.)

The latest revision (-5) of Rec. 601 standardizes an approach to widescreen SDTV sketched in Figure 11.6 above. The standard 13.5 MHz luma sampling rate for 480*i* or 576*i* component video is used, but for an image at 16:9 aspect ratio. Each sample is stretched horizontally by a ratio of $4/3$ compared to the 4:3 aspect ratio of video. Existing 480*i* or 576*i* component video infrastructure can be used directly. (Some camcorders can be equipped with anamorphic lenses to produce this form of widescreen SDTV through optical means.) A second approach, not sketched here, uses a higher sampling rate of 18 MHz (i.e., 4⁄3 times 13.5 MHz). This scheme offers somewhat increased pixel count compared to 4:3 systems; however, it is rarely used.

Progressive SDTV (480*p*/483*p*)

A progressive 483*p*59.94 studio standard has been established in SMPTE 293M, with parameters similar to Rec. 601, but without interlace and with twice the data rate. Some people consider 483*p* to provide high definition. Unquestionably, 483*p* has higher quality than 480*i*, but I cannot characterize 483*p* as HDTV. Japan's EDTV-II broadcast system is based upon 483*p* scanning. Provisions are made for 480*p* in the ATSC standards for digital television. One major U.S. network has broadcast in 480*p*29.97, one of the ATSC formats.

480*p* and 483*p* systems have either 4:2:2 or 4:2:0 chroma subsampling. The 4:2:2*p* variant is a straightforward extension of Rec. 601 subsampling to progressive scanning. The 4:2:0 variant differs from 4:2:0 used in JPEG/JFIF, and differs from 4:2:0 used in MPEG-2. This scheme is denoted 4:2:0*p*. Unfortunately, this notation appears to follow the naming convention of MPEG-2's 4:2:2 profile (denoted 422P); however, in 4:2:0*p*, the *p* is for *progressive*, not *profile!*

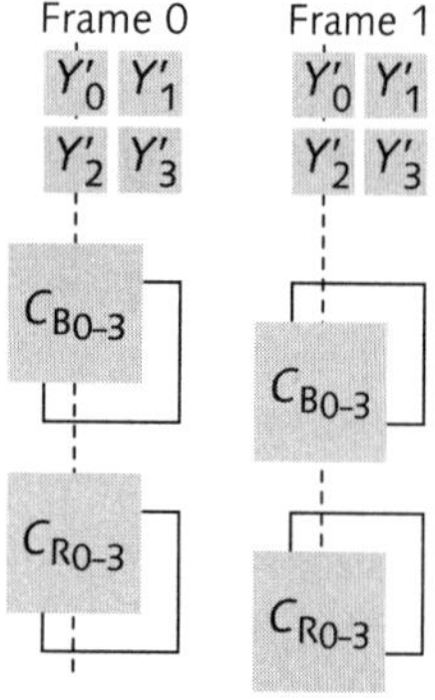

Figure 11.7 **Chroma subsampling in 4:2:0*p*** alternates frame-to-frame in a two-frame sequence, even though scanning is progressive.

Figure 11.7 depicts 4:2:0*p* chroma subsampling used in 483*p*. Although frames are progressive, chroma subsampling is not identical in every frame. Frames are denoted 0 and 1 in an alternating sequence. Chroma samples in frame 0 are positioned vertically coincident with even-numbered image rows; chroma samples in frame 1 are cosited with odd-numbered image rows. Compare this sketch with Figure 10.1, on page 90.

Quasi-interlace in consumer SDTV is comparable to *progressive segmented-frame* (PsF) in HDTV, though at 25 or 29.97 frames per second instead of 24. See page 62.

Some recent cameras implement a progressive mode – in DVC camcorders, sometimes called *movie mode*, or *frame mode* – whereby images are captured at 480*p*29.97 (720×480) or 576*p*25 (720×576). The DV compression algorithm detects no motion between the fields, so compression effectively operates on progressive frames. Interlace is imposed at the analog interface; this is sometimes called *quasi-interlace*. Excellent stillframes result; however, motion portrayal suffers.

Square and nonsquare sampling

Computer graphics equipment usually employs *square sampling* – that is, a sampling lattice where pixels are equally spaced horizontally and vertically. Square sampling of 480*i* and 576*i* is diagrammed in the top rows of Figures 11.1 and 11.2 on page 97.

See Table 13.1, on page 114, and the associated discussion.

Although ATSC's notorious Table 3 includes a 640×480 square-sampled image, no studio standard or realtime interface standard addresses square sampling of SDTV. For desktop video applications, I recommend sampling 480*i* video with exactly 780 samples per total line, for a nominal sample rate of $12\frac{3}{11}$ MHz – that is, $12.2727\overline{27}$ MHz. To accommodate full picture width in the studio, 648 samples are required; often, 640 samples are used with 480 picturelines. For square sampling of 576*i* video, I recommend using exactly 944 samples per total line, for a sample rate of exactly 14.75 MHz.

$$648 \approx 780 \cdot \left(1 - \frac{10.7\ \mu s}{63.55\overline{5}\ \mu s}\right)$$

$$767 = 944 \cdot \frac{52\ \mu s}{64\ \mu s}$$

MPEG-1, MPEG-2, DVD, and DVC all conform to Rec. 601, which specifies nonsquare sampling. Rec. 601 sampling of 480*i* and 576*i* is diagrammed in the middle rows of Figures 11.1 and 11.2.

Composite digital video systems sample at four times the color subcarrier frequency ($4f_{SC}$), resulting in nonsquare sampling whose parameters are shown in the bottom rows of Figures 11.1 and 11.2. (As I stated on page 94, composite $4f_{SC}$ systems are in decline.)

In 480*i*, the sampling rates for square-sampling, Rec. 601, and $4f_{SC}$ are related by the ratio 30:33:35. The pixel aspect ratio of Rec. 601 480*i* is exactly $^{10}/_{11}$; the pixel aspect ratio of $4f_{SC}$ 480*i* is exactly $^{6}/_{7}$.

In 576*i*, the sampling rates for square sampling and 4:2:2 are related by the ratio 59:54, so the pixel aspect ratio of 576*i* Rec. 601 is precisely $^{59}/_{54}$. Rec. 601 and $4f_{SC}$ sample rates are related by the ratio in the margin, which is fairly impenetrable to digital hardware.

$$\frac{f_{S,601}}{4f_{SC,PAL\text{-}I}} = \frac{540000}{709379}$$

Most of this nonsquare sampling business has been put behind us: HDTV studio standards call for square sampling, and it is difficult to imagine any future studio standard being established with nonsquare sampling.

Resampling

Analog video can be digitized with square sampling simply by using an appropriate sample frequency. However, SDTV already digitized at a standard digital video sampling rate such as 13.5 MHz must be *resampled* – or *interpolated*, or in PC parlance, *scaled* – when entering the square-sampled desktop video domain. If video samples at 13.5 MHz are passed to a computer graphics system and then treated as if the samples are equally spaced vertically and horizontally, then picture geometry will be distorted. Rec. 601 480*i* video will appear horizontally stretched; Rec. 601 576*i* video will appear squished. In desktop video, often resampling in both axes is needed.

The ratio $^{10}/_{11}$ relates 480*i* Rec. 601 to square sampling: Crude resampling could be accomplished by simply dropping every eleventh sample across each scan line! Crude resampling from 576*i* Rec. 601 to square sampling could be accomplished by replicating 5 samples in every 54 (perhaps in the pattern 11-*R*-11-*R*-11-*R*-11-*R*-10-*R*, where *R* denotes a repeated sample). However, such sample dropping and stuffing techniques will introduce aliasing. I recommend that you use a more sophisticated interpolator, of the type explained in *Filtering and sampling*, on page 141. Resampling could potentially be performed along either the vertical axis or the horizontal (transverse) axis; horizontal resampling is the easier of the two, as it processes pixels in raster order and therefore does not require any linestores.

Introduction to composite NTSC and PAL 12

NTSC stands for *National Television System Committee*. PAL stands for *Phase Alternate Line* (or according to some sources, *Phase Alternation* at *Line* rate, or perhaps even *Phase Alternating Line*).

SECAM is a composite technique of sorts, though it has little in common with NTSC and PAL. See page 576.

In *component* video, the three color components are kept separate. Video can use *R'G'B'* components directly, but three signals are expensive to record, process, or transmit. Luma (*Y'*) and color difference components based upon *B'–Y'* and *R'–Y'* can be used to enable subsampling: Luma is maintained at full data rate, and the two color difference components are subsampled. Even subsampled, video has a fairly high information rate (bandwidth, or data rate). To reduce the information rate further, composite NTSC and PAL color coding uses *quadrature modulation* to combine two color difference components into a *modulated chroma* signal, then uses *frequency interleaving* to combine luma and modulated chroma into a *composite* signal having roughly ⅓ the data rate – or in an analog system, ⅓ the bandwidth – of *R'G'B'*.

Composite encoding was invented to address three main needs. First, there was a need to limit transmission bandwidth. Second, it was necessary to enable black-and-white receivers already deployed by 1953 to receive color broadcasts with minimal degradation. Third, it was necessary for newly introduced color receivers to receive standard black-and-white broadcasts. Composite encoding was necessary in the early days of television, and it has proven highly effective for broadcast. NTSC and PAL are used in billions of consumer electronic devices, and broadcasting of NTSC and PAL is entrenched.

Composite NTSC or PAL encoding has three major disadvantages. First, encoding introduces some degree of mutual interference between luma and chroma. Once a signal has been encoded into composite form, the NTSC or PAL *footprint* is imposed: *Cross-luma* and *cross-color* errors are irreversibly impressed on the signal. Second, it is impossible to directly perform many processing operations in the composite domain; even to reposition or resize a picture requires decoding, processing, and reencoding. Third, digital compression techniques such as JPEG and MPEG cannot be directly applied to composite signals, and the artifacts of NTSC and PAL encoding are destructive to MPEG encoding.

The bandwidth to carry separate color components is now easily affordable; composite encoding is no longer necessary in the studio. To avoid the NTSC and PAL artifacts, to facilitate image manipulation, and to enable compression, composite video has been superseded by *component video*, where three color components $R'G'B'$, or $Y'C_BC_R$ (in digital systems), or $Y'P_BP_R$ (in analog systems), are kept separate. I hope you can manage to avoid composite NTSC and PAL, and skip this chapter!

By NTSC and PAL, I do not mean 480*i* and 576*i*, or 525/59.94 and 625/50!

The terms *NTSC* and *PAL* properly denote color encoding standards. Unfortunately, they are often used incorrectly to denote scanning standards. PAL encoding is used with both 576*i* scanning (with two different subcarrier frequencies) and 480*i* scanning (with a third subcarrier frequency); PAL alone is ambiguous.

When I use the term *PAL* in this chapter, I refer only to 576*i* PAL-B/G/H/I. Variants of PAL used for broadcasting in South America are discussed in *Analog NTSC and PAL broadcast standards*, on page 571. PAL variants in consumer devices are discussed in *Consumer analog NTSC and PAL*, on page 579.

In principle, NTSC or PAL color coding could be used with any scanning standard. However, in practice, NTSC and PAL are used only with 480*i* and 576*i* scanning, and the parameters of NTSC and PAL encoding are optimized for those scanning systems. This chapter introduces composite encoding. Three later chapters detail the principles: *NTSC and PAL chroma modulation*, on page 335; *NTSC and PAL frequency interleaving*, on page 349; and *NTSC Y'IQ system*, on page 365. Studio standards are detailed in *480i NTSC composite video*, on page 511, and *576i PAL composite video*, on page 529.

NTSC and PAL encoding

NTSC or PAL encoding involves these steps:

- *R'G'B'* component signals are matrixed and filtered, or $Y'C_BC_R$ or $Y'P_BP_R$ components are scaled and filtered, to form luma (*Y'*) and color difference signals (*U* and *V*, or in certain NTSC systems, *I* and *Q*).

- *U* and *V* (or *I* and *Q*) color difference signals are modulated onto a pair of intimately related continuous-wave color subcarriers, typically at a frequency of about 3.58 MHz in 480*i*29.97 or 4.43 MHz in 576*i*25, to produce a modulated chroma signal, *C*. (See the left side of Figure 12.1 overleaf.)

- Luma and modulated chroma are summed to form a composite NTSC or PAL signal. (See the right side of Figure 12.1.) Summation of luma and chroma is liable to introduce a certain degree of mutual interference, called *cross-luma* and *cross-color;* these artifacts can be minimized through *frequency interleaving*, to be described.

  The S-video interface bypasses the third step. The S-video interface transmits luma and modulated chroma separately: They are not summed, so cross-luma and cross-color artifacts are avoided.

NTSC and PAL decoding

NTSC or PAL decoding involves these steps:

- Luma and modulated chroma are separated. Crude separation can be accomplished using a *notch filter*. Alternatively, frequency interleaving can be exploited to provide greatly improved separation; in NTSC, such a separator is a *comb filter*. (In an S-video interface, luma and modulated chroma are already separate.)

- Chroma is demodulated to produce *UV*, *IQ*, P_BP_R, or C_BC_R baseband color difference components.

- If *R'G'B'* components are required, the baseband color difference components are interpolated, then luma and the color difference components are dematrixed.

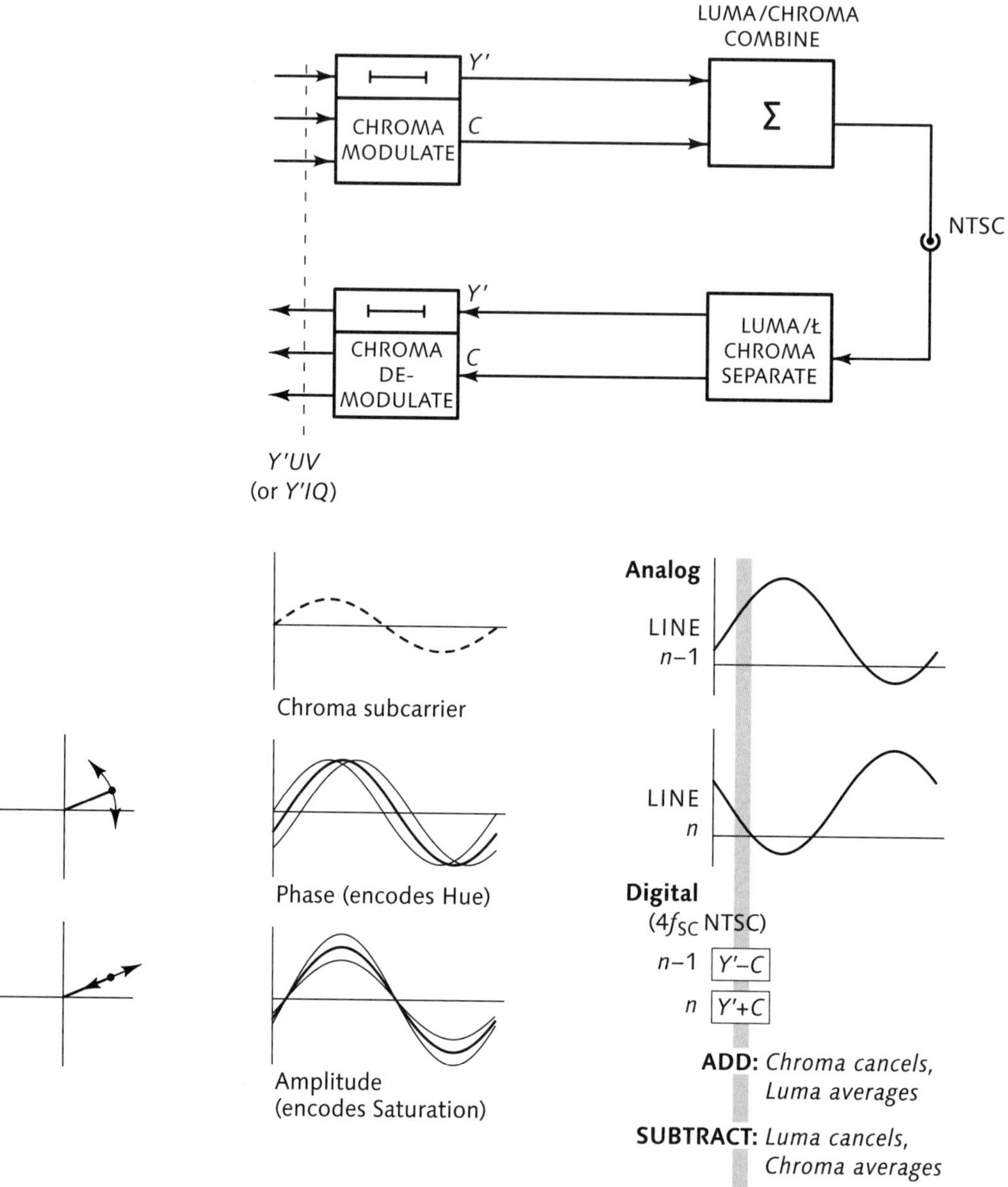

Figure 12.1 **NTSC chroma modulation and frequency interleaving** are applied, successively, to encode luma and a pair of color difference components into NTSC composite video. First, the two color difference signals are modulated onto a color subcarrier. If the two color differences are interpreted in polar coordinates, hue angle is encoded as subcarrier phase, and saturation is encoded as subcarrier amplitude. (*Burst*, a sample of the unmodulated subcarrier, is included in the composite signal.) Then, modulated chroma is summed with luma. Frequency interleaving leads to line-by-line phase inversion of the unmodulated color subcarrier, thence to the modulated subcarrier. Summation of adjacent lines tends to cause modulated chroma to cancel, and luma to average.

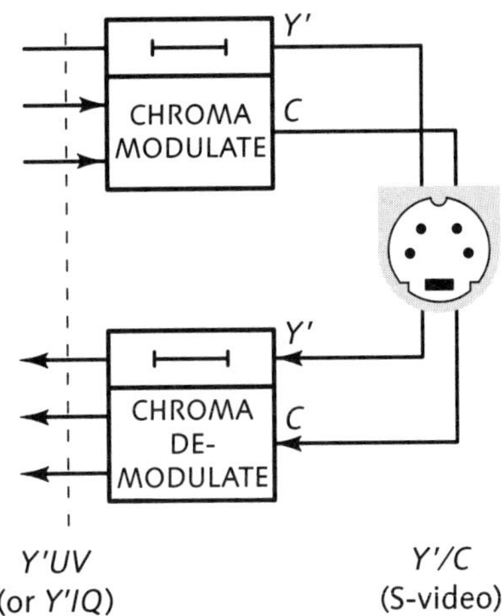

Figure 12.2 **S-video interface** involves chroma modulation; however, luma and modulated chroma traverse separate paths across the interface, instead of being summed.

S-video interface

S-video involves NTSC or PAL chroma modulation; however, luma and modulated chroma traverse separate paths across the interface instead of being summed. Figure 12.2 above sketches the encoder and decoder arrangement. S-video is common in consumer and desktop video equipment, but is rare in the studio, where either component or composite video is generally used.

Frequency interleaving

When luma and modulated chroma are summed, a certain amount of mutual interference is introduced. Interference is minimized by arranging for *frequency interleaving*, which is achieved when the color subcarrier frequency and the line rate are *coherent* – that is, when the unmodulated color subcarrier is phase-locked to a carefully chosen rational multiple of the line rate – half the line rate for NTSC, and $\frac{1}{4}$ the line rate in PAL. Coherence is achieved in the studio by deriving both sync and color subcarrier from a single master clock.

In PAL, all but the most sophisticated comb filters separate *U* and *V*, not luma and chroma. See page 341.

In NTSC, frequency interleaving enables use of a comb filter to separate luma and chroma: Adjacent lines are summed (to form vertically averaged luma) and differenced (to form vertically averaged chroma), as suggested at the bottom right of Figure 12.1.

In industrial and consumer video, subcarrier often free-runs with respect to line rate, and the advantages of frequency interleaving are lost. Most forms of analog videotape recording introduce timebase error; left uncorrected, this also defeats frequency interleaving.

Composite digital SDTV ($4f_{SC}$)

Processing of digital composite signals is simplified if the sampling frequency is a small integer multiple of the color subcarrier frequency. Nowadays, a multiple of four is used: It is standard to sample a composite NTSC or PAL signal at *four-times-subcarrier*, or $4f_{SC}$ (pronounced *four eff ess see*.)

Figure 12.3 **480*i*, $4f_{SC}$ NTSC sampling** is line-locked. If the analog sync edge were to be digitized, it would take the same set of values every line.

In $4f_{SC}$ NTSC systems sampling rate is about 14.3 MHz. Because NTSC's subcarrier is a simple rational multiple ($^{455}/_{2}$) of line rate, sampling is *line-locked.* In line-locked sampling, every line has the same integer number of sample periods. In $4f_{SC}$ NTSC, each line has 910 sample periods (S_{TL}), as indicated in Figure 12.3.

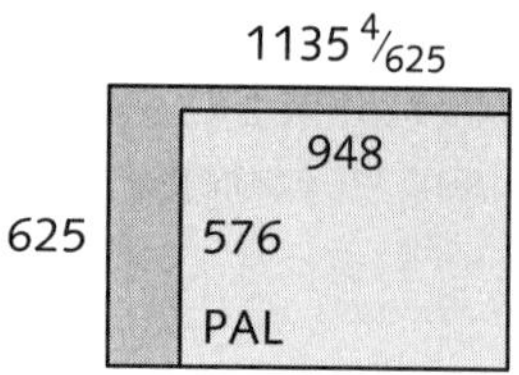

Figure 12.4 **576*i*, $4f_{SC}$ PAL sampling** is *not* line-locked.

In conventional 576*i* PAL-B/G/H/I systems, the $4f_{SC}$ sampling rate is about 17.7 MHz. Owing to the complex relationship in "mathematical PAL" between subcarrier frequency and line rate, sampling in PAL is not line-locked: There is a noninteger number ($1135\,^{4}/_{625}$) of sample periods per total line, as indicated in Figure 12.4 in the margin. (In Europe, they say that "Sampling is not precisely orthogonal.")

If you had to give $4f_{SC}$ a designation akin to 4:2:2, you might call it 4:0:0.

During the development of early studio digital standards, the disadvantages of composite video processing and recording were widely recognized. The earliest component digital video standard was Rec. 601, adopted in 1984; it specified a component video interface with 4:2:2 chroma subsampling and a sampling rate of 13.5 MHz, as I described in the previous chapter. Eight-bit sampling of Rec. 601 has a raw data rate of 27 MB/s. The first commercial DVTRs were standardized by SMPTE under the designation *D-1*. (In studio video terminology, chroma subsampling is not considered to be compression.)

Eight-bit sampling of NTSC at $4f_{SC}$ has a data rate of about 14.3 MB/s, roughly half that of 4:2:2 sampling. In 1988, four years after the adoption of the D-1 standard, Ampex and Sony commercialized $4f_{SC}$ composite digital recording to enable a cheap DVTR. This was standardized by SMPTE as *D-2*. (Despite its higher number, the format is in most ways technically inferior to D-1.) Several years later, Panasonic adapted D-2 technology to ½-inch tape in a cassette almost the same size as a VHS cassette; this became the D-3 standard.

D-2 and D-3 DVTRs offered the advantages of digital recording, but retained the disadvantages of composite NTSC or PAL: Luma and chroma were subject to cross-contamination, and pictures could not be manipulated without decoding and reencoding.

Concerning the absence of D-4 in the numbering sequence, see the caption to Table 35.2, on page 423.

D-2 and D-3 DVTRs were deployed by broadcasters, where composite encoding was inherent in terrestrial broadcasting standards. However, for high-end production work, D-1 remained dominant. In 1994, Panasonic introduced the D-5 DVTR, which records a 10-bit Rec. 601, 4:2:2 signal on ½-inch tape. Recently, VTRs using compression have proliferated.

Composite analog SDTV

Cable television is detailed in Ciciora, Walter, James Farmer, and David Large, *Modern Cable Television Technology* (San Francisco: Morgan Kaufmann, 1999).

Composite analog 480*i* NTSC and 576*i* PAL have been used for terrestrial VHF/UHF broadcasting and cable television for many decades. I will describe *Analog NTSC and PAL broadcast standards* on page 571.

Composite analog 480*i* NTSC and 576*i* PAL is widely deployed in consumer equipment, such as television receivers and VCRs. Some degenerate forms of NTSC and PAL are used in consumer electronic devices; see *Consumer analog NTSC and PAL,* on page 579.

Introduction to HDTV 13

This chapter outlines the 1280×720 and 1920×1080 image formats for high-definition television (HDTV), and introduces the scanning parameters of the associated video systems such as 720*p*60 and 1080*i*30.

Fujio, T., J. Ishida, T. Komoto, and T. Nishizawa, *High Definition Television System – Signal Standards and Transmission*, NHK Science and Technical Research Laboratories Technical Note 239 (Aug. 1979); reprinted in *SMPTE Journal*, 89 (8): 579–584 (Aug. 1980).

Fujio, T., et al., *High Definition television*, NHK Science and Technical Research Laboratories Technical Monograph 32 (June 1982).

Today's HDTV systems stem from research directed by Dr. Fujio at NHK (Nippon Hoso Kyokai, the Japan Broadcasting Corporation). HDTV was conceived to have twice the vertical and twice the horizontal resolution of conventional television, a picture aspect ratio of 5:3 (later altered to 16:9), and at least two channels of CD-quality audio. Today we can augment this by specifying a frame rate of 23.976 Hz or higher. Some people consider 480*p* systems to be HDTV, but by my definition, HDTV has ¾-million pixels or more. NHK conceived HDTV to have interlaced scanning; however, progressive HDTV systems have emerged.

Developmental HDTV systems had 1125/60.00/2:1 scanning, an aspect ratio of 5:3, and 1035 active lines. The alternate 59.94 Hz field rate was added later. Aspect ratio was changed to 16:9 to achieve international agreement upon standards. Active line count of 1080 was eventually agreed upon to provide square sampling.

Studio HDTV has a sampling rate of 74.25 MHz, 5.5 times that of the Rec. 601 standard for SDTV. HDTV has a pixel rate of about 60 megapixels per second. Other parameters are similar or identical to SDTV standards. Details concerning scanning, sample rates, and interface levels of HDTV will be presented in *1280×720 HDTV* on page 547 and *1920×1080 HDTV* on page 557. Unfortunately, the parameters for $Y'C_BC_R$ color coding for HDTV differ from the parameters for SDTV! Details will be provided in *Component video color coding for HDTV*, on page 313.

Figure 13.1 **Comparison of aspect ratios** between conventional television and HDTV was attempted using various measures: equal height, equal width, equal diagonal, and equal area. All of these comparisons overlooked the fundamental improvement of HDTV: its increased pixel count. The correct comparison is based upon equal picture detail.

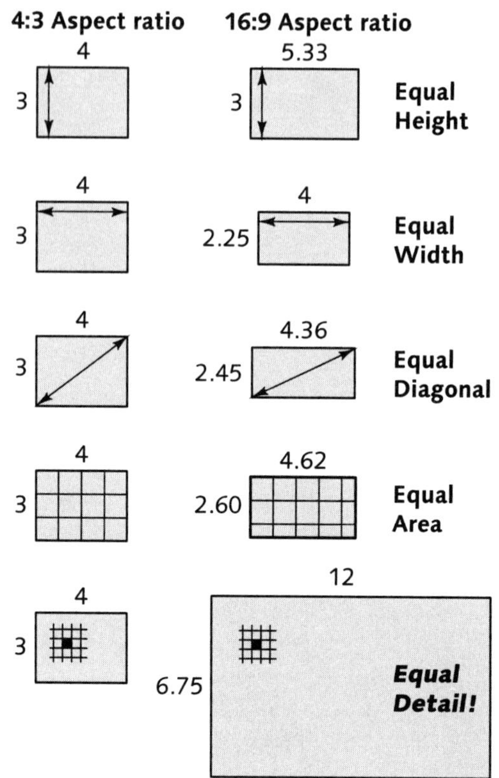

Comparison of aspect ratios

When HDTV was introduced to the consumer electronics industry in North America, SDTV and HDTV were compared using various measures, sketched in Figure 13.1 above, based upon the difference in aspect ratio between 4:3 and 16:9. Comparisons were made on the basis of equal height, equal width, equal diagonal, and equal area.

All of those measures overlooked the fundamental improvement of HDTV: Its "high definition" – that is, its resolution – does not squeeze six times the number of pixels into the same visual angle! Instead, the angular subtense of a single pixel should be maintained, and the entire image may now occupy a much larger area of the viewer's visual field. HDTV allows a greatly increased picture angle. The correct comparison between conventional television and HDTV is not based upon aspect ratio; it is based upon picture detail.

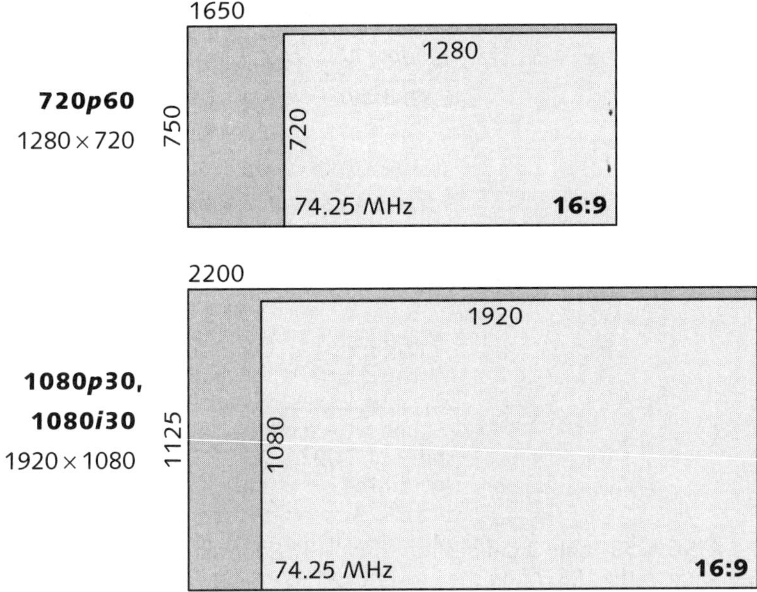

Figure 13.2 **HDTV rasters at 30 and 60 frames per second** are standardized in two formats, 1280×720 (1 Mpx, always progressive), and 1920×1080 (2 Mpx, interlaced or progressive). The latter is often denoted 1080*i*, but the standards accommodate progressive scan. These sketches are scaled to match Figures 11.1, 11.2, and 11.6; pixels in all of these sketches have identical area.

HDTV scanning

A great debate took place in the 1980s and 1990s concerning whether HDTV should have interlaced or progressive scanning. At given flicker and data rates, interlace offers some increase in static spatial resolution, as suggested by Figure 6.8 on page 59. Broadcasters have historically accepted the motion artifacts and spatial aliasing that accompany interlace, in order to gain some static spatial resolution. In the HDTV debate, the computer industry and the creative film community were set against interlace. Eventually, both interlaced and progressive scanning were standardized; to be commercially viable, a receiver must decode both formats.

In *Numerology of HDTV scanning*, on page 377, I explain the origin of the numbers in Figure 13.2.

Figure 13.2 above sketches the rasters of the 1 Mpx progressive system (1280×720, 720*p*60) and the 2 Mpx interlaced system (1920×1080, 1080*i*30) that were agreed upon. The 1920×1080 system is easily adapted to 24 and 30 Hz progressive scan (1080*i*24, 1080*i*30).

Image format	Progressive/Interlace,	‡Frame rate (Hz)	Image aspect ratio	Sampling
1920×1080	*p*	24, 30	16:9	Square
	i	30		
1280×720	*p*	24, 30, 60	16:9	Square
704×480	*p*	24, 30, 60	4:3	Nonsquare
	i	30		
	p	24, 30, 60	16:9	Nonsquare
	i	30		
640×480	*p*	24, 30, 60	4:3	Square
	i	30		

‡Frame rates modified by the ratio $^{1000}/_{1001}$ – that is, frame rates of 23.976 Hz, 29.97 Hz, and 59.94 Hz – are permitted.

Table 13.1 **ATSC A/53 Table 3** defines the so-called 18 formats – including 12 SDTV formats – for digital television in the U.S. I find the layout of ATSC's Table 3 to be hopelessly contorted, so I rearranged it. ATSC specifies 704 S_{AL} for several SDTV formats, instead of Rec. 601's 720 S_{AL}; see page 325. ATSC standard A/53 doesn't accommodate 25 Hz and 50 Hz frame rates, but A/63 does.

ATSC A/53, *Digital Television Standard.*

In addition to the 1 Mpx (progressive) and 2 Mpx (interlaced) systems, several SDTV scanning systems and several additional frame rates and were included in the ultimate ATSC standards for U.S. digital television (DTV). Table 13.1 above summarizes the "18 formats" that are found in Table 3 of the ATSC's A/53 standard.

Figure 13.2 sketched the 1920×1080 image format for frame rates of 30 Hz and 60 Hz. This image format can be carried at frame rates of 24 Hz and 25 Hz, using the standard 74.25 MHz sample rate. Figure 13.3 at the top of the facing page sketches raster structures for 24 Hz and 25 Hz systems; Table 13.2 overleaf summarizes the scanning parameters.

To carry a 1920×1080 image at a frame rate of 25 Hz, two approaches have been standardized. One approach is standardized in SMPTE 274M: 1125 total lines are retained, and S_{TL} is increased to 2640. This yields the 1080*p*25 format, using an 1125/25 raster. Scanning can be either progressive or interlaced; with progressive scanning, the signal is usually interfaced using the

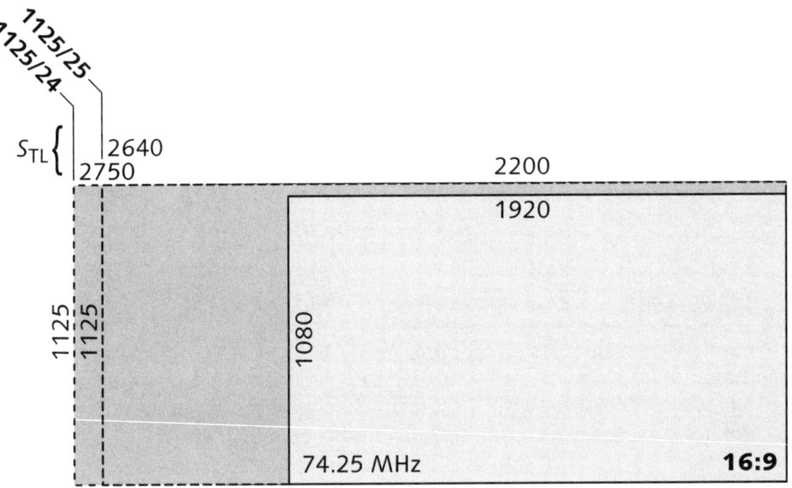

Figure 13.3 **HDTV rasters at 24 Hz and 25 Hz** carry an array of 1920×1080 active samples, using a 74.25 MHz sampling rate at the interface. For 24 Hz (1080*p*24), the 1920×1080 array is carried in an 1125/24 raster. For 25 Hz, the array is carried in an 1125/25 raster.

progressive segmented frame (PsF) scheme that I introduced on page 62.

Some European video engineers dislike 1125 lines, so in addition to the approach sketched in Figure 13.3 an alternative approach is standardized in SMPTE 295M: The 1920×1080 image is placed in a 1250/25/2:1 raster with 2376 S_{TL}. I recommend against this approach: Systems with 1125 total lines are now the mainstream.

$$\frac{24}{1.001} \approx 23.976$$

For 24 Hz, 1125 total lines are retained, and S_{TL} is increased to 2750 achieve the 24 Hz frame rate. This yields the 1080*p*24 format, in an 1125/24 raster. This system is used in emerging digital cinema (D-cinema) products. A variant at 23.976 Hz is accommodated.

In Sony's HDCAM system, the 1920×1080 image is downsampled to 1440×1080, and color differences are subsampled 3:1:1, prior to compression. This is an internal representation only; there is no corresponding uncompressed external interface standard.

System	*Scanning*	*SMPTE standard*	S_{TL}	L_T	S_{AL}	L_A
720*p*60	750/60/1:1	SMPTE 296M	1650	750	1280	720
1035*i*30‡	1125/60/2:1	SMPTE 260M	2200	1125	1920	1035
1080*i*30	1125/60/2:1	SMPTE 274M	2200	1125	1920	1080
1080*p*60¶	1125/60/1:1	SMPTE 274M	2200	1125	1920	1080
1080*p*30	1125/30/1:1	SMPTE 274M	2200	1125	1920	1080
1080*i*25	1125/25/2:1	SMPTE 274M	2640	1125	1920	1080
1080*p*25	1125/25/1:1	SMPTE 274M	2640	1125	1920	1080
1080*p*24	1125/24/1:1	SMPTE 274M	2750	1125	1920	1080

Table 13.2 **HDTV scanning parameters** are summarized. The 1035*i*30 system, flagged with ‡ above, is not recommended for new designs; use 1080*i*30 instead. SMPTE 274M includes a progressive 2 Mpx, 1080*p*60 system with 1125/60/1:1 scanning, flagged with ¶ above; this system is beyond the limits of today's technology. Each of the 24, 30, and 60 Hz systems above has an associated system at $^{1000}/_{1001}$ of that rate.

Table 13.2 summarizes the scanning parameters for 720*p*, 1080*i*, and 1080*p* systems. Studio interfaces for HDTV will be introduced in *Digital video interfaces,* on page 127. HDTV videotape recording standards will be introduced in *Videotape recording,* on page 411.

The 1035*i* (1125/60) system

The SMPTE 240M standard for 1125/60.00/2:1 HDTV was adopted in 1988. The 1125/60 system, now called 1035*i*30, had 1920×1035 image structure with nonsquare sampling: Pixels were 4% closer horizontally than vertically. After several years, square sampling was introduced into the SMPTE standards, and subsequently, into ATSC standards. 1920×1035 image structure has been superseded by 1920×1080, and square sampling is now a feature of all HDTV studio standards.

Color coding for Rec. 709 HDTV

Rec. 709 defines $Y'C_BC_R$ color coding. Unfortunately, the luma coefficients standardized in Rec. 709 – and the C_BC_R scale factors derived from them – differ from those of SDTV. $Y'C_BC_R$ coding now comes in two flavors: coding for small (SDTV) pictures, and coding for large (HDTV) pictures. I will present details concerning this troublesome issue in *SDTV and HDTV luma chaos,* on page 296.

Introduction to video compression 14

Directly storing or transmitting $Y'C_BC_R$ digital video requires immense data capacity – about 20 megabytes per second for SDTV, or about 120 megabytes per second for HDTV. First-generation studio digital VTRs, and today's highest-quality studio VTRs, store uncompressed video; however, economical storage or transmission requires compression. This chapter introduces the JPEG, M-JPEG, and MPEG compression techniques.

Data compression

Data compression reduces the number of bits required to store or convey text, numeric, binary, image, sound, or other data, by exploiting statistical properties of the data. The reduction comes at the expense of some computational effort to compress and decompress. Data compression is, by definition, lossless: Decompression recovers exactly, bit for bit (or byte for byte), the data that was presented to the compressor.

Binary data typical of general computer applications often has patterns of repeating byte strings and substrings. Most data compression techniques, including *run-length encoding* (RLE) and *Lempel-Ziv-Welch* (LZW), accomplish compression by taking advantage of repeated substrings; performance is highly dependent upon the data being compressed.

Image compression

Image data typically has strong vertical and horizontal correlations among pixels. When the RLE and LZW algorithms are applied to bilevel or pseudocolor image data stored in scan-line order, horizontal correlation among pixels is exploited to some degree, and usually results in modest compression (perhaps 2:1).

A data compression algorithm can be designed to exploit the statistics of image data, as opposed to arbitrary binary data; improved compression is then possible. For example, the ITU-T (former CCITT) fax standard for bilevel image data exploits vertical and horizontal correlation to achieve much higher average compression ratios than are possible with RLE or LZW.

Transform techniques are effective for the compression of continuous-tone (grayscale or truecolor) image data. The *discrete cosine transform* (DCT) has been developed and optimized over the last few decades; it is now the method of choice for continuous-tone compression.

Lossy compression

Data compression is lossless, by definition: The decompression operation reproduces, bit-for-bit, the data presented to the compressor. In principle, lossless data compression could be optimized to achieve modest compression of continuous-tone (grayscale or truecolor) image data. However, the characteristics of human perception can be exploited to achieve dramatically higher compression ratios if the requirement of exact reconstruction is relaxed: Image or sound data can be subject to *lossy* compression, provided that the impairments introduced are not overly perceptible. Lossy compression schemes are not appropriate for bilevel or pseudocolor images, but they are very effective for grayscale or truecolor images.

JPEG refers to a lossy compression method for still images. Its variant *M-JPEG* is used for motion sequences; DVC equipment uses an M-JPEG algorithm. *MPEG* refers to a lossy compression standard for video sequences; MPEG-2 is used in digital television distribution (e.g., ATSC and DVB), and in DVD. I will describe these techniques in subsequent sections. Table 14.1 at the top of the facing page compares typical compression ratios of M-JPEG and MPEG-2, for SDTV and HDTV.

Format	Uncompressed data rate, MB/s	Motion-JPEG compression ratio	MPEG-2 compression ratio
SDTV (480*i*30, 576*i*25)	20	15:1 (e.g., DVC)	45:1 (e.g,. DVD)
HDTV (720*p*60, 1080*i*30)	120	15:1	75:1 (e.g., ATSC)

Table 14.1 **Approximate compression ratios of M-JPEG and MPEG-2** for SDTV and HDTV

JPEG

JPEG stands for *Joint Photographic Experts Group*, constituted by ISO and IEC in collaboration with ITU-T (the former CCITT).

The JPEG committee developed a standard suitable for compressing grayscale or truecolor still images. The standard was originally intended for color fax, but it was quickly adopted and widely deployed for still images in desktop graphics and digital photography.

A JPEG compressor ordinarily transforms $R'G'B'$ to $Y'C_BC_R$, then applies 4:2:0 chroma subsampling to effect 2:1 compression. (In desktop graphics, this 2:1 factor is included in the compression ratio.) JPEG has provisions to compress $R'G'B'$ data directly, without subsampling.

Motion-JPEG

The JPEG algorithm – though not the ISO/IEC JPEG standard – has been adapted to compress motion video. Motion-JPEG simply compresses each field or frame of a video sequence as a self-contained compressed picture – each field or frame is *intra coded*. Because pictures are compressed individually, an M-JPEG video sequence can be edited; however, no advantage is taken of temporal coherence.

Video data is almost always presented to an M-JPEG compression system in $Y'C_BC_R$ subsampled form. (In video, the 2:1 factor due to chroma subsampling is generally not included in the compression ratio.)

The M-JPEG technique achieves compression ratios ranging from about 2:1 to about 20:1. The 20 MB/s data rate of digital video can be compressed to about 20 Mb/s, suitable for recording on consumer digital videotape (e.g., DVC). M-JPEG compression ratios and tape formats are summarized in Table 14.2 overleaf.

Compression ratio	Quality/application	Example tape formats
2:1	"Visually lossless" studio video	Digital Betacam
3.3:1	Excellent-quality studio video	DVCPRO50, D-9 (Digital-S)
6.6:1	Good-quality studio video; consumer digital video	D-7 (DVCPRO), DVCAM, consumer DVC, Digital8

Table 14.2 **Approximate compression ratios of M-JPEG** for SDTV applications

MPEG

Apart from scene changes, there is a statistical likelihood that successive pictures in a video sequence are very similar. In fact, it is *necessary* that successive pictures are similar: If this were not the case, human vision could make no sense of the sequence!

The M in MPEG stands for *moving*, not *motion*!

M-JPEG's compression ratio can be increased by a factor of 5 or 10 by exploiting the inherent temporal redundancy of video. The *MPEG* standard was developed by the *Moving Picture Experts Group* within ISO and IEC. In MPEG, an initial, self-contained picture provides a base value – it forms an *anchor* picture. Succeeding pictures can then be coded in terms of pixel differences from the anchor, as sketched in Figure 14.1 at the top of the facing page. The method is termed *interframe coding* (though differences between *fields* may be used).

Once the anchor picture has been received by the decoder, it provides an estimate for a succeeding picture. This estimate is improved when the encoder transmits the prediction errors. The scheme is effective provided that the prediction errors can be coded more compactly than the raw picture information.

Motion may cause displacement of scene elements – a fast-moving element may easily move 10 pixels in one frame time. In the presence of motion, a pixel at a certain location may take quite different values in successive pictures. Motion would cause the prediction error information to grow in size to the point where the advantage of interframe coding would be negated.

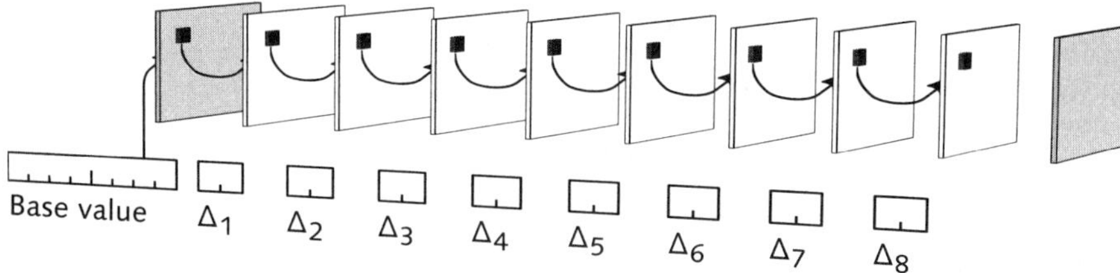

Figure 14.1 **Interpicture coding** exploits the similarity between successive pictures in video. First, a base picture is transmitted (ordinarily using intra-picture compression). Then, pixel differences to successive pictures are computed by the encoder and transmitted. The decoder reconstructs successive pictures by accumulating the differences. The scheme is effective provided that the difference information can be coded more compactly than the raw picture information.

However, objects tend to retain their characteristics even when moving. MPEG overcomes the problem of motion between pictures by equipping the encoder with *motion estimation* circuitry: The encoder computes *motion vectors*. The encoder then displaces the pixel values of the anchor picture by the estimated motion – a process called *motion compensation* – then computes prediction errors from the motion-compensated anchor picture. The encoder compresses the prediction error information using a JPEG-like technique, then transmits that data accompanied by motion vectors.

Based upon the received motion vectors, the decoder mimics the motion compensation of the encoder to obtain a predictor much more effective than the undisplaced anchor picture. The transmitted prediction errors are then applied to reconstruct the picture.

Picture coding types (I, P, B)

When encoding interlaced source material, an MPEG-2 encoder can choose to code each field as a picture or each frame as a picture, as I will describe on page 478. In this chapter, and in Chapter 40, the term *picture* can refer to either a field or a frame.

In MPEG, a video sequence is typically partitioned into successive *groups of pictures* (GOPs). The first frame in each GOP is coded independently of other frames using a JPEG-like algorithm; this is an *intra picture* or *I-picture*. Once reconstructed, an I-picture becomes an anchor picture available for use in predicting neighboring (*nonintra*) pictures. The example GOP sketched in Figure 14.2 overleaf comprises nine pictures.

A *P-picture* contains elements that are predicted from the most recent anchor frame. Once a P-picture is reconstructed, it is displayed; in addition, it becomes

Figure 14.2 **MPEG group of pictures (GOP).** The GOP depicted here has nine pictures, numbered 0 through 8. I-picture 0 is decoded from the coded data depicted in the dark gray block. Picture 9 is not in the GOP; it is the first picture of the next GOP. Here, the *intra count* (*n*) is 9.

a new anchor. I-pictures and P-pictures form a two-layer hierarchy. An I-picture and two dependent P-pictures are depicted in Figure 14.3 below.

MPEG provides an optional third hierarchical level whereby *B-pictures* may be interposed between anchor pictures. Elements of a B-picture may be bidirectionally predicted by averaging motion-compensated elements from the past anchor and motion-compensated elements from the future anchor. Each B-picture is reconstructed, displayed, and discarded: No B-picture forms the basis for any prediction. (At the encoder's discretion, elements of a B-picture may be unidirectionally forward-interpolated from the preceding anchor, or unidirectionally backward-predicted from the following anchor.) Using B-pictures delivers a substantial gain in compression efficiency compared to encoding with just I- and P-pictures.

Two B-pictures are depicted in Figure 14.4 at the top of the facing page. The three-level MPEG picture hierarchy is summarized in Figure 14.5 at the bottom of the facing page; this example has the structure IBBPBBPBB.

Figure 14.3 **An MPEG P-picture** contains elements forward-predicted from a preceding anchor picture, which may be an I-picture or a P-picture. Here, the first P-picture (3) is predicted from an I-picture (0). Once decoded, that P-picture becomes the predictor for the second P-picture (6).

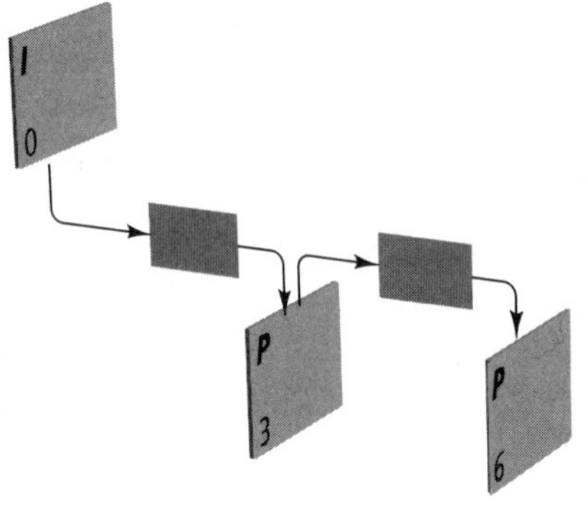

Figure 14.4 **An MPEG B-picture** is generally estimated from the average of the preceding anchor picture and the following anchor picture. (At the encoder's option, a B-picture may be unidirectionally forward-predicted from the preceding anchor, or unidirectionally backward-predicted from the following anchor.)

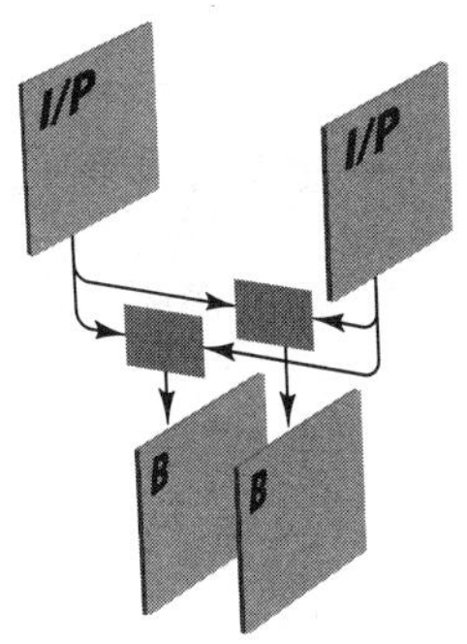

A simple encoder typically produces a bitstream having a fixed schedule of I-, P-, and B-pictures. A typical GOP structure is denoted IBBPBBPBBPBBPBB. At 30 pictures per second, there are two such GOPs per second. Regular GOP structure is described by a pair of integers n and m; n is the number of pictures from one I-picture (inclusive) to the next (exclusive), and m is the number of pictures from one anchor picture (inclusive) to the next (exclusive). If $m = 1$, there are no B-pictures. Figure 14.5 shows a regular GOP structure with an I-picture interval of $n = 9$ and an anchor-picture interval of $m = 3$. The $m = 3$ component indicates two B-pictures between anchor pictures.

Figure 14.5 **The three-level MPEG picture hierarchy.** This sketch shows a regular GOP structure with an I-picture interval of n=9, and an anchor-picture interval of m=3. This example represents a simple encoder that emits a fixed schedule of I-, B-, and P-pictures; this structure can be described as IBBPBBPBB. This example depicts an *open GOP*, where B-pictures following the last P-picture of the GOP are permitted to use backward prediction from the I-frame of the following GOP. Such prediction precludes editing of the bitstream between GOPs. A *closed GOP* permits no such prediction, so the bitstream can be edited between GOPs.

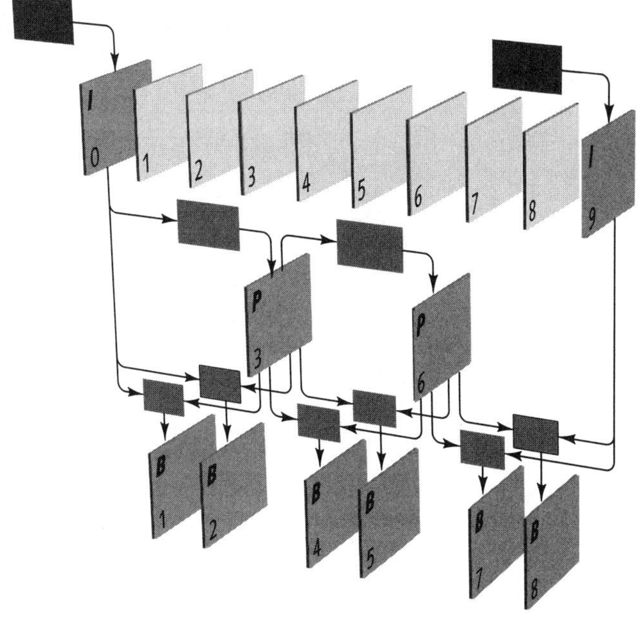

Coded B-pictures in a GOP depend upon P- and I-pictures; coded P-pictures depend upon earlier P-pictures and I-pictures. Owing to these interdependencies, an MPEG sequence cannot be edited, except at GOP boundaries, unless the sequence is decoded, edited, and subsequently reencoded. MPEG is very suitable for distribution, but owing to its inability to be edited without impairment at arbitrary points, MPEG is unsuitable for production. In the specialization of MPEG-2 called *I-frame only MPEG-2*, every GOP is a single I-frame. This is conceptually equivalent to Motion-JPEG, but has the great benefit of an international standard. (Another variant of MPEG-2, the *simple profile,* has no B-pictures.)

I have introduced MPEG as if all elements of a P-picture and all elements of a B-picture are coded similarly. But a picture that is generally very well predicted by the past anchor picture may have a few regions that cannot effectively be predicted. In MPEG, the image is tiled into *macroblocks* of 16×16 luma samples, and the encoder is given the option to code any particular macroblock in *intra* mode – that is, independently of any prediction. A compact code signals that a macroblock should be *skipped,* in which case samples from the anchor picture are used without modification. Also, in a B-picture, the encoder can decide on a macroblock-by-macroblock basis to code using forward prediction, backward prediction, or bidirectional prediction.

Reordering

In a sequence without B-pictures, I- and P-pictures are encoded and transmitted in the obvious order. However, when B-pictures are used, the decoder typically needs to access the past anchor picture and the future anchor picture to reconstruct a B-picture.

Figure 14.6 **Example GOP**

$\mathbf{I_0}B_1B_2\mathbf{P_3}B_4B_5\mathbf{P_6}B_7B_8$

Consider an encoder about to compress the sequence in Figure 14.6 (where anchor pictures I_0, P_3, and P_6 are written in boldface). The coded B_1 and B_2 pictures may be backward predicted from P_3, so the encoder must buffer the uncompressed B_1 and B_2 pictures until P_3 is coded: Only when coding of P_3 is complete can coding of B_1 start. Using B-pictures incurs a penalty in

Figure 14.7 **Example 9-frame GOP without B-pictures**

$\mathbf{I_0P_1P_2P_3P_4P_5P_6P_7P_8}$

encoding delay. (If the sequence were coded without B-pictures, as depicted in Figure 14.7, transmission of the coded information for P_1 would not be subject to this two-picture delay.) Coding delay can make MPEG with B-pictures unsuitable for realtime two-way applications such as teleconferencing.

If the coded 9-picture GOP of Figure 14.6 were transmitted in that order, then the decoder would have to hold the coded B_1 and B_2 data in a buffer while receiving and decoding P_3; only when decoding of P_3 was complete could decoding of B_1 start. The encoder must buffer the B_1 and B_2 pictures no matter what; however, to avoid the corresponding consumption of buffer memory at the decoder, MPEG-2 specifies that coded B-picture information is reordered so as to be transmitted after the coded anchor picture. Figure 14.8 indicates the pictures as reordered for transmission. I have placed I_9 in parentheses because it belongs to the next GOP; the GOP header precedes it. Here, B_7 and B_8 follow the GOP header.

Figure 14.8 **GOP reordered for transmission**

$\mathbf{I_0P_3}B_1B_2\mathbf{P_6}B_4B_5(\mathbf{I_9})B_7B_8$

MPEG-1

ISO/IEC 11172-1, *Coding of moving pictures and associated audio for digital storage media at up to about 1,5 Mbit/s – Part 1: Systems* [MPEG-1].

The original MPEG effort resulted in a standard now called MPEG-1; it comprises five parts. In the margin, I cite Part 1: *Systems*. There are additional parts – Part 2: *Video*; Part 3: *Audio*; Part 4: *Compliance testing*; and Part 5: *Software simulation*. MPEG-1 was used in consumer systems such as CD-V, and has been deployed in multimedia applications. MPEG-1 was optimized for the coding of progressive 352×240 images at 30 frames per second. MPEG-1 has no provision for interlace. When 480*i*29.97 or 576*i*25 video is coded with MPEG-1 at typical data rates, the first field of each frame is coded as if it were progressive; the second field is dropped. At its intended data rate of about 1.5 Mb/s, MPEG-1 delivers VHS-quality images.

For video broadcast, MPEG-1 has been superseded by MPEG-2. An MPEG-2 decoder must decode MPEG-1 *constrained-parameter bitstream* (CPB) sequences – to be discussed in the caption to Table 40.1, on page 475 – so I will not discuss MPEG-1 further.

MPEG-2

The MPEG-2 effort was initiated to extend MPEG-1 to interlaced scanning, to larger pictures, and to data rates much higher than 1.5 Mb/s. MPEG-2 is now widely deployed for the distribution of digital television, including standard-definition television (SDTV), DVD, and high-definition television (HDTV). MPEG-2 is defined by a series of standards from ISO/IEC.

Many MPEG terms – such as *frame*, *picture*, and *macroblock* – can refer to elements of the source video, to the corresponding elements in the coded bitstream, or to the corresponding elements in the reconstructed video. It is generally clear from context which is meant.

MPEG-2 accommodates both progressive and interlaced material. A video frame can be coded directly as a *frame-structured picture*. Alternatively, a video frame (typically originated from an interlaced source) may be coded as a pair of *field-structured pictures* – a top-field picture and a bottom-field picture. The two fields are time-offset by half the frame time, and are intended for interlaced display. Field pictures always come in pairs having opposite parity (top/bottom). Both pictures in a field pair have the same picture coding type (I, P, or B), except that an I-field may be followed by a P-field (in which case the pair is treated as an I-frame).

While the MPEG-2 work was underway, an MPEG-3 effort was launched to address HDTV. The MPEG-3 committee concluded early on that MPEG-2, at high data rate, would accommodate HDTV. Consequently, the MPEG-3 effort was abandoned. MPEG-4, MPEG-7, and MPEG-21 are underway; the numbers have no plan. MPEG-4 is concerned with coding at very low bit rates. MPEG-7, titled *Multimedia Content Description Interface,* will standardize description of various types of multimedia information (metadata). MPEG-21 seeks to establish an open framework for multimedia delivery and consumption, thereby enabling use of multimedia resources across a wide range of networks and devices." In my estimation, none of MPEGs 4, 7, or 21 are relevant to handling studio- or distribution-quality video signals.

Symes, Peter, *Video Compression Demystified* (New York: McGraw-Hill, 2000).

I will detail JPEG and motion-JPEG (M-JPEG) compression on page 447, DV compression on page 461, and MPEG-2 video compression on page 473. Video and audio compression technology is detailed in the book by Peter Symes cited in the margin.

Digital video interfaces 15

This chapter provides an overview of digital interfaces for uncompressed and compressed SDTV and HDTV.

Component digital SDTV interface (Rec. 601, "4:2:2")

ITU-R Rec. BT.601-5, *Studio encoding parameters of digital television for standard 4:3 and widescreen 16:9 aspect ratios*. Should this standard be revised, it will be denoted Rec. BT.601-6.

The notation *4:2:2* originated as a reference to a chroma subsampling scheme that I outlined on page 90. During the 1980s, it came to denote a specific component digital video interface standard incorporating 4:2:2 chroma subsampling. In the 1990s, the 4:2:2 chroma subsampling format was adopted for HDTV. As a result, the notation *4:2:2* is no longer clearly limited to SDTV, and no longer clearly denotes a scanning or interface standard. To denote the SDTV interface standard, I use the term *Rec. 601 interface* instead of *4:2:2*.

Recall from page 90 that in Rec. 601, C_B and C_R are *cosited* – each is centered on the same location as Y'_j, where j is even.

In Rec. 601, at 4:3 aspect ratio, luma is sampled at 13.5 MHz. C_B and C_R color difference components are horizontally subsampled by a factor of 2:1 with respect to luma – that is, sampled at 6.75 MHz each. Samples are multiplexed in the sequence $\{C_B, Y'_0, C_R, Y'_1\}$.

Sampling at 13.5 MHz produces a whole number of samples per total line (S_{TL}) in 480*i* systems (with 858 S_{TL}) and 576*i* systems (with 864 S_{TL}). The word rate at the interface is twice the luma sampling frequency: For each luma sampling clock, a color difference sample and a luma sample are transmitted. An 8-bit, 4:2:2 interface effectively carries 16 bits per pixel; the total data rate is 27 MB/s. A 10-bit serial interface effectively carries 20 bits per pixel, and has a total bit rate of 270 Mb/s.

Most 4:2:2 systems now accommodate 10-bit components.

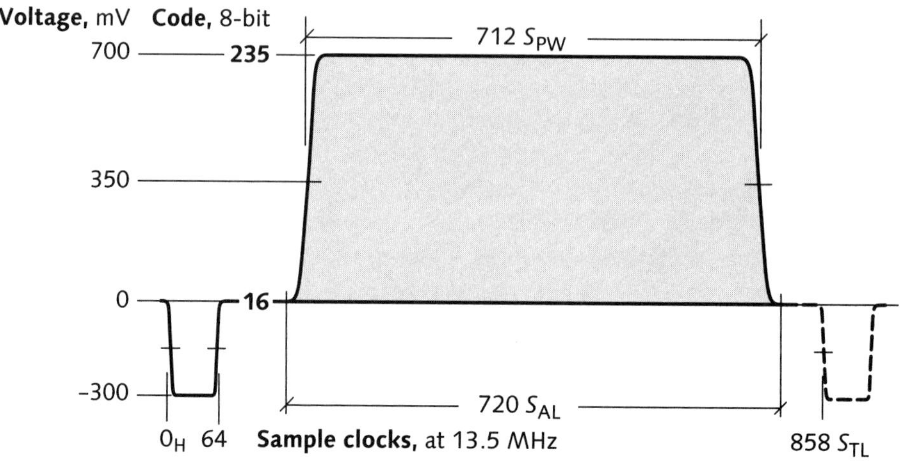

Figure 15.1 **Scan-line waveform for 480*i*29.97, 4:2:2 component luma.** EBU Tech. N10 analog levels are shown; however, these levels are rarely used in 480*i*. In analog video, sync is *blacker-than-black*, at -300 mV. (In digital video, sync is not coded as a signal level.) This sketch shows 8-bit interface levels (in bold); black is at code 16 and white is at code 235. The 720 active samples contain picture information; the remaining 138 sample intervals of the 858 comprise horizontal blanking.

Rec. 601, adopted in 1984, specified abstract coding parameters (including 4:2:2 chroma subsampling). Shortly afterwards, a parallel interface using 25-pin connectors was standardized in SMPTE 125M, EBU Tech. 3246, and Rec. 656. To enable transmission across long runs of coaxial cable, parallel interfaces have been superseded by the *serial digital interface* (SDI).

Both 480*i* and 576*i* have 720 active luma samples per line (S_{AL}). In uncompressed, 8-bit Rec. 601 video, the active samples consume about 20 MB/s.

Figure 15.1 above shows the luma (or *R'*, *G'*, or *B'*) waveform of a single scan line of 480*i* component video. The time axis shows sample counts at the Rec. 601 rate of 13.5 MHz; divide the sample number by 13.5 to derive time in microseconds. Amplitude is shown in millivolts (according to EBU Tech. N10 levels), and in 8-bit Rec. 601 digital interface code values.

Digital video interfaces convey active video framed in *timing reference signal* (TRS) sequences including *start*

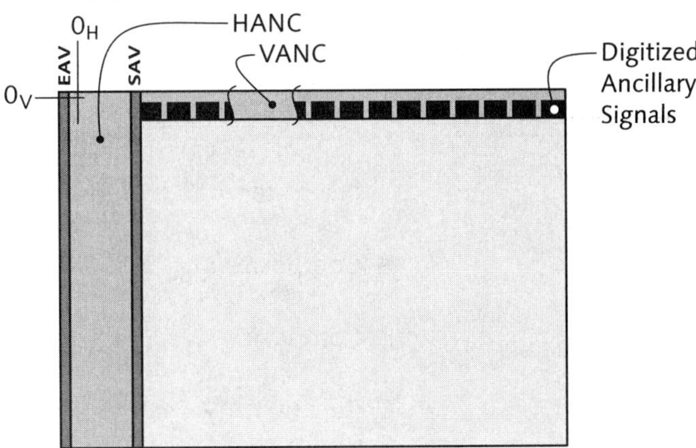

Figure 15.2 **Rec. 656 component digital interface** uses EAV to signal the start of each horizontal blanking interval, and SAV to signal the start of active video. Between EAV and SAV, ancillary data (HANC) can be carried. In a nonpicture line, the region between SAV and EAV can carry ancillary data (VANC). Digitized ancillary signals may be carried in lines other than those that convey either VANC or analog sync.

of active video (SAV) and *end of active video* (EAV). Ancillary data (ANC) and digitized ancillary signals are permitted in regions not occupied by active video. Figure 15.2 shows the raster diagram of Chapter 6, augmented with EAV, SAV, and the HANC and VANC regions. Details will be presented in *Digital sync, TRS, ancillary data, and interface,* on page 389.

Composite digital SDTV ($4f_{SC}$) interface

Composite $4f_{SC}$ digital interfaces code the entire 8- or 10-bit composite data stream, including sync edges, back porch, and burst. The interface word rate is the same as the sampling frequency, typically about half the rate of a component interface having the same scanning standard. The $4f_{SC}$ interface shares the electrical and physical characteristics of the 4:2:2 interface. Composite $4f_{SC}$ NTSC has exactly 910 sample intervals per total line (S_{TL}), and a data rate of about 143 Mb/s.

Composite $4f_{SC}$ PAL has a noninteger number of sample intervals per line: Samples in successive lines are offset to the left a small fraction ($^4/_{625}$) of the horizontal sample pitch. Sampling is not precisely *orthogonal*, although digital acquisition, processing, and display equipment treat it so. All but two lines in each frame have 1135 S_{TL}; each of the other two lines – preferably lines 313 and 625 – has 1137 S_{TL}. For 10-bit $4f_{SC}$, total data rate (including blanking) is about 177 Mb/s.

Serial digital interface (SDI)

SMPTE 259M, *10-Bit 4:2:2 Component and $4f_{SC}$ Composite Digital Signals – Serial Digital Interface.*

Serial digital interface (SDI) refers to a family of interfaces standardized by SMPTE. The Rec. 601 or $4f_{SC}$ data stream is serialized, then subjected to a scrambling technique. SMPTE 259M standardizes several interfaces, denoted by letters A through D as follows:

A Composite $4f_{SC}$ NTSC video, about 143 Mb/s

B Composite $4f_{SC}$ PAL video, about 177 Mb/s

C Rec. 601 4:2:2 component video, 270 Mb/s (This interface is standardized in Rec. 656.)

D Rec. 601 4:2:2 component video sampled at 18 MHz to achieve 16:9 aspect ratio, 360 Mb/s

Interfaces related to SMPTE 259M are standardized for the 483*p*59.94 systems specified in SMPTE 294M:

- The 4:2:2*p* system uses two 270 Mb/s SDI links ("dual link"), for a data rate of 540 Mb/s
- The 4:2:0*p* system uses a single link at 360 Mb/s

SMPTE 344M, *540 Mb/s Serial Digital Interface.*

SMPTE 344M standardizes an interface at 540 Mb/s, intended for 480*i*29.97, 4:4:4:4 component video; this could be adapted to convey 483*p*59.94, 4:2:0*p* video.

SDI is standardized for electrical transmission through coaxial cable, and for transmission through optical fiber. The SDI electrical interface uses ECL levels, 75 Ω impedance, BNC connectors, and coaxial cable. Electrical and mechanical parameters are specified in SMPTE standards and in Rec. 656; see *SDI coding* on page 396. Fiber-optic interfaces for digital SDTV, specified in SMPTE 297M, are straightforward adaptations of the serial versions of Rec. 656.

Component digital HDTV HD-SDI

The basic coding parameters of HDTV systems are standardized in Rec. 709. Various scanning systems are detailed in several SMPTE standards referenced in Table 13.2, on page 116.

Component SDTV, composite $4f_{SC}$ NTSC, and composite $4f_{SC}$ PAL all have different sample rates and different serial interface bit rates. In HDTV, a uniform sample rate of 74.25 MHz is adopted (modified by the ratio $^{1000}/_{1001}$ in applications where compatibility with 59.94 Hz frame rate is required). A serial interface bit rate of 20 times the sampling rate is used. Variations of the same standard accommodate mainstream 1080*i*30, 1080*p*24, and 720*p*60 scanning; 1080*p*30; and the obsolete 1035*i*30 system. The integer picture rates 24, 30, and 60 can be modified by the fraction $^{1000}/_{1001}$, giving rates of 23.976 Hz, 29.97 Hz, and 59.94 Hz.

The 23.976 Hz, 29.97 Hz, and 59.94 Hz frame rates are associated with a sampling rate of:

$$\frac{74.25}{1.001} \approx 74.176 \text{ Mpx/s}$$

The corresponding HD-SDI serial interface bit rate is:

$$\frac{1.485}{1.001} \approx 1.483 \text{ Gb/s}$$

The SDI interface at 270 Mb/s has been adapted to HDTV by scaling the bit rate by a factor of 5.5, yielding a fixed bit rate of 1.485 Gb/s. The sampling rate and serial bit rate for 23.976 Hz, 29.97 Hz, and 59.94 Hz interfaces are indicated in the margin. This interface is standardized for $Y'C_BC_R$, subsampled 4:2:2. Dual-link HD-SDI can be used to convey R'G'B'A, 4:4:4:4.

See Figure 13.3, on page 115.

HD-SDI accommodates 1080*i*25.00 and 1080*p*25.00 variants that might find use in Europe. This is accomplished by placing the 1920×1080 image array in a scanning system having 25 Hz rate. S_{TL} is altered from the 30 Hz standard to form an 1125/25 raster.

The standard HDTV analog interfaces use trilevel sync, instead of the bilevel sync that is used for analog SDTV. Figure 15.3 opposite shows the scan-line waveform, including trilevel sync, for 1080*i*30 HDTV.

SMPTE 292M, *Bit-Serial Digital Interface for High-Definition Television Systems.*

The HD-SDI interface is standardized in SMPTE 292M. Fiber-optic interfaces for digital HDTV are also specified in SMPTE 292M.

Interfaces for compressed video

Compressed digital video interfaces are impractical in the studio owing to the diversity of compression systems, and because compressed interfaces would require decompression capabilities in signal processing and monitoring equipment. Compressed 4:2:2 digital video studio equipment is usually interconnected through uncompressed SDI interfaces.

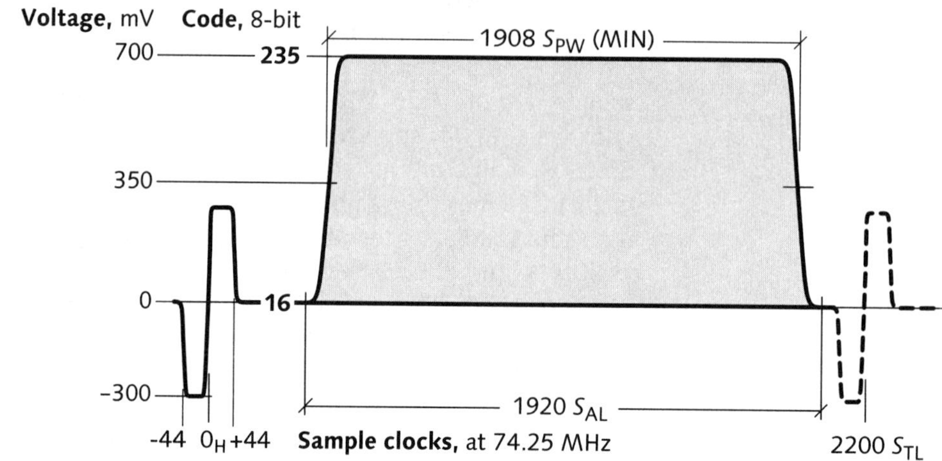

Figure 15.3 **Scan-line waveform for 1080*i*30 HDTV component luma.** Analog trilevel sync is shown, excursing ±300 mV. (In digital video, sync is not coded as a signal level.) At an 8-bit interface, black is represented by code 16 and white by 235. The indicated 1920 active samples contain picture information; the remaining sample intervals of the 2200 total comprise horizontal blanking.

Compressed interfaces can be used to transfer video into nonlinear editing systems, and to "dub" (duplicate) between VTRs sharing the same compression system. Compressed video can be interfaced directly using *serial data transport interface* (SDTI), to be described in a moment. The DVB ASI interface is widely used to convey MPEG-2 transport streams in network or transmission applications (but not in production). SMPTE SSI is an alternative, though it is not as popular as ASI. The IEEE 1394/DV interface, sometimes called *FireWire* or *i.LINK*, is widely used in the consumer electronics arena, and is beginning to be deployed in broadcast applications.

SDTI

SMPTE 305.2M, *Serial Data Transport Interface*.

SMPTE has standardized a derivative of SDI, *serial data transport interface* (SDTI), that transmits arbitrary data packets in place of uncompressed active video. SDTI can be used to transport DV25 and DV50 compressed datastreams. Despite DV bitstreams being standardized, different manufacturers have chosen incompatible techniques to wrap their compressed video data into SDTI streams. This renders SDTI useful only for interconnection of equipment from a single manufacturer.

DVB ASI and SMPTE SSI

CENELEC EN 50083-9, *Cabled distribution systems for television, sound and interactive multimedia signals – Part 9: Interfaces for CATV/SMATV headends and similar professional equipment for DVB/MPEG-2 transport streams.*

The DVB organization has standardized a high-speed serial interface for an MPEG-2 transport stream – the *asynchronous serial interface* (ASI). MPEG-2 transport packets of 188 bytes are subject to 8b–10b coding, then serialized. (Optionally, packets that have been subject to Reed-Solomon encoding can be conveyed; these packets have 204 bytes each.) The 8b–10b coding is that of the FiberChannel standard. The link operates at the SDI rate of 270 Mb/s; synchronization (filler) codes are sent while the channel is not occupied by MPEG-2 data. The standard specifies an electrical interface whose physical and electrical parameters are drawn from the SMPTE SDI standard; the standard also specifies a fiber-optic interface.

SMPTE 310M, *Synchronous Serial Interface for MPEG-2 Digital Transport Stream.*

A functional alternative to DVB-ASI is the *synchronous serial interface* (SSI), which is designed for use in environments with high RF fields. SSI is standardized in SMPTE 310M. As I write this, it is not very popular, except for interconnection of ATSC bitstreams to 8-VSB modulators.

IEEE 1394 (FireWire, i.LINK)

IEEE 1394, *Standard for a High Performance Serial Bus.*

In 1995, the IEEE standardized a general-purpose high-speed serial bus capable of connecting up to 63 devices in a tree-shaped network through point-to-point connections. The link conveys data across two shielded twisted pairs (STP), and operates at 100 Mb/s, 200 Mb/s, or 400 Mb/s. Each point-to-point segment is limited to 4.5 m; there is a limit of 72 m across the breadth of a network. Asynchronous and isochronous modes are provided; the latter accommodates realtime traffic. Apple computer refers to the interface by their trademark *FireWire*. Sony's trademark is *i.LINK*, though Sony commonly uses a 4-pin connector not strictly compliant with the IEEE standard. (The 6-pin IEEE connector provides power for a peripheral device; power is absent from Sony's 4-pin connector. A node may have either 4-pin or 6-pin connectors.)

As I write in 2002, agreement upon IEEE 1394B ("Gigabit 1394") is imminent. For STP media at a distance of 4.5 m per link, this extends the data rate to 800 Mb/s, 1.6 Gb/s, or 3.2 Gb/s. In addition, 1394B specifies four additional media:

- Plastic optical fiber (POF), for distances of up to 50 m, at data rates of either 100 or 200 Mb/s
- CAT 5 coaxial cable, for distances of up to 100 m, at 100 Mb/s
- Hard polymer-clad fiber (HPCF), for distances of up to 100 m, at 100 or 200 Mb/s
- Multimode glass optical fiber (GOF), for distances of up to 100 m at 100, 200, 400, or 800 Mb/s, or 1.6 or 3.2 Gb/s

IEC 61883-1, *Consumer audio/video equipment – Digital interface – Part 1: General.* See also parts 2 through 5.

IEC has standardized the transmission of digital video over IEEE 1394. Video is digitized according to Rec. 601, then motion-JPEG coded (using the DV standard) at about 25 Mb/s; this is colloquially known as 1394/DV25 (or DV25-over-1394). DV coding has been adapted to 100 Mb/s for HDTV (DV100); a standard for DV100-over-1394 has been adopted by IEC.

A standard for conveying an MPEG-2 transport stream over IEEE 1394 has also been adopted by IEC; however, commercial deployment of MPEG-2-over-1394 is slow, mainly owing to concerns about copy protection. The D-7 (DVCPRO50) and D-9 (Digital-S) videotape recorders use DV coding at 50 Mb/s; a standard DV50 interface across IEEE 1394 is likely to be developed.

Switching and mixing

SMPTE RP 168, *Definition of Vertical Interval Switching Point for Synchronous Video Switching.*

Switching or editing between video sources – "cutting" – is done in the vertical interval, so that each frame of the resulting video remains intact, without any switching transients. When switching between two signals in a hardware switcher, if the output signal is to be made continuous across the instant of switching, the input signals must be synchronous – the 0_V instants of both signals must match precisely in time. To prevent switching transients from disturbing vertical sync elements, switching is done somewhat later than 0_V; see SMPTE RP 168.

In a vacuum, light travels 0.299972458 m – very nearly one foot – each nanosecond.

Timing in analog facilities

Signals propagate through coaxial cable at a speed between about 0.66 and 0.75 of the speed of light in a vacuum. Time delay is introduced by long cable runs, and by processing delay through equipment. Even over a long run of 300 m (1000 ft) of cable, only a microsecond or two of delay is introduced – well under ¼ of a line time for typical video standards. (To reach a delay of one line time in 480*i* or 576*i* would take a run of about 12 km!) To compensate typical cable delay requires an adjustment of horizontal timing, by just a small fraction of a line time.

In analog video, these delays are accommodated by advancing the timing at each source, so that each signal is properly timed upon reaching the production switcher. In a medium-size or large facility, a single sync generator (or a pair of redundant sync generators) provides *house sync*, to which virtually everything else in the facility is locked with appropriate time advance or delay. To enable a seamless switch from a network source to a local source in the early days of television networks, every television station was locked to timing established by its network! Each network had an atomic clock, generating 5 MHz. This was divided to subcarrier using the relationship in the margin.

$$3.579\overline{545} = 5 \cdot \frac{63}{88}$$

Many studio sources – such as cameras and VTRs – can be driven from a *reference* input that sets the timing of the primary output. This process was historically referred to as "sync generator locking," or nowadays, as *genlock*. In the absence of a reference signal, equipment is designed to *free-run:* Its frequency will be within tolerance, but its phase will be unlocked.

In studio equipment capable of genlock, with factory settings the output signal emerges nominally synchronous with the reference. Studio equipment is capable of advancing or delaying its primary output signal with respect to the reference, by perhaps ±¼ of a line time, through an adjustment called SYSTEM PHASE. Nowadays, some studio video equipment has vertical processing that incorporates line delays; such equipment introduces delay of a line time, or perhaps a few line times.

SYSTEM PHASE advances or delays all components of the signal. Historically, HORIZONTAL PHASE (or H PHASE) altered sync and luma but left burst and subcarrier untouched.

To compensate line delays, SYSTEM PHASE must now accommodate adjustment of vertical delay as well as horizontal. The adjustment is performed by matching the timing of the 50%-points of sync. Misadjustment of SYSTEM PHASE is reflected as position error.

A studio sync generator can, itself, be genlocked. A large facility typically has several sync generators physically distributed throughout the facility. Each provides local sync, and each is timed according to its propagation delay back to the central switching or routing point.

If a piece of studio equipment originates a video signal, it is likely to have adjustable SYSTEM PHASE. However, if it processes a signal, and has no framestore, then it is likely to exhibit fixed delay: It is likely to have no genlock capability, and no capability to adjust SYSTEM PHASE. Delay of such a device can be compensated by appropriate timing of its source. For example, a typical video switcher has fixed delay, and no system phase adjustment. (It has a reference input whose sync elements are inserted onto the primary outputs of the switcher, but there is no genlock function.)

A *routing switcher* is a large matrix of crosspoint switches. A routing switcher is designed so that any path through the switcher incurs the same fixed delay.

Timing in composite analog NTSC and PAL

NTSC modulation and demodulation work properly provided that burst phase and modulated subcarrier phase remain locked: Color coding is independent of the phase relationship between subcarrier and sync.

For details concerning SCH, see page 512.

If two signals are to be switched or mixed, though, their modulated subcarrier phase (and therefore their burst phases) must match – otherwise, hue would shift as mixing took place. But the phase of luma (and therefore of the analog sync waveform) must match as well – otherwise, picture position would shift as mixing took place. These two requirements led to standardization of the relationship of subcarrier to horizontal (SCH) phase. It is standard that the zerocrossing of unmodulated subcarrier be synchronous with 0_H at line 1 of the frame, within about ±10°. In NTSC, if this requirement is met at line 1, then the zerocrossing of subcarrier will be coincident with the analog sync reference point (0_H) within the stated tolerance on *every* line. In PAL, the requirement is stated at line 1, because the phase relationship changes throughout the frame. Neither NTSC nor PAL has burst on line 1; SCH must be measureed from with regenerated subcarrier, or measured from burst on some other line (such as line 10).

SUBCARRIER PHASE is sometimes inaccurately called BURST PHASE, because the adjustment involves rotating the phase of burst. However, the primary effect is to adjust the phase of modulated chroma.

For composite analog switching, it is necessary that the signals being mixed have matching 0_V; but in addition, it is necessary that the signals have matching subcarrier phase. (If this were not the case, hue would shift during the transition.) As I have mentioned, cable delay is accommodated by back-timing. However, with imperfect cable equalization, cable delay at subcarrier frequency might be somewhat different than delay at low frequency. If the source generates zero SCH, you could match system timing, but have incorrect subcarrier phase. The solution is to have, at a composite source, a SUBCARRIER PHASE adjustment that rotates the phase of subcarrier through 360°. Equipment is timed by adjusting SYSTEM PHASE to match sync edges (and thereby, luma position), then adjusting SUBCARRIER PHASE TO match burst phase (and thereby, the phase of modulated chroma).

Timing in digital facilities

FIFO: First in, first out.

Modern digital video equipment has, at each input, a buffer that functions as a FIFO. This buffer at each input accommodates an advance of timing at that input (with respect to reference video) of up to about ±100 µs. Timing a digital facility involves advancing each signal source so that signals from all sources arrive in time at the inputs of the facility's main switcher. This timing need not be exact: It suffices to guarantee that no buffer overruns or underruns. When a routing switcher switches among SDI streams, a timing error of several dozen samples is tolerable; downstream equipment will recover timing within one or two lines after the instant of switching.

When a studio needs to accommodate an asynchronous video input – one whose frame rate is within tolerance, but whose phase cannot be referenced to house sync, such as a satellite feed – then a *framestore synchronizer* is used. This device contains a frame of memory that functions as a FIFO buffer for video. An input signal with arbitrary timing is written into the memory with timing based upon its own sync elements. The synchronizer accepts a reference video signal; the memory is read out at rates locked to the sync elements of the reference video. (Provisions are made to adjust SYSTEM PHASE – that is, the timing of the output signal with respect to the reference video.) An asynchronous signal is thereby delayed up to one frame time, perhaps even a little more, so as to match the local reference. The signal can then be used as if it were a local source.

Some video switchers incorporate digital video effects (DVE) capability; a DVE unit necessarily includes a framestore.

Some studio video devices incorporate framestores, and exhibit latency of a field, a frame, or more. Low-level timing of such equipment is accomplished by introducing time advance so that 0_V appears at the correct instant. However, even if video content is timed correctly with respect to 0_V, it may be late by a frame, or in a very large facility, by several frames. Attention must be paid to delaying audio by a similar time interval, to avoid lip-sync problems.

Part 2

Principles

Filtering and sampling 16

This chapter explains how a one-dimensional signal is filtered and sampled prior to A-to-D conversion, and how it is reconstructed following D-to-A conversion. In the following chapter, *Resampling, interpolation, and decimation,* on page 171, I extend these concepts to conversions within the digital domain. In *Image digitization and reconstruction,* on page 187, I extend these concepts to the two dimensions of an image.

My explanation describes the original sampling of an analog signal waveform. If you are more comfortable remaining in the digital domain, consider the problem of shrinking a row of image samples by a factor of n (say, $n = 16$) to accomplish image resizing. You need to compute one output sample for each set of n input samples. This is the *resampling* problem in the digital domain. Its constraints are very similar to the constraints of original sampling of an analog signal.

When a one-dimensional signal (such as an audio signal) is digitized, each sample must encapsulate, in a single value, what might have begun as a complex waveform during the sample period. When a two-dimensional image is sampled, each sample encapsulates what might have begun as a potentially complex distribution of power over a small region of the image plane. In each case, a potentially vast amount of information must be reduced to a single number.

Prior to sampling, detail within the sample interval must be discarded. The reduction of information prior to sampling is *prefiltering.* The challenge of sampling is to discard this information while avoiding the loss of information at scales larger than the sample pitch, all the time avoiding the introduction of artifacts. *Sampling theory* elaborates the conditions under which a signal can be sampled and accurately reconstructed, subject only to inevitable loss of detail that could not, in any event, be represented by a given number of samples in the digital domain.

Sampling theory was originally developed to describe one-dimensional signals such as audio, where the signal is a continuous function of the single dimension of time. Sampling theory has been extended to images, where an image is treated as a continuous function of two spatial coordinates (horizontal and vertical). Sampling theory can be further extended to the temporal sampling of moving images, where the third coordinate is time.

Sampling theorem

Assume that a signal to be digitized is well behaved, changing relatively slowly as a function of time. Consider the cosine signals shown in Figure 16.1 below, where the *x*-axis shows sample intervals. The top waveform is a cosine at the fraction 0.35 of the sampling rate f_S; the middle waveform is at $0.65 f_S$. The bottom row shows that identical samples result from sampling either of these waveforms: Either of the waveforms can masquerade as the same sample sequence. If the middle waveform is sampled, then reconstructed conventionally, the top waveform will result. This is the phenomenon of *aliasing*.

Figure 16.1 **Cosine waves less than and greater than $0.5 f_S$,** in this case at the fractions 0.35 and 0.65 of the sampling rate, produce exactly the same set of sampled values when point-sampled – they *alias*.

Symbol conventions used in this figure and following figures are as follows:

$\omega = 2\pi f_S$

$[\text{rad} \cdot \text{s}^{-1}]$

$t_S = \frac{1}{f_S}$

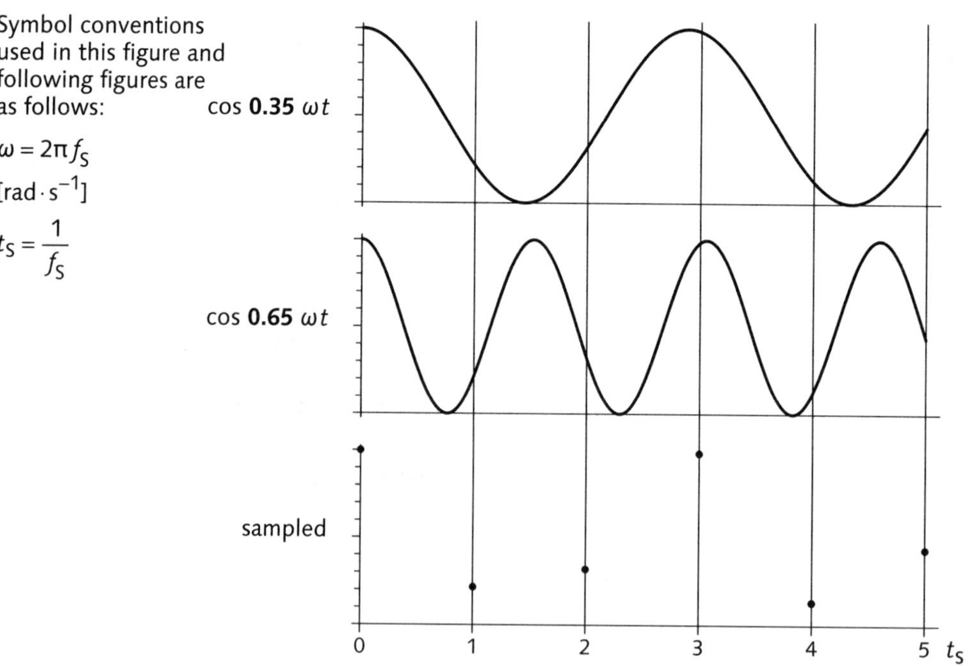

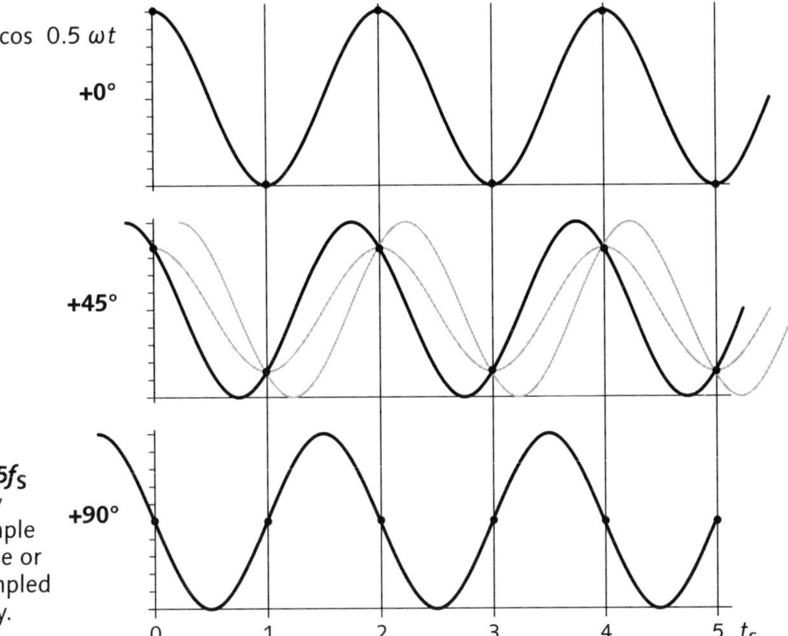

Figure 16.2 **Cosine waves at exactly 0.5f_S** cannot be accurately represented in a sample sequence if the phase or amplitude of the sampled waveform is arbitrary.

Sampling at exactly 0.5f_S

You might assume that a signal whose frequency is exactly half the sampling rate can be accurately represented by an alternating sequence of sample values, say, zero and one. In Figure 16.2 above, the series of samples in the top row is unambiguous (provided it is known that the amplitude of the waveform is unity). But the samples of the middle row could be generated from any of the three indicated waveforms, and the phase-shifted waveform in the bottom row has samples that are indistinguishable from a constant waveform having a value of 0.5. The inability to accurately analyze a signal at exactly half the sampling frequency leads to the strict "less-than" condition in the Sampling Theorem, which I will now describe.

Nyquist essentially applied to signal processing a mathematical discovery made in 1915 by E.T. Whittaker. Later contributions were made by Shannon (in the U.S.) and Kotelnikov (in Russia).

Harry Nyquist, at Bell Labs, concluded in about 1928 that to guarantee sampling of a signal without the introduction of aliases, all of the signal's frequency components must be contained strictly within half the sampling rate (now known as the *Nyquist frequency*). If a signal meets this condition, it is said to satisfy the

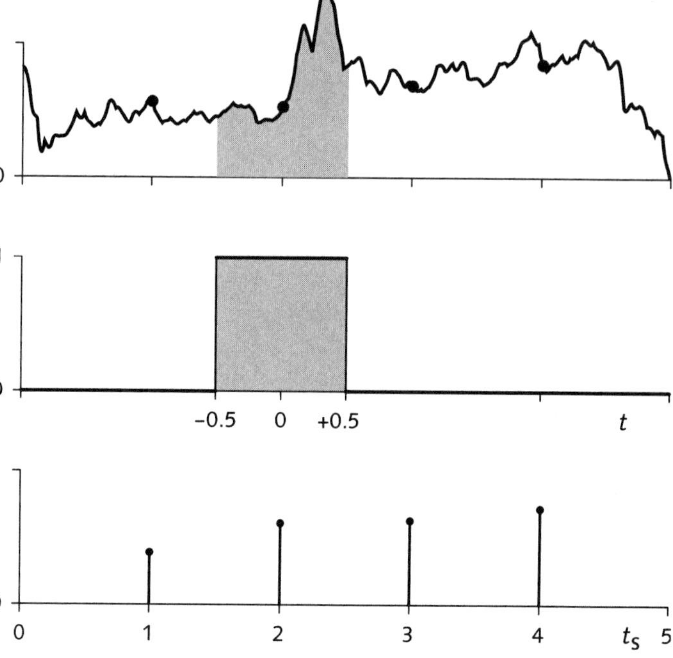

Figure 16.3 **Point sampling** runs the risk of choosing an extreme value that is not representative of the neighborhood surrounding the desired sample instant.

Figure 16.4 **Boxcar weighting function** has unity value throughout one sample interval; elsewhere, its value is zero.

Figure 16.5 **Boxcar filtering** weights the input waveform with the boxcar weighting function: Each output sample is the average across one sample interval.

Nyquist criterion. The condition is usually imposed by analog filtering, prior to sampling, that removes frequency components at $0.5f_S$ and higher. A filter must implement some sort of integration. In the example of Figure 16.1, no filtering was performed; the waveform was simply *point-sampled*. The lack of filtering admitted aliases. Figure 16.3 represents the waveform of an actual signal; point sampling at the indicated instants yields sample values that are not representative of the local neighborhood at each sampling instant.

Perhaps the most basic way to filter a waveform is to average the waveform across each sample period. Many different integration schemes are possible; these can be represented as weighting functions plotted as a function of time. Simple averaging uses the *boxcar* weighting function sketched in Figure 16.4; its value is unity during the sample period and zero outside that interval. Filtering with this weighting function is called *boxcar* filtering, since a sequence of these functions with different amplitudes resembles the profile of

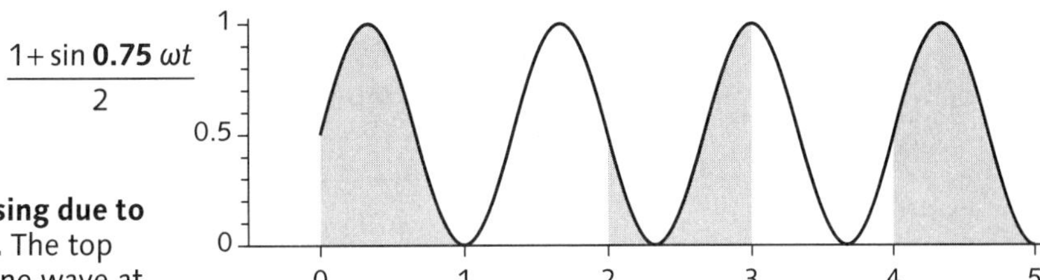

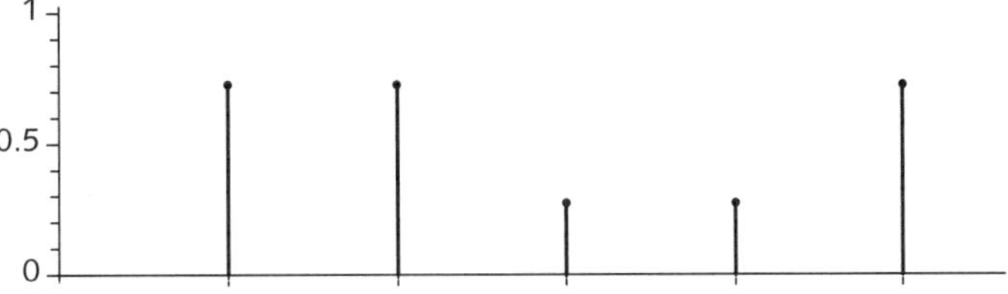

Figure 16.6 **Aliasing due to boxcar filtering.** The top graph shows a sine wave at $0.75f_S$. The shaded area under the curve illustrates its integral computed by a boxcar function. The bottom graph shows that the sequence of resulting sample points is dominated by an alias at $0.25f_S$.

a freight train. Once the weighted values are formed the signal is represented by discrete values, plotted for this example in Figure 16.5. To plot these values as amplitudes of a boxcar function would wrongly suggest that a boxcar function should be used as a reconstruction filter. The shading under the waveform of Figure 16.3 suggests box filtering.

A serious problem with boxcar filtering across each sample interval is evident in Figure 16.6 above. The top graph shows a sine wave at $0.75f_S$; the signal exceeds the Nyquist frequency. The shaded regions show integration over intervals of one sample period. For the sine wave at $0.75f_S$, sampled starting at zero phase, the first two integrated values are about 0.6061; the second two are about 0.3939. The dominant component of the filtered sample sequence, shown in the bottom graph, is one-quarter of the sampling frequency. Filtering using a one-sample-wide boxcar weighting function is inadequate to attenuate signal components above the Nyquist rate. An unwanted alias results.

Figure 16.6 is another example of *aliasing:* Owing to a poor presampling filter, the sequence of sampled values exhibits a frequency component not present in the input signal. As this example shows, boxcar integration is not sufficient to prevent fairly serious aliasing.

Magnitude frequency response

To gain a general appreciation of aliasing, it is necessary to understand signals in the *frequency domain*. The previous section gave an example of inadequate filtering prior to sampling that created an unexpected alias upon sampling. You can determine whether a filter has an unexpected response at *any* frequency by presenting to the filter a signal that sweeps through all frequencies, from zero, through low frequencies, to some high frequency, plotting the response of the filter as you go. I graphed such a frequency sweep signal at the top of Figure 7.1, on page 66. The middle graph of that figure shows a response waveform typical of a lowpass filter (LPF), which attenuates high frequency signals. The magnitude response of that filter is shown in the bottom graph.

Strictly speaking, *amplitude* is an instantaneous measure that may take a positive or negative value. *Magnitude* is properly either an absolute value, or a squared or *root mean square* (RMS) value representative of amplitude over some time interval. The terms are often used interchangeably.

Magnitude response is the RMS average response over all phases of the input signal at each frequency. As you saw in the previous section, a filter's response can be strongly influenced by the phase of the input signal. To determine response at a particular frequency, you can test all phases at that frequency. Alternatively, provided the filter is linear, you can present just two signals – a cosine wave at the test frequency and a sine wave at the same frequency. The filter's magnitude response at any frequency is the absolute value of the vector sum of the responses to the sine and the cosine waves.

See *Linearity* on page 21.

Analytic and numerical procedures called *transforms* can be used to determine frequency response. The *Laplace transform* is appropriate for continuous functions, such as signals in the analog domain. The *Fourier transform* is appropriate for signals that are sampled periodically, or for signals that are themselves periodic. A variant intended for computation on data that has been sampled is the *discrete Fourier transform* (DFT). An elegant scheme for numerical computation of the DFT is the *fast Fourier transform* (FFT). The *z-transform* is essentially a generalization of the Fourier transform. All of these transforms represent mathematical ways to determine a system's response to sine waves over a range of frequencies and phases. The result of a transform is an expression or graph in terms of frequency.

Bracewell, Ronald N., *The Fourier Transform and its Applications*, Second Edition (New York: McGraw-Hill, 1985).

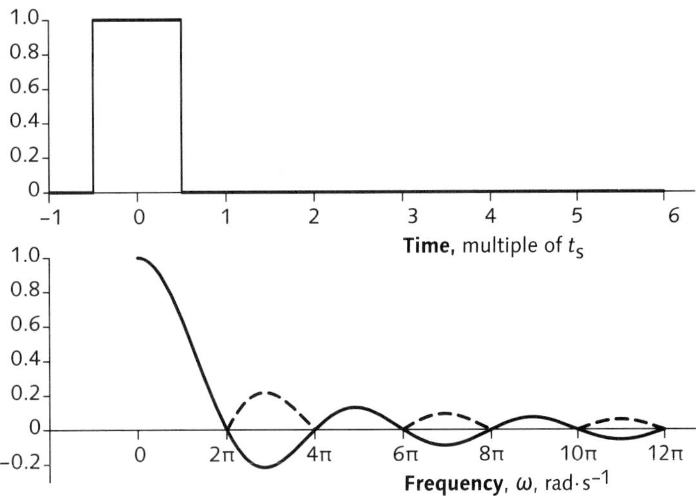

Figure 16.7 **Frequency response of a boxcar filter.** The top graph shows a boxcar weighting function, symmetrical around $t = 0$. Its frequency spectrum is a *sinc* function, shown underneath. The solid line shows that at certain frequencies, the filter causes phase inversion. Filter response is usually plotted as magnitude; phase inversion in the stopband is reflected as the absolute (magnitude) values shown in dashed lines.

$$\operatorname{sinc} \omega = \begin{cases} 1, & \omega = 0 \\ \dfrac{\sin \omega}{\omega}, & \omega \neq 0 \end{cases}$$

Eq 16.1 **sinc function** is pronounced *sink.* Formally, its argument is in radians per second (rad·s^{-1}); here I use the conventional symbol ω for that quantity. The term (sin x)/x (pronounced *sine ecks over ecks*) is often used synonymously with sinc, without mention of the units of the argument. If applied to frequency in hertz, the function could be written (sin $2\pi f$)/$2\pi f$.

sinc is unrelated to *sync* (synchronization).

Magnitude frequency response of a boxcar

The top graph of Figure 16.7 above shows the weighting function of *Point sampling* on page 144, as a function of time (in sample intervals). The Fourier transform of the boxcar function – that is, the magnitude frequency response of a boxcar weighting function – takes the shape of (sin x)/x. The response is graphed at the bottom of Figure 16.7, with the frequency axis in units of $\omega = 2\pi f_S$. Equation 16.1 in the margin defines the function. This function is so important that it has been given the special symbol *sinc*, introduced by Phillip M. Woodward in 1953 as a contraction of *sinus cardinalis*.

A presampling filter should have fairly uniform response below half the sample rate, to provide good sharpness, and needs to severely attenuate frequencies at and above half the sample rate, to achieve low aliasing. The bottom graph of Figure 16.7 shows that this requirement is not met by a boxcar weighting function. The graph of sinc predicts frequencies where aliasing can be introduced. Figure 16.6 showed an example of a sinewave at $0.75f_S$; reading the value of sinc at 1.5π from Figure 16.7 shows that aliasing is expected.

You can gain an intuitive understanding of the boxcar weighting function by considering that when the input frequency is such that an integer number of cycles lies under the boxcar, the response will be null. But when an integer number of cycles, plus a half-cycle, lies under the weighting function, the response will exhibit a local maximum that can admit an alias.

To obtain a presampling filter that rejects potential aliases, we need to pass low frequencies, up to almost half the sample rate, and reject frequencies above it. We need a frequency response that is constant at unity up to just below $0.5f_S$, whereupon it drops to zero. We need a filter function whose *frequency* response – not time response – resembles a boxcar.

The sinc weighting function

Remarkably, the Fourier transform possesses the mathematical property of being its own inverse (within a scale factor). In Figure 16.7, the Fourier transform of a boxcar *weighting* function produced a sinc-shaped *frequency* response. Figure 16.8 opposite shows a sinc-shaped *weighting* function; it produces a boxcar-shaped *frequency* response. So, sinc weighting gives the ideal lowpass filter (ILPF), and it is the ideal temporal weighting function for use in a presampling filter. However, there are several theoretical and practical difficulties in using sinc. In practice, we approximate it.

A near-ideal filter in analog video is sometimes called a *brick wall* filter, though there is no precise definition of this term.

An analog filter's response is a function of frequency on the positive real axis. In analog signal theory, there is no upper bound on frequency. But in a digital filter the response to a test frequency f_T is identical to the response at f_T offset by any integer multiple of the sampling frequency: The frequency axis "wraps" at multiples of the sampling rate. Sampling theory also dictates "folding" around half the sample rate. Signal components having frequencies at or above the Nyquist rate cannot accurately be represented.

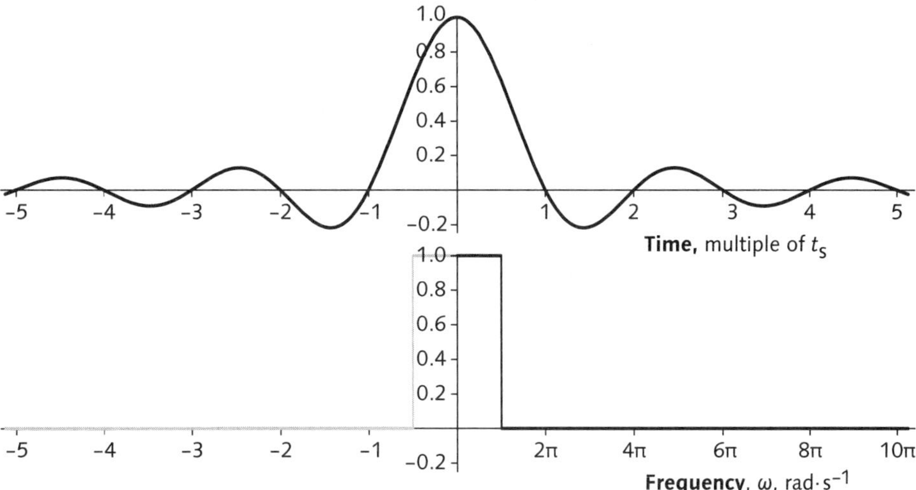

Figure 16.8 **The sin (*x*)/*x* (or sinc) weighting function** is shown in the top graph. Its frequency spectrum, shown underneath, has a boxcar shape: sinc weighting exhibits the ideal properties for a presampling filter. However, its infinite extent makes it physically unrealizable; also, its negative lobes make it unrealizable for transducers of light such as cameras, scanners, and displays. Many practical digital lowpass filters have coefficients that approximate samples of sinc.

The temporal weighting functions used in video are usually symmetrical; nonetheless, they are usually graphed in a two-sided fashion. The frequency response of a filter suitable for real signals is symmetrical about zero; conventionally, frequency response is graphed in one-sided fashion starting at zero frequency ("DC"). Sometimes it is useful to consider or graph frequency response in two-sided style.

Frequency response of point sampling

The Fourier transform provides an analytical tool to examine frequency response: We can reexamine point sampling. Taking an instantaneous sample of a waveform is mathematically equivalent to using a weighting function that is unity at the sample instant, and zero everywhere else – the weighting function is an *impulse*. The Fourier transform of an impulse function is constant, unity, at all frequencies. A set of equally spaced impulses is an *impulse train;* its transform is also unity everywhere. The sampling operation is represented as multiplication by an impulse train. An unfiltered signal sampled by a set of impulses will admit aliases equally from all input frequencies.

Clarke, R.J., *Transform Coding of Images* (Boston: Academic Press, 1985).

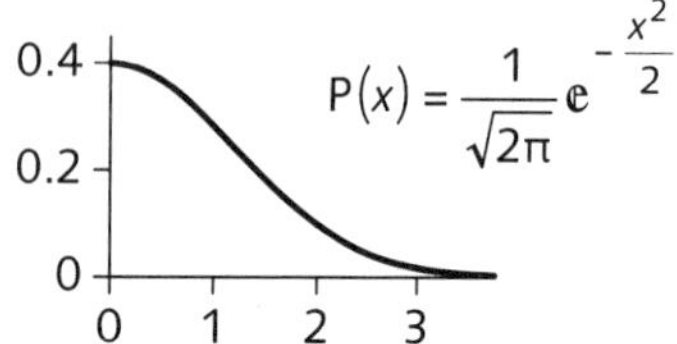

Figure 16.11 **Gaussian function** is shown here in its one-sided form, with the scaling that is usual in statistics, where the function (augmented with mean and variance terms) is known as the *normal function*. Its integral is the *error function*, erf(*x*). The frequency response of cascaded Gaussian filters is Gaussian.

Fourier transform pairs

Figure 16.9 opposite shows Fourier transform pairs for several different functions. In the left column is a set of waveforms; beside each waveform is its frequency spectrum. Functions having short time durations transform to functions with widely distributed frequency components. Conversely, functions that are compact in their frequency representation transform to temporal functions with long duration. (See Figure 16.10 overleaf.)

A Gaussian function – the middle transform pair in Figure 16.9, detailed in Figure 16.11 in the margin – is the identify function for the Fourier transform: It has the unique property of transforming to itself (within a scale factor). The Gaussian function has moderate spread both in the time domain and in the frequency domain; it has infinite extent, but becomes negligibly small more than a few units from the origin. The Gaussian function lies at the balance point between the distribution of power in the time domain and the distribution of power in the frequency domain.

Analog filters

Analog filtering is necessary prior to digitization, to bring a signal into the digital domain without aliases. I have described filtering as integration using different weighting functions; an antialiasing filter performs the integration using analog circuitry.

An analog filter performs integration by storing a magnetic field in an inductor (coil) using the electrical property of inductance (L), and/or by storing an electrical charge in a capacitor using the electrical property of capacitance (C). In low-performance filters, resistance (R) is used as well. An ordinary analog filter has an impulse response that is infinite in temporal extent.

The design of analog filters is best left to specialists.

Digital filters

Once digitized, a signal can be filtered directly in the digital domain. Design and implementation of such filters – in hardware, firmware, or software – is the domain of *digital signal processing* (DSP). Filters like the

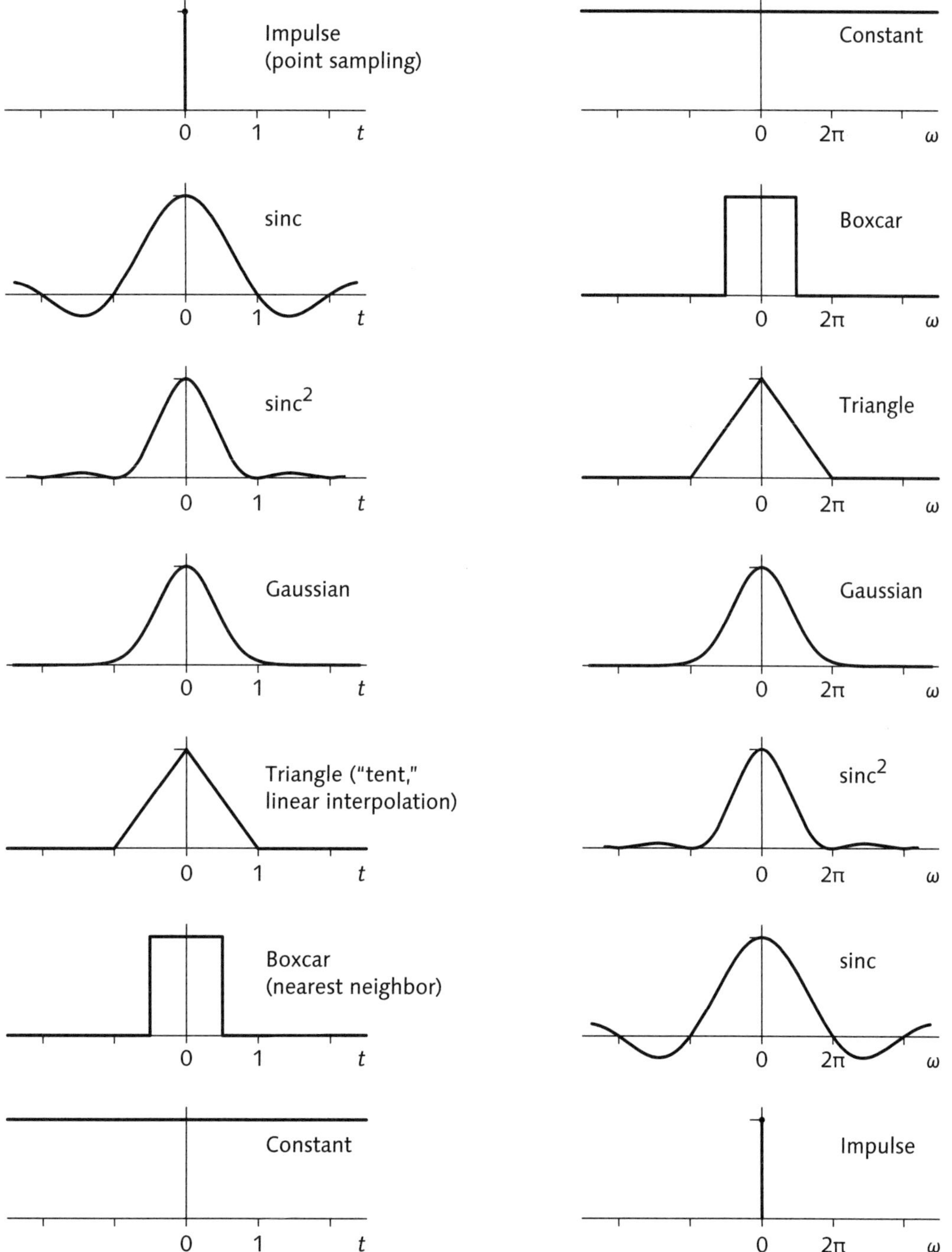

Figure 16.9 **Fourier transform pairs** for several functions are shown in these graphs. In the left column is a set of waveforms in the time domain; beside each waveform is its frequency spectrum.

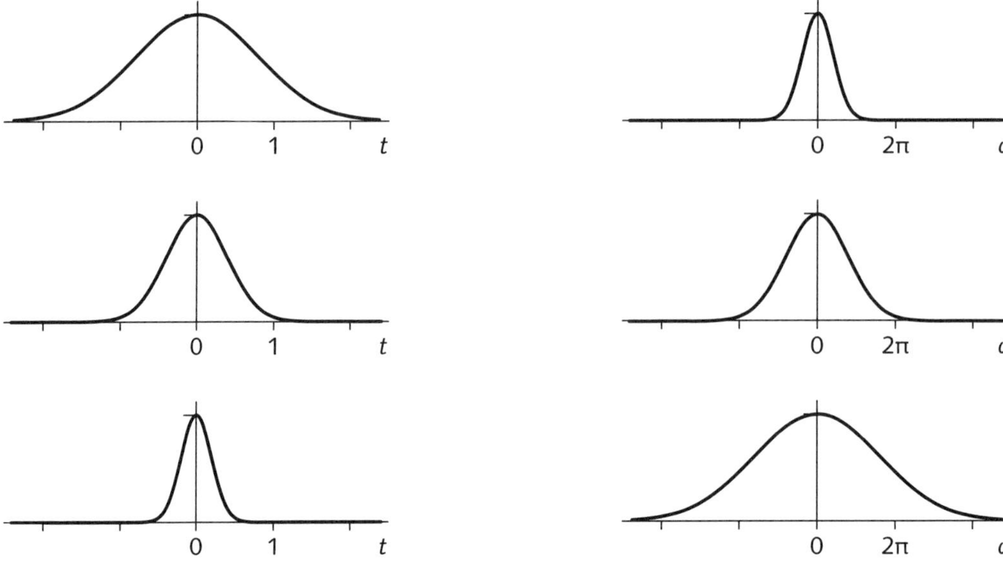

Figure 16.10 **Waveforms of three temporal extents** are shown on the left; the corresponding transforms are shown on the right. Spectral width is inversely proportional to temporal extent, not only for the Gaussians shown here, but for all waveforms.

ones that I have been describing are implemented digitally by computing weighted sums of samples.

Averaging neighboring samples is the simplest form of *moving average* (MA) filter.

Perhaps the simplest digital filter is one that just sums adjacent samples; the weights in this case are [1, 1]. Figure 16.12 on the facing page shows the frequency response of such a [1, 1] filter. This filter offers minimal attenuation to very low frequencies; as signal frequency approaches half the sampling rate, the response follows a cosine curve to zero. This is a very simple, very cheap *lowpass filter* (LPF).

I have drawn in gray the filter's response from $0.5 f_S$ to the sampling frequency. In a digital filter, frequencies in this region are indistinguishable from frequencies between $0.5 f_S$ and 0. The gain of this filter at zero frequency (DC) is 2, the sum of its coefficients. Normally, the coefficients of such a filter are normalized to sum to unity, so that the overall DC gain of the filter is one. In this case the normalized coefficients would be $[\frac{1}{2}, -\frac{1}{2}]$. However, it is inconvenient to call this a $[\frac{1}{2}, -\frac{1}{2}]$-filter; colloquially, this is a [1, 1]-filter.

Figure 16.12 **[1, 1] FIR filter** sums two adjacent samples; this forms a simple lowpass filter. I'll introduce the term *FIR* on page 157.

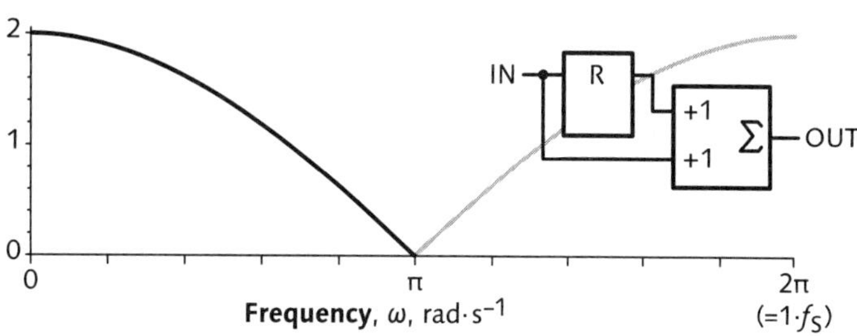

Figure 16.13 **[1, -1] FIR filter** subtracts one sample from the previous sample; this forms a simple high-pass filter.

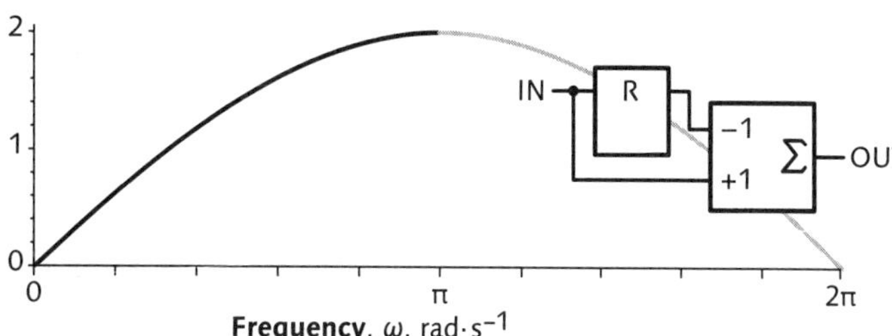

Figure 16.14 **[1, 0, 1] FIR filter** averages a sample and the second preceding sample, ignoring the sample in between; this forms a bandreject ("notch," or "trap") filter at 0.25 f_S.

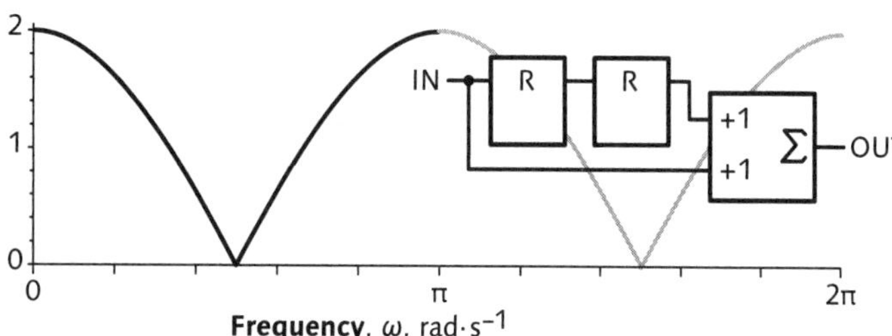

Figure 16.15 **[1, 0, -1] FIR filter** subtracts one sample from the second previous sample, ignoring the sample in between; this forms a bandpass filter centered at 0.25 f_S.

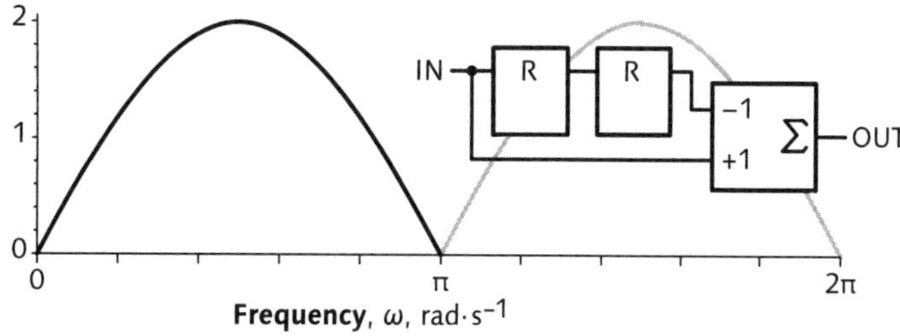

Digital filters can be implemented in software, firmware, or hardware. At the right side of each graph above, I show the block diagrams familiar to hardware designers. Each block labelled *R* designates a register; a series of these elements forms a shift register.

A simple *highpass filter* (HPF) is formed by subtracting each sample from the previous sample: This filter has weights [1, -1]. The response of this filter is graphed in Figure 16.13. In general, and in this case, a highpass

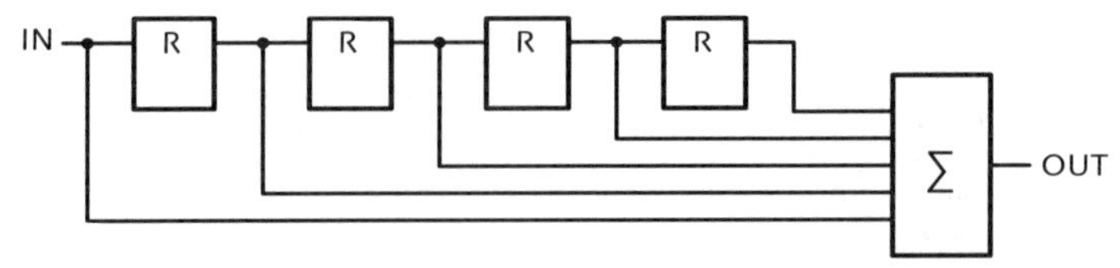

Figure 16.16 **Block diagram of 5-tap FIR filter** comprises four registers and an adder; five adjacent samples are summed. Prior to scaling to unity, the coefficients are [1, 1, 1, 1, 1].

filter is obtained when a lowpass-filtered version of a signal is subtracted from the unfiltered signal. The unfiltered signal can be considered as a two-tap filter having weights [1, 0]. Subtracting the weights [$\frac{1}{2}$, $\frac{1}{2}$] of the scaled lowpass filter from that yields the scaled weights [$\frac{1}{2}$, $-\frac{1}{2}$] of this highpass filter.

A bandpass (bandstop) filter is considered *narrowband* if its passband (stopband) covers an octave or less. (See page 19.)

Figure 16.14 shows the response of a filter that adds a sample to the second previous sample, disregarding the central sample. The weights in this case are [1, 0, 1]. This forms a simple *bandreject filter* (BRF), also known as a *bandstop* or *notch filter,* or *trap.* Here, the response has a null at one quarter the sampling frequency. The scaled filter passes DC with no attenuation. This filter would make a mess of image data – if a picket fence whose pickets happened to lie at a frequency of $0.25f_S$ were processed through this filter, the pickets would average together and disappear! It is a bad idea to apply such a filter to image data, but this filter (and filters like it) can be very useful for signal processing functions.

Figure 16.15 shows the response of a filter that subtracts a sample from the second previous sample, disregarding the central sample. Its weights are [1, 0, -1]. This forms a simple *bandpass filter* (BPF). The weights sum to zero – this filter blocks DC. The BPF of this example is complementary to the [1, 0, 1] filter.

If a filter like that of Figure 16.16 has many taps, it needs many adders. Its arithmetic can be simplified by using an accumulator to form the running sum of input samples, another accumulator to form the running sum of outputs from the shift register, and a subtractor to take the difference of these sums. This structure is called a *cascaded integrator comb* (CIC).

Figure 16.16 above shows the block diagram of a 5-tap FIR filter that sums five successive samples. As shown in the light gray curve in Figure 16.17 at the top of the facing page, this yields a lowpass filter. Its frequency response has two *zeros:* Any input signal at $0.2f_S$ or $0.4f_S$ will vanish; attenuation in the stopband reaches only about –12 dB, at $\frac{3}{10}$ of the sampling rate.

Figure 16.17 **5-tap FIR filter responses** are shown for several choices of coefficient values (tap weights).

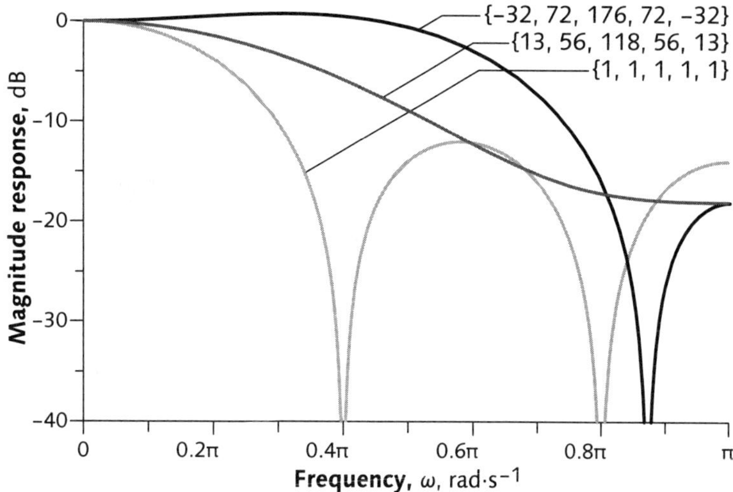

In the design of digital filters, control of frequency response is exercised in the choice of tap weights. Figure 16.18 below shows the block diagram of a filter having fractional coefficients chosen from a Gaussian waveform. The mid-gray curve in Figure 16.17 shows that this set of tap weights yields a lowpass filter having a Gaussian frequency response. By using negative coefficients, low-frequency response can be extended without deteriorating performance at high frequencies. The black curve in Figure 16.17 shows the response of a filter having coefficients [$^{-32}/_{256}$, $^{72}/_{256}$, $^{176}/_{256}$, $^{72}/_{256}$, $^{-32}/_{256}$]. This filter exhibits the same attenuation at high frequencies (about –18 dB) as the Gaussian, but has about twice the –6 dB frequency.

Negative coefficients, as in the last example here, potentially cause production of output samples that exceed unity. (In this example, output samples above unity are produced at input frequencies about ω=0.3π,

Figure 16.18 **5-tap FIR filter including multipliers** has coefficients [13, 56, 118, 56, 13], scaled by $^{1}/_{256}$. The coefficients approximate a Gaussian; so does the frequency response. The multipliers can be implemented by table lookup.

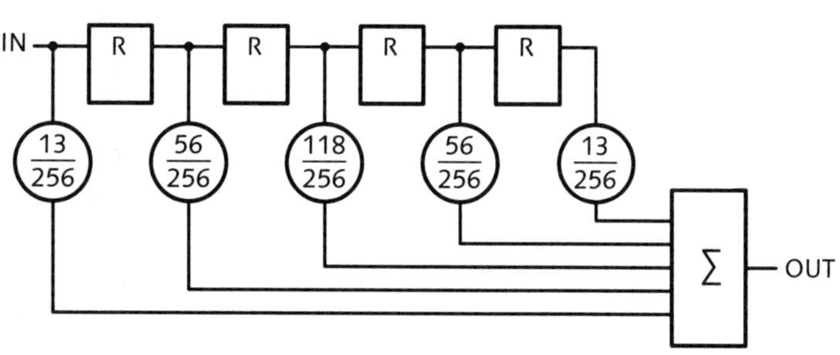

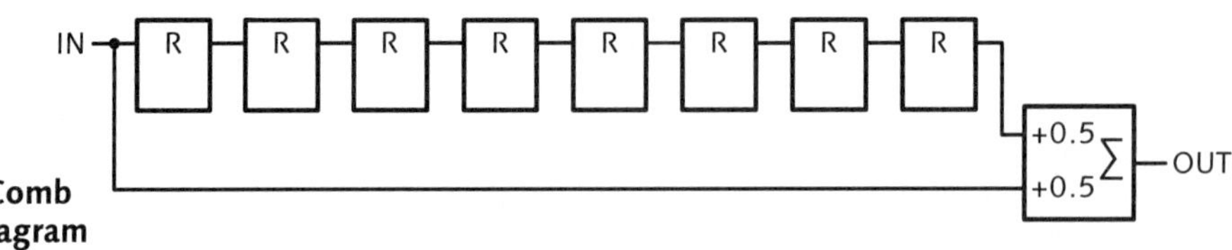

Figure 16.19 **Comb filter block diagram** includes several delay elements and an adder.

⅙ the sampling rate). If extreme values are clipped, artifacts will result. To avoid artifacts, the signal coding range must include suitable footroom and headroom.

The operation of an FIR filter amounts to multiplying a set of input samples by a set of filter coefficients (weights), and forming the appropriate set of sums of these products. The weighting can be implemented using multipliers by or using table lookup techniques. With respect to a complete set of input samples, this operation is called *convolution.* Ordinarily, convolution is conceptualized as taking place one multiplication at a time. An *n*-tap FIR filter can be implemented using a single multiplier-accumulator (MAC) component operating at *n* times the sample rate. A direct implementation with *n* multiplier components, or a multiplexed implementation with a single MAC, accepts input samples and delivers output samples in temporal order: Each coefficient needs to be presented to the filter *n* times. However, convolution is symmetrical with respect to input samples and coefficients: The same set of results can be produced by presenting filter coefficients one at a time to a MAC, and accumulating partial output sums for each output sample. FIR filters have many potential implementation structures.

For details concerning implementation structures, see the books by Lyons and Rorabaugh cited on page 170.

Figure 16.19 above shows the block diagram of an FIR filter having eight taps weighted [1, 0, 0, ..., 0, 1]. The frequency response of this filter is shown in Figure 16.20 at the top of the facing page. The response peaks when an exact integer number of cycles lie underneath the filter; it nulls when an integer-and-a-half cycles lie underneath. The peaks all have the same magnitude: The response is the same when exactly 1, 2, ..., or *n* samples are within its window. The magnitude frequency response of such a filter has a shape resembling a comb, and the filter is called a *comb filter.*

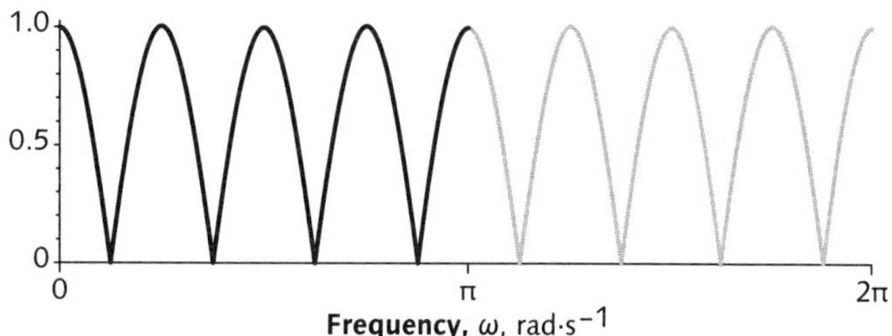

Figure 16.20 **Comb filter response** resembles the teeth of a comb. This filter has unity response at zero frequency: It passes DC. A filter having weights [½, 0, 0, …, 0, -½] blocks DC.

Impulse response

I have explained filtering as weighted integration along the time axis. I coined the term *temporal weighting function* to denote the weights. I consider my explanation of filtering in terms of its operation in the temporal domain to be more intuitive to a digital technologist than a more conventional explanation that starts in the frequency domain. But my term *temporal weighting function* is nonstandard, and I must now introduce the usual but nonintuitive term *impulse response*.

For details of the relationship between the Dirac delta, the Kronecker delta, and sampling in DSP, see page 122 of Rorabaugh's book, cited on page 170.

An analog impulse signal has infinitesimal duration, infinite amplitude, and an integral of unity. (An analog impulse is conceptually equivalent to the Dirac or Kronecker deltas of mathematics.) A digital impulse signal is a solitary sample having unity amplitude amid a stream of zeros; The *impulse response* of a digital filter is its response to an input that is identically zero except for a solitary unity-valued sample.

Finite impulse response (FIR) filters

In each of the filters that I have described so far, only a few coefficients are nonzero. When a digital impulse is presented to such a filter, the result is simply the weighting coefficients scanned out in turn. The response to an impulse is limited in duration; the examples that I have described have *finite impulse response*. They are *FIR filters*. In these filters, the impulse response is identical to the set of coefficients. The digital filters that I described on page 150 implement temporal weighting directly. The impulse responses of these filters, scaled to unity, are [½, ½], [½, -½], [½, 0, ½], and [½, 0, -½], respectively.

In Equation 16.2, g is a sequence (whose index is enclosed in square brackets), not a function (whose argument would be in parentheses). s_j is sample number j.

The particular set of weights in Figure 16.18 approximate a sampled Gaussian waveform; so, the frequency response of this filter is approximately Gaussian. The action of this filter can be expressed algebraically:

Eq 16.2

$$g[j] = \frac{13}{256}s_{j-2} + \frac{56}{256}s_{j-1} + \frac{118}{256}s_j + \frac{56}{256}s_{j+1} + \frac{13}{256}s_{j+2}$$

Symmetry:
$f(x) = f(-x)$

Antisymmetry:
$f(x) = -f(-x)$

I have described impulse responses that are symmetrical around an instant in time. You might think $t=0$ should denote the beginning of time, but it is usually convenient to shift the time axis so that $t=0$ corresponds to the central point of a filter's impulse response. A FIR (or *nonrecursive*) filter has a limited number of coefficients that are nonzero. When the input impulse lies outside this interval, the response is zero. Most digital filters used in video are FIR filters, and most have impulse responses either symmetric or antisymmetric around $t=0$.

You can view an FIR filter as having a fixed structure, with the data shifting along underneath. Alternatively, you might think of the *data* as being fixed, and the *filter* sliding across the data. Both notions are equivalent.

Physical realizability of a filter

In order to be implemented, a digital filter must be *physically realizable:* It is a practical necessity to have a temporal weighting function (impulse response) of limited duration. An FIR filter requires storage of several input samples, and it requires several multiplication operations to be performed during each sample period. The number of input samples stored is called the *order* of the filter, or its number of *taps*. If a particular filter has fixed coefficients, then its multiplications can be performed by table lookup. A straightforward technique can be used to exploit the symmetry of the impulse response to eliminate half the multiplications; this is often advantageous!

Here I use the word *truncation* to indicate the forcing to zero of a filter's weighting function beyond a certain tap. The nonzero coefficients in a weighting function may involve theoretical values that have been quantized to a certain number of bits. This *coefficient quantization* can be accomplished by *rounding* or by *truncation*. Be careful to distinguish between truncation of impulse response and truncation of coefficients.

When a temporal weighting function is truncated past a certain point, its transform – its frequency response characteristics – will suffer. The science and craft of filter design involves carefully choosing the order of the filter – that is, the position beyond which the weighting function is forced to zero. That position needs to be far enough from the center tap that the filter's high-frequency response is small enough to be negligible for the application.

Signal processing accommodates the use of impulse responses having negative values, and negative coefficients are common in digital signal processing. But image capture and image display involve sensing and generating light, which cannot have negative power, so negative weights cannot always be realized. If you study the transform pairs on page 151 you will see that your ability to tailor the frequency response of a filter is severely limited when you cannot use negative weights.

Impulse response is generally directly evident in the design of an FIR digital filter. Although it is possible to implement a boxcar filter directly in the analog domain, analog filters rarely implement temporal weighting directly, and the implementation of an analog filter generally bears a nonobvious relationship to its impulse response. Analog filters are best described in terms of Laplace transforms, not Fourier transforms. Impulse responses of analog filters are rarely considered directly in the design process. Despite the major conceptual and implementation differences, analog filters and FIR filters – and *IIR* filters, to be described – are all characterized by their frequency response.

Phase response (group delay)

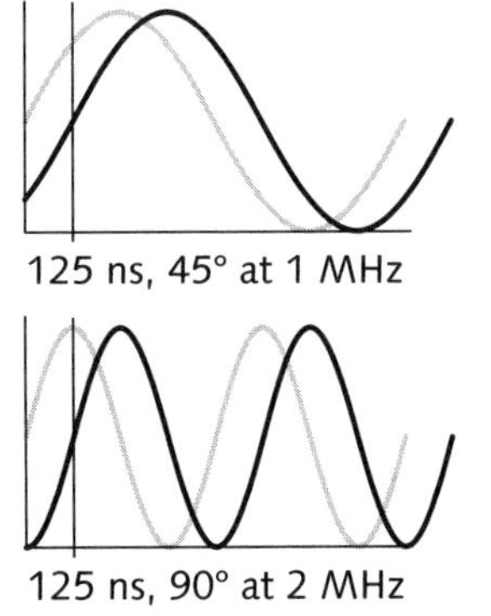

Figure 16.21 **Linear phase**

Until now I have described the magnitude frequency response of filters. *Phase frequency* response – often called phase response – is also important. Consider a symmetrical FIR filter having 15 taps. No matter what the input signal, the output will have an effective delay of 8 sample periods, corresponding to the central sample of the filter's impulse response. The time delay of an FIR filter is constant, independent of frequency.

Consider a sine wave at 1 MHz, and a second sine wave at 1 MHz but delayed 125 ns. The situation is sketched in Figure 16.21 in the margin. The 125 ns delay could be expressed as a phase shift of 45° at 1 MHz. However, if the time delay remains constant and the frequency doubles, the phase offset doubles to 90°. With constant time delay, phase offset increases in direct (linear) proportion to the increase in frequency. Since in this condition phase delay is directly proportional to frequency, its synonym is *linear phase*. A closely related condition is *constant group delay*, where the first derivative of delay is constant but a fixed time delay may be present. All FIR filters exhibit constant group delay, but only symmetric FIR filters exhibit strictly linear phase.

It is characteristic of many filters – such as IIR filters, to be described in a moment – that delay varies somewhat as a function of frequency. An image signal contains many frequencies, produced by scene elements at different scales. If the horizontal displacement of a reproduced object were dependent upon frequency, objectionable artifacts would result. Symmetric FIR filters exhibit linear phase in their passbands, and avoid this artifact. So, in image processing and in video, FIR filters are strongly preferred over other sorts of filters: Linear phase is a highly desirable property in a video system.

Infinite impulse response (IIR) filters

What a signal processing engineer calls an IIR filter is known in the finance and statistics communities as *autoregressive moving average* (ARMA).

The digital filters described so far have been members of the FIR class. A second class of digital filter is characterized by having a potentially *infinite impulse response* (IIR). An IIR (or *recursive*) filter computes a weighted sum of input samples – as is the case in an FIR filter – but adds to this a weighted sum of previous *output* samples.

A simple IIR is sketched in Figure 16.22: The input sample is weighted by $\frac{1}{4}$, and the previous output is weighted by $\frac{3}{4}$. These weighted values are summed to form the filter result. The filter result is then fed back to become an input to the computation of the next sample. The impulse response jumps rapidly upon the onset of the input impulse, and tails off over many samples. This is a simple one-tap lowpass filter; its time-domain response closely resembles an analog RC lowpass filter. A highpass filter is formed by taking the difference of the input sample from the previously stored filter result.

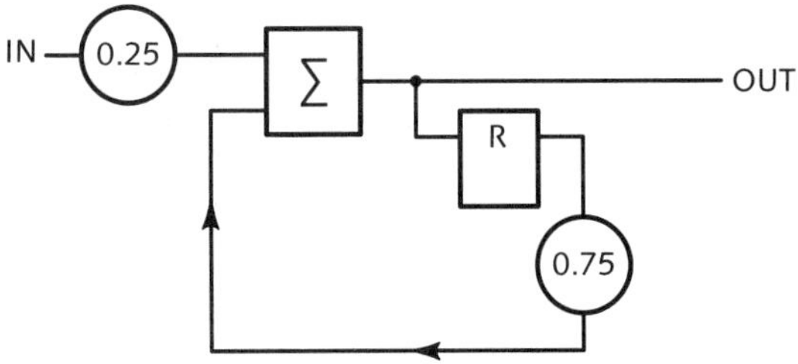

Figure 16.22 **IIR ("recursive") filter** computes a weighted sum of input samples (here, just ¼ times the current sample), and adds to this a weighted sum of previous result samples. Every IIR filter exhibits nonlinear phase response.

In an IIR filter having just one tap, the designer's ability to tailor frequency response is severely limited. An IIR filter can be extended by storing several previous filter results, and adding (or subtracting) a fraction of each to a fraction of the current input sample. In such a multi-tap IIR filter, a fine degree of control can be exercised over frequency response using just a handful of taps. Just three or four taps in an IIR filter can achieve frequency response that might take 20 taps in an FIR filter.

However, there's a catch: In an IIR filter, both attenuation and delay depend upon frequency. In the terminology of the previous section, an IIR filter exhibits nonlinear phase. Typically, low-frequency signals are delayed more than high-frequency signals. As I have explained, variation of delay as a function of frequency is potentially a very serious problem in video.

Compensation of undesired phase response in a filter is known as *equalization*. This is unrelated to the *equalization* pulses that form part of sync.

An IIR filter cannot have exactly linear phase, although a complex IIR filter can be designed to have arbitrarily small phase error. Because IIR filters usually have poor phase response, they are not ordinarily used in video. (A notable exception is the use of field- and frame-based IIR filters in temporal noise reduction, where the delay element comprises a field or frame of storage.)

The terms *nonrecursive* and *recursive* are best used to describe filter implementation structures.

Owing to the dependence of an IIR filter's result upon its previous results, an IIR filter is necessarily recursive. However, certain recursive filters have finite impulse response, so a recursive filter does *not* necessarily have infinite impulse response.

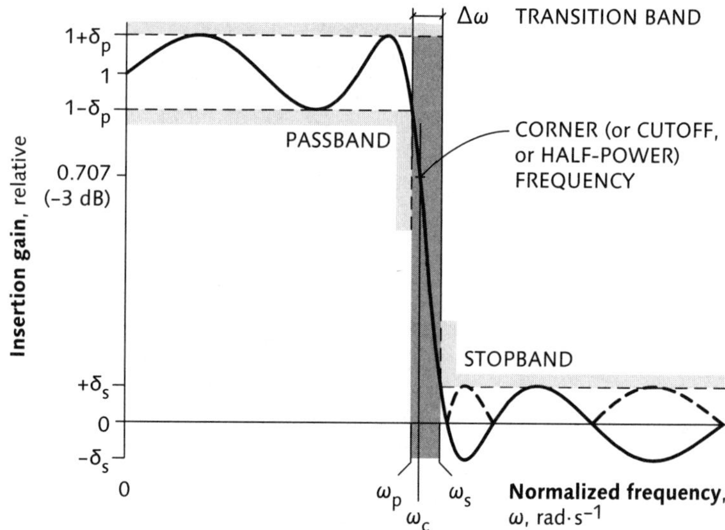

Figure 16.23 **Lowpass filter characterization.** A lowpass filter for use in video sampling or reconstruction has a corner frequency ω_C, where the attenuation is 0.707. (At the corner frequency, output power is half the input power.) In the *passband*, response is unity within δ_P, usually 1% or so. In the *stopband*, response is zero within δ_S, usually 1% or so. The *transition band* lies between the edge of the passband and the edge of the stopband; its width is $\Delta\omega$.

Here I represent frequency by the symbol ω, whose units are radians per second (rad·s^{-1}). A digital filter scales with its sampling frequency; using ω is convenient because the sampling frequency is always $\omega=2\pi$ and the half-sampling (Nyquist) frequency is always π.

Some people define bandwidth differently than I do.

Lowpass filter

A lowpass filter lets low frequencies pass undisturbed, but attenuates high frequencies. Figure 16.23 above characterizes a lowpass filter. The response has a *passband*, where the filter's response is nearly unity; a *transition band*, where the response has intermediate values; and a *stopband*, where the filter's response is nearly zero. For a lowpass filter, the *corner frequency*, ω_C – sometimes called *bandwidth*, or *cutoff frequency* – is the frequency where the magnitude response of the filter has fallen 3 dB from its magnitude at a reference frequency (usually zero, or DC). In other words, at its corner frequency, the filter's response has fallen to 0.707 of its response at DC.

The passband is characterized by the passband edge frequency ω_P and the passband ripple δ_P (sometimes denoted δ_1). The stopband is characterized by its edge frequency ω_S and ripple δ_S (sometimes denoted δ_2). The *transition band* lies between ω_P and ω_S; it has width $\Delta\omega$.

The complexity of a lowpass filter is roughly determined by its *relative transition bandwidth* (or *transition ratio*) $\Delta\omega / \omega_S$. The narrower the transition band, the more complex the filter. Also, the smaller the ripple in either the passband or the stopband, the more complex the filter. FIR filter tap count can be estimated by this formula, due to Bellanger:

Eq 16.3

$$N_e \approx \frac{\omega_S}{\Delta\omega} \cdot \frac{2}{3} \lg\left(\frac{1}{10\delta_P \delta_S}\right)$$

Bellanger, Maurice, *Digital Processing of Signals: Theory and Practice*, Third Edition (Chichester, England: Wiley, 2000). 124.

In analog filter design, frequency response is generally graphed in log–log coordinates, with the frequency axis in units of log hertz (Hz), and magnitude response in decibels (dB). In digital filter design, frequency is usually graphed linearly from zero to half the sampling frequency. The passband and stopband response of a digital filter are usually graphed logarithmically; the passband response is often magnified to emphasize small departures from unity.

The templates standardized in Rec. 601 for a studio digital video presampling filter are shown in Figure 16.24 overleaf. The response of a practical lowpass filter meeting this tremplate is shown in Figure 16.25, on page 166. This is a half-band filter, intended for use with a sampling frequency of 27 MHz; its corner frequency is $0.25 f_S$. A consumer filter might have ripple two orders of magnitude worse than this.

Digital filter design

I describe *risetime* on page 543. In response to a step input, a Gaussian filter has a risetime very close to ⅓ of the period of one cycle at the corner frequency.

A simple way to design a digital filter is to use coefficients that comprise an appropriate number of point-samples of a theoretical impulse response. Coefficients beyond a certain point – the *order* of the filter – are simply omitted. Equation 16.4 implements a 9-tap filter that approximates a Gaussian:

Eq 16.4

$$g[j] = \frac{1s_{j-4} + 9s_{j-3} + 43s_{j-2} + 110s_{j-1} + 150s_j + 110s_{j+1} + 43s_{j+2} + 9s_{j+3} + 1s_{j+4}}{476}$$

Omission of coefficients causes frequency response to depart from the ideal. If the omitted coefficients are much greater than zero, actual frequency response can depart significantly from the ideal.

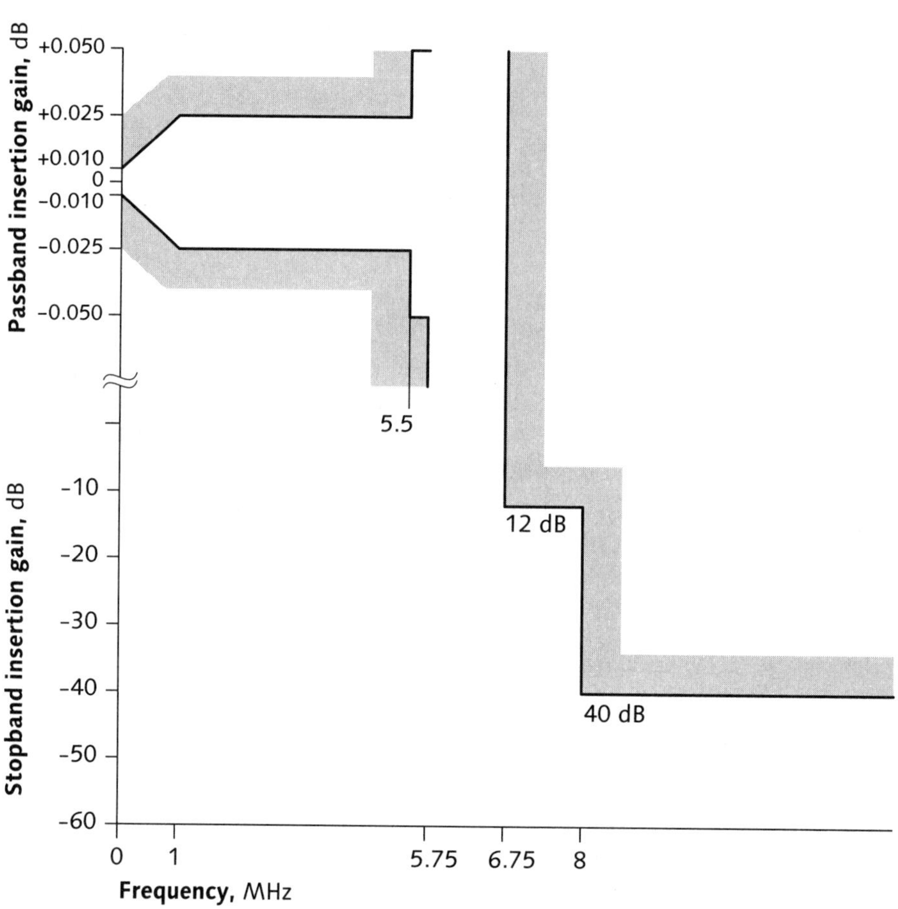

Passband insertion gain, dB
+0.050
+0.025
+0.010
0
-0.010
-0.025
-0.050
5.5
Stopband insertion gain, dB
-10
-20
-30
-40
-50
-60
12 dB
40 dB
0
1
5.75
6.75
8
Frequency, MHz

Group delay, ns
+3
+2
+1
0
-1
-2
-3
0
5.75
Frequency, MHz

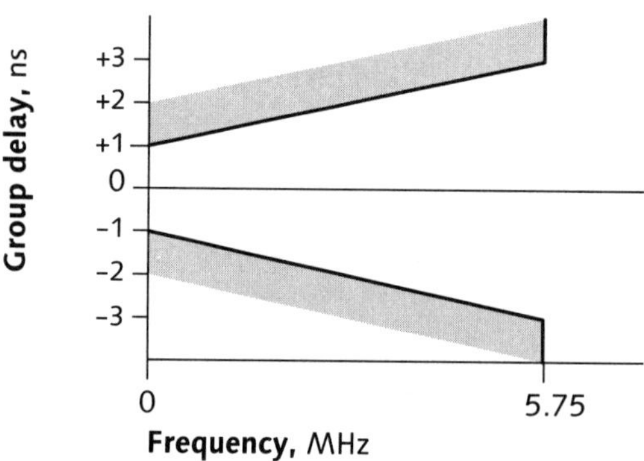

Figure 16.24 **Rec. 601 filter templates** are standardized for studio digital video systems in Rec. 601-5. The top template shows frequency response, detailing the passband (at the top) and the stopband (in the middle). The bottom template shows the group delay specification.

Another approach to digital filter design starts with the ILFP. Its infinite extent can be addressed by simply truncating the weights – that is, forcing the weights to zero – outside a certain interval, say outside the region 0±4 sample periods. This will have an unfortunate effect on the frequency response, however: The frequency response will exhibit overshoot and undershoot near the transition band.

We could use the term *weighting*, but sinc itself is a weighting function, so we choose a different word: *windowing*.

For details about windowing, see Lyons or Rorabaugh, cited on page 170, or Wolberg, George, *Digital Image Warping* (Los Alamitos, Calif.: IEEE, 1990).

Poor spectral behavior of a truncated sinc can be mitigated by applying a weighting function that peaks at unity at the center of the filter and diminishes gently to zero at the extremities of the interval. This is referred to as applying a *windowing* function. Design of a filter using the windowing method begins with scaling of sinc along the time axis to choose the corner frequency and choosing a suitable number of taps. Each tap weight is then computed as a sinc value multiplied by the corresponding window value. A sinc can be truncated through multiplication by a rectangular window. Perhaps the simplest nontrivial window has a triangular shape; this is also called the *Bartlett* window. The *von Hann* window (often wrongly called "Hanning") has a windowing function that is single cycle of a raised cosine. Window functions such as von Hann are fixed by the corner frequency and the number of filter taps; no control can be exercised over the width of the transition band. The *Kaiser* window has a single parameter that controls that width. For a given filter order, if the transition band is made narrower, then stopband attenuation is reduced. The Kaiser window parameter allows the designer to determine this tradeoff.

A windowed sinc filter has much better performance than a truncated sinc, and windowed design is so simple that there is no excuse to use sinc without windowing. In most engineering applications, however, filter performance is best characterized in the frequency domain, and the frequency-domain performance of windowed sinc filters is suboptimal: The performance of an *n*-tap windowed sinc filter can be bettered by an *n*-tap filter whose design has been suitably optimized.

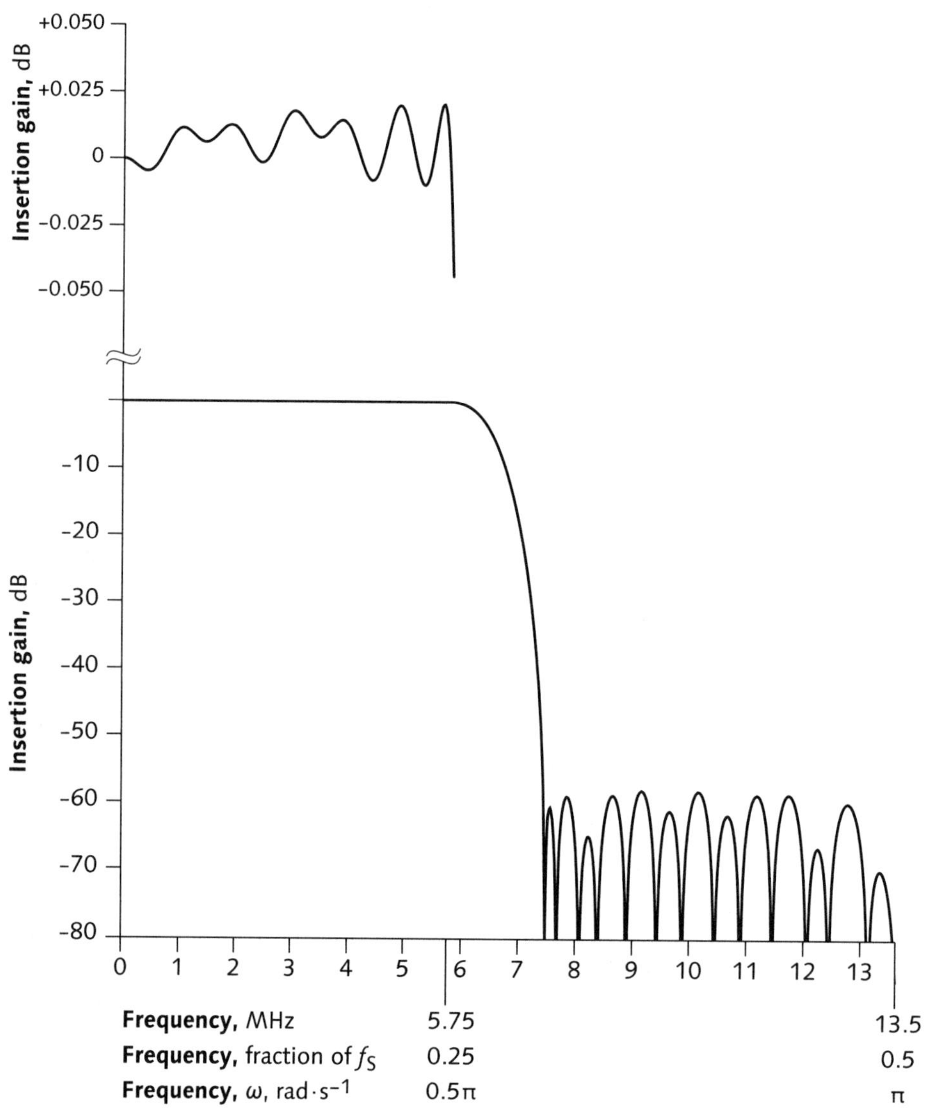

Figure 16.25 **Half-band filter.** This graph shows the frequency response of a practical filter whose corner is at one-quarter its sampling frequency of 27 MHz. The graph is linear in the abscissa (frequency) and logarithmic in the ordinate (response). The top portion shows that the passband has an overall gain of unity and a uniformity (*ripple*) of about ±0.02 dB: In the passband, its gain varies between about 0.997 and 1.003. The bottom portion shows that the stopband is rejected with an attenuation of about -60 dB: The filter has a gain of about 0.001 at these frequencies. This data, for the GF9102A halfband filter, was kindly provided by Gennum Corporation.

Figure 16.26 **FIR filter example, 25-tap lowpass**

$$
\begin{aligned}
g[i] = {} & 0.098460\, s_{i-12} \\
& +0.009482\, s_{i-11} \\
& -0.013681\, s_{i-10} \\
& +0.020420\, s_{i-9} \\
& -0.029197\, s_{i-8} \\
& +0.039309\, s_{i-7} \\
& -0.050479\, s_{i-6} \\
& +0.061500\, s_{i-5} \\
& -0.071781\, s_{i-4} \\
& +0.080612\, s_{i-3} \\
& -0.087404\, s_{i-2} \\
& +0.091742\, s_{i-1} \\
& +0.906788\, s_{i} \\
& +0.091742\, s_{i+1} \\
& -0.087404\, s_{i+2} \\
& +0.080612\, s_{i+3} \\
& -0.071781\, s_{i+4} \\
& +0.061500\, s_{i+5} \\
& -0.050479\, s_{i+6} \\
& +0.039309\, s_{i+7} \\
& -0.029197\, s_{i+8} \\
& +0.020420\, s_{i+9} \\
& -0.013681\, s_{i+10} \\
& +0.009482\, s_{i+11} \\
& +0.098460\, s_{i+12}
\end{aligned}
$$

Few closed-form methods are known to design optimum digital filters. Design of a high-performance filter usually involves successive approximation, optimizing by trading design parameters back and forth between the time and frequency domains. The classic method was published by J.H. McLellan, T.W. Parks, and L.R. Rabiner ("MPR"), based upon an algorithm developed by the Russian mathematician E.Y. Remez. In the DSP community, the method is often called the "Remez exchange."

The coefficients of a high-quality lowpass filter for studio video are shown in Figure 16.26 in the margin.

Reconstruction

Digitization involves sampling and quantization; these operations are performed in an analog-to-digital converter (ADC). Whether the signal is quantized then sampled, or sampled then quantized, is relevant only within the ADC: The order of operations is immaterial outside that subsystem. Modern video ADCs quantize first, then sample.

I have explained that filtering is generally required prior to sampling in order to avoid the introduction of aliases. Avoidance of aliasing in the sampled domain has obvious importance. In order to avoid aliasing, an analog presampling filter needs to operate prior to analog-to-digital conversion. If aliasing is avoided, then the sampled signal can, according to Shannon's theorem, be reconstructed without aliases.

To reconstruct an analog signal, an analog reconstruction filter is necessary following digital-to-analog (D-to-A) conversion. The overall flow is sketched in Figure 16.27.

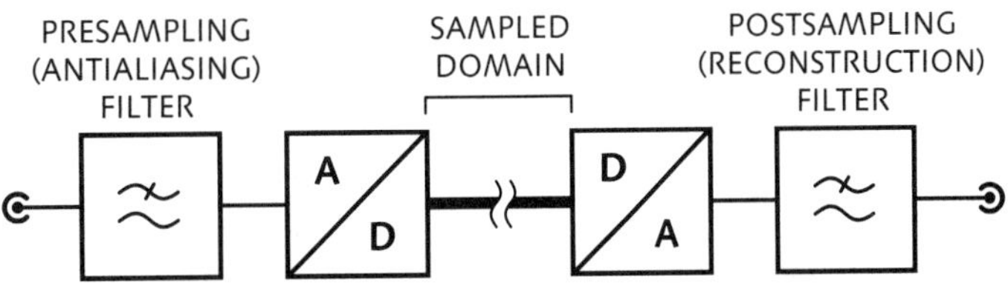

Figure 16.27 **Sampling and reconstruction**

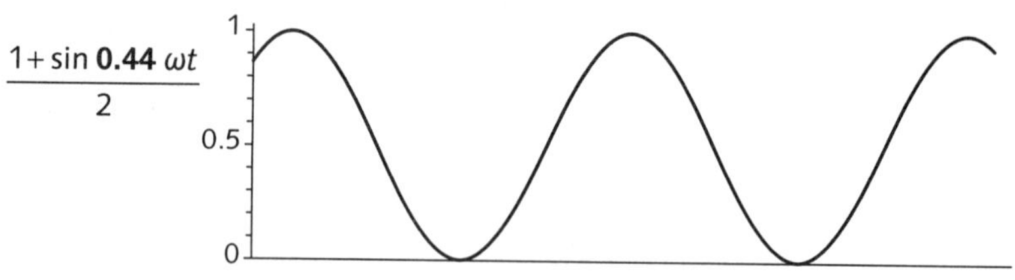

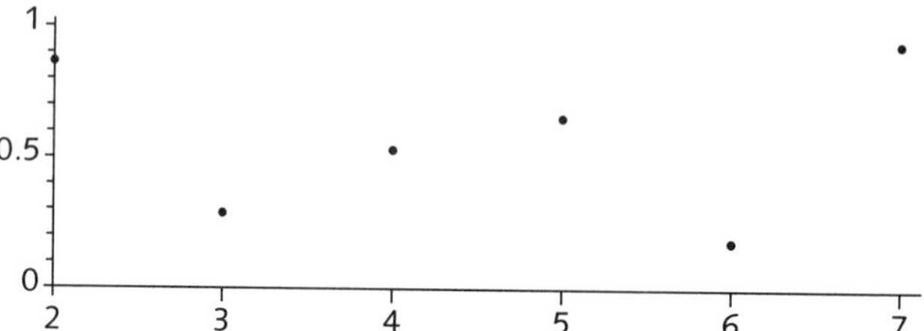

Figure 16.28 **Reconstruction close to $0.5f_S$**

Reconstruction close to $0.5f_S$

Consider the example in Figure 16.28 of a sine wave at $0.44f_S$. This signal meets the sampling criterion, and can be perfectly represented in the digital domain. However, from an intuitive point of view, it is difficult to predict the underlying sinewave from samples 3, 4, 5, and 6 in the lower graph. When reconstructed using a Gaussian filter, the high-frequency signal vanishes. To be reconstructed accurately, a waveform with a significant amount of power near half the sampling rate must be reconstructed with a high-quality filter.

(sin *x*)/*x* correction

I have described how it is necessary for an analog reconstruction filter to follow digital-to-analog conversion. If the DAC produced an impulse "train" where the amplitude of each impulse was modulated by the corresponding code value, a classic lowpass filter would suffice: All would be well if the DAC output resembled my "point" graphs, with power at the sample instants and no power in between. Recall that a waveform comprising just unit impulses has uniform frequency response across the entire spectrum.

Unfortunately for analog reconstruction, a typical DAC does not produce an impulse waveform for each sample. It would be impractical to have a DAC with an

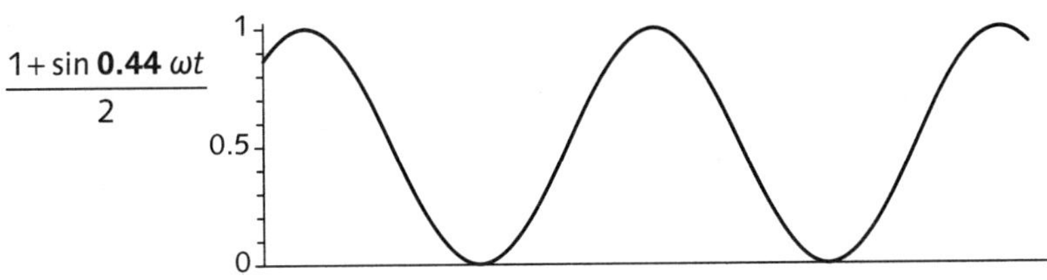

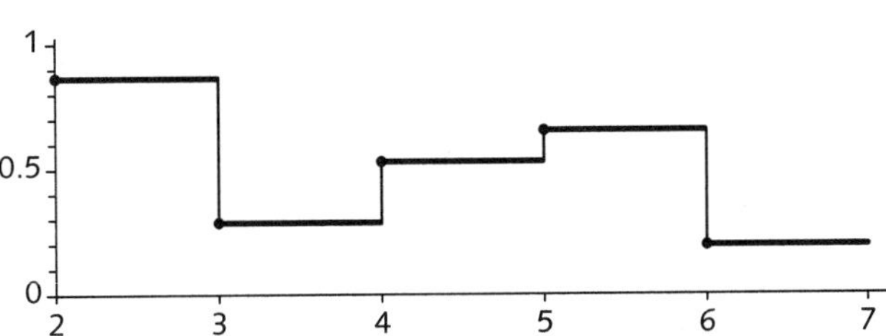

Figure 16.29 **D-to-A conversion with boxcar waveform** is equivalent to a DAC producing an impulse train followed by a boxcar filter with its (sin *x*)/*x* response. Frequencies close to $0.5 f_S$ are attenuated.

You might consider a DAC's boxcar waveform to be a "sample-and-hold" operation, but that term is normally used in conjunction with an A-to-D converter, or circuitry that lies in front of an ADC.

impulse response, because signal power is proportional to the integral of the signal, and the amplitude of the impulses would have to be impractically high for the integral of the impulses to achieve adequate signal power. Instead, each converted sample value is held for the entire duration of the sample: A typical DAC produces a boxcar waveform. A boxcar waveform's frequency response is described by the sinc function.

In Figure 16.29 above, the top graph is a sine wave at $0.44 f_S$; the bottom graph shows the boxcar waveform produced by a conventional DAC. Even with a high-quality reconstruction filter, whose response extends close to half the sampling rate, it is evident that reconstruction by a boxcar function reduces the magnitude of high-frequency components of the signal.

The DAC's holding of each sample value throughout the duration of its sample interval corresponds to a filtering operation, with a frequency response of (sin *x*)/*x*. The top graph of Figure 16.30 overleaf shows the attenuation due to this phenomenon.

The effect is overcome by (sin *x*)/*x correction:* The frequency response of the reconstruction filter is modified to include peaking corresponding to the reciprocal of (sin *x*)/*x*. In the passband, the filter's response

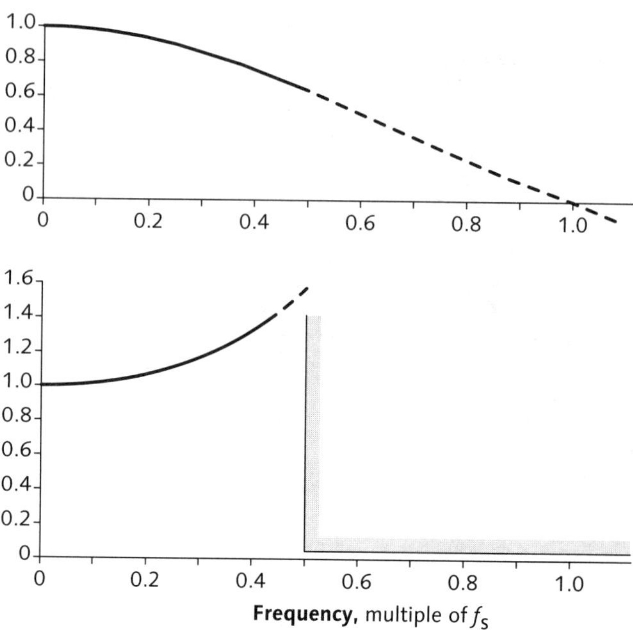

Figure 16.30 **(sin *x*)/*x* correction** is necessary following (or in principle, preceding) digital-to-analog conversion when a DAC with a typical boxcar output waveform is used. The frequency response of a boxcar-waveform DAC is shown in the upper graph. The lower graph shows the response of the (sin *x*)/*x* correction filter necessary to compensate its high frequency falloff.

increases gradually to about 4 dB above its response at DC, to compensate the loss. Above the passband edge frequency, the response of the filter must decrease rapidly to produce a large attenuation near half the sampling frequency, to provide alias-free reconstruction. The bottom graph of Figure 16.30 shows the idealized response of a filter having (sin *x*)/*x* correction.

This chapter has detailed one-dimensional filtering. In *Image digitization and reconstruction,* I will introduce two- and three-dimensional sampling and filters.

Further reading

For an approachable introduction to the concepts, theory, and mathematics of digital signal processing (DSP), see Lyons. For an alternative point of view, see Rorabaugh's book; it includes the source code for programs to design filters – that is, to evaluate filter coefficients. For comprehensive and theoretical coverage of DSP, see Mitra and Kaiser.

Lyons, Richard G., *Understanding Digital Signal Processing* (Reading, Mass.: Addison Wesley, 1997).

Rorabaugh, C. Britton, *DSP Primer* (New York: McGraw-Hill, 1999).

Mitra, Sanjit K., and James F. Kaiser, *Handbook for Digital Signal Processing* (New York: Wiley, 1993).

Resampling, interpolation, and decimation 17

In video and audio signal processing, it is often necessary to take a set of sample values and produce another set that approximates the samples that would have resulted had the original sampling occurred at different instants – at a different rate, or at a different phase. This is called *resampling.* (In PC parlance, resampling for the purpose of picture resizing is called *scaling.*) Resampling is an essential part of video processes such as these:

- Chroma subsampling (e.g., 4:4:4 to 4:2:2)
- Downconversion (e.g., HDTV to SDTV) and upconversion (e.g., SDTV to HDTV)
- Aspect ratio conversion (e.g., 4:3 to 16:9)
- Conversion among different sample rates of digital video standards (e.g., $4f_{SC}$ to 4:2:2, 13.5 MHz)
- Picture resizing in digital video effects (DVE)

One-dimensional resampling applies directly to digital audio, in applications such as changing sample rate from 48 kHz to 44.1 kHz. In video, 1-D resampling can be applied horizontally or vertically. Resampling can be extended to a two-dimensional array of samples. Two approaches are possible. A horizontal filter, then a vertical filter, can be applied in cascade (tandem) – this is the *separable* approach. Alternatively, a direct form of 2-D spatial interpolation can be implemented.

I write resampling ratios in the form *input samples*:*output samples*. With my convention, a ratio less than unity is upsampling.

Upsampling produces more result samples than input samples. In audio, new samples can be estimated at a higher rate than the input, for example when digital audio sampled at 44.1 kHz is converted to the 48 kHz professional rate used with video. In video, upsampling is required in the spatial upconversion from 1280×720 HDTV to 1920×1080 HDTV: 1280 samples in each input line must be converted to 1920 samples in the output, an upsampling ratio of 2:3.

One way to accomplish upsampling by an integer ratio of 1:n is to interpose $n-1$ zero samples between each pair of input samples. This causes the spectrum of the original signal to repeat at multiples of the original sampling rate. The repeated spectra are called "images." (This is a historical term stemming from radio; it has nothing to do with pictures!) These "images" are then eliminated (or at least attenuated) by an anti-imaging lowpass filter. In some upsampling structures, such as the Langrange interpolator that I will describe later in this chapter, filtering and upsampling are intertwined.

Downsampling produces fewer result samples than input samples. In audio, new samples can be created at a lower rate than the input. In video, downsampling is required when converting $4f_{SC}$ NTSC digital video to Rec. 601 ("4:2:2") digital video: 910 samples in each input line must be converted to 858 samples in the output, a downsampling ratio of 35:33; for each 35 input samples, 33 output samples are produced.

In an original sample sequence, signal content from DC to nearly $0.5\,f_S$ can be represented. After downsampling, though, the new sample rate may be lower than that required by the signal bandwidth. After downsampling, meaningful signal content is limited by the Nyquist criterion at the *new* sampling rate – for example, after 4:1 downsampling, signal content is limited to 1⁄8 of the original sampling rate. To avoid the introduction of aliases, lowpass filtering is necessary prior to, or in conjunction with, downsampling. The corner frequency depends upon the downsampling ratio; for example, a 4:1 ratio requires a corner less than $0.125\,f_S$. Downsampling with an integer ratio of n:1

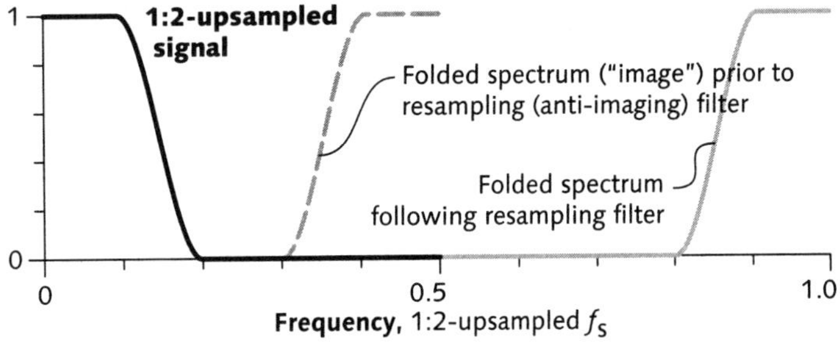

Figure 17.1 **Two-times upsampling** starts by interposing zero samples between original sample pairs. This would result in the folded spectral content of the original signal appearing in-band at the new rate. These "images" are removed by a resampling filter.

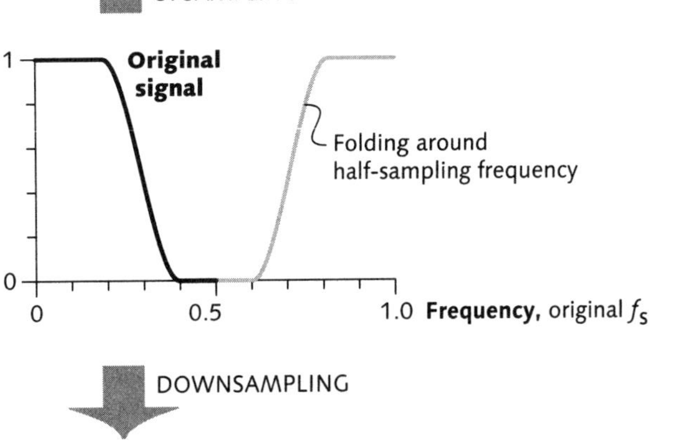

Figure 17.2 **Original signal** exhibits folding around half the sampling frequency. This is inconsequential providing that the signal is properly reconstructed. When the signal is upsampled or downsampled, the folded portion must be handled properly or aliasing will result.

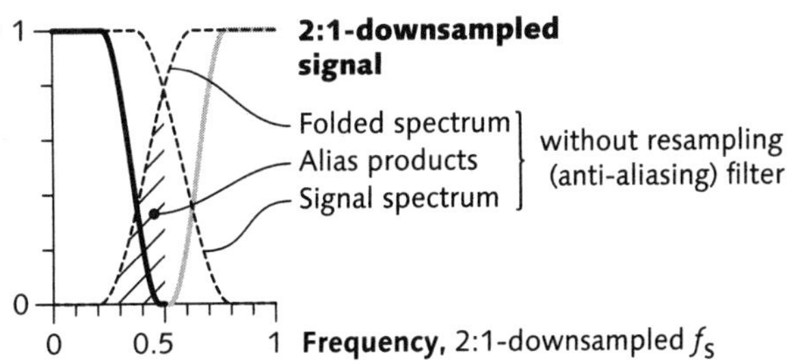

Figure 17.3 **Two-to-one downsampling** requires a resampling filter to meet the Nyquist criterion at the new sampling rate. The solid line shows the spectrum of the filtered signal; the gray line shows its folded portion. Resampling without filtering would preserve the original baseband spectrum, but folding around the new sampling rate would cause alias products shown here in the crosshatched region.

can be thought of as prefiltering (antialias filtering) for the new sampling rate, followed by the discarding of $n-1$ samples between original sample pairs.

Figure 17.2, at the center above, sketches the spectrum of an original signal. Figure 17.1 shows the frequency domain considerations of upsampling; Figure 17.3 shows the frequency domain considerations of downsampling. These examples show ratios of 1:2 and 2:1, but these concepts apply to resampling at any ratio.

2:1 downsampling

Color video originates with $R'G'B'$ components. Transcoding to $Y'C_BC_R$ is necessary if signals are to be used in the studio. The conversion involves matrixing (to $Y'C_BC_R$ in 4:4:4 form), then chroma subsampling to 4:2:2. Chroma subsampling requires a 2:1 downsampler. If this downsampling is attempted by simply dropping alternate samples, any signal content between the original 0.25 f_S and 0.5 f_S will cause aliasing in the result. Rejection of signal content at and above 0.25 f_S is required. The required filter is usually implemented as an FIR lowpass filter having its corner frequency somewhat less than one-quarter of the (original) sampling frequency. After filtering, alternate result samples can be dropped. There is no need to calculate values that will subsequently be discarded, however! Efficient chroma subsamplers take advantage of that fact, interleaving the C_B and C_R components into a single filter.

In Figure 16.12, on page 153, I presented a very simple lowpass filter that simply averages two adjacent samples. That filter has a corner frequency of $0.25f_S$. However, it makes a slow transition from passband to stopband, and it has very poor attenuation in the stopband (above $0.25f_S$). It makes a poor resampling filter. More than two taps are required to give adequate performance in studio video subsampling.

In 4:2:2 video, chroma is cosited: Each chroma sample must be located at the site of a luma sample. A symmetrical filter having an even number of (nonzero) taps does not have this property. A downsampling filter for cosited chroma must have an odd number of taps.

Oversampling

I have explained the importance of prefiltering prior to A-to-D conversion, and of postfiltering following D-to-A conversion. Historically, these filters were implemented in the analog domain, using inductors and capacitors. In discrete form, these components are bulky and expensive. It is extremely difficult to incorporate inductive and capacitive elements with suitable values and precision onto integrated circuits. However, A-to-D and D-to-A converters are operating at higher

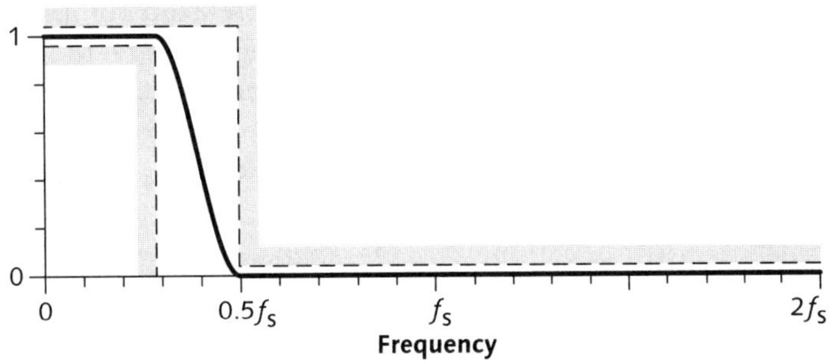

Figure 17.4 **Analog filter for direct sampling** must meet tight constraints, making it expensive.

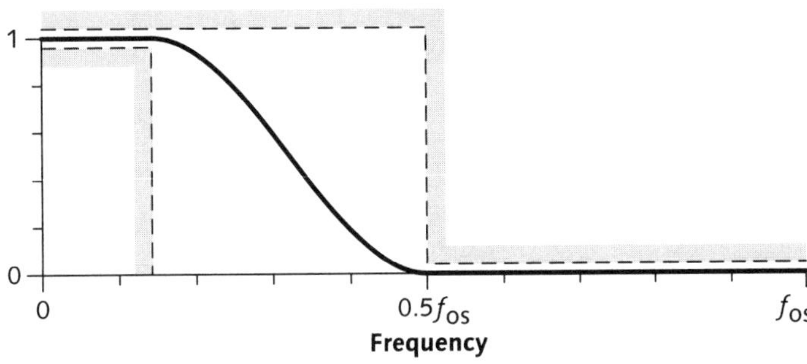

Figure 17.5 **Analog filter for 2×-oversampling** is much less demanding than a filter for direct sampling, because the difficult part of filtering – achieving a response comparable to that of Figure 17.4 – is relegated to the digital domain.

and higher rates, and digital arithmetic has become very inexpensive. These circumstances have led to the emergence of *oversampling* as an economical alternative to complex analog presampling ("antialiasing") and postsampling (reconstruction) filters.

For an explanation of transition ratio, see page 163.

The characteristics of a conventional analog presampling filter are critical: Attenuation must be quite low up to about 0.4 times the sample rate, and quite high above that. In a presampling filter for studio video, attenuation must be less than 1 dB or so up to about 5.5 MHz, and better than 40 or 50 dB above 6.75 MHz. This is a demanding transition ratio $\Delta\omega/\omega_S$. Figure 17.4 above (top) sketches the filter template of a conventional analog presampling filter.

An oversampling A-to-D converter operates at a multiple of the ultimate sampling rate – say at 27 MHz, twice the rate of Rec. 601 video. The converter is preceded by a cheap analog filter that severely attenuates components at 13.5 MHz and above. However, its characteristics between 5.5 MHz and 13.5 MHz are not critical. The demanding aspects of filtering in that region are left to a digital 2:1 downsampler. The transition ratio $\Delta\omega/\omega_S$ of the analog filter is greatly relaxed compared to direct conversion. In today's technology, the cost of the digital downsampler is less than the difference in cost between excellent and mediocre analog filtering. Complexity is moved from the analog domain to the digital domain; total system cost is reduced. Figure 17.5 (on page 175) sketches the template of an analog presampling filter appropriate for use preceding a 2x oversampled A-to-D converter.

In certain FIR filters whose corner is exactly 0.25 f_S, half the coefficients are zero. This leads to a considerable reduction in complexity.

Figure 16.25, on page 166, showed the response of a 55-tap filter having a corner frequency of 0.25 f_S. This is a *halfband* filter, intended for use following a 2×-oversampled A-to-D converter.

The approach to two-times oversampled D-to-A conversion is comparable. The D-to-A device operates at 27 MHz; it is presented with a datastream that has been upsampled by a 1:2 ratio. For each input sample, the 2×-oversampling filter computes 2 output samples. One is computed at the effective location of the input sample, and the other is computed at an effective location halfway between input samples. The filter attenuates power between 6.75 MHz and 13.5 MHz. the analog postsampling filter need only reject components at and above 13.5 MHz. As in the two-times oversampling A-to-D conversion, its performance between 6.75 MHz and 13.5 MHz isn't critical.

Interpolation

In the common case of interpolation horizontally across an image row, the argument *x* is horizontal position. Interpolating along the time axis, as in digital audio sample rate conversion, you could use the symbol *t* to represent time.

In mathematics, *interpolation* is the process of computing the value of a function or a putative function (call it $\tilde{g}$), for an arbitrary argument (x), given several function argument and value pairs $[x_i, s_i]$. There are many methods for interpolating, and many methods for constructing functions that interpolate.

Given two sample pairs $[x_0, s_0]$ and $[x_1, s_1]$, the linear interpolation function has this form:

$$\tilde{g}(x) = s_0 + \frac{x - x_0}{x_1 - x_0}(s_1 - s_0) \qquad \text{Eq 17.1}$$

In computer graphics, the linear interpolation operation is often called *LIRP*, (pronounced *lerp*).

I symbolize the interpolating function as $\tilde{g}$; the symbol f is already taken to represent frequency. I write g with a tilde ($\tilde{g}$) to emphasize that it is an approximation.

The linear interpolation function can be rewritten as a weighted sum of the neighboring samples s_0 and s_1:

$$\tilde{g}(x) = c_0(x) \cdot s_0 + c_0(x) \cdot s_1 \qquad \text{Eq 17.2}$$

The weights depend upon the x (or t) coordinate:

$$c_0(x) = \frac{x_1 - x}{x_1 - x_0}; \qquad c_1(x) = \frac{x - x_0}{x_1 - x_0} \qquad \text{Eq 17.3}$$

Lagrange interpolation

J.L. Lagrange (1736–1813) developed a method of interpolation using polynomials. A cubic interpolation function is a polynomial of this form:

$$\tilde{g}(x) = ax^3 + bx^2 + cx + d \qquad \text{Eq 17.4}$$

Julius O. Smith calls this *Waring-Lagrange* interpolation, since Waring published it 16 years before Lagrange. See Smith's *Digital Audio Resampling Home Page*, <www-ccrma.stanford.edu/~jos/resample>.

Interpolation involves choosing appropriate coefficients *a, b, c,* and *d,* based upon the given argument/value pairs $[x_j, s_j]$. Lagrange described a simple and elegant way of computing the coefficients.

Linear interpolation is just a special case of Lagrange interpolation of the first degree. (Directly using the value of the nearest neighbor can be considered zero-order interpolation.) There is a second-degree (quadratic) form; it is rarely used in signal processing.

In mathematics, to *interpolate* refers to the process that I have described. However, the same word is used to denote the property whereby an interpolating function produces values exactly equal to the original sample values (s_i) at the original sample coordinates (x_i). The Lagrange functions exhibit this property. You might guess that this property is a requirement of *any* interpolating function. However, in signal processing this is not a requirement – in fact, the interpolation functions used in video and audio rarely pass exactly through the original sample values. As a consequence of using the terminology of mathematics, in video we have the seemingly paradoxical situation that interpolation functions usually do not "interpolate"!

In principle, cubic interpolation could be undertaken for any argument x, even values outside the x-coordinate range of the four input samples. (Evaluation

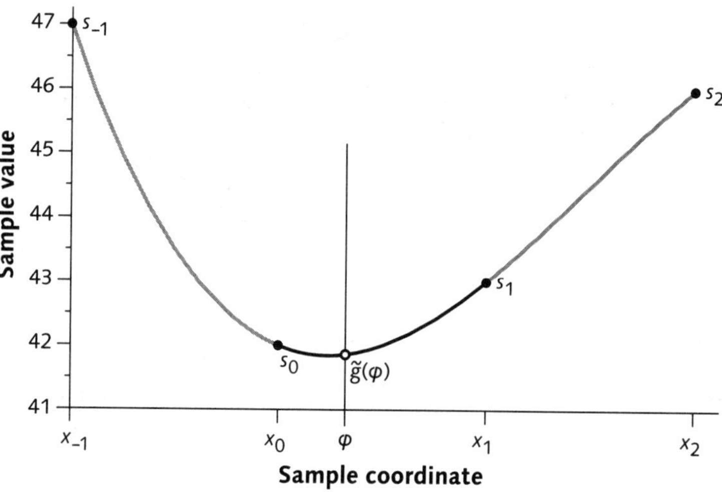

Figure 17.6 **Cubic interpolation** of a signal starts with equally spaced samples, in this example 47, 42, 43, and 46. The underlying function is estimated to be a cubic polynomial that passes through ("interpolates") all four samples. The polynomial is evaluated between the two central samples, as shown by the black segment. Here, evaluation is at phase offset φ. If the underlying function isn't a polynomial, small errors are produced.

outside the interval $[x_{-1}, x_2]$ would be called *extrapolation*.) In digital video and audio, we limit x to the range between x_0 and x_1, so as to estimate the signal in the interval between the central two samples. To evaluate outside this interval, we substitute the input sample values $[s_{-1}, s_0, s_1, s_2]$ appropriately – for example, to evaluate between s_1 and s_2, we shift the input sample values left one place.

Eq 17.5

$$\varphi = \frac{x - x_0}{x_1 - x_0}; \qquad x_0 \le \varphi \le x_1$$

With uniform sampling (as in conventional digital video), when interpolating between the two central samples the argument x can be recast as the *phase offset*, or the *fractional phase* (φ, phi), at which a new sample is required between two central samples. (See Equation 17.5.) In abstract terms, φ lies between 0 and 1; in hardware, it is implemented as a binary or a rational fraction. In video, a 1-D interpolator is usually an FIR filter whose coefficients are functions of the phase offset. The weighting coefficients (c_i) are functions of the phase offset; they can be considered as basis functions.

In signal processing, cubic (third-degree) interpolation is often used; the situation is sketched in Figure 17.6 above. In linear interpolation, one neighbor to the left and one to the right are needed. In cubic interpolation, we ordinarily interpolate in the central interval, using two original samples to the left and two to the right of the desired sample instant.

Equation 17.2 can be reformulated:

$$g(\varphi) = c_{-1}(\varphi)\cdot s_{-1} + c_0(\varphi)\cdot s_0 + c_1(\varphi)\cdot s_1 + c_2(\varphi)\cdot s_2 \qquad \text{Eq 17.6}$$

The function takes four sample values $[s_{-1}, s_0, s_1, s_2]$ surrounding the interval of interest, and the phase offset φ between 0 and 1. The coefficients (c_i) are now functions of the argument φ; The interpolator forms a weighted sum of four sample values, where the weights are functions of the parameter φ; it returns an estimated value. (If the input samples are values of a polynomial not exceeding the third degree, then the values produced by a cubic Lagrange interpolator are exact, within roundoff error: Lagrange interpolation "interpolates"!)

Smith, A.R., "Planar 2-pass texture mapping and warping," in *Computer Graphics* 21 (4): 12–19 (Jul. 1987, Proc. SIGGRAPH 87), 263–272.

If a 2-D image array is to be resampled at arbitrary *x* and *y* coordinate values, one approach is to apply a 1-D filter along one axis, then apply a 1-D filter along the other axis. This approach treats interpolation as a separable process, akin to the separable filtering that I will introduce on page 191. Surprisingly, this two-pass approach can be used to rotate an image; see Smith, cited in the margin. Alternatively, a 2×2 array (of 4 sample values) can be used for linear interpolation in 2 dimensions in one step – this is *bilinear* interpolation. A more sophisticated approach is to use a 4×4 array (of 16 sample values) as the basis for cubic interpolation in 2 dimensions – this is *bicubic* interpolation. (It is mathematically comparable to 15th-degree interpolation in one dimension.)

Bartels, Richard H., John C. Beatty, and Brian A. Barsky, *An Introduction to Splines for Use in Computer Graphics and Geometric Modeling* (San Francisco: Morgan Kaufmann, 1989).

Curves can be drawn in 2-space using a parameter *u* as the argument to each of two functions x(*u*) and y(*u*) that produce a 2-D coordinate pair for each value of *u*. Cubic polynomials can be used as x(*u*) and y(*u*). This approach can be extended to three-space by adding a third function, z(*u*). Pierre Bézier developed a method, which is now widely used, to use cubic polynomials to describe curves and surfaces. Such curves are now known as *Bézier curves* or *Bézier splines*. The method is very important in the field of computer graphics; however, Bézier splines and their relatives are infrequently used in signal processing.

Lagrange interpolation as filtering

Except for having 4 taps instead of 5, Equation 17.6 has identical form to the 5-tap Gaussian filter of Equation 16.2, on page 158! Lagrange interpolation can be viewed as a special case of FIR filtering, and can be analyzed as a filtering operation. In the previous chapter, *Filtering and sampling*, all of the examples were symmetric. Interpolation to produce samples exactly halfway between input samples, such as in a two-times oversampling DAC, is also symmetric. However, most interpolators are asymmetric.

Only symmetric FIR filters exhibit true linear phase. Other FIR filters exhibit very nearly linear phase, close enough to be considered to have linear phase in video and audio.

There are four reasons why polynomial interpolation is generally unsuitable for video signals: Polynomial interpolation has unequal stopband ripple; nulls lie at fixed positions in the stopband; the interpolating function exhibits extreme behavior outside the central interval; and signals presented to the interpolator are somewhat noisy. I will address each of these issues in turn.

- Any Lagrange interpolator has a frequency response with unequal stopband ripple, sometimes highly unequal. That is generally undesirable in signal processing, and it is certainly undesirable in video.

- A Lagrange interpolator "interpolates" the original samples; this causes a magnitude frequency response that has periodic nulls ("zeros") whose frequencies are fixed by the order of the interpolator. In order for a filter designer to control stopband attenuation, he or she needs the freedom to place nulls judiciously. This freedom is not available in the design of a Lagrange interpolator.

- Conceptually, interpolation attempts to model, with a relatively simple function, the unknown function that generated the samples. The form of the function that we use should reflect the process that underlies generation of the signal. A cubic polynomial may deliver sensible interpolated values between the two central points. However, the value of any polynomial rapidly shoots off to plus or minus infinity at arguments outside the region where it is constrained by the original sample values. That property is at odds with the behavior of signals, which are constrained to lie within a limited range of values forever (say the abstract range 0 to 1 in video, or ±0.5 in audio).

- In signal processing, there is always some uncertainty in the sample values caused by noise accompanying the signal, quantization noise, and noise due to roundoff error in the calculations in the digital domain. When the source data is imperfect, it seems unreasonable to demand perfection of an interpolation function.

These four issues are addressed in signal processing by using interpolation functions that are not polynomials and that do not come from classical mathematics. Instead, we usually use interpolation functions based upon the the sinc weighting function that I introduced on page 148. In signal processing, we usually design interpolators that do not "interpolate" the original sample values.

You can consider the entire stopband of an ideal sinc filter to contain an infinity of nulls. Mathematically, the sinc function represents the limit of Lagrange interpolation as the order of the polynomial approaches infinity. See Appendix A of Smith's *Digital Audio Resampling Home Page*, cited in the margin of page 177.

The ideal sinc weighting function has no distinct nulls in its frequency spectrum. When sinc is truncated and optimized to obtain a physically realizable filter, the stopband has a finite number of nulls. Unlike a Lagrange interpolator, these nulls do not have to be regularly spaced. It is the filter designer's ability to choose the frequencies for the zeros that allows him or her to tailor the filter's response.

Polyphase interpolators

The 720*p*60 and 1080*i*30 standards have an identical sampling rate (74.25 MHz). In the logic design of this example, there is a single clock domain.

Some video signal processing applications require upsampling at simple ratios. For example, conversion from 1280 S_{AL} to 1920 S_{AL} in an HDTV format converter requires 2:3 upsampling. An output sample is computed at one of three phases: either at the site of an input sample, or ⅓ or ⅔ of the way between input samples. The upsampler can be implemented as an FIR filter with just three sets of coefficients; the coefficients can be accessed from a lookup table addressed by φ.

Many interpolators involve ratios more complex than the 2:3 ratio of this example. For example, in conversion from $4f_{SC}$ NTSC to Rec. 601 (4:2:2), 910 input samples must be converted to 858 results. This involves a downsampling ratio of 35:33. Successive output samples are computed at an increment of $1\frac{2}{33}$ input samples. Every 33rd output sample is computed at the site of an input sample (0); other output samples are computed at input sample coordinates $1\frac{2}{33}$, $2\frac{4}{33}$, …, $16\frac{32}{33}$, $18\frac{1}{33}$, $19\frac{3}{33}$, …, $34\frac{31}{33}$. Addressing circuitry needs to increment a sample counter by one, and a fractional numerator by 2 modulo 33 (yielding the fraction $\frac{2}{33}$), at each output sample. Overflow from the fraction counter carries into the sample counter; this accounts for the missing input sample number 17 in the sample number sequence of this example. The required interpolation phases are at fractions $\varphi = 0$, $\frac{1}{33}$, $\frac{2}{33}$, $\frac{3}{33}$, …, $\frac{32}{33}$ between input samples.

In the logic design of this example, two clock domains are involved.

A straightforward approach to design of this interpolator in hardware is to drive an FIR filter at the input sample rate. At each input clock, the input sample values shift across the registers. Addressing circuitry implements a modulo-33 counter to keep track of phase – a *phase accumulator*. At each clock, one of 33 different sets of coefficients is applied to the filter. Each coefficient set is designed to introduce the appropriate phase shift. In this example, only 33 result samples are required every 35 input clocks: During 2 clocks of every 35, no result is produced.

This structure is called a *polyphase filter*. This example involves 33 phases; however, the number of *taps* required is independent of the number of *phases*. A 2×-oversampled prefilter, such I described on page 174, has just two phases. The halfband filter whose response is graphed in Figure 16.25, on page 166, would be suitable for this application; that filter has 55 taps.

Polyphase taps and phases

The number of *taps* required in a filter is determined by the degree of control that the designer needs to exercise over frequency response, and by how tightly the filters in each phase need to match each other. In many cases of consumer-grade video, cubic (4-tap) interpolation is sufficient. In studio video, eight taps or more might be necessary, depending upon the performance to be achieved.

In a direct implementation of a polyphase FIR interpolator, the number of *phases* is determined by the arithmetic that relates the sampling rates. The number of phases determines the number of coefficient sets that need to be used. Coefficient sets are typically precomputed and stored in nonvolatile memory.

On page 181, I described a polyphase resampler having 33 phases. In some applications, the number of phases is impractically large to implement directly. This is the case for the 709379:540000 ratio required to convert from $4f_{SC}$ PAL to Rec. 601 (4:2:2), from about 922 active samples per line to about 702. In other applications, such as digital video effects, the number of phases is variable, and unknown in advance. Applications such as these can be addressed by an interpolator having a number of phases that is a suitable power of two, such as 256 phases. Phase offsets are computed to the appropriate degree of precision, but are then approximated to a binary fraction (in this case having 8 bits) to form the phase offset φ that is presented to the interpolator.

$$\frac{1}{512} = \frac{1}{2} \cdot \frac{1}{2^8}$$

If the interpolator implements 8 fractional bits of phase, then any computed output sample may exhibit a positional error of up to $\pm 1/512$ of a sample interval. This is quite acceptable for component digital video. However, if the phase accumulator implements just 8 fractional bits, that positional error will accumulate as the incremental computation proceeds across the image row. In this example, with 922 active samples per line, the error could reach 3 or 4 sample intervals at the right-hand end of the line! This isn't tolerable. The solution is to choose a sufficient number of fractional bits in the phase accumulator to keep the cumulative error within limits. In this example, 13 bits are sufficient, but only 8 of those bits are presented to the interpolator.

Implementing polyphase interpolators

Polyphase interpolation is a specialization of FIR filtering; however, there are three major implementation differences. First, in a typical FIR filter, the input and output rates are the same; in a polyphase interpolator, the input and output rates are usually different.

Second, FIR filters usually have fixed coefficients; in a polyphase FIR interpolator, the coefficients vary on a sample-by-sample basis. Third, typical FIR filters are symmetrical, but polyphase interpolators are not.

Generally speaking, for a small number of phases – perhaps 8 or fewer – the cost of an interpolator is dominated by the number of multiplication operations, which is proportional to the number of taps. Beyond about 8 taps, the cost of coefficient storage begins to be significant. The cost of the addressing circuitry depends only upon the number of phases.

In the 35:33 downsampler example, I discussed a hardware structure driven by the input sample rate. Suppose the hardware design requires that the interpolator be driven by the output clock. For 31 of each 33 output clocks, one input sample is consumed; however, for 2 clocks, two input samples are consumed. This places a constraint on memory system design: Either two paths from memory must be implemented, or the extra 44 samples per line must be accessed during the blanking interval, and be stored in a small buffer. It is easier to drive this interpolator from the input clock.

Consider a 33:35 upsampler, from Rec. 601 to $4f_{SC}$ NTSC. If driven from the output side, the interpolator produces one output sample per clock, and consumes at most one input sample per clock. (For 2 of the 35 output clocks, no input samples are consumed.) If driven from the input side, for 2 of the 33 input clocks, the interpolator must produce two output samples. This is likely to present problems to the design of the FIR filter and the output side memory system.

The lesson is this: The structure of a polyphase interpolator is simplified if it is driven from the high-rate side.

Decimation

In Lagrange interpolation, no account is taken of whether interpolation computes more or fewer output samples than input samples. However, in signal processing, there is a big difference between downsampling – where lowpass filtering is necessary to prevent aliasing – and upsampling, where lowpass filtering is necessary to suppress "imaging." In signal processing, the term *interpolation* generally implies upsampling, that is, resampling to any ratio of unity or greater. (The term *interpolation* also describes phase shift without sample rate change; think of this as the special case of upsampling with a ratio of 1:1.)

Taken literally, *decimation* involves a ratio of 10:9, not 10:1.

Downsampling with a ratio of 10:9 is analogous to the policy by which the Roman army dealt with treachery and mutiny among its soldiers: One in ten of the offending soldiers was put to death. Their term *decimation* has come to describe downsampling in general.

Lowpass filtering in decimation

Earlier in this chapter, I expressed chroma subsampling as 2:1 decimation. In a decimator, samples are lowpass filtered to attenuate components at and above half the *new* sampling rate; then samples are dropped. Obviously, samples that are about to be dropped need not be computed! Ordinarily, the sample-dropping and filtering are incorporated into the same circuit.

For details of interpolators and decimators, see Crochiere, Ronald E., and Lawrence R. Rabiner, *Multirate Digital Signal Processing* (New York: Prentice-Hall, 1983).

In the example of halfband decimation for chroma subsampling, I explained the necessity of lowpass filtering to $0.25\,f_S$. In the $4f_{SC}$ NTSC to Rec. 601 example that I presented in *Polyphase interpolators*, on page 181, the input and output sample rates were so similar that no special attention needed to be paid to bandlimiting at the result sample rate. If downsampling ratio is much greater than unity – say 5:4, or greater – then the impulse response must incorporate a lowpass filtering (prefiltering, or antialiasing) function as well as phase shift. To avoid aliasing, the lowpass corner frequency must scale with the downsampling ratio. This may necessitate several sets of filter coefficients having different corner frequencies.

Image digitization and reconstruction 18

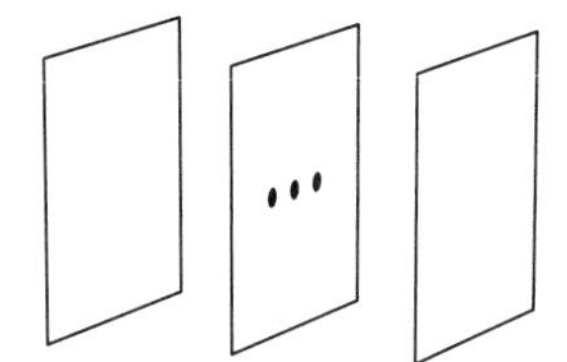
Figure 18.1 **Horizontal domain**

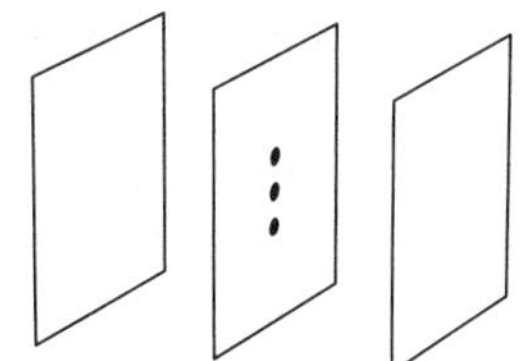
Figure 18.2 **Vertical domain**

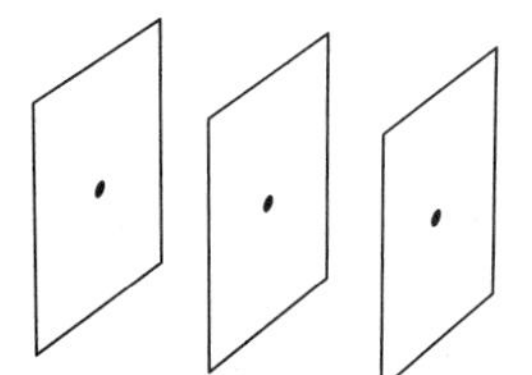
Figure 18.3 **Temporal domain**

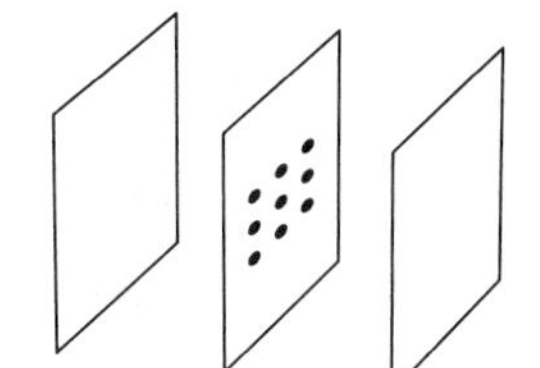
Figure 18.4 **Spatial domain**

In Chapter 16, *Filtering and sampling*, on page 141, I described how to analyze a signal that is a function of the single dimension of time, such as an audio signal. Sampling theory also applies to a signal that is a function of one dimension of space, such as a single scan line (image row) of a video signal. This is the horizontal or *transverse* domain, sketched in Figure 18.1 in the margin. If an image is scanned line by line, the waveform of each line can be treated as an independent signal. The techniques of filtering and sampling in one dimension, discussed in the previous chapter, apply directly to this case.

Consider a set of points arranged vertically that originate at the same displacement along each of several successive image rows, as sketched in Figure 18.2. Those points can be considered to be sampled by the scanning process itself. Sampling theory can be used to understand the properties of these samples.

A third dimension is introduced when a succession of images is temporally sampled to represent motion. Figure 18.3 depicts samples in the same column and the same row in three successive frames.

Complex filters can act on two axes simultaneously. Figure 18.4 illustrates spatial sampling. The properties of the entire set of samples are considered all at once, and cannot necessarily be separated into independent horizontal and vertical aspects.

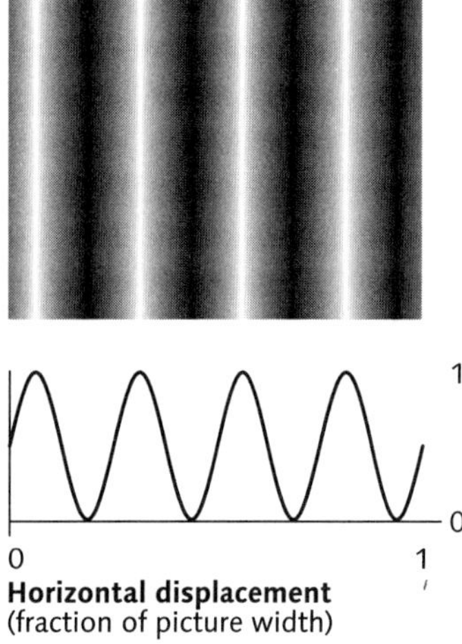

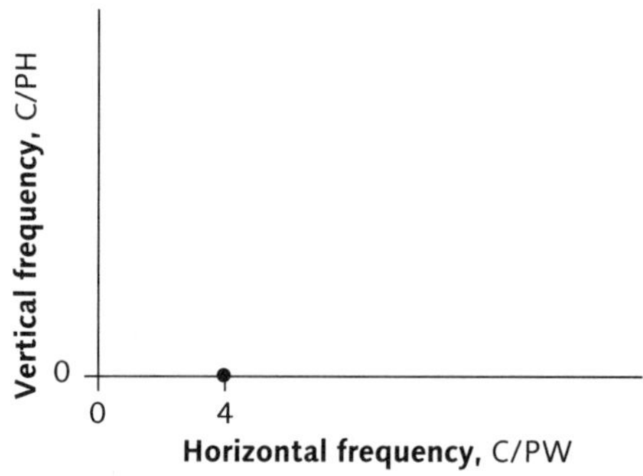

Figure 18.5 **Horizontal spatial frequency domain**

Spatial frequency domain

I explained in *Image structure,* on page 43, how a one-dimensional waveform in time transforms to a one-dimensional frequency spectrum. This concept can be extended to two dimensions: The two dimensions of space can be transformed into two-dimensional spatial frequency. The content of an image can be expressed as horizontal and vertical spatial frequency components. Spatial frequency is plotted using cycles per picture width (C/PW) as an *x*-coordinate, and cycles per picture height (C/PH) as a *y*-coordinate. You can gain insight into the operation of an imaging system by exploring its spatial frequency response.

In the image at the top left of Figure 18.5 above, every image row has identical content: 4 cycles of a sine wave. Underneath the image, I sketch the time domain waveform of every line. Since every line is identical, no power is present in the vertical direction. Considered in the spatial domain, this image contains power at a single horizontal spatial frequency, 4 C/PW; there is no power at any vertical spatial frequency. All of the power of this image lies at spatial frequency [4, 0].

Figure 18.6 opposite shows an image comprising a sinewave signal in the vertical direction. The height of the picture contains 3 cycles. The spatial frequency

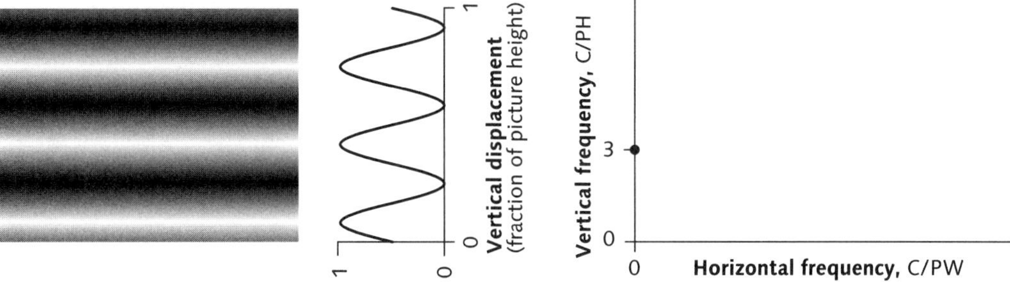

Figure 18.6 **Vertical spatial frequency domain**

graph, to the right, shows that all of the power of the image is contained at coordinates [0, 3] of spatial frequency. In an image where each image row takes a constant value, all of the power is located on the *y*-axis of spatial frequency.

If an image comprises rows with identical content, all of the power will be concentrated on the horizontal axis of spatial frequency. If the content of successive scans lines varies slightly, the power will spread to nonzero vertical frequencies. An image of diagonal bars would occupy a single point in spatial frequency, displaced from the *x*-axis and displaced from the *y*-axis.

When spatial frequency is determined analytically using the two-dimensional Fourier transform, the result is plotted in the manner of Figure 18.7, where low vertical frequencies – that is, low *y* values – are at the bottom. When spatial frequency is computed numerically using discrete transforms, such as the 2-D *discrete Fourier transform* (DFT), the *fast Fourier transform* (FFT), or the *discrete cosine transform* (DCT), the result is usually presented in a matrix, where low vertical frequencies are at the top.

The spatial frequency that corresponds to half the vertical sampling rate depends on the number of picture lines. A 480*i* system has approximately 480 picture lines: 480 samples occupy the height of the picture, and the Nyquist frequency for vertical sampling is 240 C/PH. No vertical frequency in excess of this can be represented without aliasing.

In most images, successive rows and columns of samples (of *R'*, *G'*, *B'*, or of luma) are very similar; low frequencies predominate, and image power tends to cluster toward spatial frequency coordinates [0, 0]. Figure 18.7 overleaf sketches the spatial frequency spectrum of luma in a 480*i* system. If the unmodulated NTSC color subcarrier were an image data signal, it would take the indicated location. In composite NTSC, chroma is modulated onto the subcarrier; the resulting modulated chroma can be thought of as occupying a

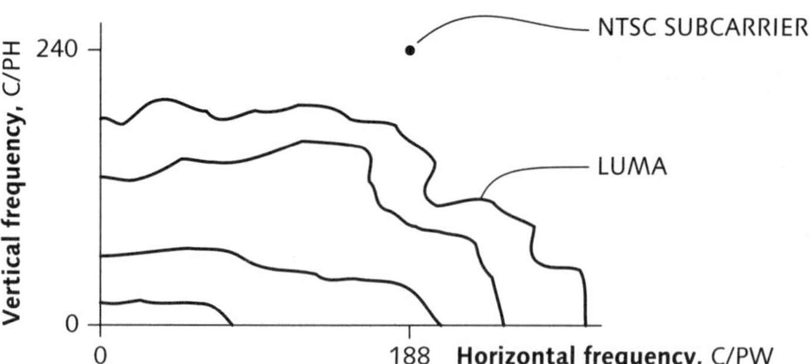

Figure 18.7 **Spatial frequency spectrum of 480*i* luma** is depicted in this plot, which resembles a topographical map. The position that unmodulated NTSC subcarrier would take if it were an image data signal is shown; see page 357.

particular region of the spatial frequency plane, as I will describe in *Spatial frequency spectrum of composite NTSC,* on page 359. In NTSC encoding, modulated chroma is then summed with luma; this causes the spectra to be overlaid. If the luma and chroma spectra overlap, cross-color and cross-luma interference artifacts can result.

Optical transfer function (OTF) includes phase. MTF is the magnitude of the OTF – it disregards phase.

In optics, the terms *magnitude frequency response* and *bandwidth* are not used. An optical component, subsystem, or system is characterized by *modulation transfer function* (MTF), a one-dimensional plot of horizontal or vertical spatial frequency response. (*Depth of modulation* is a single point quoted from this graph.) Technically, MTF is the Fourier transform of the point spread function (PSF) or line spread function (LSF). By definition, MTF relates to intensity. Since negative light power is physically unrealizable, MTF is measured by superimposing a high-frequency sinusoidal (modulating) wave onto a constant level, then taking the ratio of output modulation to input modulation.

Comb filtering

In *Finite impulse response (FIR) filters,* on page 157, I described FIR filters operating in the single dimension of time. If the samples are from a scan line of an image, the frequency response can be considered to represent horizontal spatial frequency (in units of C/PW), instead of temporal frequency (in cycles per second, or hertz).

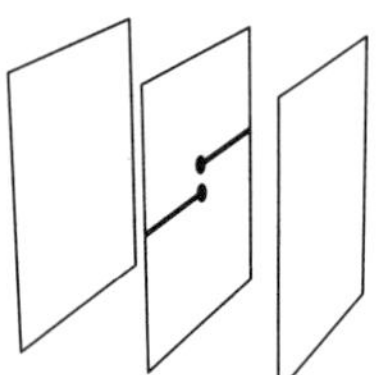

Figure 18.8 **Two samples, vertically arranged**

Consider a sample from a digital image sequence, and the sample immediately below, as sketched in Figure 18.8 in the margin. If the image has 640 active

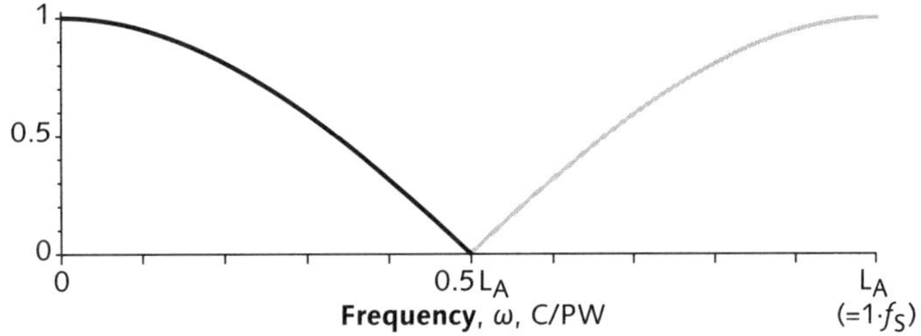

Figure 18.9 **Response of [1, 1] FIR filter** operating in the vertical domain, scaled for unity gain, is shown. This is a two-line (1*H*) comb filter. Magnitude falls as cos ω.

(picture) samples per line, and these two samples are presented to a comb filter like that of Figure 16.19, on page 156, but having 639 zero-samples between the two "ones," then the action of the comb filter will be identical to the action of a filter having two taps weighted [1, 1] operating in the vertical direction. In Figure 16.12, on page 153, I graphed the frequency response of a one-dimensional [1, 1] filter. The graph in Figure 18.9 above shows the response of the comb filter, expressed in terms of its response in the vertical direction. Here magnitude response is shown normalized for unity gain at DC; the filter has a response of about 0.707 (i.e., it is 3 db down) at one-quarter the vertical sampling frequency.

Spatial filtering

$$\begin{bmatrix} 1 & 1 \\ 1 & 1 \end{bmatrix} \qquad \begin{bmatrix} 1 & 2 & 1 \\ 2 & 4 & 2 \\ 1 & 2 & 1 \end{bmatrix}$$

Figure 18.10 **Separable spatial filter examples**

$$\begin{bmatrix} 1 & 1 & 1 \\ 1 & 1 & 1 \\ 1 & 1 & 1 \end{bmatrix} \qquad \begin{bmatrix} 0 & 0 & 1 & 0 & 0 \\ 0 & 1 & 1 & 1 & 0 \\ 1 & 1 & 1 & 1 & 1 \\ 0 & 1 & 1 & 1 & 0 \\ 0 & 0 & 1 & 0 & 0 \end{bmatrix}$$

Figure 18.11 **Inseparable spatial filter examples**

Placing a [1, 1] horizontal lowpass filter in tandem with a [1, 1] vertical lowpass filter is equivalent to computing a weighted sum of spatial samples using the weights indicated in the matrix on the left in Figure 18.10. Placing a [1, 2, 1] horizontal lowpass filter in tandem with a [1, 2, 1] vertical lowpass filter is equivalent to computing a weighted sum of spatial samples using the weights indicated in the matrix on the right in Figure 18.10. These are examples of *spatial filters*. These particular spatial filters are *separable:* They can be implemented using horizontal and vertical filters in tandem. Many spatial filters are *inseparable:* Their computation must take place directly in the two-dimensional spatial domain; they cannot be implemented using cascaded one-dimensional horizontal and vertical filters. Examples of inseparable filters are given in the matrices in Figure 18.11.

Image presampling filters

In a video camera, continuous information must be subjected to a presampling ("antialiasing") filter. Aliasing is minimized by optical spatial lowpass filtering that is effected in the optical path, prior to conversion of the image signal to electronic form. MTF limitations in the lens impose some degree of filtering. An additional filter can be implemented as a discrete optical element (often employing the optical property of birefringence). Additionally, or alternatively, some degree of filtering may be imposed by optical properties of the photosensor itself.

In resampling, signal power is not constrained to remain positive; filters having negative weights can be used. The ILPF and other sinc-based filters have negative weights, but those filters often ring and exhibit poor visual performance. Schreiber and Troxel found well-designed sharpened Gaussian filters with $\sigma = 0.375$ to have superior performance to the ILFP. A filter that is optimized for a particular mathematical criterion does not necessarily produce the best-looking picture!

Schreiber, William F., and Donald E. Troxel, "Transformations Between Continuous and Discrete Representations of Images: A Perceptual Approach," in IEEE Tr. on Pattern Analysis and Machine Intelligence, PAMI-7 (2): 178–186 (Mar. 1985).

Image reconstruction filters

On page 43, I introduced "box filter" reconstruction. This is technically known as *sample-and-hold, zero-order hold,* or *nearest-neighbor* reconstruction.

In theory, ideal image reconstruction would be obtained by using a PSF which has a two-dimensional sinc distribution. This would be a two-dimensional version of the ideal lowpass filter (ILPF) that I described for one dimension on page 148. However, a sinc function involves negative excursions. Light power cannot be negative, so a sinc filter cannot be used for presampling at an image capture device, and cannot be used as a reconstruction filter at a display device. A box-shaped distribution of sensitivity across each element of a sensor is easily implemented, as is a box-shaped distribution of intensity across each pixel of a display. However, like the one-dimensional boxcar of Chapter 16, a box distribution has significant response at high frequencies. Used at a sensor, a box filter will permit aliasing. Used in a display, scan-line or pixel

A *raised cosine* distribution is roughly similar to a Gaussian. See page 542.

Schreiber and Troxel suggest reconstruction with a sharpened Gaussian having $\sigma = 0.3$. See their paper cited in the marginal note on page 192.

structure is likely to be visible. If an external optical element such as a lens attenuates high spatial frequencies, then a box distribution might be suitable. A simple and practical choice for either capture or reconstruction is a Gaussian having a judiciously chosen half-power width. A Gaussian is a compromise that can achieve reasonably high resolution while minimizing aliasing and minimizing the visibility of the pixel (or scan-line) structure.

Spatial (2-D) oversampling

In image capture, as in reconstruction for image display, ideal theoretical performance would be obtained by using a PSF with a sinc distribution. However, a sinc function cannot be used directly in a transducer of light, because light power cannot be negative: Negative weights cannot be implemented. As in display reconstruction, a simple and practical choice for a direct presampling or reconstruction filter is a Gaussian having a judiciously chosen half-power width.

I have been describing direct sensors, where samples are taken directly from sensor elements, and direct displays, where samples directly energize display elements. In *Oversampling,* on page 174, I described a technique whereby a large number of directly acquired samples can be filtered to a lower sampling rate. That section discussed downsampling in one dimension, with the main goal of reducing the complexity of analog presampling or reconstruction filters. The oversampling technique can also be applied in two dimensions: A sensor can directly acquire a fairly large number of samples using a crude optical presampling filter, then use a sophisticated digital spatial filter to downsample.

The advantage of interlace – reducing scan-line visibility for a given bandwidth, spatial resolution, and flicker rate – is built upon the assumption that the sensor (camera), data transmission, and display all use identical scanning. If oversampling is feasible, the situation changes. Consider a receiver that accepts progressive image data (as in the top left of Figure 6.8, on page 59), but instead of displaying this data directly, it

Oversampling to double the number of lines displayed during a frame time is called *line doubling*.

synthesizes data for a larger image array (as in the middle left of Figure 6.8). The synthetic data can be displayed with a spot size appropriate for the larger array, and all of the scan lines can be illuminated in each $1/60$ s instead of just half of them. This technique is *spatial oversampling*. For a given level of scan-line visibility, this technique enables closer viewing distance than would be possible for progressive display.

If such oversampling had been technologically feasible in 1941, or in 1953, then the NTSC would have undoubtedly chosen a progressive transmission standard. However, oversampling is not economical even in today's SDTV studio systems, let alone HDTV or consumer electronics. So interlace continues to have an economic advantage. However, this advantage is eroding. It is likely that all future video system standards will have progressive scanning.

Oversampling provides a mechanism for a sensor PSF or a display PSF to have negative weights, yielding a spatially "sharpened" filter. For example, a sharpened Gaussian PSF can be obtained, and can achieve performance better than a Gaussian. With a sufficient degree of oversampling, using sophisticated filters having sinc-like PSFs, the interchange signal can come arbitrarily close to the Nyquist limit. However, mathematical excellence does not necessarily translate to improved visual performance. Sharp filters are likely to ring, and thereby produce objectionable artifacts.

If negative weights are permitted in a PSF, then negative signal values can potentially result. Standard studio digital interfaces provide footroom so as to permit moderate negative values to be conveyed. Using negative weights typically improves filter performance even if negative values are clipped after downsampling.

Similarly, if a display has many elements for each digital sample, a sophisticated digital upsampler can use negative weights. Negative values resulting from the filter's operation will be clipped for presentation to the display itself, but again, improved performance could result.

Perception and visual acuity 19

Properties of human vision are central to image system engineering. They determine how many bits are necessary to represent luminance (or tristimulus) levels, and how many pixels need to be provided per degree of picture angle. This chapter introduces the intensity discrimination and spatial properties of vision.

Retina

The human retina has four types of photoreceptor cells that respond to incident radiation with different spectral response curves. A retina has about 100 million *rod* cells, and about 5 million *cone* cells (of three types).

Rods are effective only at extremely low light levels. Since there is only one type of rod cell, what is loosely called *night vision* cannot discern colors.

Boynton, Robert M., *Human Color Vision* (New York: Holt, Rinehart and Winston, 1979).

Wandell, Brian A., *Foundations of Vision* (Sunderland, Mass.: Sinauer Associates, 1995).

The cone cells are sensitive to longwave, mediumwave, and shortwave light – roughly, light in the red, green, and blue portions of the spectrum. Because there are just three types of color photoreceptors, three numerical components are necessary and sufficient to describe a color: Color vision is inherently *trichromatic*. To arrange for three components to mimic color vision, suitable spectral sensitivity functions must be used; this topic will be discussed in *The CIE system of colorimetry,* on page 211.

Adaptation

Vision operates over a remarkable range of luminance levels – about eight orders of magnitude (decades) sketched in Figure 19.1. For about four decades at the low end of the range, the rods are active; vision at these light levels is called *scotopic*. For the top five or six decades, the cones are active; vision at these light levels is called *photopic*.

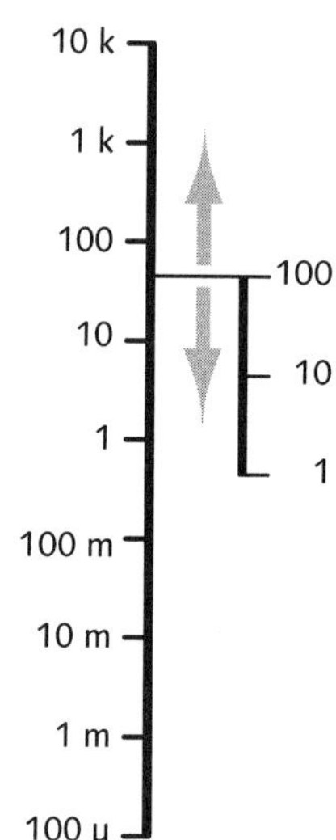

Figure 19.1 **Luminance range of vision**

Mesopic vision takes place in the range of luminance levels where there is some overlap between rods and cones. Considered from the bottom of the photopic region, this is called *rod intrusion*. It is a research topic whether the rods have significance to color image reproduction at usual luminance levels (such as in the cinema). Today, for engineering purposes, the effect of rod intrusion is discounted.

Vision adapts throughout this luminance range, as sketched in Figure 19.2. From sunlight to moonlight, illuminance changes by a factor of about 200000; adaptation causes the sensitivity of the visual system to increase by about a factor of 1000. About one decade of adaptation is effected by the eye's iris – that is, by changes in pupil diameter. (Pupil diameter varies from about 2 mm to 8 mm.) Adaptation involves a photochemical process involving the *visual pigment* substance contained in the rods and the cones; it also involves neural mechanisms in the visual pathway.

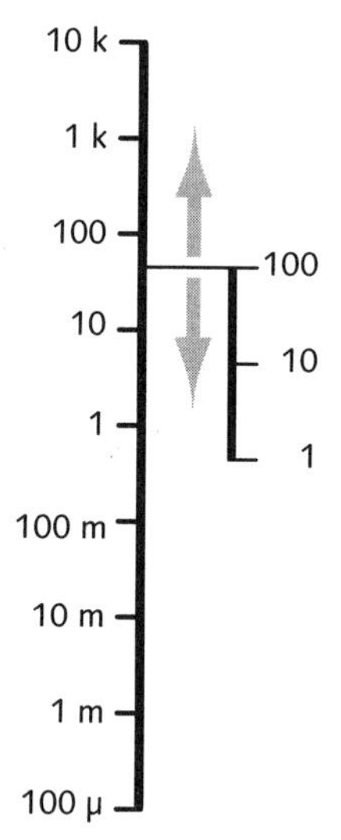

Figure 19.2 **Adaptation**

Dark adaptation, to low luminance, is slow: Adaptation from a bright sunlit day to the darkness of a cinema can take a few minutes. Adaptation to higher luminance is rapid but can be painful, as you may have experienced when walking out of the cinema back into daylight.

Adaptation is a low-level phenomenon within the visual system; it is mainly controlled by total retinal illumination. Your adaptation state is closely related to the mean luminance in your field of view. In a dark viewing environment, such as a cinema, the image itself controls adaptation.

At a particular state of adaptation, vision can discern different luminances across about a 1000:1 range. When viewing a real scene, adaptation changes depending upon where in the scene your gaze is directed.

Diffuse white was described on page 83. This wide range of luminance levels is sometimes called *dynamic range*, but nothing is in motion!

For image reproduction purposes, vision can distinguish different luminances down to about 1% of diffuse white; in other words, our ability to distinguish luminance differences extends over a ratio of luminance of about 100:1. Loosely speaking, luminance levels less than 1% of peak white appear just "black": Different luminances below that level can be measured, but they cannot be visually distinguished.

Contrast ratio

Contrast ratio is the ratio of luminances of the lightest and darkest elements of a scene, or an image. In print and photography, the term need not be qualified. However, image content in motion picture film and video changes with time. *Simultaneous contrast ratio* (or *on-off contrast ratio*) refers to contrast ratio at one instant. *Sequential contrast ratio* measures light and dark elements that are separated in time – that is, not part of the same picture. Sequential contrast ratio in film can reach 10000:1. Such a high ratio may be useful to achieve an artistic effect, but performance of a display system is best characterized by simultaneous contrast ratio.

Simultaneous contrast ratio is sometimes shortened to *simultaneous contrast*, which unfortunately has a second (unrelated) meaning. See *Surround effect*, on page 82. Contrast ratio without qualification should be taken as simultaneous.

In practical imaging systems, many factors conspire to increase the luminance of black, thereby lessening the contrast ratio and impairing picture quality. On an electronic display or in a projected image, simultaneous contrast ratio is typically less than 100:1 owing to spill light (stray light) in the ambient environment or flare in the display system. Typical simultaneous contrast ratios are shown in Table 19.1 overleaf. Contrast ratio is a major determinant of subjective image quality, so much so that an image reproduced with a high simultaneous contrast ratio may be judged sharper than another image that has higher measured spatial frequency content.

Viewing environment	*Max. luminance, cd·m^{-2}*	*Typical simul. contrast ratio*	*L* range*
Cinema	40	80:1	11...100
Television (living room)	100	20:1	27...100
Office	200	5:1	52...100

Table 19.1 **Typical simultaneous contrast ratios** in image display are summarized.

During the course of the day we experience a wide range of illumination levels; adaptation adjusts accordingly. But in video and film, we are nearly always concerned with viewing at a known adaptation state, so a simultaneous contrast ratio of 100:1 is adequate.

Contrast sensitivity

Within the two-decade range of luminance that is useful for image reproduction, vision has a certain threshold of discrimination. It is convenient to express the discrimination capability in terms of *contrast sensitivity*, which is the ratio of luminances between two adjacent patches of similar luminance.

Y_0: Adaptation (surround) luminance

Y: Test luminance

ΔY: Increment in test luminance

Figure 19.3 below shows the pattern presented to an observer in an experiment to determine the contrast sensitivity of human vision. Most of the observer's field of vision is filled by a *surround* luminance level, Y_0, which fixes the observer's state of adaptation. In the central area of the field of vision are placed two adjacent patches having slightly different luminance

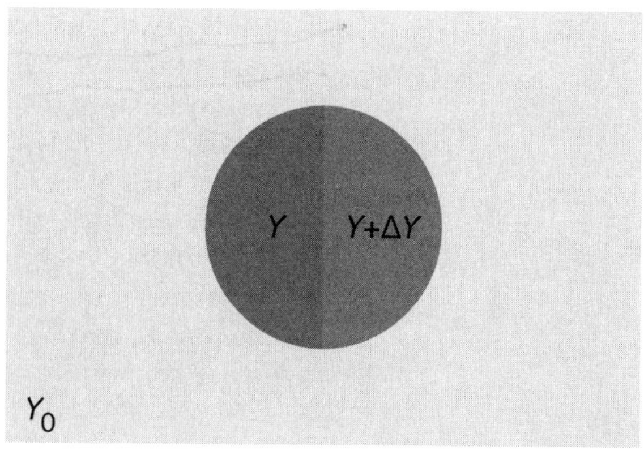

Figure 19.3 **Contrast sensitivity test pattern** is presented to an observer in an experiment to determine the contrast sensitivity of human vision. The experimenter adjusts ΔY; the observer reports whether he or she detects a difference in lightness between the two patches.

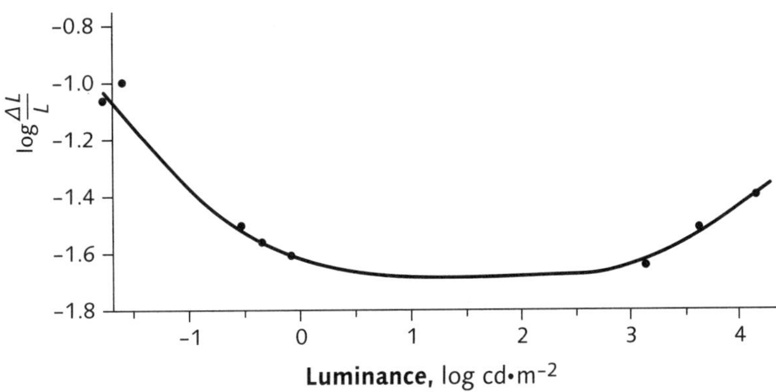

Figure 19.4 **Contrast sensitivity.** This graph is redrawn, with permission, from Figure 3.4 of Schreiber's *Fundamentals of Electronic Imaging Systems*. Over a range of intensities of about 300:1, the discrimination threshold of vision is approximately a constant ratio of luminance. The flat portion of the curve shows that the perceptual response to luminance – termed *lightness* – is approximately logarithmic.

levels, Y and $Y + \Delta Y$. The experimenter presents stimuli having a wide range of test values with respect to the surround, that is, a wide range of Y/Y_0 values. At each test luminance, the experimenter presents to the observer a range of luminance increments with respect to the test stimulus, that is, a range of $\Delta Y/Y$ values.

Schreiber, William F., *Fundamentals of Electronic Imaging Systems*, Third Edition (Berlin: Springer-Verlag, 1993).

When this experiment is conducted, the relationship graphed in Figure 19.4 above is found: Plotting $\log(\Delta Y/Y)$ as a function of $\log Y$ reveals an interval of more than two decades of luminance over which the discrimination capability of vision is about 1% of the test luminance level. This leads to the conclusion that – for *threshold* discrimination of two adjacent patches of nearly identical luminance – the discrimination capability is very nearly logarithmic.

$$\frac{\lg 100}{\lg 1.01} \approx 463; \quad 1.01^{463} \approx 100$$

NTSC documents from the early 1950s used a contrast sensitivity of 2% and a contrast ratio of 30:1 to derive 172 steps:

$$\frac{\lg 30}{\lg 1.02} = 172$$

See Fink, Donald G., ed., *Color Television Standards* (New York: McGraw-Hill, 1955), p. 201.

The contrast sensitivity function begins to answer this question: What is the minimum number of discrete codes required to represent relative luminance over a particular range? In other words, what luminance codes can be thrown away without the observer noticing? On a linear luminance scale, to cover a 100:1 range with an increment of 0.01 takes 10000 codes, or about 14 bits. If codes are spaced according to a *ratio* of 1.01, then only about 463 codes are required. This number of codes can be represented in 9 bits. (For video distribution, 8 bits suffice.)

ISO 5-1, *Photography – Density measurements – Terms, symbols, and notations.* See also parts 2 through 4.

In transmissive film media, *transmittance* (τ) is the fraction of light transmitted through the medium. Transmittance is usually measured in logarithmic units: *Optical density* – or just *density* – is the negative of the logarithm of transmittance. (Equivalently, optical density is the logarithm of incident power divided by transmitted power.) The term stems from the physical density of developed silver (or in color film, developed dye) in the film. In reflective media, *reflectance* (ρ) is similarly expressed in density units. In motion picture film, logarithms are used not only for measurement, but also for image coding (in the Kodak Cineon system, and the SMPTE DPX standard).

SMPTE 180M, *File Format for Digital Moving-Picture Exchange (DPX).*

The logarithmic relationship relates to contrast sensitivity *at threshold:* We are measuring the ability of the visual system to discriminate between two nearly identical luminances. If you like, call this a *just-noticeable difference* (JND), defined where the difference between two stimuli is detected as often as it is undetected. Logarithmic coding rests on the assumption that the threshold function can be extended to large luminance ratios. Experiments have shown that this assumption does not hold very well. At a given state of adaptation, the discrimination capability of vision degrades at low luminances, below several percent of diffuse white. Over a wider range of luminance, strict adherence to logarithmic coding is not justified for perceptual reasons. Coding based upon a power law is found to be a better approximation to lightness response than a logarithmic function. In video, and in computing, power functions are used instead of logarithmic functions. Incidentally, other senses behave according to power functions, as shown in Table 19.2.

When two stimuli differ by 1 JND, 75% of guesses will be right and 25% will be wrong.

Stevens, S.S., *Psychophysics* (New York: Wiley, 1975).

Percept	*Physical quantity*	*Power*
Loudness	Sound pressure level	0.67
Saltiness	Sodium chloride concentration	1.4
Smell	Concentration of aromatic molecules	0.6

Table 19.2 **Power functions in perception**

Figure 19.5 **Contrast sensitivity function (CSF)** varies with retinal illuminance, here shown in units of troland (Td). The curve at 9 Td, which typifies television viewing, peaks at about 4 cycles per degree (CPD, or ∿/°). Below that spatial frequency, the eye acts as a differentiator; above it, the eye acts as an integrator.

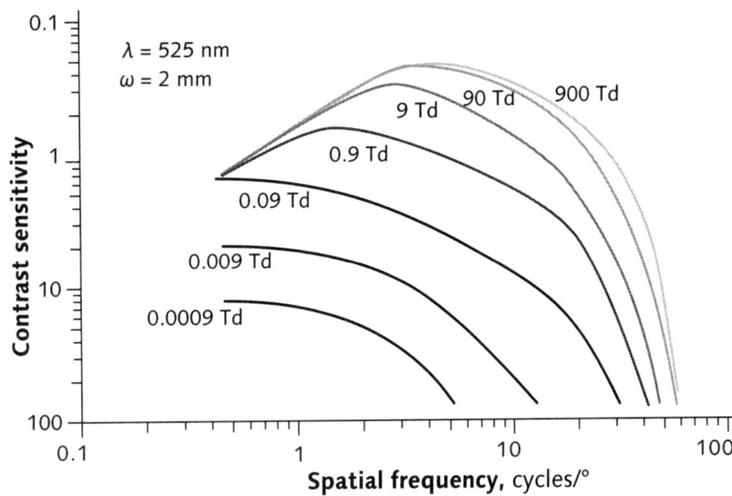

Contrast sensitivity function (CSF)

van Nes, F. L., and M. A. Bouman, "Spatial modulation transfer in the human eye," in *J. Opt. Soc. Am.* 57: 419–423 (1967).

The contrast sensitivity of vision is about 1% – that is, vision cannot distinguish two luminance levels if the ratio between them is less than about 1.01. That threshold applies to visual features of a certain angular extent, about ⅛°, for which vision has maximum ability to detect luminance differences. However, the contrast sensitivity of vision degrades for elements having angular subtense smaller or larger than about ⅛°.

Barten, Peter G. J., *Contrast Sensitivity of the Human Eye and its Effect on Image Quality* (Knegsel, Netherlands: HV Press, 1999).

In vision science, rather than characterizing vision by its response to an individual small feature, we place many small elements side by side. The spacing of these elements is measured in terms of spatial frequency, in units of *cycles per degree*. Each cycle comprises a dark element and a white element. At the limit, a cycle comprises two samples or two pixels; in the vertical dimension, the smallest cycle corresponds to two scan lines.

Troland (Td) is a unit of retinal illuminance equal to object luminance (in $cd \cdot m^{-2}$) times pupillary aperture area (in mm^2).

Figure 19.5 above shows a graph of the dependence of contrast sensitivity (on the *y*-axis, expressed in percentage) upon spatial frequency (on the *x*-axis, expressed in cycles per degree). The graph shows a family of curves, representing different adaptation levels, from very dark (0.0009 Td) to very bright (900 Td). The curve at 90 Td is representative of electronic or projected displays.

For video engineering, three features of this graph are important:

- First, the 90 Td curve has fallen to a contrast sensitivity of 100 at about 60 cycles per degree. Vision isn't capable of perceiving spatial frequencies greater than this; a display need not reproduce detail higher than this frequency. This limits the resolution (or bandwidth) that must be provided.
- Second, the peak of the 90 Td curve has a contrast sensitivity of about 1%; luminance differences less than this can be discarded. This limits the number of bits per pixel that must be provided.
- Third, the curve falls off at spatial frequencies below about one cycle per degree. In a consumer display, luminance can diminish (within limits) toward the edges of the image without the viewer's noticing.

Campbell, F.W., and V.G. Robson, "Application of Fourier analysis to the visibility of gratings," in *J. Physiol.* (London) 197: 551–566 (1968).

In traditional video engineering, the spatial frequency and contrast sensitivity aspects of this graph are used independently. The JPEG and MPEG compression systems exploit the interdependence of these two aspects, as will be explained in *JPEG and motion-JPEG (M-JPEG) compression*, on page 447.

Luminance and lightness 20

Nonlinear coding of luminance is essential to maximize the perceptual performance of an image coding system. This chapter introduces luminance and lightness, or what is loosely called *brightness*.

In *Color science for video*, on page 233, I will describe how spectral power distributions (SPDs) in the range 400 nm to 700 nm are related to colors.

Luminance, denoted Y, is what I call a *linear-light* quantity; it is directly proportional to physical intensity weighted by the spectral sensitivity of human vision. Luminance involves light having wavelengths in the range of about 400 nm to 700 nm; luminance can be computed as a properly weighted sum of linear-light red, green, and blue tristimulus components, according to the principles and standards of the CIE.

Lightness, denoted L^*, is defined by the CIE as a nonlinear transfer function of luminance that approximates the perception of brightness.

The term *luminance* is often carelessly and incorrectly used to refer to *luma*. See *Relative luminance*, on page 206, and Appendix A, *YUV and luminance considered harmful*, on page 595.

In video, we do not compute the linear-light luminance of color science; nor do we compute lightness. Instead, we compute an approximation of lightness, *luma* (denoted Y') as a weighted sum of *nonlinear* (gamma-corrected) R', G', and B' components. Luma is only loosely related to true (CIE) luminance. In *Constant luminance*, on page 75, I explained why video systems approximate lightness instead of computing it directly. I will detail the nonlinear coding used in video in *Gamma*, on page 257. In *Luma and color differences*, on page 281, I will outline how luma is augmented with color information.

Radiance, intensity

Image science concerns optical power incident upon the image plane of a sensor device, and optical power emergent from the image plane of a display device.

See *Introduction to radiometry and photometry*, on page 601.

Radiometry concerns the measurement of radiant optical power in the electromagnetic spectrum from 3×10^{11} Hz to 3×10^{16} Hz, corresponding to wavelengths from 1 mm down to 10 nm. There are four fundamental quantities in radiometry:

- Radiant optical power, *flux*, is expressed in units of watts (W).
- Radiant flux per unit area is *irradiance;* its units are watts per meter squared ($W\cdot m^{-2}$).
- Radiant flux in a certain direction – that is, radiant flux per unit of solid angle – is *radiant intensity;* its units are watts per steradian ($W\cdot sr^{-1}$).
- Flux in a certain direction, per unit area, is *radiance;* its units are watts per steradian per meter squared ($W\cdot sr^{-1}\cdot m^{-2}$).

Radiance is measured with an instrument called a *radiometer.* A *spectroradiometer* measures spectral radiance – that is, radiance per unit wavelength. A *spectroradiometer* measures incident light; a *spectrophotometer* incorporates a light source, and measures either spectral reflectance or spectral transmittance.

Photometry is essentially radiometry as sensed by human vision: In photometry, radiometric measurements are weighted by the spectral response of human vision (to be described). This involves wavelengths (λ) between 360 nm to 830 nm, or in practical terms, 400 nm to 700 nm. Each of the four fundamental quantities of radiometry – flux, irradiance, radiant intensity, and radiance – has an analog in photometry. The photometric quantities are *luminous flux, illuminance, luminous intensity,* and *luminance.* In video engineering, luminance is the most important of these.

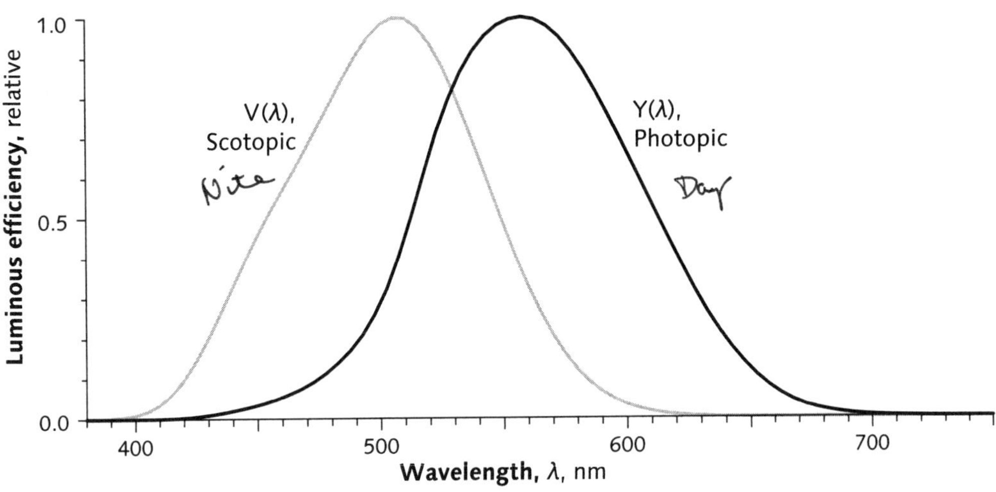

Figure 20.1 **Luminous efficiency functions.** The solid line indicates the luminance response of the cone photoreceptors – that is, the CIE *photopic* response. A monochrome scanner or camera must have this spectral response in order to correctly reproduce lightness. The peak occurs at about 555 nm, the wavelength of the brightest possible monochromatic 1 mW source. (The lightly shaded curve shows the *scotopic* response of the rod cells – loosely, the response of night vision. The increased relative luminance of blue wavelengths in scotopic vision is called the *Purkinje shift*.)

Luminance

I presented a brief introduction to *Lightness terminology* on page 11.

The *Commission Internationale de L'Éclairage* (CIE, or International Commission on Illumination) is the international body responsible for standards in the area of color. The CIE defines brightness as *the attribute of a visual sensation according to which an area appears to exhibit more or less light*. Brightness is, by the CIE's definition, a subjective quantity: It cannot be measured.

Publication CIE 15.2, *Colorimetry*, Second Edition (Vienna, Austria: Commission Internationale de L'Éclairage, 1986); reprinted with corrections in 1996.

The CIE has defined an objective quantity that is related to brightness. *Luminance* is defined as radiance weighted by the spectral sensitivity function – the sensitivity to power at different wavelengths – that is characteristic of vision. The *luminous efficiency* of the CIE Standard Observer, denoted Y(λ), is graphed as the black line of Figure 20.1 above. It is defined numerically, is everywhere positive, and peaks at about 555 nm. When a spectral power distribution (SPD) is integrated using this weighting function, the result is *luminance*, denoted *Y*. In continuous terms, luminance is an integral of spectral radiance across the spectrum. In discrete terms, it is a dot product. The magnitude of

Until 2000, *Y*(λ) had the symbol $\bar{y}$, pronounced *WYE-bar*. The luminous efficiency function has also been denoted V(λ), pronounced *VEE-lambda*.

luminance is proportional to physical power; in that sense it is like intensity. However, its spectral composition is intimately related to the lightness sensitivity of human vision. Luminance is expressed in units of $cd \cdot m^{-2}$ ("nits"). Relative luminance, which I will describe in a moment, is a pure number without units.

The *luminous efficiency function* is also known as the *Y(λ) color-matching function* (CMF). Luminance, *Y*, is one of three distinguished tristimulus values. The other two distinguished tristimulus values, *X* and *Z*, and various *R*, *G*, and *B* tristimulus values, will be introduced in *Color science for video,* on page 233.

You might intuitively associate pure luminance with gray, but a spectral power distribution having the shape of Figure 20.1 would *not* appear neutral gray! In fact, an SPD of that shape would appear distinctly green. As I will detail in *The CIE system of colorimetry,* on page 211, it is very important to distinguish analysis functions – called *color-matching functions*, or CMFs – from spectral power distributions. The luminous efficiency function takes the role of an analysis function, not an SPD.

Relative luminance

In image reproduction – including photography, cinema, video, and print – we rarely, if ever, reproduce the absolute luminance of the original scene. Instead, we reproduce luminance approximately proportional to scene luminance, up to the maximum luminance available in the reproduction medium. We process or record an approximation to *relative luminance*. To use the unqualified term *luminance* would suggest that we are processing or recording absolute luminance.

SMPTE RP 71, *Setting Chromaticity and Luminance of White for Color Television Monitors Using Shadow-Mask Picture Tubes.*

In image reproduction, luminance is usually normalized to 1 or 100 units relative to a specified or implied *reference white*; we assume that the viewer will adapt to white in his or her ambient environment. SMPTE has standardized studio video monitors to have a reference white luminance of 103 $cd \cdot m^{-2}$, and a reference white chromaticity of CIE D_{65}. (I will introduce CIE D_{65} on page 224.)

Luminance from red, green, and blue

The luminous efficiency of vision peaks in the medium-wave (green) region of the spectrum: If three mono-chromatic sources appear red, green, and blue, and have the same radiant power in the visible spectrum, then the green will appear the brightest of the three; the red will appear less bright, and the blue will be the darkest of the three. As a consequence of the luminous efficiency function, the most saturated blue colors are quite dark, and the most saturated yellows are quite light.

If the luminance of a scene element is to be sensed by a scanner or camera having a single spectral filter, then the spectral response of the scanner's filter must – in theory, at least – correspond to the luminous efficiency function of Figure 20.1. However, luminance can also be computed as a weighted sum of suitably chosen red, green, and blue tristimulus components. The coeffi-cients are functions of vision, of the white reference, and of the particular red, green, and blue spectral weighting functions employed. For realistic choices of white point and primaries, the green coefficient is quite large, the blue coefficient is the smallest of the three, and the red coefficient has an intermediate value.

The primaries of contemporary CRT displays are stan-dardized in Rec. ITU-R BT.709. Weights computed from these primaries are appropriate to compute relative luminance from red, green, and blue tristimulus values for computer graphics, and for modern video cameras and modern CRT displays in both STDV and HDTV:

$$^{709}Y = 0.2126\,R + 0.7152\,G + 0.0722\,B \qquad \text{Eq 20.1}$$

My notation is outlined in Figure 24.5, on page 289. The coefficients are derived in *Color science for video*, on page 233.

Luminance comprises roughly 21% power from the red (longwave) region of the spectrum, 72% from green (mediumwave), and 7% from blue (shortwave).

To compute luminance using $(R+G+B)/3$ is at odds with the spectral response of vision.

Blue has a small contribution to luminance. However, vision has excellent color discrimination among blue hues. If you give blue fewer bits than red or green, then blue areas of your images are liable to exhibit contouring artifacts.

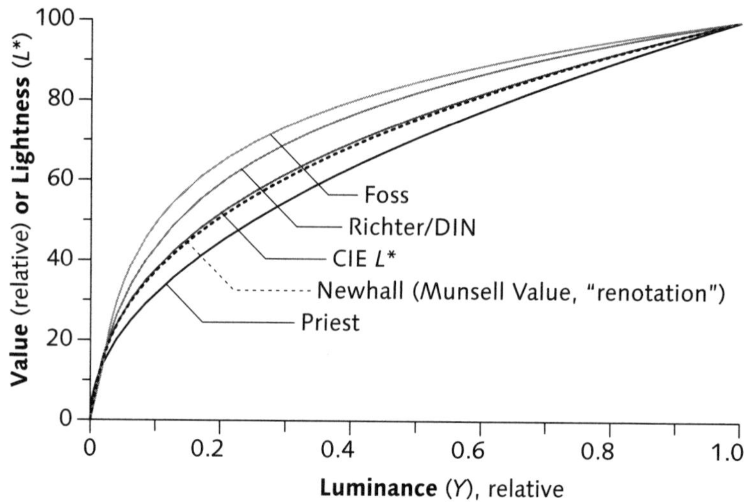

Figure 20.2 **Luminance and lightness.** The dependence of lightness (L^*) or value (V) upon relative luminance (Y) has been modeled by polynomials, power functions, and logarithms. In all of these systems, 18% "mid-gray" has lightness about halfway up the perceptual scale. For details, see Fig. 2 (6.3) in Wyszecki and Stiles, *Color Science* (cited on page 231).

Lightness (CIE *L**)

In *Contrast sensitivity*, on page 198, I explained that vision has a nonlinear perceptual response to luminance. Vision scientists have proposed many functions that relate relative luminance to perceived lightness; several of these functions are graphed in Figure 20.2.

The L^* symbol is pronounced *EL-star*.

In 1976, the CIE standardized the L^* function to approximate the lightness response of human vision. Other functions – such as Munsell *Value* – specify alternate lightness scales, but the CIE L^* function is widely used and internationally standardized.

L^* is a power function of relative luminance, modified by the introduction of a linear segment near black:

$$L^* = \begin{cases} 903.3\dfrac{Y}{Y_n}; & \dfrac{Y}{Y_n} \le 0.008856 \\ 116\left(\dfrac{Y}{Y_n}\right)^{\frac{1}{3}} - 16; & 0.008856 < \dfrac{Y}{Y_n} \end{cases} \qquad \text{Eq 20.2}$$

L^* has a range of 0 to 100. Y is CIE luminance (proportional to intensity). Y_n is the luminance of reference white. The quotient Y/Y_n is relative luminance. (If you normalize luminance to unity, then you need not compute the quotient.)

A linear segment is defined near black: For Y/Y_n values 0.008856 or less, L^* is proportional to Y/Y_n. The parameters have been chosen such that the breakpoint occurs at an L^* value of 8. This value corresponds to less than 1% on the relative luminance scale! In a display system having a contrast ratio of 100:1, the entire reproduced image is confined to L^* values between 8 and 100! The linear segment is important in color specification; however, Y/Y_n values that small are rarely encountered in video. (If you don't use the linear segment, make sure that you prevent L^* from ranging below zero.)

To compute L^* from optical density D in the range 0 to 2, use this relation:

$$L^* = 116 \cdot 10^{-D/3} - 16$$

The linear and power function segments are defined to maintain function and tangent continuity at the breakpoint between the two segments. The exponent of the power function segment is ⅓, but the scale factor of 116 and the offset of –16 modify the pure power function such that a 0.4-power function best approximates the overall curve. Roughly speaking, lightness is 100 times the 0.4-power of relative luminance.

ΔL^* is pronounced *delta EL-star*.

The difference between two L^* values, denoted ΔL^*, is a measure of perceptual "distance." A difference of less than unity between two L^* values is generally imperceptible – that is, ΔL^* of unity is taken to lie at the threshold of discrimination. L^* provides one component of a *uniform color space*. The term *perceptually linear* is not appropriate: Since we cannot directly measure the quantity in question, we cannot assign to it any strong properties of mathematical linearity.

In Chapter 8, *Constant luminance*, I described how video systems encode a luma signal (Y') that is an engineering approximation to lightness. That signal is only indirectly related to the relative luminance (Y) or the lightness (L^*) of color science.

The CIE system of colorimetry 21

The *Commission Internationale de L'Éclairage* (CIE) has defined a system that maps a *spectral power distribution* (SPD) of physics into a triple of numerical values – CIE *XYZ* tristimulus values – that form the mathematical coordinates of color space. In this chapter, I describe the CIE system. In the following chapter, *Color science for video,* I will explain how these *XYZ* tristimulus values are related to linear-light *RGB* values.

Figure 21.1 **Example coordinate system**

Color coordinates are analogous to coordinates on a map (see Figure 21.1). Cartographers have different map projections for different functions: Some projections preserve areas, others show latitudes and longitudes as straight lines. No single map projection fills all the needs of all map users. There are many "color spaces." As in maps, no single coordinate system fills all of the needs of users.

For an approachable, nonmathematical introduction to color physics and perception, see Rossotti, Hazel, *Colour: Why the World Isn't Grey* (Princeton, N.J.: Princeton Univ. Press, 1983).

In Chapter 20, *Luminance and lightness*, I introduced the linear-light quantity *luminance*. To reiterate, I use the term *luminance* and the symbol *Y* to refer to CIE luminance. I use the term *luma* and the symbol *Y'* to refer to the video component that conveys an approximation to lightness. Most of the quantities in this chapter, and in the following chapter *Color science for video*, involve values that are proportional to intensity. In Chapter 8, *Constant luminance*, I related the theory of color science to the practice of video. To approximate perceptual uniformity, video uses quantities such as *R'*, *G'*, *B'*, and *Y'* that are *not* proportional to intensity.

Fundamentals of vision

About 8% of men and 0.4% of women have deficient color vision, called *color blindness*. Some people have fewer than three types of cones; some people have cones with altered spectral sensitivities.

As I explained in *Retina,* on page 195, human vision involves three types of color photoreceptor *cone* cells, which respond to incident radiation having wavelengths (λ) from about 400 nm to 700 nm. The three cell types have different spectral responses; color is the perceptual result of their absorption of light. Normal vision involves three types of cone cells, so three numerical values are necessary and sufficient to describe a color: Normal color vision is inherently *trichromatic*.

Power distributions exist in the physical world; however, color exists only in the eye and the brain. Isaac Newton put it this way, in 1675:

"Indeed rays, properly expressed, are not coloured."

Definitions

In *Lightness terminology,* on page 11, I defined brightness, intensity, luminance, value, lightness, and tristimulus value. In Appendix B, *Introduction to radiometry and photometry,* on page 601, I give more rigorous definitions. In color science, it is important to use these terms carefully. It is especially important to differentiate physical quantities (such as intensity and luminance), from perceptual quantities (such as lightness and value).

Hue is the attribute of a visual sensation according to which an area appears to be similar to one of the perceived colors, red, yellow, green, and blue, or a combination of two of them. Roughly speaking, if the dominant wavelength of a spectral power distribution shifts, the hue of the associated color will shift.

Saturation is the colorfulness of an area, judged in proportion to its brightness. Saturation is a perceptual quantity; like brightness, it cannot be measured.

Bill Schreiber points out that the words *saturation* and *purity* are often used interchangeably, to the dismay of purists.

Purity is the ratio of the amount of a monochromatic stimulus to the amount of a specified achromatic stimulus which, when mixed additively, matches the color in question. Purity is the objective correlate of saturation.

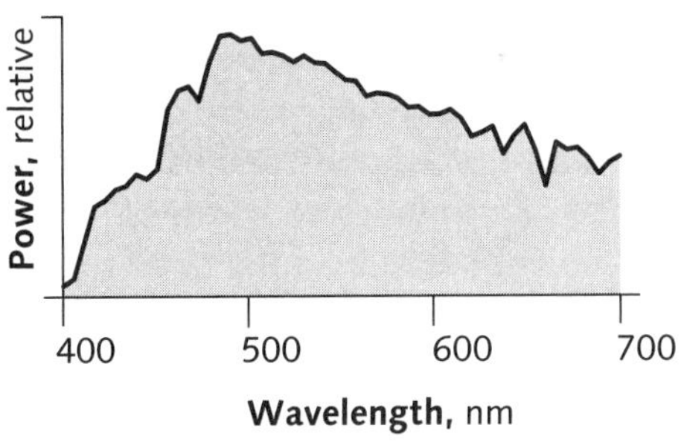

Figure 21.2 **Spectral and tristimulus color reproduction.** A color can be represented as a spectral power distribution (SPD), perhaps in 31 components representing power in 10 nm bands over the range 400 nm to 700 nm. However, owing to the trichromatic nature of human vision, if appropriate spectral weighting functions are used, three components suffice to represent color. The SPD shown here is the CIE D_{65} daylight illuminant.

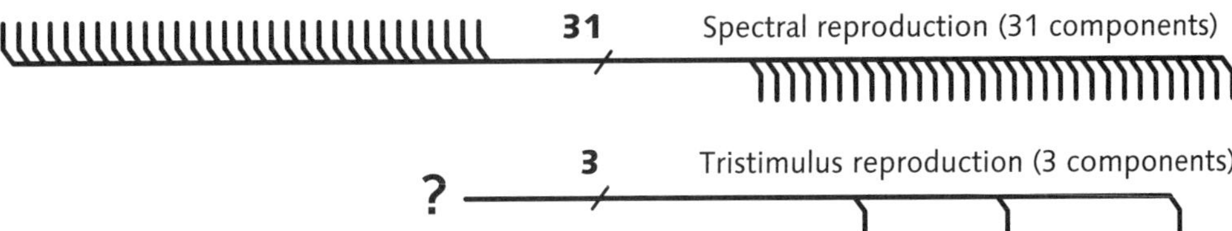

Spectral power distribution (SPD) and tristimulus

The more an SPD is concentrated near one wavelength, the more saturated the associated color will be. A color can be desaturated by adding light with power at all wavelengths.

The physical wavelength composition of light is expressed in a *spectral power distribution* (SPD, or *spectral radiance*). An SPD representative of daylight is graphed at the upper left of Figure 21.2 above.

One way to reproduce a color is to directly reproduce its spectral power distribution. This approach, termed *spectral reproduction*, is suitable for reproducing a single color or a few colors. For example, the visible range of wavelengths from 400 nm to 700 nm could be divided into 31 bands, each 10 nm wide. However, using 31 components for each pixel is an impractical way to code an image. Owing to the trichromatic nature of vision, if suitable spectral weighting functions are used, any color can be described by just three components. This is called *tristimulus reproduction*.

Strictly speaking, *colorimetry* refers to the measurement of color. In video, *colorimetry* is taken to encompass the transfer functions used to code linear *RGB* to *R'G'B'*, and the matrix that produces luma and color difference signals.

The science of *colorimetry* concerns the relationship between SPDs and color. In 1931, the Commission Internationale de L'Éclairage (CIE) standardized weighting curves for a hypothetical *Standard Observer.* These curves – graphed in Figure 21.4, on page 216 – specify how an SPD can be transformed into three *tristimulus values* that specify a color.

To specify a color, it is not necessary to specify its spectrum – it suffices to specify its tristimulus values. To reproduce a color, its spectrum need not be reproduced – it suffices to reproduce its tristimulus values. This is known as a *metameric* match. *Metamerism* is the property of two spectrally different stimuli having the same tristimulus values.

Pronounced *mehta-MAIR-ik* and *meh-TAM-er-ism*.

The colors produced in reflective systems – such as photography, printing, or paint – depend not only upon the colorants and the substrate (media), but also on the SPD of the illumination. To guarantee that two colored materials will match under illuminants having different SPDs, you may have to achieve a spectral match.

Scanner spectral constraints

The relationship between spectral distributions and the three components of a color value is usually explained starting from the famous color-matching experiment. I will instead explain the relationship by illustrating the practical concerns of engineering the spectral filters required by a color scanner or camera, using Figure 21.3 opposite.

For a textbook lowpass filter, see Figure 16.23 on page 162.

The top row shows the spectral sensitivity of three wideband optical filters having uniform response across each of the longwave, mediumwave, and shortwave regions of the spectrum. Most filters, whether for electrical signals or for optical power, are designed to have responses as uniform as possible across the passband, to have transition zones as narrow as possible, and to have maximum possible attenuation in the stopbands.

At the top left of Figure 21.3, I show two monochromatic sources, which appear saturated orange and red, analyzed by "textbook" bandpass filters. These two different wavelength distributions, which are seen as different colors, report the identical *RGB* triple [1, 0, 0]. The two SPDs are perceived as having different colors; however, this filter set reports identical *RGB* values. The wideband filter set senses color incorrectly.

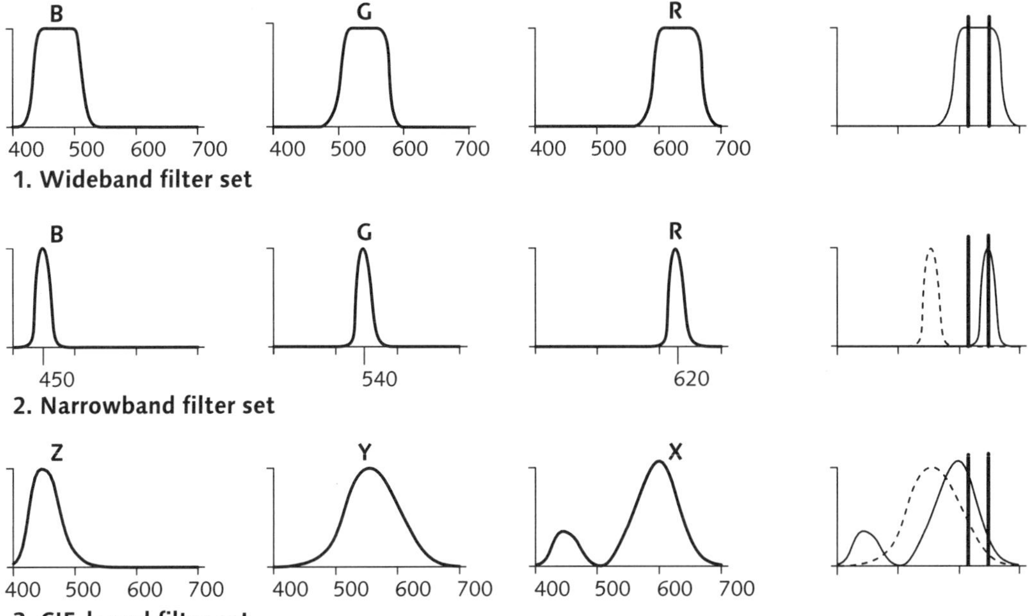

Figure 21.3 **Spectral constraints** are associated with scanners and cameras. **1. Wideband filter set** of the top row shows the spectral sensitivity of filters having uniform response across the shortwave, mediumwave, and longwave regions of the spectrum. Two monochromatic sources seen by the eye to have different colors – in this case, a saturated orange and a saturated red – cannot be distinguished by the filter set. **2. Narrowband filter set** in the middle row solves that problem, but creates another: Many monochromatic sources "fall between" the filters, and are sensed as black. To see color as the eye does, the filter responses must closely relate to the color response of the eye. **3. CIE-based filter set** in the bottom row shows the *color-matching functions* (CMFs) of the CIE Standard Observer.

At first glance it may seem that the problem with the wideband filters is insufficient wavelength discrimination. The middle row of the example attempts to solve that problem by using three narrowband filters. The narrowband set solves one problem, but creates another: Many monochromatic sources "fall between" the filters. Here, the orange source reports an *RGB* triple of [0, 0, 0], identical to the result of scanning black.

Although my example is contrived, the problem is not. Ultimately, the test of whether a camera or scanner is successful is whether it reports distinct *RGB* triples if and only if human vision sees two SPDs as being

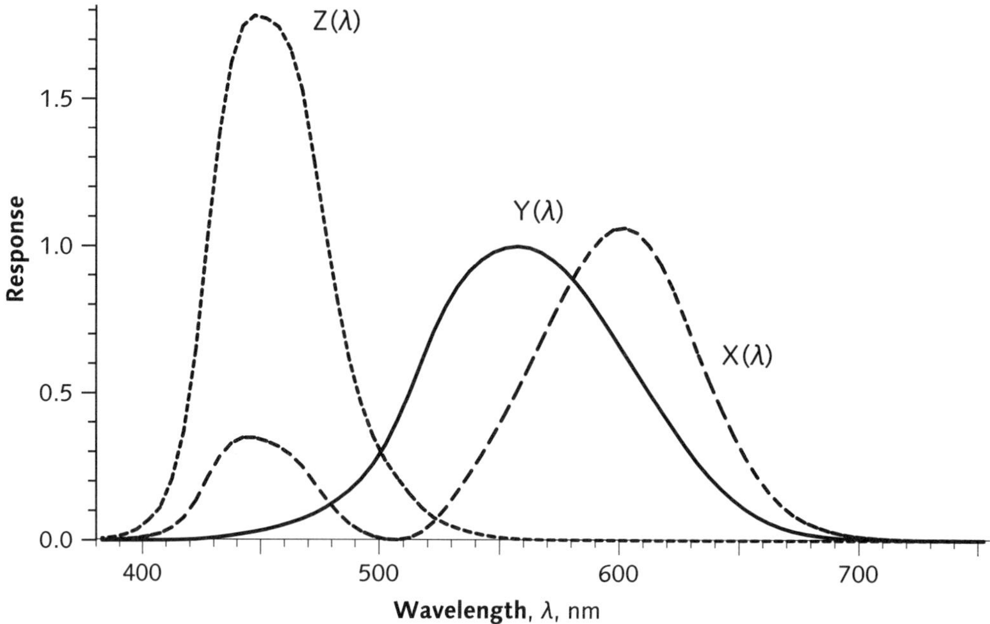

Figure 21.4 **CIE 1931, 2° color-matching functions.** A camera with 3 sensors must have these spectral response curves, or linear combinations of them, in order to capture all colors. However, practical considerations make this difficult. These analysis functions are *not* comparable to spectral power distributions!

different colors. For a scanner or a camera to see color as the eye does, the filter sensitivity curves must be intimately related to the response of human vision.

CIE Nº 15.2, *Colorimetry*, Second Edition (Vienna, Austria: Commission Internationale de L'Éclairage, 1986); reprinted with corrections in 1996.

In CIE Nº 15.2, color matching functions are denoted $\bar{x}(\lambda)$, $\bar{y}(\lambda)$, and $\bar{z}(\lambda)$ [pronounced *ECKS-bar, WYE-bar, ZEE-bar*]. CIE Nº 15.3 is in draft status, and I have adopted its new notation $X(\lambda)$, $Y(\lambda)$, and $Z(\lambda)$.

Some authors refer to CMFs as *color mixture curves*, or CMCs. That usage is best avoided, because CMC denotes a particular color difference formula defined in British Standard BS:6923.

The famous "color-matching experiment" was devised during the 1920s to characterize the relationship between physical spectra and perceived color. The experiment measures mixtures of different spectral distributions that are required for human observers to match colors. From statistics obtained from experiments involving observers participating in these experiments, in 1931 the CIE standardized a set of spectral weighting functions that models the perception of color.

These curves are called the $X(\lambda)$, $Y(\lambda)$, and $Z(\lambda)$ *color-matching functions* (CMFs) for the CIE Standard Observer. They are illustrated at the bottom of Figure 21.3, and are graphed at a larger scale in Figure 21.4 above. They are defined numerically; they are everywhere nonnegative.

The CIE 1931 functions are appropriate to estimate the visual response to stimuli subtending angles of about 2° at the eye. In 1964, the CIE standardized a set of CMFs suitable for stimuli subtending about 10°; this set is generally unsuitable for image reproduction.

The term *sharpening* is used in the color science community to describe certain 3×3 transforms of cone fundamentals. This terminology is unfortunate, because in image science, *sharpening* refers to spatial phenomena.

The functions of the CIE Standard Observer were standardized based upon experiments with visual color matching. Research since then revealed the spectral absorbance of the three types of cone cells – the *cone fundamentals*. We would expect the CIE CMFs to be intimately related to the properties of the retinal photoreceptors; many experimenters have related the cone fundamentals to CIE tristimulus values through 3×3 linear matrix transforms. None of the proposed mappings is very accurate, apparently owing to the intervention of high-level visual processing. For engineering purposes, the CIE functions suffice.

The $Y(\lambda)$ and $Z(\lambda)$ CMFs each have one peak – they are "unimodal." However, the $X(\lambda)$ CMF has a secondary peak, between 400 nm and 500 nm. This does not directly reflect any property of the retinal response; instead, it is a consequence of the mathematical process by which the $X(\lambda)$, $Y(\lambda)$, and $Z(\lambda)$ curves are constructed.

CIE *XYZ* tristimulus

X, *Y*, and *Z* are pronounced *big-X*, *big-Y*, and *big-Z*, or *cap-X*, *cap-Y*, and *cap-Z*, to distinguish them from little *x* and little *y*, to be described in a moment.

Weighting an SPD under the $Y(\lambda)$ color-matching function yields luminance (symbol Y), as I described on page 205. When luminance is augmented with two other values, computed in the same manner as luminance but using the $X(\lambda)$ and $Z(\lambda)$ color-matching functions, the resulting values are known as *XYZ tristimulus* values (denoted X, Y, and Z). *XYZ* values correlate to the spectral sensitivity of human vision. Their amplitudes – always positive – are proportional to intensity.

Tristimulus values are computed from a continuous SPD by integrating the SPD under the $X(\lambda)$, $Y(\lambda)$, and $Z(\lambda)$ color-matching functions. In discrete form, tristimulus values are computed by a matrix multiplication, as illustrated in Figure 21.5 overleaf.

$$
\begin{bmatrix} X \\ Y \\ Z \end{bmatrix} =
\begin{bmatrix}
0.0143 & 0.0004 & 0.0679 \\
0.0435 & 0.0012 & 0.2074 \\
0.1344 & 0.0040 & 0.6456 \\
0.2839 & 0.0116 & 1.3856 \\
0.3483 & 0.0230 & 1.7471 \\
0.3362 & 0.0380 & 1.7721 \\
0.2908 & 0.0600 & 1.6692 \\
0.1954 & 0.0910 & 1.2876 \\
0.0956 & 0.1390 & 0.8130 \\
0.0320 & 0.2080 & 0.4652 \\
0.0049 & 0.3230 & 0.2720 \\
0.0093 & 0.5030 & 0.1582 \\
0.0633 & 0.7100 & 0.0782 \\
0.1655 & 0.8620 & 0.0422 \\
0.2904 & 0.9540 & 0.0203 \\
0.4334 & 0.9950 & 0.0087 \\
0.5945 & 0.9950 & 0.0039 \\
0.7621 & 0.9520 & 0.0021 \\
0.9163 & 0.8700 & 0.0017 \\
1.0263 & 0.7570 & 0.0011 \\
1.0622 & 0.6310 & 0.0008 \\
1.0026 & 0.5030 & 0.0003 \\
0.8544 & 0.3810 & 0.0002 \\
0.6424 & 0.2650 & 0.0000 \\
0.4479 & 0.1750 & 0.0000 \\
0.2835 & 0.1070 & 0.0000 \\
0.1649 & 0.0610 & 0.0000 \\
0.0874 & 0.0320 & 0.0000 \\
0.0468 & 0.0170 & 0.0000 \\
0.0227 & 0.0082 & 0.0000 \\
0.0114 & 0.0041 & 0.0000
\end{bmatrix}^{\mathbf{T}}
\bullet
\begin{bmatrix}
82.75 \\ 91.49 \\ 93.43 \\ 86.68 \\ 104.86 \\ 117.01 \\ 117.81 \\ 114.86 \\ 115.92 \\ 108.81 \\ 109.35 \\ 107.80 \\ 104.79 \\ 107.69 \\ 104.41 \\ 104.05 \\ 100.00 \\ 96.33 \\ 95.79 \\ 88.69 \\ 90.01 \\ 89.60 \\ 87.70 \\ 83.29 \\ 83.70 \\ 80.03 \\ 80.21 \\ 82.28 \\ 78.28 \\ 69.72 \\ 71.61
\end{bmatrix}
\begin{matrix}
\text{400 nm} \\ \\ \\ \\ \\ \text{450 nm} \\ \\ \\ \\ \\ \text{500 nm} \\ \\ \\ \\ \\ \text{550 nm} \\ \\ \\ \\ \\ \text{600 nm} \\ \\ \\ \\ \\ \text{650 nm} \\ \\ \\ \\ \\ \text{700 nm}
\end{matrix}
$$

Figure 21.5 **Calculation of tristimulus values by matrix multiplication** starts with a column vector representing the SPD. The 31-element column vector in this example is a discrete version of CIE Illuminant D_{65}, at 10 nm intervals. The SPD is matrix-multiplied by a discrete version of the CIE $X(\lambda)$, $Y(\lambda)$, and $Z(\lambda)$ color-matching functions of Figure 21.4, here in a 31×3 matrix. The superscript **T** denotes the matrix transpose operation. The result of the matrix multiplication is a set of *XYZ* tristimulus components.

Grassmann's Third Law:

Sources of the same color produce identical effects in an additive mixture regardless of their spectral composition.

Human color vision follows a principle of superposition known as Grassmann's Third Law: The tristimulus values computed from the sum of a set of SPDs is identical to the sum of the tristimulus values of each SPD. Due to this linearity of additive color mixture, any set of three components that is a nontrivial linear combination of X, Y, and Z – such as R, G, and B – is also a set of tristimulus values. (In *Transformations between RGB and CIE XYZ,* on page 251, I will introduce related CMFs that produce R, G, and B tristimulus values.)

Thornton, William A., "Spectral Sensitivities of the Normal Human Visual System, Color-Matching Functions and Their Principles, and How and Why the Two Sets Should Coincide," in *Color Research and Application* 24 (2): 139–156 (April 1999).

This chapter accepts the CIE Standard Observer rather uncritically. Although the CIE Standard Observer is very useful and widely used, some researchers believe that it exhibits some problems and ought to be improved. For one well-informed and provocative view, see Thornton.

CIE [*x*, *y*] chromaticity

The x and y symbols are pronounced *little-x* and *little-y*.

It is convenient, for both conceptual understanding and for computation, to have a representation of "pure" color in the absence of lightness. The CIE standardized a procedure for normalizing XYZ tristimulus values to obtain two *chromaticity* values x and y.

Chromaticity values are computed by this projective transformation:

$$x = \frac{X}{X+Y+Z}; \qquad y = \frac{Y}{X+Y+Z} \qquad \text{Eq 21.1}$$

A third chromaticity coordinate, z, is defined, but is redundant since $x + y + z = 1$. The x and y chromaticity coordinates are abstract values that have no direct physical interpretation.

A color can be specified by its chromaticity and luminance, in the form of an xyY triple. To recover X and Z tristimulus values from [x, y] chromaticities and luminance, use the inverse of Equation 21.1:

$$X = \frac{x}{y}Y; \qquad Z = \frac{1-x-y}{y}Y \qquad \text{Eq 21.2}$$

A color plots as a point in an [x, y] *chromaticity diagram,* plotted in Figure 21.6 overleaf.

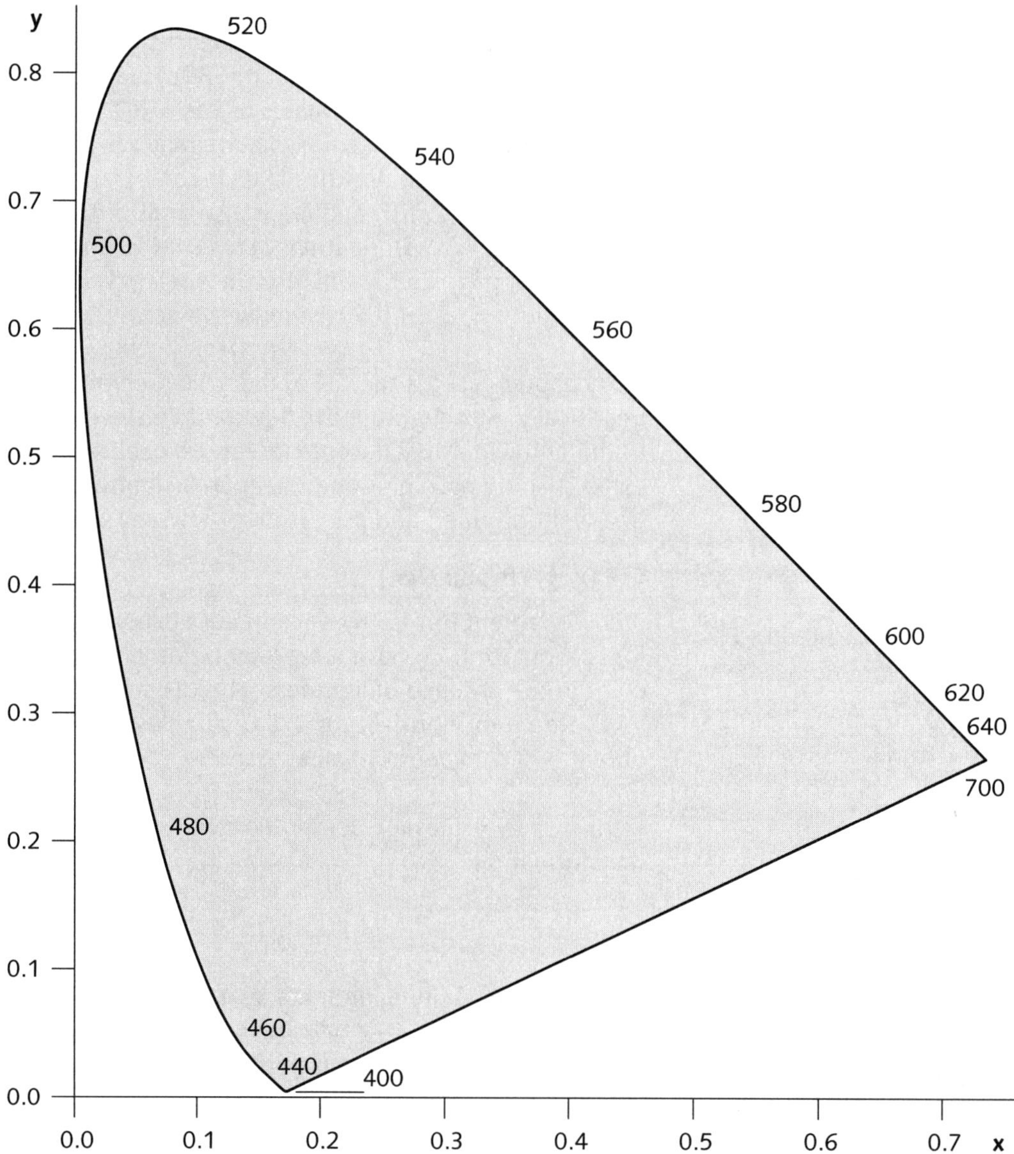

Figure 21.6 **CIE 1931 2° [x, y] chromaticity diagram.** The spectral locus is a shark-fin-shaped path swept by a monochromatic source as it is tuned from 400 nm to 700 nm. The set of all colors is closed by the *line of purples,* which traces SPDs that combine longwave and shortwave power but have no mediumwave power. All colors lie within the shark-fin-shaped region: Points outside this region are not colors.

This diagram is not a slice through [*X*, *Y*, *Z*] space! Instead, points in [*X*, *Y*, *Z*] project onto the plane of the diagram in a manner comparable to the perspective projection. White has [*X*, *Y*, *Z*] values near [1, 1, 1]; it projects to a point near the center of the diagram, in the region of [⅓, ⅓]. Attempting to project black, at [0, 0, 0], would require dividing by zero: Black has no place in this diagram.

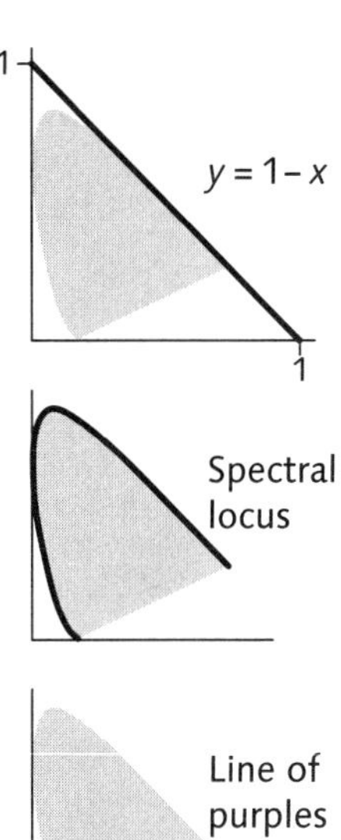

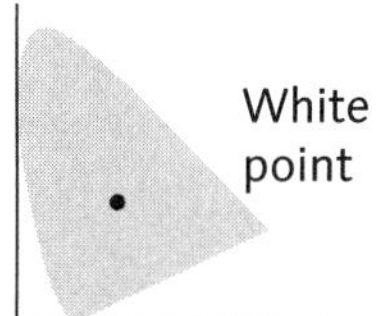

Figure 21.7 **CIE [x, y] chart features**

In Figure 21.7 in the margin, I sketch several features of the [*x*, *y*] diagram. The important features lie on, or below and to the left, of the line $y = 1 - x$.

When a narrowband (monochromatic) SPD comprising power at just one wavelength is swept across the range 400 nm to 700 nm, it traces the inverted-U-shaped *spectral locus* in [*x*, *y*] coordinates.

The sensation of purple cannot be produced by a single wavelength; it requires a mixture of shortwave and longwave light. The *line of purples* on a chromaticity diagram joins the chromaticity of extreme blue (violet), containing only shortwave power, to the chromaticity of extreme red, containing only longwave power.

There is no unique physical or perceptual definition of white. Many important sources of illumination are blackbody radiators, whose chromaticity coordinates lie on the *blackbody locus* (sometimes called the *Plankian locus*). The SPDs of blackbody radiators will be discussed in the next section.

An SPD that appears white has CIE [*X*, *Y*, *Z*] values of about [1, 1, 1], and [*x*, *y*] coordinates in the region of [$\frac{1}{3}$, $\frac{1}{3}$]: White plots in the central area of the chromaticity diagram. In the section *White*, on page 223, I will describe the SPDs associated with white.

Any all-positive (*physical*, or *realizable*) SPD plots as a single point in the chromaticity diagram, within the region bounded by the spectral locus and the line of purples. All colors lie within this region; points outside this region are not associated with colors. It is silly to qualify "color" by "visible," because color is itself defined by vision – if it's invisible, it's not a color!

In the projective transformation that forms *x* and *y*, any additive mixture (linear combination) of two SPDs – or two tristimulus values – plots on a straight line in the [*x*, *y*] plane. However, distances are not preserved, so chromaticity values do not combine linearly. Neither [*X*, *Y*, *Z*] nor [*x*, *y*] coordinates are perceptually uniform.

Figure 21.8 **SPDs of blackbody radiators** at several temperatures are graphed here. As the temperature increases, the absolute power increases and the peak of the spectral distribution shifts toward shorter wavelengths.

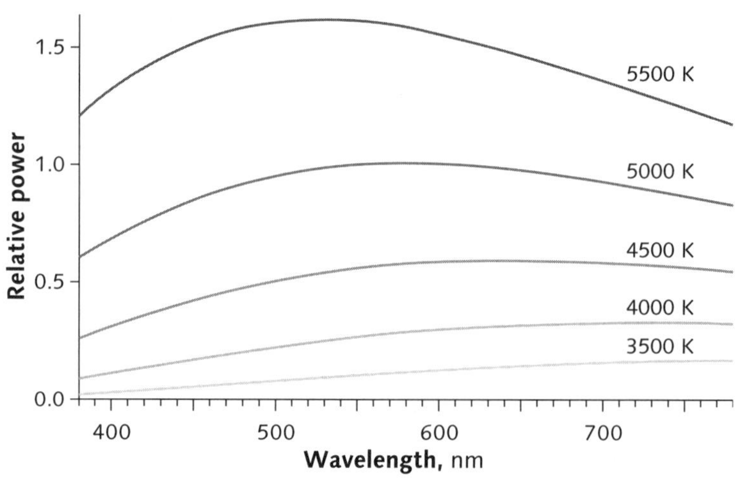

Blackbody radiation

Max Planck determined that the SPD radiated from a hot object – a *blackbody radiator* – is a function of the temperature to which the object is heated. Figure 21.8 above shows the SPDs of blackbody radiators at several temperatures. As temperature increases, the absolute power increases and the spectral peak shifts toward shorter wavelengths. If the power of blackbody radiators is normalized at an arbitrary wavelength, dramatic differences in spectral character become evident, as illustrated in Figure 21.9 opposite.

The symbol for Kelvin is properly written *K* (with no degree sign).

Many sources of illumination have, at their core, a heated object, so it is useful to characterize an illuminant by specifying the absolute temperature (in units of kelvin, K) of a blackbody radiator having the same hue.

The *blackbody locus* is the path traced in [*x*, *y*] coordinates as the temperature of a blackbody source is raised. At low temperature, the source appears red ("red hot"). When a viewer is adapted to a white reference of CIE D_{65}, which I will describe in a moment, at about 2000 K, the source appears orange. Near 4000 K, it appears yellow; at about 6000 K, white. Above 10000 K, it is blue-hot.

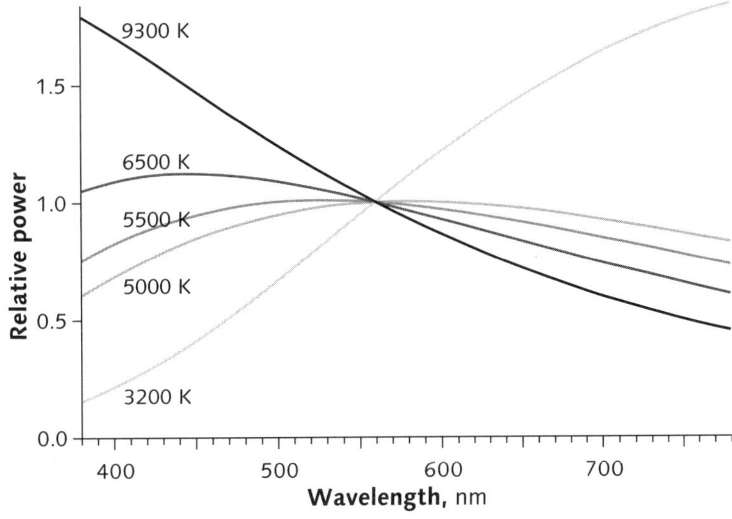

Figure 21.9 **SPDs of blackbody radiators, normalized** to equal power at 555 nm, are graphed here. The dramatically different spectral character of blackbody radiators at different temperatures is evident.

Color temperature

An illuminant may be specified by a single color temperature number, also known as *correlated color temperature* (CCT). However, it takes two numbers to specify chromaticity! To address this deficiency, color temperature is sometimes augmented by a second number giving the closest distance in the deprecated CIE 1960 [*u*, *v*] coordinates of the color from the blackbody locus – the arcane "minimum perceptible color difference" (MPCD) units. It is more sensible to directly specify [*x*, *y*] or [*u*′, *v*′] chromaticity coordinates.

The 1960 [*u*, *v*] coordinates are described in the marginal note on page 226.

White

As I mentioned a moment ago, there is no unique definition of white: To achieve accurate color, you must specify the SPD or the chromaticity of white. In additive mixture, to be detailed on page 234, the *white point* is the set of tristimulus values (or the luminance and chromaticity coordinates) of the color reproduced by equal contributions of the red, green, and blue primaries. The color of white is a function of the ratio – or *balance* – of power among the primary components. (In subtractive reproduction, the color of white is determined by the SPD of the illumination, multiplied by the SPD of the uncolored media.)

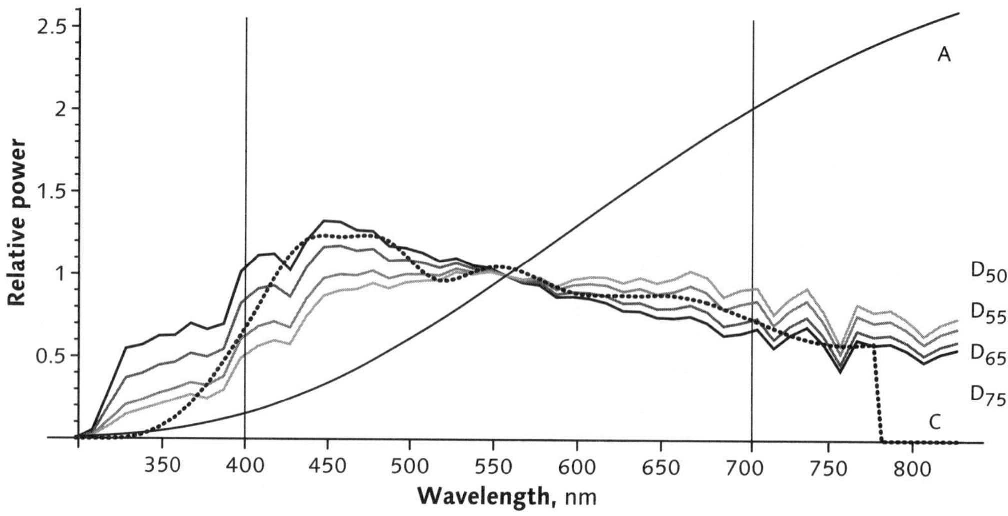

Figure 21.10 **CIE illuminants** are graphed here. Illuminant A is an obsolete standard representative of tungsten illumination; its SPD resembles the blackbody radiator at 3200 K shown in Figure 21.9, on page 223. Illuminant C was an early standard for daylight; it too is obsolete. The family of D illuminants represents daylight at several color temperatures.

It is sometimes convenient for purposes of calculation to define white as an SPD whose power is uniform throughout the visible spectrum. This white reference is known as the *equal-energy illuminant*, denoted *CIE Illuminant E;* its CIE [x, y] coordinates are [$\frac{1}{3}$, $\frac{1}{3}$].

The CIE D illuminants are properly denoted with a two-digit subscript. CIE Illuminant D_{65} has a correlated color temperature of about 6504 K.

A more realistic reference, approximating daylight, has been numerically specified by the CIE as Illuminant D_{65}. You should use this unless you have a good reason to use something else. The print industry commonly uses D_{50} and photography commonly uses D_{55}; these represent compromises between the conditions of indoor (tungsten) and daylight viewing. Figure 21.10 above shows the SPDs of several standard illuminants; chromaticity coordinates are given in Table 21.1 opposite.

Concerning 9300 K, see page 254.

Many computer monitors and many consumer television receivers have a default color temperature setting of 9300 K. That white reference contains too much blue to achieve acceptable image reproduction in Europe or America. However, there is a cultural preference in Asia for a more bluish reproduction than D_{65}; 9300 K is common in Asia (e.g., in studio monitors in Japan).

Tungsten illumination can't have a color temperature higher than tungsten's melting point, 3680 K.

Human vision adapts to the viewing environment. An image viewed in isolation – such as a 35 mm slide, or motion picture film projected in a dark room – creates its own white reference; a viewer will be quite tolerant of variation in white point. However, if the same image is viewed alongside an external white reference, or with a second image, differences in white point can be objectionable. Complete adaptation seems to be confined to color temperatures from about 5000 K to 6500 K. Tungsten illumination, at about 3200 K, almost always appears somewhat yellow.

Table 21.1 enumerates the chromaticity coordinates of several common white references:

Notation	x	y	z	u'_n	v'_n
CIE Ill. A (obsolete)	0.4476	0.4074	0.1450	0.2560	0.5243
CIE Ill. B (obsolete)	0.3484	0.3516	0.3000	0.2137	0.4852
CIE Ill. C (obsolete)	0.3101	0.3162	0.3737	0.2009	0.4609
CIE Ill. D_{50}	0.3457	0.3587	0.2956	0.2091	0.4882
CIE Ill. D_{55}	0.3325	0.3476	0.3199	0.2044	0.4801
CIE Ill. D_{65}	0.312727	0.329024	0.358250	0.1978	0.4683
CIE Ill. E (equi-energy)	0.333334	0.333330	0.333336	0.2105	0.4737
9300 K (discouraged, but used in studio standards in Japan)	0.283	0.298	0.419	0.1884	0.4463

Table 21.1 **White references**

Perceptually uniform color spaces

As I outlined in *Perceptual uniformity,* on page 21, a system is perceptually uniform if a small perturbation to a component value is approximately equally perceptible across the range of that value.

Luminance is not perceptually uniform. On page 208, I described how luminance can be transformed to lightness, denoted L^*, which is nearly perceptually uniform:

$$L^* = \begin{cases} 903.3\dfrac{Y}{Y_n}; & \dfrac{Y}{Y_n} \le 0.008856 \\ 116\left(\dfrac{Y}{Y_n}\right)^{\frac{1}{3}} - 16; & 0.008856 < \dfrac{Y}{Y_n} \end{cases} \qquad \text{Eq 21.3}$$

$L^*u^*v^*$ and $L^*a^*b^*$ are sometimes written CIELUV and CIELAB; they are pronounced *SEA-love* and *SEA-lab*. The u^* and v^* quantities of color science – and the u' and v' quantities, to be described – are unrelated to the U and V color difference components of video.

Extending this concept to color, *XYZ* and *RGB* tristimulus values, and *xyY* (chromaticity and luminance), are far from perceptually uniform. Finding a transformation of *XYZ* into a reasonably perceptually uniform space occupied the CIE for a decade, and in the end no single system could be agreed upon. In 1976, the CIE standardized two systems, $L^*u^*v^*$ and $L^*a^*b^*$, which I will now describe.

CIE $L^*u^*v^*$

Computation of CIE $L^*u^*v^*$ involves a projective transformation of $[X, Y, Z]$ into intermediate u' and v' quantities:

$$u' = \frac{4\,X}{X + 15\,Y + 3\,Z}; \qquad v' = \frac{9\,Y}{X + 15\,Y + 3\,Z} \qquad \text{Eq 21.4}$$

Equivalently, u' and v' can be computed from x and y chromaticity:

$$u' = \frac{4\,x}{3 - 2\,x + 12\,y}; \qquad v' = \frac{9\,y}{3 - 2\,x + 12\,y} \qquad \text{Eq 21.5}$$

The primes in the CIE 1976 u' and v' quantities denote the successor to the obsolete 1960 CIE u and v quantities. $u = u'$; $v = \frac{2}{3}v'$. The primes are not formally related to the primes in R', G', B', and Y', though all imply some degree of perceptual uniformity.

Since u' and v' are formed by a projective transformation, u' and v' coordinates are associated with a chromaticity diagram similar to the *CIE 1931 2° [x, y] chromaticity diagram* on page 220. You should use the $[u', v']$ diagram if your plots are intended to be suggestive of perceptible differences.

To recover X and Z tristimulus values from u' and v', use these relations:

$$X = \frac{9u'}{4v'}Y; \qquad Z = \frac{12 - 3u' - 20v'}{4v'}Y \qquad \text{Eq 21.6}$$

To recover x and y chromaticity from u' and v', use these relations:

$$x = \frac{9u'}{6u' - 16v' + 12}; \qquad y = \frac{4v'}{6u' - 16v' + 12} \qquad \text{Eq 21.7}$$

To compute u^* and v^*, first compute L^*. Then compute u'_n and v'_n from your reference white X_n, Y_n, and Z_n. (The subscript n suggests *normalized*.) The u'_n and v'_n coordinates for several common white points are given in Table 21.1, *White references,* on page 225. Finally, compute u^* and v^*:

$$u^* = 13L^*\left(u' - u'_n\right); \qquad v^* = 13L^*\left(v' - v'_n\right) \qquad \text{Eq 21.8}$$

For gamuts typical of image reproduction, each u^* and v^* value ranges approximately ±100.

ΔE^* is pronounced *DELTA E-star*.

Euclidean distance in $L^*u^*v^*$ – denoted ΔE^*_{uv} – is taken to measure perceptibility of color differences:

$$\Delta E^*_{uv} = \sqrt{\left(L^*_2 - L^*_1\right)^2 + \left(u^*_2 - u^*_1\right)^2 + \left(v^*_2 - v^*_1\right)^2} \qquad \text{Eq 21.9}$$

If ΔE^*_{uv} is unity or less, the color difference is taken to be imperceptible. However, $L^*u^*v^*$ does not achieve perceptual uniformity, it is merely an approximation. ΔE^*_{uv} values between about 1 and 4 may or may not be perceptible, depending upon the region of color space being examined. ΔE^*_{uv} values greater than 4 are likely to be perceptible; whether such differences are objectionable depends upon circumstances.

A polar-coordinate version of the $[u^*, v^*]$ pair can be used to express chroma and hue:

$$C^*_{uv} = \sqrt{u^{*2} + v^{*2}}; \qquad h_{uv} = \tan^{-1}\frac{v^*}{u^*} \qquad \text{Eq 21.10}$$

In addition, there is a "psychometric saturation" term:

$$s_{uv} = \frac{C^*}{L^*} \qquad \text{Eq 21.11}$$

Chroma, hue, and saturation defined here are not directly related to saturation and hue in the *HSB, HSI, HSL, HSV, and IHS* systems used in computing and in digital image processing: Most of the published descriptions of these spaces, and most of the published formulae, disregard the principles of color science. In particular, the quantities called *lightness* and *value* are wildly inconsistent with their definitions in color science.

CIE $L^*a^*b^*$

Providing that all of X/X_n, Y/Y_n, and Z/Z_n are greater than 0.008856, a^* and b^* are computed as follows:

Eq 21.12

$$a^* = 500\left[\left(\frac{X}{X_n}\right)^{\frac{1}{3}} - \left(\frac{Y}{Y_n}\right)^{\frac{1}{3}}\right]; \qquad b^* = 200\left[\left(\frac{Y}{Y_n}\right)^{\frac{1}{3}} - \left(\frac{Z}{Z_n}\right)^{\frac{1}{3}}\right]$$

As in the L^* definition, the transfer function incorporates a linear segment. For any quantity X/X_n, Y/Y_n, or Z/Z_n that is 0.008856 or smaller, denote that quantity t, and instead of the cube root, use this quantity:

Eq 21.13

$$7.787t + \frac{16}{116}$$

For details, consult CIE Publication Nº 15.2, cited in the margin of page 216.

As in $L^*u^*v^*$, one unit of Euclidean distance in $L^*a^*b^*$ – denoted ΔE^*_{ab} – approximates the perceptibility of color differences:

Eq 21.14

$$\Delta E^*_{ab} = \sqrt{\left(L^*_2 - L^*_1\right)^2 + \left(a^*_2 - a^*_1\right)^2 + \left(b^*_2 - b^*_1\right)^2}$$

If ΔE^*_{ab} is unity or less, the color difference is taken to be imperceptible. However, $L^*a^*b^*$ does not achieve perceptual uniformity: It is merely an approximation.

A polar-coordinate version of the [a^*, b^*] pair can be used to express chroma and hue:

Eq 21.15

$$C^*_{ab} = \sqrt{a^{*2} + b^{*2}}; \qquad h_{ab} = \tan^{-1}\frac{b^*}{a^*}$$

The equations that form a^* and b^* coordinates are not projective transformations; straight lines in [x, y] do not transform to straight lines in [a^*, b^*]. [a^*, b^*] coordinates can be plotted in two dimensions, but such a plot is not a chromaticity diagram.

CIE $L^*u^*v^*$ and CIE $L^*a^*b^*$ summary

Both $L^*u^*v^*$ and $L^*a^*b^*$ improve the 80:1 or so perceptual nonuniformity of XYZ to about 6:1. Both systems transform tristimulus values into a lightness component ranging from 0 to 100, and two color components ranging approximately ±100. One unit of Euclidean distance in $L^*u^*v^*$ or $L^*a^*b^*$ corresponds roughly to a just-noticeable difference (JND) of color.

McCamy argues that under normal conditions 1,875,000 colors can be distinguished. See McCamy, C.S.,"On the Number of Discernable Colors," in *Color Research and Application*, 23 (5): 337 (Oct. 1998).

Consider that L^* ranges 0 to 100, and each of u^* and v^* range approximately ±100. A threshold of unity ΔE^*_{uv} defines four million colors. About one million colors can be distinguished by vision, so CIE $L^*u^*v^*$ is somewhat conservative. A million colors – or even the four million colors identified using a ΔE^*_{uv} or ΔE^*_{ab} threshold of unity – are well within the capacity of the 16.7 million colors available in a 24-bit truecolor system that uses perceptually appropriate transfer functions, such as the function of Rec. 709. (However, 24 bits per pixel are far short of the number required for adequate performance with linear-light coding.)

The $L^*u^*v^*$ or $L^*a^*b^*$ systems are most useful in color specification. Both systems demand too much computation for economical realtime video processing, although both have been successfully applied to still image coding, particularly for printing. The complexity of the CIE $L^*u^*v^*$ and CIE $L^*a^*b^*$ calculations makes these systems generally unsuitable for image coding. The nonlinear $R'G'B'$ coding used in video is quite perceptually uniform, and has the advantage of being suitable for realtime processing. Keep in mind that $R'G'B'$ typically incorporates significant gamut limitation, whereas $L^*u^*v^*$ and CIE $L^*a^*b^*$ represent all colors. $L^*a^*b^*$ is sometimes used in desktop graphics with $[a^*, b^*]$ coordinates ranging from –128 to +127 (e.g., Photoshop). The ITU-T Rec. T.42 standard for color fax accommodates $L^*a^*b^*$ coding with a^* ranging $^-85$ to 85, and b^* ranging $^-75$ to 125. Even with these restrictions, CIE $L^*a^*b^*$ covers nearly all of the colors.

ITU-T Rec. T.42, *Continuous-tone colour representation for facsimile*.

Color specification

A color specification system needs to be able to represent any color with high precision. Since few colors are handled at a time, a specification system can be computationally complex. A system for color specification must be intimately related to the CIE system.

The systems useful for color specification are CIE XYZ and its derivatives xyY, $L^*u^*v^*$, and $L^*a^*b^*$.

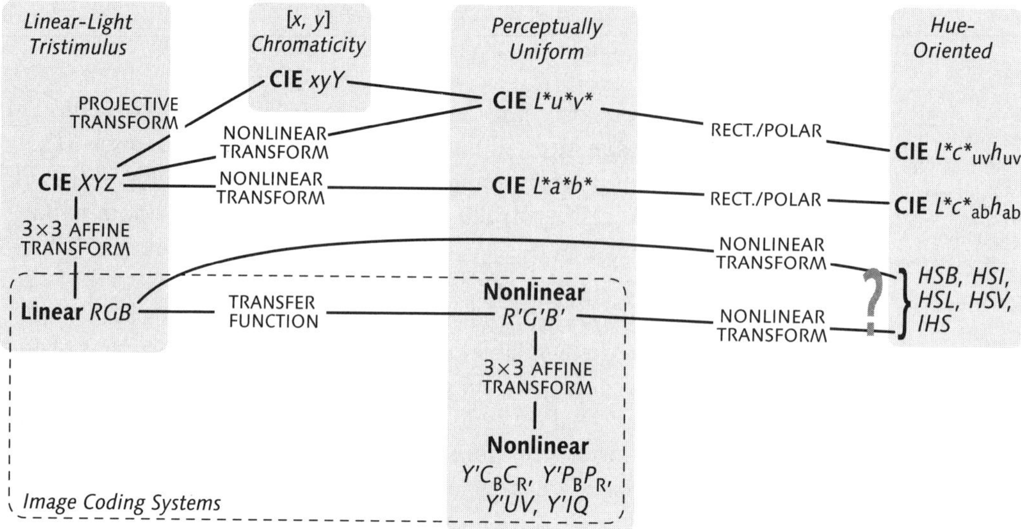

Figure 21.11 **Color systems** are classified into four groups that are related by different kinds of transformations. Tristimulus systems, and perceptually uniform systems, are useful for image coding. (I flag *HSB, HSI, HSL, HSV,* and *IHS* with a question mark: These systems lack objective definition of color.)

Color image coding

A color image is represented as an array of pixels, where each pixel contains three values that define a color. As you have learned in this chapter, three components are necessary and sufficient to define any color. (In printing it is convenient to add a fourth, black, component, giving CMYK.)

In theory, the three numerical values for image coding could be provided by a color specification system. However, a practical image coding system needs to be computationally efficient, cannot afford unlimited precision, need not be intimately related to the CIE system, and generally needs to cover only a reasonably wide range of colors and not all possible colors. So image coding uses different systems than color specification.

The systems useful for image coding are linear *RGB;* nonlinear *RGB* (usually denoted *R'G'B'*, and including sRGB); nonlinear *CMY;* nonlinear *CMYK;* and derivatives of *R'G'B'*, such as $Y'C_BC_R$ and $Y'P_BP_R$. These are summarized in Figure 21.11.

If you manufacture cars, you have to match the paint on the door with the paint on the fender; color specification will be necessary. You can afford quite a bit of computation, because there are only two colored elements, the door and the fender. To convey a picture of the car, you may have a million colored elements or more: Computation must be quite efficient, and an image coding system is called for.

Further reading

The bible of colorimetry is *Color Science*, by Wyszecki and Styles. But it's daunting. For a condensed version, read Judd and Wyszecki's *Color in Business, Science, and Industry*. It is directed to the color industry: ink, paint, and the like.

Wyszecki, Günter, and W.S. Styles, *Color Science: Concepts and Methods, Quantitative Data and Formulae*, Second Edition (New York: Wiley, 1982).

Judd, Deane B., and Günter Wyszecki, *Color in Business, Science, and Industry*, Third Edition (New York: Wiley, 1975).

For an approachable introduction to color theory, accompanied by practical descriptions of image reproduction, consult Hunt's classic work.

Hunt, R.W.G., *The Reproduction of Colour in Photography, Printing & Television*, Fifth Edition (Tolworth, England: Fountain Press, 1995).

Color science for video 22

Classical color science, explained in the previous chapter, establishes the basis for numerical description of color. But color science is intended for the *specification* of color, not for image coding. Although an understanding of color science is necessary to achieve good color performance in video, its strict application is impractical. This chapter explains the engineering compromises necessary to make practical cameras and practical coding systems.

Video processing is generally concerned with color represented in three components derived from the scene, usually red, green, and blue, or components computed from these. Accurate color reproduction depends on knowing exactly how the physical spectra of the original scene are transformed into these components, and exactly how the components are transformed to physical spectra at the display. These issues are the subject of this chapter.

Once red, green, and blue components of a scene are obtained, these components are transformed into other forms optimized for processing, recording, and transmission. This will be discussed in *Component video color coding for SDTV,* on page 301, and *Component video color coding for HDTV,* on page 313. (Unfortunately, color coding differs between SDTV and HDTV.)

The previous chapter explained how to analyze SPDs of scene elements into *XYZ* tristimulus values representing color. The obvious way to reproduce those colors is to arrange for the reproduction system to reproduce those *XYZ* values. That approach works in many applications of color reproduction, and it's the basis for color in video. However, in image reproduction, direct recreation of the *XYZ* values is unsuitable for perceptual reasons. Some modifications are necessary to achieve subjectively acceptable results. Those modifications were described in *Constant luminance*, on page 75.

Should you wish to skip this chapter, remember that accurate description of colors expressed in terms of *RGB* coordinates depends on the characterization of the *RGB* primaries and their power ratios (white reference). If your system is standardized to use a fixed set of primaries throughout, you need not be concerned about this; however, if your images use different primary sets, it is a vital issue.

Additive reproduction (*RGB*)

In the previous chapter, I explained how a physical SPD can be analyzed into three components that represent color. This section explains how those components can be mixed to reproduce color.

The simplest way to reproduce a range of colors is to mix the beams from three lights of different colors, as sketched in Figure 22.1 opposite. In physical terms, the spectra from each of the lights add together wavelength by wavelength to form the spectrum of the mixture. Physically and mathematically, the spectra add: The process is called *additive reproduction*.

If you are unfamiliar with the term *luminance*, or the symbols *Y* or *Y'*, refer to *Luminance and lightness*, on page 203.

I described Grassmann's Third Law on page 219: Color vision obeys a principle of superposition, whereby the color produced by any additive mixture of three primary SPDs can be predicted by adding the corresponding fractions of the *XYZ* tristimulus components of the primaries. The colors that can be formed from a particular set of *RGB* primaries are completely determined by the colors – tristimulus values, or luminance values and chromaticity coordinates – of the individual primaries. Subtractive reproduction, used in photography, cinema film, and commercial printing, is much more complicated: Colors in subtractive mixtures are

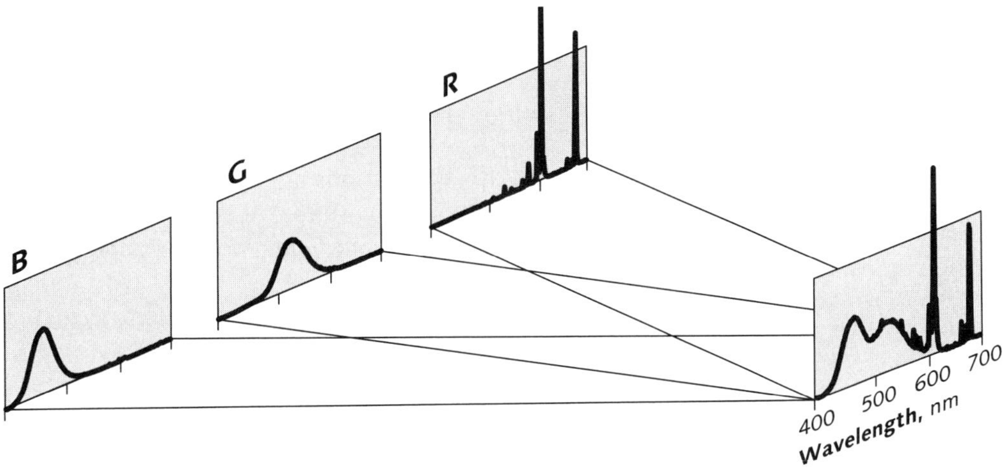

Figure 22.1 **Additive reproduction.** This diagram illustrates the physical process underlying additive color mixture, as is used in video. Each primary has an independent, direct path to the image. The spectral power of the image is the sum of the spectra of the primaries. The colors of the mixtures are completely determined by the colors of the primaries; analysis and prediction of mixtures is reasonably simple. The SPDs shown here are those of a Sony Trinitron monitor.

not determined by the *colors* of the individual primaries, but by their *spectral* properties.

Additive reproduction is employed directly in a video projector, where the spectra from a red beam, a green beam, and a blue beam are physically summed at the surface of the projection screen. Additive reproduction is also employed in a direct-view color CRT, but through slightly indirect means. The screen of a CRT comprises small phosphor dots (triads) that, when illuminated by their respective electron beams, produce red, green, and blue light. When the screen is viewed from a sufficient distance, the spectra of these dots add at the retina of the observer.

The widest range of colors will be produced with primaries that individually appear red, green, and blue. When color displays were exclusively CRTs, *RGB* systems were characterized by the chromaticities of their phosphors. To encompass newer devices that form colors without using phosphors, we refer to *primary chromaticities* rather than *phosphor chromaticities*.

Characterization of *RGB* primaries

An additive *RGB* system is specified by the chromaticities of its primaries and its white point. The extent – or *gamut* – of the colors that can be mixed from a given set of *RGB* primaries is given in the [*x*, *y*] chromaticity diagram by a triangle whose vertices are the chromaticities of the primaries. Figure 22.2 opposite plots the primaries of several contemporary video standards that I will describe.

In computing there are no standard primaries or white point chromaticities, though the sRGB standard is becoming increasingly widely used. (I will describe sRGB below, along with Rec. 709.) If you have *RGB* image but have no information about its primary chromaticities, you cannot accurately reproduce the image.

CIE *RGB* primaries

CIE standards established in 1964 were based upon monochromatic primaries at 444.4, 526.3, and 645.2 nm.

Color science researchers in the 1920s used monochromatic primaries – that is, primaries whose chromaticity coordinates lie on the spectral locus. The particular primaries that led to the CIE standard in 1931 became known as the *CIE primaries;* their wavelengths are 435.8 nm, 546.1 nm, and 700.0 nm, as documented in the CIE publication *Colorimetry* (cited on page 216). These primaries, ennumerated in Table 22.1, are historically important; however, they are not useful for image coding or image reproduction.

Table 22.1 **CIE primaries** were established for the CIE's color-matching experiments; they are unsuitable for image coding or reproduction.

	Red, 700.0 nm	*Green, 546.1 nm*	*Blue, 435.8 nm*	*White CIE Ill. B*
x	0.73469	0.27368	0.16654	0.34842
y	0.26531	0.71743	0.00888	0.35161
z	0	0.00890	0.82458	0.29997

NTSC primaries (obsolete)

In 1953, the NTSC standardized a set of primaries used in experimental color CRTs at that time. Those primaries and white reference are still documented in ITU-R Report 624. But phosphors changed over the years, primarily in response to market pressures for brighter receivers, and by the time of the first videotape recorder the primaries actually in use were quite

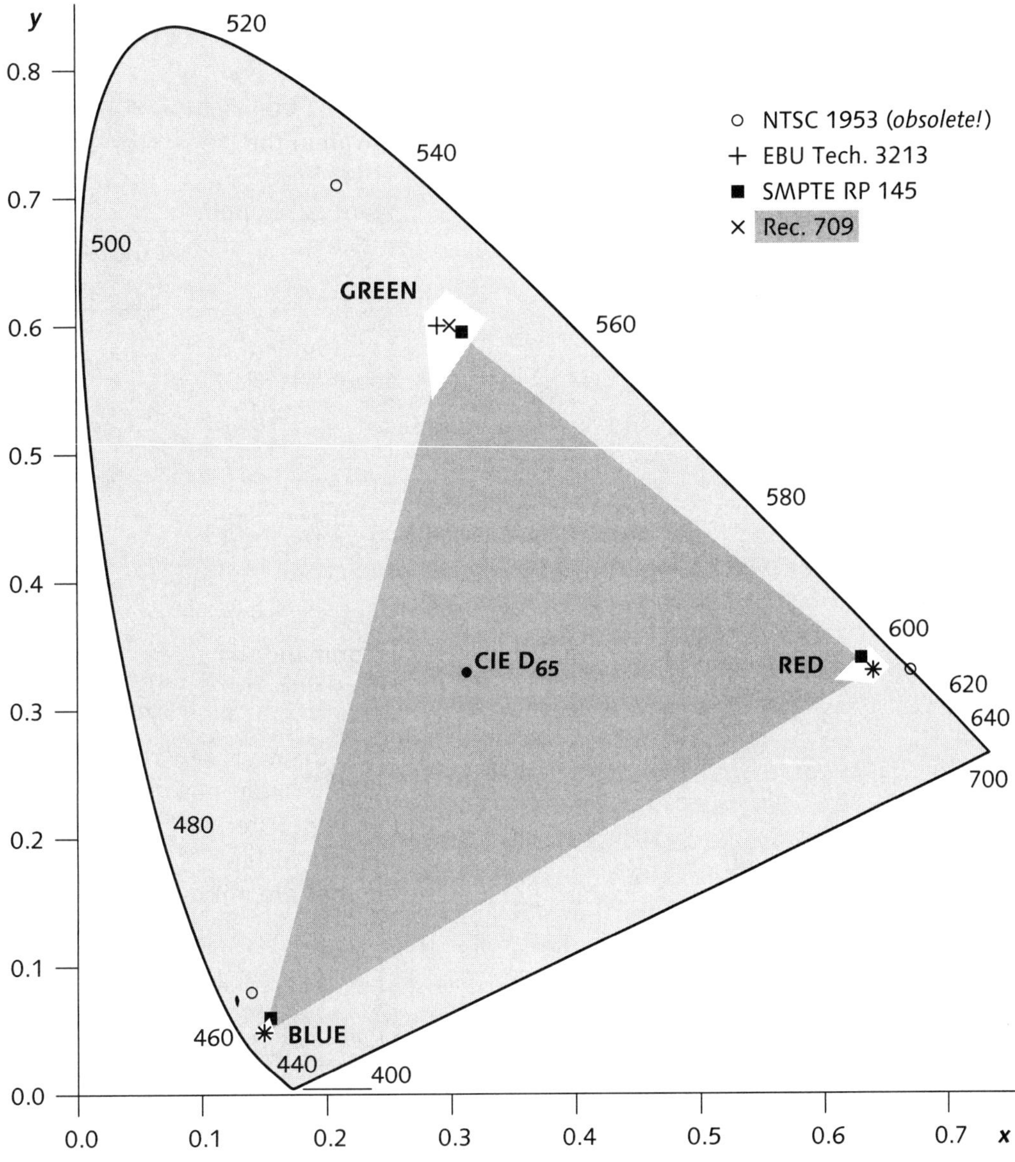

Figure 22.2 **Primaries of video standards** are plotted on the CIE 1931, 2° [*x*, *y*] chromaticity diagram. The colors that can be represented in positive *RGB* values lie within the triangle joining a set of primaries; here, the gray triangle encloses the Rec. 709 primaries. The Rec. 709 standard specifies no tolerance. SMPTE tolerances are specified as ±0.005 in *x* and *y*. EBU tolerances are shown as white quadrilaterals; they are specified in *u'*, *v'* coordinates related to the color discrimination of vision. The EBU tolerance boundaries are not parallel to the [*x*, *y*] axes.

different from those "on the books." So although you may see the NTSC primary chromaticities documented – even in contemporary textbooks, and in standards for image exchange! – they are of absolutely no practical use today. I include them in Table 22.2, so you'll know what primaries to avoid:

Table 22.2 **NTSC primaries (obsolete)** were once used in 480*i* SDTV systems, but have been superseded by SMPTE RP 145 and Rec. 709 primaries.

	Red	*Green*	*Blue*	*White CIE Ill. C*
x	0.67	0.21	0.14	0.310
y	0.33	0.71	0.08	0.316
z	0	0.08	0.78	0.374

The luma coefficients chosen for the NTSC system – 0.299, 0.587, and 0.114 – were chosen in 1953, based upon these primaries. Decades later, in 1984, these luma coefficients were standardized in Rec. 601 (described on page 291). Rec. 601 is silent concerning primary chromaticities. The primaries in use by 1984 were quite different from the 1953 NTSC primaries. The luma coefficients in use for SDTV are no longer matched to the primary chromaticities. The discrepancy has little practical significance.

EBU Tech. 3213 primaries

Phosphor technology improved considerably in the decade following the adoption of the NTSC standard. In 1966, the European Broadcasting Union (EBU) standardized 576*i* color video – then denoted 625/50, or just *PAL*. The primaries in Table 22.3 below are standardized by EBU Tech. 3213. They are in use today for 576*i* systems, and they are very close to the Rec. 709 primaries that I will describe in a moment:

EBU Tech. 3213, *EBU standard for chromaticity tolerances for studio monitors* (Geneva: European Broadcasting Union, 1975; reissued 1981).

Table 22.3 **EBU Tech. 3213 primaries** apply to 576*i* SDTV systems.

	Red	*Green*	*Blue*	*White*, D_{65}
x	0.640	0.290	0.150	0.3127
y	0.330	0.600	0.060	0.3290
z	0.030	0.110	0.790	0.3582

The EBU retained, for PAL, the well-established NTSC luma coefficients. Again, the fact that the underlying primaries had changed has little practical significance.

SMPTE RP 145, *SMPTE C Color Monitor Colorimetry.*

SMPTE RP 145 primaries

For 480*i* SDTV, the primaries of SMPTE RP 145 are standard, as specified in Table 22.4:

Table 22.4 **SMPTE RP 145 primaries** apply to 480*i* SDTV systems, and to early 1035*i*30 HDTV systems.

	Red	*Green*	*Blue*	*White*, D_{65}
x	0.630	0.310	0.155	0.3127
y	0.340	0.595	0.070	0.3290
z	0.030	0.095	0.775	0.3582

RP 145 primaries are specified in SMPTE 240M for 1035*i*30 HDTV, and were once included as the "interim implementation" provision of SMPTE standards for 1280×720, and 1920×1080 HDTV. The most recent revisions of SMPTE standards for 1280×720 and 1920×1080 have dropped provisions for the "interim implementation," and now specify only the Rec. 709 primaries, which I will now describe.

Rec. 709/sRGB primaries

ITU-R Rec. BT.709, *Basic parameter values for the HDTV standard for the studio and for international programme exchange.*

International agreement was obtained in 1990 on primaries for high-definition television (HDTV). The standard is formally denoted *Recommendation ITU-R BT.709* (formerly CCIR Rec. 709). I'll call it *Rec. 709*. Implausible though this sounds, the Rec. 709 chromaticities are a political compromise obtained by choosing EBU red, EBU blue, and a green which is the average (rounded to 2 digits) of EBU green and SMPTE green! These primaries are closely representative of contemporary monitors in studio video, computing, and computer graphics. The Rec. 709 primaries and its D_{65} white point are specified in Table 22.5:

Table 22.5 **Rec. 709 primaries** apply to 1280×720 and 1920×1080 HDTV systems; they are incorporated into the sRGB standard for desktop PCs.

	Red	*Green*	*Blue*	*White*, D_{65}
x	0.640	0.300	0.150	0.3127
y	0.330	0.600	0.060	0.3290
z	0.030	0.100	0.790	0.3582

Rec. 601 does not specify primary chromaticities. It is implicit that SMPTE RP 145 primaries are used with 480*i*, and that EBU 3213 primaries are used with 576*i*.

Video standards specify *RGB* chromaticities that are closely matched to practical monitors. Physical display devices involve tolerances and uncertainties, but if you have a monitor that conforms to Rec. 709 within some tolerance, you can think of the monitor as being device-independent.

IEC FDIS 61966-2-1, *Multimedia systems and equipment – Colour measurement and management – Part 2-1: Colour management – Default RGB colour space – sRGB.*

The Rec. 709 primaries are incorporated into the sRGB specification used in desktop computing. Beware that the sRGB transfer function is somewhat different from the transfer functions standardized for studio video.

The importance of Rec. 709 as an interchange standard in studio video, broadcast television, and HDTV, and the firm perceptual basis of the standard, assures that its parameters will be used even by such devices as flat-panel displays that do not have the same physics as CRTs. However, there is no doubt that emerging display technologies will soon offer a wider color gamut.

CMFs and SPDs

You might guess that you could implement a display whose primaries had spectral power distributions with the same shape as the CIE spectral analysis curves – the color-matching functions for *XYZ*. You could make such a display, but when driven by *XYZ* tristimulus values, it would not properly reproduce color. There are display primaries that reproduce color accurately when driven by *XYZ* tristimuli, but the SPDs of those primaries do not have the same shape as the $X(\lambda)$, $Y(\lambda)$, and $Z(\lambda)$ CMFs. To see why requires understanding a very subtle and important point about color reproduction.

To find a set of display primaries that reproduces color according to *XYZ* tristimulus values would require constructing three SPDs that, when analyzed by the $X(\lambda)$, $Y(\lambda)$, and $Z(\lambda)$ color-matching functions, produced [1, 0, 0], [0, 1, 0], and [0, 0, 1], respectively. The $X(\lambda)$, $Y(\lambda)$, and $Z(\lambda)$ CMFs are positive across the entire spectrum. Producing [0, 1, 0] would require positive contribution from some wavelengths in the required primary SPDs. We could arrange that; however, there is no wavelength that contributes to *Y* that does not also contribute positively to *X* or *Z*.

The solution to this dilemma is to force the *X* and *Z* contributions to zero by making the corresponding SPDs have negative power at certain wavelengths. Although this is not a problem for mathematics, or even for signal processing, an SPD with a negative portion is not physically realizable in a transducer for light, because light power cannot go negative. So we cannot build a real display that responds directly to *XYZ*. But as you will see, the concept of negative SPDs – and *nonphysical SPDs* or *nonrealizable primaries* – is very useful in theory and in practice.

To understand the mathematical details of color transforms, described in this section, you should be familiar with linear (matrix) algebra. If you are unfamiliar with linear algebra, see Strang, Gilbert, *Introduction to Linear Algebra*, Second Edition (Boston: Wellesley-Cambridge, 1998).

There are many ways to choose nonphysical primary SPDs that correspond to the $X(\lambda)$, $Y(\lambda)$, and $Z(\lambda)$ color-matching functions. One way is to arbitrarily choose three display primaries whose power is concentrated at three discrete wavelengths. Consider three display SPDs, each of which has some amount of power at 600 nm, 550 nm, and 470 nm. Sample the $X(\lambda)$, $Y(\lambda)$, and $Z(\lambda)$ functions of the matrix given earlier in *Calculation of tristimulus values by matrix multiplication,* on page 218, at those three wavelengths. This yields the tristimulus values shown in Table 22.6:

Table 22.6 **Example primaries** are used to explain the necessity of signal processing in accurate color reproduction.

	Red, 600 nm	*Green, 550 nm*	*Blue, 470 nm*
X	1.0622	0.4334	0.1954
Y	0.6310	0.9950	0.0910
Z	0.0008	0.0087	1.2876

These coefficients can be expressed as a matrix, where the column vectors give the *XYZ* tristimulus values corresponding to pure red, green, and blue at the display, that is, [1, 0, 0], [0, 1, 0], and [0, 0, 1]. It is conventional to apply a scale factor in such a matrix to cause the middle row to sum to unity, since we wish to achieve only relative matches, not absolute:

Eq 22.1 This matrix is based upon *R, G,* and *B* components with unusual spectral distributions. For typical *R, G,* and *B,* see Eq 22.8.

$$\begin{bmatrix} X \\ Y \\ Z \end{bmatrix} = \begin{bmatrix} 0.618637 & 0.252417 & 0.113803 \\ 0.367501 & 0.579499 & 0.052999 \\ 0.000466 & 0.005067 & 0.749913 \end{bmatrix} \bullet \begin{bmatrix} R_{600\,\mathrm{nm}} \\ G_{550\,\mathrm{nm}} \\ B_{470\,\mathrm{nm}} \end{bmatrix}$$

That matrix gives the transformation from *RGB* to *XYZ*. We are interested in the inverse transform, from *XYZ* to *RGB*, so invert the matrix:

Eq 22.2

$$\begin{bmatrix} R_{600\,\mathrm{nm}} \\ G_{550\,\mathrm{nm}} \\ B_{470\,\mathrm{nm}} \end{bmatrix} = \begin{bmatrix} 2.179151 & -0.946884 & -0.263777 \\ -1.382685 & 2.327499 & 0.045336 \\ 0.007989 & -0.015138 & 1.333346 \end{bmatrix} \bullet \begin{bmatrix} X \\ Y \\ Z \end{bmatrix}$$

The column vectors of the matrix in Equation 22.2 give, for each primary, the weights of each of the three discrete wavelengths that are required to display unit *XYZ* tristimulus values. The color-matching functions for CIE *XYZ* are shown in Figure 22.3, *CMFs for CIE XYZ primaries*, on page 244. Opposite those functions, in Figure 22.4, is the corresponding set of primary SPDs. As expected, the display primaries have some negative spectral components: The primary SPDs are nonphysical. Any set of primaries that reproduces color from *XYZ* tristimulus values is necessarily *supersaturated*, more saturated than any realizable SPD could be.

To determine a set of physical SPDs that will reproduce color when driven from *XYZ*, consider the problem in the other direction: Given a set of physically realizable display primaries, what CMFs are suitable to directly reproduce color using mixtures of these primaries? In this case the matrix that relates *RGB* components to CIE *XYZ* tristimulus values is all-positive, but the CMFs required for analysis of the scene have negative portions: The analysis filters are nonrealizable.

Michael Brill and R.W.G. Hunt argue that *R*, *G*, and *B* tristimulus values have no units. See Hunt, R.W.G., "The Heights of the CIE Colour-Matching Functions," in *Color Research and Application*, 22 (5): 337 (Oct. 1997).

Figure 22.6 shows a set of primary SPDs conformant to SMPTE 240M, similar to Rec. 709. Many different SPDs can produce an exact match to these chromaticities. The set shown is from a Sony Trinitron monitor. Figure 22.5 shows the corresponding color-matching functions. As expected, the CMFs have negative lobes and are therefore not directly realizable.

We conclude that we can use physically realizable analysis CMFs, as in the first example, where *XYZ* components are displayed directly. But this requires nonphysical display primary SPDs. Or we can use physical display primary SPDs, but this requires nonphysical analysis CMFs. As a consequence of the way color vision works, there is no set of nonnegative display primary SPDs that corresponds to an all-positive set of analysis functions.

The escape from this conundrum is to impose a 3×3 matrix multiplication in the processing of the camera signals, instead of using the camera signals to directly drive the display. Consider these display primaries: monochromatic red at 600 nm, monochromatic green at 550 nm, and monochromatic blue at 470 nm. The 3×3 matrix of Equation 22.2 can be used to process *XYZ* values into components suitable to drive that display. Such signal processing is not just desirable; it is a necessity for achieving accurate color reproduction!

A sensor element is a *photosite.*

Every color video camera or digital still camera needs to sense the image through three different spectral characteristics. Digital still cameras and consumer camcorders typically have a single area array CCD sensor ("one chip"); each 2×2 tile of the array has sensor elements covered by three different types of filter. Typically, filters appearing red, green, and blue are used; the green filter is duplicated onto two of the photosites in the 2×2 tile. This approach loses light, and therefore sensitivity. A studio video camera separates incoming light using dichroic filters operating as beam splitters; each component has a dedicated CCD sensor ("3 CCD"). Such an optical system separates different wavelength bands without absorbing any light, achieving high sensitivity.

In a "one-chip" camera, hardware or firmware performs spatial interpolation to reconstruct *R, G,* and *B* at each photosite. In a "three-chip" camera, the dichroic filters are mounted on one or two glass blocks. In optical engineering, a glass block is called a prism, but it is not the prism that separates the colors, it is the dichroic filters.

Figure 22.7 shows the set of spectral sensitivity functions implemented by the beam splitter and filter ("prism") assembly of an actual video camera. The functions are positive everywhere across the spectrum, so the filters are physically realizable. However, rather poor color reproduction will result if these signals are used directly to drive a display having Rec. 709 primaries. Figure 22.8 shows the same set of camera analysis functions processed through a 3×3 matrix transform. The transformed components will reproduce color more accurately – the more closely these curves resemble the ideal Rec. 709 CMFs of Figure 22.5, the more accurate the camera's color reproduction will be.

In theory, and in practice, using a linear matrix to process the camera signals can capture and reproduce *all* colors correctly. However, capturing all of the colors is seldom necessary in practice, as I will explain in the *Gamut* section below. Also, capturing the entire range of colors would incur a noise penalty, as I will describe in *Noise due to matrixing,* on page 252.

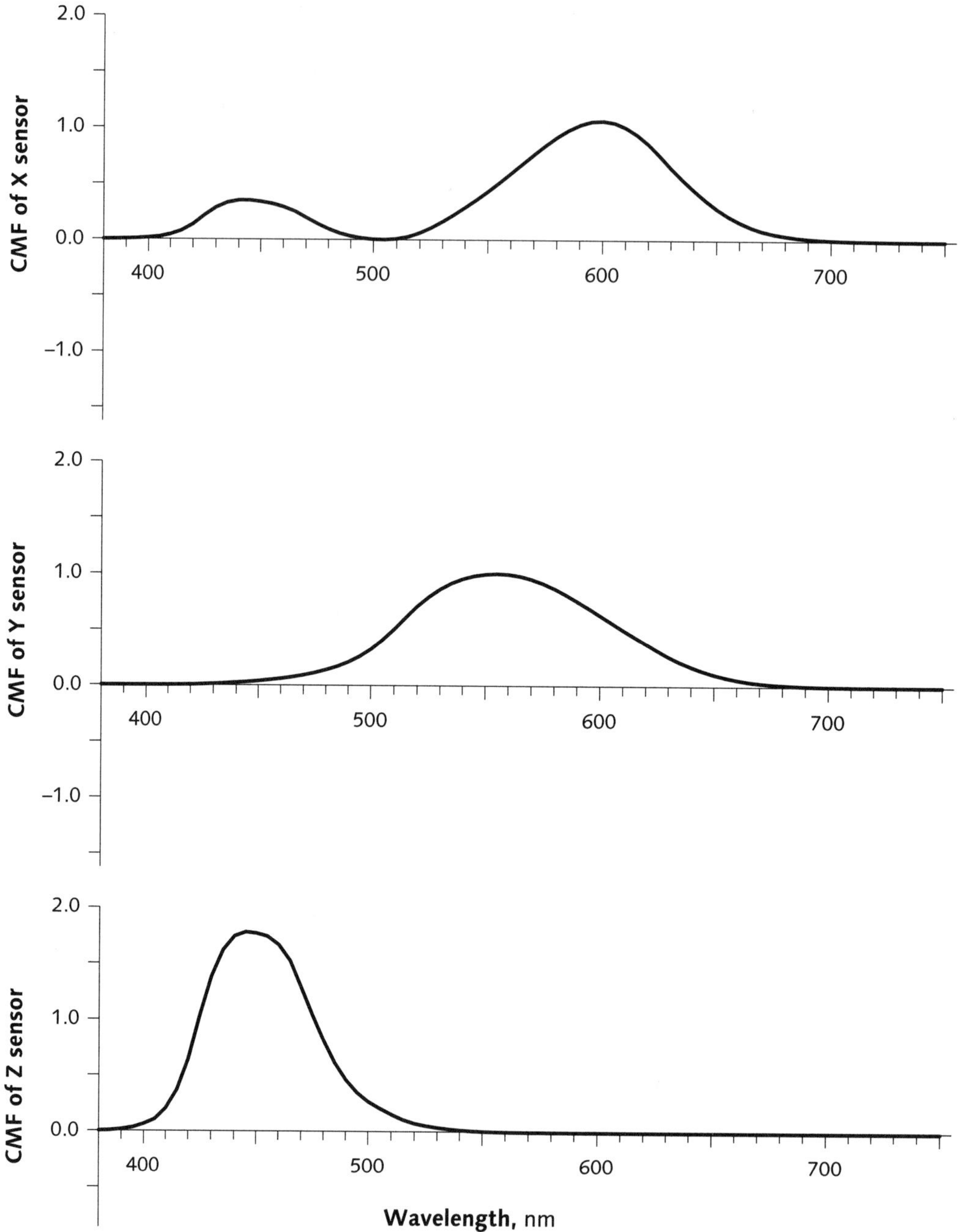

Figure 22.3 **CMFs for CIE XYZ primaries.** To acquire all colors in a scene requires filters having the CIE $X(\lambda)$, $Y(\lambda)$, and $Z(\lambda)$ spectral sensitivities. The functions are nonnegative, and therefore could be realized in practice. However, these functions are seldom used in actual cameras or scanners, for various engineering reasons.

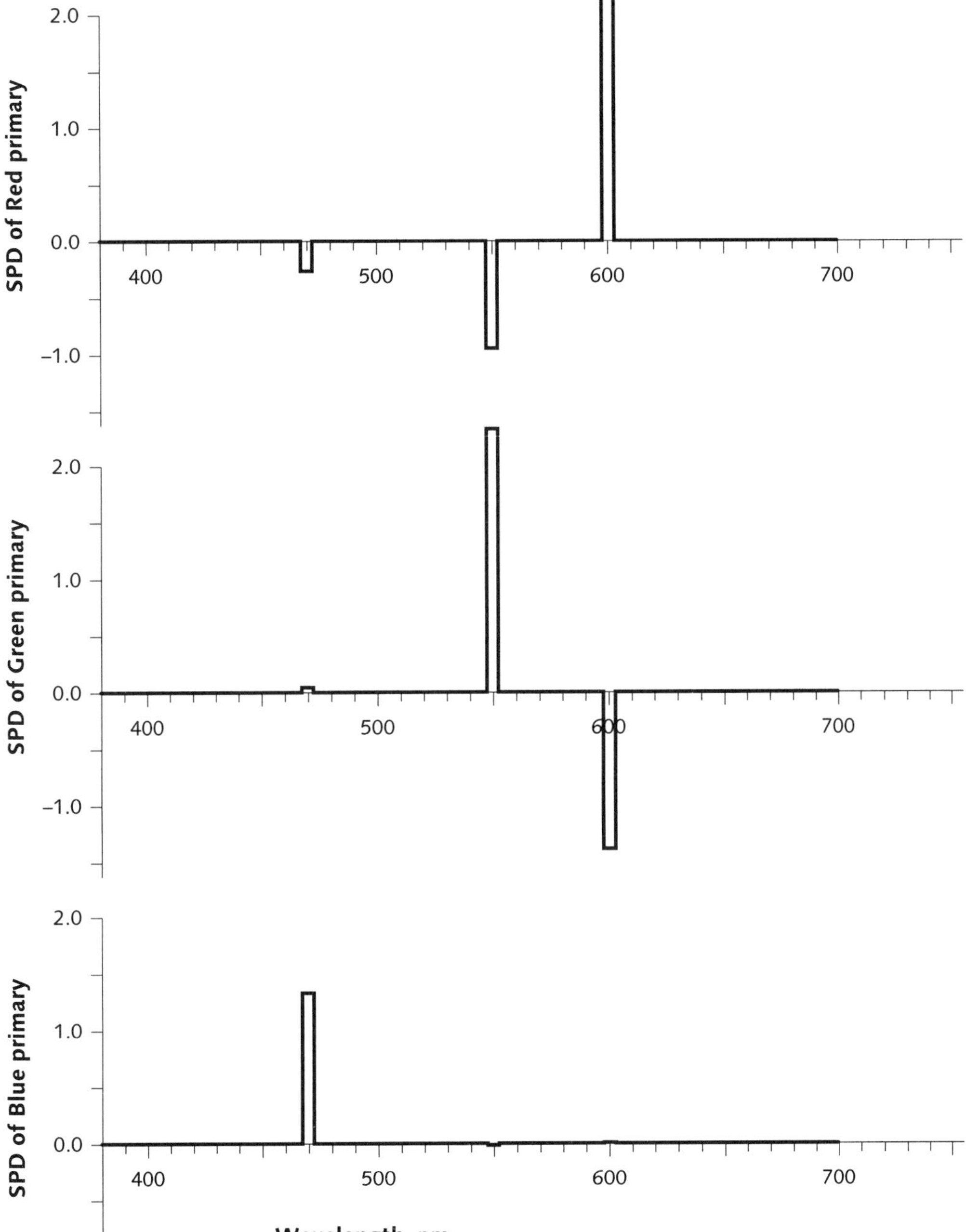

Figure 22.4 **SPDs for CIE XYZ primaries.** To directly reproduce a scene that has been analyzed using the CIE color-matching functions requires *nonphysical* primaries having negative excursions, which cannot be realized in practice. Many different sets are possible. In this hypothetical example, the power in each primary is concentrated at the same three discrete wavelengths, 470, 550, and 600 nm.

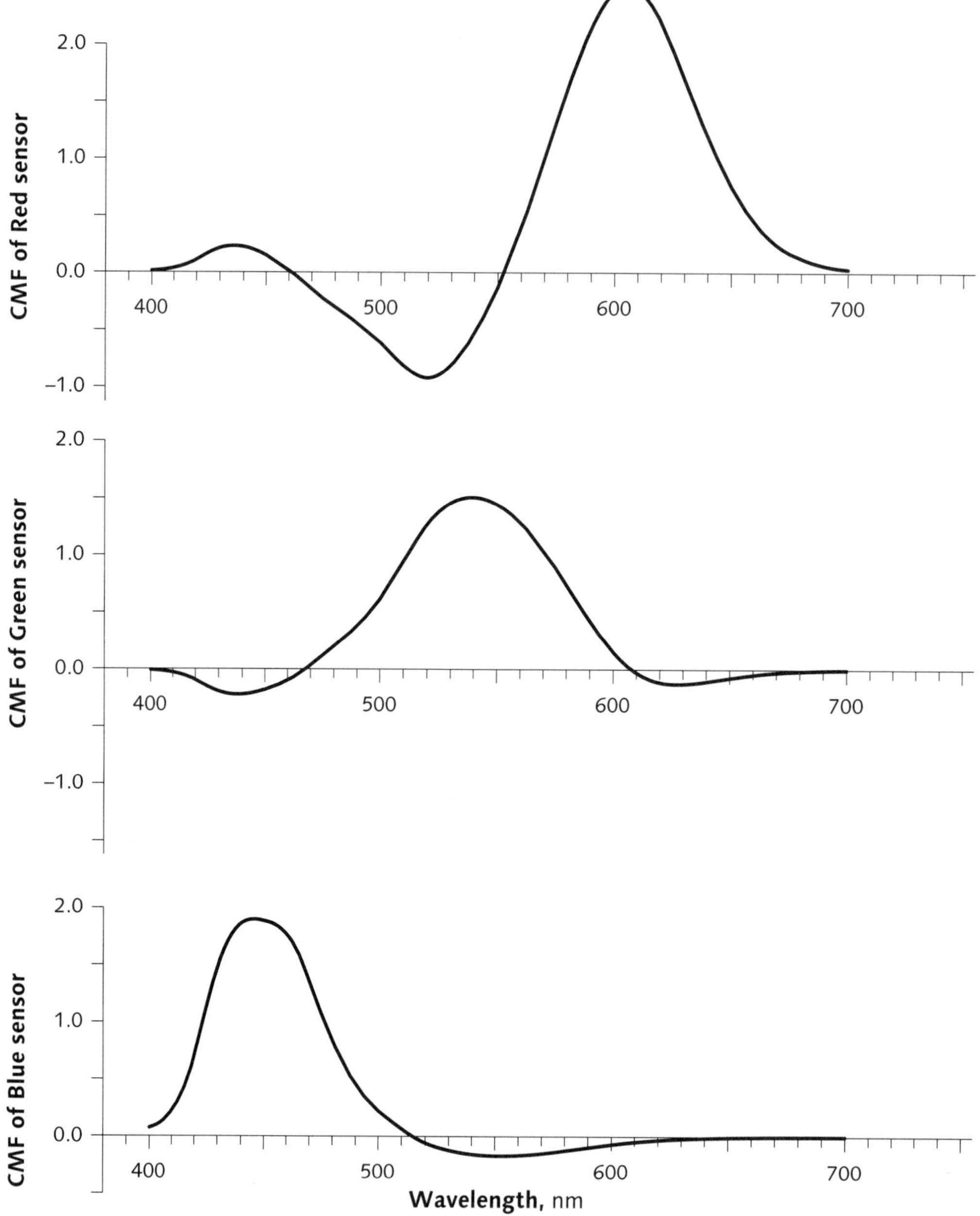

Figure 22.5 **CMFs for Rec. 709 primaries.** These analysis functions are theoretically correct to acquire *RGB* components for display using Rec. 709 primaries. The functions are not directly realizable in a camera or a scanner, due to their negative lobes. But they can be realized by a 3×3 matrix transformation of the CIE *XYZ* color-matching functions of Figure 22.3.

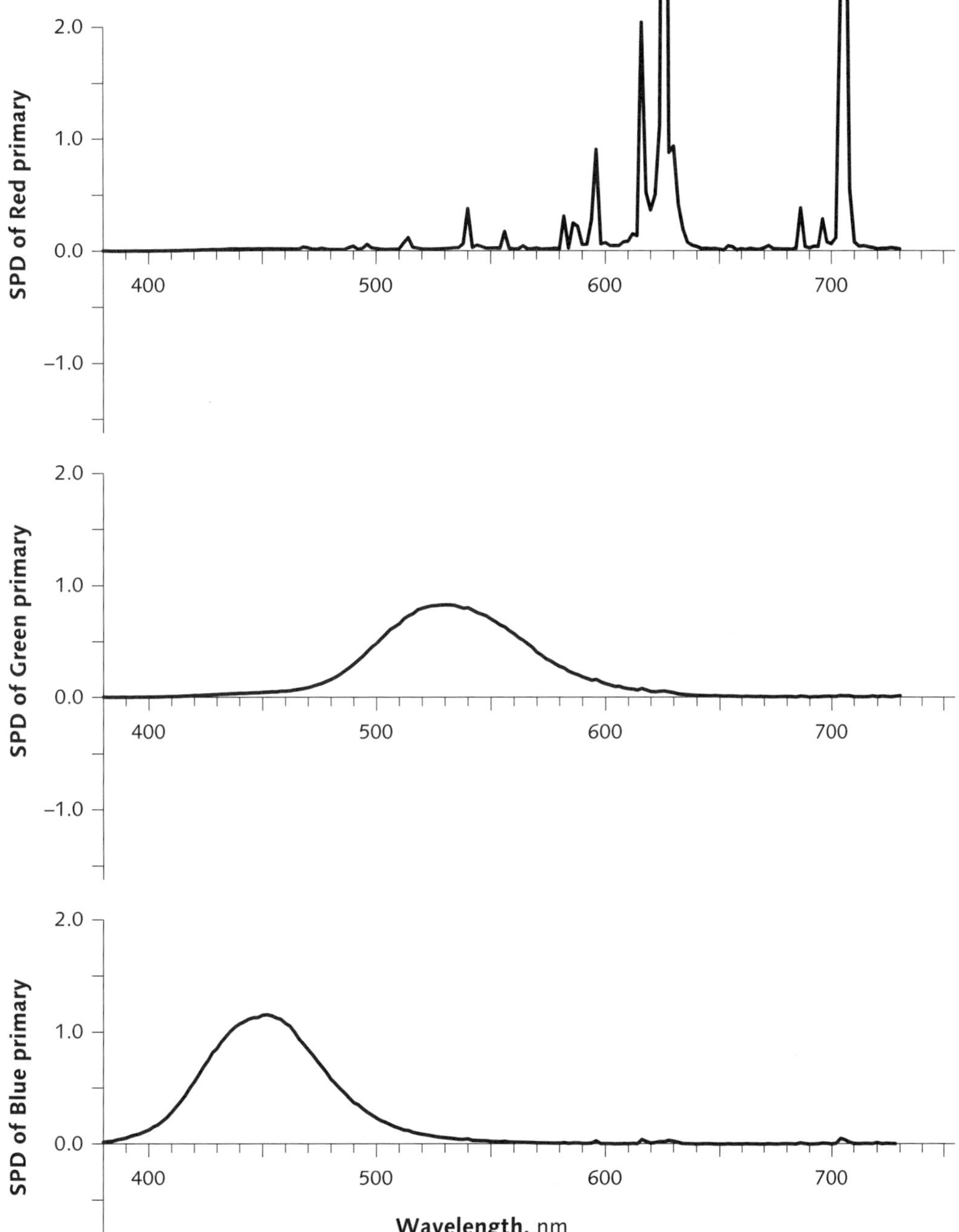

Figure 22.6 **SPDs for Rec. 709 primaries.** This set of SPDs has chromaticity coordinates that conform to SMPTE RP 145, similar to Rec. 709. Many SPDs could produce the same chromaticity coordinates; this particular set is produced by a Sony Trinitron monitor. The red primary uses *rare earth* phosphors that produce very narrow spectral distributions, different from the phosphors used for green or blue.

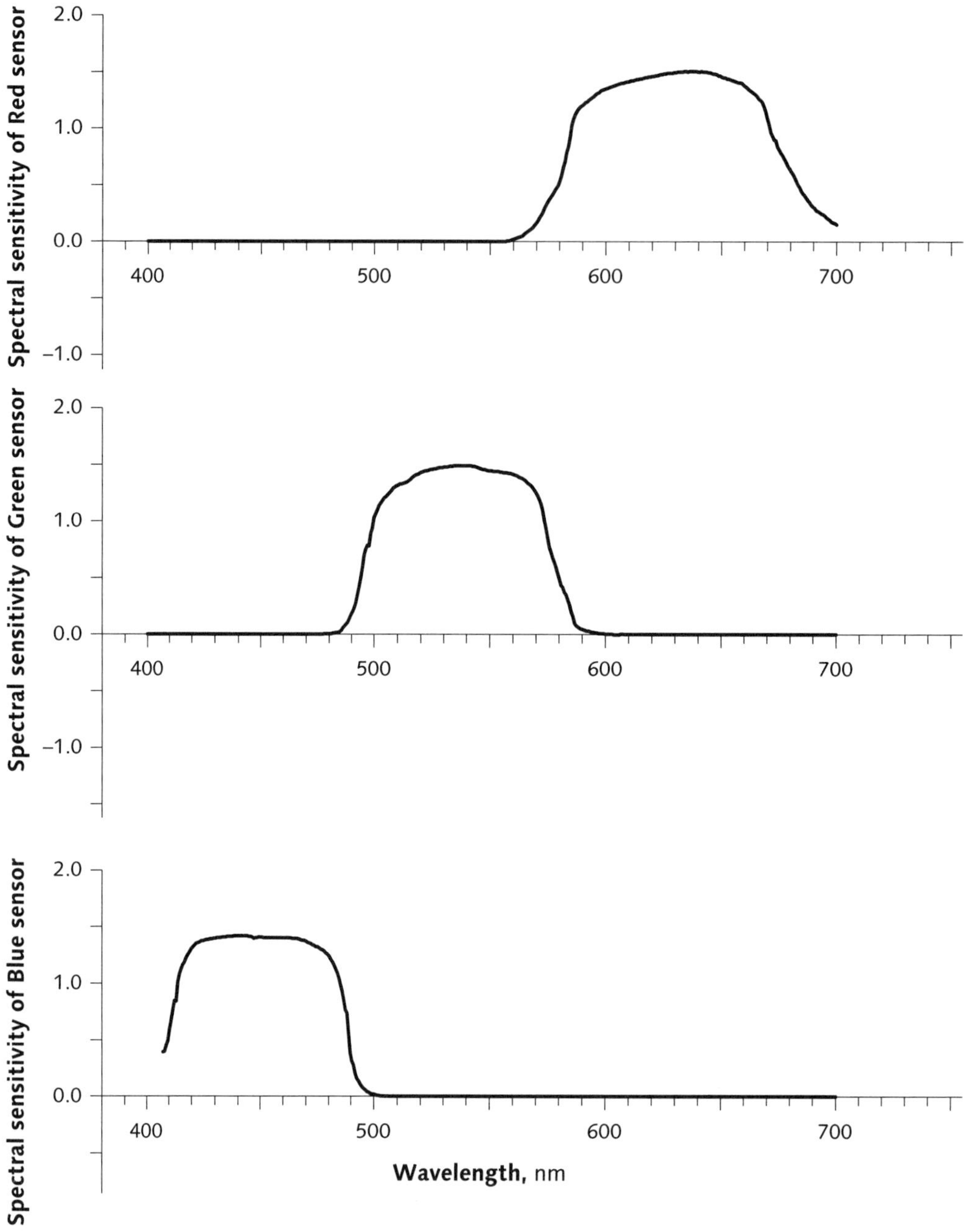

Figure 22.7 **Analysis functions for a real camera.** This set of spectral sensitivity functions is produced by the dichroic color separation filters (*prism*) of a state-of-the-art CCD studio camera.

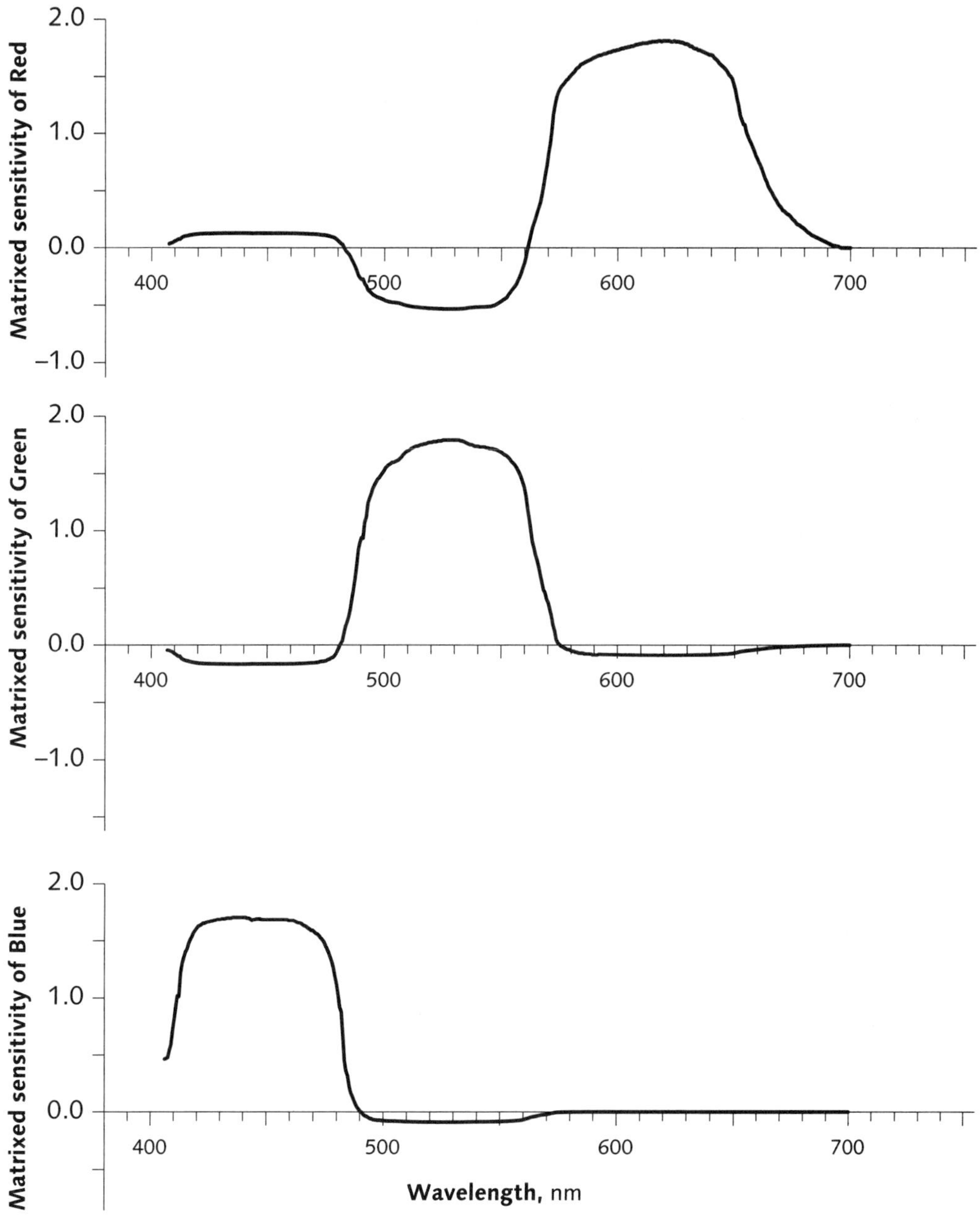

Figure 22.8 **CMFs of an actual camera after matrixing** for Rec. 709 primaries. These curves result from the analysis functions of Figure 22.7, opposite, being processed through a 3×3 matrix. Colors as "seen" by this camera will be accurate to the extent that these curves match the ideal CMFs for Rec. 709 primaries shown in Figure 22.5.

Luminance coefficients

Relative luminance can be formed as a properly weighted sum of *RGB* tristimulus components. The luminance coefficients can be computed starting with the chromaticities of the *RGB* primaries, here expressed in a matrix:

$$\mathbf{C} = \begin{bmatrix} x_r & x_g & x_b \\ y_r & y_g & y_b \\ z_r & z_g & z_b \end{bmatrix} \qquad \text{Eq 22.3}$$

Coefficients J_r, J_g, and J_b are computed from the chromaticities, and the white reference, as follows:

For the D_{65} reference now standard in video, $\boldsymbol{C}^{-1}$ is multiplied by the vector [0.95, 1, 1.089].

$$\begin{bmatrix} J_r \\ J_g \\ J_b \end{bmatrix} = \mathbf{C}^{-1} \bullet \begin{bmatrix} x_w \\ y_w \\ z_w \end{bmatrix} \bullet \frac{1}{y_w} \qquad \text{Eq 22.4}$$

Luminance can then be computed as follows:

$$Y = \begin{bmatrix} J_r y_r & J_g y_g & J_b y_b \end{bmatrix} \bullet \begin{bmatrix} R \\ G \\ B \end{bmatrix} \qquad \text{Eq 22.5}$$

This calculation can be extended to compute [*X, Y, Z*] from [*R, G, B*] of the specified chromaticity. First, compute a matrix ***T***, which depends upon the primaries and the white point of the [*R, G, B*] space:

$$\boldsymbol{T} = \boldsymbol{C} \bullet \begin{bmatrix} J_r & 0 & 0 \\ 0 & J_g & 0 \\ 0 & 0 & J_b \end{bmatrix} \qquad \text{Eq 22.6}$$

The elements J_r, J_g, and J_b of the diagonal matrix have the effect of scaling the corresponding rows of the chromaticity matrix, balancing the primary contributions to achieve the intended chromaticity of white. CIE tristimulus values [*X, Y, Z*] are then computed from the specified [*R, G, B*] as follows:

$$\begin{bmatrix} X \\ Y \\ Z \end{bmatrix} = \boldsymbol{T} \bullet \begin{bmatrix} R \\ G \\ B \end{bmatrix} \qquad \text{Eq 22.7}$$

See *Rec. 601 luma*, *SMPTE 240M-1988 luma*, and *Rec. 709 luma*, on pages 291 and following.

As I explained in *Constant luminance,* on page 75, video systems compute luma as a weighted sum of nonlinear *R'G'B'* components. Even with the resulting nonconstant-luminance errors, there is a second-order benefit in using the "theoretical" coefficients. The standard coefficients are computed as above, from the 1953 FCC NTSC primaries and CIE Illuminant C (for SDTV and computer graphics), from SMPTE RP 145 primaries and CIE D_{65} (for 1035*i* HDTV), and from Rec. 709 primaries and CIE D_{65} (for other HDTV standards).

Transformations between *RGB* and CIE *XYZ*

RGB values in a particular set of primaries can be transformed to and from CIE *XYZ* by a 3×3 matrix transform. These transforms involve tristimulus values, that is, sets of three linear-light components that approximate the CIE color-matching functions. CIE *XYZ* represents a special case of tristimulus values. In *XYZ*, any color is represented by an all-positive set of values. SMPTE has standardized a procedure for computing these transformations.

SMPTE RP 177, *Derivation of Basic Television Color Equations*.

To transform from Rec. 709 *RGB* (with its D_{65} white point) into CIE *XYZ*, use the following transform:

Eq 22.8

$$\begin{bmatrix} X \\ Y \\ Z \end{bmatrix} = \begin{bmatrix} 0.412453 & 0.357580 & 0.180423 \\ 0.212671 & 0.715160 & 0.072169 \\ 0.019334 & 0.119193 & 0.950227 \end{bmatrix} \bullet \begin{bmatrix} R_{709} \\ G_{709} \\ B_{709} \end{bmatrix}$$

When constructing such a matrix for fixed-point calculation, take care when rounding to preserve unity sum of the middle (luminance) row.

The middle row of this matrix gives the luminance coefficients of Rec. 709. Because white is normalized to unity, the middle row sums to unity. The column vectors are the *XYZ* tristimulus values of pure red, green, and blue. To recover primary chromaticities from such a matrix, compute little x and y for each *RGB* column vector. To recover the white point, transform $RGB = [1, 1, 1]$ to *XYZ*, then compute x and y according to Equation 21.1.

To transform from CIE *XYZ* into Rec. 709 *RGB*, use the inverse of Equation 22.8:

Eq 22.9

$$\begin{bmatrix} R_{709} \\ G_{709} \\ B_{709} \end{bmatrix} = \begin{bmatrix} 3.240479 & -1.537150 & -0.498535 \\ -0.969256 & 1.875992 & 0.041556 \\ 0.055648 & -0.204043 & 1.057311 \end{bmatrix} \bullet \begin{bmatrix} X \\ Y \\ Z \end{bmatrix}$$

I'll describe gamut on page 255.

This matrix has some negative coefficients: *XYZ* colors that are *out of gamut* for Rec. 709 *RGB* transform to

RGB components where one or more components are negative or greater than unity.

Any *RGB* image data, or any matrix that purports to relate *RGB* to *XYZ*, should indicate the chromaticities of the *RGB* primaries involved. If you encounter a matrix transform or image data without reference to any primary chromaticities, be very suspicious! Its originator may be unaware that *RGB* values must be associated with chromaticity specifications in order to have meaning for accurate color.

Noise due to matrixing

Even if it were possible to display colors in the outer reaches of the chromaticity diagram, there would be a great practical disadvantage in doing so. Consider a camera that acquires *XYZ* tristimulus components, then transforms to Rec. 709 *RGB* according to Equation 22.9. The coefficient 3.240479 in the upper left-hand corner of the matrix in that equation determines the contribution from *X* at the camera into the red signal. An *X* component acquired with 1 mV of noise will inject 3.24 mV of noise into red: There is a noise penalty associated with the larger coefficients in the transform, and this penalty is quite significant in the design of a high-quality camera.

Transforms among *RGB* systems

RGB values in a system employing one set of primaries can be transformed to another set by a 3×3 linear-light matrix transform.

[*R*, *G*, *B*] tristimulus values in a source space (denoted with the subscript *s*) can be transformed into [*R*, *G*, *B*] tristimulus values in a destination space (denoted with the subscript *d*), using matrices $\mathbf{T}_s$ and $\mathbf{T}_d$ computed from the corresponding chromaticities and white points:

Eq 22.10

$$\begin{bmatrix} R_d \\ G_d \\ B_d \end{bmatrix} = \mathbf{T}_d^{-1} \bullet \mathbf{T}_s \bullet \begin{bmatrix} R_s \\ G_s \\ B_s \end{bmatrix}$$

As an example, here is the transform from SMPTE RP 145 *RGB* (e.g., SMPTE 240M) to Rec. 709 *RGB*:

Eq 22.11

$$\begin{bmatrix} R_{709} \\ G_{709} \\ B_{709} \end{bmatrix} = \begin{bmatrix} 0.939555 & 0.050173 & 0.010272 \\ 0.017775 & 0.965795 & 0.016430 \\ -0.001622 & -0.004371 & 1.005993 \end{bmatrix} \bullet \begin{bmatrix} R_{145} \\ G_{145} \\ B_{145} \end{bmatrix}$$

This matrix transforms EBU 3213 RGB to Rec. 709:

Eq 22.12

$$\begin{bmatrix} R_{709} \\ G_{709} \\ B_{709} \end{bmatrix} = \begin{bmatrix} 1.044036 & -0.044036 & 0 \\ 0 & 1 & 0 \\ 0 & 0.011797 & 0.988203 \end{bmatrix} \bullet \begin{bmatrix} R_{\text{EBU}} \\ G_{\text{EBU}} \\ B_{\text{EBU}} \end{bmatrix}$$

To transform typical Sony Trinitron *RGB*, with D_{65} white reference, to Rec. 709, use this transform:

Eq 22.13

$$\begin{bmatrix} R_{709} \\ G_{709} \\ B_{709} \end{bmatrix} = \begin{bmatrix} 1.068706 & -0.078595 & 0.009890 \\ 0.024110 & 0.960070 & 0.015819 \\ 0.001735 & 0.029748 & 0.968517 \end{bmatrix} \bullet \begin{bmatrix} R_{\text{SONY}} \\ G_{\text{SONY}} \\ B_{\text{SONY}} \end{bmatrix}$$

Transforming among *RGB* systems may lead to an *out of gamut RGB* result, where one or more *RGB* components are negative or greater than unity.

These transformations produce accurate results only when applied to tristimulus (linear-light) components. In principle, to transform nonlinear *R'G'B'* from one primary system to another requires application of the inverse transfer function to recover the tristimulus values, computation of the matrix multiplication, then reapplication of the transfer function. However, the transformation matrices of Equations 22.11, 22.12, and 22.13 are similar to the identity matrix: The diagonal terms are nearly unity, and the off-diagonal terms are nearly zero. In these cases, if the transform is computed in the nonlinear (gamma-corrected) *R'G'B'* domain, the resulting errors will be small.

Camera white reference

There is an implicit assumption in television that the camera operates as if the scene were illuminated by a source having the chromaticity of CIE D_{65}. In practice, television studios are often lit by tungsten lamps, and scene illumination is often deficient in the shortwave (blue) region of the spectrum. This situation is compensated by *white balancing* – that is, by adjusting the gain of the red, green, and blue components at the camera so that a diffuse white object reports the values that would be reported if the scene illumination had the same tristimulus values as CIE D_{65}. In studio cameras, controls for white balance are available. In consumer cameras, activating WHITE BALANCE causes the camera to integrate red, green, and blue over the picture, and to adjust the gains so as to equalize the sums. (This approach to white balancing is sometimes called *integrate to gray*.)

Monitor white reference

SMPTE RP 71, *Setting Chromaticity and Luminance of White for Color Television Monitors Using Shadow-Mask Picture Tubes*.

In additive mixture, the illumination of the reproduced image is generated entirely by the display device. In particular, reproduced white is determined by the characteristics of the display, and is not dependent on the environment in which the display is viewed. In a completely dark viewing environment, such as a cinema theater, this is desirable; a wide range of chromaticities is accepted as "white." However, in an environment where the viewer's field of view encompasses objects other than the display, the viewer's notion of "white" is likely to be influenced or even dominated by what he or she perceives as "white" in the ambient. To avoid subjective mismatches, the chromaticity of white reproduced by the display and the chromaticity of white in the ambient should be reasonably close. SMPTE has standardized the chromaticity of reference white in studio monitors; in addition, the standard specifies that luminance for reference white be reproduced at 103 $cd \cdot m^{-2}$.

Modern blue CRT phosphors are more efficient with respect to human vision than red or green phosphors. Until recently, brightness was valued in computer monitors more than color accuracy. In a quest for a small brightness increment at the expense of a loss of color accuracy, computer monitor manufacturers adopted a white point having a color temperature of about 9300 K, producing a white having about 1.3 times as much blue as the standard CIE D_{65} white reference used in television. So, computer monitors and computer pictures often look excessively blue. The situation can be corrected by adjusting or calibrating the monitor to a white reference with a lower color temperature. (Studio video standards in Japan call for viewing with a 9300 K white reference; this is apparently due to a cultural preference regarding the reproduction of skin tones.)

Gamut

Analyzing a scene with the CIE analysis functions produces distinct component triples for all colors. But when transformed into components suitable for a set of physical display primaries, some of those colors – those colors whose chromaticity coordinates lie outside the triangle formed by the primaries – will have negative component values. In addition, colors outside the triangle of the primaries may have one or two primary components that exceed unity. These colors cannot be correctly displayed. Display devices typically clip signals that have negative values and saturate signals whose values exceed unity. Visualized on the chromaticity diagram, a color outside the triangle of the primaries is reproduced at a point on the boundary of the triangle.

If a scanner is designed to capture all colors, its complexity is necessarily higher and its performance is necessarily worse than a camera designed to capture a smaller range of colors. Thankfully, the range of colors encountered in the natural and man-made world is a small fraction of all of the colors. Although it is necessary for an instrument such as a colorimeter to measure all colors, in an imaging system we are generally concerned with colors that occur frequently.

Pointer, M.R., "The Gamut of Real Surface Colours," in *Color Research and Application* 5 (3): 143–155 (Fall 1980).

M.R. Pointer characterized the distribution of frequently occurring *real surface colors*. The naturally occurring colors tend to lie in the central portion of the chromaticity diagram, where they can be encompassed by a well-chosen set of physical primaries. An imaging system performs well if it can display all or most of these colors. Rec. 709 does reasonably well; however, many of the colors of conventional offset printing – particularly in the cyan region – are not encompassed by all-positive Rec. 709 *RGB*. To accommodate such colors requires wide-gamut reproduction.

Wide-gamut reproduction

Poynton, Charles, "Wide Gamut Device-Independent Colour Image Interchange," in Proc. International Broadcasting Convention, 1994 (IEE Conference Pub. No. 397), 218–222.

For much of the history of color television, cameras were designed to incorporate assumptions about the color reproduction capabilities of color CRTs. But nowadays, video production equipment is being used to originate images for a much wider range of applications than just television broadcast. The desire to make digital cameras suitable for originating images for this wider range of applications has led to proposals for video standards that accommodate a wider gamut.

Levinthal and Porter introduced a coding system to accommodate linear-light (tristimulus) values below zero and above unity. See Levinthal, Adam, and Thomas Porter, "Chap: A SIMD Graphics Processor," in *Computer Graphics*, 18 (3): 77–82 (July 1984, Proc. SIGGRAPH '84).

I will introduce the *Rec. 1361 transfer function*, on page 265. That transfer function is intended to be the basis for wide-gamut reproduction in future HDTV systems. The Rec. 1361 function is intended for use with *RGB* tristimulus values having Rec. 709 primaries. However, the *RGB* values can occupy a range from -0.25 to +1.33, well outside the range 0 to 1. The excursions below zero and above unity allow Rec. 1361 *RGB* values to represent colors outside the triangle enclosed by the Rec. 709 primaries. When the extended *R'G'B'* values are matrixed, the resulting $Y'C_BC_R$ values lie within the "valid" range: Regions of $Y'C_BC_R$ space outside the "legal" *RGB* cube are exploited to convey wide-gamut colors. For details, see *C_BC_R components for Rec. 1361 HDTV*, on page 318.

Further reading

For a highly readable short introduction to color image coding, consult DeMarsh and Giorgianni. For a terse, complete technical treatment, read Schreiber (cited in the margin of page 20).

DeMarsh, LeRoy E., and Edward J. Giorgianni, "Color Science for Imaging Systems," in *Physics Today*, September 1989, 44–52.

Lindbloom, Bruce, "Accurate Color Reproduction for Computer Graphics Applications," in *Computer Graphics*, 23 (3): 117–126 (July 1989).

Hall, Roy, *Illumination and Color in Computer Generated Imagery* (New York: Springer-Verlag, 1989). Sadly, it's out of print.

For a discussion of nonlinear *RGB* in computer graphics, read Lindbloom's *SIGGRAPH* paper.

In a computer graphics system, once light is on its way to the eye, any tristimulus-based system can accurately represent color. However, the interaction of light and objects involves spectra, not tristimulus values. In computer-generated imagery (CGI), the calculations actually involve sampled SPDs, even if only three components are used. Roy Hall discusses these issues.

Gamma 23

In photography, video, and computer graphics, the *gamma* symbol, γ, represents a numerical parameter that describes the nonlinearity of luminance reproduction. Gamma is a mysterious and confusing subject, because it involves concepts from four disciplines: physics, perception, photography, and video. This chapter explains how gamma is related to each of these disciplines. Having a good understanding of the theory and practice of *gamma* will enable you to get good results when you create, process, and display pictures.

Luminance is proportional to intensity. For an introduction to the terms *brightness, intensity, luminance*, and *lightness*, see page 11.

This chapter focuses on electronic reproduction of images, using video and computer graphics techniques and equipment. I deal mainly with the reproduction of luminance, or, as a photographer would say, *tone scale*. Achieving good tone reproduction is one important step toward achieving good color reproduction. (Other issues specific to color reproduction were presented in the previous chapter, *Color science for video*.)

Electro-optical transfer function (EOTF) refers to the transfer function of the device that converts from the electrical domain of video into light – a display.

A *cathode-ray tube* (CRT) is inherently nonlinear: The luminance produced at the screen of a CRT is a nonlinear function of its voltage input. From a strictly physical point of view, *gamma correction* in video and computer graphics can be thought of as the process of compensating for this nonlinearity in order to achieve correct reproduction of relative luminance.

As introduced in *Nonlinear image coding*, on page 12, and detailed in *Luminance and lightness*, on page 203, the human perceptual response to luminance is quite nonuniform: The *lightness* sensation of vision is roughly the 0.4-power function of luminance. This characteristic needs to be considered if an image is to be coded to minimize the visibility of noise, and to make effective perceptual use of a limited number of bits per pixel.

Combining these two concepts – one from physics, the other from perception – reveals an amazing coincidence: The nonlinearity of a CRT is remarkably similar to the *inverse* of the lightness sensitivity of human vision. Coding luminance into a gamma-corrected signal makes maximum perceptual use of the channel. If gamma correction were not already necessary for physical reasons at the CRT, we would have to invent it for perceptual reasons.

Opto-electronic transfer function (OETF) refers to the transfer function of a scanner or camera.

I will describe how video draws aspects of its handling of gamma from all of these areas: knowledge of the CRT from physics, knowledge of the nonuniformity of vision from perception, and knowledge of viewing conditions from photography. I will also discuss additional details of the CRT transfer function that you will need to know if you wish to calibrate a CRT or determine its nonlinearity.

Gamma in CRT physics

The physics of the electron gun of a CRT imposes a relationship between voltage input and light output that a physicist calls a *five-halves power law:* The luminance of light produced at the face of the screen is proportional to voltage input raised to $5/2$ power. Luminance is roughly between the square and cube of the voltage. The numerical value of the exponent of this power function is represented by the Greek letter γ (gamma). CRT monitors have voltage inputs that reflect this power function. In practice, most CRTs have a numerical value of gamma quite close to 2.5.

Olson, Thor, "Behind Gamma's Disguise," in *SMPTE Journal*, 104 (7): 452–458 (July 1995).

Figure 23.1 opposite is a sketch of the power function that applies to the electron gun of a grayscale CRT, or to each of the red, green, and blue electron guns of a color CRT. The three guns of a color CRT exhibit very similar, but not necessarily identical, responses.

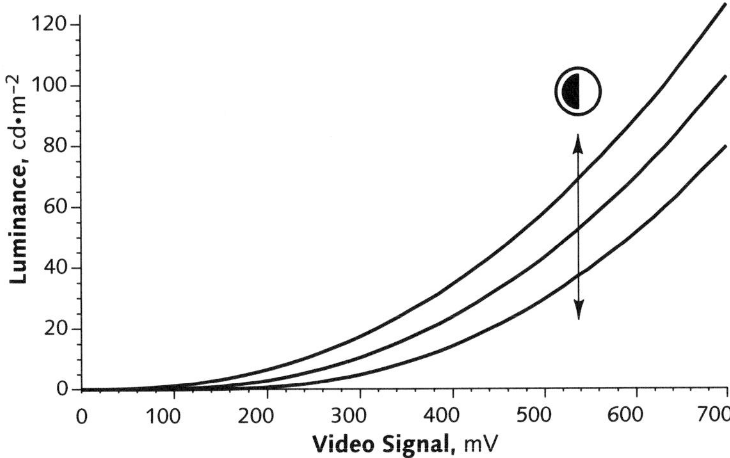

Figure 23.1 **CRT transfer function** involves a nonlinear relationship between video signal and luminance, graphed here for an actual CRT at three different settings of the CONTRAST control. Luminance is approximately proportional to input signal voltage raised to the 2.5 power. The *gamma* of a display system – or more specifically, a CRT – is the numerical value of the exponent of the power function. Here I show the CONTRAST control varying luminance, on the *y*-axis; however, owing to the mathematical properties of a power function, scaling the voltage input would yield the identical effect.

The nonlinearity in the voltage-to-luminance function of a CRT originates with the electrostatic interaction between the cathode, the grid, and the electron beam. The function is influenced to a small extent by the mechanical structure of the electron gun. Contrary to popular opinion, the CRT phosphors themselves are quite linear, at least up to the onset of saturation at a luminance of about eight-tenths of maximum. I denote the exponent the *decoding gamma,* γ_D.

Gamma correction involves a *power* function, which has the form $y = x^a$ (where *a* is constant). It is sometimes incorrectly claimed to be an *exponential* function, which has the form $y = a^x$ (where *a* is constant).

Gamma correction is unrelated to the gamma function $\Gamma(x)$ of mathematics.

In a video camera, we precompensate for the CRT's nonlinearity by processing each of the *R, G,* and *B* tristimulus signals through a nonlinear transfer function. This process is known as gamma correction. The function required is approximately a square root. The curve is often not precisely a power function; nonetheless, I denote the best-fit exponent the *encoding gamma,* γ_E. In video, gamma correction is accomplished by analog (or sometimes digital) circuits at the camera. In computer graphics, gamma correction is usually accomplished by incorporating the nonlinear transfer function into a framebuffer's lookup table.

Roberts, Alan, "Measurement of display transfer characteristic (gamma, γ)," in *EBU Technical Review* 257: 32–40 (Autumn 1993).

The value of decoding gamma (γ_D) for a typical, properly adjusted CRT ranges from about 2.35 to 2.55. Computer graphics practitioners sometimes claim numerical values of gamma wildly different from 2.5; however, such measurements often disregard two issues. First, the largest source of variation in the nonlinearity of a monitor is careless setting of the BRIGHTNESS (or BLACK LEVEL) control. Before a sensible measurement of gamma can be made, this control must be adjusted, as outlined on page 26, so that black elements in the picture are correctly reproduced. Second, computer systems often have lookup tables (LUTs) that effect control over transfer functions. A gamma value dramatically different from 2.5 is often due to the function loaded into the LUT. A Macintosh is often said to have a gamma of 1.8; however, this value is a consequence of the default Macintosh LUT! The Macintosh monitor itself has gamma between about 2.35 and 2.55.

Getting the physics right is an important first step toward proper treatment of gamma, but it isn't the whole story, as you will see.

The amazing coincidence!

In *Luminance and lightness,* on page 203, I described the nonlinear relationship between luminance (a physical quantity) and lightness (a perceptual quantity): Lightness is approximately luminance raised to the 0.4-power. The previous section described how the nonlinear transfer function of a CRT relates a voltage signal to luminance. Here's the surprising coincidence: The CRT voltage-to-luminance function is very nearly the *inverse* of the luminance-to-lightness relationship.

In analog systems, we represent lightness information as a voltage, to be transformed into luminance by a CRT's power function. In a digital system, we simply digitize analog voltage. To minimize the perceptibility of noise, we should use a perceptually uniform code. Amazingly, the CRT function is a near-perfect inverse of vision's lightness sensitivity: CRT voltage is effectively a perceptually uniform code!

Gamma in video

Many video engineers are unfamiliar with color science. They consider only the first of these two purposes, and disregard, or remain ignorant of, the great importance of perceptually uniform coding.

In a video system, gamma correction is applied at the camera for the dual purposes of precompensating the nonlinearity of the display's CRT and coding into perceptually uniform space. Figure 23.2 summarizes the image reproduction situation for video. At the left, gamma correction is imposed at the camera; at the right, the display imposes the inverse function.

Coding into a perceptual domain was important in the early days of television because of the need to minimize the noise introduced by over-the-air analog transmission. However, the same considerations of noise visibility apply to analog videotape recording. These considerations also apply to the quantization error that is introduced upon digitization, when a signal representing luminance is quantized to a limited number of bits. Consequently, it is universal to convey video signals in gamma-corrected form.

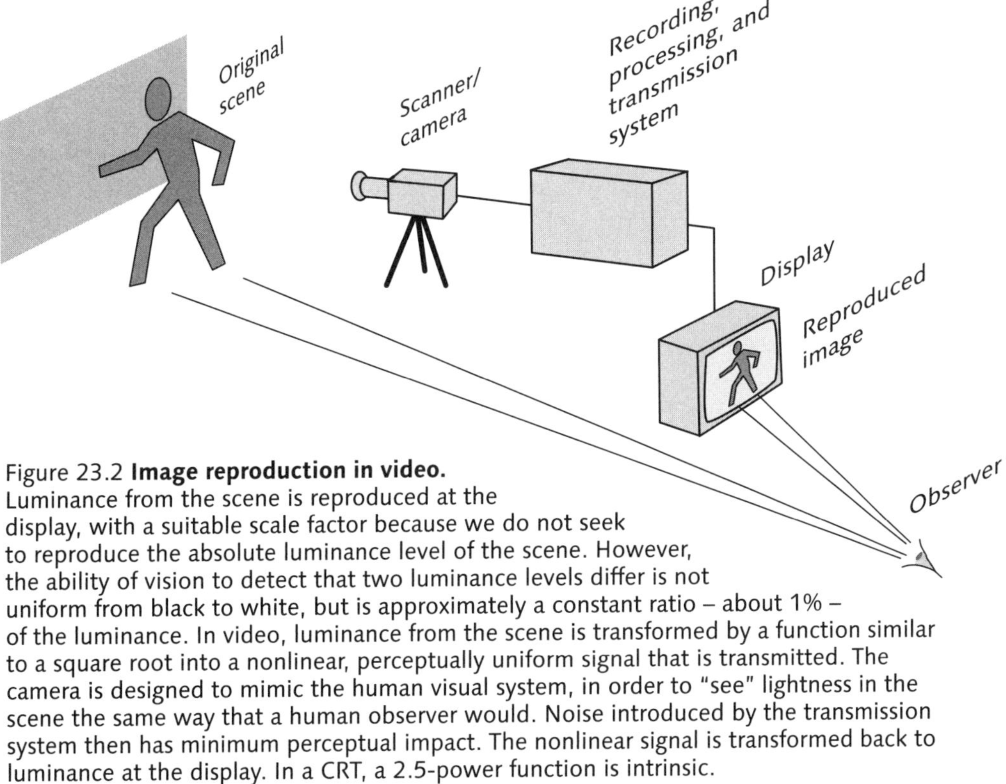

Figure 23.2 **Image reproduction in video.** Luminance from the scene is reproduced at the display, with a suitable scale factor because we do not seek to reproduce the absolute luminance level of the scene. However, the ability of vision to detect that two luminance levels differ is not uniform from black to white, but is approximately a constant ratio – about 1% – of the luminance. In video, luminance from the scene is transformed by a function similar to a square root into a nonlinear, perceptually uniform signal that is transmitted. The camera is designed to mimic the human visual system, in order to "see" lightness in the scene the same way that a human observer would. Noise introduced by the transmission system then has minimum perceptual impact. The nonlinear signal is transformed back to luminance at the display. In a CRT, a 2.5-power function is intrinsic.

The importance of rendering intent, and the consequent requirement for different exponents for encoding (γ_D) and decoding (γ_D), has been poorly recognized and poorly documented in the development of video.

As I explained in *Rendering intent*, on page 81, it is important for perceptual reasons to alter the tone scale of an image reproduced at a luminance substantially lower than that of the original scene, reproduced with limited contrast ratio, or viewed in a dim surround. The dim surround condition is characteristic of television viewing. In video, the alteration is accomplished at the camera by slightly undercompensating the actual power function of the CRT, to obtain an end-to-end power function whose exponent is about 1.25, as indicated in Equation 23.1 in the margin. This achieves end-to-end reproduction that is subjectively correct (though not mathematically linear).

Eq 23.1

$$\gamma_E \approx 0.5; \gamma_D \approx 2.5;$$
$$\gamma_E \cdot \gamma_D \approx 1.25$$

Optoelectronic transfer functions (OETFs)

Unfortunately, several different transfer functions have been standardized and are in use. In the sections to follow, I will detail these transfer function standards:

- Rec. 709 is an international standard that specifies the basic parameters of HDTV. Although the Rec. 709 transfer function is intended for HDTV, it is representative of current SDTV technology, and it is being retrofitted into SDTV studio standards.
- SMPTE 240M was the first studio HDTV standard; its transfer function remains in use in some HDTV equipment deployed today. Recent revisions of SMPTE standards call for the Rec. 709 transfer function, but previous revisions allowed an "interim implementation" using the transfer function of SMPTE 240M-1988.
- Rec. 1361 extends the Rec. 709 coding to accommodate a wide color gamut; it is not yet deployed.
- sRGB refers to a transfer function used in PCs.
- The transfer function of the original 1953 NTSC specification, often written $^1/_{2.2}$, has been effectively superseded by Rec. 709.
- The transfer function of European specifications for 576*i*, often written $^1/_{2.8}$, has been effectively superseded by Rec. 709.

Figure 23.3 **Rec. 709 transfer function** is used in SDTV and HDTV.

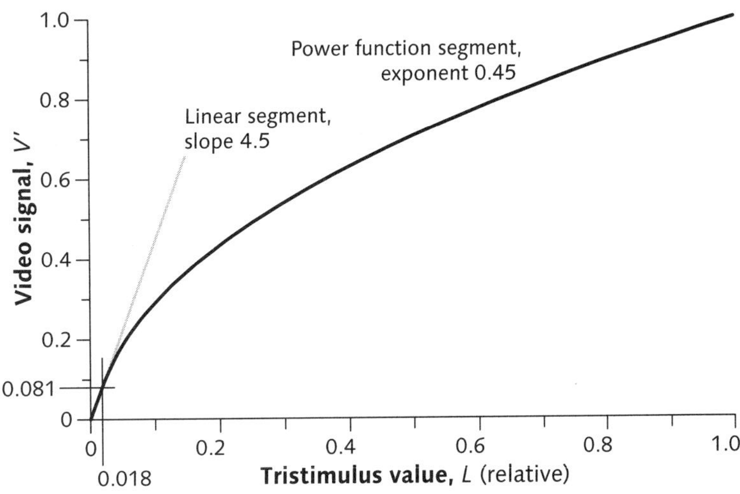

Rec. 709 transfer function

ITU-R Rec. BT.709, *Basic parameter values for the HDTV standard for the studio and for international programme exchange.*

Figure 23.3 illustrates the transfer function defined by the international Rec. 709 standard for high-definition television (HDTV). It is based upon a pure power function with an exponent of 0.45. Theoretically, a pure power function suffices for gamma correction; however, the slope of a pure power function (whose exponent is less than unity) is infinite at zero. In a practical system such as a television camera, in order to minimize noise in dark regions of the picture it is necessary to limit the slope (gain) of the function near black. Rec. 709 specifies a slope of 4.5 below a tristimulus value of +0.018, and scales and offsets the pure power function segment of the curve to maintain function and tangent continuity at the breakpoint.

The symbol L suggests *linear*. Take care not to confuse it with lightness, L^*. The symbol V' suggests voltage, or video.

In this equation the tristimulus (linear light) component is denoted L, and the resulting gamma-corrected video signal – one of R', G', or B' components – is denoted with a prime symbol, V'_{709}. R, G, and B are processed through identical functions to obtain R', G', and B':

$$V'_{709} = \begin{cases} 4.5L; & 0 \le L < 0.018 \\ 1.099L^{0.45} - 0.099; & 0.018 \le L \le 1 \end{cases} \qquad \text{Eq 23.2}$$

The Rec. 709 equation includes an exponent of 0.45. However, the effect of the scale factor and offset terms makes the overall power function very similar to a square root ($\gamma_E \approx 0.5$). For this reason, it is misleading to describe Rec. 709 as having "gamma of 0.45."

Rec. 709 encoding assumes that encoded *R'G'B'* signals will be converted to tristimulus values at a CRT (or some other display device) with a 2.5-power function ($\gamma_D \approx 2.5$):

$$L = \left(V'\right)^{2.5} \qquad \text{Eq 23.3}$$

The product of the effective 0.5 exponent at the camera and the 2.5 exponent at the display produces an end-to-end power of about 1.25, suitable for typical television display environment, as I explained in *Rendering intent,* on page 81. Should you wish to recover the *RGB* scene tristimulus values, invert Equation 23.2:

$$L = \begin{cases} \dfrac{V'_{709}}{4.5}; & 0 \le V'_{709} < 0.081 \\ \left(\dfrac{V'_{709} + 0.099}{1.099}\right)^{\frac{1}{0.45}}; & 0.081 \le V'_{709} \le 1 \end{cases} \qquad \text{Eq 23.4}$$

Equation Eq 23.4 does not incorporate correction for rendering intent: The recovered values are proportional to the *scene* tristimulus values, not to the intended *display* tristimulus values. Rec. 709 is misleading in its failure to discuss – or even mention – rendering intent.

See *Headroom and footroom,* on page 22.

I have described signals in the abstract range 0 to 1. When *R'G'B'* or *Y'* components are interfaced in 8 bits, the 0 to 1 values are scaled by 219 and offset by +16. Interface codes below 16 and above 235 are used for footroom and headroom. (Codes 0 and 255 are used for synchronization, and are otherwise prohibited.)

For interfaces having more than 8 bits, the reference black and white levels are multiplied by 2^{k-8}, where k is the number of bits at the interface. For example, when *R'G'B'* or *Y'* components are interfaced in 10 bits, the 0 to 1 values are scaled by 219·4 (i.e., 876), and offset by +64. (At the interface, codes having the 8 most-significant bits all zero, or all one, are prohibited from video data.)

SMPTE 240M, *1125-Line High-Definition Production Systems – Signal Parameters*.

SMPTE 240M transfer function

SMPTE Standard 240M for 1125/60, 1035*i*30 HDTV was adopted two years before Rec. 709 was adopted. Virtually all HDTV equipment deployed between 1988 and 1998 uses the SMPTE 240M parameters. SMPTE and ATSC standards for HDTV now specify Rec. 709 parameters; however, the standards previously accommodated an "interim implementation" having the identical transfer function to SMPTE 240M. SMPTE 240M's transfer function is this:

$$V'_{240} = \begin{cases} 4.0L; & 0 \le L < 0.0228 \\ 1.1115L^{0.45} - 0.1115; & 0.0228 \le L \le 1 \end{cases} \qquad \text{Eq 23.5}$$

To recover scene tristimulus values, use this relation:

$$L = \begin{cases} \dfrac{V'_{240}}{4.0}; & 0 \le V'_{240} < 0.0913 \\ \left(\dfrac{V'_{240} + 0.1115}{1.1115}\right)^{\frac{1}{0.45}}; & 0.0913 \le V'_{240} \le 1 \end{cases} \qquad \text{Eq 23.6}$$

In 1993, CCIR was renamed ITU-R.

The difference between the SMPTE 240M and Rec. 709 transfer functions is negligible for real images. It is a shame that international agreement could not have been reached on the SMPTE 240M parameters that were widely implemented in 1990, when the CCIR discussions were taking place. The transfer function of Rec. 709 is closely representative of current studio practice, and should be used for all but very unusual conditions.

Rec. 1361 transfer function

ITU-R Rec. BT.1361, *Worldwide unified colorimetry and related characteristics of future television and imaging systems*.

Rec. 1361 is intended to enable future HDTV systems to achieve wider color gamut than Rec. 709, through use of tristimulus signals having negative values and values greater than unity. The Rec. 1361 transfer function is identical to Rec. 709's for *RGB* tristimulus values within Rec. 709's range, that is, between 0 and 1. Tristimulus values from $-\frac{1}{4}$ to zero are subject to a transfer function that is Rec. 709's function mirrored, and scaled by a factor of $\frac{1}{4}$, on both axes. Tristimulus values from unity to $+\frac{4}{3}$ are subject to a straightforward extension of the Rec. 709 curve.

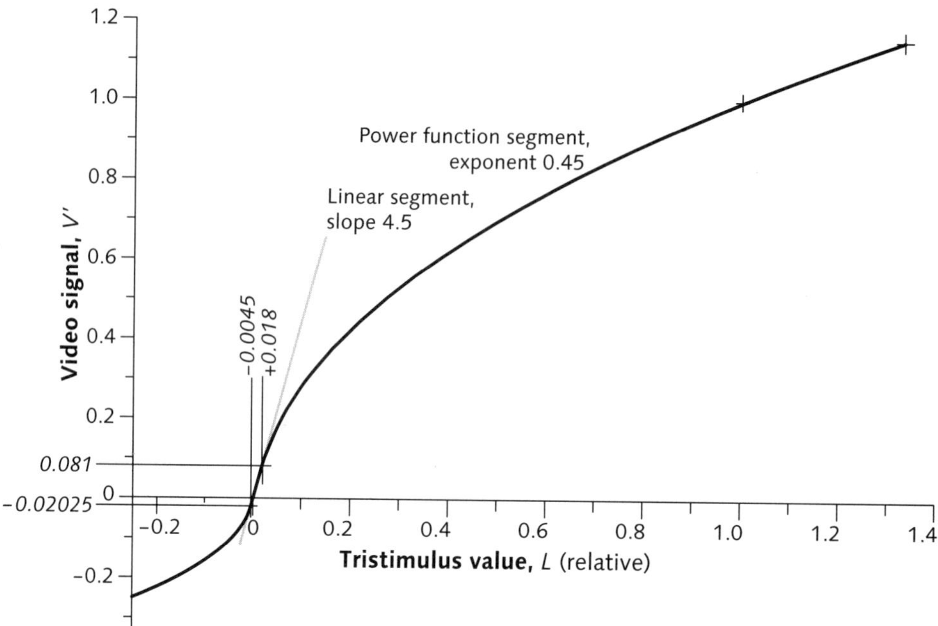

Figure 23.4 **Rec. 1361 transfer function**

Encoding for Rec. 1361 is expressed in Equation 23.7:

Eq 23.7

$$V'_{1361} = \begin{cases} -\dfrac{1.099(-4L)^{0.45} - 0.099}{4}; & -0.25 \le L < -0.004 \\ 4.5L; & -0.0045 \le L < 0.018 \\ 1.099L^{0.45} - 0.099; & 0.018 \le L < 1.33 \end{cases}$$

The function is graphed in Figure 23.4 above.

For positive values of V'_{1361}, it is assumed that a conventional display will apply a 2.5-power function to produce display tristimulus values. A wide-gamut display is expected to do whatever signal processing is necessary to deliver the colors within its gamut.

$$\frac{160}{219} = \frac{2^5 \cdot 5}{73 \cdot 3}$$

The gamma-corrected *R'G'B'* components of Rec. 1361 lie in the range [-0.25 … +1.152]. Their black-to-white excursion is reduced by the ratio $^{160}/_{219}$ from that of Rec. 709, SMPTE 274M, or SMPTE 296M *R'G'B'* components: Scaled by 160 for 8-bit coding, they would occupy the range [–40 … 184.3]. If subsequently offset +48 at an 8-bit interface, they would lie in the range [8 … 232.3]. However, Rec. 1361 is intended for use with 10-bit components, at minimum. As in Rec. 709, the reference black and white levels are multiplied by 2^{k-8}, where k is the number of bits at the interface. When scaled and offset for 10-bit 4:4:4 interface, Rec. 1361 *R'G'B'* ranges 192 through 832 (compared to a range of 64 through 940 for 10-bit Rec. 709).

sRGB transfer function

IEC FDIS 61966-2-1, *Multimedia systems and equipment – Colour measurement and management – Part 2-1: Colour management – Default RGB colour space – sRGB.*

The notation *sRGB* refers to a specification for color image coding for personal computers, and for image exchange on the Internet. The FlashPix file format for digital still cameras incorporates sRGB coding (there called NIFRGB). The sRGB specification calls for a transfer function very similar to – but regrettably not identical to – Rec. 709. The encoding is this:

$$V'_{\mathrm{sRGB}} = \begin{cases} 12.92L; & 0 \le L \le 0.0031308 \\ 1.055L^{\left(\frac{1}{2.4}\right)} - 0.055; & 0.0031308 < L \le 1 \end{cases} \qquad \text{Eq 23.8}$$

Although the equation contains the exponent $1/2.4$, the the scale factor and the offset cause the overall function to approximate a pure 0.45-power function ($\gamma_E \approx 0.45$). It is misleading to describe sRGB as having "gamma of 0.42."

Stokes, Michael, and Matthew Anderson, Srinivasan Chandrasekar, and Ricardo Motta, *A Standard Default Color Space for the Internet – sRGB.* Internet: www.color.org.

See *Rendering intent,* on page 81.

sRGB encoding assumes that conversion of the encoded *R'G'B'* signals will be accomplished at a CRT with a nominal 2.5-power function, as in Rec. 709 and SMPTE 240M coding. However, the sRGB specification anticipates a higher ambient light level for viewing than Rec. 709 and SMPTE 240M: sRGB's effective 0.45-power function, displayed on a monitor with a 2.5-power, results in an end-to-end power of 1.125. This is considerably lower than the 1.25 value produced by Rec. 709 encoding.

$$\gamma_E \approx 0.45 \approx \frac{1}{2.22}$$

$$\gamma_D \approx 2.5$$

$$0.45 \cdot 2.5 \approx 1.125$$

It is standard to code sRGB components in 8-bit form from 0 to 255, with no footroom and no headroom.

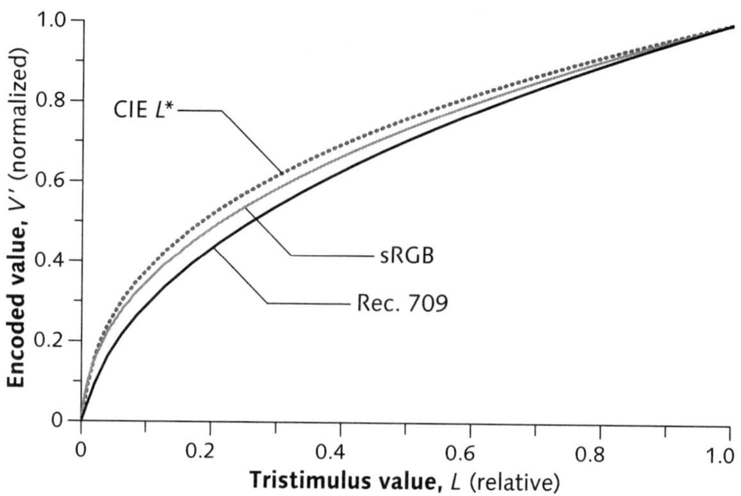

Figure 23.5 **Rec. 709, sRGB, and CIE L^* transfer functions** are compared. They are all approximately perceptually uniform; however, they are not close enough to be interchangeable.

Use this relation to recover scene tristimulus values – but not display tristimulus values! – from sRGB:

$$L = \begin{cases} \frac{1}{12.92} V'_{\text{sRGB}}; & 0 \le V'_{\text{sRGB}} \le 0.03928 \\ \left(\frac{V'_{\text{sRGB}} + 0.055}{1.055} \right)^{2.4}; & 0.03928 < V'_{\text{sRGB}} \le 1 \end{cases} \qquad \text{Eq 23.9}$$

Figure 23.5 sketches the sRGB transfer function, alongside the Rec. 709 and CIE L^* functions.

Transfer functions in SDTV

Historically, transfer functions for 480*i* SDTV have been very poorly specified. The FCC NTSC standard has, since 1953, specified *R'G'B'* encoding for a display with a "transfer gradient (gamma exponent) of 2.2." However, modern CRTs have power function laws very close to 2.5! The FCC statement is widely interpreted to suggest that *encoding* should approximate a power of $1/2.2$; the reciprocal of $1/2.2$, 0.45, appears in modern standards such as Rec. 709. However, as I mentioned on page 263, Rec. 709's overall curve is very close to a square root. The FCC specification should not be taken too seriously: Use Rec. 709 for encoding.

Standards for 576*i* STDV also have poorly specified transfer functions. An "assumed display power function" of 2.8 is mentioned in BBC specifications; some people interpret this as suggesting an encoding exponent of $1/2.8$. However, the 2.8 value is unrealistically high. In fact, European displays are comparable to displays in other parts of the world, and encoding to Rec. 709 is appropriate.

Although there are standards to specify viewing conditions in the studio, no standard specifies the transfer function of an idealized studio monitor! With studio monitor transfer functions unspecified, it is no surprise that there is no standard for consumer monitors. Implicitly, a 2.5-power function is assumed.

Bit depth requirements

In Figure 8.1 on page 76, as part of Chapter 8's discussion of constant luminance, I indicated that conveying relative luminance directly would require about 11 bits. That observation stems from two facts. First, studio video experience proves that 8 bits is just sufficient to convey gamma-corrected $R'G'B'$ – that is, 2^8 (or 256) nonlinear levels are sufficient. Second, the transfer function used to derive gamma-corrected $R'G'B'$ has a certain maximum slope; a maximum slope of 4.5 is specified in Rec. 709. The number of codes necessary in a linear-light representation is the product of these two factors: 256 times 4.5 is 1152, which requires 11 bits.

In Rec. 601 coding with 8 bits, the black-to-white range without footroom or headroom encompasses 220 levels. For linear-light coding of this range, 10 bits would suffice:

$$4.5 \cdot 220 = 990; \quad 990 < 2^{10}$$

In studio video, 8 bits per component barely suffice for distribution purposes. Some margin for roundoff error is required if the signals are subject to processing operations. For this reason, 10-bit studio video is now usual. To maintain 10-bit Rec. 709 accuracy in a linear-light system would require 12 bits per component; to achieve 10-bit L^* or sRGB performance would require 14 bits per component in a linear-light representation.

$$4.5 \cdot 880 = 3960; \quad 3960 < 2^{12}$$

The Rec. 709 transfer function is suitable for video intended for display in the home, where contrast ratio is limited by the ambient environment. For higher-quality video, such as home theater, or for the adaptation of HDTV to digital cinema, we would like a higher maximum gain. When scaled to a lightness range of unity, CIE L^* has a maximum gain of 9.033; sRGB has a gain limit of 12.92. For these systems, linear-light representation requires 4 bits in excess of 10 on the nonlinear scale – that is, 14 bits per component.

If *RGB* or *XYZ* tristimulus components were conveyed directly, then 16 bits in each component would suffice for any realistic image-reproduction purpose. Linear-light 16-bit coding might be practical in a decade, but for now, for most purposes, we exploit the nonlinear characteristics of perception to achieve an efficient image data coding.

Gamma in emerging display devices

PDP and DLP devices are commonly described as employing PWM. However, it is not quite the width of the pulses that is being modulated, but the number of unit pulses per frame.

Emerging display devices, such as liquid crystal displays (LCDs), have different transfer functions than CRTs. Plasma display panels (PDPs) and Digital Light Processors (DLPs) both achieve apparent continuous tone through *pulse width modulation* (PWM): They are intrinsically linear-light devices, with straight-line transfer functions. Linear-light devices, such as PDPs and DLPs, potentially suffer from the "code 100" problem explained on page 12: In linear-light, more than 8 bits per component are necessary to achieve high quality.

No matter what transfer function characterizes the display, it is economically important to encode image data in a manner that is well matched to perceptual requirements. The most important aspect of Rec. 709 encoding is not that it is well matched to CRTs, but that it is well matched to perception! The performance advantage of perceptual coding, the wide deployment of equipment that encodes to Rec. 709, and the huge amount of program material already encoded to this standard preclude any attempt to establish new standards optimized to particular devices.

A display device whose transfer function differs from a CRT must incorporate local correction, to adapt from its intrinsic transfer function to the transfer function that has been standardized for image interchange.

CRT transfer function details

To calibrate your monitor, or to determine the transfer function of your CRT, you must be familiar with the

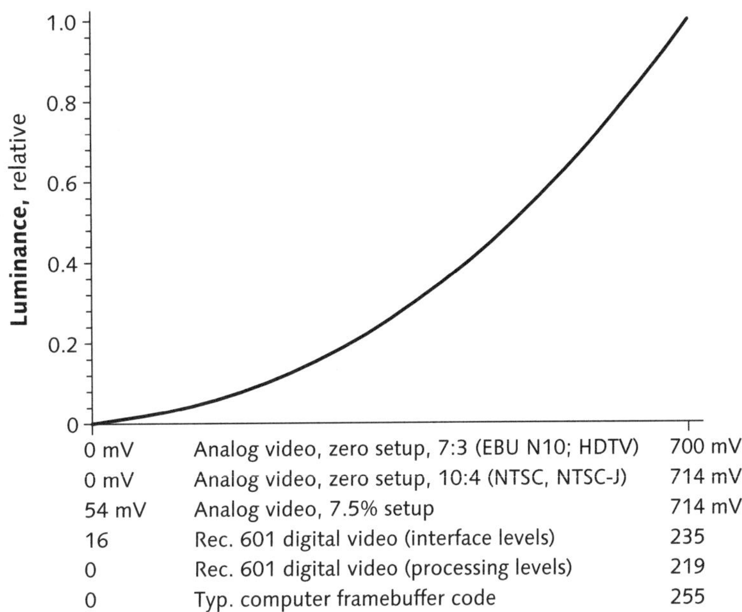

Figure 23.6 **CRT signal levels and luminance.** An analog video signal may be coded between 0 and 700 mV, between 0 and 714 mV, or between 54 mV and 714 mV. A digital signal may be coded from 16 to 235 (for Rec. 601 studio video interface), from 0 to 219 (for Rec. 601-related studio video signal processing), or from 0 to 255 (as is typical in computer graphics).

electrical interface between a computer framebuffer and a monitor.

Figure 23.6 illustrates the function that relates signal input to a CRT monitor to the light luminance produced at the face of the screen. The graph characterizes a grayscale monitor, or each of the red, green, and blue components of a color monitor. The *x*-axis of the graph shows the input signal level, from reference black to reference white. The input signal can be presented as a digital code, or as an analog voltage according to one of several standards. The *y*-axis shows the resulting relative luminance.

Details will be presented in *Setup (pedestal)*, on page 327.

For analog voltage signals, three standards are in use. The range 54 mV to 714 mV is used in video systems that have *7.5% setup*, including composite 480*i* systems such as NTSC, and computer video systems that conform to the levels of the archaic EIA RS-343-A standard. Computer framebuffer digital-to-analog converters often have 7.5% setup; these almost universally have very loose tolerance – about ±5% of full scale – on the analog voltage associated with reference black. This induces black-level errors, which in turn cause serious errors in the luminance reproduced for black. In the absence of a display calibrator, you must compensate these framebuffer black-level errors by adjusting the BLACK LEVEL (or BRIGHTNESS) control on your monitor. This act effectively marries the monitor to the framebuffer.

The accuracy of black-level reproduction is greatly improved in newer analog video standards that have *zero setup*. The voltage range 0 to 700 mV is used in zero-setup standards, including 480*i* video in Japan, 576*i* video in Europe, and HDTV.

Concerning the conversion between Rec. 601 levels and the full-range levels used in computing, see Figure 27.3, on page 329.

For the 8-bit digital *RGB* components that are ubiquitous in computing, reference black and white correspond to digital codes 0 and 255. The Rec. 601 interface for studio digital video places black at code 16 and white at code 235. Either of these digital coding standards can be used in conjunction with an analog interface having either 7.5% setup or zero setup.

Knowing that a CRT is intrinsically nonlinear, and that its response is based on a power function, many researchers have attempted to summarize the nonlinearity of a CRT display in a single numerical parameter γ using this relationship, where V' is code (or voltage) and L is luminance (or tristimulus value):

$$L = \left(V'\right)^{\gamma_D} \qquad \text{Eq 23.10}$$

The model forces zero voltage to map to zero luminance for *any* value of gamma. Owing to the model being "pegged" at zero, it cannot accommodate black-level errors: Black-level errors that displace the transfer function upward can be "fit" only by an estimate of gamma that is much smaller than 2.5. Black-level errors that displace the curve downward – saturating at zero over some portion of low voltages – can be "fit" only with an estimate of gamma that is much larger than 2.5. The only way the single gamma parameter can fit a black-level variation is to alter the curvature of the

Berns, R.S., R.J. Motta, and M.E. Gorzynski, "CRT Colorimetry, in *Color Research and Application* 18: 299–325 (1993).

function. The apparent wide variability of gamma under this model has given gamma a bad reputation.

A much better model is obtained by fixing the exponent of the power function at 2.5, and using the single parameter to accommodate black-level error, ϵ:

$$L = \left(V' + \epsilon\right)^{2.5} \qquad \text{Eq 23.11}$$

This model fits the observed nonlinearity much better than the variable-gamma model.

Cowan, William B., "An Inexpensive Scheme for Calibration of a Colour Monitor in terms of CIE Standard Coordinates," in *Computer Graphics* 17 (3): 315–321 (July 1983).

If you want to determine the nonlinearity of your monitor, consult the article by Cowan. In addition to describing how to measure the nonlinearity, he describes how to determine other characteristics of your monitor – such as the chromaticity of its white point and its primaries – that are important for accurate color reproduction.

Gamma in video, CGI, SGI, and Macintosh

Transfer functions in video (and PC), computer-generated imagery, SGI, and Macintosh are sketched in the rows of Figure 23.7 overleaf. Each row shows four function blocks; from left to right, these are a camera or scanner LUT, an image storage device, an output LUT, and a monitor.

In video, sketched in the top row, the camera applies a transfer function to accomplish gamma correction. Signals are then maintained in a perceptual domain throughout the system until conversion to tristimulus values at the monitor. I show the output LUT with a ramp that leaves data unaltered: Video systems conventionally use no LUT, but the comparison is clarified if I portray the four rows with the same blocks.

PC graphics hardware ordinarily implements lookup tables at the output of the framestore, as I detailed in *Raster images,* on page 34. However, most PC software accommodates display hardware without lookup tables. When the LUT is absent, code values map directly to voltage, and the situation is equivalent to video. So, the top row in the diagram pertains to PCs.

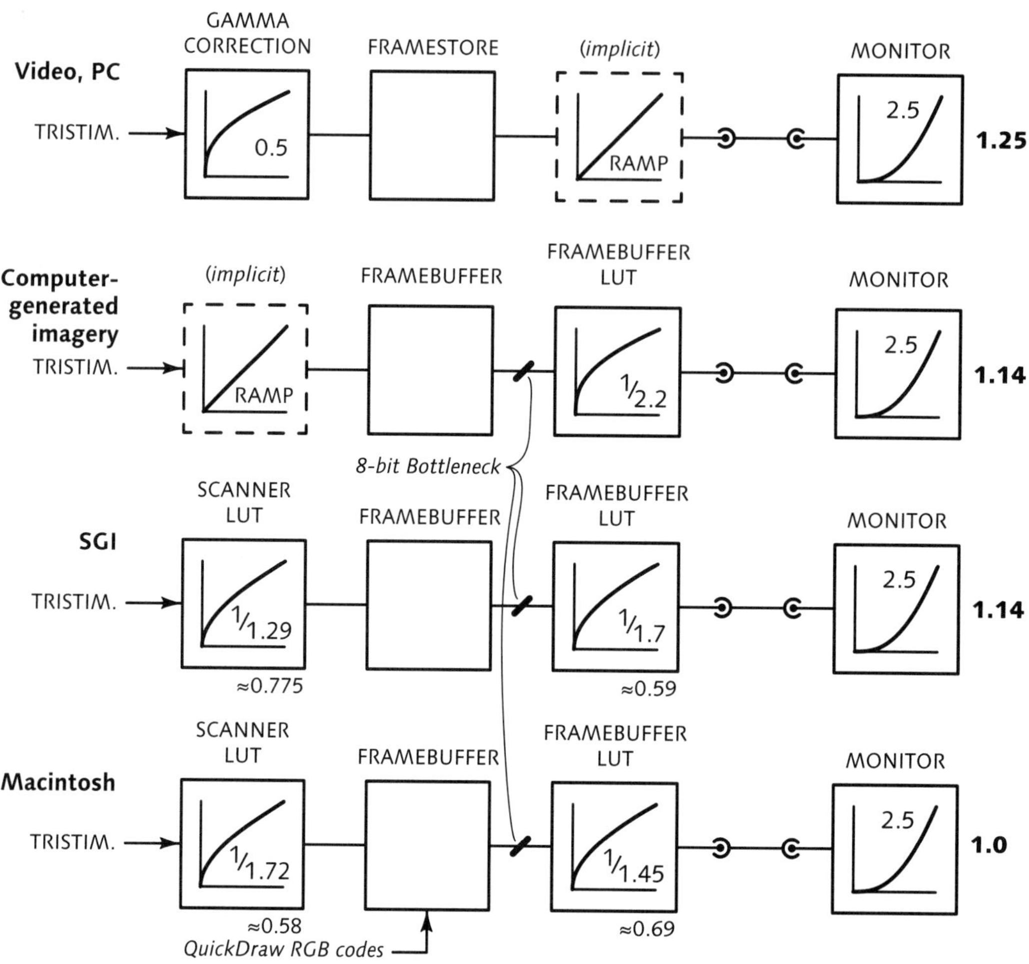

Figure 23.7 **Gamma in video, CGI, SGI, and Macintosh** are summarized in the rows of this diagram. Tristimulus signals enter from the left; the columns show the transfer functions of (respectively) a camera or scanner; the image storage device (framestore or framebuffer); output LUT; and the monitor.

In video, sketched in the top row, a transfer function that mimics vision is applied at the camera ("gamma correction"); the signal remains in perceptual space until the encoding is reversed by the monitor. (PCs have comparable signal encoding.) In computer graphics, sketched in the second row, calculations are performed in the linear-light domain, and gamma correction is applied in a LUT at the output of the framebuffer. SGI computers take a hybrid approach: Part of the correction is accomplished at the camera or scanner, and part is accomplished through a $1/1.7$-power function that is loaded into the LUT. Macintosh computers, sketched in the bottom row, also take a hybrid approach: The camera or scanner applies a $1/1.72$ power, and a $1/1.45$-power function is loaded into the LUT. Using $\gamma_E \approx 1/1.72$ is appropriate for prerendered imagery, to produce an end-to-end exponent of 1.0.

The end-to-end power function exponent, or *rendering intent* (see page 81), is shown for each row by the number at the extreme right. This number is the product of the exponents across the system. Some people call this "system gamma," but that term is so widely misused that I reject it.

Computer graphics systems generally store tristimulus values in the framebuffer, and use hardware LUTs, in the path to the display, to gamma-correct on the fly. This is illustrated in the second row. Typically, a $\frac{1}{2.2}$-power function is loaded into the output LUT; in this case, rendering intent of 1.14 is achieved.

The Macintosh computer by default implements a $\frac{1}{1.45}$-power function at the output LUT. John Knoll's *Gamma* Control Panel can load the output LUT. When set to a gamma value g, the Control Panel loads an output LUT with a power function whose exponent is $\frac{2.61}{g}$. Strangely, gamma on Macintosh computers has come to be quoted as the exponent applied prior to the framebuffer (whereas in other computers it is the exponent of the table loaded into the output LUT). So, the Mac's default gamma is said to be 1.8, not 1.45.

A Macintosh can be set to handle video (or PC) $R'G'B'$ data by loading a ramp into its output LUT. Using Knoll's control panel, this is accomplished by setting gamma to 2.61.

JFIF files originated on Macintosh ordinarily represent R, G, and B display tristimulus values raised to the $\frac{1}{1.72}$ power.

Macintosh computers use the approach shown in the bottom row. The output LUT is, by default, loaded with a $\frac{1}{1.45}$-power function. The combination of the default LUT and the usual 2.5-power monitor function results in a 1.72-power function that relates QuickDraw $R'G'B'$ values (such as the values stored in a PICT file or data structure) to displayed tristimulus values.

If a desktop scanner is to produce QuickDraw $R'G'B'$ values that display relative luminance correctly, then a 1.72-power function must be loaded to the scanner LUT. In the typical Macintosh situation, the $\frac{1}{1.72}$, $\frac{1}{1.45}$, and 2.5 exponents combine to achieve an end-to-end exponent of unity. This is suitable for scanning photographs or offset printed matter, where a suitable rendering intent is already incorporated into the image.

For QuickDraw $R'G'B'$ values originated by application software, part of Macintosh gamma correction must be effected by application software prior to presentation of $R'G'B'$ values to the QuickDraw graphics subsystem; the remainder is accomplished in the output LUTs. When scanning, part of Macintosh gamma correction is effected by the LUT in the scanner driver, and the remainder is accomplished in the output LUTs.

Halftoned printing has a builtin nonlinearity, owing to the phenomenon of dot gain. Reflectance from the printed page is approximately proportional to the 1.8-power of *CMYK* code values. QuickDraw $R'G'B'$ values are not perceptually optimum; however, apparently by serendipity, QuickDraw $R'G'B'$ coding is nearly perfectly matched to the dot gain of halftone printing. This has led to the dominance of Macintosh computers in graphic arts and prepress, and has made "gamma 1.8" image coding a de facto standard.

An SGI workstation can be set to handle video (or PC) $R'G'B'$ data by setting gamma to 1.

SGI (formerly Silicon Graphics) computers, by default, use an output LUT containing a 1.7-power function; this is shown in the third row. If a scanner is to produce images for display on an SGI system (without imposing any rendering intent), it must incorporate a transfer function whose exponent is approximately $1/1.47$.

At the right-hand end of each row of Figure 23.7, on page 274, I have indicated in boldface type the rendering intent usually used. In video, I have shown an end-to-end power function of 1.25. For computer-generated imagery and SGI, I have shown the typical value of 1.14. For Macintosh, I have sketched the usual situation where prerendered images are being scanned; in this case, the end-to-end power function is unity.

To correct PC image data for display on a Mac, apply a 1.45-power function. To correct Mac image data for display on a PC, apply a 0.69-power function – that is, $1/1.45$.

Correct display of computer image data depends upon knowing the transfer function that will be applied at the output of the graphics subsystem. If an image originates on a PC, after traversing the default $1/1.45$-power function in a Mac LUT, midtones will display too light: Code 128 will produce luminance 1.6 times higher than intended. Conversely, if an image originates on a Mac (where the $1/1.45$-power function is expected), but is displayed on a PC (without this function), midtones will display much too dark. The relationship between default $R'G'B'$ code values and reproduced luminance factors is graphed in Figure 23.8.

Gamma in computer graphics

Computer-generated imagery (CGI) software systems generally perform calculations for lighting, shading, depth-cueing, and antialiasing using approximations to tristimulus values, so as to model the physical mixing of light. Values stored in the framebuffer are processed by hardware lookup tables on the fly on their way to the display. If linear-light values are stored in the framebuffer, the LUTs can accomplish gamma-correction. The power function at the CRT acts on the gamma-corrected signal voltages to reproduce the correct luminance values at the face of the screen. Software systems usually provide a default gamma value and some method to change the default.

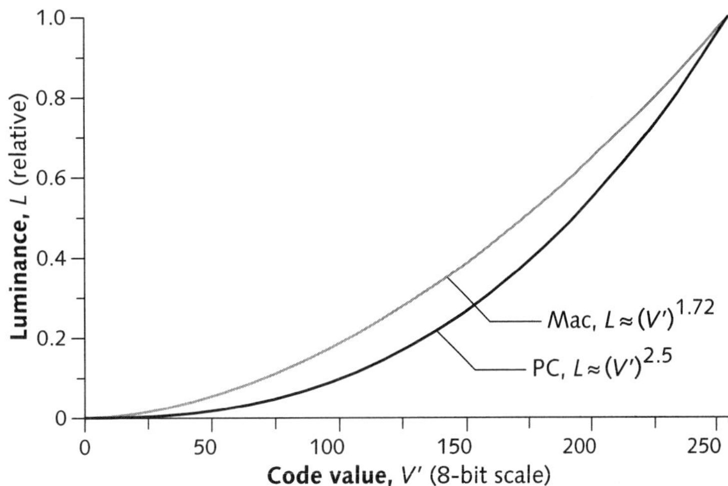

Figure 23.8 **Gamma in Mac and PC** are different, owing to the interpretation of *RGB* code values by the display system. On a PC, the output LUT is either absent or programmed as if absent, and code values are subject to the 2.5-power function of the display (sketched in the lower curve). On a Mac, the default output LUT imposes a $1/1.45$-power function on the code values, then the display imposes its usual 2.5-power function; the concatenation of these two functions results in a 1.72-power function that relates Mac code value to displayed relative luminance, as sketched in the upper curve.

You can construct a gamma-correction lookup table to apply Rec. 709 to 8-bit tristimulus data, using this C code:

```
#define CLIP(b,t,v) ((v) <= (b) ? (b) : (v) >= (t) ? (t) : v)
#define REC_709(L) ((L) <= 0.018 ? (L) * 4.5 : \
  (1.099 * pow((L), 0.45) - 0.099))
int rec_709[256], i;
for (i=0; i<256; i++)
  rec_709[i] = CLIP(0, 255,
    (int)(0.5 + 255.0 * REC_709(i / 255.)));
```

Loading this table into the hardware lookup table at the output side of a framebuffer will cause integer *RGB* tristimulus values r, g, and b between 0 and 255 to be gamma-corrected by the hardware as if by the following C code:

```
red_signal = rec_709[r];
green_signal = rec_709[g];
blue_signal = rec_709[b];
```

The Rec. 709 function is suitable for viewing in a dim surround. For viewing in other environments, see the comments on page 84: In a bright surround, cascade Rec. 709 with a 0.9-power function; in a dark surround, cascade it with a 1.2-power function.

The framebuffer's LUTs enable software to perform tricks to manipulate the appearance of the image data without changing the image data itself. To allow the user to make use of features such as accurate color reproduction, applications should access lookup tables in the structured ways that are provided by the graphics system, and not by direct manipulation of the LUTs.

Gamma in pseudocolor

In *Pseudocolor,* on page 38, I described how the color lookup table (CLUT) in a pseudocolor system contains values that are directly mapped to voltage at the display. It is conventional for a pseudocolor application program to provide, to a graphics system, *R'G'B'* color values that are already gamma corrected for a typical monitor and typical viewing conditions. A pseudocolor image stored in a file is accompanied by a *colormap* whose *R'G'B'* values incorporate gamma correction.

Limitations of 8-bit linear coding

As mentioned in *Gamma in computer graphics,* on page 276, computer graphics systems that render synthetic imagery usually perform computations in the linear-light – or loosely, intensity – domain. Low-end graphics accelerators often perform Gouraud shading in the linear-light domain, and store 8-bit components in the framebuffer. In *The "code 100" problem,* on page 12, I explained that linear-light representation cannot achieve high-quality images with just 8 bits per component: The images will exhibit contouring. The visibility of contouring is enhanced by a perceptual effect called *Mach bands*; consequently, the contouring artifact is sometimes called *banding*.

High-end systems for computer-generated imagery (CGI) usually do not depend on hardware acceleration. Rendering software operates in the linear-light domain using more than 8 bits per component (often floating

Figure 23.9 **Linear and nonlinear coding in computer graphics standards.** In the PHIGS and CGM standards, code [128, 128, 128] produces luminance halfway up the *physical* scale, a relative luminance of 0.5. In JPEG, code [128, 128, 128] produces luminance halfway up the *perceptual* scale, only about 0.18 in relative luminance. Values are denoted *RGB* in both cases; however, the values are not comparable. This exemplifies a serious problem in the exchange of image files.

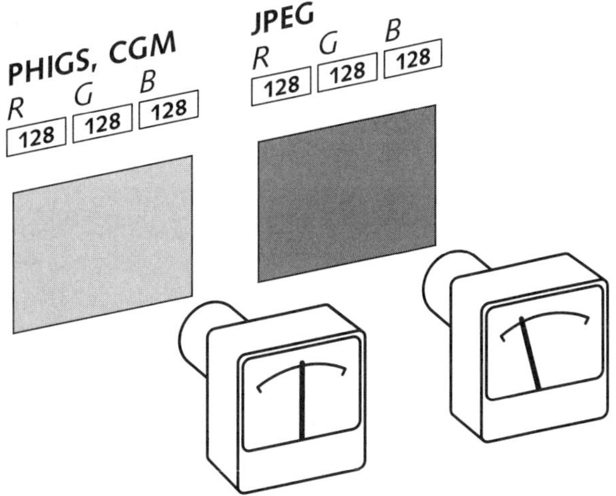

point), performs gamma correction in software, then writes gamma-corrected values into the framebuffer. A unity ramp is loaded into the LUT of the framebuffer associated with the image. This arrangement maximizes perceptual performance, and produces rendered imagery without the quantization artifacts of 8-bit linear-light coding.

Professional video software on Macintosh or SGI platforms ordinarily loads the output LUT with a ramp function; code values are then interpreted as in video. Unfortunately, colors are altered in image data or interface elements that assume the default gamma of the platform.

Linear and nonlinear coding in CGI

Computer graphic standards such as PHIGS and CGM make no mention of transfer function, but linear-light coding is implicit. In the JPEG standard there is also no mention of transfer function, but *nonlinear* (video-like) coding is implicit: Unacceptable results are obtained when JPEG is applied to linear-light data. All of these standards deal with *RGB* quantities; you might consider their *RGB* values to be comparable, but they're not!

Figure 23.9 sketches two systems displaying the same *RGB* triple, [128, 128, 128]. A photometer reading the luminance displayed by a PHIGS or CGM system is

What are loosely called *JPEG files* use the *JPEG File Interchange Format* (JFIF), cited in the margin of page 459. Version 1.02 of that specification states that linear-light coding (gamma 1.0) is used. That is seldom the case in practice; instead, encoding power laws of 0.45 (sRGB) or 0.58 (i.e., $^{1.45}/_{2.5}$) are usually used. See page 273.

shown at the left; a photometer reading luminance displayed by a JPEG system is shown at the right. In PHIGS and CGM, the displayed luminance is halfway up the *physical* scale, a relative luminance of 0.5. In the JPEG case, displayed luminance is halfway up the *perceptual* scale, only about 0.18 in relative luminance. The PHIGS and CGM standards are obsolete; however, the problem persists that many graphics image files do not carry any transfer function information. If you exchange *RGB* image data without regard for transfer functions, huge differences will result when image data is displayed.

The digital image-processing literature rarely discriminates between linear and nonlinear coding. Also, when *intensity* is mentioned, be suspicious: Image data may be represented in linear-light form, *proportional* to intensity. However, a pixel component value is usually associated with a small area of a sensor or a display, so its units should include a per square meter ($\cdot m^{-2}$) term. Pixel component values are ordinarily properly represented as radiance, luminance, relative luminance, or tristimulus value.

Luma and color differences 24

This chapter describes color coding systems that are used to convey image data derived from additive (*RGB*) primaries. I outline nonlinear *R'G'B'*, explain the formation of *luma*, denoted *Y'*, as a weighted sum of these nonlinear signals, and introduce the *color difference* (chroma) components [*B'–Y'*, *R'–Y'*], [C_B, C_R], and [P_B, P_R].

The design of a video coding system is necessarily rooted in detailed knowledge of human color perception. However, once this knowledge is embodied in a coding system, what remains is physics, mathematics, and signal processing. This chapter concerns only the latter domains.

Color acuity

A monochrome video system ideally senses relative luminance, described on page 205. Luminance is then transformed by the gamma correction circuitry of the camera, as described in *Gamma in video,* on page 261, into a signal that takes into account the properties of lightness perception. At the receiver, the CRT itself imposes the required inverse transfer function.

A color image is sensed in three components, red, green, and blue, according to *Additive reproduction (RGB),* on page 234. To minimize the visibility of noise or quantization, the *RGB* components should be coded nonlinearly.

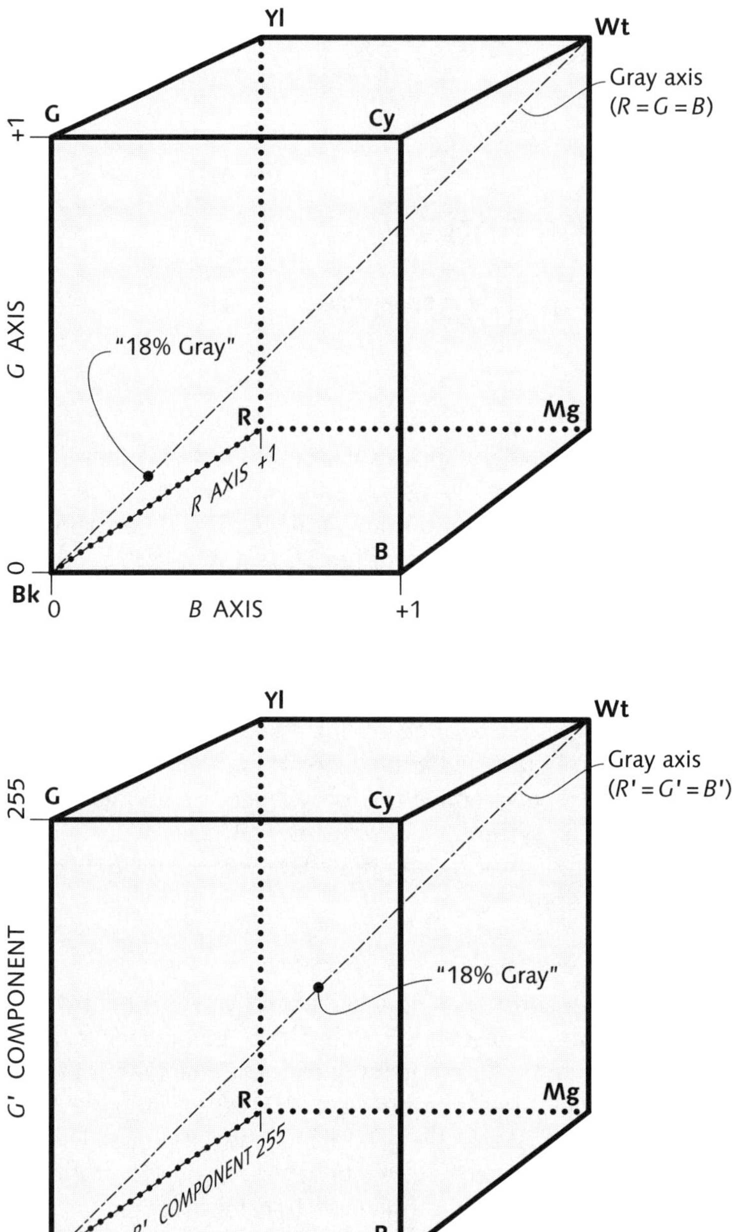

Figure 24.1 ***RGB* and *R'G'B'* cubes.** *RGB* components form the coordinates of a three-dimensional color space; coordinate values between 0 and 1 define the unit cube. Linear coding, sketched at the top, has poor perceptual performance. In video, *RGB* components are subject to *gamma correction;* this yields perceptually uniform *R'G'B'* that exhibits good performance with 8-bit components.

RGB and *R'G'B'* color cubes

Red, green, and blue tristimulus (linear light) primary components, as detailed in *Color science for video*, on page 233, can be considered to be the coordinates of a three-dimensional color space. Coordinate values between zero and unity define the unit cube of this space, as sketched at the top of Figure 24.1 opposite. Linear-light coding is used in CGI, where physical light is simulated. However, as I explained in the previous chapter, *Gamma in video*, 8-bit linear-light coding performs poorly for images to be viewed: 12 or 14 bits per component are necessary to achieve excellent quality. The best perceptual use is made of a limited number of bits by using nonlinear coding that mimics the nonlinear lightness response of human vision. As introduced on page 12, and detailed in the previous chapter, in video, JPEG, MPEG, computing, digital still photography, and in many other domains a nonlinear transfer function is applied to *RGB* tristimulus signals to give nonlinearly coded (*gamma-corrected*) components, denoted with prime symbols: *R'G'B'*. Excellent image quality is obtained with 10-bit nonlinear coding with a transfer function similar to that of Rec. 709 or sRGB.

In PC graphics, 8-bit nonlinear coding is common: Each of *R'*, *G'*, and *B'* ranges from 0 through 255, inclusive, following the quantizer transfer function sketched in Figure 2.1, on page 17. The resulting *R'G'B'* cube is sketched at the bottom of Figure 24.1 opposite. A total of 2^{24} colors – that is, 16777216 colors – are representable. Not all of them can be distinguished visually; not all are perceptually useful; but they are all colors. Studio video uses headroom and footroom, as I explained in *Headroom and footroom,* on page 22: 8-bit *R'G'B'* has 219 codes between black and white, for a total of 10648000 codewords.

In video, *codeword* (or *codepoint*) refers to a combination of three integer values such as [*R'*, *G'*, *B'*] or [*Y'*, C_B, C_R].

The drawback of conveying *R'G'B'* components of an image is that each component requires relatively high spatial resolution: Transmission or storage of a color image using *R'G'B'* components requires a capacity three times that of a grayscale image. Human vision has considerably less spatial acuity for color information than for lightness. Owing to the poor color acuity of vision, a color image can be coded into a wideband monochrome component representing lightness, and two narrowband components carrying color information, each having substantially less spatial resolution than lightness. In analog video, each color channel has bandwidth typically one-third that of the monochrome channel. In digital video, each color channel has half the data rate (or data capacity) of the monochrome channel, or less. There is strong evidence that the human visual system forms an achromatic channel and two chromatic color-difference channels at the retina.

Here the term *color difference* refers to a signal formed as the difference of two gamma-corrected color components. In other contexts, the term can refer to a numerical measure of the perceptual distance between two colors.

Green dominates luminance: Between 60% and 70% of luminance comprises green information. Signal-to-noise ratio is maximized if the color signals on the other two components are chosen to be blue and red. The simplest way to"remove" lightness from blue and red is to subtract it, to form a pair of *color difference* (or loosely, *chroma*) components.

The monochrome component in color video could have been based upon the luminance of color science (a weighted sum of R, G, and B). Instead, as I explained in *Constant luminance,* on page 75, luma is formed as a weighted sum of R', G', and B', using coefficients similar or identical to those that would be used to compute luminance. Expressed in abstract terms, luma ranges 0 to 1. Color difference components $B'-Y'$ and $R'-Y'$ are bipolar; each ranges nearly ±1.

In component analog video, $B'-Y'$ and $R'-Y'$ are scaled to form P_B and P_R components. In abstract terms, these range ±0.5. Figure 24.2 opposite shows the unit $R'G'B'$ cube transformed into luma [Y', P_B, P_R]. (Various interface standards are in use; see page 303.) In component digital video, $B'-Y'$ and $R'-Y'$ are scaled to form C_B and C_R components. In 8-bit $Y'C_BC_R$ prior to the application of the interface offset, the luma axis of Figure 24.2 would be scaled by 219, and the chroma axes by 112.

I introduced interface offsets on page 23.

Once color difference signals have been formed, they can be subsampled to reduce bandwidth or data capacity, without the observer's noticing, as I will explain in *Chroma subsampling, revisited,* on page 292.

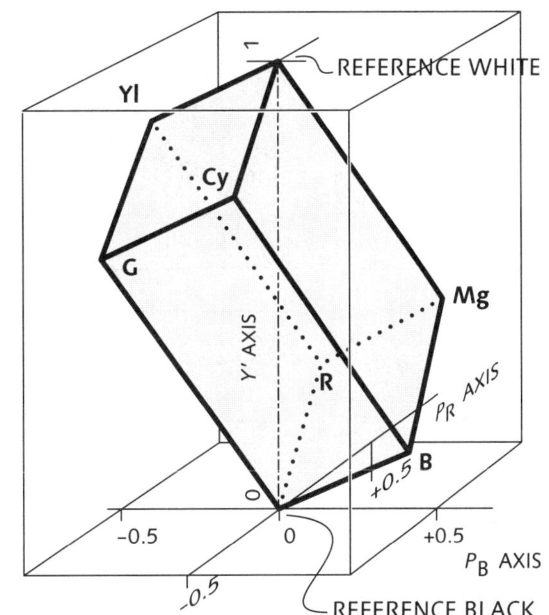

Figure 24.2 ***Y'P_BP_R* cube** is formed when *R'*, *G'*, and *B'* are subject to a particular 3×3 matrix transform. The *valid R'G'B'* unit cube occupies about one-quarter of the volume of the $Y'P_BP_R$ unit cube. (The volume of the $Y'P_BP_R$ unit cube, the outer boundary of this sketch, is the same as the volume of the *R'G'B'* cube in Figure 24.1 on page 282; however, the useful codes occupy only the central prism here.) Luma and color difference coding incurs a penalty in signal-to-noise ratio, but this disadvantage is compensated by the opportunity to subsample.

Izraelevitz, David, and Joshua L. Koslov, "Code Utilization for Component-coded Digital Video," in *Tomorrow's Television*, Proc. 16th Annual SMPTE Television Conference (White Plains, N.Y.: SMPTE, 1982), 22–30.

It is evident from Figure 24.2 that when *R'G'B'* signals are transformed into the $Y'P_BP_R$ space of analog video, the unit *R'G'B'* cube occupies only part of the volume of the unit $Y'P_BP_R$ cube: Only ¼ of the $Y'P_BP_R$ volume corresponds to *R'G'B'* values all between 0 and 1. Consequently, $Y'P_BP_R$ exhibits a loss of signal-to-noise ratio compared to *R'G'B'*. However, this disadvantage is compensated by the opportunity to subsample.

A *legal* signal is one in which no component exceeds its reference excursion. Combinations that are *R'G'B'*-legal are termed *valid.* Signals within the $Y'P_BP_R$ unit cube are $Y'P_BP_R$-legal. However, about ¾ of these combinations correspond to *R'G'B'* combinations outside the *R'G'B'* unit cube: Although legal, these $Y'P_BP_R$ combinations are *invalid* – that is, they are *R'G'B'*-illegal.

$$\frac{\frac{1}{4}\cdot 220 \cdot 225^2}{220^3} = \frac{2784375}{10648000} \approx 0.261$$

In digital video, we refer to *codewords* instead of combinations. There are about 2.75 million valid codewords in 8-bit $Y'C_BC_R$, compared to 10.6 million in 8-bit studio *R'G'B'*. If *R'G'B'* is transcoded to $Y'C_BC_R$, then transcoded back to *R'G'B'*, the resulting *R'G'B'* cannot have any more than 2.75 million colors.

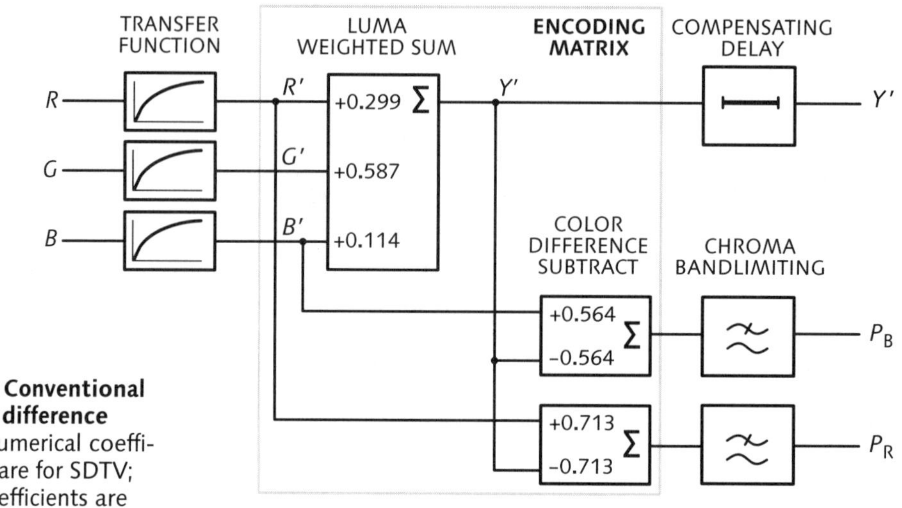

Figure 24.3 **Conventional luma/color difference encoder.** Numerical coefficients here are for SDTV; different coefficients are standard for HDTV.

Conventional luma/color difference coding

I explained constant luminance on page 75. True constant luminance coding remains an intriguing possibility, but at present all video systems use nonconstant luminance coding, which I will now describe.

Figure 24.3 shows a time delay element in the luma path. Luma is delayed by a time interval equal to the transit delay of chroma through the chroma bandlimiting filters.

A conventional luma/color difference encoder is shown in Figure 24.3 above. First, a nonlinear transfer function is applied to each of the red, green, and blue linear (tristimulus) components. Then luma is formed as a weighted sum of gamma-corrected *R'*, *G'*, and *B'* components. *B'–Y'* and *R'–Y'* color difference components are formed by subtraction; in Figure 24.3, scaling to analog P_B and P_R components is indicated. Finally, the color difference components are lowpass filtered.

Eq 24.1 Rec. 601 $Y'P_BP_R$ encoding matrix (for SDTV)

$$\mathbf{P} = \begin{bmatrix} 0.299 & 0.587 & 0.114 \\ -0.169 & -0.331 & 0.5 \\ 0.5 & -0.419 & -0.081 \end{bmatrix}$$

The gray rectangle in Figure 24.3 groups together the weighted adder that forms luma with the pair of color difference subtractors; the combination is equivalent to matrix multiplication by the 3×3 matrix ***P*** shown in Equation 24.1 in the margin. The numerical values used in Equation 24.1, in Figure 24.3, and in subsequent figures in this chapter all reflect the Rec. 601 luma coefficients used in SDTV. Unfortunately, the coefficients for HDTV are different; as I will describe in *Component video color coding for HDTV,* on page 313.

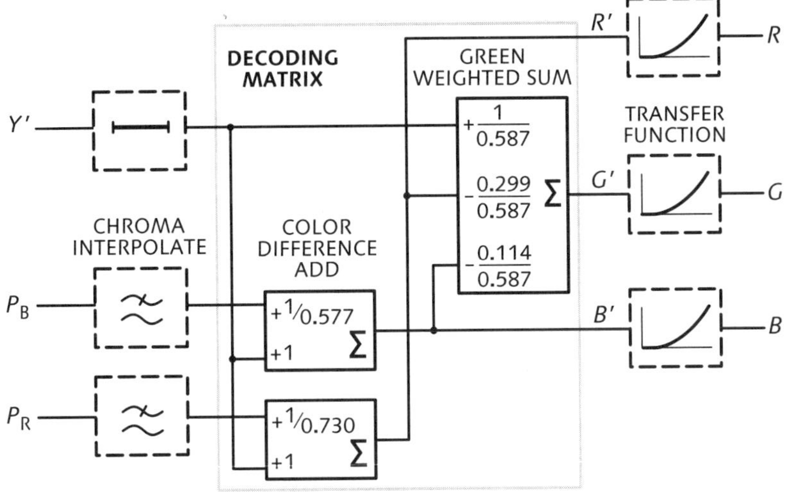

Figure 24.4 **Conventional luma/color difference decoder**

Figure 24.4 illustrates a conventional luma/color difference decoder. In a digital decoder, the color difference (chroma) components are horizontally (and, in some applications, spatially) interpolated; in an analog decoder, no circuitry is required to perform this function. Luma is added to the color difference components to reconstruct nonlinear blue and red components. A weighted sum of luma, blue, and red is then formed to reconstruct the nonlinear green component.

Eq 24.2 Rec. 601 $Y'P_BP_R$ decoding matrix (for SDTV)

$$\boldsymbol{P}^{-1} = \begin{bmatrix} 1 & 0 & 1.402 \\ 1 & -0.344 & -0.714 \\ 1 & 1.772 & 0 \end{bmatrix}$$

The blue and red color difference adders and the weighted adder that recovers green, all enclosed by the gray rectangle of Figure 24.4, can be considered together as multiplication by the 3×3 matrix $\boldsymbol{P}^{-1}$ shown in Equation 24.2. These values are for SDTV; the matrix for HDTV is different.

To produce linear-light tristimulus components, all three components are subject to the inverse transfer function sketched at the right with dashed outlines. Usually, a decoder is used with a CRT that has an intrinsic 2.5-power function, or with some other display that incorporates a 2.5-power function; in either case, the transfer function need not be explicitly computed.

Luminance and luma notation

In *Luminance from red, green, and blue*, on page 207, I described how relative (linear-light) luminance, proportional to intensity, can be computed as an appropriately weighted sum of *RGB*.

In video, the luminance of color science isn't computed. Instead, we compute a nonlinear quantity *luma* as a weighted sum of nonlinear (gamma-corrected) *R'G'B'*. The weights – or *luma coefficients* – are related to the luminance coefficients. The luma coefficients specified in Rec. 601 have been ubiquitous for SDTV, but new and different weights have been introduced in HDTV standards. In my opinion, the luma coefficients need not and should not have been changed for HDTV: Complexity is added to upconversion and downconversion in the studio and consumer equipment, for no improvement in performance or quality.

See Appendix A, *YUV and luminance considered harmful*, on page 595.

Television standards documents historically used the prime symbol (′) – often combined with the letter *E* for voltage – to denote a component that incorporates gamma correction. For example, E'_{R} historically denoted the gamma-corrected red channel. Gamma correction is nowadays so taken for granted in video that the *E* and the prime symbol are usually elided. This has led to much confusion among people attempting to utilize video technology in other domains.

The existence of several standard sets of primary chromaticities, the introduction of new coefficients, and continuing confusion between luminance and luma all beg for a notation to distinguish among the many possible combinations. In the absence of any standard notation, I was compelled to invent my own. Figure 24.5 at the top of the facing page sketches the notation that I use. The base symbol is *Y, R, G, or B.* The subscript denotes the standard that specifies the chromaticities of the primaries and white. An unprimed letter indicates a linear-light tristimulus component (*R*, *G*, or *B*), or relative luminance (*Y*). A prime symbol (′) indicates a nonlinear (gamma-corrected) component (*R*′, *G*′, and *B*′), or luma (*Y*′).

Figure 24.5 **Luminance and luma notation** is necessary because different primary chromaticity sets, different luma coefficients, and different component scale factors are in use. Unity scaling suffices for components in this chapter; in succeeding chapters, other scale factors will be introduced.

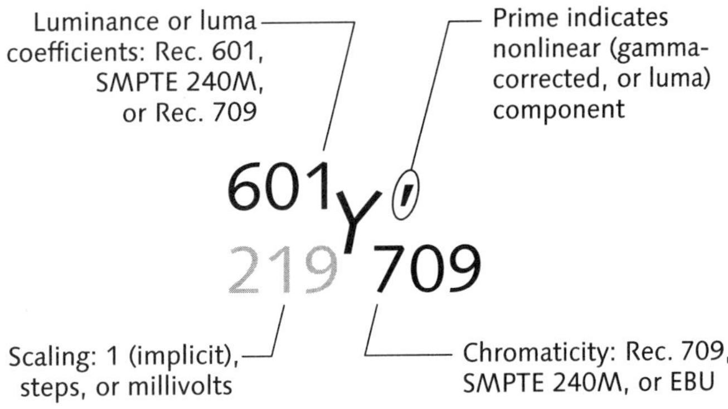

For luminance or luma, a leading superscript indicates the standard specifying the weights used; historically, the weights of Rec. 601 were implicit, but recent HDTV standards such as Rec. 709 and SMPTE 240M call for different weights. Finally, the leading subscript indicates the overall scaling of the signal. If omitted, an overall scaling of unity is implicit, otherwise an integer such as 219, 255, or 874 specifies the black-to-white excursion in a digital system, or a number such as 661, 700 or 714 specifies the analog excursion in millivolts.

Typesetting $Y'C_BC_R$ (or $Y'P_BP_R$) is a challenge! I illustrate the main points in Figure 24.6 below. Y' is augmented with shaded leading superscript and subscript and a trailing subscript, according to the conventions of Figure 24.5. Without these elements, the intended color cannot be determined with certainty.

Figure 24.6 **Typesetting $Y'C_BC_R$** is a challenge! Luma coefficient set, scaling, and chromaticities are set out as in Figure 24.5 above. The prime should always be present, to distinguish *luma* from the *luminance* of color science. *C* is appropriate for digital signals, *P* for analog. Subscripts B and R serve as tags, not variables: They should be in Roman type, not italics. B comes before R.

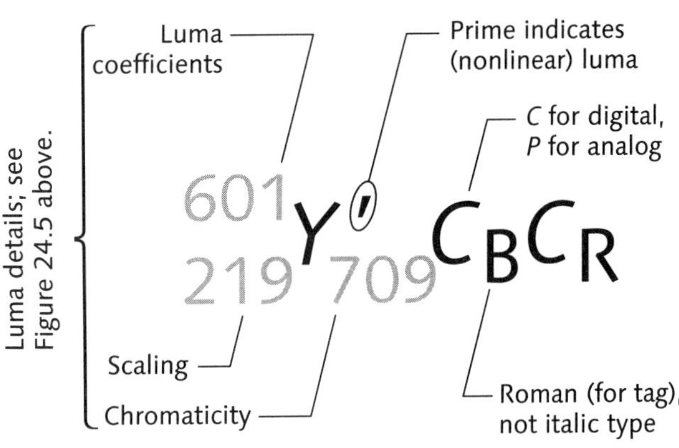

Nonlinear red, green, blue ($R'G'B'$)

Now that I have explained the overall signal flow of video, and introduced my notation for the basic components, I will detail the encoding of luma and color difference signals, starting with the formation of nonlinear R', G', and B' primary components.

Video originates with approximations of linear-light (*tristimulus*) *RGB* primary components, usually represented in abstract terms in the range 0 (black) to +1 (white). In order to meaningfully determine a color from an *RGB* triple, the colorimetric properties of the primaries and the reference white – such as their CIE $[x, y]$ chromaticity coordinates – must be known. Colorimetric properties of *RGB* components were discussed in *Color science for video,* on page 233. In the absence of any specific information, use the Rec. 709 primaries and the CIE D_{65} white point.

In *Gamma,* on page 257, I described how lightness information is coded nonlinearly, in order to achieve good perceptual performance from a limited number of bits. In a color system, the nonlinear transfer function described in that chapter is applied individually to each of the three *RGB* tristimulus components: From the set of *RGB* tristimulus (linear-light) values, three gamma-corrected primary signals are computed; each is approximately proportional to the square-root of the corresponding scene tristimulus value.

I detailed the *Rec. 709 transfer function* on page 263. Although standardized for HDTV, it is now applied to conventional video as well. For tristimulus values greater than a few percent, use these equations:

$$
\begin{aligned}
R'_{709} &= 1.099R^{0.45} - 0.099 \\
G'_{709} &= 1.099G^{0.45} - 0.099 \\
B'_{709} &= 1.099B^{0.45} - 0.099
\end{aligned}
\qquad \text{Eq 24.3}
$$

The obsolete SMPTE 240M standard for 1035*i*30 HDTV specified transfer function parameters slightly different from those of Rec. 709. For tristimulus values greater than a few percent, use these equations:

$$R'_{240} = 1.1115R^{0.45} - 0.1115$$
$$G'_{240} = 1.1115G^{0.45} - 0.1115 \qquad \text{Eq 24.4}$$
$$B'_{240} = 1.1115B^{0.45} - 0.1115$$

The sRGB specification for desktop computing uses numerical values slightly different again (page 267). For tristimulus values greater than a few percent:

$$R'_{sRGB} = 1.055R^{\frac{1}{2.4}} - 0.055$$
$$G'_{sRGB} = 1.055R^{\frac{1}{2.4}} - 0.055 \qquad \text{Eq 24.5}$$
$$B'_{sRGB} = 1.055R^{\frac{1}{2.4}} - 0.055$$

Rec. 601 luma

The following luma equation is standardized in Rec. 601 for SDTV, and also applies to JPEG/JFIF (in computing) and Exif (in digital still photography):

$$^{601}Y' = 0.299\,R' + 0.587\,G' + 0.114\,B' \qquad \text{Eq 24.6}$$

As mentioned a moment ago, the *E* and prime symbols originally used for video signals have been elided over the course of time, and this has led to ambiguity of the *Y* symbol between color science and television.

The coefficients in the luma equation are based upon the sensitivity of human vision to each of the *RGB* primaries standardized for the coding. The low value of the blue coefficient is a consequence of saturated blue colors having low lightness. The luma coefficients are also a function of the white point, or more properly, the *chromaticity of reference white*.

The Rec. 601 luma coefficients were computed using the technique that I explained in *Luminance coefficients*, on page 250, using the NTSC primaries and white point of Table 22.2, on page 238.

In principle, luma coefficients should be derived from the primary and white chromaticities. The Rec. 601 luma coefficients of Equation 24.6 were established in 1953 by the NTSC from the primaries and white point then in use. Primaries have changed over the years since the adoption of NTSC. The primaries in use for 480*i* today are approximately those specified in SMPTE RP 145; the primaries in use for 576*i* are approximately those specified in EBU Tech. 3213. (These

The mismatch between the primaries and the luma coefficients of SDTV has little practical significance; however, the mismatch of luma coefficients between SDTV and HDTV has great practical significance!

primary sets are slightly different; both sets very nearly match the primaries of Rec. 709.) Despite the change in primaries, the luma coefficients for 480*i* and 576*i* video have remained unchanged from the values that were established in 1953. As a consequence of the change in primaries, the luma coefficients in SDTV no longer theoretically match the primaries. The mismatch has little practical significance.

Rec. 709 luma

International agreement on Rec. 709 was achieved in 1990 on the basis of "theoretically correct" luma coefficients derived from the Rec. 709 primaries:

$$^{709}Y' = 0.2126\,R' + 0.7152\,G' + 0.0722\,B' \qquad \text{Eq 24.7}$$

SMPTE 240M-1988 luma

Two years before Rec. 709 was adopted, SMPTE standardized luma coefficients for 1035*i*30 HDTV that were "theoretically correct" for the SMPTE RP 145 primaries in use at the time:

$$^{240}Y' = 0.212\,R' + 0.701\,G' + 0.087\,B' \qquad \text{Eq 24.8}$$

Following the establishment of Rec. 709, the successors to SMPTE 240M – such as SMPTE 274M for 1920×1080 HDTV – specified the primaries, transfer function, and luma coefficients of Rec. 709. However, provisions were made in these standards to accommodate the 240M parameters as an "interim implementation," and the 240M parameters remain in use in some of the HDTV equipment that is deployed as I write this. The most recent revision of SMPTE 274M dispenses with the"interim implementation," and embraces Rec. 709.

Chroma subsampling, revisited

The purpose of color difference coding is to enable subsampling. In analog video, the color difference components are subject to bandwidth reduction through the use of analog lowpass filters; horizontal color detail is removed. In digital video, the chroma components are subsampled, or *decimated*, by filtering followed by the discarding of samples. Figure 10.3, *Chroma subsampling*, on page 90, sketches several digital subsampling schemes. In 4:2:2 subsampling, after filtering, alternate color difference samples are discarded at the encoder. In 4:2:0, vertical chroma detail is removed as well. At the decoder, the missing samples are approximated by interpolation.

In analog chroma bandlimiting, and in digital subsampling, some color detail is lost. However, owing to the poor color acuity of vision, the loss cannot be detected by a viewer *at normal viewing distance*.

Some low-end digital video systems simply drop chroma pixels at the encoder without filtering, and replicate chroma pixels at the decoder. Discarding samples can be viewed as point sampling; that operation runs the risk of introducing aliases. Proper decimation and interpolation filters should be used; these should be designed according to the principles explained in *Filtering and sampling,* on page 141.

Luma/color difference summary

When luma and color difference coding is used for image interchange, it is important for the characteristics of red, green, and blue to be maintained from the input of the encoder to the output of the decoder. The chromaticities of the primaries were detailed in *Color science for video,* on page 233, and mentioned in this chapter as they pertain to the encoding and decoding of luma. I have assumed that the characteristics of the primaries match across the whole system. The primaries upon which luma and color difference coding are based are known as the *interchange* (or *transmission*) *primaries*.

In practice, a camera sensor may produce *RGB* components whose chromaticities do not match the interchange primaries. To achieve accurate color reproduction in such a camera, it is necessary to insert a 3×3 matrix that transforms tristimulus signals from the image capture primaries to the interchange primaries. (This is the "linear matrix" built into the camera.) Similarly, a decoder may be required to drive a display whose primaries are different from the interchange primaries; at the output of the decoder, in may be

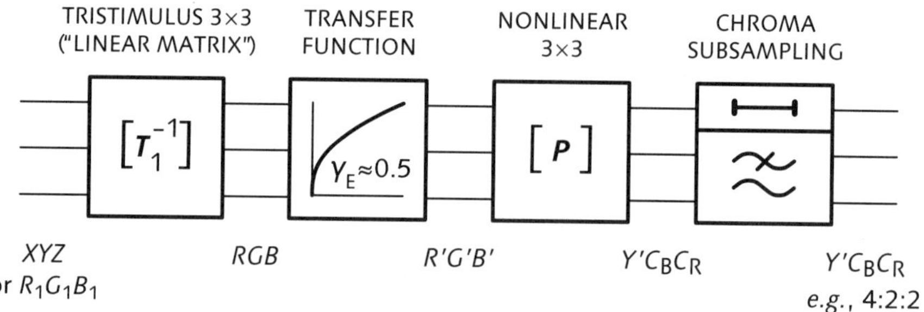

Figure 24.7 **Luma/color difference encoder.** involves the four stages summarized in this block diagram. First, linear-light (tristimulus) input signals are transformed through the "linear" matrix $\boldsymbol{T}_1^{-1}$ to produce *RGB* coded to the interchange primaries. Gamma correction is then applied. The matrix $\boldsymbol{P}$ then produces luma and two color differences. The color difference (chroma) signals are then subsampled; luma undergoes a compensating delay.

necessary to insert a 3×3 matrix that transforms from the interchange primaries to the image display primaries. (See page 252.)

I use $\boldsymbol{T}_1^{-1}$ to denote the encoding "linear matrix," to conform to the notation of *Luminance coefficients,* on page 250.

Figure 24.7 above summarizes luma/color difference encoding. If image data originated in linear *XYZ* components, a 3×3 matrix transform ($\boldsymbol{T}_1^{-1}$) would be applied to obtain linear *RGB* having chromaticities and white reference of the interchange primaries. For Rec. 709 interchange primaries standard for SDTV and HDTV, the matrix would be that of Equation 22.9, on page 251. More typically, image data originates in some device-dependent space that I denote $R_1G_1B_1$, and the 3×3 "linear matrix" transform ($\boldsymbol{T}_1^{-1}$) is determined by the camera designer. See the sequence of Figures 22.3 through 22.8, starting on page 244, and the accompanying text and captions, to gain an appreciation for how such a matrix might be crafted. Practical cameras do not have spectral sensitivities that are linear combinations of the CIE color matching functions, so they are not properly characterized by chromaticities. Nonetheless, once a linear matrix to a set of interchange primaries has been chosen, Equation 22.10 can be used to derive equivalent sensor primaries (the "taking primaries").

Interchange primaries are also called transmission primaries.

Once the linear matrix has been applied, each of the components is subject to a nonlinear transfer function (gamma correction) that produces nonlinear *R'G'B'*. These components are transformed through a 3×3

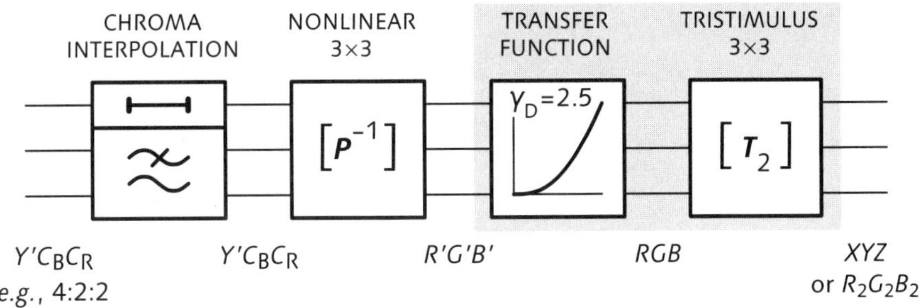

Figure 24.8 **Luma/color difference decoder** involves the inverse of the four stages of Figure 24.7 in opposite order. First, subsampled color difference (chroma) signals are interpolated; luma undergoes a compensating delay. The matrix $\boldsymbol{P}^{-1}$ then recovers $R'G'B'$ from luma and two color differences. A transfer function having an exponent of about 2.5 is then applied, which produces linear-light (tristimulus) signals RGB. If the display's primaries differ from the interchange primaries, RGB are transformed through the matrix $\boldsymbol{T}_2$ to produce appropriate $R_2G_2B_2$.

matrix ($\boldsymbol{P}$), to obtain luma and color difference components $Y'C_BC_R$ or $Y'P_BP_R$. (This matrix depends upon the luma coefficients in use, and upon color difference scale factors.) Then, if necessary, a chroma subsampling filter is applied to obtain subsampled color difference components; luma is subject to a compensating delay.

A decoder uses the inverse operations of the encoder, in the opposite order, as sketched in Figure 24.8. In a digital decoder, the chroma interpolation filter reconstructs missing chroma samples; in an analog decoder, no explicit operation is needed. The 3×3 color difference matrix ($\boldsymbol{P}^{-1}$) reconstructs nonlinear red, green, and blue primary components. The transfer functions restore the primary components to their linear-light tristimulus values. Finally, the tristimulus 3×3 matrix ($\boldsymbol{T}_2$) transforms from the primaries of the interchange standard to the primaries implemented in the display device.

Figures 24.7 and 24.8 show 3×3 matrix transforms being used for two distinctly different tasks. When someone hands you a 3×3, you have to ascertain whether it is intended for a linear or nonlinear task.

When a decoder is intimately associated with a CRT monitor, the decoder's transfer function is performed by the nonlinear voltage-to-luminance relationship intrinsic to the CRT: No explicit operations are required for this step. However, to exploit this transfer function, the display primaries must be the same as – or at least very similar to – the interchange primaries.

The transfer functions of the decoder (or the CRT) are intertwined with gamma correction. As I explained on page 81, an end-to-end power function having an exponent of about 1.25 is appropriate for typical television viewing in a dim surround. The encoder of Figure 24.7 imposes a 0.5-power function; the decoder of Figure 24.8 imposes a 2.5-power. The product of these implements the end-to-end power function.

Owing to the dependence of the optimum end-to-end power function upon viewing conditions, there here ought to be a user control for rendering intent – perhaps even replacing BRIGHTNESS and CONTRAST – but there isn't!

When viewing in a light surround, a 1.125 end-to-end power is appropriate; when driving a CRT, a 0.9-power function should intervene. When viewing in a dark surround, a 1.5 end-to-end power is appropriate; a 1.2-power function should intervene. If the transfer function of a display device differs from that of a CRT, then decoding should include a transfer function that is the composition of a 2.5-power function and the inverse transfer function of the display device.

If the display primaries match the interchange primaries, the decoder's 3×3 tristimulus matrix is not needed. If a CRT display has primaries not too different from the interchange primaries, then it may be possible to compensate the primaries by applying a 3×3 matrix in the nonlinear domain. But if the primaries are quite different, it will be necessary to apply the transform between primaries in the tristimulus domain; see *Transforms among RGB systems*, on page 252.

SDTV and HDTV luma chaos

Although the concepts of $Y'P_BP_R$ and $Y'C_BC_R$ coding are identical in SDTV and HDTV, the Rec. 709 standard has – unfortunately, in my opinion – established a new set of luma coefficients for HDTV. That set differs dramatically from the luma coefficients for SDTV specified in Rec. 601. There are now two flavors of $Y'C_BC_R$ coding, as suggested by Figure 24.9 in the margin; I denote the flavors $^{601}Y'C_BC_R$ for SDTV, and $^{709}Y'C_BC_R$ for HDTV. Similarly, there are two flavors of $Y'P_BP_R$ for analog systems, $^{601}Y'P_BP_R$ for SDTV, and $^{709}Y'P_BP_R$ for HDTV. (A third luma coefficient set was specified in SMPTE 240M-1988; though obsolete, that set continues to be used in legacy 1035*i* equipment.)

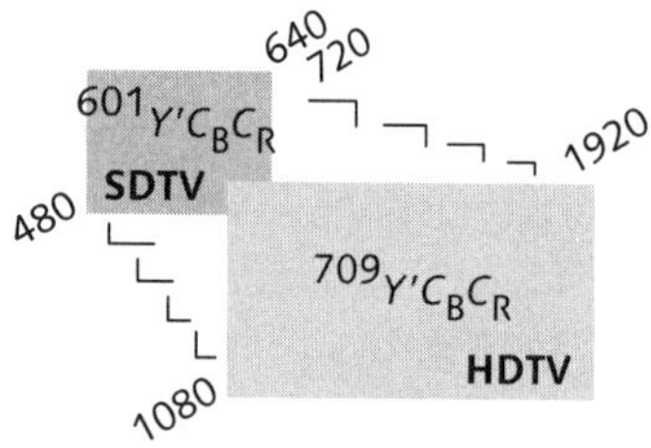

Figure 24.9 **Luma/color difference flavors**

System	Primary chromaticity	Transfer function	Luma coefficients
480*i*	SMPTE RP 145	Rec. 709	Rec. 601
576*i*	EBU Tech. 3213	Rec. 709	Rec. 601
1035*i*	SMPTE RP 145	SMPTE 240M	SMPTE 240M
720*p*, 1080*i*, 1080*p*	Rec. 709	Rec. 709	Rec. 709

Table 24.1 **Chromaticity, transfer function, and luma combinations** circa 2002 are summarized.

In my view, it is extremely unfortunate that different coding has been adopted: Image coding and decoding now depend on whether the picture is small (conventional video, SDTV) or large (HDTV); that dependence erodes the highly useful concept of resolution-independent production in the $Y'C_BC_R$ 4:2:2 and 4:2:0 domains. In my opinion, $Y'C_BC_R$ should have been standardized with C_B and C_R having identical excursion to luma, and HDTV should have been standardized with the Rec. 601 luma coefficients. With things as they stand, the smorgasbord of color-encoding parameters makes accurate image interchange extremely difficult. The situation is likely to get worse with time, not better.

Table 24.1 above summarizes the standards for primary chromaticities, transfer functions, and luma coefficients that are either implicit or explicit in several SDTV and HDTV standards. When video is converted among these standards, appropriate processing should be performed in order to preserve the intended color.

It's sensible to use the term colorbar test *signal* (or *pattern*) instead of colorbar test *image*: The image is not standardized.

It is a problem that the colorbar test signal is standardized in the $R'G'B'$ domain, without any reference to primaries, transfer function, or luma coefficients. The colors of the bars depend upon which primary chromaticities are in use; the luma and color difference levels of the bars depend upon which luma coefficients are in use. When color conversions and standards conversions are properly performed, the colors and levels of the colorbar test signal will change!

Luma/color difference component sets

These color difference component sets, all based upon $B'-Y'$ and $R'-Y'$, are in use:

- $Y'P_BP_R$ coding is used in component analog video; P_B and P_R are scaled to have excursion nominally identical to that of luma. $Y'P_BP_R$ can be potentially based upon any of three sets of luma coefficients: Rec. 601 for SDTV, SMPTE 240M ("interim implementation") for HDTV, or Rec. 709 for HDTV. In 480*i*29.97 SDTV, three different analog interface standards are in use: EBU N10 "SMPTE," Sony, and Panasonic.

- $Y'C_BC_R$ coding is used for component digital video; C_B and C_R are scaled to have excursion $^{224}/_{219}$ that of luma. A "full-range" variant is used in JPEG/JFIF. $Y'C_BC_R$ can be potentially based upon Rec. 601, SMPTE 240M, or Rec. 709 luma coefficients.

In *NTSC and PAL chroma modulation*, on page 335, I will detail two additional component sets, whose proper use is limited to composite NTSC and PAL SDTV:

- $Y'UV$ components are only applicable to composite NTSC and PAL systems. $B'-Y'$ and $R'-Y'$ are scaled so as to limit the excursion of the composite (luma plus modulated chroma) signal. $Y'UV$ coding is always based upon Rec. 601 luma coefficients.

- $Y'IQ$ components are only applicable to certain composite NTSC systems. UV components are rotated 33°, and axis-exchanged, to enable wideband-I transmission. This is an obsolete technique that is rarely, if ever, practiced nowadays. $Y'IQ$ coding is always based upon Rec. 601 luma coefficients.

The bewildering set of scale factors and luma coefficients in use is set out in Table 24.2A opposite for analog SDTV, Table 24.2B overleaf for digital SDTV and computing systems, and Table 24.2C for analog and digital HDTV. The following two chapters detail component color coding for SDTV and HDTV, respectively.

	System	Notation	Color difference scaling
1	Component analog video, 480*i* (EIA/CEA-770 and "SMPTE") and 576*i* EBU N10; also, 480*i* Panasonic M-II, zero setup (Japan)[a]	${}^{601}_{700}Y'_{145}P_BP_R$, ${}^{601}_{700}Y'_{EBU}P_BP_R$	The EBU N10 standard calls for 7:3 picture-to-sync ratio, 700 mV luma excursion with zero setup. P_B and P_R components are scaled individually to range ±350 mV, an excursion identical to luma.
2	Component analog video, 480*i* Sony, 7.5% setup[a]	${}^{601}_{661}Y'_{145}P_BP_R$	Sony de facto standards call for 10:4 picture-to-sync ratio, 7.5% setup, and black-to-white luma excursion of approximately 661 mV. P_B and P_R components are scaled individually to range 4⁄3 times ±350 mV, that is, ±466 2⁄3 mV.
3	Component analog video, 480*i* Sony, zero setup (Japan)[a]	${}^{601}_{714}Y'_{145}P_BP_R$	Sony de facto standards call for 10:4 picture-to-sync ratio, zero setup, and black-to-white luma excursion of approximately 714 mV. P_B and P_R components are scaled individually to range 4⁄3 times ±350 mV, that is, ±466 2⁄3 mV.
4	Component analog video, 480*i* Panasonic, 7.5% setup[a]	${}^{601}_{674}Y'_{145}P_BP_R$	Panasonic de facto standards call for 10:4 picture-to-sync ratio, zero setup, and black-to-white luma excursion of approximately 674.5 mV. P_B and P_R components are scaled individually to range 37⁄40 times ±350 mV, that is, ±323.75 mV.
5	Composite analog NTSC, PAL video (incl. S-video, *Y'/C*688, etc.)	various, typ. ${}^{601}_{700}Y'_{EBU}UV$, ${}^{601}_{714}Y'_{145}IQ$	*U* and *V* are scaled to meet a joint constraint: Scaling is such that peak composite video – luma plus modulated chroma – is limited to 4⁄3 of the blanking-to-white excursion. Rotation and exchange of axes (e.g., *I* and *Q*) cannot be distinguished after analog encoding. There is no standard component interface.

Table 24.2A **Color difference systems for analog SDTV.** The EBU N10 levels indicated in the shaded (first) row are sensible but unpopular. Designers of 480*i* SDTV studio equipment are forced to implement configuration settings for three interface "standards": EBU N10 ("SMPTE"), Sony, and Panasonic.

a The component analog interface for consumer equipment (such as DVD players) is properly scaled $Y'P_BP_R$, according to EIA/CEA-770.2, cited on page 509. Some consumer equipment has been engineered and deployed with incorrect $Y'P_BP_R$ scaling. Certain consumer devices have rear-panel connectors labelled *Y, B–Y, R–Y,* or *YUV*; these designations are plainly wrong.

	System	Notation	Color difference scaling
6	Component digital video: 4:2:0, 4:1:1, Rec. 601 4:2:2 (incl. M-JPEG, MPEG, DVD, DVC)	${}^{601}_{219}Y'_{145}C_BC_R$	Rec. 601 calls for luma range 0…219, offset +16 at the interface. C_B and C_R are scaled individually to range ±112, an excursion $^{224}/_{219}$ of luma, offset +128 at the interface. Codes 0 and 255 are prohibited.
7	Component digital stillframe JPEG (incl. JFIF 1.02), typical desktop publishing and www. Transfer functions vary; see the marginal note on page 280.	${}^{601}_{255}Y'_{709}C_BC_R$	There is no comprehensive standard. Luma reference range is typically 0 through 255. C_B and C_R are typically scaled individually to a "full range" of ±128, an excursion $^{256}/_{255}$ that of luma. C_B and C_R codes +128 are clipped; fully saturated blue and fully saturated red cannot be represented.
8	Composite digital video: $4f_{SC}$ 576*i* PAL	${}^{601}_{147}Y'_{EBU}UV$	*U* and *V* are scaled to meet a joint constraint such that peak composite video – luma plus modulated chroma – is limited to $^4/_3$ of the blanking-to-white excursion. Obsolescent.
9	Composite digital video: $4f_{SC}$ 480*i* NTSC (7.5% setup)	${}^{601}_{129.5}Y'_{145}IQ$	Scaling is identical to *Y'UV*, but axes are rotated 33°, exchanged, and denoted *I* and *Q*. Obsolescent.
10	Composite digital video: $4f_{SC}$ 480*i* NTSC-J (zero setup)	${}^{601}_{140}Y'_{145}IQ$	Scaling is identical to *Y'UV*, but axes are rotated 33°, exchanged, and denoted *I* and *Q*. Obsolescent.

Table 24.2B **Color difference systems for digital SDTV and computing.** The scaling indicated in the shaded (first) row is recommended for new designs.

	System	Notation	Color difference scaling
11	Component analog HDTV	${}^{709}_{700}Y'_{709}P_BP_R$	7:3 picture-to-sync ratio, 700 mV luma excursion with zero setup. P_B and P_R components are scaled individually to range ±350 mV, an excursion identical to luma.
12	Component digital HDTV (Rec. 709)	${}^{709}_{219}Y'_{709}C_BC_R$	Rec. 709 calls for luma range 0…219, offset +16 at the interface. C_B and C_R are scaled individually to range ±112, an excursion $^{224}/_{219}$ of luma, offset +128 at the interface. Codes 0 and 255 are prohibited.
13	Component digital HDTV (Rec. 1361)	${}^{1361}_{219}Y'_{709}C_BC_R$	Rec. 1361 $Y'C_BC_R$ is identical to Rec. 709 $Y'C_BC_R$, except that some codewords outside the *R'G'B'* unit cube represent wide-gamut colors.

Table 24.2C **Color difference systems for HDTV.** The luma coefficients for HDTV differ dramatically from those of SDTV.

Component video color coding for SDTV 25

Various scale factors are applied to the basic color difference components $B'-Y'$ and $R'-Y'$ for different applications. In the previous chapter, I introduced luma and color difference coding; in this chapter, I will detail the following coding systems:

- $B'-Y'$, $R'-Y'$ components form the numerical basis for all the other component sets; otherwise, they are not directly used.
- P_BP_R components are used for component analog video (including DVD player analog interfaces).
- C_BC_R components as defined in Rec. 601 are used for component digital video, including studio video, M-JPEG, and MPEG.
- "Full range" C_BC_R components are used in JPEG/JFIF.
- UV components are used for NTSC or PAL, as I will describe on page 336.
- IQ components were historically used for NTSC, as I will describe on page 367.

Video uses the symbols U and V to represent certain color difference components. The CIE defines the pairs $[u, v]$, $[u', v']$, and $[u^*, v^*]$. All of these pairs represent *chromatic* or chroma information, but they are all numerically and functionally different. Video $[U, V]$ components are neither directly based upon, nor superseded by, any of the CIE color spaces.

$Y'UV$ and $Y'IQ$ are intermediate quantities toward the formation of composite NTSC, PAL, and S-video. Neither $Y'UV$ nor $Y'IQ$ has a standard component interface, and neither is appropriate when the components are kept separate. Unfortunately, the $Y'UV$ nomenclature has come to be used rather loosely, and to some people it now denotes *any* scaling of $B'-Y'$ and $R'-Y'$. I will detail the formation of true $Y'UV$ and $Y'IQ$ in *NTSC and PAL chroma modulation*, on page 335.

For a discussion of primary chromaticities, see page 236.

The coding systems described in this chapter can be applied to various *RGB* primary sets – EBU 3213, SMPTE RP 145 (or potentially even Rec. 709). Rec. 601 does not specify primary chromaticities: SMPTE RP 145 primaries are implicit in 480*i* systems, and EBU 3213 primaries are implicit in 576*i* systems.

The equations for $[Y', B'-Y', R'-Y']$, $Y'P_BP_R$, and $Y'C_BC_R$ can be based upon either the Rec. 601 luma coefficients of SDTV or the Rec. 709 coefficients of HDTV. The equations and figures of this chapter are based upon the Rec. 601 coefficients. Unfortunately, the luma coefficients that have been standardized for HDTV are different from those of Rec. 601. Concerning the HDTV luma coefficients, see *Rec. 709 luma* on page 292; for details of HDTV color difference components, see *Component video color coding for HDTV,* on page 313. Surprisingly, broadcasters in Japan apparently intend to retrofit their SDTV broadcast plant with Rec. 709 luma coefficients according to the equations that I will detail in the following chapter, *Component video color coding for HDTV*.

Chroma components are properly ordered $B'-Y'$ then $R'-Y'$; or P_B then P_R; or C_B then C_R. Blue associates with U, and red with V; U and V are ordered alphabetically. The subscripts in C_BC_R and P_BP_R are often written in lowercase. In my opinion, this compromises readability, so I write them in uppercase. The B in C_B serves as a tag, not a variable, so I set it in Roman type (not italics). Authors with great attention to detail sometimes "prime" C_BC_R and P_BP_R to indicate their nonlinear origin, but because no practical image coding system employs linear-light color differences, I consider it safe to omit the primes.

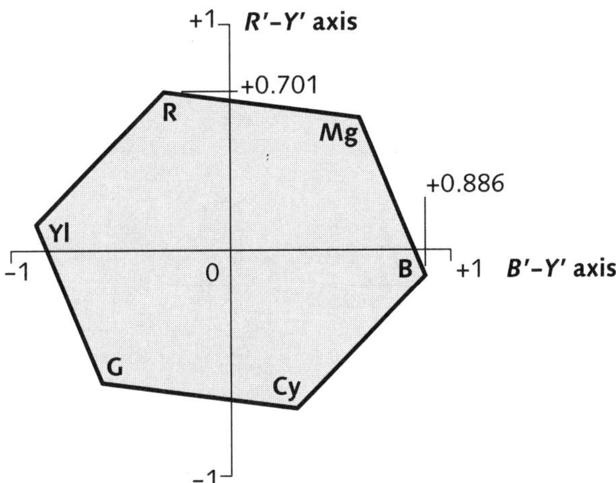

Figure 25.1 **B'–Y', R'–Y' components for SDTV**

B'–Y', R'–Y' components for SDTV

To obtain [Y', B'–Y', R'–Y'] components from R'G'B', for Rec. 601 luma, use this matrix equation:

$$\begin{bmatrix} {}^{601}Y' \\ B'-{}^{601}Y' \\ R'-{}^{601}Y' \end{bmatrix} = \begin{bmatrix} 0.299 & 0.587 & 0.114 \\ -0.299 & -0.587 & 0.886 \\ 0.701 & -0.587 & -0.114 \end{bmatrix} \bullet \begin{bmatrix} R' \\ G' \\ B' \end{bmatrix} \qquad \text{Eq 25.1}$$

Figure 25.1 shows a plot of the [B'–Y', R'–Y'] color difference plane.

ITU-R Rec. BT.601-5, *Studio encoding parameters of digital television for standard 4:3 and wide-screen 16:9 aspect ratios.*

As I described on page 291, the Rec. 601 luma coefficients are used for SDTV. With these coefficients, the B'–Y' component reaches its positive maximum at pure blue ($R' = 0$, $G' = 0$, $B' = 1$; $Y' = 0.114$; $B'-Y' = +0.886$) and its negative maximum at pure yellow ($B'-Y' = -0.886$). Analogously, the extrema of R'–Y' take values ±0.701, at pure red and cyan. These are inconvenient values for both digital and analog systems. The P_BP_R, C_BC_R, and *UV* color difference components all involve versions of [Y', B'–Y', R'–Y'] that are scaled to place the extrema of the component values at more convenient values.

P_BP_R components for SDTV

P_B and P_R denote color difference components having excursions nominally identical to the excursion of the

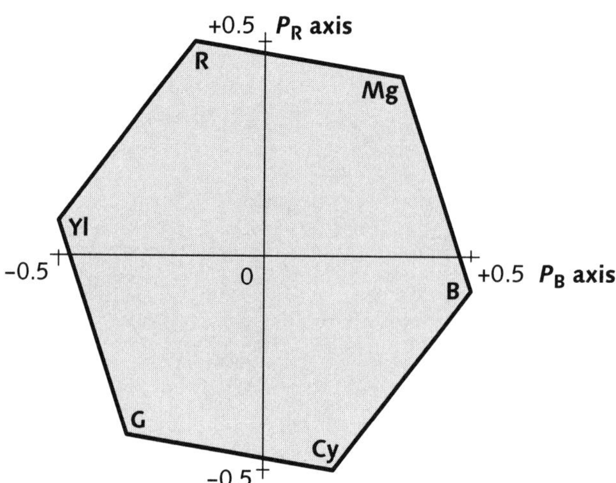

Figure 25.2 **P_BP_R components for SDTV**

accompanying luma component. For Rec. 601 luma, the equations are these:

Eq 25.2

$$P_B = \frac{0.5}{1-0.114}\left(B' - {}^{601}Y'\right) = \frac{1}{1.772}\left(B' - {}^{601}Y'\right) \approx 0.564\left(B' - {}^{601}Y'\right)$$
$$P_R = \frac{0.5}{1-0.299}\left(R' - {}^{601}Y'\right) = \frac{1}{1.402}\left(R' - {}^{601}Y'\right) \approx 0.713\left(R' - {}^{601}Y'\right)$$

These scale factors are chosen to limit the excursion of *each* color difference component to the range -0.5 to +0.5 with respect to unity luma excursion: 0.114 in the first expression above is the luma coefficient of blue, and 0.299 in the second is for red. Figure 25.2 above shows a plot of the $[P_B, P_R]$ plane.

Expressed in matrix form, the $B'-Y'$ and $R'-Y'$ rows of Equation 25.1 are scaled by $^{0.5}/_{0.886}$ and $^{0.5}/_{0.701}$. To encode from $R'G'B'$ where reference black is zero and reference white is unity:

Eq 25.3

$$\begin{bmatrix} {}^{601}Y' \\ P_B \\ P_R \end{bmatrix} = \begin{bmatrix} 0.299 & 0.587 & 0.114 \\ -0.168736 & -0.331264 & 0.5 \\ 0.5 & -0.418688 & -0.081312 \end{bmatrix} \bullet \begin{bmatrix} R' \\ G' \\ B' \end{bmatrix}$$

The first row of Equation 25.3 comprises the luma coefficients; these sum to unity. The second and third rows each sum to zero, a necessity for color difference components. The two entries of 0.5 reflect the reference excursions of P_B and P_R, at the blue and red primaries [0, 0, 1] and [1, 0, 0]. The reference excursion is ±0.5; the peak excursion may be slightly larger, to accommodate analog undershoot and overshoot. There are no standards for how much analog footroom and headroom should be provided.

The inverse, decoding matrix is this:

$$\begin{bmatrix} R' \\ G' \\ B' \end{bmatrix} = \begin{bmatrix} 1 & 0 & 1.402 \\ 1 & -0.344136 & -0.714136 \\ 1 & 1.772 & 0 \end{bmatrix} \bullet \begin{bmatrix} {}^{601}Y' \\ P_B \\ P_R \end{bmatrix} \qquad \text{Eq 25.4}$$

See Table 24.2A on page 299; *Component analog $Y'P_BP_R$ interface, EBU N10*, on page 508; and *Component analog $Y'P_BP_R$ interface, industry standard*, on page 509.

$Y'P_BP_R$ is employed by 480*i* and 576*i* component analog video equipment such as that from Sony and Panasonic, where P_B and P_R are conveyed with roughly half the bandwidth of luma. Unfortunately, three different analog interface level standards are used: $Y'P_BP_R$ is ambiguous with respect to electrical interface.

P_B and P_R are properly written in that order, as I described on page 302. The *P* stands for *parallel*, stemming from a failed effort within SMPTE to standardize a parallel electrical interface for component analog video. In C_BC_R, which I will now describe, *C* stands for *chroma*. The C_BC_R notation predated P_BP_R.

C_BC_R components for SDTV

A straightforward scaling of $Y'P_BP_R$ components would have been suitable for digital interface. Scaling of luma to the range [0 … 255] would have been feasible; this "full range" scaling of luma is used in JPEG/JFIF used in computing, as I will describe on page 310. However, for studio applications it is necessary to provide signal-processing footroom and headroom to accommodate ringing from analog and digital filters, and to accommodate signals from misadjusted analog equipment.

For an 8-bit interface, luma could have been scaled to an excursion of 224; $B'-Y'$ and $R'-Y'$ could have been scaled to ±112. This would have left 32 codes of footroom and headroom for each component. Although sensible, that approach was not taken when Rec. 601 was adopted in 1984. Instead – and unfortunately, in my opinion – different excursions were standardized for luma and chroma. Eight-bit luma excursion was standardized at 219; chroma excursion was standardized at 224. Each color difference component has as excursion $^{224}/_{219}$ that of luma. Since video component amplitudes are usually referenced to luma excursion, this condition is more clearly stated the opposite way: In $Y'C_BC_R$, each color difference component has $^{224}/_{219}$ the excursion of the luma component. The notation C_BC_R distinguishes this set from P_BP_R, where the luma and chroma excursions are nominally identical: Conceptually, $Y'P_BP_R$ and $Y'C_BC_R$ differ only in scaling.

The $Y'P_BP_R$ and $Y'C_BC_R$ scaling discrepancy is unfortunate enough, but it is compounded by "full range" $Y'C_BC_R$ used in JPEG/JFIF, scaled similarly but not identically to $Y'P_BP_R$; see page 310. Confusion is compounded by the EBU referring in Technical Standard N10-1998 to C_BC_R analog color difference components, when they are properly denoted P_BP_R.

Historically, $Y'P_BP_R$ scaling was used at analog interfaces, and $Y'C_BC_R$ was used at digital interfaces. Nowadays so many different scale factors and offsets are in use in both the analog and digital domains that the dual nomenclature is more a hindrance than a help.

To provide footroom to accommodate luma signals that go slightly negative, an offset is added to luma at a $Y'C_BC_R$ interface. At an 8-bit interface, an offset of +16 is added; this places black at code 16 and white at code 235. At an 8-bit interface, codes 0 and 255 are used for synchronization purposes; these codes are prohibited from video data. Codes 1 through 15 are interpreted as signal levels $-^{15}/_{219}$ through $-^{1}/_{219}$ (respectively), relative to unity luma excursion; codes 236 through 254 are interpreted as signal levels $^{220}/_{219}$ through $^{238}/_{219}$ (respectively), relative to unity excursion. Unfortunately, luma footroom and headroom are asymmetrical.

C_BC_R color difference components are conveyed in offset binary form: An offset of +128 is added. In studio $Y'C_BC_R$, chroma reference levels are 16 and 240, and codes 0 and 255 are prohibited from chroma data.

Rec. 601 provides for 10-bit components; 10-bit studio video equipment is now commonplace. At a 10-bit interface, the 8-bit interface levels and prohibited codes are maintained; extra bits are appended as least-significant bits to provide increased precision. The prohibited codes respect the 8-bit interface: Codes having all 8 most-significant bits either all zeros or all ones are prohibited from video data across a 10-bit interface.

Figure 25.3 **C_BC_R components for SDTV** are shown in their mathematical form. The range outside [–112 … +112] is available for undershoot and overshoot. At an 8-bit interface, an offset of +128 is added to each color difference component.

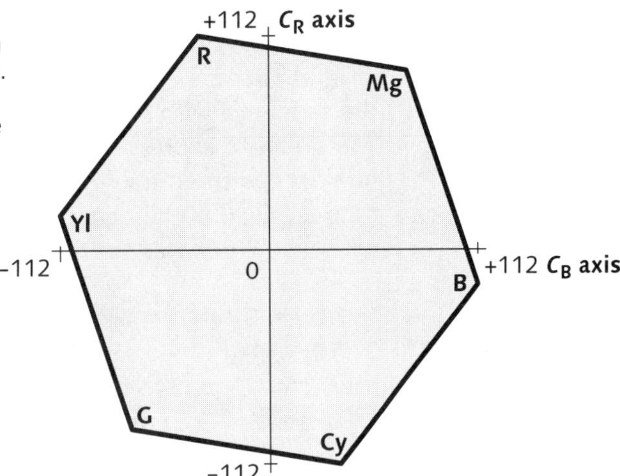

For signal-processing arithmetic operations such as gain adjustment, Y', C_B, and C_R must be zero for black: The interface offsets must be removed. For 8-bit luma arithmetic, it is convenient to place reference black at code 0 and reference white at code 219. Color difference signals are most conveniently handled in two's complement form, scaled so that reference color difference signals (at pure yellow, cyan, red, and blue) are ±112. Figure 25.3 above shows the C_BC_R color difference plane scaled in this manner, without offsets.

As far as I am concerned, the offsets should be treated as an interface feature. Most descriptions of $Y'C_BC_R$, though – including SMPTE and ITU standards – take the $Y'C_BC_R$ notation to include the offset. In the equations to follow, I include the offset terms in gray. If your goal is to compute abstract, mathematical quantities suitable for signal processing, omit the offsets. If you are concerned with the interface, include them.

These equations form Rec. 601 $Y'C_BC_R$ components from [Y', $B'-Y'$, $R'-Y'$] components ranging [0 … +1]:

The numerical values used in this equation, and in those to follow, are based on the Rec. 601 luma coefficients. The coefficients for HDTV are, unfortunately, different. See *Rec. 601 luma*, on page 291.

$$\begin{aligned} {}^{601}_{219}Y' &= 16 + \left(219 \cdot {}^{601}Y'\right) \\ C_B &= 128 + \frac{112}{0.886}\left(B' - {}^{601}Y'\right) \\ C_R &= 128 + \frac{112}{0.701}\left(R' - {}^{601}Y'\right) \end{aligned} \qquad \text{Eq 25.5}$$

To extend Marginal note to 10 bits, append to each of Y', C_B, and C_R two low-order bits having binary weights $\frac{1}{2}$ and $\frac{1}{4}$. To extend $Y'C_BC_R$ beyond 10 bits, continue the sequence with LSBs weighted $\frac{1}{8}$, $\frac{1}{16}$, and so on. If you prefer to express these quantities as whole numbers, without fractional bits, multiply Marginal note (and all of the equations to follow) by 2^{k-8}, where $k \geq 8$ denotes the number of bits.

To obtain 8-bit Rec. 601 $Y'C_BC_R$ from $R'G'B'$ ranging 0 to 1, scale the rows of the matrix in Equation 25.3 by the factors 219, 224, and 224, corresponding to the excursions of each of Y', C_B, and C_R, respectively:

Eq 25.6

$$\begin{bmatrix} {}^{601}_{219}Y' \\ C_B \\ C_R \end{bmatrix} = \begin{bmatrix} 16 \\ 128 \\ 128 \end{bmatrix} + \begin{bmatrix} 65.481 & 128.553 & 24.966 \\ -37.797 & -74.203 & 112 \\ 112 & -93.786 & -18.214 \end{bmatrix} \bullet \begin{bmatrix} R' \\ G' \\ B' \end{bmatrix}$$

Summing the top row of this matrix yields 219, the luma excursion. The lower two rows sum to zero. The two entries of 112 reflect the positive C_B and C_R extrema, at the blue and red primaries.

To recover $R'G'B'$ in the range [0…+1] from 8-bit Rec. 601 $Y'C_BC_R$, invert Equation 25.6:

Eq 25.7

$$\begin{bmatrix} R' \\ G' \\ B' \end{bmatrix} = \begin{bmatrix} 0.00456621 & 0 & 0.00625893 \\ 0.00456621 & -0.00153396 & -0.00318811 \\ 0.00456621 & 0.00791071 & 0 \end{bmatrix} \bullet \left(\begin{bmatrix} {}^{601}_{219}Y' \\ C_B \\ C_R \end{bmatrix} - \begin{bmatrix} 16 \\ 128 \\ 128 \end{bmatrix} \right)$$

You can determine the excursion that an encoding matrix is designed to produce – often 1, 219, 255, or 256 – by summing the coefficients in the top row. In Equation 25.8, the sum is 256. If you find an unexpected sum, suspect an error in the matrix.

For implementation in binary arithmetic, the multiplication by $\frac{1}{256}$ can be accomplished by shifting. The entries of 256 in this matrix indicate that the corresponding component can simply be added; there is no need for a multiplication operation. This matrix contains entries larger than 256; the corresponding multipliers will need capability for more than 8 bits.

When rounding the matrix coefficients, take care to preserve the intended row sums, in this case, [1, 0, 0]. You must take care to prevent overflow due to roundoff error or other conditions: Use saturating arithmetic.

At the interface, after adding the offsets, clip all three components to the range 1 through 254 inclusive, to avoid the prohibited codes 0 and 255.

$Y'C_BC_R$ from studio *RGB*

In studio equipment, 8-bit $R'G'B'$ components usually have the same 219 excursion as the luma component of $Y'C_BC_R$. To encode 8-bit Rec. 601 $Y'C_BC_R$ from $R'G'B'$ in the range [0...219], scale the encoding matrix of Equation 25.6 by 256⁄219:

Eq 25.8

$$\begin{bmatrix} {}^{601}_{219}Y' \\ C_B \\ C_R \end{bmatrix} = \begin{bmatrix} 16 \\ 128 \\ 128 \end{bmatrix} + \frac{1}{256} \begin{bmatrix} 76.544 & 150.272 & 29.184 \\ -44.182 & -86.740 & 130.922 \\ 130.922 & -109.631 & -21.291 \end{bmatrix} \bullet \begin{bmatrix} {}_{219}R' \\ {}_{219}G' \\ {}_{219}B' \end{bmatrix}$$

To decode to $R'G'B'$ in the range [0...219] from 8-bit Rec. 601 $Y'C_BC_R$, invert Equation 25.8:

Eq 25.9

$$\begin{bmatrix} {}_{219}R' \\ {}_{219}G' \\ {}_{219}B' \end{bmatrix} = \frac{1}{256} \begin{bmatrix} 256 & 0 & 350.901 \\ 256 & -86.132 & -178.738 \\ 256 & 443.506 & 0 \end{bmatrix} \bullet \left(\begin{bmatrix} {}^{601}_{219}Y' \\ C_B \\ C_R \end{bmatrix} - \begin{bmatrix} 16 \\ 128 \\ 128 \end{bmatrix} \right)$$

These transforms assume that the $R'G'B'$ components incorporate gamma correction, such as that specified by Rec. 709; see page 276.

$Y'C_BC_R$ from computer *RGB*

In computing it is conventional to use 8-bit $R'G'B'$ components, with no headroom and no footroom: Black is at code 0 and white is at 255. To encode 8-bit Rec. 601 $Y'C_BC_R$ from $R'G'B'$ in this range, scale the matrix of Equation 25.6 by 256⁄255:

Eq 25.10

$$\begin{bmatrix} {}^{601}_{219}Y' \\ C_B \\ C_R \end{bmatrix} = \begin{bmatrix} 16 \\ 128 \\ 128 \end{bmatrix} + \frac{1}{256} \begin{bmatrix} 65.738 & 129.057 & 25.064 \\ -37.945 & -74.494 & 112.439 \\ 112.439 & -94.154 & -18.285 \end{bmatrix} \bullet \begin{bmatrix} {}_{255}R' \\ {}_{255}G' \\ {}_{255}B' \end{bmatrix}$$

To decode $R'G'B'$ in the range [0...255] from 8-bit Rec. 601 $Y'C_BC_R$, use the transform of Equation 25.11:

Eq 25.11

$$\begin{bmatrix} {}_{255}R' \\ {}_{255}G' \\ {}_{255}B' \end{bmatrix} = \frac{1}{256} \begin{bmatrix} 298.082 & 0 & 408.583 \\ 298.082 & -100.291 & -208.120 \\ 298.082 & 516.411 & 0 \end{bmatrix} \bullet \left(\begin{bmatrix} {}^{601}_{219}Y' \\ C_B \\ C_R \end{bmatrix} - \begin{bmatrix} 16 \\ 128 \\ 128 \end{bmatrix} \right)$$

Rec. 601 $Y'C_BC_R$ uses the extremes of the coding range to handle signal overshoot and undershoot. Clipping is required when decoding to an $R'G'B'$ range that has no headroom or footroom.

"Full-range" $Y'C_BC_R$

The $Y'C_BC_R$ coding used in JPEG/JFIF stillframes in computing conventionally has no footroom or headroom. Luma (Y') is scaled to an excursion of 255 and represented in 8 bits: Black is at code 0 and white is at code 255. Obviously, luma codes 0 and 255 are not prohibited! Color difference components are scaled to an excursion of ±128, so each color difference component nominally has an excursion $^{256}/_{255}$ that of luma. However, a mid-tread quantizer necessarily uses an odd number of codes; to represent integers ranging ±128 takes 257 code values. In JPEG/JFIF, 8-bit codes are used; neither C_B code +128 (for example, at fully saturated blue) nor C_R code +128 (for example, at fully saturated red) can be exactly represented. Figure 25.4 shows the transfer function of the color difference quantizer, emphasizing that code +128 (pure blue, or pure red) is clipped.

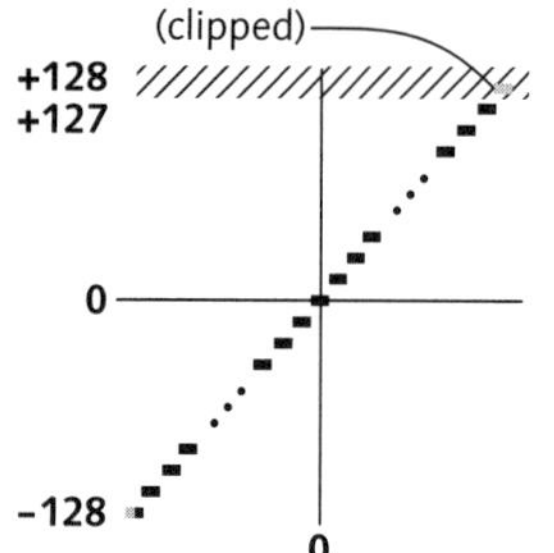

Figure 25.4 **C_BC_R "full range" quantizer** is used in JPEG/JFIF. Code +128 is clipped.

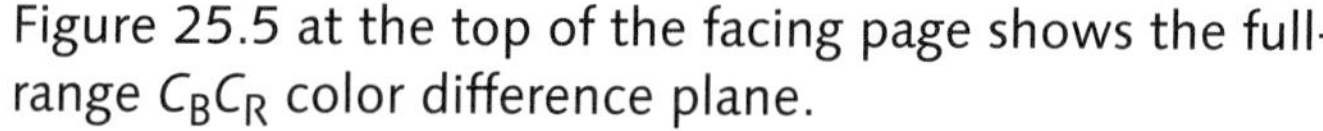

Figure 25.5 at the top of the facing page shows the full-range C_BC_R color difference plane.

To encode from $R'G'B'$ in the range [0...255] into 8-bit $Y'C_BC_R$, with luma in the range [0...255] and C_B and C_R each ranging ±128, use the transform in Equation 25.12:

Eq 25.12

$$\begin{bmatrix} {}^{601}_{255}Y' \\ C_B \\ C_R \end{bmatrix} = \frac{1}{256} \begin{bmatrix} 76.544 & 150.272 & 29.184 \\ -43.027 & -84.471 & 127.498 \\ 127.498 & -106.764 & -20.734 \end{bmatrix} \bullet \begin{bmatrix} {}_{255}R' \\ {}_{255}G' \\ {}_{255}B' \end{bmatrix}$$

To decode into $R'G'B'$ in the range [0...255] from full-range 8-bit $Y'C_BC_R$, use the transform in Equation 25.13:

Eq 25.13

$$\begin{bmatrix} {}_{255}R' \\ {}_{255}G' \\ {}_{255}B' \end{bmatrix} = \frac{1}{256} \begin{bmatrix} 256 & 0 & 357.510 \\ 256 & -87.755 & -182.105 \\ 256 & 451.860 & 0 \end{bmatrix} \bullet \begin{bmatrix} {}^{601}_{255}Y' \\ C_B \\ C_R \end{bmatrix}$$

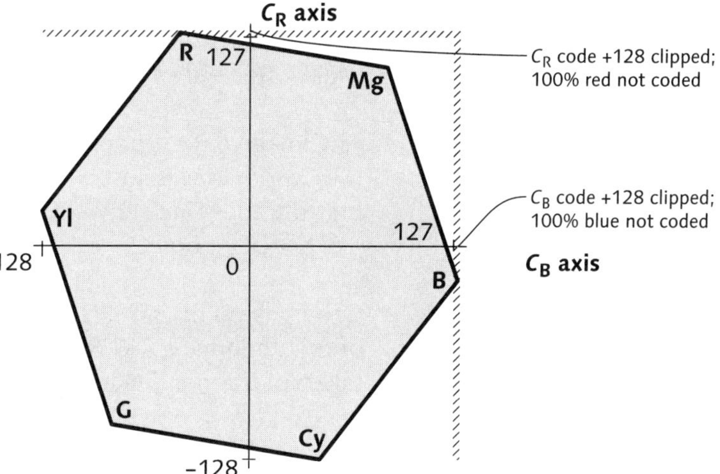

Figure 25.5 **C_BC_R "full range" components** used in JPEG/JFIF are shown, ranging from –128 to +127. Chroma code +128 is clipped so that fully saturated blue and red cannot be preserved. No provision is made for undershoot or overshoot. The accompanying luma signal ranges 0 through 255.

Y'UV, Y'IQ confusion

I have detailed $Y'P_BP_R$ and $Y'C_BC_R$. These are both based on [$B'-Y'$, $R'-Y'$] components, but they have different scale factors suitable for component analog and component digital interface, respectively.

In *NTSC and PAL chroma modulation*, on page 335, I will describe [U, V] and [I, Q] color differences. These components are also based on $B'-Y'$ and $R'-Y'$, but have yet another set of scale factors. *UV* scaling – or *IQ* scaling and rotation – is appropriate only when the signals are destined for composite encoding, as in NTSC or PAL.

Unfortunately, the notation *Y'UV* – or worse, *YUV* – is sometimes loosely applied to *any* form of color difference coding based on [$B'-Y'$, $R'-Y'$]. Do not be misled by video equipment having connectors labelled *Y'UV* or Y', $B'-Y'$, $R'-Y'$, or these symbols without primes, or by JPEG being described as utilizing *Y'UV* coding. In fact the analog connectors convey signals with $Y'P_BP_R$ scaling, and the JPEG standard itself specifies what I would denote ${}^{601}_{255}Y'C_BC_R$.

When the term *Y'UV* (or *YUV*) is encountered in a computer graphics or image-processing context, usually Rec. 601 $Y'C_BC_R$ is meant, but beware!

- Any image data supposedly coded to the original 1953 NTSC primaries is suspect, because it has been about four decades since any equipment using these primaries has been built.

- Generally no mention is made of the transfer function of the underlying *R'G'B'* components, and no account is taken of the nonlinear formation of luma.

When the term *Y'IQ* (or *YIQ*) is encountered, beware!

- Image data supposedly coded in *Y'IQ* is suspect since no analog or digital interface for *Y'IQ* components has ever been standardized.

- Nearly all NTSC encoders and decoders built since 1970 have been based upon *Y'UV* components, not *Y'IQ*.

Component video color coding for HDTV 26

In the previous chapter, *Component video color coding for SDTV*, I detailed various component color coding systems that use the luma coefficients specified in Rec. 601. Unfortunately, for no good technical reason, Rec. 709 for HDTV standardizes different luma coefficients. Deployment of HDTV requires upconversion and downconversion capabilities both at the studio and at consumers' premises; this situation will persist for a few decades. Owing to this aspect of conversion between HDTV and SDTV, if you want to be an HDTV expert, you have to be an SDTV expert as well!

Today's computer imaging systems – for still frames, desktop video, and other applications – use the Rec. 601 parameters, independent of the image's pixel count ("resolution independence"). As I write, it isn't clear whether Rec. 601 or Rec. 709 coding will be used when computer systems start performing HDTV editing. To me, it is sensible to retain the Rec. 601 coefficients.

In this chapter, I assume that you're familiar with the concepts of *Luma and color differences*, described on page 281. I will detail these component sets:

- $B'-Y'$, $R'-Y'$ components, the basis for P_BP_R and C_BC_R
- P_BP_R components, used for analog interface
- C_BC_R components, used for digital interface

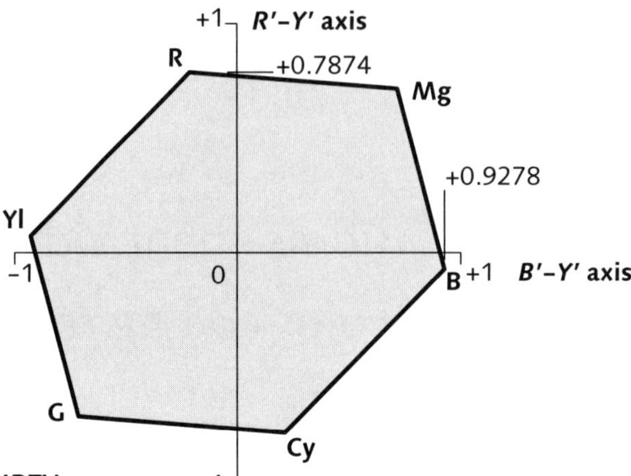

Figure 26.1 ***B′–Y′*, *R′–Y′* components for Rec. 709 HDTV**

B′–Y′, *R′–Y′* components for Rec. 709 HDTV

The $B'–Y'$ component reaches its positive maximum at blue ($R'=0$, $G'=0$, $B'=1$). With Rec. 709 luma coefficients, the maximum of $B'–Y' = +0.9278$ occurs at $Y'=0.0722$. The $B'–Y'$ component reaches its negative maximum at yellow ($B'–Y' = -0.9278$). Analogously, the extrema of $R'–Y'$ occur at red and cyan at values ±0.7874. (See Figure 26.1 above). These are inconvenient values for both digital and analog systems. The $^{709}Y'P_BP_R$ and $^{709}Y'C_BC_R$ systems to be described both employ versions of [Y', $B'–Y'$, $R'–Y'$] that are scaled to place the extrema of the component values at more convenient values.

To obtain [Y', $B'–Y'$, $R'–Y'$], from $R'G'B'$, for Rec. 709 luma coefficients, use this matrix equation:

$$\begin{bmatrix} ^{709}Y' \\ B'-{}^{709}Y' \\ R'-{}^{709}Y' \end{bmatrix} = \begin{bmatrix} 0.2126 & 0.7152 & 0.0722 \\ -0.2126 & -0.7152 & 0.9278 \\ 0.7874 & -0.7152 & -0.0722 \end{bmatrix} \bullet \begin{bmatrix} R' \\ G' \\ B' \end{bmatrix} \qquad \text{Eq 26.1}$$

P_BP_R components for Rec. 709 HDTV

If two color difference components are to be formed having excursions identical to luma, then P_B and P_R

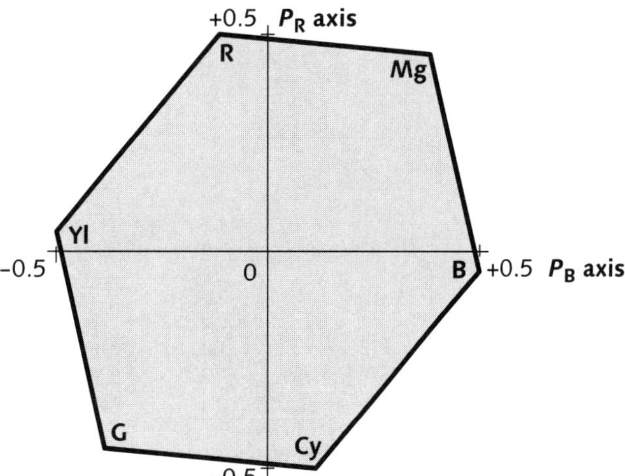

Figure 26.2 **$P_B P_R$ components for Rec. 709 HDTV**

color difference components are used. For Rec. 709 luma, the equations are these:

Eq 26.2

$$\begin{aligned}
{}^{709}P_B &= \frac{0.5}{1-0.0722}\left(B' - {}^{709}Y'\right) &= \frac{1}{1.8556}\left(B' - {}^{709}Y'\right) &\approx 0.5389\left(B' - {}^{709}Y'\right) \\
{}^{709}P_R &= \frac{0.5}{1-0.2126}\left(R' - {}^{709}Y'\right) &= \frac{1}{1.5748}\left(R' - {}^{709}Y'\right) &\approx 0.6350\left(R' - {}^{709}Y'\right)
\end{aligned}$$

These scale factors limit the excursion of each color difference component to the range -0.5 to +0.5 with respect to unity luma excursion: 0.0722 in the first expression above is the luma coefficient of blue, and 0.2126 in the second is for red. At an HDTV analog interface, luma ranges from 0 mV (black) to 700 mV (white), and P_B and P_R analog components range ±350 mV. Figure 26.2 above shows a plot of the $[P_B, P_R]$ plane.

Expressed in matrix form, the $B'-Y'$ and $R'-Y'$ rows of Equation 26.1 are scaled by $^{0.5}/_{0.9278}$ and $^{0.5}/_{0.7874}$. To encode from $R'G'B'$ where reference black is zero and reference white is unity:

Eq 26.3

$$\begin{bmatrix} {}^{709}Y' \\ P_B \\ P_R \end{bmatrix} = \begin{bmatrix} 0.2126 & 0.7152 & 0.0722 \\ -0.114572 & -0.385428 & 0.5 \\ 0.5 & -0.454153 & -0.045847 \end{bmatrix} \bullet \begin{bmatrix} R' \\ G' \\ B' \end{bmatrix}$$

Figure 26.3 **C_BC_R components for Rec. 709 HDTV** are shown in their mathematical form. At an 8-bit interface, an offset of +128 is added to each color difference component.

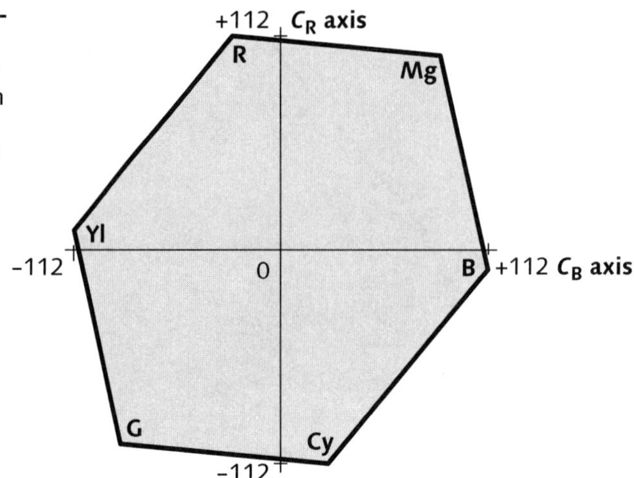

The inverse, decoding matrix is this:

$$\begin{bmatrix} R' \\ G' \\ B' \end{bmatrix} = \begin{bmatrix} 1 & 0 & 1.5748 \\ 1 & -0.187324 & -0.468124 \\ 1 & 1.8556 & 0 \end{bmatrix} \bullet \begin{bmatrix} {}^{709}Y' \\ P_B \\ P_R \end{bmatrix} \qquad \text{Eq 26.4}$$

C_BC_R components for Rec. 709 HDTV

${}^{709}Y'C_BC_R$ coding is used in component digital HDTV equipment. In 8-bit systems, luma has an excursion of 219. Color differences C_B and C_R are coded in 8-bit offset binary form, with excursions of ±112. The [C_B, C_R] plane of HDTV is plotted in Figure 26.3.

In 8-bit systems, a luma offset of +16 is added at the interface, placing black at code 16 and white at code 235; an offset of +128 is added to C_B and C_R, yielding a range of 16 through 240 inclusive. (Following the convention of the previous chapter, in the equations to follow I write the offset terms in gray.) HDTV standards provide for 10-bit components, and 10-bit studio video equipment is commonplace. In a 10-bit interface, the 8-bit interface levels and prohibited codes are maintained; the extra two bits are appended as least-significant bits to provide increased precision.

To form ${}^{709}Y'C_BC_R$ from $[Y', B'-Y', R'-Y']$ components in the range [0…+1], use these equations:

Eq 26.5

$$
\begin{aligned}
{}^{709}_{219}Y' &= 16 + \left(219 \cdot {}^{709}Y'\right) \\
C_B &= 128 + \frac{112}{0.9278}\left(B' - {}^{709}Y'\right) \\
C_R &= 128 + \frac{112}{0.7874}\left(R' - {}^{709}Y'\right)
\end{aligned}
$$

To obtain ${}^{709}Y'C_BC_R$ from $R'G'B'$ ranging 0 to 1, scale the rows of the matrix in Equation 26.3 by the factors [219, 224, 224], corresponding to the excursions of each of the components:

Eq 26.6

$$
\begin{bmatrix} {}^{709}_{219}Y' \\ C_B \\ C_R \end{bmatrix} = \begin{bmatrix} 16 \\ 128 \\ 128 \end{bmatrix} + \begin{bmatrix} 46.559 & 156.629 & 15.812 \\ -25.664 & -86.336 & 112 \\ 112 & -101.730 & -10.270 \end{bmatrix} \bullet \begin{bmatrix} R' \\ G' \\ B' \end{bmatrix}
$$

Summing the first row of the matrix yields 219, the luma excursion from black to white. The two entries of 112 reflect the positive C_BC_R extrema at blue and red.

To recover $R'G'B'$ in the range [0…+1] from ${}^{709}Y'C_BC_R$, use the inverse of Equation 26.6:

Eq 26.7

$$
\begin{bmatrix} R' \\ G' \\ B' \end{bmatrix} = \begin{bmatrix} 0.00456621 & 0 & 0.00703036 \\ 0.00456621 & -0.00083627 & -0.00208984 \\ 0.00456621 & 0.00828393 & 0 \end{bmatrix} \bullet \left(\begin{bmatrix} {}^{709}_{219}Y' \\ C_B \\ C_R \end{bmatrix} - \begin{bmatrix} 16 \\ 128 \\ 128 \end{bmatrix} \right)
$$

The ${}^{709}Y'C_BC_R$ components are integers in 8 bits; reconstructed $R'G'B'$ is scaled to the range [0…+1].

Figure 24.2 (on page 285) illustrated that when $R'G'B'$ components are transformed to luma and color differences, the unit $R'G'B'$ cube occupies only a small fraction of the volume of the enclosing cube. In digital video, only about ¼ of $Y'C_BC_R$ codewords correspond to $R'G'B'$ values between zero and unity. Certain signal-processing operations (such as filtering) may produce $Y'C_BC_R$ codewords that lie outside the *RGB*-legal cube. These codewords cause no difficulty in the $Y'C_BC_R$ domain, but potentially present a problem when decoded to $R'G'B'$. Generally, $R'G'B'$ values are clipped between 0 and 1.

C_BC_R components for Rec. 1361 HDTV

One method of extending the color gamut of an $R'G'B'$ system is to allow components to excurse below zero and above unity. In *Rec. 1361 transfer function*, on page 265, I explained one approach. Rec. 1361 is based upon Rec. 709 primaries, but enables the RGB tristimulus components to excurse from $-\frac{1}{4}$ to $+\frac{4}{3}$.

Concerning Pointer, see the marginal note on page 255.

When transformed to Rec. 709 $Y'C_BC_R$, all of the real surface colors documented by Pointer – that is, all the colors in Pointer's gamut – produce values that are $Y'C_BC_R$-valid. Though Rec. 1361 was needed to specify the $R'G'B'$ representation of wide-gamut colors, no special provisions are necessary to carry those colors across a ${}^{709}Y'C_BC_R$ interface. The notation "Rec. 1361 $Y'C_BC_R$," or as I write it, ${}^{1361}Y'C_BC_R$, makes it explicit that codewords outside the unit $R'G'B'$ cube are to be interpreted as wide-gamut colors, instead of being treated as RGB-illegal.

Equipment conforming to Rec. 1361 is not yet deployed, and is not anticipated for several years. Wide-gamut acquisition and production equipment will begin to replace film over the next decade or so; however, wide-gamut consumer displays are not expected in that time frame. When these begin to be deployed, it is unlikely that they will all have the same gamut; electronics associated with each display will have to process the color signals according to the properties of each display. In the long term, gamut mapping strategies comparable to those in the desktop color management community will have to be deployed.

$Y'C_BC_R$ from studio RGB

In studio equipment, 8-bit $R'G'B'$ components usually use the same 219 excursion as the luma component of $Y'C_BC_R$. To encode $Y'C_BC_R$ from $R'G'B'$ in the range [0...219] using 8-bit binary arithmetic, scale the encoding matrix of Equation 26.6 by $\frac{256}{219}$:

Eq 26.8

$$\begin{bmatrix} {}^{709}_{219}Y' \\ C_B \\ C_R \end{bmatrix} = \begin{bmatrix} 16 \\ 128 \\ 128 \end{bmatrix} + \frac{1}{256}\begin{bmatrix} 54.426 & 183.091 & 18.483 \\ -30.000 & -100.922 & 130.922 \\ 130.922 & -118.918 & -12.005 \end{bmatrix} \bullet \begin{bmatrix} {}_{219}R' \\ {}_{219}G' \\ {}_{219}B' \end{bmatrix}$$

To decode to $R'G'B'$ in the range [0...219] from $Y'C_BC_R$ using 8-bit binary arithmetic:

Eq 26.9

$$\begin{bmatrix} R' \\ G' \\ B' \end{bmatrix} = \begin{bmatrix} 0.00456621 & 0 & 0.00703036 \\ 0.00456621 & -0.00083627 & -0.00208984 \\ 0.00456621 & 0.00828393 & 0 \end{bmatrix} \bullet \left(\begin{bmatrix} {}^{709}_{219}Y' \\ C_B \\ C_R \end{bmatrix} - \begin{bmatrix} 16 \\ 128 \\ 128 \end{bmatrix} \right)$$

$Y'C_BC_R$ from computer *RGB*

In computing it is conventional to use 8-bit $R'G'B'$ components, with no headroom or footroom: Black is at code 0 and white is at 255. To encode $Y'C_BC_R$ from $R'G'B'$ in the range [0...255] using 8-bit binary arithmetic, the matrix of Equation 26.6 is scaled by $^{256}/_{255}$:

Eq 26.10

$$\begin{bmatrix} {}^{709}_{219}Y' \\ C_B \\ C_R \end{bmatrix} = \begin{bmatrix} 16 \\ 128 \\ 128 \end{bmatrix} + \frac{1}{256} \begin{bmatrix} 65.738 & 129.057 & 25.064 \\ -37.945 & -74.494 & 112.439 \\ 112.439 & -94.154 & -18.285 \end{bmatrix} \bullet \begin{bmatrix} {}_{255}R' \\ {}_{255}G' \\ {}_{255}B' \end{bmatrix}$$

To decode $R'G'B'$ in the range [0...255] from Rec. 601 $Y'C_BC_R$ using 8-bit binary arithmetic:

Eq 26.11

$$\begin{bmatrix} {}_{255}R' \\ {}_{255}G' \\ {}_{255}B' \end{bmatrix} = \frac{1}{256} \begin{bmatrix} 298.082 & 0 & 458.942 \\ 298.082 & -54.592 & -136.425 \\ 298.082 & 540.775 & 0 \end{bmatrix} \bullet \left(\begin{bmatrix} {}^{709}_{219}Y' \\ C_B \\ C_R \end{bmatrix} - \begin{bmatrix} 16 \\ 128 \\ 128 \end{bmatrix} \right)$$

Conversions between HDTV and SDTV

The differences among the EBU, SMPTE, and Rec. 709 primaries are negligible for practical purposes. New equipment should be designed to Rec. 709. Also, SDTV and HDTV have effectively converged to the transfer function specified in Rec. 709. Consequently, $R'G'B'$ coding uses essentially identical parameters worldwide, for SDTV and HDTV. (The sRGB standard for desktop computing uses the primaries of Rec. 709, but uses a different transfer function.)

Unfortunately, as I have mentioned, the luma coefficients differ dramatically between SDTV and HDTV. This wouldn't matter if HDTV systems were isolated! However, in practice, SDTV is upconverted and HDTV is downconverted, both at the studio and at consumers' premises. Serious color reproduction errors arise if differences among luma coefficients are not taken into account in conversions.

In principle, downconversion can be accomplished by decoding ${}^{709}Y'C_BC_R$ to $R'G'B'$ using a suitable 3×3 matrix (such as that in Equation 26.7, on page 317), then encoding $R'G'B'$ to ${}^{601}Y'C_BC_R$ using another 3×3 matrix (such as that in Equation 25.6, on page 308). The two 3×3 matrices can be combined so that the conversion can take place in one step:

$$\begin{bmatrix} {}^{601}_{219}Y' \\ C_B \\ C_R \end{bmatrix} = \begin{bmatrix} 1 & 0.101579 & 0.196076 \\ 0 & 0.989854 & -0.110653 \\ 0 & -0.072453 & -0.983398 \end{bmatrix} \bullet \begin{bmatrix} {}^{709}_{219}Y' \\ C_B \\ C_R \end{bmatrix} \qquad \text{Eq 26.12}$$

In the first row of the matrix, the coefficient 0.101579 adds about one tenth of Rec. 709's C_B into Rec. 601's luma, as consequence of Rec. 709's blue luma coefficient being just 0.0722, compared to 0.114 for Rec. 601. The coefficient 0.196076 adds about one fifth of Rec. 709's C_R into Rec. 601's luma, as consequence of Rec. 709's red luma coefficient being 0.2126, compared to 0.299 for Rec. 601. Clearly, failure to perform this color transform produces large color errors.

To convert from SD to HD, the matrix of Equation 26.12 is inverted:

$$\begin{bmatrix} {}^{709}_{219}Y' \\ C_B \\ C_R \end{bmatrix} = \begin{bmatrix} 1 & -0.118188 & -0.212685 \\ 0 & 1.018640 & -0.114618 \\ 0 & 0.075049 & 1.025327 \end{bmatrix} \bullet \begin{bmatrix} {}^{601}_{219}Y' \\ C_B \\ C_R \end{bmatrix} \qquad \text{Eq 26.13}$$

Equations 26.12 and 26.13 are written without interface offsets of +16 for luma and +128 for of C_B and C_B: If these are present, remove them, transform, and reapply them.

Unfortunately, to upconvert or downconvert a subsampled representation such as 4:2:2 or 4:2:0 requires chroma interpolation, color transformation, then chroma subsampling. This is computationally intensive.

SMPTE 240M-1988 luma

For details of SMPTE 240M-1988 luma, see page 292.

The coding systems that I have described are based upon the luma coefficients of Rec. 709. Before Rec. 709 was established, SMPTE 240M-1988 for 1035*i*30 HDTV established luma coefficients based upon the SMPTE RP 145 primaries. In 1990, international agreement was reached in Rec. 709 on a new transfer function, a new set of primaries, and new luma coefficients. SMPTE 274M for 1920×1080 HDTV adopted the Rec. 709 parameters, but made provisions for the SMPTE 240M parameters as the "interim implementation." Much equipment has been deployed using the 240M parameters. The most recent revision of SMPTE 274M eliminates the provision for the "interim implementation," and specifies Rec. 709 parameters.

I recommend that you use the Rec. 709 parameters for new equipment. However, if your equipment must interoperate with the "interim implementation," or with SDTV equipment, you must pay very careful attention to conversion. Although the differences in transfer functions and primary sets are evident in test signals, they are negligible for actual pictures. However, the differences among luma coefficients are significant.

To convert from legacy SMPTE 240M $Y'C_BC_R$ components to Rec. 709 $Y'C_BC_R$, use this transform:

Eq 26.14

$$\begin{bmatrix} {}^{709}_{219}Y' \\ C_B \\ C_R \end{bmatrix} = \begin{bmatrix} 0.999400 & 0.000534 & 0.000066 \\ -0.000314 & 0.981134 & 0.019180 \\ -0.003437 & -0.011363 & 1.014800 \end{bmatrix} \bullet \begin{bmatrix} {}^{240}_{219}Y' \\ C_B \\ C_R \end{bmatrix}$$

Color coding standards

ITU-R Rec. BT.709, *Basic parameter values for the HDTV standard for the studio and for international programme exchange.*

SMPTE 274M, *1920×1080 Scanning and Analog and Parallel Digital Interfaces for Multiple Picture Rates.*

SMPTE 296M, *1280×720 Progressive Image Sample Structure – Analog and Digital Representation and Analog Interface.*

ITU-R Rec. BT.709 defines $Y'P_BP_R$ for component analog HDTV and $Y'C_BC_R$ for component digital HDTV.

The parameters of $Y'P_BP_R$ and $Y'C_BC_R$ for the 1280×720 and 1920×1080 systems are defined by the SMPTE standards cited in the margin.

Video signal processing 27

This chapter presents several diverse topics concerning the representation and processing of video signals.

Transition samples

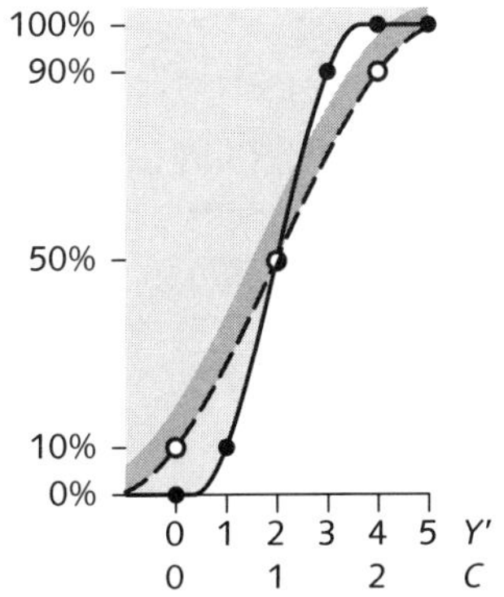

Figure 27.1 **Transition samples.** The solid line, dots (•), and light shading show the luma transition; the dashed line, open circles (o), and heavy shading show 4:2:2 chroma

In *Scanning parameters,* on page 54, I mentioned that it is necessary to avoid an instantaneous transition from blanking to picture at the start of a line. It is also necessary to avoid an instantaneous transition from picture to blanking at the end of a line. In studio video, the first and the last few active video samples on a line are blanking transition samples. I recommend that the first luma (*Y'*) sample of a line be black, and that this sample be followed by three transition samples clipped to 10%, 50%, and 90% of the full signal amplitude. In 4:2:2, I recommend that the first three color difference (*C*) samples on a line be transition samples, clipped to 10%, 50%, and 90%. Figure 27.1 sketches the transition samples. The transition values should be applied by clipping, rather than by multiplication, to avoid disturbing the transition samples of a signal that already has a proper blanking transition.

Edge treatment

If an image row of 720 samples is to be processed through a 25-tap FIR filter (such as that of Figure 16.26, on page 167) to produce 720 output samples, the calculations for 12 output samples at each end of the line will refer to input samples outside the image. One approach to this problem is to produce just those output samples – 696 in this example – that can be computed from the available input samples. However, filtering operations are frequently cascaded, particularly in the studio, and it is unacceptable to repeatedly narrow the image width upon application of a sequence of FIR filters. A strategy is necessary to deal with filtering at the edges of the image.

Some digital image-processing textbooks advocate considering the area outside the pixel array to contain replicated edge samples. I consider this to be quite unrealistic, because a small feature that happens to lie at the edge of the image will exert undue influence into the interior of the pixel array. Other digital image-processing textbooks consider the image to wrap in a cylinder: Missing samples outside the left-hand edge of the image are copied from the *right-hand* edge of the image! This concept draws from Fourier transform theory, where a finite data set is treated as being cyclic. In practice, I consider the wrapping strategy to be even worse than edge replication.

See *Scanning parameters*, on page 54, and *Transition samples*, on page 323.

In video, we treat the image as lying on a field of black: Unavailable samples are taken to be zero. With this strategy, repeated lowpass filtering causes the implicit black background to intrude to some extent into the image. In practice, few problems are caused by this intrusion. Video image data nearly always includes some black (or blanking) samples, as I outlined in the discussion of samples per picture width and samples per active line. In studio standards, a region lying within the pixel array is designated as the *clean aperture*, as sketched in Figure 6.4, on page 55. This region is supposed to remain subjectively free from artifacts that originate from filtering at the picture edges.

Picture lines

In *480i line assignment*, on page 500, I will detail how 480*i* studio standards provide up to 487 picture lines. In *576i line assignment*, on page 520, I detail how 576*i* studio standards provide 574 full lines and two halflines.

Historically, the count of picture lines (image rows, L_A) has been poorly standardized in 480*i* systems. Various standards have specified between 480 and 487 picture lines. It is pointless to carry picture on line 21/284 or earlier, because in NTSC transmission this line is reserved for closed caption data: 482 full lines, plus the bottom halfline, now suffice. With 4:2:0 chroma subsampling, as used in JPEG, MPEG-1, and MPEG-2, a multiple of 16 picture lines is required. MPEG compression is now so important that a count of 480 lines has become *de rigeur* for 525-line MPEG video. In *576i* scanning, a rigid standard of 576 picture lines has always been enforced; fortuitously for MPEG in *576i*, this is a multiple of 16.

MPEG-2 accommodates the 1920×1080 image format, but 1080 is not a multiple of 16. In MPEG-2 coding, eight black lines are appended to the bottom of each 1920×1080 picture, to form a 1920×1088 array that is coded. The extra 8 lines are discarded upon decoding.

Traditionally, the image array of 480*i* and 576*i* systems had halflines, as sketched in Figures 11.3 and 11.4 on page 98: Halfline blanking was imposed on picture information on the top and bottom lines of each frame. Neither JPEG nor MPEG provides halfline blanking: When halfline-blanked image data is presented to a JPEG or MPEG compressor, the blank image data is compressed. Halflines have been abolished from HDTV.

Active lines (vertically) encompass the picture height. *Active samples* (horizontally) encompass not only the picture width, but also up to about a dozen blanking transition samples.

Studio video standards have no transition samples on the vertical axis: An instantaneous transition from vertical blanking to full picture is implied. However, nonpicture vertical interval information coded like video – such as VITS or VITC – may precede the picture lines in a field or frame. Active lines comprise only picture lines (and exceptionally, in 480*i* systems, closed caption data). L_A excludes vertical interval lines.

Computer monitor interface standards, such as those from VESA, make no provision for nonpicture (vertical interval) lines other than blanking.

Choice of S_{AL} and S_{PW} parameters

In *Scanning parameters,* on page 54, I characterized two video signal parameters, *samples per active line* (S_{AL}) and *samples per picture width* (S_{PW}). Active sample counts in studio standards have been chosen for the convenience of system design; within a given scanning standard, active sample counts standardized for different sampling frequencies are not exactly proportional to the sampling frequencies.

Historically, "blanking width" was measured instead of picture width. Through the decades, there has been considerable variation in blanking width of studio standards and broadcast standards. Also, blanking width was measured at levels other than 50%, leading to an unfortunate dependency upon frequency response.

HDTV standards specify that the 50%-points of picture width must lie no further than 6 samples inside the production aperture.

Most modern video standards do not specify picture width: It is implicit that the picture should be as wide as possible within the production aperture, subject to reasonable blanking transitions. Figure 11.1, on page 96 indicates S_{AL} values typical of studio practice.

720 S_{AL} accommodates 714 S_{PW}, corresponding to 10.7 µs of analog blanking in the studio, conformant to SMPTE 170M. 704 S_{PW} corresponds to 11.4 µs of analog blanking, outside SMPTE 170M.

For digital terrestrial broadcasting of 480*i* and 480*p*, the ATSC considered the coding of transition samples to be wasteful. Instead of specifying 720 S_{AL}, ATSC established 704 S_{AL}. This created an inconsistency between production standards and broadcast standards: MPEG-2 macroblocks are misaligned between the two.

Computer monitor interface standards, such as those from VESA, do not accommodate blanking transition samples. In these standards, S_{PW} and S_{AL} are equal.

Video levels

I introduced 8-bit studio video levels on page 22. Studio video coding provides headroom and footroom. At an 8-bit interface, luma has reference black at code 16 and reference white at code 235; color differences are coded in offset binary, with zero at code 128, the negative reference at code 16, and the positive reference at code 240. (It is a nuisance that the positive reference levels differ between luma and chroma.) I use the term *reference* instead of *peak:* the peaks of transient excursions may lie outside the reference levels. All studio interfaces today accommodate 10-bit signals, and most equipment today implements 10 bits. In 10-bit systems, the reference levels just mentioned are multiplied by 4; the two LSBs add precision.

In 480*i systems* with setup, *picture excursion* refers to the range from blanking to white, even though strictly speaking the lowest level of the picture signal is 7.5 IRE, not 0 IRE.

Video levels in 480*i* systems are expressed in *IRE units*, sometimes simply called *units*. IRE refers to the Institute of Radio Engineers in the United States, the predecessor of the IEEE. Reference blanking level is defined as 0 IRE; reference white level is 100 IRE. The range between these values is the *picture excursion*.

In the analog domain, sync is coded at voltage level more negative than black; sync is "blacker than black." The ratio of picture excursion to sync amplitude is the *picture:sync ratio*. Two different ratios are standard: 10:4 is predominant in 480*i* and computing; 7:3 is universal in 576*i* and HDTV, occasionally used in 480*i*, and rarely used in computing.

Setup (pedestal)

In 480*i* composite NTSC video in North America, reference black is offset above blanking by 7.5% ($^3/_{40}$) of the picture excursion. *Setup* refers to this offset, expressed as a fraction or percentage of the picture excursion. In a 480*i* system with setup, there are nominally 92.5 IRE units from black to white.

Back porch is described in *Analog horizontal blanking interval*, on page 405.

Blanking level at an analog interface is established by a back porch clamp. However, in a system with setup, no signal element is present that enables a receiver to accurately recover black level. If an interface has poor tolerance, calibration error, or drift, setup causes problems in maintaining accurate black-level reproduction. Consequently, setup has been abolished from modern video systems: *Zero setup* is a feature of EBU N10 component video, all variants of 576*i* video, and HDTV. In all of these systems, blanking level also serves as the reference level for black.

480*i* video in Japan originally used setup. However, in about 1985, zero setup was adopted; 10:4 picture-to-sync ratio was retained. Consequently, there are now three level standards for analog video interface. Figure 27.2 overleaf shows these variations.

The archaic EIA RS-343-A standard specifies monochrome operation, 2:1 interlace with 60.00 Hz field rate, 7 μs horizontal blanking, and other parameters that have no place in modern video systems. Unfortunately, Most PC graphics display standards have inherited RS-343-A's 10:4 picture-to-sync ratio and 7.5% setup. (Some high-end workstations have zero setup.)

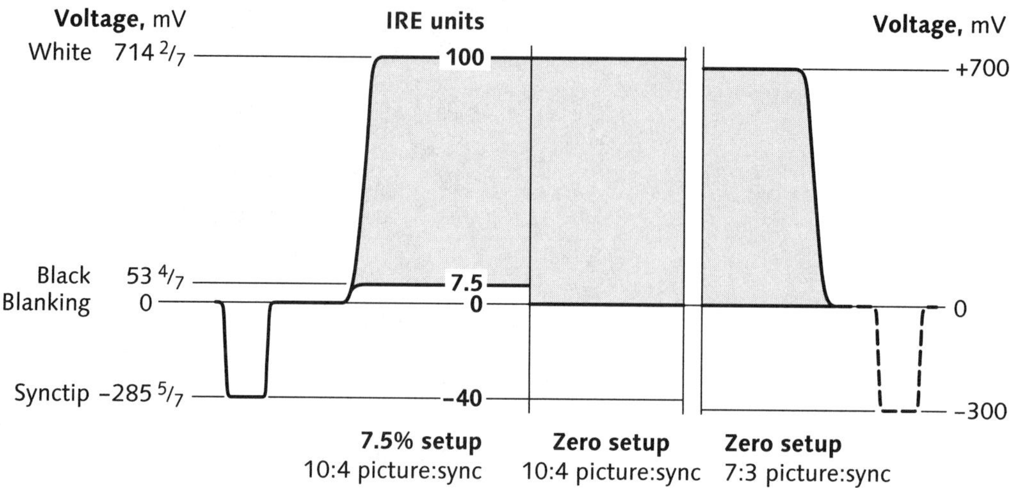

Figure 27.2 **Comparison of 7.5% and zero setup.** The left-hand third shows the video levels of composite 480*i* video, with 7.5% setup and 10:4 picture-to-sync ratio. This coding is used in some studio equipment and in most computer monitor interfaces. The middle third shows zero setup and 10:4 picture-to-sync, as used in 480*i* video in Japan. EBU N10 component video, 576*i* systems, and HDTV use zero setup, 700 mV picture, and 300 mV sync, as shown at the right.

The term *pedestal* refers to the absolute value of the offset from blanking level to black level, in IRE units or millivolts: Composite 480*i* NTSC incorporates a pedestal of 7.5 IRE. Pedestal includes any deliberate offset added to *R'*, *G'*, or *B'* components, to luma, or to a composite video signal, to achieve a desired technical or aesthetic intent. In Europe, this is termed *lift*. (I prefer the term *black level* to either *pedestal* or *lift*.)

Rec. 601 to computing

The coding difference between computer graphics and studio video necessitates image data conversion at the interface. Figure 27.3 opposite shows the transfer function that converts 8-bit Rec. 601 studio *R'G'B'* into computer *R'G'B'*. The footroom and headroom regions of Rec. 601 are clipped, and the output signal omits 36 code values. This coding difference between computer graphics and studio video is one of many challenges in taking studio video into the computer domain.

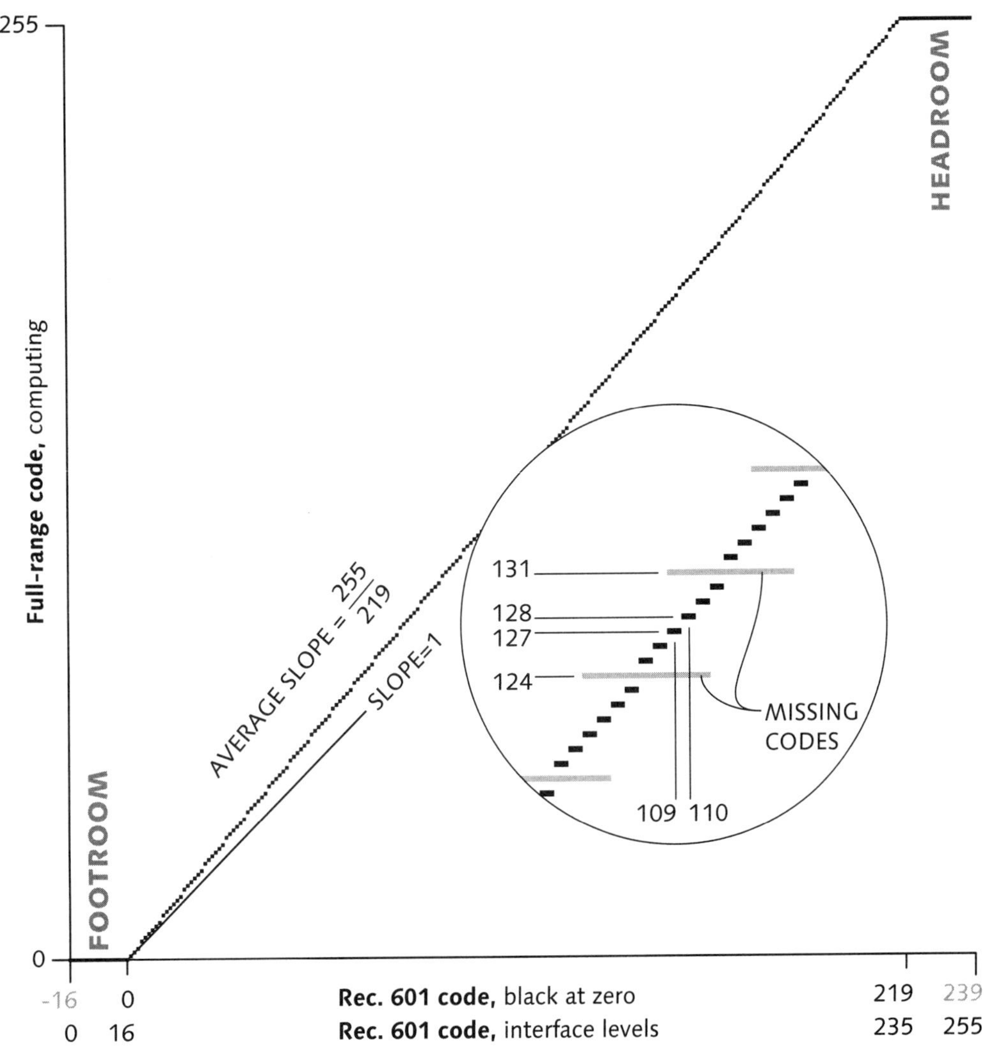

Figure 27.3 **8-bit Rec. 601 to full-range (computer) *R'G'B'* conversion** involves multiplying by a scale factor of $^{255}/_{219}$, to account for the difference in range. This causes the footroom and headroom regions of the studio video signal to be clipped, and causes the output signal to be missing several code values. The detail shows the situation at mid-scale; the transfer function is symmetrically disposed around input pair [109, 110] and output pair [127, 128]. This graph shows a linear relationship from black to white. The linear relationship is suitable in computer systems where a ramp is loaded into the lookup table (LUT) between the framebuffer and the display; in that case, *R'G'B'* data is displayed on the computer monitor comparably to the way *R'G'B'* is displayed in video; see *Gamma,* on page 257.

Enhancement

This section and several subsequent sections discuss enhancement, median filtering, coring, chroma transition improvement (CTI), and scan-velocity modulation (SVM). Each of these operations superficially resembles FIR filtering: A "window" involving a small set of neighboring samples slides over the input data. For each new input sample, the filtering operation delivers one output sample that has been subject to some fixed time delay with respect to the input. Unlike FIR filtering, with the exception of the most benign forms of enhancement these operations are nonlinear. They cannot, in general, be undone.

The term "enhancement" is widely used in image processing and video. It has no precise meaning. Evidently, the goal of enhancement is to improve, in some sense, the quality of an image. In principle, this can be done only with knowledge of the process or processes that degraded the image's quality. In practice, it is extremely rare to have access to any history of the processes to which image data has been subject, so no systematic approach to enhancement is possible.

In some applications, it may be known that image data has been subject to processes that have introduced specific degradations or artifacts. In these cases, enhancement may refer to techniques designed to reduce these degradations. A common example involves degraded frequency response due to aperture effects. Enhancement in this case, also known as *aperture correction*, is accomplished by some degree of highpass filtering, either in the horizontal direction, the vertical direction, or both. Compensation of loss of optical MTF should be done in the linear-light domain; however, it is sometimes done in the gamma-corrected domain. Historically, vertical aperture correction in interlaced tube cameras (vidicons and plumbicons) was done in the interlaced domain.

The SHARPNESS control in consumer receivers effects horizontal "enhancement" on the luma signal.

More generally, enhancement is liable to involve nonlinear processes that are based on some assumptions about the properties of the image data. Unless signal flow is extremely well controlled, there is a huge danger in using such operations: Upon receiving image data that has *not* been subject to the expected process, "enhancement" is liable to degrade the image, rather than improve it. For this reason, I am generally very strongly opposed to "enhancement."

Median filtering

In a median filter, each output sample is computed as the median value of the input samples under the window. Ordinarily, an odd number of taps are used; the median is the central value when the input samples are sorted by value. Median filtering usually involves a horizontal window with 3 taps. Occasionally, 5 taps are used; rarely, 3×3 spatial median filters are used.

Any isolated extreme value, such as a large-valued sample due to impulse noise, will not appear in the output sequence of a median filter: Median filtering can be useful to reduce noise. However, a legitimate extreme value will not be included either! I urge you to use great caution in imposing median filtering: If your filter is presented with image data whose statistics are not what you expect, you are very likely to degrade the image instead of improving it.

Coring

Coring assumes that any low-magnitude, high-frequency signal components are noise. The input signal is separated into low- and high-frequency components using complementary filters. The low-frequency component is passed to the output. The magnitude of the high-frequency component is estimated, and the magnitude is subject to a thresholding operation. If the magnitude is below threshold, then the high-frequency component is discarded; otherwise, it is passed to the output through summation with the low-frequency component. Coring can be implemented by the block diagram shown in Figure 27.4 overleaf.

Like median filtering, coring depends upon the statistical properties of the image data. If the image is a flat-shaded cartoon having large areas of uniform color with rapid transitions between them, then coring will eliminate noise below a certain magnitude. However, if the

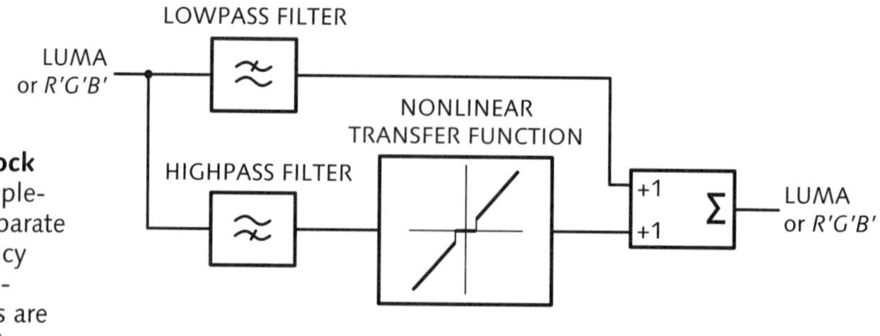

Figure 27.4 **Coring block diagram** includes complementary filters that separate low- and high-frequency components. The high-frequency components are processed by the nonlinear transfer function in the sketch.

input is *not* a cartoon, you run the risk that coring will cause it to look like one! In a close-up of a face, skin texture produces a low-magnitude, high-frequency component that is *not* noise. If coring eliminates this component, the face will take on the texture of plastic.

Coring is liable to introduce spatial artifacts into an image. Consider an image containing a Persian carpet that recedes into the distance. The carpet's pattern will produce a fairly low spatial frequency in the foreground (at the bottom of the image); as the pattern recedes into the background, the spatial frequency of the pattern becomes higher and its magnitude becomes lower. If this image is subject to coring, beyond a certain distance, coring will cause the pattern to vanish. The viewer will perceive a sudden transition from the pattern of the carpet to no pattern at all. The viewer may conclude that beyond a certain distance there is a different carpet, or no carpet at all.

Chroma transition improvement (CTI)

Color-under VCRs exhibit very poor color difference bandwidth (evidenced as poor chroma resolution in the horizontal direction). A localized change in luma may be faithfully reproduced, but the accompanying change in color difference components will be spread horizontally. If you assume that colored areas tend to be uniformly colored, one way of improving image quality is to detect localized changes in luma, and use that information to effect repositioning of color difference information. Techniques to accomplish this are collectively known as *chroma transition improvement* (CTI).

If you use CTI, you run the risk of introducing excessive emphasis on edges. Also, CTI operates only on the horizontal dimension: Excessive CTI is liable to become visible owing to perceptible (or even objectionable) differences between the horizontal and vertical characteristics of the image. CTI works well on cartoons, and on certain other types of images. However, it should be used cautiously.

Scan-velocity modulation (SVM)

CRT displays are subject to limitations of how fast the electron beam can change from one state to another (for example, from on to off). These limitations are imposed by limited bandwidth of the video amplifiers and by the electrical capacitance that the CRT's cathode or grid presents to the driving circuitry. These limitations are reflected as limited spatial resolution of the reproduced image: An edge is reproduced across a horizontal dimension wider than desired.

One way to reduce the dimension of an edge involves making the electron beam position responsive to changes in beam intensity. If intensity is increasing rapidly as the beam goes left-to-right, the beam can be accelerated. If intensity is decreasing rapidly, the beam can be decelerated so that it dwells longer on areas of the screen that require high intensity. This process is *scan-velocity modulation* (SVM). Luma (or some comparable quantity) is processed through a high-pass filter; the result is amplified and applied to the horizontal deflection circuit of the CRT.

Note that all of the red, green, and blue beams are deflected together: The technique is effective only on black-to-white or white-to-black transitions. In a magenta-to-green transition, both red and blue are negative-going, even though luma is increasing: In this example, SVM has unintended effects on red and blue.

Mixing and keying

Mixing video signals together to create a transition, or a layered effect – for example, to mix or wipe – is called *compositing.* In America, a piece of equipment that performs such effects is a *production switcher.* In

Europe, the equipment – or the person that operates it! – is called a *vision mixer.*

Accomplishing mix, wipe, or key effects in hardware also requires synchronous video signals – that is, signals whose timing matches perfectly in the vertical and horizontal domains. (In composite video, it is also necessary to match subcarrier phase, as I will describe.)

Porter, Thomas, and Tom Duff, "Compositing Digital Images," in *Computer Graphics,* 18 (3): 253–259 (July 1984, Proc. SIGGRAPH '84). The terms *composite* and *compositing* are overused in video!

SMPTE RP 157, *Key Signals.*

Keying (or *compositing*) refers to superimposing a foreground (FG, or *fill video*) image over a background (BG) image. Keying is normally controlled by a *key* (or *matte*) signal, coded like luma, that indicates the transparency of the accompanying foreground image data, coded between black (fully transparent) and white (fully opaque). In computer graphics, the key signal (data) is called *alpha* (α), and the operation is called *compositing.*

Eq 27.1

$$R = \alpha \cdot FG + \left(1 - \alpha\right) \cdot BG$$

The keying (or compositing) operation is performed as in Equation 27.1. Foreground image data that has been premultiplied by the key is called *shaped* in video, or *associated, integral,* or *premultiplied* in computer graphics. Foreground image data that has not been premultiplied by the key is called *unshaped* in video, or *unassociated* or *nonpremultiplied* in computer graphics.

The most difficult part of keying is extracting ("pulling") the matte. For review from a computer graphics perspective, see Smith, Alvy Ray, and James F. Blinn, "Blue Screen Matting," in *Computer Graphics,* Annual Conference Series 1996 (Proc. SIGGRAPH 96), 259–268.

The multiplication of foreground and background data in keying is equivalent to modulation: This can produce signal components above half the sampling rate, thereby producing alias components. Aliasing can be avoided by upsampling the foreground, background, and key signals; performing the keying operation at twice the video sampling rate; then suitably filtering and downsampling the result. Most keyers operate directly at the video sampling rate without upsampling or downsampling, and so exhibit some aliasing.

To mimic optical compositing, keying should be performed in the linear-light domain. However, keying in video is usually done in the gamma-corrected domain. (A key signal in video is sometimes called *linear key;* this does not refer to linear light, but to a key signal representing opacity with more than just the two levels fully transparent and fully opaque.)

NTSC and PAL chroma modulation 28

In *Introduction to composite NTSC and PAL,* on page 103, I outlined composite NTSC and PAL color encoding. This chapter details how an encoder forms *U* and *V* color difference components, how modulated chroma (*C*) is formed, and how a decoder demodulates back to *U* and *V*. The following chapter, *NTSC and PAL frequency interleaving,* on page 349, explains how an encoder sums luma and chroma to form a composite NTSC or PAL signal, and how a decoder separates luma and modulated chroma prior to chroma demodulation.

The designers of NTSC color television intended that chroma would be based upon *I* and *Q* components. Nowadays, *I* and *Q* components are essentially obsolete, and *U* and *V* components are generally used. For details, see *NTSC Y'IQ system,* on page 365.

See Appendix A, *YUV and luminance considered harmful,* on page 595.

Y'UV coding is unique to composite NTSC and PAL: It is has no place in component video, HDTV, or computing. If chroma components are to be kept separate, it is incorrect to apply the *U* and *V* scaling, or to use *U* and *V* notation. Unfortunately, the *Y'UV* notation – or, carelessly written, *YUV* – is often used nowadays to denote *any* component system involving two scaled color difference components based upon *B'–Y'* and *R'–Y'* where the scaling is unknown or implicit. Even worse, the notation *YUV* is sometimes used: The unprimed *Y* suggests luminance, but no *YUV* system uses linear-light luminance, and if luminance were actually used, the *UV* scaling would be incorrect.

Figure 28.1 ***UV* components** are scaled so as to limit the composite (Y'+C) excursion. *UV* scaling is inappropriate if the components are kept separate. This sketch reflects the display of a colorbar test signal on an NTSC vectorscope; the colorbar signal is described on page 535. If the figure rotates with respect to burst, a chroma phase error has occurred; upon display, this will manifest itself as a hue error.

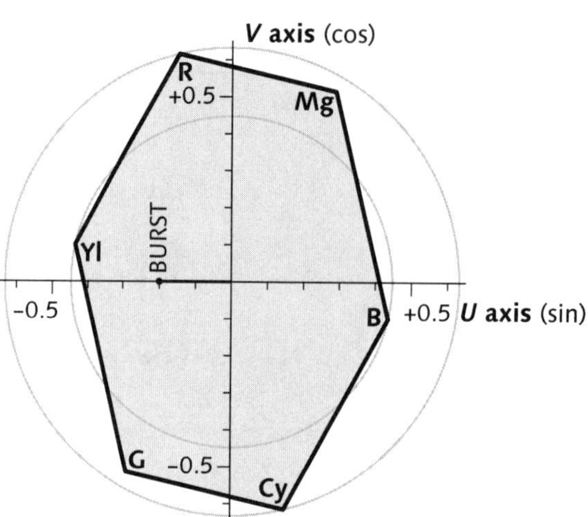

UV components

In *Component video color coding for SDTV,* on page 301, I outlined the formation of luma and color difference components. In encoding NTSC, PAL, or S-video, the color difference components are scaled so that the eventual composite signal is contained within the amplitude limits of VHF and UHF television transmitters. It is standard to limit the composite excursion to the range [-⅓ ... +4⁄3] of unity luma excursion. To this end, the $B'-Y'$ and $R'-Y'$ components are scaled according to Equation 28.1 by factors k_B and k_R to form U and V components depicted in Figure 28.1.

$$U = k_B\left(B' - {}^{601}Y'\right); \qquad V = k_R\left(R' - {}^{601}Y'\right) \qquad \text{Eq 28.1}$$

The scale factors are chosen to satisfy this constraint:

$$-\frac{1}{3} \le {}^{601}Y' \pm \sqrt{U^2 + V^2} \le \frac{4}{3} \qquad \text{Eq 28.2}$$

The exact values are these:

$$k_B = \frac{1}{3}\sqrt{\frac{209556997}{96146491}}$$

$$k_R = \sqrt{\frac{221990474}{288439473}}$$

Incidentally, the ratio $k_B : k_R$ is almost exactly 9:16.

I described *B'-Y', R'-Y' components for SDTV,* on page 303. The maximum excursions of the individual color difference components occur at the blue and red primaries. Since these points are not located on the axes where scaling takes place, the scale factors are derived from two simultaneous equations involving $B'-Y'$ and $R'-Y'$. The scale factors were once standardized to three digits, rounded to 0.493 and 0.877; in the contemporary SMPTE 170M standard, they are expressed to 6 digits. B'–Y' and R'–Y' components are transformed to UV through these relations:

Eq 28.3

$$\begin{aligned} U &= 0.492111\left(B' - {}^{601}Y'\right) &\approx \frac{1}{2.03}\left(B' - {}^{601}Y'\right) \\ V &= 0.877283\left(R' - {}^{601}Y'\right) &\approx \frac{1}{1.14}\left(R' - {}^{601}Y'\right) \end{aligned}$$

The scaling can be expressed in matrix form:

Eq 28.4

$$\begin{bmatrix} {}^{601}Y' \\ U \\ V \end{bmatrix} = \begin{bmatrix} 1 & 0 & 0 \\ 0 & 0.492111 & 0 \\ 0 & 0 & 0.877283 \end{bmatrix} \bullet \begin{bmatrix} {}^{601}Y' \\ B' - {}^{601}Y' \\ R' - {}^{601}Y' \end{bmatrix}$$

To obtain $Y'UV$ from $R'G'B'$, concatenate the matrix of Equation 28.4 above with the matrix of Equation 25.1, on page 303:

Eq 28.5

$$\begin{bmatrix} {}^{601}Y' \\ U \\ V \end{bmatrix} = \begin{bmatrix} 0.299 & 0.587 & 0.114 \\ -0.147141 & -0.288869 & 0.436010 \\ 0.614975 & -0.514965 & -0.100010 \end{bmatrix} \bullet \begin{bmatrix} R' \\ G' \\ B' \end{bmatrix}$$

To recover $R'G'B'$ from $Y'UV$, invert Equation 28.5:

Eq 28.6

$$\begin{bmatrix} R' \\ G' \\ B' \end{bmatrix} = \begin{bmatrix} 1 & 0 & 1.139883 \\ 1 & -0.394642 & -0.580622 \\ 1 & 2.032062 & 0 \end{bmatrix} \bullet \begin{bmatrix} {}^{601}Y' \\ U \\ V \end{bmatrix}$$

$$-233\tfrac{1}{3} = -\tfrac{1}{3} \cdot 700$$

$$933\tfrac{1}{3} = +\tfrac{4}{3} \cdot 700$$

The k_B and k_R scale factors apply directly to PAL: For a luma excursion of 700 mV, the PAL composite signal ranges about -233 mV to +933 mV.

The IRE unit is introduced on page 326.

For details, see page 516.

As I will detail in *Setup (pedestal),* on page 327, NTSC (except in Japan) has 7.5% setup. Setup reduces luma excursion by the fraction $^{37}/_{40}$, and places luma on a pedestal of 7.5 IRE. The k_B and k_R scale factors were computed disregarding setup, so the NTSC composite signal has an excursion -23⅓ IRE to +130⅚ IRE, not quite the -33⅓ IRE to +133⅓ IRE excursion implied by the range -⅓ … +4⁄3.

The +4⁄3 limit applies to composite analog or digital studio equipment, and to PAL transmission. However, a hard limit of +1.2 (120 IRE) applies to terrestrial (VHF/UHF) NTSC transmitters, and a practical limit of

Figure 28.2 **Spectra of *U*, *V*, and modulated chroma** are sketched for 1.3 MHz baseband chroma bandwidth typical of the studio. Modulated chroma (*C*) consumes 2.6 MHz of bandwidth, centered on the color subcarrier frequency. The crosshatching suggests that information from both the *U* and *V* components is found across the 2.6 MHz band.

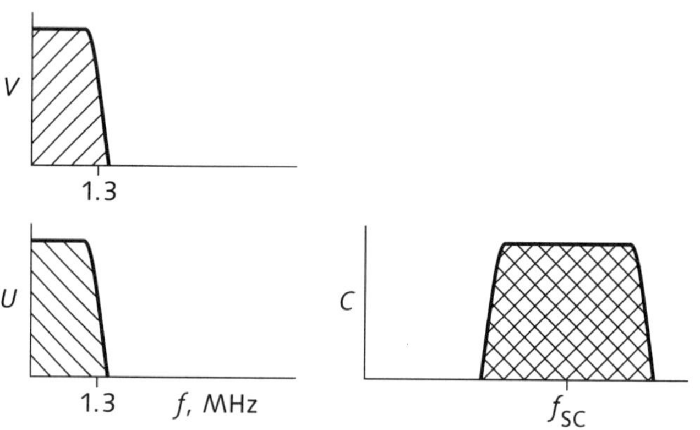

Not all *RGB*-legal colors are NTSC-legal: Some *RGB*-legal saturated yellow and cyan colors fall outside NTSC transmitter limits. An algorithm to reduce chroma saturation in *R'G'B'* images is described in Martindale, David, and Alan W. Paeth, "Television color encoding," in *Graphics Gems II*, edited by James Arvo (Boston: Academic Press, 1991).

about +1.15 is appropriate to avoid interference problems with sound in old television receivers. Many computer graphics systems have provisions to check or limit chroma excursion. If the composite signal is simply clipped, artifacts will result: Chroma clipping must be accomplished by more sophisticated techniques.

NTSC chroma modulation

Once *U* and *V* components are formed, in studio video each component is lowpass-filtered to about 1.3 MHz, as sketched at the left-hand side of Figure 28.2 above. (Luma is processed through a matching delay.) Historically, in analog encoders, only horizontal filtering was done. Vertical filtering ought to be performed also, to enable good performance from comb filter decoders. However, despite the potential for improved quality, vertical filtering is very rarely performed at encoders.

In the rare cases that vertical filtering is performed prior to NTSC or PAL encoding, this is called *precombing*.

After matrixing, scaling, and filtering, *U* and *V* components are combined into a single *modulated chroma* signal *C*, using quadrature modulation onto a continuous-wave color subcarrier. Chroma modulation is achieved by simultaneously multiplying *U* by sine of the subcarrier and multiplying *V* by cosine of the subcarrier, then summing the products:

$$C = U \sin \omega t + V \cos \omega t; \qquad \omega = 2\pi f_{SC} \qquad \text{Eq 28.7}$$

In Equation 28.7, sin ωt represents the subcarrier, typically about 3.58 MHz for NTSC or 4.43 MHz for PAL.

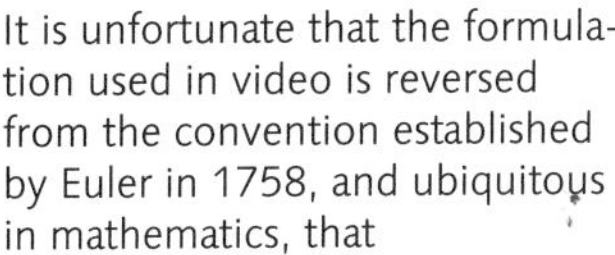

It is unfortunate that the formulation used in video is reversed from the convention established by Euler in 1758, and ubiquitous in mathematics, that

$$e^{i\theta} = \cos\theta + i\sin\theta, \quad i^2 = -1$$

where i is associated with the y-axis. The video formulation also opposes convention in communications theory, where the carrier is considered to be a cosine wave, not a sine wave.

The exact subcarrier frequency is not important to quadrature modulation, but it is critical to frequency interleaving, as I will detail in *NTSC and PAL frequency interleaving,* on page 349. The spectrum of the modulated chroma is sketched at the right of Figure 28.2.

The sum of the sine and cosine terms is then bandpass filtered, producing the modulated chroma spectrum sketched at the right of Figure 28.2. Modulated chroma is centered on the subcarrier. With *U* and *V* bandwidth of 1.3 MHz, the lower sideband extends 1.3 MHz below the subcarrier frequency, and the upper sideband extends 1.3 MHz above. (In *NTSC and PAL frequency interleaving,* on page 349, I will discuss how much chroma bandwidth is preserved in transmission.)

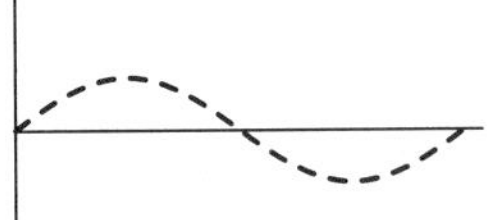

Chroma subcarrier

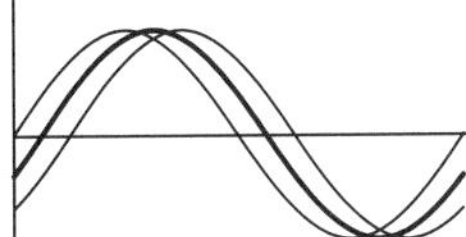

Phase (encodes Hue)

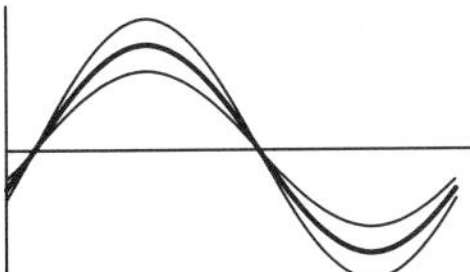

Amplitude
(encodes Saturation)

Figure 28.3 **Quadrature modulation** can be viewed as simultaneous phase and amplitude modulation.

If you transform the two color differences *U* and *V* from rectangular to polar coordinates, you can think of *U* and *V* as being conveyed by a combination of phase and amplitude modulation, as suggested by Figure 28.3 in the margin. Consider the point in the chroma plane plotted at coordinates [*U*, *V*]. The angle from the *x*-axis to the point relates to the hue attribute of the associated color; this quantity effectively modulates subcarrier phase. The distance from the origin to the point [*U*, *V*] relates to the saturation of the color; this quantity effectively modulates subcarrier amplitude.

It is standard to sample digital composite video at four times the subcarrier frequency, $4f_{SC}$. Early digital NTSC systems sampled on the [*B'–Y'*, *R'–Y'*] axes – that is, sampling took place at the 0°, 90°, 180°, and 270° phases of subcarrier, so the sine subcarrier took values chosen cyclically from {0, 1, 0, –1}; the cosine subcarrier took values chosen cyclically from {1, 0, –1, 0}.

In early $4f_{SC}$ NTSC systems, multiplying sine by *U* and cosine by *V*, and adding the two products, gave digital modulated chroma samples {*V*, *U*, –*V*, –*U*}. However, when the SMPTE 244M standard was established for $4f_{SC}$ NTSC, it called for sampling on the [*I*, *Q*] axes – that is, at the 33° phase of subcarrier. In modern $4f_{SC}$ NTSC equipment, digital modulated chroma samples take values chosen cyclically from {*I*, *Q*, –*I*, –*Q*}. In the

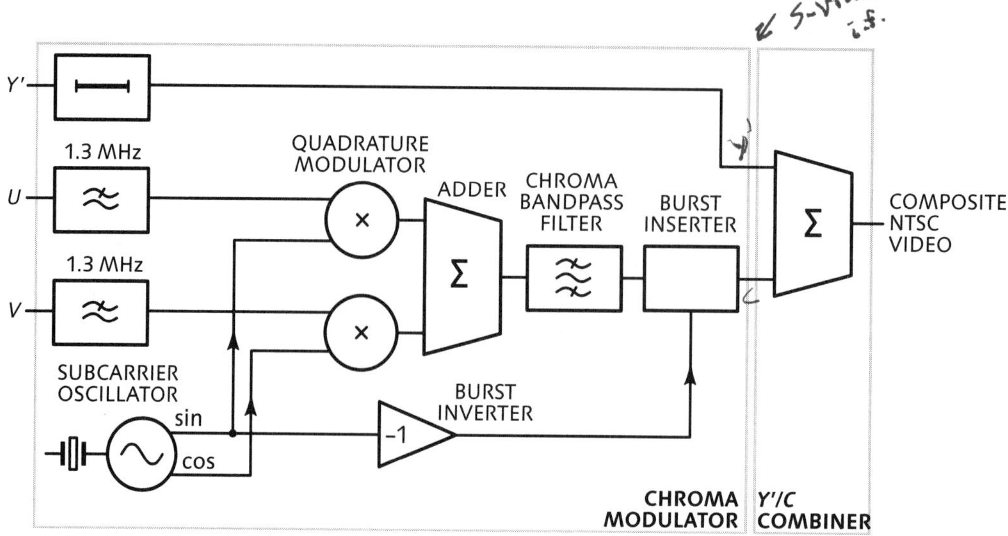

Figure 28.4 **NTSC encoder block diagram.** A subcarrier oscillator generates *sin* and *cos* continuous waves. Quadrature modulation is performed on lowpass-filtered *U* and *V* components by a pair of 4-quadrant multipliers. An adder forms modulated chroma, *C*. Chroma and luma *Y'* are summed to form composite video. Frequency interleaving is achieved when subcarrier is coherent with scanning.

following chapter, I will detail how luma is added to modulated chroma; adding luma yields the $4f_{SC}$ NTSC sample sequence {*Y'*+*I*, *Y'*+*Q*, *Y'*–*I*, *Y'*–*Q*}.

If the phase of burst is altered, and the phase of modulated subcarrier is altered by the same amount, an analog chroma demodulator will still produce the correct color. What matters is the phase relationship between the two. An analog decoder cannot determine the phase at which chroma modulation was performed by an encoder.

Chroma demodulation depends on the decoder having access to the continuous-wave color subcarrier used in encoding. To this end, an encoder inserts a brief *burst* of the inverted sine subcarrier into the horizontal blanking interval. (See Figure 42.1, on page 512.)

Figure 28.4 above shows the block diagram of an NTSC encoder. An S-video interface provides *Y'* and *C* signals after modulation but prior to summation. In S-video, burst is inserted onto the modulated chroma signal.

NTSC chroma demodulation

An NTSC decoder is shown in Figure 28.5 at the top of the facing page. Decoding begins with separation of the luma and modulated chroma components – *Y'/C separation*, which I will detail in the following chapter, *NTSC and PAL frequency interleaving*. For an S-video input signal, the *Y'/C* separator is bypassed.

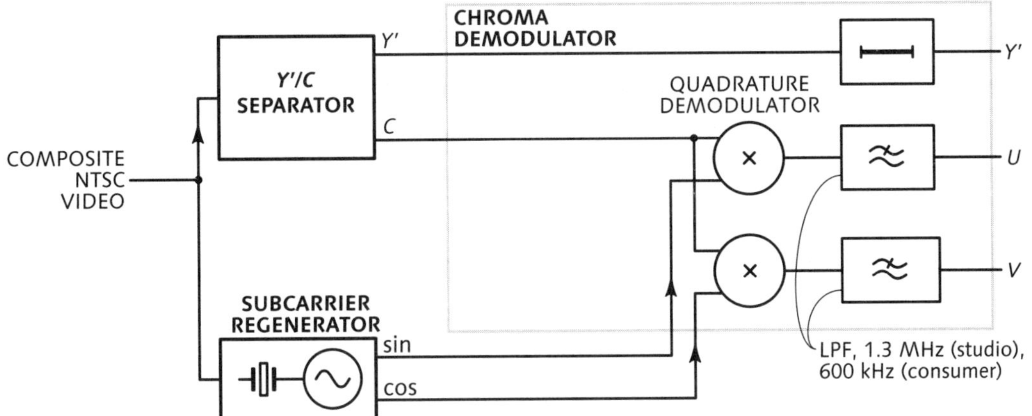

Figure 28.5 **NTSC decoder block diagram.** *Y'/C* separation is accomplished using a "notch" filter or a comb filter. Subcarrier is regenerated from burst. Separated chroma is independently multiplied by continuous *sin* and *cos* waves in quadrature; the products are lowpass filtered to recover *U* and *V*. To recover wideband *U* and *V* in the studio, use 1.3 MHz filters. To recover narrowband *U* and *V* in consumer applications, use 600 kHz filters. For VHS VCRs, use 300 kHz filters.

The decoder reconstructs the continuous-wave color subcarrier that was used at encoding. I will describe that process in *Subcarrier regeneration,* on page 344.

In *NTSC Y'IQ system,* on page 365, I will explain why it is futile to attempt to recover more than about 600 kHz of chroma bandwidth from terrestrial VHF/UHF NTSC.

The separated modulated chroma is then multiplied simultaneously by sine and cosine of the regenerated subcarrier. The products are lowpass filtered to recover the baseband *U* and *V* components. Luma is processed through a matching delay.

Provided that *U* and *V* are limited in bandwidth to less than half the subcarrier frequency, chroma modulation is reversible without information loss. In practice, chroma modulation itself introduces no significant impairments, although the bandwidth limitation of the color difference signals removes color detail.

Even in NTSC, modulated chroma inverts phase on alternate lines! The *A* in *PAL* refers not to this alternation, but to the line by line alternation of phase of the *V* chroma component.

PAL chroma modulation

Analog transmission is susceptible to *differential phase error,* whereby the phase of modulated chroma is influenced by luma (as I will describe on page 541). In NTSC, these errors cause incorrectly decoded hue; vision is quite sensitive to hue errors. PAL augments the NTSC system with a *V-axis inverter,* which alternates the phase of the modulated *V* component line-by-line. (PAL

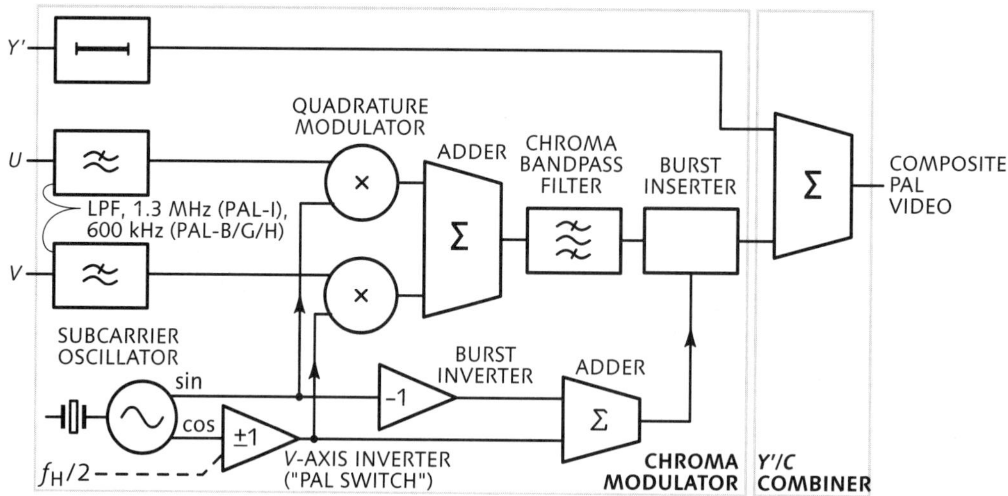

Figure 28.6 **PAL encoder block diagram** augments the NTSC encoder of Figure 28.4 with a *V*-axis inverter. Also, the alternating cosine phase of subcarrier makes a contribution to burst.

derives its acronym from this *Phase Alternation at Line rate*.) The *V*-axis alternation causes any phase error in modulated chroma to take alternate directions on alternate lines. These phase errors average at the receiver, and thereby cancel. Chroma phase error causes loss of saturation, but that is less objectionable than hue shift. PAL is inherently insensitive to DP-induced hue error. Figure 28.6 shows the block diagram of a PAL encoder.

Old texts refer to a *PAL-S* (simple PAL) decoder, which operates without a delay element, and a *PAL-D* (deluxe PAL) decoder, which uses a 1*H* line delay. Nowadays, virtually all PAL receivers are deluxe PAL. This use of S and D is unrelated to the letters B, D, G, H, I, M, or N that may follow PAL; those refer to transmission standards. PAL-D, in the second sense, is used for broadcasting in China.

A PAL decoder – sketched in Figure 28.7 opposite – is essentially an NTSC decoder augmented by a *V*-axis inverter and a *U/V* separator. The *U/V* separator produces modulated chroma components that I denote C_U and C_V, based upon PAL's *V*-axis alternation, as I will detail in the following chapter, *NTSC and PAL frequency interleaving*. In modern PAL decoders, *U/V* separation uses a comb filter with at least a one line (1*H*) delay. Unlike an NTSC comb filter, PAL's comb filter separates *U* and *V*; it does *not* separate luma from chroma! (*U/V* separation is intrinsic in NTSC's quadrature demodulator; no circuitry is dedicated to that function.)

In $4f_{SC}$ digital PAL, it is standard to sample on the [*U*+*V*, *U*–*V*] axes, at 45° with respect to subcarrier (i.e.,

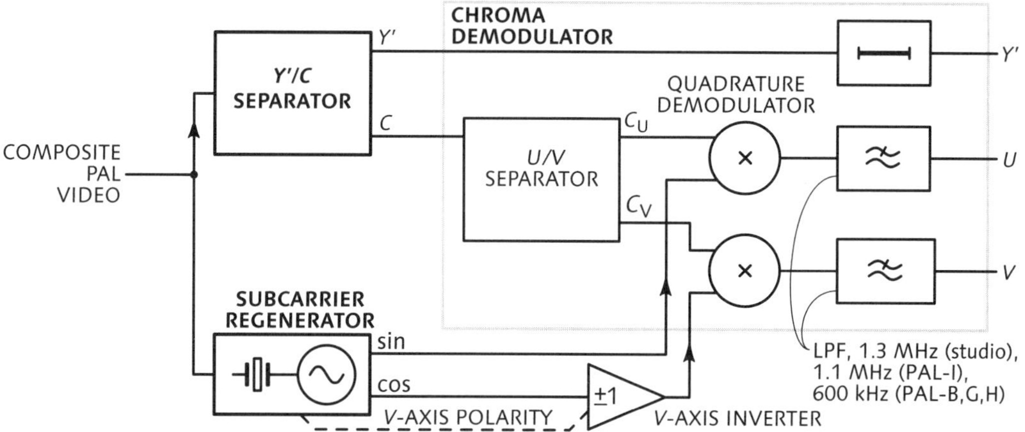

Figure 28.7 **PAL decoder block diagram** begins with *Y'/C* separation, usually accomplished by a "notch" filter. Modulated *U* and *V* chroma components are separated, usually by a comb filter. Regenerated subcarrier is processed through PAL's *V*-axis inverter prior to demodulating chroma.

0° with respect to PAL burst). This results in modulated chroma samples chosen cyclically from these values:

$$\{U \pm V,\ -U \pm V,\ -U \mp V,\ U \mp V\} \qquad \text{Eq 28.8}$$

The $\pm$ symbol designates addition on lines where *V* is normal ("NTSC lines") and subtraction on lines where *V* is inverted ("PAL lines"). The $\mp$ symbol designates subtraction on lines where *V* is normal and addition on lines where *V* is inverted.

The *V*-axis switch causes a vectorscope display of the color test pattern to display two hexagons, as sketched in Figure 28.8 overleaf. Associated with PAL's *V*-axis switch, burst alternates at line rate, between +135° and -135° with respect to subcarrier (compared to a fixed 180° burst phase for NTSC). This is called *Brüch burst* or *swinging burst*. Burst alternation enables a PAL decoder to recover the *V*-switch polarity.

PAL differs from NTSC in several other aspects to be detailed in *Frequency interleaving in PAL,* on page 355.

The advantage of PAL's *V*-axis inverter is offset by increased complexity both at the encoder and the decoder. While PAL's modifications to NTSC once

Figure 28.8 ***UV* components in PAL** display two overlaid hexagons on a vectorscope. One portion is identical to the NTSC pattern in Figure 28.1, on page 336; the associated lines (where PAL burst takes +135° phase) are sometimes called *NTSC lines*. The other lines, where the *V*-component is inverted (and PAL burst takes -135° phase) are sometimes called *PAL lines*.

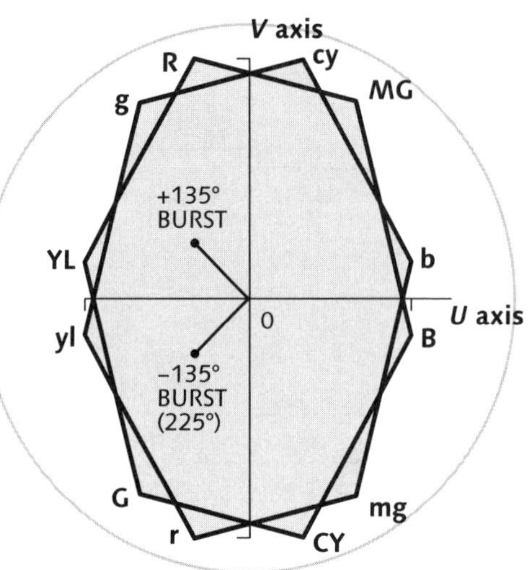

conferred an incremental performance advantage, that advantage has long since been subverted by the great difficulty of exchanging program material between countries, and by the expense of producing professional, industrial, and consumer equipment that operates with both standards. PAL's differences must now be seen as premature optimization. I hope that European television engineers will think twice before again adopting a uniquely European standard.

Subcarrier regeneration

Subcarrier regeneration in the digital domain requires a *digital phase-locked loop* (DPLL), one component of which is a *number-controlled oscillator* (NCO) or a *direct digital synthesizer* (DDS).

An analog NTSC or PAL decoder regenerates subcarrier using a specialized phase-locked loop (PLL) circuit like that shown in Figure 28.9 at the top of the facing page. Continuous-wave cosine and sine wave signals are generated in a crystal oscillator; their frequency and phase are updated once per line by a phase comparator, based on a comparison with the signal's burst. The loop filter is a lowpass filter with a time constant of about 10 lines.

The most straightforward way to generate burst would be to sample the sine phase of subcarrier directly. However, the NTSC worried that if a receiver had poor blanking, burst might become visible. The potential for burst visibility was minimized by using the inverted sine subcarrier: A burst inverter is included in the NTSC

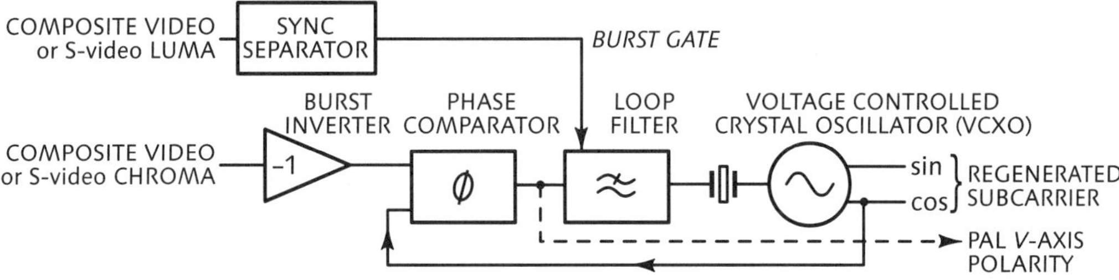

Figure 28.9 **Subcarrier regeneration**

encoder of Figure 28.4, and in the PAL encoder of Figure 28.6. In Figure 28.9, I indicate regeneration of subcarrier itself (at 0°), but keep in mind that the sine phase of subcarrier is inverted from burst phase. SMPTE 170M uses the term "burst-locked sinewave"; this reflects the preference of some decoder designers to regenerate a continuous wave at burst phase (180°).

Techniques to regenerate subcarrier from consumer devices are described in *Consumer analog NTSC and PAL*, on page 579.

The circuit of Figure 28.9 can be directly used to reconstruct PAL color subcarrier: The two burst phases average in the loop filter to 180°. The *V*-switch polarity is derived from the phase error, or from demodulated *V*, during burst. Alternatively, a more sophisticated circuit can process the +135° and –135° burst phases explicitly.

Although $4f_{SC}$ NTSC systems sample on the [*I*, *Q*] *axes*, narrowband *Q* is rarely used. See *NTSC Y'IQ system*, on page 365.

The obvious choices of sampling phase in a composite digital $4f_{SC}$ system are 0°, 90°, 180°, and 270°, so that subcarrier samples take the values {0, 1, 0, –1}. But no! It is standard to sample composite $4f_{SC}$ NTSC on the [*I*, *Q*] axes, at 33°, 123°, 213°, and 303° with respect to the sine (0°) subcarrier; it is standard to sample composite $4f_{SC}$ PAL systems on the [*U*+*V*, *U*–*V*] axes, at 45°, 135°, 225°, and 315° with respect to the sine subcarrier.

Burst is present on virtually all composite video signals nowadays, even black and white signals. However, if the subcarrier regenerator detects that burst is absent, then a *color killer* should force demodulated *U* and *V* to zero so as to reproduce a grayscale ("black-and-white") picture.

S-video interface

The S-video interface – sometimes denoted *Y'/C*, *Y'/C*3.58, or *Y'/C*4.43 – is a hybrid of component and composite systems. The *S* stands for *separate:* In S-video, luma and modulated chroma signals are conveyed across the interface on separate wires. There are three different versions of the S-video interface: S-video-525, S-video-525-J (for NTSC-J, in Japan), and S-video-625. The S-video interface was first introduced in S-VHS VCRs, and S-video remains a feature of virtually all S-VHS and Hi8 VCRs. However, the S-video *interface* is quite independent of S-VHS *recording* technology.

The S-video connector is sketched on page 409. Electrical and mechanical details are presented in *S-video-525 (Y'/C3.58)*, on page 515, and *S-video-625 (Y'/C4.43)*, on page 531.

Quadrature modulation is intrinsic to S-video, so chroma suffers some bandwidth reduction. However, S-video does not use frequency interleaving: Luma and chroma are not summed, so cross-luma and cross-color artifacts are completely avoided. Because S-video avoids the NTSC or PAL "footprint," it offers substantially better performance than composite NTSC or PAL. S-video is widely used in desktop video and consumer video. It is rarely used in the studio.

Decoder controls

A few decades ago, consumer receivers had unstable circuitry: User adjustment was necessary to produce acceptable color. Modern circuits are so stable that user controls are no longer necessary, but consumers continue to expect them. This is a shame, because consumer adjustment of these controls is more likely to degrade the picture than to improve it. Developers of desktop video systems typically provide an excess of controls; perhaps they believe that this relieves them of implementing correct signal-processing arithmetic.

I described the BRIGHTNESS and CONTRAST controls in Chapter 3, on page 25. These controls operate in the *R'G'B'* domain; they are found in television receivers and in computer monitors. Two other controls, which I will now describe, are associated with NTSC and PAL decoders.

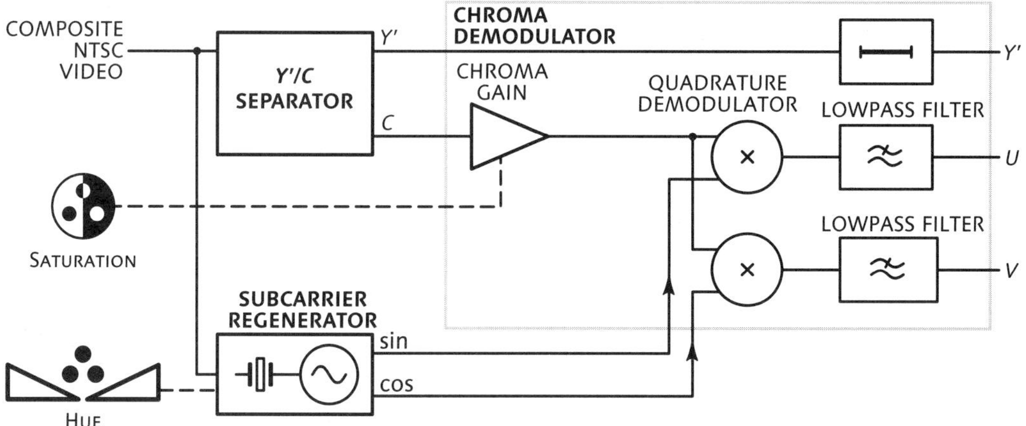

Figure 28.10 **NTSC decoder controls.** SATURATION alters chroma gain. HUE rotates the [*U*, *V*]-plane as viewed on a vectorscope. These controls were necessitated by the instability of analog receivers. Modern circuits are sufficiently stable that user adjustment of these controls is no longer necessary.

Figure 28.10 shows the block diagram of an NTSC or PAL decoder, augmented to reflect the places in the signal flow where the these controls are effected.

Figure 28.11 **SATURATION control** in a decoder alters chroma gain. The comparable control in processing equipment is CHROMA GAIN.

The SATURATION control, whose icon is shown in Figure 28.11, alters the gain of modulated chroma prior to demodulation. (Alternatively, the control can be implemented by altering the gain of both decoded color difference components.) This control is sometimes called COLOR, but SATURATION is preferred because it is ambiguous whether COLOR should adjust *which* color (hue) or the *amount* of color (saturation). This control is found in both NTSC and PAL decoders.

Figure 28.12 **HUE control** is usually implemented in a decoder by altering phase of regenerated subcarrier, so as to rotate the demodulated [*U*, *V*] components. The comparable control in processing equipment is CHROMA PHASE.

The HUE control, whose icon is shown in Figure 28.12, rotates the decoded colors around the [*U*, *V*] plot of Figure 28.1; it is implemented by altering the phase of regenerated subcarrier. This control is sometimes called TINT. That name is misleading and should be avoided, because to an artist, *tint* refers to adding white to increase lightness and decrease saturation – to an artist, to tint a color *preserves* its hue! As I mentioned on page 342, PAL has inherent immunity to hue errors arising from differential phase errors; consequently, the HUE control is usually omitted from PAL decoders.

NTSC and PAL frequency interleaving 29

I introduced the concepts of composite encoding in *Introduction to composite NTSC and PAL*, on page 103. In the previous chapter, *NTSC and PAL chroma modulation*, I detailed the formation of modulated chroma. In the S-video interface used in consumer equipment, luma and modulated chroma are conveyed separately. However, in most applications of NTSC and PAL, luma and modulated chroma are summed to form a single composite NTSC or PAL signal. In studio-quality or broadcast composite video, summation of these signals is based upon the frequency-interleaving principle.

The frequency-interleaving scheme devised by the NTSC places chroma at frequencies that are little-used by luma: The NTSC scheme enabled transmission of 1.3 MHz of chroma signal interleaved with – or if you like, overlaid upon – a 4.2 MHz luma signal. In NTSC, frequency interleaving is exploited by a *comb filter*. I will describe frequency interleaving in a moment, but first, I will discuss some aspects of notch filtering.

Notch filtering

When *U* and *V* components are filtered to 1.3 MHz and then modulated, chroma is centered on the color subcarrier frequency, as I sketched in Figure 28.2, on page 338. In NTSC, color subcarrier frequency is about 3.6 MHz, so modulated chroma extends from about 2.3 MHz to 4.9 MHz. Conventional PAL's color subcarrier frequency is about 4.4 MHz, so modulated chroma extends from about 3.1 MHz to 5.7 MHz.

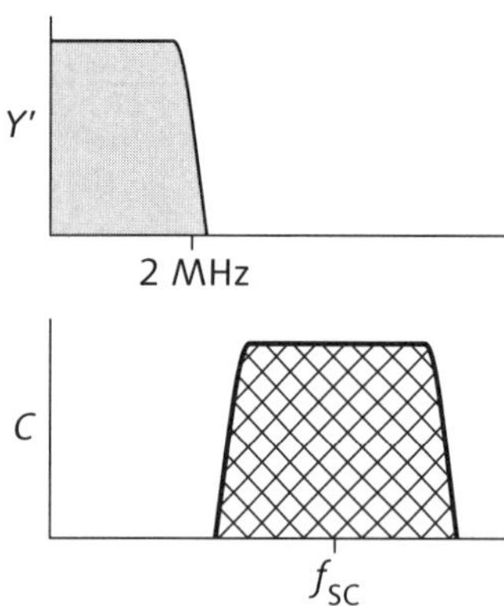

Figure 29.1 ***Y'/C* spectra** are disjoint if luma is limited to 2 MHz.

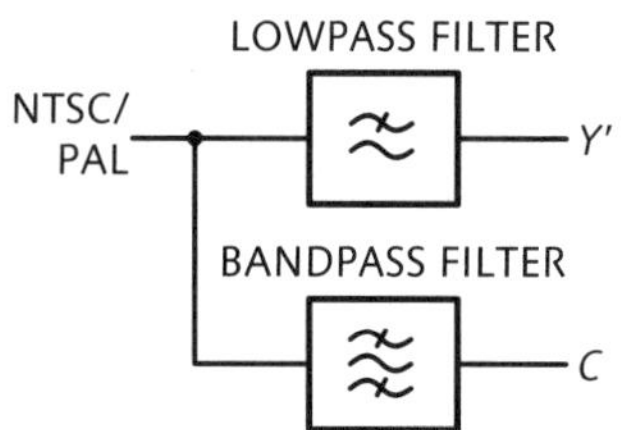

Figure 29.2 ***Y'/C* separation using notch filtering** involves a lowpass filter to extract luma and a bandpass filter to extract modulated chroma. The term *notch* is a misnomer, as explained in the text.

If luma were bandwidth limited to 2 MHz prior to summing with chroma, frequency occupancy of the two signals would be disjoint, as sketched in Figure 29.1. A cheap decoder could then accomplish separation using the simple scheme sketched in Figure 29.2: A lowpass filter extracts luma, and a bandpass filter centered on the color subcarrier frequency extracts chroma. This scheme is called *notch filtering;* it is used in VHS VCRs. This scheme has the obvious disadvantage of offering at most 2.3 MHz of luma bandwidth in NTSC (or 3.1 MHz in conventional PAL). The pictures suffer poor sharpness compared to the frequency interleaving scheme that I will describe, whereby luma and chroma share frequencies between 2.3 MHz (or 3.1 MHz) and the top of the luma band.

I described the simple-minded scheme, and sketched Figure 28.2, as if 1.3 MHz of baseband chroma could be decoded. In the studio, composite bandwidth of 5.5 MHz or more is available, so modulated chroma bandwidth of about 1.3 MHz is attainable. In conventional PAL, the color subcarrier is about 4.4 MHz; with 1.3 MHz chroma, the upper sideband of modulated chroma would extend to about 5.7 MHz. However, PAL-B/G/H transmission is limited to 5.0 MHz of video bandwidth, so just 600 kHz of chroma bandwidth is recoverable. (The PAL-I system, used in the U.K., has 5.5 MHz of composite video bandwidth; in PAL-I, about 1.1 MHz of chroma is recoverable.)

In the NTSC studio, about 1.3 MHz of modulated chroma bandwidth is available, but for NTSC transmission the situation is more complicated. NTSC chroma is modulated onto a 3.58 MHz subcarrier, and an NTSC transmitter is limited to 4.2 MHz: Only about 600 kHz is available for the upper sideband of modulated chroma. The designers of NTSC devised a scheme whereby chroma bandwidth of 1.3 MHz could be achieved for one of the two color difference components. Sadly, the scheme fell into disuse. I will detail the scheme, and its demise, in the following chapter, *NTSC Y'IQ system*. Today, chroma bandwidth in the studio is typically 1.3 MHz, but chroma bandwidth of terrestrial NTSC broadcast is effectively limited to 600 kHz.

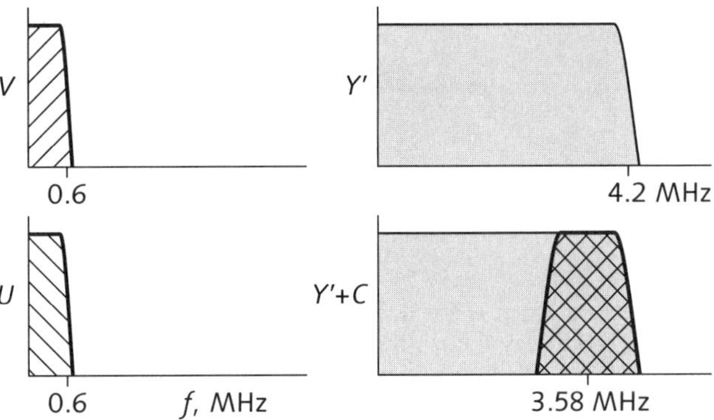

Figure 29.3 **NTSC chroma is limited to 600 kHz** upon terrestrial VHF/UHF broadcast, even if wideband components are presented to the encoder. (The original NTSC *Y'IQ* scheme allowed 1.3 MHz bandwidth for one chroma component, but that scheme is now abandoned.) In the studio, chroma bandwidth of 1.3 MHz is available.

Today's NTSC situation is sketched in Figure 29.3: *U* and *V* signals limited to 600 kHz are shown at the left. Luma, and the composite signal, are shown at the right. So, a decoder for terrestrial VHF/UHF NTSC should bandlimit demodulated chroma to about 600 kHz. You might think that *all* other components of the composite signal should be presumed to be luma, and the word *notch* suggests that a complimentary bandstop filter should be used to recover luma. There are two problems with that approach. One problem relates to broadcast NTSC signals, the other to VHS recording.

- Broadcast NTSC video is bandlimited to about 4.2 MHz. A notch filter that rejects components within 600 kHz of the 3.58 MHz subcarrier will reject everything up to the top of the luma band! There is no reason to reject only frequencies centered on subcarrier – all high frequencies might as well be rejected. A lowpass filter ought to be used for luma, instead of a notch filter.

- In VHS recording, luma is limited to a bandwidth of about 2 MHz, and baseband chroma is limited to about 300 kHz. The situation of Figure 29.1 pertains, and there is no need for a luma notch filter!

A notch filter is sometimes called a *trap*.

So, the term *notch filter* is a misnomer. In both broadcast and consumer VHS video, unless comb filtering is used, a decoder should use a lowpass filter to extract luma and a bandpass filter to extract chroma. However, much better separation is obtained by using a comb filter to exploit frequency interleaving.

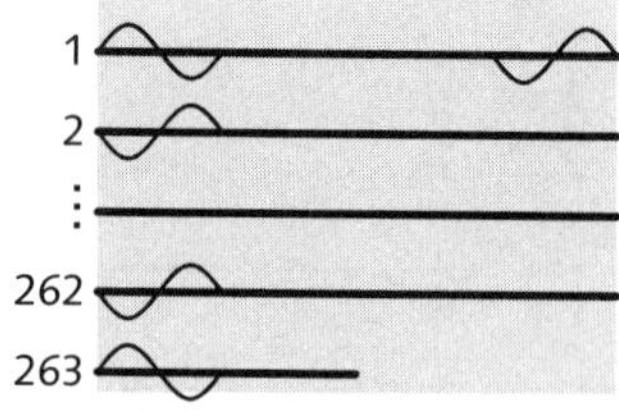

Figure 29.4 **Color subcarrier in NTSC** has its frequency chosen so that subcarrier phase inverts line-to-line. If *U* and *V* color difference components are constant line-to-line, then the phase of modulated chroma will invert line-to-line; this enables a comb filter to separate luma and chroma. A field comprises an odd integer number of halflines; it contains an odd integer number of half-cycles of subcarrier. Thus, subcarrier inverts phase frame-to-frame. This leads to NTSC color-frames *A* and *B*.

Frequency interleaving in NTSC

In studio video, the frequency of unmodulated NTSC color subcarrier is an odd multiple of half the line rate. This relationship causes subcarrier to invert phase line to line with respect to sync, as sketched in Figure 29.4 above. The luma and modulated chroma components sketched at the bottom right of the composite NTSC spectrum in Figure 29.3 appear, at the macro scale, to overlay each other. However, the line-to-line inversion of subcarrier phase produces frequency interleaving: Viewed at a finer scale, the spectra interleave.

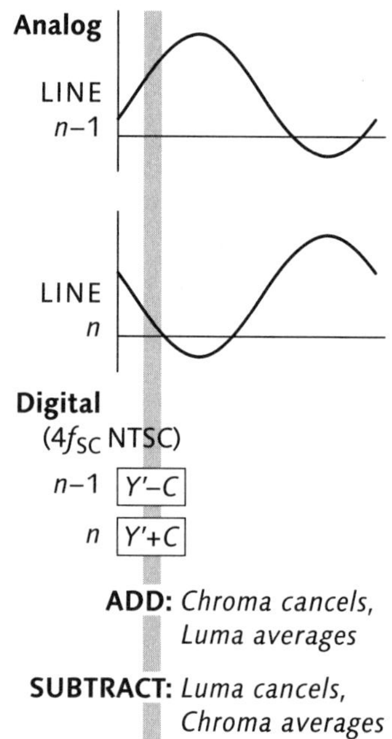

Figure 29.5 ***Y'/C* separation** in a 2-line (1*H*) NTSC comb filter is based upon line-by-line inversion of subcarrier phase.

Frequency interleaving enables separation of luma and chroma using a comb filter. A simple ("2-line," or 1*H*) comb filter has storage for one line of composite video. Provided that luma and chroma are similar line-to-line, if vertically adjacent samples are summed, chroma tends to cancel and luma tends to average. If vertically adjacent samples are differenced, luma tends to cancel and chroma tends to average. This interpretation is sketched in Figure 29.5 in the margin. Figure 29.6 at the top of the facing page sketches the implementation of a 2-line comb filter in NTSC. A digital comb filter uses digital memory; the memory element of an analog comb filter is typically an ultrasonic glass delay line.

In $4f_{SC}$ NTSC, if the composite signal comprises the sample sequence {*Y'*+*I*, *Y'*+*Q*, *Y'*−*I*, *Y'*−*Q*} on one line, NTSC's subcarrier frequency interleaving causes it to take the values {*Y'*−*I*, *Y'*−*Q*, *Y'*+*I*, *Y'*+*Q*} on the next. The

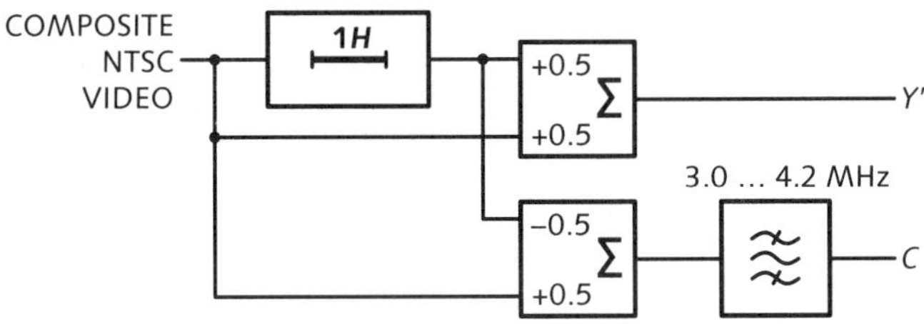

Figure 29.6 **NTSC 2-line comb filter** separates *Y′* and *C* using a 1*H* delay element. This is more complex than a notch filter; however, cross-luma and cross-color artifacts are greatly reduced.

sum of two vertically adjacent samples approximates luma; their difference approximates modulated chroma.

In a decoder that uses a notch filter, NTSC chroma inverts in phase line-by-line even if mistakenly decoded as luma. When integrated vertically by large spot size at the display, and when integrated vertically in the viewer's eye, luma tends to average (that is, to be reinforced) and chroma tends to cancel. This visual filtering is what allowed color to be retrofitted into black-and-white television: The newly added modulated chroma component averaged out – and thereby was not very visible – when viewed on a black-and-white receiver.

In *Consumer analog NTSC and PAL*, on page 579, I will discuss the decoding of video from consumer devices.

Proper operation of a comb filter depends upon the video signal having stable timebase and coherent subcarrier. In addition, comb filtering is only sensible if the video signal has luma content above 3 MHz. All of these conditions hold for broadcast signals, and luma/chroma separation should use comb filtering. If any of these conditions fails, as is likely with video originating from a consumer device, then comb filtering is likely to introduce artifacts and it should be defeated; a notch filter should be used instead.

In later sections of this chapter, I will explain comb filtering in the spatial frequency (two-dimensional) domain and in the one-dimensional frequency domain.

Cross-luma and cross-color

If neither luma nor chroma changes vertically, vertical summing and differencing in a comb filter can perfectly separate luma and chroma! In a solid-colored area of an image, comb filtering works well. However, to the extent that either luma or chroma changes vertically, chroma leaks ("crosses") into luma, and luma leaks ("crosses") into chroma. A decoder with a notch filter will produce *cross-color* artifacts that may appear as swirling rainbows, when luma occupying frequencies in the range of subcarrier "crosses into" – and is mistakenly decoded as – chroma. A notch filter can also introduce *cross-luma* artifacts, when chroma "crosses into" – and is mistakenly decoded as – luma.

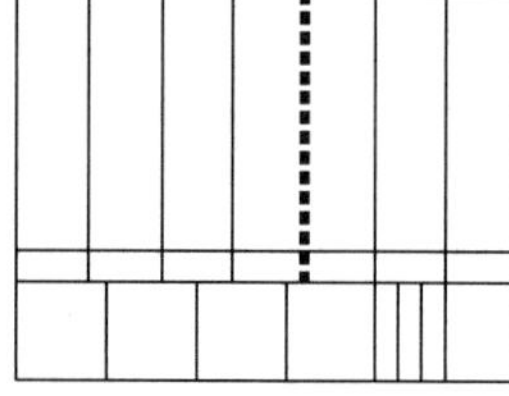

Figure 29.7 **Dot crawl** is exhibited when saturated colors side-by-side are subject to NTSC decoding. Dot crawl is most evident on the green-magenta transition of the colorbar signal.

Consider a set of image rows, each containing the same large, abrupt change in color – say from one colored vertical bar to another in the colorbar test pattern to be explained in *Colorbars*, on page 535. Most decoders will mistakenly interpret some of the power in this transition to be luma. The mistakenly decoded luma will not only invert in phase line to line, it will also invert frame to frame. The frame-rate inversion, combined with interlace, produces a fine pattern of dots, depicted in Figure 29.7. The dots apparently travel upward along the transition at a rate of one image row per field time. (In 480*i*, each dot takes about eight seconds to traverse the height of the image.) This particular cross-luma artifact is called *dot crawl*. It can be avoided in an NTSC decoder by the use of a comb filter.

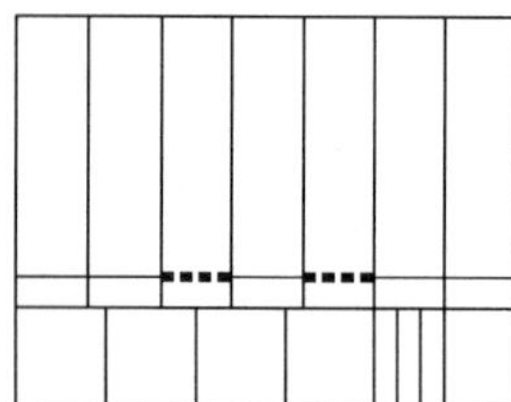

Figure 29.8 **Hanging dots** are evident when the colorbar signal has been subject to NTSC decoding by a simple two-line nonadaptive comb filter.

Another cross-luma artifact is apparent when the SMPTE colorbar test pattern is decoded using a simple 2-line (1*H*) comb filter. About ⅔ of the way down the pattern, the image contains highly saturated complementary colors that abut vertically: There is an abrupt change from a line containing a set of saturated colors to a line containing the same colors in a different order. When decoded by a simple 2-line NTSC comb filter, each abrupt vertical transition contains power that decodes to a strong luma component at the subcarrier frequency. On a monitor with sufficiently high resolution, stationary, horizontal patterns of *hanging dots*, depicted schematically in Figure 29.8, are displayed at several of the transitions. The artifact is strikingly obvious when colorbars are displayed on a studio monitor equipped with a comb filter.

The introduction of cross-luma and cross-color artifacts at an NTSC decoder can be minimized by using a comb filter. However, *encoders* rarely perform any processing (beyond bandpass filtering of modulated chroma) on luma and chroma prior to their being summed. If luma and chroma components overlap in spatial frequency, they will be confused upon summation at the *encoder*, and no subsequent processing in a decoder can possibly repair the damage: The composite *footprint* is said to be imposed on the signal by the first encoder.

Highly sophisticated encoders include comb filter preprocessing to prevent the introduction, at the encoder, of severe cross-color and cross-luma artifacts. However, broadcasters have never deployed these encoders in any significant numbers. This has placed an upper bound on the quality of video delivered to those consumers having high-quality receivers.

Frequency interleaving in PAL

In *PAL chroma modulation*, on page 341, I described the *V*-axis switch, which introduces line-by-line phase inversion of the *V* chroma component. PAL differs from NTSC in two other significant ways that I will describe in this section; other minor differences will be described in *576i PAL composite video*, on page 529.

$$f_{SC,PAL\text{-}B/G/H/I} \approx \frac{1135}{4} f_{H,576i}$$

In studio NTSC, subcarrier frequency is an odd multiple of one-half the line rate. In PAL, subcarrier frequency is based on an odd multiple of one-*quarter* the line rate. On its own, this would lead to roughly a 90° delay of subcarrier phase line-by-line; see Figure 29.9 overleaf.

In PAL-M, the offset is absent.

See *576i PAL color subcarrier*, on page 375. PAL was developed in Hannover [*sic*], Germany, at the research labs of Telefunken. In most video literature, the name of the city is Anglicized and spelled with a single *n*.

In standard 576*i* (625/50) PAL, a +25 Hz frequency offset is added to the basic subcarrier frequency to reduce the visibility of a cross-luma artifact called *Hannover bars*. The +25 Hz offset contributes a +0.576° phase advance (0.0016 of a subcarrier cycle) to subcarrier phase line-by-line. This phase advance leads to the nonlinelocked characteristic, and the noninteger number of samples per total line, of 576*i*, $4f_{SC}$ PAL. Since the offset adds exactly one subcarrier cycle over the duration of a frame, it has no impact on the four-frame sequence. Historically, some 576*i* PAL test signal

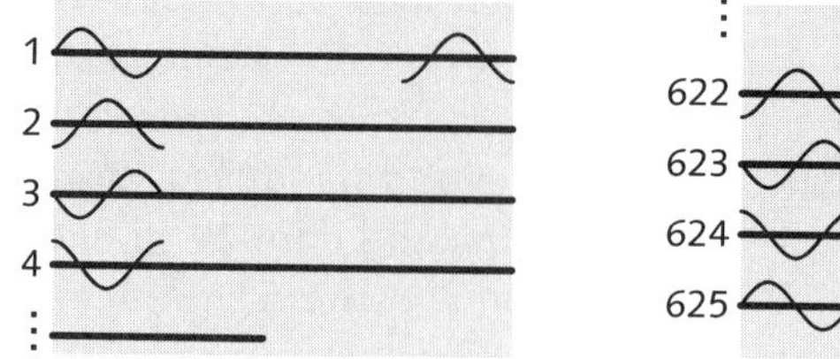

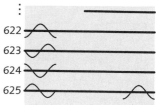

Figure 29.9 **Color subcarrier in 576*i* PAL** has a line-to-line phase delay of about ¼-cycle – that is, 90°. A frame comprises an odd number of lines, so it contains an odd integer number of quarter-cycles of subcarrier: Subcarrier is delayed 90° frame-to-frame. This leads to PAL colorframes *I*, *II*, *III*, and *IV*. A +25 Hz offset is added to this basic frequency; the offset alters the line-to-line phase delay very slightly, to 90.576°, but does not alter the frame-to-frame sequence.

generators were simplified by omitting the +25 Hz offset. A PAL signal without the +25 Hz offset is called *nonmathematical*. (PAL signals where scanning and color subcarrier are incoherent, such as the signals to be described in *Degenerate analog NTSC and PAL*, on page 581, can also be considered nonmathematical.)

In 576*i* PAL sampled at $4f_{SC}$, the near-90° line-to-line delay of subcarrier phase, combined with the inversion of the modulated *V* component, cause a 4×4 block of chroma samples in a field to take values such as those of Figure 29.10:

Figure 29.10 **Chroma arrangement in $4f_{SC}$ PAL.** In "mathematical" 576*i* PAL, this diagram applies at just one location in a field; however, successive lines have a +0.576° phase offset. In nonmathematical PAL, this pattern tiles each field.

$U+V$	$U-V$	$-U-V$	$-U+V$
$-U-V$	$U-V$	$U+V$	$-U+V$
$-U-V$	$-U+V$	$U+V$	$U-V$
$U+V$	$-U+V$	$-U-V$	$U-V$

An ideal *U*/*V* separator for PAL would incorporate a delay element having a duration of exactly one line time: This would make available vertically aligned data. (In 576*i* PAL, one line time is almost exactly 283¾ cycles of subcarrier.) However, with exactly one line of delay, the modulated chroma samples are in the wrong vertical arrangement for easy separation: Summing two vertically adjacent samples yields neither *U* nor *V*. In addition to a line delay, a *U*/*V* separator ideally needs a 90° phase shift element to advance the phase of modulated chroma by 90°. Vertical summation would then extract the *V* component; differencing would extract the U component. In this ideal arrangement, modulated chroma would be averaged vertically.

In digital signal processing, a 90° phase shifter is called a *Hilbert transformer*.

In practice, the 90° phase shift element is rarely – if ever – implemented. Instead, the delay element is engineered to have a duration ¼-cycle short of a line time; the theoretically required *phase* advance is approximated by a ¼-cycle *time* advance. Separation of modulated U and V takes place as depicted by Figure 29.11:

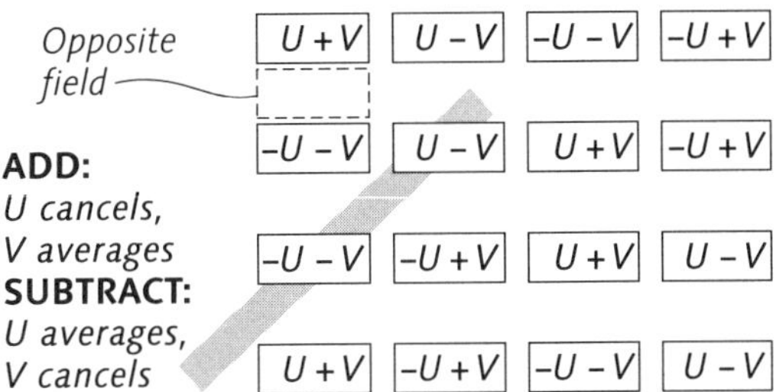

Figure 29.11 **Separation of modulated U and V in PAL** typically involves a delay of 283½ cycles, just shy of the 283¾-cycle delay that would arrange samples vertically. Summing and differencing produce the indicated modulated chroma components.

With this arrangement, modulated chroma is averaged somewhat off-vertical (at about 22°). The ¼-cycle time advance is precisely 90° at the subcarrier frequency. However, modulated chroma occupies frequencies from about 3.4 MHz to 5.4 MHz. Across that range, the ¼-cycle time advance causes phase advance to vary from about 70° to about 110°, so errors are introduced at higher chroma frequencies.

See also *576i PAL composite video*, on page 529. For further details, consult these texts:

Hutson, Geoffrey, Peter Shepherd, and James Brice, *Colour Television: System Principles, Engineering Practice, and Applied Technology*, Second Edition (London: McGraw-Hill, 1990).

Sandbank, C.P. (Editor), *Digital Television* (Chichester, England: Wiley, 1990).

I have described U/V separation in digital PAL sampled at $4f_{SC}$. The same concepts apply to separation of U and V in an analog PAL decoder. Figure 29.12 overleaf sketches an implementation of PAL's classic Y'/C separator (using a notch filter) and U/V separator (using a two-line comb filter).

Spatial frequency spectra of NTSC

Unmodulated NTSC subcarrier in studio and broadcast video has exactly 227½ cycles per total line. Its frequency is an odd multiple of half the line rate, so its phase inverts line to line. Viewed in the spatial frequency domain, its power is concentrated at a vertical frequency corresponding to exactly half the scan-line pitch. NTSC has 480 picture lines, so subcarrier corresponds to a vertical frequency of 240 C/PH. In

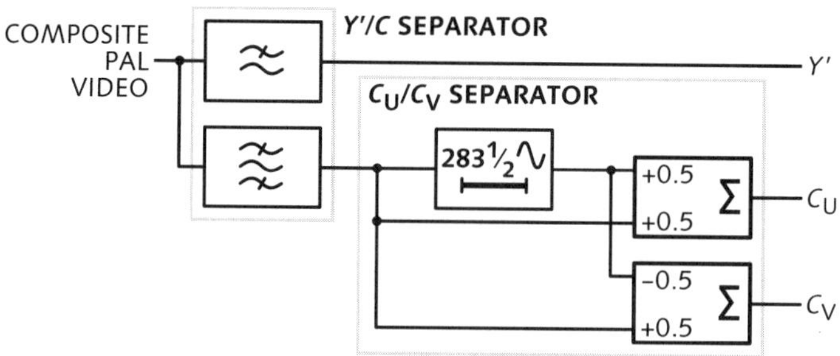

Figure 29.12 **Typical PAL Y'/C and C_U/C_V separator** includes a notch filter that separates luma and modulated chroma. (More sophisticated separators are sometimes used.) Virtually every PAL decoder includes a two-line (1*H*) comb filter, not to separate luma and chroma, but to separate modulated chroma components C_U and C_V based upon the line-by-line *V*-axis inversion.

the vertical domain, the situation resembles Figure 16.2, on page 143, where the sample instants correspond to the scan-line pitch. All of the power in this signal is contained at a spatial frequency corresponding to the vertical Nyquist frequency. On page 143, I explained that a signal at $0.5f_S$, with arbitrary phase and amplitude, cannot be sampled without ambiguity. But the amplitude and phase of unmodulated subcarrier are fixed, and untouched by picture information. Modulation is not exactly sampling, and the usual restriction of sampling theory doesn't apply.

With horizontal blanking removed, about 188 NTSC subcarrier cycles lie across the width of a 480*i* picture. In terms of horizontal spatial frequency, all of the power of this signal is located at 188 C/PW. Consequently, NTSC subcarrier is located at coordinates [188, 240], near the upper-right corner of Figure 18.7, on page 190.

Viewed in the spatial frequency domain, each unmodulated color difference component clusters around [0, 0] like luma. Quadrature modulation causes the color difference components to be translated in the spatial frequency domain so as to be centered at the subcarrier. Color detail in the image causes modulated chroma to spread out in spatial frequency from subcarrier, in the same manner that luma spreads from [0, 0]. The spread of modulated chroma in the spatial frequency domain is limited by the horizontal filtering – and vertical filtering,

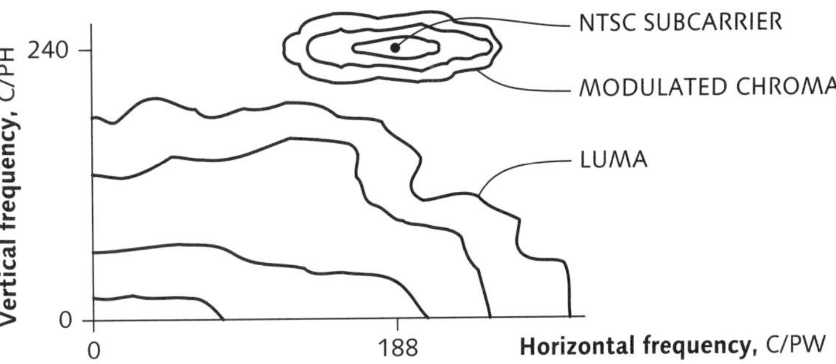

Figure 29.13 **Spatial frequency spectrum of composite NTSC** includes luma, which spreads from [0, 0], color subcarrier at [188, 240], and modulated chroma, which spreads from [188, 240].

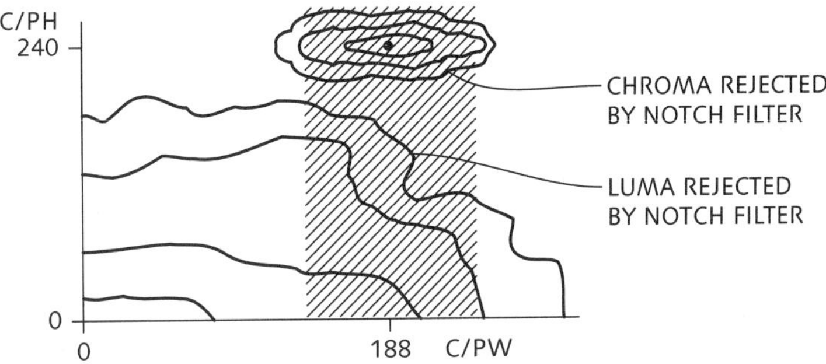

Figure 29.14 **Spatial frequency response of NTSC "notch" filter** shows that a large portion of the luma spectrum is wrongly decoded as chroma. In areas of fine periodic luma detail, cross-color artifacts such as swirling color rainbows are liable to appear.

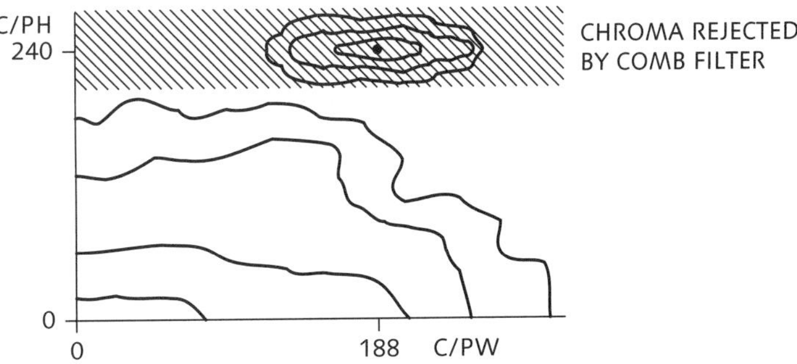

Figure 29.15 **Spatial frequency response of NTSC comb filter** exhibits greatly improved luma response, and reduced cross-color artifacts, compared to a "notch" filter.

if any – that has been applied to the baseband color difference components. Spectra of luma and chroma in NTSC are depicted in Figure 29.13 at the top of this page.

The challenge of NTSC decoding is to separate luma and modulated chroma. A bandpass (notch) filter operates only in the horizontal domain. Figure 29.14 indicates the spatial frequencies that are rejected by a chroma notch filter. Although chroma is rejected, a significant amount of luma is eliminated as well.

In *Comb filtering*, on page 190, I explained how to construct a filter that operates in the vertical dimension; in Figure 18.9, on page 191, I graphed the response of a comb filter in the vertical domain having coefficients [1, 1]. Figure 29.15 shows the region of spatial frequency that is rejected by this two-line comb filter. It is clear from this graph that horizontal luma detail in the range of subcarrier frequencies is retained.

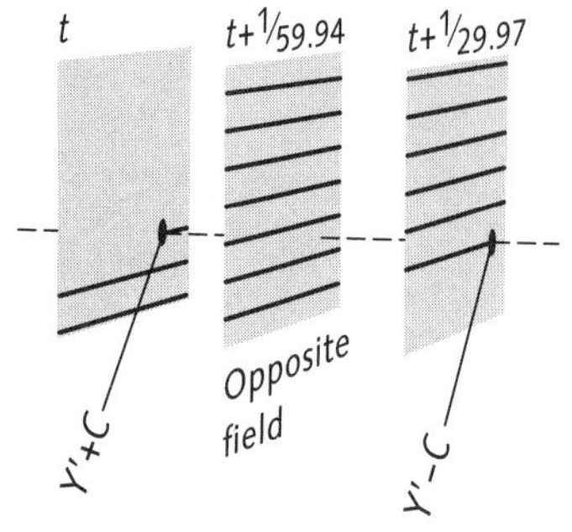

Figure 29.16 **Frame comb** accesses successive temporal samples at the same location in the image array. Because modulated chroma inverts frame-to-frame, summing the indicated samples tends to average luma and cancel chroma.

The concept of two-dimensional spatial frequency can be extended to three-dimensional spatiotemporal frequency. Consider the luma component of Figure 29.15 to be clustered at zero temporal frequency, and imagine a third, temporal axis extending into the page. In addition to inverting line by line, NTSC subcarrier inverts frame by frame. This causes subcarrier to be located at 29.97 Hz in the third coordinate, and causes chroma to cluster around this point in spatiotemporal frequency. A *frame comb* filter (or *3-D comb filter*) uses a frame of memory to operate along this axis, as sketched in Figure 29.16. Providing luma and chroma are constant, summing the indicated samples rejects chroma. Motion presents a serious problem for this arrangement: If a scene element moves ½ of a subcarrier cycle horizontally in a frame time, or one image row vertically, or any odd multiple of these displacements, separation fails completely and interchanges luma and chroma! To be practical, the frame comb technique must be combined with motion adaptivity.

Spatial frequency spectra of PAL

In 576*i* PAL, about 230 subcarrier cycles lie across the picture width; subcarrier is located at a horizontal spatial frequency of 230 C/PW. Subcarrier is based on an odd multiple of one-*quarter* the line rate; subcarrier is thereby placed at ¼ of the vertical sampling rate, 144 C/PH in the vertical frequency domain. Modulated PAL chroma surrounds subcarrier. PAL luma and chroma are plotted in Figure 29.17 at the top of the facing page. Unless chroma is prefiltered at the encoder, luma and chroma spectra overlap much more severely than in NTSC. The line-alternate *V*-axis inversion causes the C_U and C_V spectra to be separated if phase is taken into account, though phase is not shown in this plot.

Figure 29.17 **Spatial frequency spectrum of PAL** shows that chroma is displaced vertically compared to NTSC. Modulated chroma interferes with luma much more severely than it does in NTSC, unless luma is spatially filtered prior to encoding.

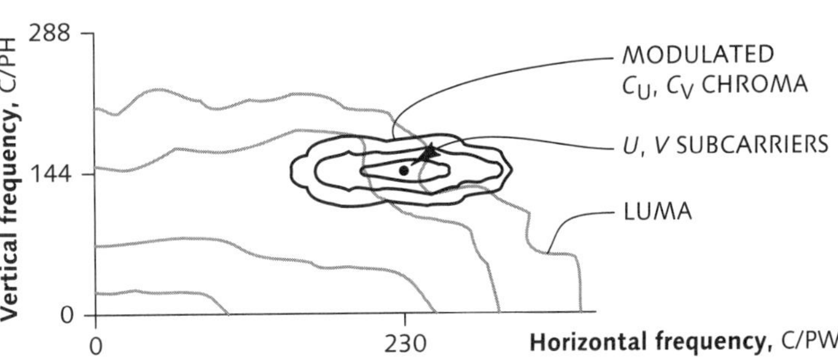

One-dimensional frequency spectrum of NTSC

In *Filtering and sampling*, on page 141, I explained how a one-dimensional waveform in time transforms to a one-dimensional frequency spectrum.

The theory of spatial frequency hadn't been invented when the NTSC system was devised. In this section, I recast the explanation of the NTSC spectrum into the one-dimensional frequency domain that was familiar in 1953, at the time of the NTSC. In an image where every scan line is identical, its one-dimensional waveform is periodic at the line rate, and its power is thus concentrated at multiples of the line rate: 0 (DC, or zero frequency), f_H (the line rate), $2f_H$, $3f_H$, and so on. In a typical image, power tends to concentrate at low frequencies, and diminishes toward higher frequencies.

If the content of successive scan lines varies, the effect is to broaden the spectral lines in the one-dimensional frequency spectrum: Power is centered at 0, f_H, $2f_H$, $3f_H$, and so on, but spreads into nearby frequencies. A graph of the luma component of a typical image is graphed at the top of Figure 29.18 overleaf.

Consider a video signal where every scan line contains a sinewave of frequency f_T chosen such that its phase inverts on alternate lines. This signal is periodic at half the line rate: All of the power in this signal lies at multiples of $f_H/2$. Furthermore, owing to symmetry, the power lies *only* at odd multiples.

In studio and broadcast NTSC, the color subcarrier frequency is coherent with the line rate. Subcarrier has 227.5 cycles per total line, so subcarrier is located at $227.5f_H$. That frequency is an odd multiple of half the line rate, so subcarrier phase inverts on alternate lines.

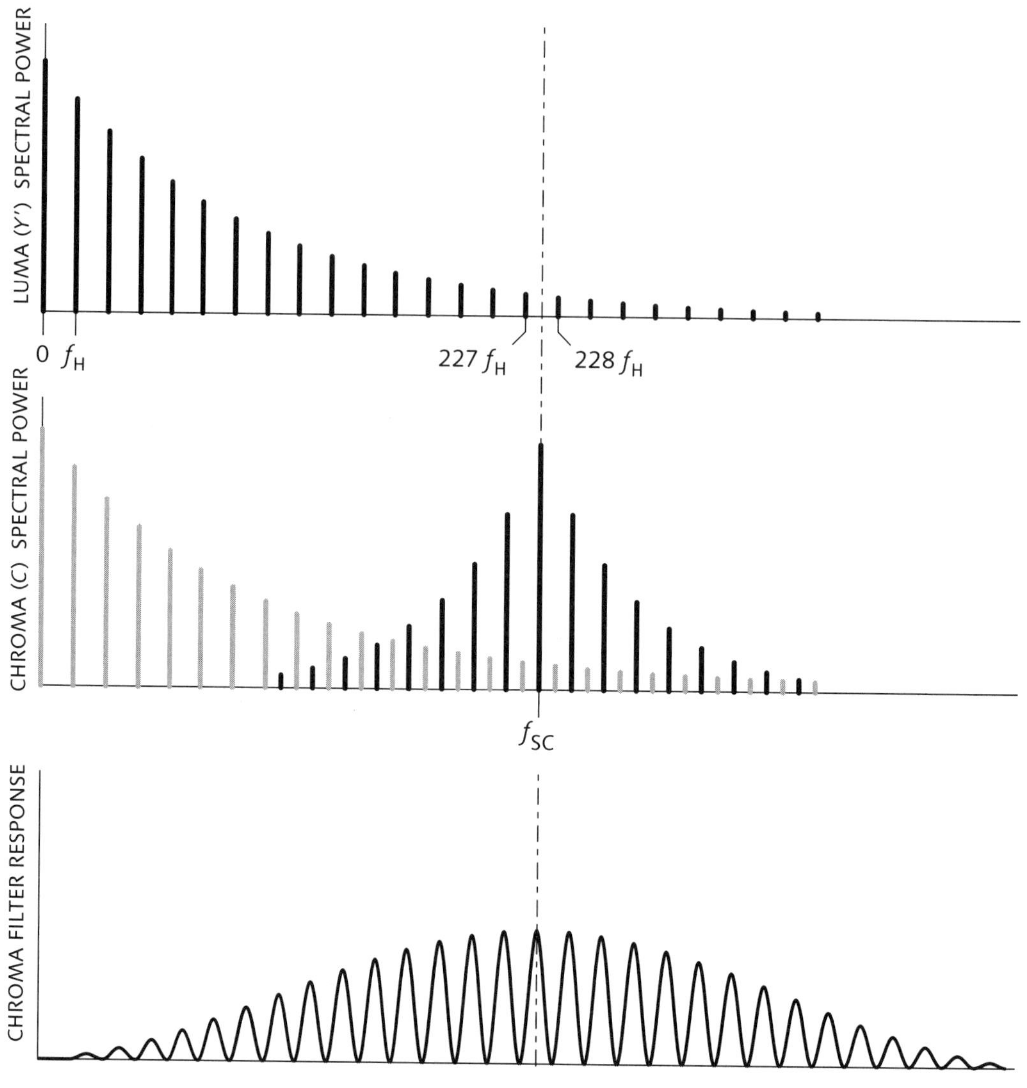

Figure 29.18 **Frequency spectrum of NTSC.** The top graph shows the power spectrum of luma in a typical picture. Luma power clusters at integer multiples of the line rate (here exaggerated). The middle graph shows the spectrum of chroma after modulation onto the subcarrier, whose frequency is $227.5 f_H$, an odd multiple of one-half the line rate. Modulated chroma also clusters at multiples of the line rate, but the choice of subcarrier frequency causes modulated color information to cluster halfway between the luma spectral lines. The bottom graph shows the frequency response of a two-line [1, –1] comb filter in tandem with a [1, 0, –1] transverse (horizontal) bandpass filter; this combination separates chroma with relatively little contamination from luma.

In composite NTSC and PAL video, color information is subject to quadrature modulation that imposes color information onto the color subcarrier, as I described in *NTSC and PAL chroma modulation,* on page 335. (Quadrature modulation suppresses the unmodulated subcarrier.) An encoder then sums luma and modulated chroma. Low-frequency chroma information lies very near the subcarrier frequency; higher-frequency color detail causes the modulated information to spread out in frequency around odd $f_H/2$ multiples, in the same manner that luma spreads from f_H multiples. The middle graph of Figure 29.18 shows the spectrum of modulated NTSC chroma in a typical image.

One way to accomplish separation of luma and chroma in an NTSC decoder is to use a band reject (notch) filter operating in the horizontal domain. The *a* band reject filter rejects signals in the region of subcarrier frequency. In Figure 16.14, at the bottom of page 153, I showed the response of a [1, 0, 1] filter, which has a notch at one-quarter of the sampling frequency. In a system sampled at four times the color subcarrier frequency ($4f_{SC}$), this filter would reject chroma. Although a notch filter eliminates chroma, luma that happens to occupy similar horizontal frequencies is eliminated as well: A notch filter reduces picture detail.

In *Comb filtering,* on page 190, I described a filter that produces notches at regular intervals of the one-dimensional frequency spectrum. If a comb filter such as the one in Figure 16.19, on page 156, has a total delay corresponding to exactly one line time, the peaks will pass luma and the notches will reject modulated chroma. A comb filter rejects chroma as effectively as a notch filter, but it has the great advantage that luma detail in the range of subcarrier frequencies is retained.

If luma that has been separated from a composite signal is subtracted from the composite signal, chroma remains! Prior to subtraction, the composite signal must be delayed to compensate the delay of luma through the separation filter. The bottom graph of Figure 29.18 shows the chroma response of a comb filter cascaded with a bandpass filter.

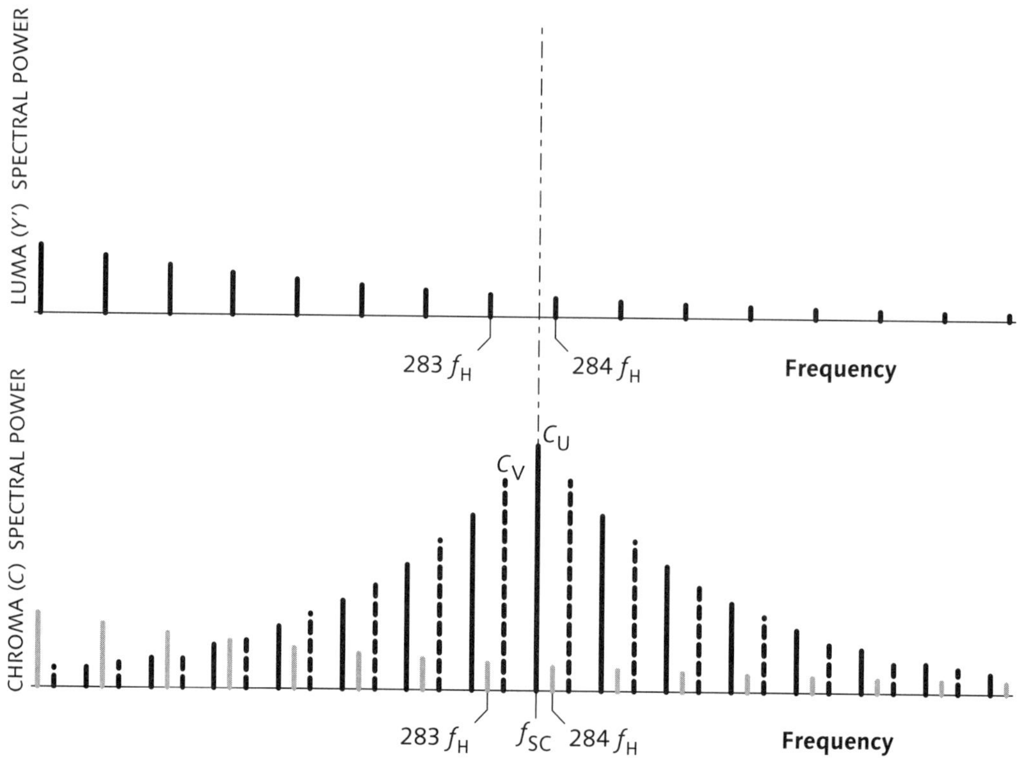

Figure 29.19 **Frequency spectrum of 576*i* PAL.** The top graph depicts the power spectrum of luma in the neighborhood of the PAL color subcarrier frequency, $283.7516 f_H$. The bottom graph shows the spectrum of the two modulated chroma components after modulation onto the PAL color subcarrier. The *U* color difference component after modulation is denoted C_U; its spectrum peaks at $283.7516 f_H$, and it has content surrounding $(k+0.75) f_H$. Modulation of the *V* color difference component includes line-by-line phase alternation, which offsets the C_V spectrum from the subcarrier by one-half the line rate. Spectral peaks of C_V thereby surround $(k+0.25) f_H$, halfway between C_U peaks. A two-line (1*H*) comb filter cannot be used to separate luma from chroma in PAL, but a suitably arranged two-line comb filter can be used to separate C_U and C_V.

One-dimensional frequency spectrum of PAL

The situation in PAL is more complicated than NTSC. Figure 29.19 shows the one-dimensional frequency spectrum of a 576*i* PAL signal in the vicinity of the color subcarrier. Modulated chroma is not located halfway between luma spectral peaks, so a two-line (1*H*) NTSC-style comb filter cannot be used to separate luma from chroma. However, if luma is first removed using a notch filter, then a specialized form of a two-line comb filter can be used to separate C_U and C_V.

NTSC *Y'IQ* system 30

See *Notch filtering,* on page 349.

In the NTSC studio, 5.5 MHz of composite bandwidth is available; wideband chroma of about 1.3 MHz can be easily maintained. However, only 4.2 MHz of composite bandwidth is available for NTSC broadcast. If equiband *U* and *V* components are modulated onto a 3.58 MHz color subcarrier, only 600 kHz of chroma bandwidth is achieved. The designers of NTSC considered 600 kHz of chroma bandwidth to be insufficient, and they devised a scheme to form modulated chroma from *I* and *Q* components, where *Q* was bandlimited to about 600 kHz, but where *I* preserves a higher bandwidth of about 1.3 MHz. NTSC's wideband *I* scheme incurred some increase in complexity over equiband *U* and *V* encoding; however, the NTSC decided in 1953 that the improved color detail would be worthwhile.

Television receiver manufacturers found the NTSC's *I* and *Q* scheme costly, however, and the scheme never reached significant deployment in receivers. In the 1950s and 1960s, studio encoders generated wide-band *I* signals, without the benefits being realized by consumers. During the 1970s and 1980s, equiband *U* and *V* encoders became dominant. In 1990, SMPTE adopted standard 170M, which endorsed *U* and *V* encoding. Sadly, that act effectively banished wideband chroma from terrestrial broadcasting: Chroma band-width for NTSC broadcast is now effectively limited to 600 kHz. Virtually no equipment today uses NTSC's *Y'IQ* scheme. However, it is historically and theoretically important, and it is very widely – and inaccurately – documented. So, I feel obliged to cover it here.

Because an analog demodulator cannot determine whether an encoder was operating at 0° or 33° phase, in analog usage the terms *Y'UV* and *Y'IQ* are often used somewhat interchangeably. See also *Y'UV, Y'IQ confusion*, on page 311.

Y'IQ coding is unique to composite NTSC: It has no place in PAL, component video, HDTV, or computing. If color components are kept separate, it is incorrect to apply *I* and *Q* (or *U* and *V*) scaling or notation. PAL and SECAM are based upon equiband *U* and *V* components; component analog systems use equiband $Y'P_BP_R$; and component digital systems use equiband $Y'C_BC_R$.

Composite digital $4f_{SC}$ NTSC systems defined in SMPTE 244M sample on the [*I*, *Q*] axes. These systems are properly described as *Y'IQ*, but there is no requirement for narrowband *Q* filtering, and it is rarely (if ever) used.

Narrowband *Q*

Hazeltine Corporation, *Principles of Color Television*, by the Hazeltine Laboratories staff, compiled and edited by Knox McIlwain and Charles E. Dean (New York: Wiley, 1956).

With subcarrier at about 3.6 MHz, and baseband chroma component bandwidth of 1.3 MHz, the upper sideband of modulated chroma extends to about 4.9 MHz. The designers of NTSC were faced with a channel bandwidth of 4.2 MHz, insufficient to convey the upper sideband of modulated chroma. Bandwidth limitation of the composite signal would cause *quadrature crosstalk* – that is, cross-contamination of the chroma components above 600 kHz.

Vision has less spatial acuity for purple-green transitions than it does for orange-cyan. The *U* and *V* signals of *Y'UV* must be carried with equal bandwidth, albeit less than that of luma, because neither aligns with the minimum color acuity axis. However, if signals *I* and *Q* are formed from *U* and *V*, as I will describe, then the *Q* signal can be more severely filtered than *I* – to about 600 kHz, compared to about 1.3 MHz – without any loss in chroma resolution being perceived by a viewer at typical viewing distance.

The NTSC's desire for 1.3 MHz orange-cyan detail led to the narrowband *Q* scheme. *I* and *Q* color difference components are formed from *U* and *V* by a 33° rotation and an exchange of axes. The *Q* axis is aligned with the NTSC's estimate of the minimum color acuity axis of vision. *Q* can thereby be more severely bandlimited than *I*. The NTSC decided to bandlimit *I* to 1.3 MHz and *Q* to 0.6 MHz (600 kHz). Quadrature modulation is then performed with subcarrier phase-shifted 33°.

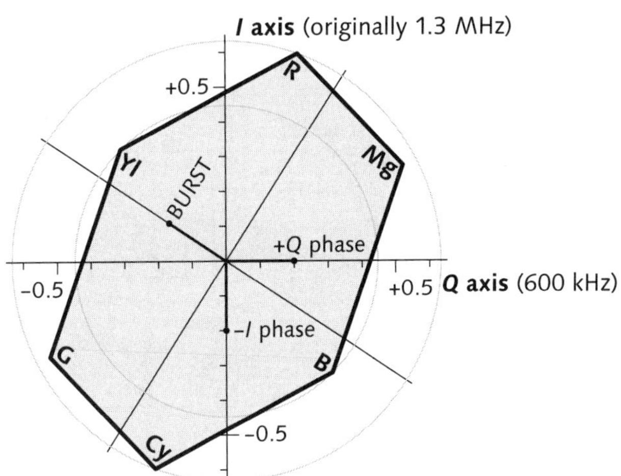

Figure 30.1 ***IQ* components** are formed by rotating, by 33°, the [*U*, *V*] components depicted in Figure 28.1, on page 336. According to the conventions of communications theory, *I* (for *in-phase*) should be aligned with the *x*-axis, and *Q* (for *quadrature*) should be aligned with the *y*-axis; however, in video the rotation is followed by an exchange of axes. This sketch includes –*I* and +*Q* vectors, at burst amplitude, that are elements of SMPTE colorbars; see page 537.

IQ components

Figure 30.1 shows a plot of the *IQ* color difference plane. The rotation and exchange from [*U*, *V*] to [*I*, *Q*] is accomplished by this matrix transform of *Y'UV* components:

Eq 30.1

$$\begin{bmatrix} {}^{601}Y' \\ I \\ Q \end{bmatrix} = \begin{bmatrix} 1 & 0 & 0 \\ 0 & -0.544639 & 0.838671 \\ 0 & 0.838671 & 0.544639 \end{bmatrix} \bullet \begin{bmatrix} {}^{601}Y' \\ U \\ V \end{bmatrix}$$

Some authors mistakenly omit the exchange of *B'–Y'* and *R'–Y'* axes in describing *Y'IQ* coding. Some authors wrongly state or suggest that *Y'IQ* is in use with linear-light coding.

Owing to the exchange of axes, the matrix is its own inverse: The same matrix recovers *Y'UV* from *Y'IQ*.

To encode *Y'IQ* from *R'G'B'*, the rotation and exchange above are concatenated with the matrix of Equation 28.4, on page 337:

Eq 30.2

$$\begin{bmatrix} {}^{601}Y' \\ I \\ Q \end{bmatrix} = \begin{bmatrix} 0.299 & 0.587 & 0.114 \\ 0.595901 & -0.274557 & -0.321344 \\ 0.211537 & -0.522736 & 0.311200 \end{bmatrix} \bullet \begin{bmatrix} R' \\ G' \\ B' \end{bmatrix}$$

To recover *R'G'B'* from *Y'IQ*, invert Equation 30.2:

Eq 30.3

$$\begin{bmatrix} R' \\ G' \\ B' \end{bmatrix} = \begin{bmatrix} 1 & 0.955986 & 0.620825 \\ 1 & -0.272013 & -0.647204 \\ 1 & -1.106740 & 1.704230 \end{bmatrix} \bullet \begin{bmatrix} {}^{601}Y' \\ I \\ Q \end{bmatrix}$$

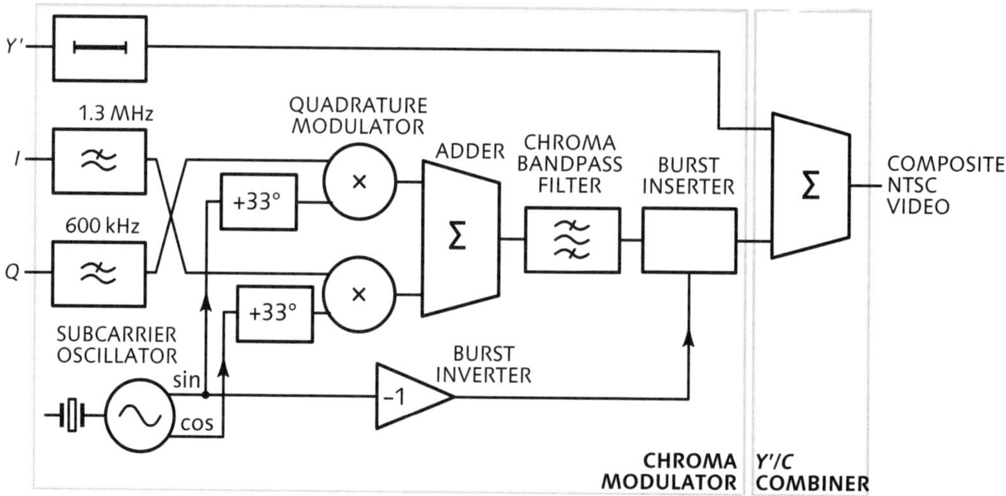

Figure 30.2 **NTSC encoder using *Y'IQ*** is similar to the NTSC encoder using *Y'UV* components presented in Figure 28.4, on page 340. Here, *I* and *Q* components are presented to the encoder. Historically, the *I* and *Q* filters had unequal bandwidths as indicated in this diagram, but today's $4f_{SC}$ NTSC studio encoders use equiband 1.3 MHz filters. The continuous-wave sine and cosine color subcarrier signals are phase-shifted 33° prior to being presented to the quadrature multipliers.

Y'IQ encoding

The block diagram of a *Y'IQ* encoder is shown in Figure 30.2. The *I* and *Q* components are lowpass filtered to 1.3 MHz and 0.6 MHz respectively, then modulated in a manner similar to Equation 28.7 on page 338:

$$C = Q \sin\left(\omega t + 33°\right) + I \cos\left(\omega t + 33°\right);\ \omega = 2\pi f_{SC} \qquad \text{Eq 30.4}$$

A decoder for *Y'IQ* is shown in Figure 30.3 at the top of the facing page. *Q* is decoded using a 600 kHz lowpass filter. Wideband *I* is decoded using a *Nyquist* filter: The low-frequency component of *I* (from 0 to 0.6 MHz) is recovered from both sidebands of modulated chroma, and its high-frequency component (from 0.6 MHz to 1.3 MHz) is recovered from the lower sideband alone. Filtering at the encoder and decoder are sketched in Figure 30.4 at the bottom of the facing page.

A *Y'IQ* decoder recovers wideband *I* and narrowband *Q* only if the signal was encoded on the [*I*, *Q*] axes from wideband *I* and narrowband *Q* components. Until 1960s, it was reasonable to assume that an NTSC signal was encoded in this way, as the NTSC intended.

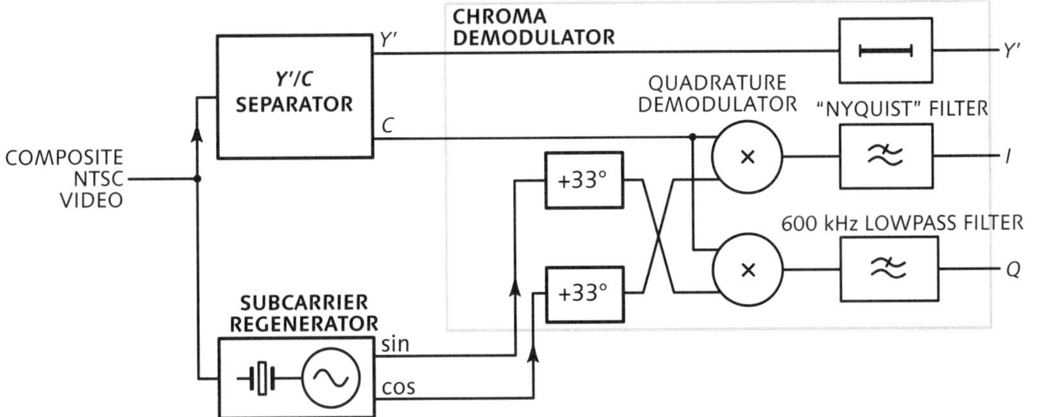

Figure 30.3 **NTSC decoder using *Y′IQ*** is similar to the decoder using *Y′UV* that I presented in Figure 28.5, on page 341. Phase shifts of 33° are applied to the sine and cosine phases of subcarrier. The *Q* lowpass filter has a corner of 600 kHz; the *I* lowpass filter has a special "Nyquist" shape detailed in Figure 30.4 overleaf. The 33° phase shifters and the Nyquist filter are useful only if the signal was encoded on [*I*, *Q*] axes with wideband *I* and narrowband *Q*. Because proper *Y′IQ* encoding has not been practiced since about 1970, using this textbook *Y′IQ* decoder is pointless.

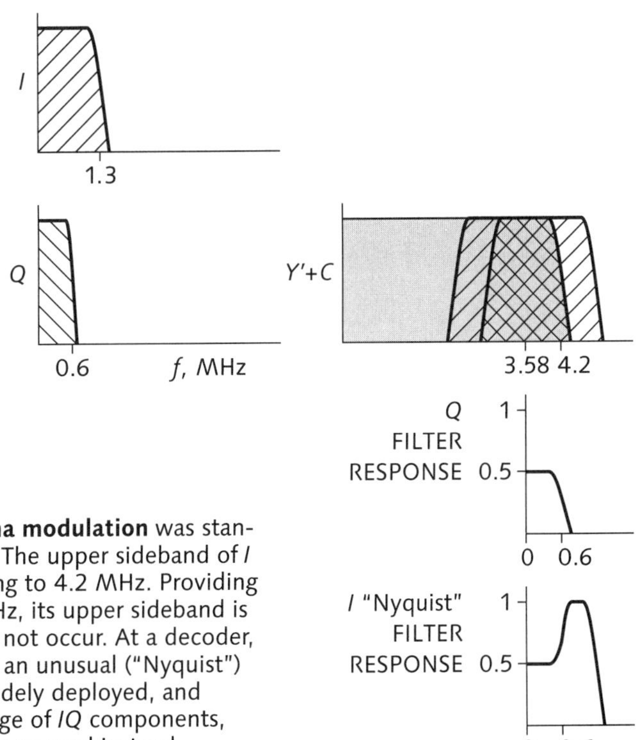

Figure 30.4 **Wideband *I* chroma modulation** was standardized by the NTSC in 1953. The upper sideband of *I* chroma is lost upon bandlimiting to 4.2 MHz. Providing that *Q* is bandlimited to 600 kHz, its upper sideband is retained, and *IQ* crosstalk does not occur. At a decoder, recovering wideband *I* requires an unusual ("Nyquist") filter. The scheme was never widely deployed, and despite the theoretical advantage of *IQ* components, equiband *UV* components are now used instead.

A decoder cannot determine whether a source was encoded with narrowband or wideband components. An analog decoder cannot determine which axes were used by the encoder.

However, recovery of the wideband *I* component was rarely implemented even in early consumer receivers, so the promise of NTSC's design was never fulfilled. Later, the low chroma bandwidth realizable in consumer VCRs had the effect of limiting the maximum usable color difference bandwidth to less than 600 kHz in both components. To recover color differences up to 600 kHz in an analog decoder, it is pointless to use the *Y'IQ* scheme: a *Y'UV* decoder fitted with 600 kHz filters is less complex, and might as well be used instead.

Owing to the technical difficulty of encoding *Y'IQ* properly in the studio, and because few consumer receivers recovered wideband chroma in any event, *Y'IQ* encoding was gradually abandoned for studio encoders during the 1970s and 1980s. In the studio, it became common to encode *U* and *V* components both having 1.3 MHz bandwidth. In NTSC transmission, the composite signal bandwidth cannot exceed 4.2 MHz. This restriction is ordinarily imposed by naive lowpass filtering. For a composite signal encoded with wideband *U* and *V*, 4.2 MHz lowpass filtering caused cross-contamination of all chroma components above 600 kHz. As these poor studio practices proliferated, recovery of wideband *I* by a high-quality receiver became more and more problematic: Cross-contamination above 600 kHz at the transmitter became more and more likely, and by about 1980, any prospect of wideband chroma at the consumers' premises was lost.

With wideband *U* and *V* components in the studio, full *I* bandwidth could have been retained in NTSC broadcast if wideband chroma had been decoded, then reencoded using wideband *I* and narrowband *Q* prior to lowpass filtering of the composite signal to 4.2 MHz. Such decoding and reencoding has virtually never been done.

When SMPTE adopted the 170M standard in 1990, wideband *I* and narrowband *Q* encoding was ostensibly permitted. However, equiband 1.3 MHz encoding of *U* and *V* components was permitted as well. A decoder cannot possibly determine whether narrowband or wideband components were encoded. In any event, proper *Y'IQ* encoding as envisaged by the NTSC in 1953 was extremely rare by 1990 and is virtually unseen today. Although wideband chroma is ubiquitous in the studio, the establishment of SMPTE 170M had the effect of permanently enshrining narrowband chroma for broadcast: Upon lowpass filtering at the transmitter, only narrowband chroma can be reliably recovered.

Frame, field, line, and sample rates 31

This chapter outlines the field, frame, line, and sampling rates of 480*i* video, 576*i* video, and HDTV. The standard sampling frequency for component digital video is exactly 13.5 MHz; this rate produces an integer number of samples per line in both 480*i* and 576*i*. Modern systems such as HTDV sample at multiples of this rate.

Field rate

Television systems originated with field rates based on the local AC power line frequency: 60 Hz for North America, and 50 Hz for Europe. In the 1940s and 1950s, coupling of the ripple of a receiver's power-supply into circuitry – such as video amplifiers and high-voltage supplies – had an effect on the instantaneous brightness of the display. If the vertical scanning frequency was different from the power line frequency, interference caused artifacts called *hum bars*, at the difference in frequency – the beat frequency – between the two. Their visibility was minimized by choosing a field rate the same as the power line frequency, so as to make the hum bars stationary. There was no requirement to have an exact frequency match, or to lock the phase: As long as the pattern was stationary, or drifting very slowly, it was not objectionable. The power supply interactions that were once responsible for hum bars no longer exist in modern circuitry, but the vertical scan rates that were standardized remain with us.

Line rate

The total number of raster lines chosen for the 525-line television is the product of a few small integers: 525 is $7 \times 5^2 \times 3$. The choice of small integer factors arose from the use of vacuum tube divider circuits to derive the field rate from the line rate: Such dividers were stable only for small divisors. The total number of scan lines per frame is odd. Equivalently, the field rate is an odd multiple of half the line rate. This relationship generates the 2:1 interlace that I introduced in *Interlaced scanning*, on page 56. These factors combined to give monochrome 525/60 television a line rate of $30 \times (7 \times 5^2 \times 3)$, or exactly 15.750 kHz.

$$\frac{525 \cdot 60}{2} = 15750$$

For 525-line receivers, a scheme was invented to develop high voltage for the picture tube using a transformer operating at the horizontal scanning frequency, 15.750 kHz, rather than the AC line frequency. This permitted a lightweight transformer, which became known as the *flyback transformer*. (The scheme is still used today; it can be considered as a precursor to the switch-mode power supply.) The flyback transformer was a complex component, and it was tuned to the horizontal frequency.

When European engineers began to consider the design of receivers for Europe, it was a practical necessity to fix the field rate at 50 Hz, matching the power line frequency. Rather than develop flyback transformers from scratch, European engineers imported them from North America! This constrained the horizontal frequency to a narrow range around 15.750 kHz. The total line count was chosen as 625, that is, 5^4. Monochrome 625-line television had – and continues to have – a line rate of 5^6, or exactly 15.625 kHz.

Sound subcarrier

In about 1941, the first NTSC recognized that visibility of sound-related patterns in the picture could be minimized by making the picture line rate and the sound subcarrier rest frequency were coherent. In monochrome 525/60 television the sound subcarrier was placed at 4.5 MHz, exactly $2000/7$ (i.e., $285\,5/7$) times the line rate. Sound in conventional television is frequency modulated, and with an analog sound modulator even perfect silence cannot be guaranteed to generate an FM carrier of exactly 4.5 MHz. Nonetheless, making the FM sound carrier average out to 4.5 MHz was thought to have some value.

Addition of composite color

NTSC and PAL color coding both employ the frequency-interleaving technique to achieve compatibility with monochrome systems. With frequency interleaving, the color subcarrier frequency is chosen to alternate phase line by line, so as to minimize the visibility of encoded color on a monochrome receiver. This line-to-line phase relationship makes it possible to accurately separate chroma from luma in an NTSC decoder that incorporates a comb filter (although a cheaper notch filter can be used instead).

NTSC color subcarrier

For details, consult the Hazeltine Laboratories publication cited on page 366.

In 1953, the second NTSC decided to choose a color subcarrier frequency of approximately 3.6 MHz. They recognized that any nonlinearity in the processing of the composite color signal with sound – such as limiting in the *intermediate frequency* (IF) stages of a receiver – would result in intermodulation distortion between the sound subcarrier and the color subcarrier. The difference, or *beat frequency,* between the two subcarriers, about 920 kHz, falls in the luminance bandwidth and could potentially have been quite visible.

The NTSC recognized that the visibility of this pattern could be minimized if the beat frequency was line-interlaced. Since the color subcarrier is necessarily an odd multiple of half the line rate, the sound subcarrier had to be made an integer multiple of the line rate.

$$f_{SC,NTSC} = \frac{455}{2} f_{H,480i}$$

The NTSC decided that the color subcarrier should be exactly $^{455}\!/_{2}$ times the line rate. Line interlace of the beat could be achieved by increasing the sound-to-line rate ratio (previously $285\,^{5}\!/_{7}$) by the fraction $^{1001}\!/_{1000}$ to the next integer (286).

Setting broadcast standards was (and is) the responsibility of the Federal Communications Commission. The

FCC could have allowed the sound subcarrier rest frequency to be increased by the fraction $^{1001}/_{1000}$ – that is, increased it by 4.5 kHz to about 4.5045 MHz. Had the FCC made this choice, the color subcarrier in NTSC would have been exactly 3.583125 MHz; the original 525/60 line and field rates would have been unchanged; we would have retained exactly 60 frames per second – and NTSC would have no dropframes! Since sound is frequency modulated, the sound carrier was never crystal-stable at the subcarrier frequency anyway – not even during absolute silence – and the tolerance of the rest frequency was already reasonably large (±1 kHz). The deviation of the sound subcarrier was – and remains – 25 kHz, so a change of 4.5 kHz could easily have been accommodated by the intercarrier sound systems of the day.

$$525 \times \left(\frac{60}{2}\,\text{Hz}\right) \times \frac{1000}{1001} \times \frac{455}{2} = \frac{315}{88}\,\text{MHz} \approx 3.579\overline{545}\,\text{MHz}$$

However, the FCC refused to alter the sound subcarrier. Instead, the color/sound constraint was met by reducing both the line rate and field rate by the fraction $^{1001}/_{1000}$, to about 15.734 kHz and 59.94 Hz. Color subcarrier was established as $3.579\overline{545}$ MHz. What was denoted 525/60 scanning became 525/59.94, though unfortunately the 525/60 notation is still used loosely to refer to 525/59.94.

The factors of 1001 are 7, 11, and 13. This numerical relationship was known in ancient times: The book *1001 Arabian Nights* is based on it. The numbers 7, 11, and 13 are considered to be very unlucky. Unfortunately the field rate of $^{60}/_{1.001}$, about 59.94 Hz, means that 60 fields consume slightly more than one second: Counting 30 fields per second does not agree with clock time. Dropframe timecode was invented to alleviate this difficulty; see *Timecode,* on page 381.

$$525 \times \left(\frac{60}{2}\,\text{Hz}\right) \times \frac{1000}{1001} \times 455 \times 2 = \frac{315}{22}\,\text{MHz} \approx 14.318\overline{181}\,\text{MHz}$$

NTSC sync generators generally use a master oscillator of $14.31\overline{818}$ MHz. This clock is divided by 4 to obtain color subcarrier, and simultaneously divided by 7 to obtain a precursor of line rate. Prior to the emergence of framestore synchronizers in the 1980s, each major broadcast network in the United States had an atomic clock to provide 5 MHz, followed by a rate multiplier of $^{63}/_{22}$ to derive its master $14.31\overline{818}$ MHz clock.

576*i* PAL color subcarrier

In 576*i* PAL, the color subcarrier frequency is based on an odd multiple of one-quarter the line rate, using the factor $^{1135}/_{4}$ (or for PAL-N, $^{909}/_{4}$). The odd multiple of one-quarter, combined with the line-to-line alternation of the phase of the *V* color difference component, causes the *U* and *V* color components to occupy separate parts of the composite signal spectrum. This makes the PAL signal immune to the hue errors that result when an NTSC signal is subject to differential phase distortion.

$$625 \times \left(\frac{50}{2}\,\text{Hz}\right) \times \left(\frac{1135}{4} + \frac{1}{625}\right)$$
$$= 4.433618750\ \text{MHz}$$

In standard PAL-B, PAL-G, PAL-H, and PAL-I, an offset of +25 Hz is added to the basic subcarrier frequency so as to minimize the visibility of the Hannover bar effect. The 25 Hz offset means that the phase relationship of subcarrier to horizontal advances exactly +0.576° each line. Consequently, subcarrier-locked sampling in PAL is not line-locked: The subcarrier phase, modulo 90°, of vertically aligned samples is not identical! The introduction of the +25 Hz offset destroyed the simple integer ratio between subcarrier and line rate: The ratio is quite complex, as shown in the margin. The prime factor 64489 is fairly impenetrable to digital techniques.

$$\frac{1135}{4} + \frac{1}{625} = \frac{709379}{2500} = \frac{11 \times 64489}{2^2 \times 5^3}$$

$4f_{SC}$ sampling

The earliest digital television equipment sampled composite NTSC or PAL video signals. It was convenient for composite digital NTSC equipment to operate at a sampling frequency of exactly four times the color subcarrier frequency, or about 14.318 MHz, denoted $4f_{SC}$. This rate is sometimes sloppily referred to as *D-2*, although that term properly refers to the corresponding videotape format, not the sampling structure.

Any significant processing of a picture, such as repositioning, resizing, rotating, and so on, requires that the signal be represented in components. For this reason, component video equipment is preferred in production and postproduction. But $4f_{SC}$ equipment has half the data rate of Rec. 601 equipment; $4f_{SC}$ equipment is cheaper than component equipment, and continues to dominate broadcast operations.

Sampling NTSC at $4f_{SC}$ gives 910 samples per total line (S_{TL}). A count of 768 samples (3×2^8) encompasses the active samples of a line, including the blanking transitions. A count of 512 (2^9) lines is just slightly more than the number of nonblanked lines in 480*i* scanning. The numbers 768 and 512 were convenient for early memory systems: 512 is the ninth power of 2, and 768 is 3 times the eighth power of 2. In the early days of digital television, this combination – 768 and 512 – led to very simple memory and addressing circuits for framestores. The importance of this special combination of 768 and 512 is now irrelevant: Framestore systems usually have more than a single frame of memory, memory devices have much higher capacities, and total memory capacity is now a more important constraint than active sample and line counts. In any case, the binary numbers 768 and 512 were never any help in the design of 576*i* framestores.

In a $4f_{SC}$ system, the digital version of the unmodulated color subcarrier contains only four unique sample values: Chroma demodulation can be implemented simply, using fixed multipliers or ROMs. However, this approach is susceptible to *cycle-hopping* when the subcarrier-to-horizontal relationship is unlocked or not carefully controlled; color-under signals cannot be processed; and system timing cannot be easily implemented without shifting the horizontal picture position.

Common sampling rate

The designers of the NTSC and PAL systems chose video parameters based on simple integer ratios. When component digital sampling became feasible it came as a surprise that the ratio of line duration of 480*i* and 576*i* systems turned out to be the ratio of 144 to 143, derived as shown in Table 31.1.

The lowest common sampling frequency corresponding to these factors is 2.25 MHz, half of the now-familiar NTSC sound subcarrier frequency of 4.5 MHz. Any multiple of 2.25 MHz could have been used as the basis for line-locked sampling of both 480*i* and 576*i*. The most practical sampling frequency is 6 times 2.25 MHz, or 13.5 MHz; this multiplier is a compromise between

$f_{H,480i}$	:	$f_{H,576i}$
$525\times\frac{60}{2}\times\frac{1000}{1001}$	:	$625\times\frac{50}{2}$
$7\times5^2\times3\times\frac{5\cdot3\cdot2^2}{2}\times\frac{5^3\cdot2^3}{13\cdot11\cdot7}$	:	$5^4\times\frac{5^2\times2}{2}$
$3\times3\times2^4$	:	13×11
144	:	143

Table 31.1 **Derivation of 13.5 MHz common sampling rate**

a rate high enough to ease the design of analog anti-aliasing filters and low enough to minimize data rate and memory requirements.

ITU-R Rec. BT.601-5, *Studio encoding parameters of digital television for standard 4:3 and wide-screen 16:9 aspect ratios.*

At 13.5 MHz, 480*i* video has 858 samples per total line, and 576*i* video has 864 S_{TL}. Fortunately, the blanking tolerances between NTSC and PAL accommodate a choice of 720 samples per active line (S_{AL}) in both systems. Standardization of this number of active samples results in a high degree of commonality in the design of video processing equipment, since only the difference in active line counts needs to be accommodated to serve both 525 and 625 markets. Also the technically difficult problem of standards conversion is eased somewhat with a common sampling frequency, since horizontal interpolation becomes unnecessary. However, blanking must be treated differently in the two systems to meet studio interchange standards.

Numerology of HDTV scanning

Figure 31.1 overleaf gives a graphic representation of the development of the magic numbers in HDTV. At the upper left is the AC power line frequency in North America, and the small integer factors of 525. Next to that is indicated the AC power frequency in Europe, and the small integer factors of 625. HDTV was originally conceived as having twice the horizontal and twice the vertical resolution of conventional television: At the top right is the conceptual origin of the total number of HDTV scanning lines as twice the geometric mean of 525 and 625. North America would have preferred twice 525 and Europe twice 625; the

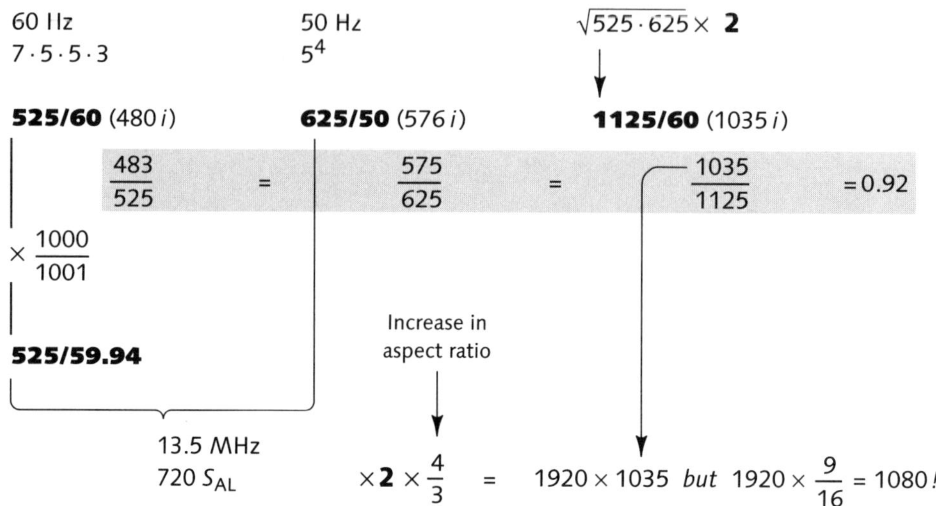

Figure 31.1 **Numerology of HDTV scanning**

designers choose a total line count of 1125 (i.e., $5^3 \times 3^2$) that was thought to be politically acceptable on both sides of the Atlantic Ocean.

Figure 31.1 indicates 575 active lines in 625/50 systems; this constitutes 287 full lines, plus a halfline, in each field. Counting each halfline as a full line, the total is 576.

Underneath the scanning designations 525/60, 625/50, and 1125/60 is a gray bar containing the ratio of picture lines to total lines in each system. The count of lines per total vertical (L_T) for each of these systems is the fraction $^{23}/_{25}$ of the total. This led to the original choice of 1035 picture lines for 1125/60 HDTV. The addition of color to the NTSC system introduced the ratio $^{1000}/_{1001}$, and led to the 525/59.94 system.

The desire for a common sampling frequency for component digital video led to the synthesis of line rates of 480*i* and 576*i* into a common sampling frequency, 13.5 MHz, and a common count of samples per active line (S_{AL}), 720. For HDTV, the active pixel count was doubled to increase the horizontal resolution; then multiplied by the $^4/_3$ increase in aspect ratio (from 4:3 to 16:9), netting 1920.

A raster structure 1920×1035 results from these choices, and SMPTE standardized that in 1988. However, in about 1991 it became clear that the 1920×1035 structure had a sample pitch unequal in the horizontal and vertical dimensions – nonsquare sampling. The degree of inequality was small, just 4%, but for many applications any departure from equal spacing imposes a burden. In about 1995, the standard was adapted to achieve square pixels by choosing a count of active lines $\frac{9}{16}$ times 1920, that is, 1080 lines. SMPTE, and subsequently ATSC, enshrined square sampling in the 1920×1080 image array. The system has about two million pixels per frame; the exact number is very slightly less than 2^{21}, a neat fit into binary-sized memory components.

NHK planned to operate the 1920×1035 system at a frame rate of exactly 30 Hz ("30.00 Hz"), and early 1035*i* equipment operated only at that rate. However, the discrepancy of about one frame every 16 seconds between 1035*i*30.00 and 480*i*29.97 is a big nuisance in standards conversion. To ease this problem, and engineering difficulties associated with digital audio sample rates, current 1080*i* HDTV standards accommodate both 29.97 Hz and 30 Hz frame rates.

While NHK and others were developing 1125/60 interlaced HDTV, progressive-scan systems having nearly identical pixel rate were being developed by other organizations, mainly in the United States. Technology permitted a rate of about 60 megapixels per second, whether the scanning was interlace or progressive. With interlace scanning, 60 Mpx/s at 30 Hz frame rate allows a two-megapixel image structure. With progressive scanning, 60 Mpx/s at 60 Hz frame rate allows just one megapixel. Partitioning one megapixel into a square lattice yields an image structure of 1280×720; this led to the 720*p* family of standards.

Audio rates

Digital audio has two standard sample rates: 48 kHz, for professional applications, and 44.1 kHz, for consumer applications. In the standardization of digital audio, manufacturers decided to adopt two different standards in order that professional and consumer equipment could be differentiated! That goal failed miserably, and now the dichotomy in sample rates is a major nuisance in video and audio production.

$3 \cdot 588 \cdot 25\ \text{Hz} = 44100\ \text{Hz}$

$$3 \cdot 490 \cdot \frac{30\ \text{Hz}}{1.001} = \frac{44100}{1.001}\ \text{kHz} \approx 44.056\ \text{kHz}$$

The 44.1 kHz sampling rate for consumer digital audio originated from an early PCM recording system that recorded three, 16-bit stereo sample pairs on 588 active lines of a 625/50 U-matic VCR. In 525/59.94 countries, the original rate was $^{44100}/_{1.001}$: Three 16-bit stereo sample pairs were recorded on each of 490 active lines per frame. Eventually, the 44.1 kHz rate was standardized worldwide.

The professional audio sampling rate was chosen to be 48 kHz. The time interval of one video picture at 50 fields or frames per second corresponds to exactly 960 audio samples at 48 kHz. An AES/EBU audio frame comprises 192 left/right sample pairs, with 16 bits in each sample: In 50 Hz video standards, a video frame occupies exactly the same time interval as five audio frames.

In video at 59.94 fields or frames per second, the timing relationships are unfortunate. There are $1601\,^3/_5$ audio sample intervals in one picture time: This noninteger number is very inconvenient. The timing relationship of audio samples to video pictures aligns just once every five pictures. There are $^{1001}/_{240}$ (i.e., $4.17083\overline{3}$) AES/EBU audio frames in a video picture time.

At the consumer audio rate, there are 882 samples in $^1/_{50}$ s; an integer. There are exactly 1471.47 samples in $^1/_{59.94}$ s; again, the noninteger ratio causes havoc.

Timecode 32

This chapter gives technical details concerning timecode, as used in video, film, audio recording, editing, and sequencing equipment.

Introduction

Timecode systems assign a number to each frame of video analogously to the way that film is manufactured with edge numbers to allow each frame to be uniquely identified. Time data is coded in binary-coded decimal (BCD) digits in the form HH:MM:SS:FF, in the range 00:00:00:00 to 23:59:59:29. There are timecode variants for 24, 25, 29.97, and 30 frames per second. Timecode data is digitally recorded with the associated image. *Burnt-in timecode* (BITC) refers to a recording with timecode numbers keyed over the picture content (that is, embedded in the image data).

SMPTE 262M, *Binary Groups of Time and Control Codes – Storage and Transmission of Data Control Codes.*

SMPTE RP 169, *Television, Audio and Film Time and Control Code – Auxiliary Time Address Data in Binary Group – Dialect Specification of Directory Index Locations.*

In addition to approximately 32 bits required for eight-digit time data, timecode systems accommodate an additional 32 *user bits* per frame. User bits may convey one of several types of information: a second timecode stream, such as a timecode from an original recording; a stream of ASCII/ISO characters; motion picture production data, as specified in SMPTE 262M; auxiliary BCD numerical information, such as tape reel number; or nonstandard information. A group of 4 user bits is referred to as a *binary group*. The information portion of timecode thus totals 64 bits per frame.

A number of synchronization bits are appended to the 64 information bits of timecode in order to convey timecode through a recording channel. Sixteen synchronization bits are appended to form 80-bit *linear timecode* (LTC). Eighteen sync bits and 8 CRC bits are appended to form 90-bit *vertical interval timecode* (VITC) that can be inserted into a video signal.

BCD coding of time data has two implications. First, since no BCD digit can contain all ones, the all-ones code is available for other purposes. Second, the high-order bits of certain timecode digits are available for use as flags; these flag bits are described on page 388.

The colorframe flag is asserted when the least significant bit of the timecode frame number is intentionally locked to the colorframe sequence of the associated video – in 480*i* systems, locked to Colorframes A and B of SMPTE 170M. See *NTSC two-frame sequence*, on page 512.

Dropframe timecode

In 25 Hz video, such as in 576*i* video systems, and in 24 Hz film, there is an exact integer number of frames in each second. In these systems, timecode has an exact correspondence with clock time.

See *Frame, field, line, and sample rates*, on page 371.

In consumer 480*i*29.97 DV, dropframe timecode is mandatory.

During the transition from monochrome to color television in the United States, certain interference constraints needed to be satisfied among the horizontal scanning, sound, and color frequencies. These constraints were resolved by reducing the 60.00 Hz field rate of monochrome television by a factor of exactly $^{1000}/_{1001}$ to create the color NTSC field rate of about 59.94 Hz. This leads to a noninteger number of frames per second in 29.97 Hz or 59.94 Hz systems. The *dropframe* (DF) mechanism can be used to compensate timecode to obtain a very close approximation to clock time. Dropframes are not required or permitted when operating at exact integer numbers of frames per second. Dropframe timecode is optional in 29.97 Hz or 59.94 Hz systems; operation with a straight counting sequence is called *nondropframe* (NDF).

The final field in an hour of 480*i*29.97 video has DF code *hh*:59:59;29 and NDF code *hh*:59:56:23.

Counting frames at the NTSC frame rate of 29.97 Hz is slower than realtime by the factor $^{1000}/_{1001}$, which, in NDF code, would result in an apparent cumulative error of about +3.6 seconds in an hour. To make timecode correspond to clock time, approximately once every 1000 frames a frame number is dropped – that is, omitted from the counting sequence. Of course, it is only the *number* that is dropped, not the video frame! Frame numbers are dropped in pairs in order to maintain the relationship of timecode (even or odd frame number) to NTSC colorframe (A or B).

hh:mm: ss: ff
xx:x0:00:00
xx:x1:06:20
xx:x2:13:10
xx:x3:20:00
xx:x4:26:20
xx:x5:33:10
xx:x6:40:00
xx:x7:46:20
xx:x8:53:10

Figure 32.1
Periodic dropped timecode numbers

Dropping a pair of frames every 66 ⅔ seconds – that is, at an interval of 1 minute, 6 seconds, and 20 frames – would result in dropping the codes indicated in Figure 32.1 in the margin. Although this sequence is not easily recognizable, it repeats after exactly ten minutes! This is a consequence of the ratios of the numbers: Two frames in 2000 accumulates 18 frames in 18000, and there are 18000 intervals of $^{1}/_{30}$ second in 10 minutes (30 frames, times 60 seconds, times 10 minutes). To produce a sequence that is easy to compute and easy to remember, instead of dropping numbers strictly periodically, this rule was adopted: *Drop frame numbers 00:00 and 00:01 at the start of every minute, except the tenth minute.* In effect, a dropped pair that is due is delayed until the beginning of the next minute.

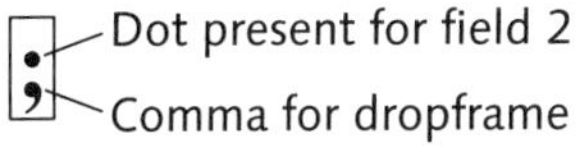

Dot present for field 2
Comma for dropframe

Figure 32.2 **Timecode displayed,** or represented in ASCII, has the final delimiter (separating seconds from frames) selected from colon, semicolon, period, and comma, to indicate dropframe code and field 2.

Figure 31.2 depicts the convention that has emerged to represent field identification and of the use of dropframe code in timecode displays.

Dropframe does not achieve a perfect match to clock time, just a very good match: Counting dropframe code at $^{30}/_{1.001}$ frames per second results in timecode that is about 86.4 ms late (slow) over 24 hours. If the residual error were to accumulate, after 11 or 12 days timecode would fall about one second later than clock time. If a timecode sequence is to be maintained longer than 24 hours, timecode should be jammed daily to reference clock time at an innocuous moment. No standard recommends when this should take place; however, the usual technique is to insert duplicate timecode numbers

00:00:00;00 and 00:00:00;01. Editing equipment treats the duplicate codes as a timecode interruption.

Editing

SMPTE 258M, *Television – Transfer of Edit Decision Lists.*

Timecode is basic to video editing. An edit is denoted by its *in point* (the timecode of the first field or frame to be recorded) and its *out point* (the timecode of the first field or frame beyond the recording). An edited sequence can be described by the list of edits used to produce it: Each entry in an *edit decision list* (EDL) contains the in and out points of the edited material, the in and out points of the source, and tape reel number or other source and transition identification.

An edited tape is invariably recorded with continuous "nonbroken" timecode. Nearly all editing equipment treats the boundary between 23:59:59:29 and 00:00:00:00 as a timecode discontinuity; consequently, it is conventional to start the main program segment on tape with the code 01:00:00:00. If the tape includes the usual 1.5 minutes of bars and tone leader, then the tape will start near timecode 00:58:30:00.

Linear timecode (LTC)

Timecode was historically recorded on studio videotape and audiotape recorders on longitudinal tracks having characteristics similar or identical to those of audio tracks. This became known as *longitudinal timecode* (LTC). The word *longitudinal* became unfashionable, and LTC was renamed *linear timecode* – thankfully, it retains its acronym. LTC is interfaced in the studio as an audio signal pair using a three-pin XLR connector.

Each frame time is divided into 80 bit-cells; at 30 Hz frame rate, the bit rate of timecode data is nominally 2.4 kb/s. LTC is recorded using the *binary FM* technique, also known as *Manchester* code: Each bit cell has a transition at its start; a 1-bit has a transition in the middle of the cell and a 0-bit does not. This coding is immune to the polarity reversals that sometimes occur in audio distribution equipment.

LTC is transmitted bit serially, in 4-bit *nibbles*; first a timecode nibble, then a user nibble, least significant bit first. This 64-bit stream is followed by a 16-bit sync word pattern that comprises the fixed sequence 0, 0, twelve ones, 0, and 1. The sync pattern is distinguished from any data pattern, since the combination of BCD timecode digit coding and time/user digit interleaving inherently excludes any run of 11 or more successive 1-bits. The sync pattern also identifies whether timecode is being read in the forward or reverse direction, so that timecode can be recovered whether the tape is moving forward or backward.

At normal play speed, LTC can be decoded from tape as long as the playback system (heads, preamps) has an audio bandwidth out to about 2.4 kHz. To recover timecode at the shuttle rates of a high-quality studio VTR – about 60 times play speed – requires an audio bandwidth about 60 times higher. Due to the limitations of stationary head magnetic recording, longitudinal timecode from a VTR (or ATR) cannot be read at very slow speeds or with the tape stopped.

Vertical interval timecode (VITC)

SMPTE RP 164, *Location of Vertical Interval Time Code.*

Vertical interval timecode overcomes the disadvantage that LTC cannot be read with videotape stopped or moving slowly. With VITC, one or two video scan lines in the vertical interval of the video signal contain timecode data. In 480*i* systems, VITC should be conveyed on lines 14 and 277; in 576*i* systems, VITC should be conveyed on lines 19 and 332. For videotape recording it is advisable to record VITC redundantly on two nonconsecutive lines, in case one line suffers a tape dropout. SMPTE recommends that the redundant copy in 480*i* systems be placed on line 16 (279). VITC identifies each field of video; a *field mark* bit is asserted for the second field (field 2).

Each VITC line conveys 90 bits as 9 serialized bytes of eight bits each, each preceded by a 2-bit sync code [1, 0]. The first 8 bytes contain the timecode information and user bits in LTC order. The ninth byte contains a cyclic redundancy check (CRC) code that may be used for error detection (and possibly correction). CRC is computed as $G(x) = x^8 + 1$ across the 64 information bits and the 18 VITC sync bits. The CRC can be generated by an 8-bit shift register and an exclusive-or (XOR) gate. The CRC is independently computed by the receiver from the information and sync bits; if the computed CRC does not match the transmitted CRC, then an error is known to have occurred in transmission or recording.

The IRE unit is introduced on page 326.

The bit rate of VITC for 480*i* systems is one-half of the NTSC color subcarrier frequency, that is, one-half of $^{315}/_{88}$ MHz. A 0-bit is coded at blanking level (0 IRE), and a 1-bit is coded at 80 IRE. The 0-to-1 transition of the first (start) bit occurs 10.5 µs from the 50%-point of the line sync datum (0_H). A decoder must use the sync bit transition at the start of the line to establish a decoder phase reference; it may or may not use the other sync transitions.

Timecode structure

Table 32.1A opposite illustrates the structure of timecode data. The 8×8 block of bits at the upper left comprises the main set of information bits. In LTC, these 64 bits are transmitted serially, followed by 16 LTC sync bits; bits transmitted with LTC are indicated by shaded entries in the table. In VITC, each group of 8 bits is preceded by two VITC sync bits; these ten words are followed by a final pair of VITC sync bits and a CRC.

The information bits include a flag bit *polarity/field* (whose function differs between LTC and VITC), and three *binary group flags* BGF_0, BGF_1, and BGF_2; they are interpreted in Table 32.1B and Table 32.1 overleaf. A clumsy error was made when SMPTE standards were adapted to 25 Hz timecode: The positions of flag bits BGF_0, BGF_2, and Polarity/Field were jumbled. Flag bit interpretation now sadly depends upon whether the timecode is 25 Hz-related. The timecode information bits provide no explicit indication of frame rate; frame rate must be determined after a one-second delay, or from parameters outside timecode.

Table 32.1A **Timecode bit assignment table** Transmission order is right to left, top to bottom – that is, least significant to most significant. For LTC, transmit the shaded entries below; bit numbers 0 through 79 are obtained by adding the row number (0, 8, …, 72) to the column number (0 through 7, reading right to left). For VITC, include the rightmost column of fixed *VITC sync* bits. The jumbled flag bits of 25 Hz systems are enclosed in braces:

col 7 6 5 4	3	2	1 ⇐ 0	*row*	⇐ *VITC sync*	
1st binary group			Frames units 0–9	*0*	**0**	**1**
2nd binary group *(or character 0)*	Color-frame flag	Drop-frame flag	Frame tens 0–2	*8*	**0**	**1**
3rd binary group			Seconds units 0–9	*16*	**0**	**1**
4th binary group *(or character 1)*	Polarity /Field {BGF_0}		Seconds tens 0–5	*24*	**0**	**1**
5th binary group			Minutes units 0–9	*32*	**0**	**1**
6th binary group *(or character 2)*	BGF_0 {BGF_2}		Minutes tens 0–5	*40*	**0**	**1**
7th binary group			Hours units 0–9	*48*	**0**	**1**
8th binary group *(or character 3)*	BGF_2 {Polarity / Field}	BGF_1	Hours tens 0–2	*56*	**0**	**1**

In vertical interval code, the VITC sync and information bits are followed by a final 2 VITC sync bits, then 8 cyclic redundancy check (CRC) bits computed across the preceding 82 bits:

7 6 5 4 3 2 1 ⇐ 0	⇐ *VITC sync*	
$G(x) = x^8 + 1$	**0**	**1**

In LTC, the 64 information bits are followed by 16 fixed LTC synchronization bits, here arranged in two rows, *sync A* and *sync B*:

7	*6*	*5*	*4*	*3*	*2*	*1*	⇐ *0*	*row*	
1	**1**	**1**	**1**	**1**	**1**	**0**	**0**	*64*	sync A
1	**0**	**1**	**1**	**1**	**1**	**1**	**1**	*72*	sync B

Dropframe flag	Asserted for dropframe timecode mode in 59.94 Hz systems only
Colorframe flag	Asserted when timecode is locked to the colorframe sequence of the associated video
Polarity (LTC only)	Computed such that the complete 80-bit LTC timecode for a frame contains an even number of zero bits (a.k.a. parity, or biphase mark polarity correction)
Field mark (VITC only)	Asserted for the second field

Table 32.1B **Timecode flag bits**

BGF_2	BGF_1	BGF_0	*User-bit interpretation*
0	0	0	Unspecified characters or data
0	0	1	ISO 646 and ISO 2202 eight-bit characters
1	0	1	SMPTE RP 135 data ("page/line")
all other combinations			Unassigned

Table 32.1C **Timecode binary group flags**

Further reading

SMPTE 12M, *Time and Control Code.*

Timecode for 480*i* television is standardized in ANSI/SMPTE 12M. Timecode for 576*i* is described in IEC 60461, with additional information provided in European Broadcasting Union document EBU N12.

SMPTE RP 136, *Time and Control Codes for 24, 25 or 30 Frame-per-Second Motion-Picture Systems.*

SMPTE RP 136 standardizes magnetic recording of timecode on motion picture film at 24, 25, 29.97, or 30 frames per second. SMPTE 262M, cited on page 381, standardizes a method of structuring user-bit data.

SMPTE 266M, *4:2:2 Digital Component Systems – Digital Vertical Interval Time Code.*

SMPTE 266M standardizes a version of VITC, *Digital Vertical Interval Timecode* (DVITC), to be transported across a Rec. 601, 4:2:2 interface.

SMPTE RP 196, *Transmission of LTC and VITC Data as HANC Packets in Serial Digital Television Interfaces.*

SMPTE RP 196 standardizes a mechanism to encode LTC and VITC data in ancillary (ANC) packets of the SDI.

Digital sync, TRS, ancillary data, and interface 33

Along with picture information, a video system needs to convey information about which time instants – or which digital samples – are associated with the start of each frame and the start of each line. In digital video, this information is conveyed by *timing reference signals* (TRS) that I will explain in this chapter.

I outlined the *Serial digital interface (SDI),* on page 130. SDI has capacity to transmit ancillary (ANC) data. The *serial data transport interface* (SDTI) resembles SDI, but has no uncompressed active video – instead, the full data capacity of the link is dedicated to carrying ANC packets. Compressed digital video, such as DV25 or DV50, can be conveyed in these ANC packets.

In *Digital video interfaces,* on page 127, I introduced DVB-ASI, SMPTE SSI, and IEEE 1394/DV. These interfaces have no ancillary data, and do not use TRS.

Standard serial interfaces transmit 10-bit samples; a transmitter must encode all 10 bits (even if the two LSBs are zero).

I use the subscript h to denote a hexadecimal (base 16) integer. Sample values in this chapter are expressed in 10 bits.

TRS and ANC sequences are introduced by 10-bit codewords 0 and $3FF_h$. For compatibility with legacy parallel interfaces such as SMPTE RP 125 and EBU Tech. 3246, a receiver must ignore the two LSBs in identifying TRS and ANC. Apart from their use to delimit TRS and ANC, codewords 0, 1, 2, 3, and $3FC_h$, $3FD_h$, $3FE_h$, and $3FF_h$, are prohibited from digital video data.

TRS in 4:2:2 component SDTV

In *Component digital SDTV interface (Rec. 601, "4:2:2")*, on page 127, I explained that 4:2:2 samples are multiplexed in the sequence $\{C_B, Y'_0, C_R, Y'_1\}$ onto the serial digital interface (SDI). Rec. 601 defines the abstract signal coding parameters; Rec. 656 defines the interface.

Active luma samples are numbered from zero to $S_{AL}-1$; active chroma samples are numbered from zero to $(S_{AL}/2)-1$. The interface transmits two words for each luma sample clock: Even-numbered words convey chroma samples; odd-numbered words convey luma samples. The sample structure aligns with 0_H: If analog sync were digitized, a particular digitized luma sample would precisely reflect the 50% value of sync.

In 4:2:2 video, a four-word TRS sequence immediately precedes active video, indicating *start* of *active video* (SAV). SAV is followed by C_B sample zero. Immediately following the last active sample of the line is another four-word TRS sequence, *end* of *active video* (EAV). The TRS sequence comprises a word of all ones (codeword $3FF_h$), a word of all zeros, another word of all zeros, and finally a word including flag bits *F* (Field), *V* (Vertical), *H* (Horizontal), P_3, P_2, P_1, and P_0 (Parity). SAV is indicated by $H=0$; EAV has $H=1$. Table 33.1 at the top of the facing page shows the elements of TRS.

The *V* and *H* bits are asserted during the corresponding blanking intervals. The *F* bit denotes field, not frame.

The *F* and *V* bits change state in the EAV prior to the start of the associated line; rather than calling it EAV, you might call it *start of horizontal interval.* In interlaced systems, *F* is asserted during the second field. In 480*i* systems, *F* changes at lines 4 and 266; in other scanning systems, including 576*i* and HDTV, *F* changes state at line 1. In progressive systems, *F* is always zero – except in 483*p*59.94, where *F* encodes frame parity.

In Rec. 601-4 (1994) and in SMPTE RP 125-1992, in 480*i* systems, an SAV with *V*=0 could occur prior to the first active (picture) line – as early as line 10 or line 273. To be compatible with legacy equipment, do not rely upon the 1-to-0 transition of *V*.

The vertical blanking (*V*) bit is zero in every line that is defined by the associated scanning standard to contain active (picture) video; it is asserted elsewhere – that is, in the vertical interval.

Word	Value	MSB 9	8	7	6	5	4	3	2	1	LSB 0
0	$3FF_h$	1	1	1	1	1	1	1	1	1	1
1	0	0	0	0	0	0	0	0	0	0	0
2	0	0	0	0	0	0	0	0	0	0	0
3		1	F	V	H	P_3	P_2	P_1	P_0	0	0

Table 33.1 **Timing reference sequence (TRS)** for 4:2:2 comprises 4 codewords. Start of active video (SAV) is indicated by $H = 0$; end of active video (EAV) has $H = 1$. For compatibility with 8-bit equipment, the 2 LSBs are ignored in decoding TRS.

Value		F	V	H	$P_3 = V \oplus H$	$P_2 = F \oplus H$	$P_1 = F \oplus V$	$P_0 = F \oplus V \oplus H$		
200_h	1	0	0	0	0	0	0	0	0	0
274_h	1	0	0	1	1	1	0	1	0	0
$2AC_h$	1	0	1	0	1	0	1	1	0	0
$2DB_h$	1	0	1	1	0	1	1	0	0	0
$31C_h$	1	1	0	0	0	1	1	1	0	0
368_h	1	1	0	1	1	0	1	0	0	0
380_h	1	1	1	0	1	1	0	0	0	0
$3C4_h$	1	1	1	1	0	0	0	1	0	0

Table 33.2 **Protection bits for SAV and EAV** are computed as the exclusive-or (⊕) of various combinations of *F*, *V*, and *H*. The code can correct 1-bit errors, and can detect 2-bit errors. The error-correction capability is arguably useful for the parallel interface. However, it is useless for SDI, because a single-bit error in the SDI bitstream, when descrambled, corrupts up to 5 bits.

The *F*, *V*, and *H* bits are protected by parity bits P_3, P_2, P_1, and P_0, formed as indicated in Table 33.2 above by an exclusive-or across two or three of *F*, *V*, and *H*.

SMPTE standards are inconsistent in their numbering of words outside the active region. EAV functions as the start of a digital line with regard to state changes to the *F* and *V* bits, so I number words from 0 at EAV. In this scheme, SAV starts at word $S_{TL}-S_{AL}-4$. Another reason for numbering EAV as word 0 is that the proposed SMPTE standard for HD-SDTI anticipates a scheme to advance the timing of SAV codes. Word and sample numbering is strictly notational: Neither word nor sample numbers appear at the interface.

SMPTE 348M, *High Data-Rate Serial Data Transport Interface (HD-SDTI).*

The horizontal blanking interval at the interface, from EAV to SAV, can contain ancillary data (HANC). In each active (picture) line, the interval from SAV to EAV contains active video. Outside the active picture lines, the interval between SAV and EAV can be used for ancillary data (VANC) packets. If a line outside the active picture is not carrying VANC, and the line isn't associated with analog sync elements*, the interval from SAV to EAV can carry a digitized ancillary signal coded like active video. Intervals not used for EAV, SAV, active video, digitized ancillary signals, or ancillary (ANC) data are filled by alternating codes {chroma 200_h, luma 40_h}, which, in active picture, would represent blanking.

* 1250/50 is an exception; see SMPTE 295M. I recommend that you avoid 1250/50, and use 1125/50 instead.

TRS in HD-SDI

HD-SDI is similar to 4:2:2 SDTV SDI; however, the single link carries two logical streams, one carrying chroma, the other carrying luma. Each stream has TRS sequences; independent ANC packets can be carried in each stream. The two streams are word multiplexed; the multiplexed stream is serialized and scrambled. Four words indicated in Table 33.3 below are appended to each EAV. Each bit 9 is the complement of bit 8. Words 4 and 5 convey line number (LN0, LN1). Words 6 and 7 provide CRC protection for the stream's active video. Each stream has a CRC generator that implements a characteristic function $x^{18}+x^5+x^4+1$. Each generator is reset to zero immediately after SAV, and accumulates words up to and including LN1.

SMPTE 260M describes a scheme, now deprecated, to convey line numbers in ANC packets.

Word	*Value*	*MSB 9*	*8*	*7*	*6*	*5*	*4*	*3*	*2*	*1*	*LSB 0*
4	*LN0*	$\overline{L_6}$	L_6	L_5	L_4	L_3	L_2	L_1	L_0	**0**	**0**
5	*LN1*	**1**	**0**	**0**	**0**	L_{10}	L_9	L_8	L_7	**0**	**0**
6	*CR0*	$\overline{CRC_8}$	CRC_8	CRC_7	CRC_6	CRC_5	CRC_4	CRC_3	CRC_2	CRC_1	CRC_0
7	*CR1*	$\overline{CRC_{17}}$	CRC_{17}	CRC_{16}	CRC_{15}	CRC_{14}	CRC_{13}	CRC_{12}	CRC_{11}	CRC_{10}	CRC_9

Table 33.3 **Line number and CRC in HD-SDI** comprises four words immediately following EAV; the package is denoted EAV+LN+CRC. Bit 9 of each word is the complement of bit 8. Line number is coded in 11 bits L_{10} through L_0, conveyed in two words. The CRC covers the first active sample through the line number. An HD-SDI interface conveys two streams, each including EAV+LN+CRC and SAV sequences; one stream carries chroma-aligned words, the other carries luma-aligned words.

Word	Value	MSB 9	8	7	6	5	4	3	2	1	LSB 0
0	$3FF_h$	**1**	**1**	**1**	**1**	**1**	**1**	**1**	**1**	**1**	**1**
1	0	**0**	**0**	**0**	**0**	**0**	**0**	**0**	**0**	**0**	**0**
2	0	**0**	**0**	**0**	**0**	**0**	**0**	**0**	**0**	**0**	**0**
3	0	**0**	**0**	**0**	**0**	**0**	**0**	**0**	**0**	**0**	**0**
4	*ID*	$\overline{PAR}$	*PAR*	X_4	X_3	X_2	X_1	X_0	FR_1	FR_0	*F*

Table 33.4 **TRS-ID in $4f_{SC}$** comprises five words. Line number is coded in word 4, in 5 bits X_4 through X_0; these bits count from 1 to 31 in each field, then saturate at 31. Bits FR_1 and FR_1 identify colorframes; bit *F* is asserted for the second field.

TRS-ID in $4f_{SC}$ composite video

I introduced the *Composite digital SDTV ($4f_{SC}$) interface,* on page 129. In composite $4f_{SC}$, active video is digitized and transmitted across the interface with one word for each sample clock. Sync edges and the back porch (including burst) are included among the samples.

In composite $4f_{SC}$ NTSC, sampling is at [*I*, *Q*] phase, as I will detail in Chapter 42, on page 511. No sample precisely coincides with 0_H in the analog domain.

In composite $4f_{SC}$ PAL, sampling is at [*U*+*V*, *U*–*V*] phase, as I will detail in Chapter 44, on page 529. Owing to $4f_{SC}$ PAL not being line-locked, the position of 0_H changes line-by-line. The relationship between sync and subcarrier in PAL causes a further complexity: Each line has 1135 samples, except for two lines per frame which contain 1137 samples each.

Ideally, these are lines 313 and 625; see page 533.

In $4f_{SC}$, the synchronization sequence is called *TRS-ID*; it is located in the analog synctip interval, commencing several samples after 0_H. TRS-ID structure is shown in Table 33.4 above. The SAV and EAV codes of Rec. 601 are not used. The first four words, denoted *TRS*, contain the fixed sequence {$3FF_h$, 0, 0, 0}. The final word, denoted *ID*, conveys line number and field/frame data.

Line number is coded in 5 bits, X_4 through X_0; the count runs from 1 to 31, then saturates at 31.

See *NTSC two-frame sequence*, on page 512, and *PAL four frame sequence*, on page 529.

Bits FR_1, FR_0, and F encode field and frame information. The F bit functions identically to the F bit of the 4:2:2 interface: It is negated (zero) during the first field, and asserted during the second field. In NTSC, FR_1 is fixed at 0; FR_0 is zero during colorframe A, and asserted during colorframe B. In PAL, FR_1 and FR_0 are encoded 00, 01, 10, and 11 to indicate PAL colorframes I, II, III, and IV, respectively.

If the set $\{X_4, X_3, X_2, X_1, X_0, FR_1, FR_0, F\}$ contains an odd number of 1-bits, PAR is asserted; otherwise, it is negated. $\overline{PAR}$ is the complement of PAR.

Digital to analog timing relationships

The relationship between the digital and analog domains is established by the position of 0_H with respect to some TRS element. Table 33.5 below summarizes several standards for digital representation of component 4:2:2 video; the rightmost column gives the number of luma sample intervals between the first word of EAV and the 0_H sample (if it were digitized).

System	*AR*	*Scanning*	*SMPTE Standard*	S_{TL}	S_{AL}	*EAV to* 0_H
483*i*29.97		525/59.94/2:1	SMPTE 125M, Rec. 601	858	720	12
576*i*25		625/50/2:1	EBU 3246, Rec. 601	864	720	16
483*i*29.97	16:9	525/59.94/2:1	SMPTE 267M, Rec. 601-5	1144	960	16
483*p*59.94	16:9	525/59.94/1:1	SMPTE 293M	1144	960	16
576*i*25	16:9	625/50/2:1	EBU 3246, Rec. 601-5	1152	960	21
720p60	16:9	750/60/1:1	SMPTE 296M	1650	1280	110
1035*i*30‡	16:9	1125/60/2:1	SMPTE 260M	2200	1920	88
1080*i*30	16:9	1125/60/2:1	SMPTE 274M	2200	1920	88
1080*p*30	16:9	1125/30/1:1	SMPTE 274M	2200	1920	88
1080*p*25	16:9	1125/25/1:1	SMPTE 274M	2640	1920	192
1080*p*24	16:9	1125/24/1:1	SMPTE 274M	2750	1920	192

Table 33.5 **Digital to analog timing relationships** for several scanning standards are summarized. The 1035*i*30 systems (flagged with a double-dagger symbol, ‡) are not recommended for new designs; I suggest that you use 1080*i*30. The rightmost column relates TRS to 0_H; it gives the count of luma sample intervals from EAV word 0 ($3FF_h$) to the 0_H sample (if it were digitized).

Ancillary data

To determine whether a line that is a candidate for a digitized ancillary signal actually contains such a signal, examine every chroma/luma pair for $\{200_h, 40_h\}$: If any pair is unequal to these values, a digitized ancillary signal is present.

In 4:2:2 SDTV, and in HDTV, ancillary data is permitted immediately after any EAV (HANC), or immediately after SAV (VANC) on a line containing neither active picture nor digitized ancillary data. (In 576*i*, ancillary data is limited to lines 20 through 22 and 333 through 335.) An ancillary packet is introduced by an ancillary data flag (ADF) comprising the three-word sequence $\{0, 3FF_h, 3FF_h\}$.

In $4f_{SC}$ SDTV, ancillary packets are permitted in the synctip interval, immediately following the five-word TRS-ID sequence. Ancillary packets are also permitted in certain regions of the vertical interval; see SMPTE 259M. An ancillary packet is introduced by an ADF comprising the single word $3FF_h$.

SMPTE 291M, *Ancillary Data Packet and Space Formatting.*

An ANC packet must not interfere with active video, or with any TRS, SAV, or EAV. Multiple ANC packets are allowed, provided that they are contiguous. Certain ANC regions are reserved for certain purposes; consult SMPTE 291M.

An ancillary packet comprises the 3-word (4:2:2) or 1-word ($4f_{SC}$) ADF, followed by these elements:

- A one-word data ID (DID)
- A one-word data block number (DBN) or secondary DID (SDID)
- A one-word data count (DC), from 0 to 255
- Zero to 255 user data words (UDW)
- A one-word checksum (CS)

Each header word – DID, DBN/SDID, and DC – carries an 8-bit value. Bit 8 of each header word is parity, asserted if an odd number of bits 7 through 0 is set, and deasserted if an even number of bits is set. Bit 9 is coded as the complement of bit 8. (Codewords having 8 MSBs all-zero or all-one are thereby avoided; this prevents collision with the 0_h and $3FF_h$ codes used to introduce TRS and ANC sequences.)

Two types of ANC packet are differentiated by bit 7 of the DID word. If DID_7 is asserted, the packet is Type 1; DID is followed by data block number (DBN). There are 128 DID codes available for Type 1 packets. The DBN value indicates continuity: If zero, it is inactive; otherwise, it counts packets within each DID from 1 through 255, modulo 255.

If DID_7 is negated, the packet is Type 2: The DID is followed by a secondary data ID (SDID), giving $127 \cdot 255$ (i.e., 32385) ID codes for Type 2 packets.

SMPTE 260M describes a scheme, now deprecated, to convey line numbers in ANC packets where DID=0. That value is now "undefined."

Three DID values, 004_h, 008_h, and $00C_h$ indicate a Type 2 ANC packet coded with 8-bit data; other DID values in the range 001_h through $00F_h$ are prohibited. DID 80_h marks a packet for deletion. DID 84_h marks the last ANC packet in a VANC or HANC region.

The data count (DC) word contains a value from 0 through 255 (protected by two parity bits), indicating the count of words in the user data area. The DC word spans all ten bits of the interface. Even if an 8-bit DID is indicated, SMPTE standards imply that the two least significant bits of the DC word are meaningful. (If they were not, then the count of user data words could not be uniquely determined.)

The checksum (CS) word provides integrity checking for the contents of an ancillary packet. In every word from DID through the last word of UDW, the MSB is masked out (to zero); these values are summed modulo 512. The 9-bit sum is transmitted in bits 8 through 0 of CS; bit 9 is coded as the complement of bit 8.

SDI coding

In the obsolete Rec. 656 parallel interface that I mentioned on page 128, a dedicated clock accompanied the data. In the serial interface it is necessary for a receiver to recover the clock from the coded bitstream. The coded bitstream must therefore contain significant power at the coded bit rate. Coaxial cable attenuates high-frequency information; equalization is necessary to overcome this loss. Because equalizers involve high-frequency AC circuits, the coded bitstream should contain little power at very low frequencies: The code must be *DC-free*. To enable economical equalizers, the frequency range required for correct recovery of the signal should be as small as possible. A ratio of the highest to lowest frequency components of about 2:1 – where the coded signal is contained in one octave of bandwidth – is desirable. These considerations argue for a high clock rate. But it is obviously desirable to have a low clock rate so as to minimize cost. The choice of a clock rate is a compromise between these demands.

Details of the application of SDI in the studio are found in Chapter 7 of Robin, Michael, and Michel Poulin, *Digital Television Fundamentals: Design and Installation of Video and Audio Systems*, Second Edition (New York: McGraw-Hill, 2000).

The SDI uses scrambled coding, where the data stream is serialized, then passed through a shift register arrangement with exclusive-or taps implementing a characteristic function $x^9 + x^4 + 1$.

Scrambling techniques using a single scrambler are well known. But the SDI and HD-SDI scrambler has a second-stage scrambler, whose characteristic function is $x + 1$. The two cascaded stages offer improved performance over a conventional single-stage scrambler. The scrambling technique is self-synchronizing; there is no need for initialization.

A previous version of Rec. 656 specified *8b9b* coding: Each 8-bit word of the Rec. 601 stream was mapped through a lookup table to a 9-bit code, and that code was serialized. The scheme is now abandoned.

The data rate at the interface is the word rate times the number of bits per word. It is standard to serialize 10-bit data; when coding 8-bit video, the two LSBs are forced to zero.

No provision is made to avoid data sequences that would result, after serialization and scrambling, in serial bit sequences with long runs of zeros or long runs of ones. But a long run of zeros or ones provides no signal transitions to enable a receiver to recover the clock! In practice, such *pathological sequences* are rare.

SDI is standardized for electrical transmission at ECL levels through coaxial cable, using a BNC connector as depicted in Figure 33.1. Distances between 200 m and 400 m are practical. SDI is also standardized for transmission through optical fiber. Fiber-optic interfaces for digital SDTV are straightforward adaptations of the SDI.

Figure 33.1
BNC connector

SMPTE 292M, *Bit-Serial Digital Interface for High-Definition Television Systems.*

HD-SDI coding

The SDI interface at 270 Mb/s has been adapted to HDTV by scaling the bit rate by a factor of 5.5, yielding a bit rate of 1.485 Gb/s (or in 24.976, 29.97, or 59.94 Hz systems, $^{1.485}/_{1.001}$ Gb/s). HD-SDI is standardized in SMPTE 292M. The interface is modeled after SDTV SDI, but there are two significant changes:

- Chroma and luma are encoded in separate streams, each with its own TRS sequence. The streams are multiplexed, then scrambled.
- Coded line number and a CRC are appended to the EAV potion of the TRS sequence (giving what is called EAV+LN+CRC).

In 1080*i* and 1080*p* standards documents, samples are numbered with respect to 0_H (unlike SDTV, standards documents, where samples are numbered with respect to the zeroth active sample of the line).

Summary

Table 33.6 summarizes SDTV and HDTV digital interface standards.

ITU-R Rec. BT.656, *Interfaces for digital component video signals in 525-line and 625-line television systems operating at the 4:2:2 level of Recommendation ITU-R BT.601.*

SMPTE 125M, *Component Video Signal 4:2:2 – Bit-Parallel Digital Interface.*

SMPTE 259M, *10-Bit 4:2:2 Component and $4f_{SC}$ Composite Digital Signals – Serial Digital Interface.*

SMPTE 267M, *Bit-Parallel Digital Interface – Component Video Signal 4:2:2 16×9 Aspect Ratio.*

SMPTE 292M, *Bit-Serial Digital Interface for High-Definition Television Systems.*

SMPTE 297M, *Serial Digital Fiber Transmission System for ANSI/SMPTE 259M Signals.*

Table 33.6 **SDTV and HDTV interface standards**

Analog SDTV sync, genlock, and interface 34

In analog SDTV, sync is combined with video and conveyed by levels "blacker than black." This chapter explains the construction of analog sync, and explains *sync separation*, which recovers the significant timing instants associated with an analog video signal, and *genlock*, which reconstructs a sampling clock.

In analog interlaced video, 0_V denotes the start of either field. In digital video, 0_V for the second field is unimportant; some people use 0_V to denote the start of a frame.

In analog video, line sync is achieved by associating, with every scan line, a line sync (horizontal) datum denoted 0_H (pronounced *zero-H*) defined at the midpoint of the leading (falling) edge of sync. Field and frame sync is achieved by associating, with every field, a vertical sync datum denoted 0_V (pronounced *zero-V*).

Analog sync

Figure 34.1 overleaf illustrates the development of the combined (vertical and horizontal) sync waveform. Every line outside the vertical interval starts with a normal sync pulse having a duration of 4.7 µs. Vertical sync is identified by a sequence of *broad pulses*, each having a duration of half the line time less a full sync width. The broad pulses are *serrated* so that a receiver can maintain horizontal sync during the vertical interval.

When analog sync separators comprised just a few resistors and capacitors, imperfect vertical sync separation was prone to exhibit *line pairing,* where scan lines from the second field were not laid exactly halfway between lines of the first field. Line pairs were prone to be visible. Achieving good interlace required interposing narrow *equalization* pulses, each having half

A **Naive combined sync** establishes horizontal timing using a relatively narrow pulse each line time. Here, the duration of the line sync pulse is about 7.5% of the line time. Vertical sync is signaled by a wide pulse. The vertical pulse here, having a duration of one line time, has poor noise immunity.

B **Noise immunity is improved** by stretching the vertical pulse to three lines. However, line sync is now absent during vertical sync: Horizontal scanning could become unlocked during this time. If accurate line sync wasn't reestablished by the first picture line, the top of the picture would be disturbed.

C **Line sync during vertical blanking** is maintained by *serrating* the vertical pulse, and by appending a narrow pulse at its end. Every line now commences with a negative-going sync edge. The vertical pulses are *broad* pulses; the start of each broad pulse is aligned with the associated line sync datum, 0_H.

D **Interlace is achieved** by offsetting the first broad pulse of the second field to start halfway between line syncs. If simple analog circuits were used with this waveform, proximity of the neighboring line syncs would disturb recovery of the first negative-going vertical pulse.

E **Twice line-rate pulses** are introduced before, during, and after vertical sync, so that sync information in within a few lines of the vertical pulses has an identical pattern in both fields. The lines of the second field are thereby accurately placed between lines in the first field, preventing *line pairing*.

F **Fully developed sync** for the second field of 480*i*29.97 video is shown here; sync for 576*i*25 differs in several details described in the text. This is the *sync* waveform – some people call it *composite sync*, but that's confusing because sync is independent of the composite color-coding scheme.

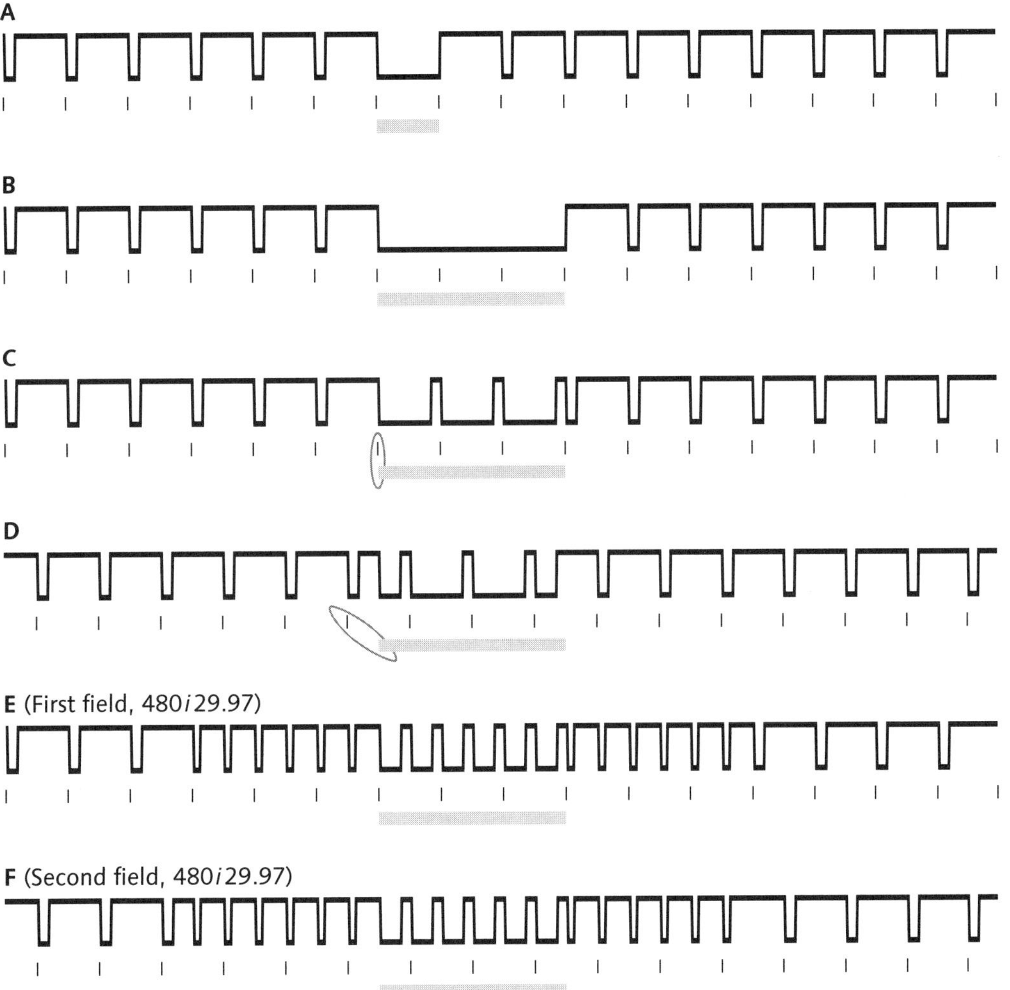

Figure 34.1 **Origin of sync elements** is demonstrated in the sequence of sketches above, annotated by the captions opposite. Each 0_H is marked with a tick. Each gray bar shows the position and duration of vertical drive (VD); the start of each gray bar is at 0_V. The sequence culminates in the sync waveforms for the first field and the second field of 480*i* video. Sync in 576*i* is conceptually equivalent, but differs in detail.

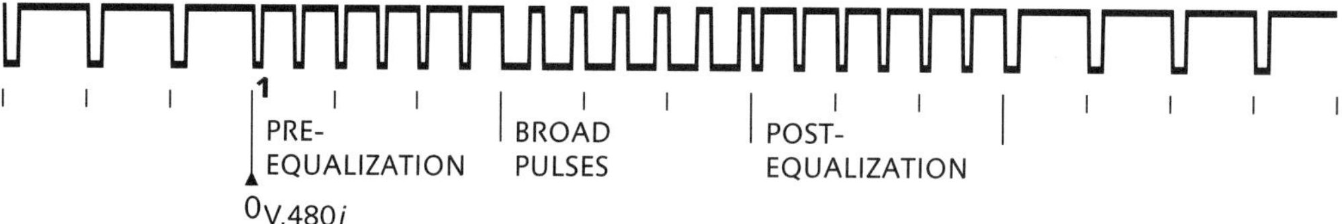

Figure 34.2 **Sync waveform of 480*i*** for the first field, during the vertical sync interval.

the duration of normal sync, between line syncs. Also, the duration of line syncs during the vertical interval was halved. (The term *equalization* now refers to all the narrow pulses, not just the interposed ones.)

The interval between the end of a broad pulse and the start of the following sync has the width of a sync pulse; it was historically called *serration*. If you consider field sync to be a single pulse asserted for several lines, serration is the negation of that pulse at twice the line rate. In digital technology it is more intuitive to consider the pulses that are present than the ones that are absent, so the term serration is now unpopular: Vertical sync is considered to be established by a series of *broad* pulses. The vertical sync datum, 0_V, is defined with respect to the sequence of equalization and broad pulses.

Equalization pulses are unrelated to the process of *equalization* that is used to compensate poor frequency response of coaxial cable, or poor frequency or phase response of a filter.

Figure 34.2 above illustrates sync in the vertical interval of analog 480*i*. There are three lines of *preequalization* pulses, three lines of broad pulses, and three lines of *postequalization* pulses. In 480*i*, line 1 and 0_V are defined by first equalization pulse of a field. (In other scanning standards, including HDTV, line 1 and 0_V are defined by the first *broad* pulse of a field, or frame.)

The first field in 480*i* was historically denoted *odd*, and the second field was historically denoted *even*. Those terms should now be avoided, and *first* and *second* used instead. Historically, 0_V was defined for each field, and lines were numbered from 1 in each field. Nowadays, 0_V for the second field is largely irrelevant, and lines are numbered through the frame. 0_V for the 480*i* frame is defined by first equalization pulse coincident with 0_H.

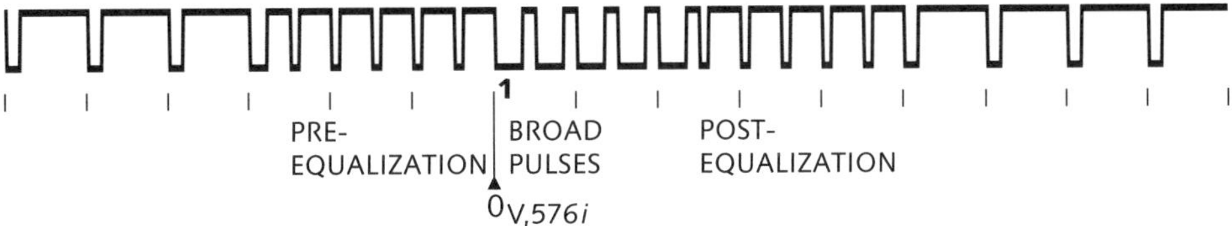

Figure 34.3 **Sync waveform of 576*i*** for the first field, during the vertical sync interval.

In analog 480*i*, lines were historically numbered in each field; the first field had 263 lines and the second field had 262. Nowadays, lines are numbered through the frame. In interlaced digital video and HDTV, the second field has one more line than the first field.

In 480*i* and 576*i*, the top and bottom picture lines each contain half a line of blanking, as I mentioned in Figure 11.3, on page 98. See *480i component video*, on page 499, and *576i component video* on page 519.

Figure 34.3 above illustrates sync in the vertical interval of analog 576*i*. The sync structure of 576*i* has several gratuitous differences from 480*i*. There are two and one-half lines (five pulses) each of preequalization, broad, and postequalization pulses. In 576*i* – and in HDTV – lines count through the frame; line 1 and 0_V are defined by the first broad pulse coincident with 0_H. The relationship between line numbers and vertical sync components differs between 576*i* and 480*i*. Finally, the temporal sequence of halflines differs. MPEG-2 assimilates both systems into a common notation, and denotes fields as *top* and *bottom;* see *Interlacing in MPEG-2,* on page 98.

"Phantom" sync traces, sketched in Figure 34.4 overleaf, arise from infrequent equalization and broad pulses when analog sync is displayed on a waveform monitor.

Odd/even, first/second, top/bottom

Historically, in composite NTSC, editing took place on color-frame (2-frame) boundaries. In 2-3 pulldown, picture content changes between the fields of an M-frame. A film edit may be present at this point.

In interlaced scanning, it is implicit that the first field and the second field convey information from the same source – that is, temporally coherent information. In principle, an edit could cause the underlying image to change between the first field and the second field. Studio equipment is designed and configured to edit between the second and first fields only. A video sequence having edits between the first field and the second field is said to have a *field dominance* problem.

Most lines have a single normal-width sync pulse.

About a dozen lines of each frame contain equalization pulses.

About half a dozen lines of each frame contain broad pulses.

The equalization and broad pulses display on a waveform monitor as faint "phantom" traces.

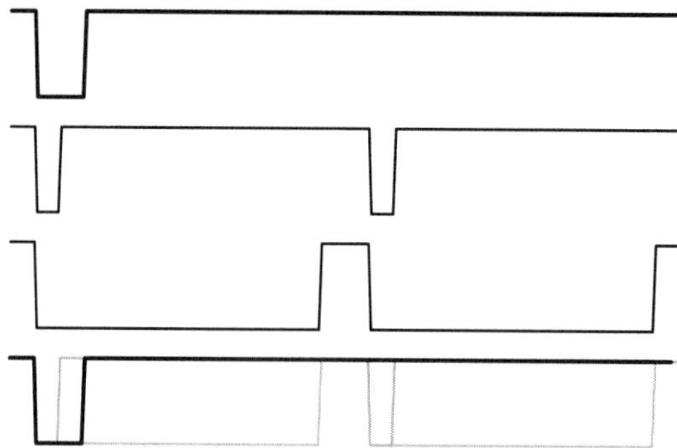

Figure 34.4 **"Phantom" sync traces**

Sync distribution

The term *composite* is overused in video. In the context of sync, it refers to combined horizontal and vertical elements, and is unrelated to the combining of luma and modulated chroma!

Synchronization was once achieved in studio and network facilities by distributing multiple pulse signals, usually having amplitudes of 4 V_{PP} or 2 V_{PP}. Figure 6.7, on page 58, sketched the *horizontal drive* (HD) and *vertical drive* (VD) pulses that were once common. Nowadays, composite sync has amplitude of either 285$\frac{5}{7}$ mV (in 480*i* systems with 10:4 picture:sync ratio) or 300 mV (in 480*i* systems with EBU N10 (curiously called "SMPTE") levels, 576*i*, and HDTV). Sync can be regarded as a legitimate video signal, with zero setup, no burst, and picture information that is entirely black.

When *R'G'B'* is accompanied by separate HD and VD signals, this is denoted *RGBHV*. When separate "composite" sync accompanies *R'G'B'*, this is denoted *RGBS.*

SMPTE 318M, *Reference Signals for the Synchronization of 59.94- or 50-Hz Related Video and Audio Systems in Analog and Digital Areas.*

To distribute timing information among component analog video equipment, it is conventional to distribute a *blackburst* or *colorblack* reference signal comprising sync, blanking, and burst (and optionally, setup). Blackburst represents an entirely black picture, with zero luma and zero chroma everywhere. SMPTE 318M defines a colorframe pulse signal that may be included on lines 15 and 278 in 480*i* systems.

Although a component video signal *per se* has no burst, it is common to include burst on the reference video signals of SDTV component video systems.

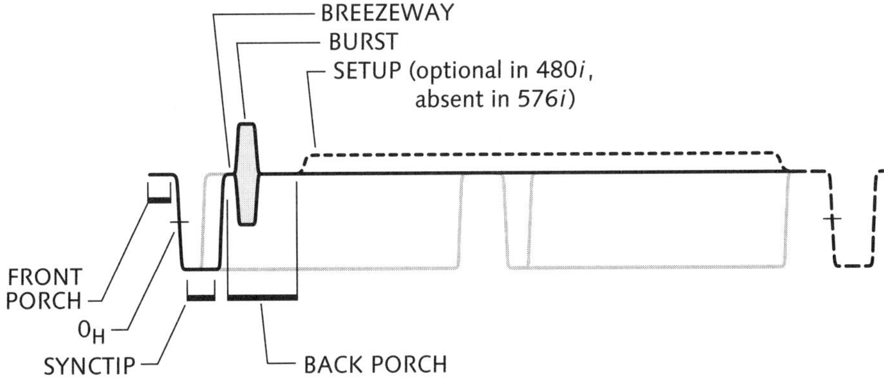

Figure 34.5 **Sync features**

Genlock

Different pieces of video processing and recording equipment have their sync structures (and so, their video timing) brought into synchronism by having their sync generators locked – *genlock*. This requires that each piece of equipment contain a voltage-controlled crystal oscillator (VCXO), a kind of phase-locked loop (PLL). The frequency swing of a VCXO is typically about 100 parts per million, or perhaps 1.5 kHz at 14.318 MHz. This is ten times better than the tolerance of typical PC video, and several times better than the tolerance of typical workstation video. Studio equipment cannot usually genlock to a PC or workstation.

Studio video equipment SDI inputs are typically equipped with digital delays, of a line time or so, to accommodate timing differences between inputs.

Analog horizontal blanking interval

Features of the analog horizontal blanking interval are shown in Figure 34.5 above, using as an example the blackburst signal that is the ubiquitous timing reference for both analog and digital equipment in the studio. Blackburst is used not only in analog systems, but also in digital video. This example indicates, with a dashed line, the 7.5% setup that is optional in 480*i* systems; setup is not required for use of this signal as a timing reference. I show with a dashed line the sync pulse of the next line, following its 0_H.

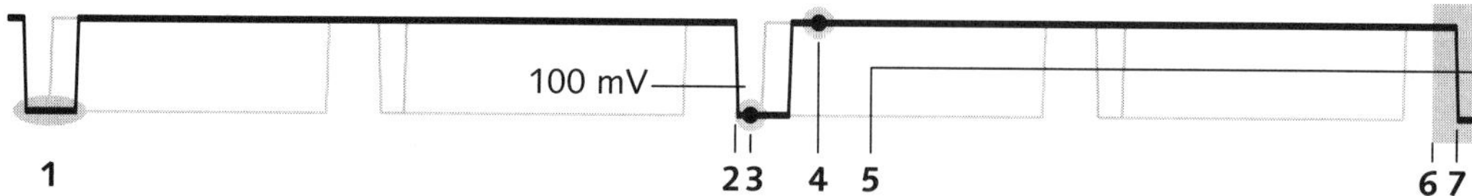

Figure 34.6 **Sync separation** process is not standardized, but it is usually accomplished using the seven steps detailed in the text.

Sync separation

In Figure 34.6, I sketch the steps of recovering (or *separating*) horizontal timing from lowpass-filtered SDTV sync or composite or component video. Sync separation must be accomplished without interference from any picture information that may be present.

1 A coarse synctip level is established as the most negative excursion of the signal.

2 Coarse sync timing is established when the waveform crosses about 100 mV above synctip; this slice level achieves maximum immunity to degenerate and noisy signals. From this instant, three intervals are timed out: synctip (3), back porch (4), and a 1*H* window (6).

3 Synctip window opens; synctip level is sampled.

4 Back porch window opens; back porch level is sampled.

5 The 50% level midway between synctip and back porch levels is established.

6 The 1*H* window opens.

7 Fine sync is sliced at the 50% level; this establishes a precise 0_H datum.

After line sync is established, sync pulse widths can be measured to identify normal sync pulses, broad pulses, and equalization pulses; their sequence can then be decoded to establish vertical sync. A high-quality genlock circuit will validate its reference signal timing and sync structure before switching to it. This may necessitate two counter chains.

Component analog levels

Analog video is conveyed as voltage, with a range of 1 V from synctip to reference white. (Transient excursions slightly above reference white are permitted.)

In 576*i* systems, and in HDTV, picture:sync ratio is 7:3, and there is no setup. Picture excursion is exactly 700 mV; sync amplitude is exactly 300 mV. The reference levels are exactly specified in millivolts. In 576*i* systems, the IRE unit is rarely used. If the IRE unit were used in 576*i*, it would correspond to exactly 7 mV.

SMPTE failed to standardize a component luma/color difference analog interface, so 480*i* component analog equipment was deployed using two different interface standards, both having variations of 7.5% setup. These interfaces will be detailed in *Component analog Y'P_BP_R interface, industry standard,* on page 509. Some 480*i* component analog systems use 7:3 picture:sync ratio, and zero setup – *EBU N10 levels*. Details will be presented in *Component analog Y'P_BP_R interface, EBU N10,* on page 508. (Paradoxically, this has become known in North America as "SMPTE levels"!)

Composite analog levels

CVBS refers to composite video, blanking, and sync; the term is used in Europe.

Composite 576*i* PAL systems have a picture-to-sync ratio of 7:3, and zero setup. Picture excursion is exactly 700 mV, and sync amplitude is exactly 300 mV. No chroma amplitude limit is inherent in PAL transmission.

Composite 480*i* systems usually have picture-to-sync ratio of 10:4. Sync level is $-285\frac{5}{7}$ mV, or –40 IRE; the composite signal never falls below that level. Reference white is $714\frac{2}{7}$ mV, or 100 IRE. In the studio, positive chroma peaks can reach $+133\frac{1}{3}$ IRE; however, an NTSC transmitter limits positive peaks to +120 IRE, as I discussed on page 337.

In composite 480*i* video with setup, the excursion from reference black to reference white is nominally $660\frac{5}{7}$ mV, or 92.5 IRE. NTSC-J in Japan has zero setup; the excursion from reference black to reference white is nominally $714\frac{2}{7}$ mV, or 100 IRE.

Analog electrical interface

Analog video is usually conveyed in the studio as a voltage on an unbalanced coaxial cable into a pure-resistive impedance of 75 Ω. At equipment output, video is DC-coupled. Reference blanking level (zero in the equations used in Chapters 41 through 44) corresponds to a level of 0 V_{DC}. Reference black is also at 0 V_{DC}, except in 480*i* systems with 7.5% setup, where it is at $^3/_{56}$ V, or about 54 mV. Reference white (unity in the equations in Part 4) corresponds to 700 mV, except for "NTSC-related" signals having 10:4 picture-to-sync ratio, where white is $^5/_7$ V, or about 714 mV.

Analog video is ordinarily AC-coupled at equipment input; DC level is blocked by capacitive coupling. A *clamp* or *DC restoration* circuit is used to establish blanking level within the equipment. Clamping or DC restoration is accomplished by introducing an offset which forces the back-porch level of each component to zero (or some other fixed level). Once the signal containing sync is DC-restored, accurate sync can be obtained, and this fine sync can be used to improve the accuracy of DC restoration.

Analog mechanical interface

Figure 34.7
BNC connector

It is standard for studio analog video to use a *BNC* connector, depicted in Figure 34.7, that conforms to IEC 169-8. That standard defines a 50 Ω connector, but video systems use an impedance of 75 Ω, and video standards encourage the use of connectors whose impedance is 75 Ω. A set of three connectors is used for *R'G'B'* interface. In video, sync is usually inserted on the green component (*sync on green*, "RG_SB"), or on the luma component. In computing, separate sync is common ("RGBS").

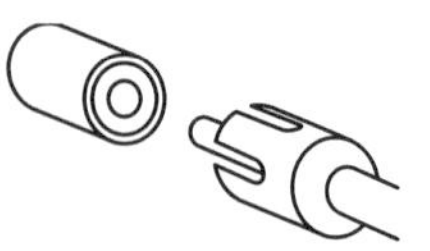

Figure 34.8
RCA phono connector

Industrial and consumer equipment interfaces composite video at *baseband*, directly as a voltage from DC to about 5 MHz, using an *RCA phono* connector, called *Cinch* in Europe, depicted in Figure 34.8. An accompanying audio signal uses a separate phono connector; accompanying stereo audio uses a separate pair of phono connectors.

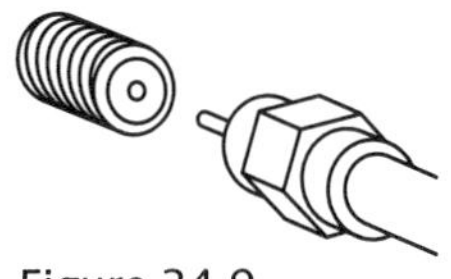

Figure 34.9
Type-F connector

Consumer NTSC, PAL, and SECAM interfaces often use *radio frequency (RF) modulation*, where the composite video signal is modulated onto a VHF radio frequency carrier. In NTSC countries, the frequencies used correspond to channel 3 or channel 4. Output level is typically 750 µV into 75 Ω. Audio is modulated onto the associated audio subcarrier; no separate audio interface is necessary. This interface uses a *type-F* connector, depicted in Figure 34.9.

S-video electrical and mechanical interface

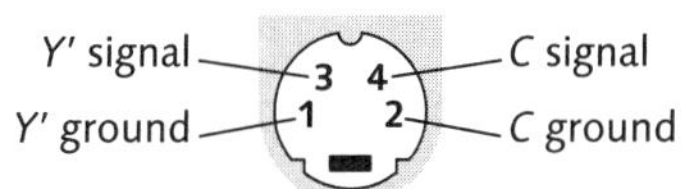

Figure 34.10
S-video connector
looking into cable.

I introduced the consumer S-video interface on page 107. The *Y′* and *C* signals at an S-video interface have structure and levels identical to the constituent signals of analog NTSC or PAL: If *Y′* and *C* are summed, a legal NTSC or PAL signal results. Details about levels will be presented in *S-video-525 (Y′/C3.58),* on page 515, and *S-video-625 (Y′/C4.43),* on page 531. S-video uses a mini-DIN-4 connector; the connector pinout is sketched in Figure 34.10 in the margin.

Historically, S-video has conveyed pictures with the 4:3 aspect ratio of conventional 480*i* and 576*i* video. An emergent industry standard conveys widescreen signalling information along with the chroma signal. The format options are sketched in Figure 34.11 below. Zero offset, compatible with legacy equipment, indicates the usual 4:3 aspect ratio. A DC offset of +2.3 V (through 10 kΩ resistive impedance) indicates letterbox format: The full raster has 4:3 aspect ratio, but the central portion of the raster height contains a 16:9 aspect ratio picture (having 362 picture lines in 480*i*, or 430 picture lines in 576*i*); the top and bottom margins are black. A DC offset of +5 V indicates widescreen 525 or 625 video: The full raster contains an ("anamorphic") image at 16:9 aspect ratio.

In 576*i* or 576*p* systems, the central 430 lines are used, not 432 lines (¾ of 576): This calculation assumes that the top and bottom halflines in the full-frame picture are cropped.

Figure 34.11 **S-video widescreen signalling**

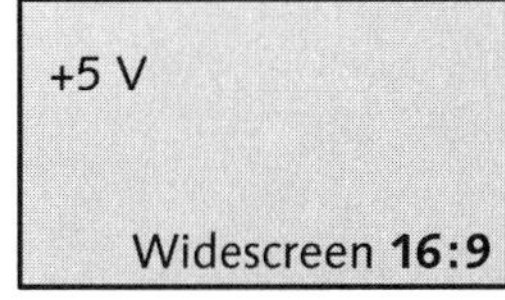

Videotape recording 35

The last decade has seen an astonishing improvement in the data capacity of magnetic disks. It is now feasible to record many hours of highly compressed digital video on fairly inexpensive disks. However, magnetic tape remains the mainstay of video recording.

Magnetic tape cannot be transported past a recording or playback head fast enough to accommodate the high bit rate of digital video recording (or the high frequencies of analog video recording). Instead of moving the *tape* rapidly, videotape tape recorders (VTRs) move the *head* rapidly, across slow-moving tape. In modern VTRs, the tape is wrapped around a drum that is tilted several degrees with respect to the edge of the tape. The drum incorporates a rotating head that scans a helical path across the wrapped tape, as sketched in Figure 35.1 below. (The tape exits the scanner at a different elevation than it enters.) The technique is known as *helical scanning;* it is used in all modern videotape recorders – consumer analog (e.g., VHS), consumer digital (e.g., DVC), and professional.

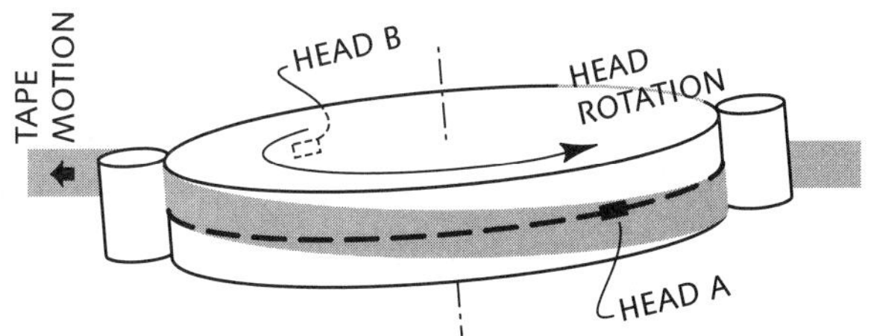

Figure 35.1 **A videotape recorder (VTR)** or videocassette recorder (VCR) wraps magnetic tape around a drum that is tilted at several degrees. The video head scans a diagonal swath across the slow-moving tape. This sketch shows a scanner having 180° wrap and two heads (on opposite sides of the drum). Some scanners have two stationary drum halves separated by a rotating head-wheel; some scanners affix the heads to a rotating upper drum.

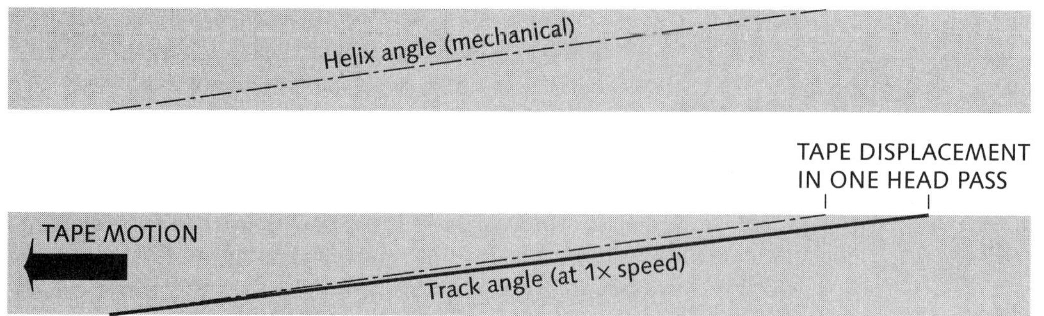

Figure 35.2 **VTR helix angle** defines a diagonal path across the stationary tape, as shown (exaggerated) in the upper diagram. When tape moves past the head at normal (1×) speed, as sketched in the lower diagram, the recorded track angle is slightly shallower (if the drum rotates against the tape, as shown here), or slightly steeper (if the drum rotates in the direction of tape motion). In recording at 1×, and in playback at 1×, the angle is fixed. In playback when the tape is stopped, or moving at speeds other than 1×, the change in effective angle is liable to cause signal disturbances.

The 180° wrap yields a U-shaped tape path. This, combined with the ease of automatic threading compared to near-360° wrap, led to the term *U-matic*.

In a conventional analog VTR, each pass of the head records or plays back one field of video. In the 180° wrap shown in Figure 35.1, a second head (on the opposite side of the drum) records or plays the opposite field. The 180° wrap angle simplifies tape threading, compared to the near-360° wrap that would be necessary if just one head were provided. In a typical digital VTR, the head is tilted at a steeper angle from the vertical, the wrap angle is reduced, and several passes and several heads are used to record each field.

Videotape track angles depend upon whether the tape is moving or stationary. Figure 35.2 above, at the top, sketches the *helix angle* that the head traces when the tape is stationary. The bottom sketch shows that when the head rotates against the tape moving at play speed, the *track angle* is shallower. If a recording is made at normal speed, and played back at normal speed, the recorded track is at this (shallower) angle.

It is a challenge to read information using helical scan when the tape is stopped, because the head trace aligns with the center of the recorded track at only one position on each head pass.

Trick mode (or *stunt mode*) refers to playback of stills and playback within a limited range of speeds around normal play speed. In consumer analog VCRs, trick modes are possible with just 2 heads, but much better performance is obtained by installing a second set of heads with narrow track width (giving a *4-head VCR*). The narrow heads can produce good-quality playback signal even when not aligned precisely with the center of the recorded track. (There remain short intervals when the head is passing between tracks.) In the VHS format, the narrow-track heads can be used for recording at higher density, giving *extended play* (EP) time of 6 hours. Compared to regular 2 hour, *standard play* (SP) recordings, EP recordings have poor SNR and exhibit poor quality in trick mode playback.

In consumer VCR search mode playback (e.g., 2×, 4×), tape is moved an integer number of fields per head rotation. This causes an integer number of fields to be scanned in each head pass. The noisy signal reproduced between tracks is made stationary. This is less annoying than noise at irregular positions.

In broadcast VTRs, playback at still, and playback within a limited range of speeds around normal play speed, typically -1× to +3× normal speed, can be accomplished by mounting the head on an arm that can be mechanically deflected to position the heads vertically. Usually this is accomplished by using a piezoelectric material arranged in a *bimorph*; sometimes, moving coil magnetic actuators are used. This electromechanical transducer can be displaced up and down through electrical control. Control circuitry deflects each playback head so that it remains centered on the recorded track as it scans. Track-following is assisted by introducing a deliberate wobble or *dither*, typically with a frequency of about half a dozen cycles along the track length. Playback signal magnitude is detected and correlated with the wobble, so as to allow the electronics to estimate the center of the recorded track.

This is called *automatic scan tracking*, AST (Ampex), or *dynamic tracking*, DT (Sony).

Playback in shuttle

It is also a challenge to read information from the tape at speeds faster than normal play speed; in *shuttle mode,* the head trace aligns with the centers of several recorded tracks at several positions on each head pass; each alignment lasts just a short time, and produces just a short burst of video information.

When the tape is in shuttle, the head traverses each track for only a brief interval. In an analog VTR, a few lines of each track appear; information from adjacent tracks is concatenated. The scanner rotates at nominal field rate, however; at ⅓ of its rotation through the wrap angle, the head is reading information located ⅓ of the way down the picture. Playback in shuttle produces what is structured as a field of video, but with lines collected from many adjacent fields. This video forms a useful picture.

A consumer VCR is designed to play the same field (always first, or always second) in pause and in slow-speed trick modes. This avoids field-tearing in pause, and vertical judder in slow play, which would be judged as annoying by the consumer.

Recording

Head rotation during recording is synchronized to the field rate of the input video. The scanner is equipped with a tachometer (sometimes called a *frequency generator*, FG) based upon optical or magnetic pickup from the rotating scanner. Tach (or FG) pulses are presented to one input of a phase comparator; the other input is derived from the field rate of input video. The phase error is filtered, and the error signal drives the head motor: If tach pulses are arriving more frequently than field sync pulses, the head motor is sped up; if less frequently, the motor is slowed down. Once frequency lock is established, the circuit seeks phase lock: If tach pulses are arriving later than field sync pulses, the motor is sped up momentarily; if earlier, it is slowed down momentarily. This process constitutes the *head servo;* it keeps playback video locked to reference video.

Tape is pulled through the scanner by a *capstan*. In low-cost VTRs, the capstan has a small diameter, and mates with a pinch roller on the opposite side of the tape. The pinch roller is released when the VTR is placed in shuttle mode (rewind or fast forward); tape motion is then obtained by driving the supply and takeup reel motors. In high-quality VTRs, the capstan has a larger diameter; it contacts sufficient tape area that the resulting friction makes a pinch roller unnecessary. This type of capstan can drive the tape in shuttle modes without requiring use of the supply and takeup reel motors. This yields improved tape control compared to a pinch roller.

When recording blank tape, the capstan is driven at fixed, precise speed. A longitudinal *control track* (CT) is recorded with a regular pulse sequence that is locked to the video field rate (and thereby to scanner rotation).

Playback

In a studio VTR, playback video is ordinarily locked to a reference video signal. This allows a playback VTR to be locked to local video; allows several playback VTRs to be locked together; and allows a VTR to switch into record mode to accomplish a videotape edit. To lock playback to a reference signal, the capstan is equipped with a servo. Off-tape CT pulses during playback are compared to field pulses from reference video; the capstan servo uses the capstan motor to drive the tape to the correct speed and positional relationship.

Heads for other longitudinal tracks, such as audio or timecode, are typically located in the same *head stack* (or *head block*) as the CT head.

If it were mechanically possible, the control track head would be mounted right at the scanner, so that a CT pulse would be recorded at a position on tape immediately adjacent to the start of each recorded track. In practice, mechanical constraints demand that the CT head be located some distance away from the scanner. The distance is set to an integer multiple of the distance that the tape advances during one field. In locked playback, with no tape stretch, this yields the same result as if the CT head were located at the scanner. In practice, some mechanical uncertainty and some tape stretch occurs, and *tracking* adjustment – either manual or automatic – is necessary to align the head trace with the recorded tracks. Automatic tracking slews the tape position, searching for maximum playback signal magnitude.

Tape motion during normal play and record, and in slow-speed trick modes, is controlled by the capstan. However, tape is delivered from the supply reel and is taken up by the takeup reel. Obviously, these need to be driven. The performance of a studio VTR strongly depends upon tight control of tape tension. In a studio VTR, each reel has a motor that is driven by a reel servo that is controlled by tape tension. (Tension can be measured by an arm with a spring.) In a consumer VCR, tension is controlled more crudely, often by a passive friction mechanism.

Editing

Mechanical synchronization is called *servo lock*, or *lock*.

I mentioned that when recording blank tape, the CT is recorded. *Assemble edit* refers to switching (at a field boundary) from synchronized playback into record, such that the resulting pattern of tracks on tape is continuous. Subsequent playback is continuous across the edit. An assemble-mode edit records the control track.

When assembly recording ends, if the tape was previously recorded, there will almost certainly be a discontinuity between the track just recorded and the tracks previously recorded. Subsequent playback across this point would suffer a disruption in playback video while the playback circuits reestablished synchronization.

Certain tape formats have no control track – its function is accomplished by sophisticated processing of special *tracking* signals recorded on the helical tracks.

An *insert edit* begins identically to an assemble edit; however, the control track is not recorded. Instead, it is played back – the playback CT information locks the capstan servo, exactly as in play mode, so that the tape advances in accordance with the previously recorded tracks. When insert recording ends, the boundary between new material and previously recorded material is continuous; playback across that boundary will suffer no disruption.

You might be tempted to insert-edit all the time. However, insert editing requires previously recorded video: You'll have to use prerecorded tape (typically recorded with black) instead of blank tape.

Many studio recorders are capable of *confidence play*, whereby video is read immediately upon being recorded on tape. Confidence playback is achieved through a set of playback heads different from the record heads. Often the playback heads can be deflected for track-following in trick modes. (Record heads are always affixed to the scanner.)

In most consumer VCRs, audio is recorded on a longitudinal track. This severely limits audio performance, and prevents digital audio recording. Studio

DVTRs record digital audio with helical scanning, using the same heads that are used to record digital video.

Studio VTRs need the capability to record audio and video independently – for example, to replace one or more audio tracks associated with a previous video recording. This is done by recording audio on a different portion of the tape than video.

Digital VTRs

All of the processes that I have described are used for both analog and digital VTRs. In this section, I will outline features specific to digital VTRs.

The minimum wavelength that can be recorded on modern videotape is about 1 μm. One wavelength can represent two bits. Each field of uncompressed Rec. 601 SDTV requires about 5 Mb. If each field were recorded in a single track, the track length would be about 2.5 m! This would obviously lead to an unmanageable drum diameter. The dilemma is resolved by *segmented recording*, whereby each field is recorded in several passes. (In a D-1 VTR operating at 480*i*29.97, there are 10 passes, called *video sectors*.)

The term *sync* in *sync block* is unrelated to sync pulses.

In a digital VTR, data is arranged in small packets called *sync blocks*, each short enough to be recoverable in its entirety even at fast forward or rewind speed. Each sync block has a few bytes of identification (ID) information giving the picture coordinates associated with the data. In shuttle modes, any successfully decoded sync block has its picture data written, at the appropriate coordinates, into a framebuffer. The framebuffer contains a usable picture at all times.

Timebase error

Instabilities in mechanical scanning during recording and playback introduce timebase error into the reproduced video signal. In a digital VTR, timebase error is removed through FIFOs built into the signal path. In analog VTRs, a *timebase corrector* (TBC), to be discussed, removes this error. Nearly all studio VTRs have TBCs. Consumer television receivers can tolerate timebase error, so consumer VCRs have no TBCs.

Channel coding

Magnetic recording cannot easily deal with recording DC, or with recording a wide range of frequencies. Different techniques are used to eliminate DC, and to limit the range of frequencies that must be recorded.

In analog audio recording, DC is eliminated through use of a high-frequency bias signal, above the range of hearing. In analog video recording, the recorded signal is frequency-modulated onto an RF carrier.

Watkinson, John, *Coding for Digital Recording* (Oxford: Focal Press, 1990).

In digital recording, channel coding limits the range of frequencies that are recorded and reproduced to about one octave. The scrambled NRZ scheme is common: serial data is presented to a shift register that includes XOR feedback. (A similar scheme is used in the SDI interface.) For details, see Watkinson.

Analog VTR signal processing

Three analog video recording methods are dominant: *component*, *direct color*, and *color-under* (or *heterodyne*). For studio recording, analog VTRs are obsolete (though many Betacam VTRs remain in service).

The *direct color* technique was used in composite analog studio VTRs (such as "Type-C," 1-inch). The analog NTSC or PAL signal was frequency-modulated onto a high-frequency carrier that was recorded on tape. Long-term (field-to-field) timebase error of a few line times, and short-term (line-to-line) timebase jitter of up to perhaps ±500 ns, was introduced. The short-term frequency variation made it impossible to phase-lock a color subcarrier crystal upon playback; consequently, a direct-color videotape playback signal had to be processed through a TBC before viewing or further processing. Since the signal was in composite form, the combined luma and chroma components underwent the same distortion; coherence between subcarrier and scanning (SCH) was maintained.

In *component analog* recording, three components – Y', P_B, and P_R – are recorded separately using FM. Luma is recorded on its own track. Advantage is taken of subsampling: The P_B, and P_R components are each time-

Notation	SMPTE type	Method	Tape width[a]	Resolution, TVL/PH (approx.)
Type-B	B	Direct color, segmented scan	1 inch	430
Type-C	C	Direct color	1 inch	430
U-matic	E	Color-under	¾ inch	250
U-matic SP		Color-under	¾ inch	320
Betacam	L	Component analog (CTDM)	½ inch (Beta)	320
Betacam SP	L	Component analog (CTDM)	½ inch (Beta, MP)	360
M-II	M-2	Component analog (CTDM)	½ inch (VHS, MP)	400
Betamax		Color-under	½ inch (Beta)	240
VHS, VHS-C	H	Color-under	½ inch	240
S-VHS	H	Color-under	½ inch	400
Video-8 (8 mm)		Color-under	8 mm	280
Hi8		Color-under	8 mm MP/ME	400

Table 35.1 **Analog videotape formats for SDTV** are summarized. At the top are studio formats; the shaded rows at the bottom are consumer formats.

a Tape is metal oxide, unless indicated as MP (metal particle).

Component analog VTRs are ordinarily equipped with NTSC or PAL decoders and encoders, so as to accept and produce NTSC and PAL signals.

compressed by a factor of 2:1; the time-compressed chroma waveforms for each line are concatenated and then recorded on a second track. (This is called *component time-division multiplexing*, CTDM.) The recorded signal has no subcarrier, and although timebase correction is necessary, no subcarrier-related processing is associated with recording or playback.

Heterodyne (color-under) recording is used in ¾-inch (U-matic) VTRs, and in consumer Betamax, VHS, S-VHS, Video-8 (8 mm), and Hi8 VCRs. (See page 583.)

Analog videotape formats

M-2 is an exception to SMPTE's usual single-letter designation.

Table 35.1 summarizes SDTV analog videotape formats. SMPTE has jurisdiction to standardize studio formats; surprisingly, SMPTE has also documented the VHS and S-VHS consumer formats. SMPTE designates an analog videotape format with a single letter.

Digital VTR signal processing

Error correction refers to perfect correction, by playback or receiver circuits, of errors introduced in recording or transmission. Redundant *forward error-correction* (FEC) information is inserted by the recorder or transmitter; correction is effected by the decoder's using that information to perfectly reconstruct the errored bits.

This is sometimes called *error checking and correction* (ECC).

Uncorrectable errors may be introduced in recording or playback, perhaps due to physical media problems such as scratches or dropouts of the magnetic coating on the tape. These errors are detected by playback circuits, but they are beyond the code's correction capability. *Error concealment* refers to masking, by playback or receiver circuits, of such errors. Concealment is accomplished by replacing errored samples with values estimated by interpolation.

Error checking and correction in DVTRs is ordinarily accomplished by two concatenated processes, an *outer code*, and an *inner code*, so named for their positions in a block diagram of encoding and decoding with the magnetic tape at the center.

In outer coding, video data is arranged in arrays called *outer code blocks* that are related to the image array. Outer coding appends one or more rows of check bytes to each outer code block. The check bytes are capable of correcting a small number of errored bytes in each column. In the D-1 standard, the array has 12 columns and 30 rows of 8-bit bytes; outer coding appends two rows of check bytes that enable correction of up to two errored bytes in each column.

Inner coding appends columns of check bytes. In the D-1 standard, four bytes are appended to each 60-byte row. The code is capable of correcting any single errored byte. The code has a very high probability of detecting errors in excess of one byte; such errors are flagged for treatment by the outer decoder. A severe error in one row, perhaps caused by a long tape dropout, might invalidate the entire row. However, this causes only a one-byte error in each column of the outer code, so these errors are likely to be correctable.

Even if playback errors are so severe that correction is defeated, the error locations are known. Concealment uses correct data to interpolate sample values that are unavailable owing to uncorrectable errors. Concealment is ineffective for clustered error samples, so data is *shuffled* between outer and inner coding to cause neighboring samples to be widely dispersed on tape.

Compressed DVTRs can afford a much higher budget of bits allocated to forward error correction. However, in the face of uncorrectable errors, entire blocks or macroblocks are lost, not individual samples as in uncompressed DVTRs. It is necessary to conceal erred blocks or macroblocks. This cannot be accomplished spatially: Interfield or interframe interpolation is necessary.

Digital videotape formats

Many digital videotape formats – some would say too many! – have been standardized. They are summarized in Table 35.2 overleaf. SMPTE designates a digital videotape standard by the letter *D* followed by a dash and an integer. Several widely used formats have been deployed without benefit of SMPTE standardization.

D-1

The D-1 format records uncompressed Rec. 601 (4:2:2) SDTV data onto 19 mm tape, at a video bit rate of about 172 Mb/s. (The designation *D-1* properly applies to the tape format, not to the Rec. 601 signal interface.)

D-2

In *Composite digital SDTV* ($4f_{SC}$), on page 108, I outlined the circumstances that led to the introduction of uncompressed composite $4f_{SC}$ DVTRs. In 1988, Ampex introduced the D-2 format, which records uncompressed $4f_{SC}$ video onto 19 mm metal particle tape in a D-1-style cassette, at a bit rate of about 94 Mb/s. (Again, the designation *D-2* properly applies to the tape format, not the $4f_{SC}$ signal interface.)

D-3

Several years later, Panasonic adapted D-2 technology to ½-inch tape in a cassette almost the same size as a VHS cassette; this became the D-3 standard. (In addition to the VHS-size cassette, D-3 accommodates a large cassette with a recording time of 4 hours.)

D-5

Panasonic's D-5 DVTR was introduced in 1994, and is now standardized by SMPTE. It records uncompressed 10-bit Rec. 601, 4:2:2 video, at a video bit rate of about 220 Mb/s, onto ½-inch tape in VHS-style cassettes.

Digital Betacam

Sony's Digital Betacam system compresses 480*i*29.97 or 576*i*25 SDTV to about 90 Mb/s, for recording onto ½-inch tape in a Betacam-style cassette. Its compression uses a motion-JPEG-style algorithm that is unrelated to DV; details are in IEC 61904.

DV family

In the mid-1990s, about a dozen consumer electronics manufacturers developed a set of standards for consumer *digital video cassette* (DVC) products. Their technical agreement was documented in the "blue book" cited below, which later evolved into a set of IEC standards. The "blue book" and the IEC standards specify compression of Rec. 601 SDTV to about 25 Mb/s (SD mode), using an algorithm of the motion-JPEG type. The consumer DVC standard is promulgated by IEC; it is not in SMPTE's *D* series.

The *C* in *DVC* initially stood for *cassette;* the tape format could be distinguished from the compression system. Lately, the *C* has been dropped, and *DV* stands for both the format and the compression system. Consumer DV variants are discussed on page 468.

The DVC system was developed for consumer use, with a data rate of 25 Mb/s (DV25). The compression system, now known generically as *DV*, was later adapted to 50 Mb/s for studio SDTV (DV50), and to 100 Mb/s for studio HDTV (DV100). In the following sections, I will describe DV as recorded on tape; details of the compression system will be presented in *DV compression*, on page 461.

HD Digital VCR Conference, *Specifications of consumer-use digital VCRs using 6.3 mm magnetic tape* (Tokyo: HD Digital VCR Conference, Dec. 1995) ["Blue Book"].

IEC 61834-1, *Recording – Helical-scan digital video cassette recording system using 6,35 mm magnetic tape for consumer use (525-60, 625-50, 1125-60 and 1250-50 systems) – Part 1: General specifications.* See also parts 2 through 10.

In consumer DVC, the cassette is referred to as *MiniDV;* it measures about 2×2.2 inches, and contains 6.35 mm tape. Its outline is shown at actual size in the margin. A MiniDV tape comes in two tape lengths; the shorter length records 30 minutes in SDL mode to be described (a data capacity of about 8.5 GB), and the longer length records 60 minutes (about 17 GB).

Professional DV products offer a large cassette size as well; it measures 4.9×3 inches, and records up to 4.5 hours (about 38 GB).

Notation	Method	Tape width (track pitch)[a]	Data rate video/all, Mb/s	Notes
D-1	Component 4:2:2	19 mm (45 μm)	172/225	8-bit video
D-2	Composite $4f_{SC}$ NTSC, PAL	19 mm (35 μm MP)	94/127 (NTSC)	8-bit video
D-3	Composite $4f_{SC}$ NTSC, PAL	½ inch (VHS, 18 μm MP)	94/125 (NTSC)	8-bit video
D-5	Component 4:2:2	½ inch (VHS, 18 μm MP)	220/300	10-bit video
Digital Betacam	Component compressed, 4:2:2, M-JPEG-like compression	½ inch (Beta, 21.7 μm MP)	90/128	(Sony)
Betacam SX	Component compressed, 4:2:2, MPEG-2 422P@ML (I-B GOP)	½ inch (Beta, 32 μm)	18.7/44	(Sony)
DVC	Component compressed; 4:1:1 for 480*i*, 4:2:0 for 576*i*	6.35 mm (10 μm ME)	25/41.85	Consumer format, DV25
Digital8	Component compressed; 4:1:1 for 480*i*, 4:2:0 for 576*i*	8 mm (16.3 μm ME/MP)	25/41.85	Consumer format, DV25 (Sony)
DVCAM	Component compressed; 4:1:1 for 480*i*, 4:2:0 for 576*i*	6.35 mm (15 μm ME)	25/41.85	DV25 (Sony)
D-7 (DVCPRO)	Component compressed; 4:1:1 for 480*i*, 4:2:0 for 576*i*[b]	6.35 mm (18 μm MP)	25/41.85	DV25
DVCPRO50	Component compressed, 4:2:2	6.35 mm (18 μm MP)	50/80	DV50
D-9 (Digital-S)	Component compressed, 4:2:2	½ inch (VHS, 20 μm MP)	50/80	DV50 (JVC)
D-10 (MPEG IMX)	Component compressed, MPEG-2 422P@ML (I-frame only)	½ inch (Beta, 21.7 μm)	50/105	(Sony)
DVCPRO P (DVCPRO50 P)	Component compressed, 4:2:0	6.35 mm (18 μm MP)	50/80	DV50 (480*p*)

Table 35.2 **Digital videotape formats for SDTV** Those formats above the line are "uncompressed" (although subject to chroma subsampling); those below the line use compression. The shaded rows are consumer formats. D-4 is unused by SMPTE, owing to the number 4 being inauspicious in Asian cultures. D-8 is unused by SMPTE, to avoid potential confusion with Video-8, 8 mm, or Digital8. SMPTE has decided to leave D-13 unassigned (owing to 13 being inauspicious in Western cultures), and is likely to leave D-16 unassigned (to avoid confusion with Quantel's D16 format for digital film).

a Tape type is metal oxide, unless indicated as MP (metal particle) or ME (metal evaporated).

b At its introduction, DVCPRO used 4:2:0 chroma subsampling in its 576*i* version, conformant with the consumer DVC standard. However, SMPTE D-7 specifies 4:1:1 chroma subsampling for both 480*i* and 576*i* at 25 Mb/s. SMPTE D-7 specifies 4:2:2 chroma subsampling for DV50.

Concerning the formation of coded macroblocks in DV, see *DV compression*, on page 461.

DV recording

For recording on tape, a video sync block is assembled from 5 bytes of sync/ID information, a compressed ("coded") macroblock (CM), and an inner error detection and correction (EDC) code. The ID portion of the sync block header encodes the position in the image of the associated CM.

A sequence of 135 video sync blocks, augmented by *video auxiliary* (VAUX) data and outer EDC codes, forms a video sector. All of the elements of the sector are randomized through a prescribed pattern of exclusive-or operations. The serialized bitstream is augmented by an *extra bit* (EB) every 24th data bit; the extra bit is used to insert pilot tones (*F*0, *F*1, *F*2) used for tracking.

An audio sector is constructed similarly, but using audio samples and *audio auxiliary* (AAUX) data.

Video and audio are recorded on separate sectors, with an *intersector gap;* the gap enables video and audio to be edited separately. A track commences with a short *insert and track information* (ITI) sector that provides control information to enable insert editing. Every track ends with a *subcode* sector that provides control and timecode functions.

For DV25, the aggregate data rate on tape is about about 40 Mb/s. DV25 480*i* SDTV requires 10 tracks (i.e., head passes) per frame; DV25 576*i* SDTV requires 12 tracks per frame. In consumer DV, such a recording (with standard 10 µm track pitch) is termed *standard definition* (SD) mode.

LP refers to *long play* mode, sometimes referred to as *LP mode, narrow track pitch*. LP mode is virtually identical to SD mode, except that track pitch is reduced from the usual 10 µm to 6.67 µm, and tape speed is correspondingly reduced. This yields 1.5 times the recording time of SD for a given tape length. Not all consumer DV products offer this mode.

Sony has adapted DV25 coding to the 8 mm tape format, for consumer use; this is called *Digital8*. Tape runs twice the speed of 480*i* Hi8, or 1.5 times the speed of 576*i* Hi8, leading to a corresponding reduction in the record time indicated on a Hi8 cassette.

Studio adaptation of DV technology

DV technology has been adapted to professional use.

D-7 (DVCPRO), DVCAM

The DVCPRO format (developed by Panasonic, and standardized by SMPTE as D-7) and the DVCAM format (developed by Sony) both use DV25 coding identical to consumer DVC; their tape cassettes are virtually identical to those of DVC. However, the formats are different: Both use wider track pitch than DVC, to obtain more robust operation. DVCAM has 1.5 times the track pitch (and track width) of DV, and 1.5 times higher tape speed, resulting in ⅔ the recording time for a given tape length. DVCPRO has 1.8 times the track pitch and speed, resulting in 55% of the recording time for a given tape length.

DV coding has been adapted to a data rate of 50 Mb/s (*DV50*), to achieve higher quality for studio SDTV.

D-9 (Digital-S)

JVC adapted the DV50 scheme to ½-inch tape in a VHS-size cassette. This was introduced as *Digital-S*, then subsequently standardized by SMPTE as D-9.

DVCPRO50

Equipment using DV50 coding for 480*i* and 576*i* was introduced by Panasonic as DVCPRO50. The format was subsequently incorporated into a new revision of SMPTE's D-7 series of standards, which formerly applied just to DV25.

DVCPRO P (DVCPRO50 P)

Equipment using DV50 coding for 480*p* has been introduced by Panasonic, and denoted DVCPRO P or DVCPRO50 P. A medium-sized cassette augments the small and large cassettes used for DVCPRO.

D-10 (MPEG IMX)

Unrelated to the DV developments, Sony developed a videotape format, introduced as *MPEG IMX*, that compresses 480*i*29.97 or 576*i*25 SDTV to about 50 Mb/s, for recording onto ½-inch tape in a Betacam-style cassette. The format was standardized by SMPTE as *D-10*. I-frame only MPEG-2 compression is used.

Notation	Method	Tape	Data rate, Mb/s	Notes
D-6	Component 4:2:2 HDTV	19 mm	1188	
D-5 HD (HD-D5)	Component compressed, 4:2:2 HDTV	½ inch (VHS-derived)	270	(Panasonic)
D-11 (HDCAM)	Component compressed, M-JPEG-like, 1440×1080, 3:1:1 HDTV	½ inch (Beta-derived, MP)	135	(Sony)
D-12 (DVCPRO HD)	Component compressed, DV100, 1280×1080 (or 960×720), 4:2:2 HDTV	6.35 mm	100	DV100
DV HD	Component compressed, DV50, 1008×1024, 3:1:1 HDTV	6.35 mm	50	DV50 (not deployed/ obsolescent)

Table 35.3 **Digital videotape formats for HDTV** The D-6 format is "uncompressed" (although subject to chroma subsampling); all of the other formats (below the line) use compression. The shaded row describes a consumer format that is standardized but unlikely to be deployed.

HDTV videotape formats

Table 35.3 summarizes HDTV digital videotape formats.

D-6

SMPTE D-6 defines a videotape format that records uncompressed, 8-bit, 4:2:2 HDTV, at a bit rate of 1.188 Gb/s. This equipment has superb performance, and is very expensive.

D-5 HD (HD-D5)

The SMPTE D-5 standard, mentioned earlier, records uncompressed SDTV video at 270 Mb/s. Panasonic adapted the D-5 format to HDTV by equipping it with a motion-JPEG codec having a compression ratio of about 5:1. This variant of the D-5 VTR is denoted D-5 HD or (in SMPTE standards) HD-D5.

D-11 (HDCAM)

What is now the D-11 format was introduced by Sony as *HDCAM*. Interlaced or progressive HDTV video with 1440×1080 image format and 3:1:1 chroma subsampling is subject to M-JPEG-style compression comparable to that of DV, coded at about 135 Mb/s. D-11 equipment accepts and delivers 1080*i* or 1080*p* video at any of several different frame rates; see page 471. This format uses a tape cassette derived from Betacam, with ½-inch tape.

D-12 (DVCPRO HD)

The DV standard was adapted to accommodate 1080*i*30 HDTV signals downsampled to 1280×1080 image format (or 720*p*60 downsampled to 960×720), with 4:2:2 chroma subsampling in the downsampled domain, compressed to a bit rate of about 100 Mb/s (DV100). This format was introduced by Panasonic as DVCPRO HD, and was later standardized as SMPTE D-12; it shares many of the mechanical and signal processing elements of the DV25 and DV50 formats.

The "blue book" and the IEC standard for DVC, both referenced earlier, define an adaptation of DV coding at 50 Mb/s for consumer HDTV. Details will be presented in *Consumer DV variants – SD, LP, SDL, HD,* on page 468. The format is unlikely to be commercialized; it is likely to be rendered obsolete by direct recording of DTV broadcast MPEG-2 transport bitstreams.

Consumer bitstream recording – DV ATV, DV DVB

The ATSC bitstream, to be outlined in *Digital television broadcast standards,* on page 587, has a data rate of about 19.39 Mb/s. A scheme has been defined to map two 188-byte ATSC transport packets onto five sync blocks of a modified DV25 stream. A comparable scheme has been defined to record DVB bitstreams.

An MPEG-2 transport stream is not designed to be robust in the presence of channel errors. ATSC and DVB have standardized schemes to augment the transport stream with *error checking and correction* (ECC) information. For DV recording, the transport stream is augmented by an ECC scheme suitable for videotape.

Unlike a DV-encoded bitstream, an MPEG-2 bitstream does not provide for picture-in-shuttle. DV standards provide modest capacity in the recorded bitstream to store *trick mode at low speed* (TPL) and *trick mode at high speed* (TPH) data. The on-tape location of this data is chosen to enable recovery during slow-speed play (TPL) and during shuttle (TPH). Consumer recorders are supposed to extract, encode, and record data from MPEG I-frames. The standards do not specify exactly what data is to be recorded, so such data is unlikely to be interchangeable among different manufacturers.

DV ATV and DVB modes provide data rate of about 25 Mb/s at DV SD standard tape speed of 18.831 mm/s. Half-rate (12.5 Mb/s) and quarter-rate (6.25 Mb/s) modes are provided, tape speeds are correspondingly reduced (to 9.4242 mm/s and 4.7143 mm/s respectively), and play time doubled and quadrupled.

Digital VHS (D-VHS) is a scheme for recording bitstreams (such as DTV broadcast bitstreams) up to a data rate of about 28.2 Mb/s to S-VHS-class, ½-inch tape in a VHS-style cassette. Details have until recently been proprietary to JVC, but a standards proposal has been submitted to IEC.

Further reading

Gregory, Stephen, *Introduction to the 4:2:2 Digital Video Recorder* (London: Pentech Press, 1988).

Watkinson, John, *The D-2 Digital Video Recorder* (London: Focal Press, 1990).

Gregory's book details the D-1 format, and discusses Sony's first implementation. Watkinson's book discusses some fundamental aspects of video and audio recording, and outlines their application to the D-2 format.

2-3 pulldown 36

Motion picture film originates at 24 frames per second. Many television programs, including the majority of prime-time programs, originate on film at this rate. This chapter discusses the conversion of film to video at frame rates different from the native 24 Hz of film.

Film has historically been transferred to 480*i*29.97 video using a technique called *2-3 pulldown*, whereby successive film frames are scanned first twice then three times to produce five video fields. The process is then repeated, reversing the roles of the first and second fields. The scheme is sketched in Figure 36.1:

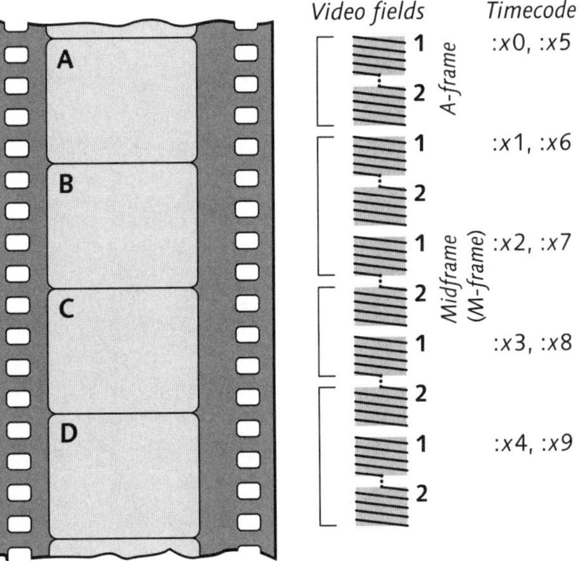

Figure 36.1 **"2-3 pulldown"** refers to transfer of film at about 24 frames per second to video at about 60 fields per second. The first film frame is transferred to two video fields; the second frame is transferred to three. The 2-3 cycle repeats. SMPTE RP 197 denotes film frames as A, B, C, and D. The A-frame is unique in being associated with exactly two fields, first then second, of a single video frame. ("A-frame" denotes both a film frame *and* a video frame.) According to SMPTE RP 201, this video frame should have timecode ending in 0 or 5. The *midframe* (M-frame) is the video frame which comprises one field from each of two film frames.

A piece of equipment that performs this film-to-video conversion in realtime is called a *telecine*. (The term *film scanner* ordinarily implies nonrealtime operation.)

In 480*i*29.97 systems, the film is run 0.1% slow, at about 23.976 Hz, so that the $5/2$ ratio of 2-3 pulldown results in a field rate of exactly 59.94 Hz. Figure 36.1 sketches four film frames; beside the set of film frames is the sequence of video fields produced by 2-3 pulldown. The *1* and *2* labels at the right indicate the first and second fields in an interlaced system.

This scheme is often called *3-2 pulldown*. However, SMPTE standards assign letters A, B, C, and D to sets of four film frames; the A-frame is associated with the frame without a duplicate (redundant) field, so the sequence is best described as *2-3*, not *3-2*.

When a 2-3 sequence is associated with nondropframe timecode, it is standard for the A-frames to take timecode numbers ending in 0 and 5.

In a sequence containing 2-3 pulldown, *cadence* refers to the temporal regularity of the A-frames. Careful editing preserves cadence; careless editing disrupts it.

EBU Tech. R62, *Recommended dominant field for 625-line 50-Hz video processing*.

In an interlaced sequence, *field dominance* refers to the field parity (first or second) where temporal coherence is susceptible to interruption due to editing. In principle, video edits can be made at any field; however, it is poor practice to make edits anywhere except the beginning of field one. (See page 403.)

In 480*i* consumer laserdiscs (now obsolete), video sequences incorporating 2-3 pulldown were fully recorded on the disc, despite the 20% waste of storage capacity. Stepping through disc frames would result in certain frames displaying content from two different film frames, in the manner of the static lattice of Figure 6.12 on page 61. A "white flag" was encoded on the disc, in the vertical interval associated with each new film frame; the flag allowed laserdisc players to correctly weave fields together for playback of stills.

Film is transferred to 576*i*25 video by simply running the film 4% fast, scanning each film frame to two video fields. This is called *2-2 pulldown*. The 0.1% speed change of 2-3 pulldown has no significant effect on the accompanying audio; however, the 4% speed change of 2-2 pulldown necessitates audio pitch correction.

I have described transfer to interlaced video. The 2-3 pulldown technique can be used to produce progressive video at 60 Hz. In this case, what I have described as first and second fields are first and second frames.

Engineers are prone to think that better-quality motion results from higher frame rates. Proposals have been made to shoot film for television – even to shoot movies – at 30 frames per second instead of 24. The 24 Hz rate is obviously the world standard for cinema, but it is also uniquely suited to conversion to both 50 Hz systems (through 2-2 pulldown, 4% fast) and 59.94 Hz systems (through 2-3 pulldown, 0.1% slow). Choosing a film frame rate other that 24 Hz would compromise this widely accepted method of conversion, and make it difficult for film producers to access international markets.

Conversion of film to different frame rates

When an image sequence originated with 2-3 pulldown is displayed in video, motion portrayal is impaired to a certain degree. The impairment is rarely objectionable. However, if a 2-3 sequence is naively converted to a different frame rate, or if a still frame is extracted from a 2-3 sequence, the resulting impairments are liable to be objectionable. Prior to frame rate conversion from a film original, original film frames need to be reconstructed by weaving together the appropriate pair of fields. Despite the fact that 2-3 pulldown has been used for half a century, no information to aid this weaving accompanies the video signal.

A simple method to convert from the 24 Hz film frame rate to any other rate could write successive film lines into a dual port framebuffer at film scan rate, then read successive lines out of the buffer at video scan rate. But if a scene element is in motion with respect to the

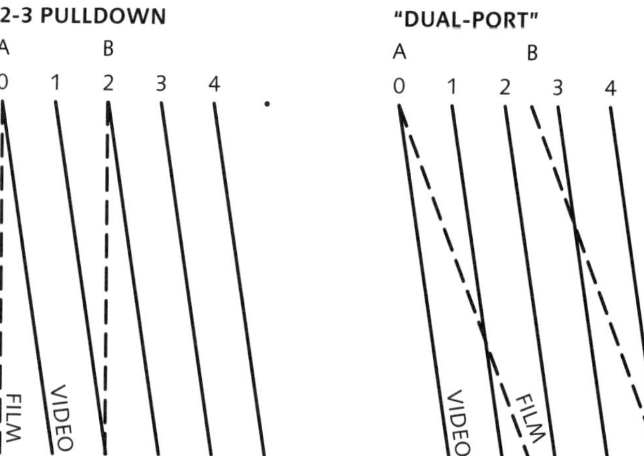

Figure 36.2 **Vertical/temporal relationships of 2-3 pull-down.** Time is on the *x*-axis; vertical displacement is on the *y*-axis. 2-3 pulldown, shown on the left, introduces temporal discontinuities. The "dual-port" approach, on the right, introduces spatial discontinuities.

camera, this technique won't work. The right portion of Figure 36.2 indicates lines scanned from film being written into a framebuffer. The slanted dashed lines intersect the video scanning; at the vertical coordinate where the lines intersect, the resulting picture switches abruptly from one field frame to another. This results in output fields that contain spatial discontinuities. (Although this description refers to interlaced scanning, none of these effects are directly related to interlace: Exactly the same effects are found in progressive systems.)

Figure 36.2 shows the vertical-temporal ($V{\cdot}T$) relationships of 2-3 pulldown, with time on the horizontal axis, and vertical dimension of scanning on the vertical axis. Dashed lines represent film sampling; solid lines represent video sampling. Film capture samples the entire picture at the same instant. The staggered sequence introduced by 2-3 pulldown is responsible for the irregular spacing of the film sample lines. In video, sampling is delayed as the scan proceeds down the field; this is reflected in the slant of the lines of Figure 36.2.

In deinterlacing for a dedicated display, the output frame rate can be locked to the input video frame rate of 59.94 Hz or 50 Hz. But in desktop computing applications of deinterlacing, the output rate cannot be forced to match the native video rate: the output is generally higher than 60 Hz, and asynchronous to the

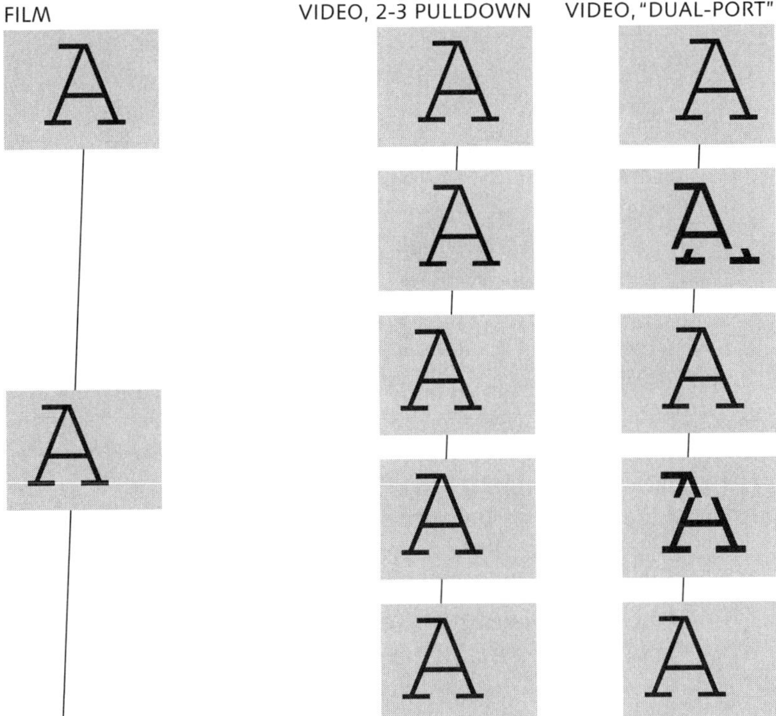

Figure 36.3 **2-3 pulldown, spatial view.** These sketches show the effect on the picture of two schemes to transfer film frames at 24 Hz, shown in the left column, into five video fields at 60 Hz. The center column shows the result of 2-3 pulldown. The right column shows the naive approach of writing into a framebuffer at film rate and reading at video rate.

video rate. In this case, progressive reading from memory is faster than, and asynchronous to, the interlaced writing. If a single framestore is used, at some point the "fast" read pointer will cross the "slow" write pointer. If a "pointer crossing" event occurs on a scan line containing an element in motion, a spatial disturbance will be introduced into the picture. These disturbances can be prevented by using three fields of memory.

Figure 36.3 shows the effect in the spatial domain. Two intact film frames are shown at the left. The 2-3 pulldown technique introduces temporal irregularity into the video sequence, shown in the center column of five video fields, but the individual images are still intact. The result of the naive framebuffer approach is shown the right column: Spatial discontinuities are introduced into two of the five fields. With conversion from 24 Hz to 60 Hz, depending on the phase alignment of film and video, either two or three discontinuities will be evident to the viewer. With conversion from film at exactly 24 Hz to video at 59.94 Hz, the discontinuities will drift slowly down the screen.

Using a pair of buffers – *double buffering* – and synchronizing the writing and reading of the buffers with the start of the film and video frames, keeps each frame intact and removes the spatial discontinuities. However, the delays involved in this technique reintroduce exactly the same temporal stutter as 2-3 pulldown!

Although 2-3 pulldown introduces a temporal artifact into the video stream, acceptable motion portrayal is obtained when the 2-3 video is displayed at video rate. However, if the frame rate is altered a second time, temporal artifacts of the two cascaded conversions may become objectionable; this is especially true when the image is displayed with a wide picture angle.

SMPTE RP 197, *Film-to-Video Transfer List.*

SMPTE RP 201, *Encoding Film Transfer Information Using Vertical Interval Time Code.*

If transfer from film to video is carefully done, pictures ending with timecode digits 0 or 5 are A-frames. Aside from A-frame-locked timecode, there are no standards that convey, along with a video signal, information concerning film origination. Absent locked timecode, the only way to detect 2-3 pulldown is to compare data in successive, like fields: If two successive first fields contain identical luma and chroma, within a certain noise tolerance, and the repeat pattern follows the characteristic 2-3 sequence, then the material can be assumed to have originated from film. Once the original film frames have been identified, conversion to the ultimate display rate can be accomplished with minimal introduction of motion artifacts. Identifying film frames using this method is feasible for dedicated hardware, but it is impractical for today's desktop computers.

Native 24 Hz coding

Traditionally, 2-3 pulldown is imposed in the studio, at the point of transfer from film to video. The repeated fields are redundant, and consume media capacity to no good effect except compatibility with native 60 field-per-second equipment: When a movie is recorded on Laserdisc, or on VHS tape, fully 20% of the media capacity is wasted. In the studio, it is difficult to recover original film frames from a 2-3 sequence; information about the repeated fields is not directly available, and decoding equipment attempts to reconstruct the sequence by comparing pixel values in successive fields.

MPEG-2 coding can handle coding of progressive material at 24 frames per second; it is inefficient to encode a sequence with 2-3 pulldown. Some MPEG-2 encoders are equipped to detect, and remove, 2-3 pulldown, to reconstruct 24 progressive frames per second to be coded. However, this process – called *inverse telecine* – is complex and trouble-prone.

Ordinarily, repeated fields in 2-3 pulldown are omitted from an MPEG-2 bitstream. However, the bitstream can include flags that indicate to the decoder that these fields should be repeated; this allows the decoder to reconstruct the 2-3 sequence. If an image sequence is coded directly in 24 Hz progressive mode, a decoder used with 60 Hz interlace display can impose 2-3 pull-down during decompression; however, the same sequence can be decompressed for display at 72 Hz progressive by flashing each frame thrice.

Conversion to other rates

In 2-3 pulldown from 24 Hz to 60 Hz, information from successive film frames is replicated in the fixed sequence {2, 3, 2, 3, 2, 3, ...}. The frequency of the repeat pattern – the *beat frequency* – is fairly high: The {2, 3} pattern repeats 12 times per second, so the beat frequency is 12 Hz. The ratio of frame rates in this case is $^5/_2$ – the small integers in this fraction dictate the high beat frequency.

When PCs are to display 480*i*29.97 video that originated on film – whether from laserdisc, DVD, or digital satellite – the situation is more complicated, and motion impairments are more likely to be introduced.

In conversion to a rate that is related to 24 Hz by a ratio of larger integers, the frequency of the repeated pattern falls. For example, converting to 75 Hz involves the fraction $^{25}/_{8}$; this creates the sequence {3, 3, 3, 3, 3, 3, 3, 4}, which repeats three times per second. Converting to 76 Hz involves the fraction $^{17}/_{6}$; this creates the sequence {2, 3, 3, 3, 3, 3}, which repeats four times per second. The susceptibility of the human visual system to motion artifacts peaks between 4 and 6 beats per second. The temporal artifacts introduced upon conversion to 75 Hz or 76 Hz are likely to be quite visible. Motion estimation and motion-compensated interpolation could potentially be used to reduce the severity of these conversion artifacts, but these techniques are highly complex, and will remain out of reach for desktop computing for several years.

When 24 Hz material is to be displayed in a computing environment with wide viewing angle and good ambient conditions, the best short-term approach is to choose a display rate that is intimately related to 24 Hz. Displaying at 60 Hz reproduces the situation with video display, and we know well that the motion portrayal is quite acceptable. However, 60 Hz is somewhat low as a refresh rate in a high ambient brightness, and flicker could result. Obviously, 72 Hz is ideal for motion portrayal of film; however, a refresh rate of 72 Hz is too low to unconditionally meet ergonomics requirements worldwide.

Deinterlacing 37

In *Interlace artifacts*, on page 60, I explained that when a scene element in motion relative to the camera is captured in an interlaced system, the scene element appears at different positions in the two fields. Reconstruction of progressive frames is necessary for certain image-processing operations, such as upconversion, downconversion, or standards conversion. Also, computer displays use progressive scanning: Integrating video imagery into computer displays also requires deinterlacing. This chapter describes deinterlacing techniques.

I will introduce deinterlacing in the spatial domain. Then I will describe the vertical-temporal domain, and outline practical deinterlacing algorithms. I will discuss the problem of deinterlacing, and the algorithms, in reference to the test scene sketched in Figure 37.1. The test scene comprises a white background, partially occluded by a black disk that is in motion with respect to the camera.

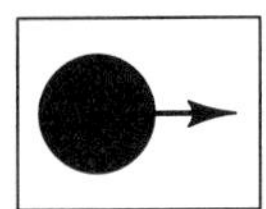

Figure 37.1 **Test scene**

Spatial domain

Video captures 60 unique fields per second. If a scene contains an object in motion with respect to the camera, each field will carry half the spatial information in of the object, but the information in the second field will be displaced according to the object's motion. The situation is illustrated in Figure 37.2, which shows the first and second fields, respectively. The example is typical of capture by a CCD camera set for a short exposure time; the example neglects capture blur due to

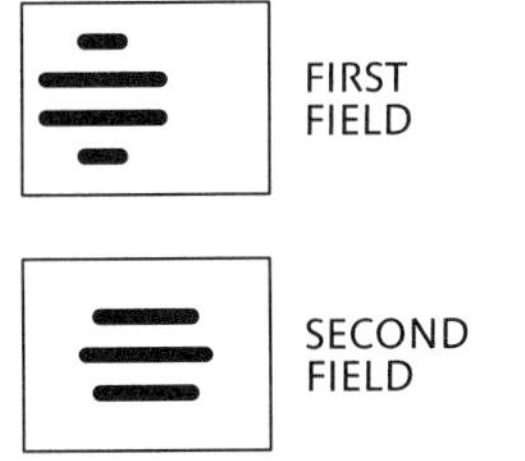

Figure 37.2 **Interlaced capture**

Poynton, Charles, "Motion portrayal, eye tracking, and emerging display technology," in Proc. 30th SMPTE Advanced Motion Imaging Conference (New York: SMPTE, 1996), 192-202.

nonzero exposure time at the camera. (For details of temporal characteristics of image acquisition and display, see my SMPTE paper.)

You can think of an interlaced video signal as having its lines in permuted order, compared to a progressive signal. An obvious way to accomplish deinterlacing is to write into two fields of video storage – the first field, then the second – in video order, then read out the assembled frame progressively (in spatial order). This method is sometimes given the sophisticated name *field replication*, or *weave*. This method is quite suitable for a stationary scene, or a scene containing only slow-moving elements. However, the image of the second field is delayed with respect to the first, by half the frame time (typically $\frac{1}{60}$ s or $\frac{1}{50}$ s). If the scene contains an element in fairly rapid motion, such as the disk in our test scene, the object will exhibit *field tearing:* It will be reproduced with jagged edges, either when viewed as a still frame or when viewed in motion. The effect is sketched in Figure 37.3.

Figure 37.3 **Static lattice**

Field tearing can be avoided by *intrafield* processing, using only information from a single field of video. The simplest intrafield technique is to replicate each line upon progressive readout. This method will reproduce a stationary element with at most half of its potential vertical resolution. Also, line replication introduces a blockiness into the picture, and an apparent down-ward shift of one image row. The effect is sketched in Figure 37.4.

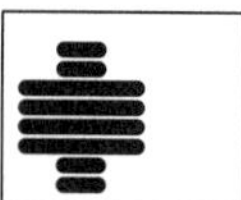

Figure 37.4 **Line replication**

The blockiness of the line replication approach can be avoided by synthesizing information that is apparently located spatially in the opposite field, but located temporally coincident with the same field. This can be accomplished by averaging vertically adjacent samples in one field, to create a synthetic intermediate line, as depicted in Figure 37.5. (In the computer industry, this is called "bob.") The averaging can be done prior to writing into the video memory, or upon reading, depending on which is more efficient for the memory system. Averaging alleviates the disadvantage of blocki-ness, but does not compensate the loss of vertical reso-

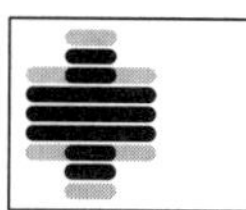

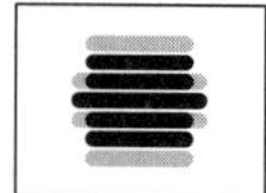

Figure 37.5 **Interfield averaging**

For a modest improvement over 2-tap averaging, use 4 taps with coefficients [$\frac{1}{16}$, $\frac{7}{16}$, $\frac{7}{16}$, $\frac{1}{16}$].

lution. Nonetheless, the method performs well for VHS-grade images, which lack resolution in any case. Rather than simply averaging two lines, improved performance can be attained by using longer FIR filters with suitable tap weights; see *Filtering and sampling*, on page 141.

Vertical-temporal domain

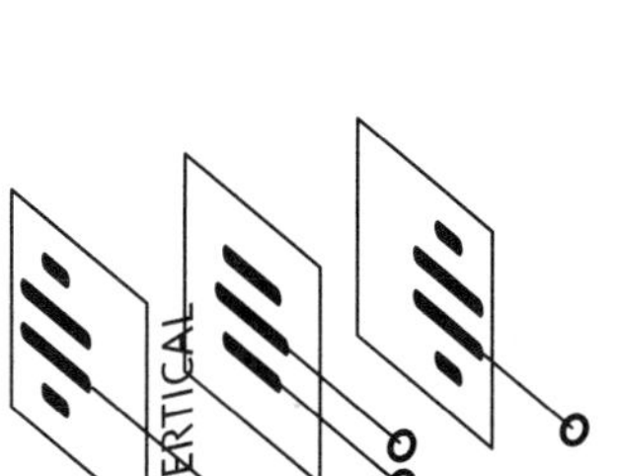

Figure 37.6 ***V·T* development**

Interlace-to-progressive conversion can be considered in the vertical-temporal (*V·T*) domain. Figure 37.6 in the margin sketches the *Interlaced capture* fields of Figure 37.2, in a 3-dimensional view. Viewed from the "side," along the axis of the scan lines, the vertical-temporal domain is projected. The temporal samples are at discrete times corresponding to the field instants; the vertical samples are at discrete intervals of space determined by the scan-line pitch. The four open disks represent samples of original picture information that are available at a certain field instant and line number. A calculation on these samples can synthesize the missing sample value at the center of the pattern. In the diagrams to follow, the reconstructed sample will be drawn as a filled disk. (A similar calculation is performed for every sample along the scan line at the given vertical and temporal coordinate: For Rec. 601 digital video, the calculation is performed 720 times per scan line.)

Figure 37.7 shows the block diagram of a storage system that can be used to implement interlace-to-progressive conversion.

Figure 37.7 **Storage system to implement deinterlacing** can be implemented with two fields of memory. This drawing suggests 525 lines of storage, but it suffices to store just the active lines.

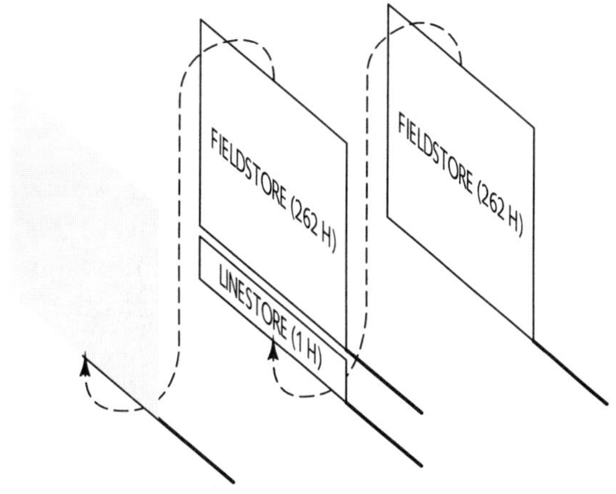

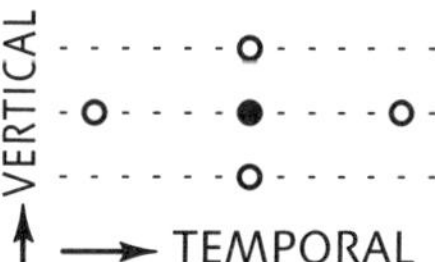

Figure 37.8 ***V·T* domain**

In Figure 37.8, I sketch the vertical-temporal domain, now in a 2-D view. Conversion from interlace to progressive involves computing some combination of the four samples indicated by open disks, to synthesize the sample at the center of the four (indicated by the filled disk). Techniques utilizing more than these four samples are possible, but involve more complexity than is justified for desktop video.

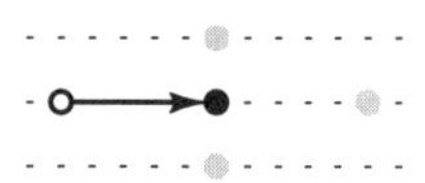

Figure 37.9 **Static lattice in the *V·T* domain**

In Figure 37.9, I sketch the field replication (or *weave*) technique in the *V·T* domain. The sample to be computed is simply copied from the previous field. The result is correct spatially, but if the corresponding area of the picture contains an element in motion, tearing will be introduced, as indicated in Figure 37.3.

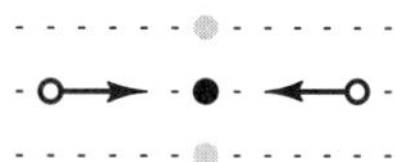

Figure 37.10 **Interframe averaging in the *V·T* domain**

Instead of copying information forward from the previous field, the previous field and the following field can be averaged. This approach is sketched in Figure 37.10. This technique also suffers from a form of field tearing, but it is useful in conjunction with an adaptive approach to be discussed in a moment.

Figure 37.11 **Line replication in the *V·T* domain**

The line replication technique is sketched in the *V·T* domain in Figure 37.11. The central sample is simply copied from the line above. Because the copied sample is from the same field, no temporal artifacts are introduced. The line replication technique causes a downward shift of one image row. The shift is evident from Figure 37.4: The disk in the test scene is vertically centered, but in Figure 37.4 it appears off-center.

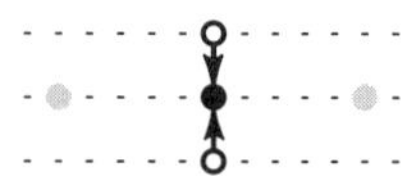

Figure 37.12 **Interfield averaging in the *V·T* domain**

Intrafield averaging – what some people call the *bob* technique – is sketched in Figure 37.12. The central sample is computed by averaging samples from lines above and below the desired location. The information being averaged originates at the same instant in time, so no temporal artifact is introduced. Also, the one-row downward shift of line replication is avoided. However, the vertical resolution of a static scene is reduced.

Motion adaptivity

Analyzing the conversion in the *V·T* domain suggests that an improvement could be made by converting stationary scene elements using the static technique, but converting elements in motion using line averaging. This improvement can be implemented by detecting, for each result pixel, whether that pixel is likely to belong to a scene element in motion. If the element is likely to be in motion, then intrafield averaging is used (avoiding spatial artifacts). If the element is likely to be stationary, then interfield averaging is used (avoiding resolution loss).

Motion can be detected by comparing one field to a previous field. Ideally, a like field would be used – if motion is to be estimated for field 1, then the previous field 1 should be used as a point of reference. However, this approach demands that a full framestore be available for motion detection. Depending on the application, it may suffice to detect motion from the opposite field, using a single field of memory.

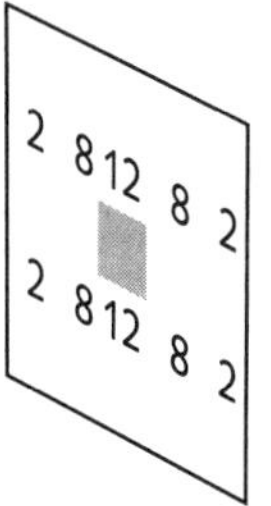

Figure 37.13 **Interstitial spatial filter coefficients**

Whether a field or a frame of memory is used to detect motion, it is important to apply a spatial lowpass filter to the available picture information, in order to prevent small details, or noise, from causing abrupt changes in the estimated motion. Figure 37.13 shows the coefficients of a spatial-lowpass filter that computes a spatial sample halfway between the scan lines. The shaded square indicates the effective location of the result. This filter requires a linestore (or a dual-ported memory). The weighted sums can be implemented by three cascaded [1, 1] sections, each of which requires a single adder.

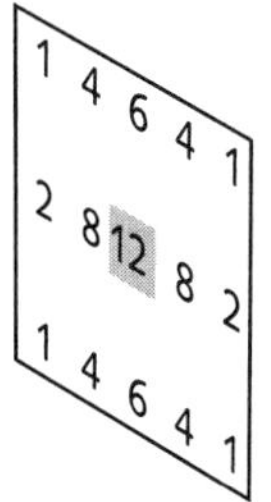

Figure 37.14 **Cosited spatial filter coefficients**

A low-pass filtered sample cosited (spatially coincident) with a scan line can be computed using the weights indicated in Figure 37.14. Again, the shaded square indicates the central sample, whose motion is being detected. This filter can also be implemented using just linestores and cascaded [1, 1] sections. The probability of motion is estimated as the absolute value of the difference between the two spatial filter results.

The spatial filters of Figure 37.13 and Figure 37.14 incorporate transverse filters having coefficients [1, 4, 6, 4, 1]. Because of the particular coefficients

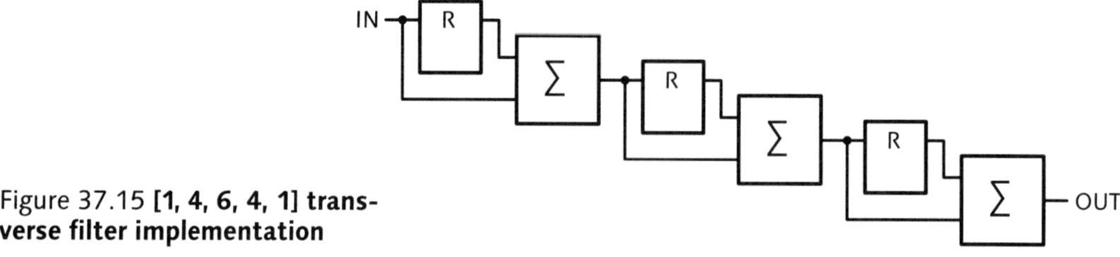

Figure 37.15 **[1, 4, 6, 4, 1] transverse filter implementation**

chosen, each of these transverse filters can be implemented using the structure shown in Figure 37.15 above, which employs three registers and three adders. The [2, 8, 12, 8, 2] filter is identical, but has its final sum shifted left one place to accomplish the multiplication by 2.

The 2-line spatial filter of Figure 37.13 can be implemented using a linestore, two [1, 4, 6, 4, 1] transverse filters, and an adder, as shown in Figure 37.16 below.

The 3-line spatial filter of Figure 37.14 can be implemented using two linestores, three [1, 4, 6, 4, 1] transverse filters – one of them having its result doubled to implement coefficients 2, 8, 12, 8, 2 – and two adders, as shown in Figure 37.17 at the top of the facing page.

A simple adaptive filter switches from interframe averaging to interfield averaging when the motion estimate exceeds some threshold. However, abrupt switching can result in artifacts: Two neighboring samples may have very similar values, but if one is judged to be stationary and the other judged to be in motion, the samples computed by the deinterlace filter may have dramatically different values. These differences can be visually

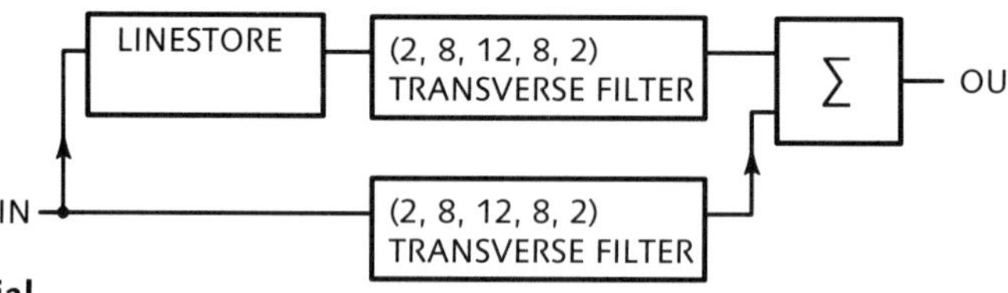

Figure 37.16 **Interstitial spatial filter implementation**

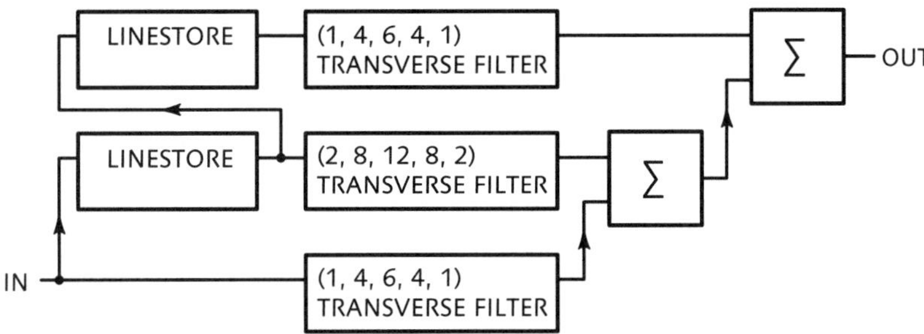

Figure 37.17 **Cosited spatial filter implementation**

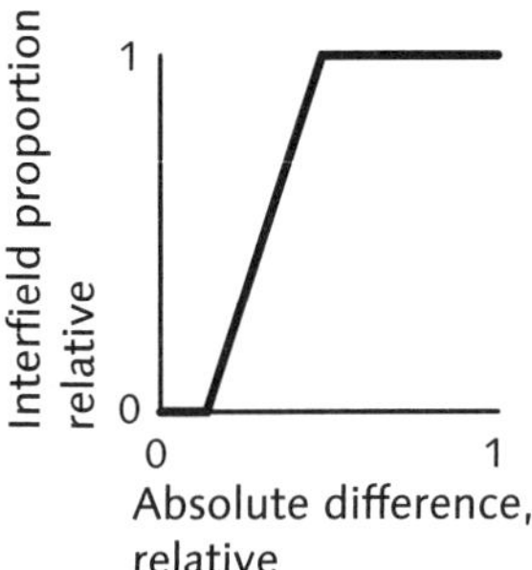

Figure 37.18 **Window function** in deinterlacing

objectionable. These artifacts can be reduced by mixing proportionally – in other words, fading – between the interframe and interfield averages instead of switching abruptly. Mixing can be controlled by a window function of the motion difference, as sketched in Figure 37.18 in the margin.

Part 3

Video compression

JPEG and motion-JPEG (M-JPEG) compression 38

This chapter describes *JPEG*, a standard for lossy compression of still images based upon the discrete cosine transform (DCT). JPEG is rarely used directly in video, but it forms the basis of M-JPEG (used in desktop video editing) and DV compression. Also, JPEG techniques form the core of MPEG.

Motion-JPEG (M-JPEG) refers to the use of a JPEG-like algorithm to compress each field or frame in a sequence of video fields or frames. M-JPEG systems use the methods of JPEG, but rarely (if ever) conform to the ISO/IEC JPEG standard. DV is a specific type of M-JPEG, which is well standardized; it is described in the following chapter, *DV compression*, on page 461. The *I-frame-only* variant of MPEG-2 is conceptually equivalent to M-JPEG, but again has a well-respected standard; see Chapter 40, on page 473.

ISO/IEC 10918, *Information Technology – Digital compression and coding of continuous-tone still images.*

The JPEG standard, cited in the margin, defines four modes: *sequential, hierarchical, progressive,* and *lossless*. The JPEG standard accommodates DCT coefficients having from 2 to 16 bits, and accommodates two different entropy coders (*Huffman* and *arithmetic*). *Baseline* refers to a defined subset of JPEG's sequential mode that is restricted to 8-bit coefficients and restricted to Huffman coding. Only baseline JPEG is commercially important. JPEG's other modes are mainly of academic interest, and won't be discussed here.

Four 8×8 Luma (Y') blocks

8×8 C_B block

8×8 C_R block

Figure 38.1 **A JPEG 4:2:0 minimum coded unit** (MCU) comprises six 8×8 blocks: a luma block, a block of C_B, and a block of C_R. The six constituent blocks result from nonlinear $R'G'B'$ data being matrixed to $Y'C_BC_R$, then subsampled according to the 4:2:0 scheme; chroma subsampling is effectively the first stage of compression. The blocks are processed independently.

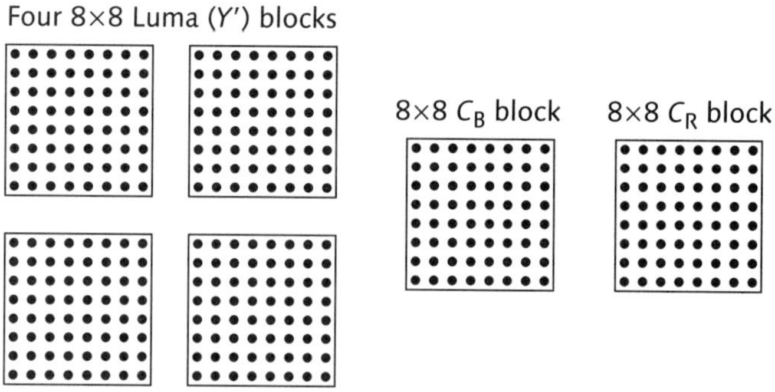

JPEG blocks and MCUs

In MPEG, a macroblock is the area covered by a 16×16 array of luma samples. In DV, a macroblock comprises the Y', C_B, and C_R blocks covered by an 8×8 array (block) of chroma samples. In JPEG, an MCU comprises those blocks covered by the minimum-sized tiling of Y', C_B, and C_R blocks. For 4:2:0 subsampling, all of these definitions are equivalent; they differ for 4:1:1 and 4:2:2 (or for JPEG's other rarely used patterns).

In desktop graphics, saving JPEG at high quality may cause $R'G'B'$ to be compressed without subsampling.

An 8×8 array of sample data is known in JPEG terminology as a *block*. Prior to JPEG compression of a color image, normally the nonlinear $R'G'B'$ data is matrixed to $Y'C_BC_R$, then subsampled 4:2:0. According to the JPEG standard (and the JFIF standard, to be described), other color subsampling schemes are possible; strangely, different subsampling ratios are permitted for C_B and C_R. However, only 4:2:0 is widely deployed, and the remainder of this discussion assumes 4:2:0. Four 8×8 luma blocks, an 8×8 block of C_B, and an 8×8 block of C_R are known in JPEG terminology as a *minimum coded unit* (MCU); this corresponds to a *macroblock* in DV or MPEG terminology. The 4:2:0 macroblock arrangement is shown in Figure 38.1 above.

Quantizer matrices and VLE tables will be described in the example starting on page 452.

The luma and color difference blocks are processed independently by JPEG, using virtually the identical algorithm. The only significant difference is that the quantizer matrix and the VLE tables used for chroma blocks are usually different from the quantizer matrix and VLE tables used for luma blocks.

I use zero-origin array indexing.

As I explained in *Spatial frequency domain* on page 188, typical images are dominated by power at low spatial frequencies. In Figure 38.4, on page 452, I present an example 8×8 array of luma samples from an image. In Figure 38.2 at the top of the facing page, I show an 8×8 array the spatial frequencies computed from this luma array through the DCT. The [0, 0] entry (the *DC term*), at the upper left-hand corner of that array

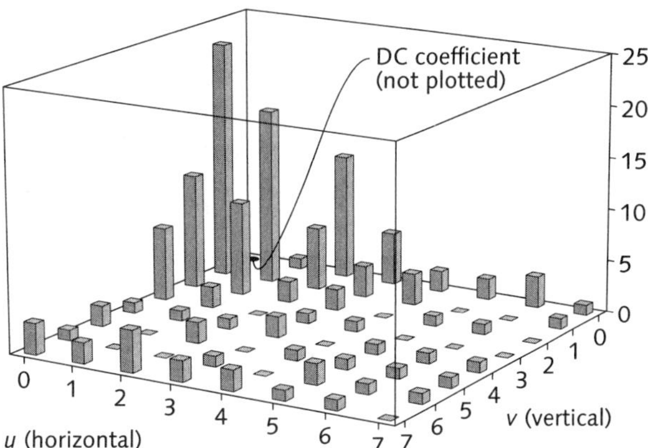

Figure 38.2 **DCT concentrates image power** at low spatial frequencies. In Figure 38.4, on page 452, I give an example 8×8 array of luma samples from an image. The magnitudes of the spatial frequency coefficients after the DCT transform are shown in this plot. Most of the image power is collected in the [0, 0] ("DC") coefficient, whose value is so large that it is omitted from this plot. Only a handful of other ("AC") coefficients are much greater than zero.

represents power at zero frequency. That entry typically contains quite a large value; it is not plotted here. Coefficients near that one tend to have fairly high values; coefficients tend to decrease in value further away from [0, 0]. Depending upon the image data, a few isolated high-frequency coefficients may have high values, as sketched at the bottom.

This typical distribution of image power, in the spatial frequency domain, represents the redundancy present in the image. The redundancy is reduced by coding the image in that domain, instead of coding the sample values of the image directly.

In addition to its benefit of removing redundancy from typical image data, representation in spatial frequency has another advantage. The lightness sensitivity of the visual system depends upon spatial frequency: We are more sensitive to low spatial frequencies than high, as can be seen from the graph in Figure 19.5, on page 201. Information at high spatial frequencies can be degraded to a large degree, without having any objectionable (or perhaps even perceptible) effect on image quality. Once image data is transformed by the DCT, high-order coefficients can be approximated – that is, coarsely quantized – to discard data corresponding to spatial frequency components that have little contribution to the perceived quality of the image.

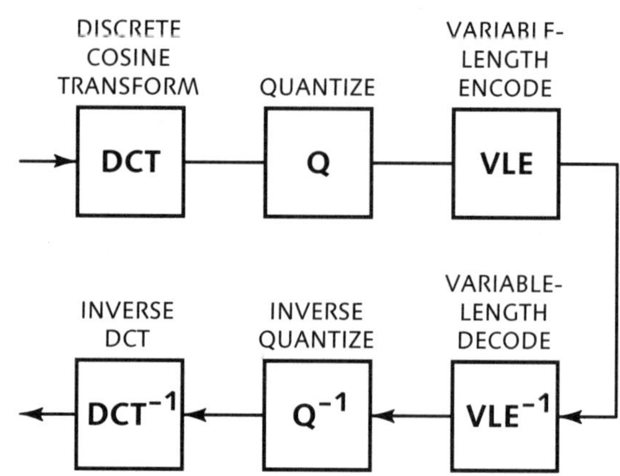

Figure 38.3 **JPEG block diagram** shows the encoder (at the top), which performs the *discrete cosine transform* (DCT), *quantization* (Q), and *variable-length encoding* (VLE). The decoder (at the bottom) performs the inverse of each of these operations, in reverse order.

In principle, the DCT algorithm could be applied to any block size, from 2×2 up to the size of the whole image, perhaps 512×512. (DCT is most efficient when applied to a matrix whose dimensions are powers of two.) The choice of 8×8 blocks of luma for the application of DCT in video represents a compromise between a block size small enough to minimize storage and processing overheads, but large enough to effectively exploit image redundancy.

The DCT operation discards picture information to which vision is insensitive. Surprisingly, though, the JPEG standard itself makes no reference to perceptual uniformity. Because JPEG's goal is to represent visually important information, it is important that so-called *RGB* values presented to the JPEG algorithm are first subject to a nonlinear transform such as that outlined in *Nonlinear image coding,* on page 12, that mimics vision.

JPEG block diagram

The JPEG block diagram in Figure 38.3 shows, at the top, the three main blocks of a JPEG encoder: the *discrete cosine transform* (DCT) computation (sometimes called *forward DCT*, FDCT), quantization (Q), and *variable-length encoding* (VLE). The decoder (at the bottom of Figure 38.3) performs the inverse of each of these operations, in reverse order. The inverse DCT is sometimes denoted *IDCT*; inverse quantization is sometimes denoted *IQ*.

Inverse quantization (IQ) has no relation to *IQ* color difference components.

Owing to the eight-line-high vertical transform, eight lines of image memory are required in the DCT subsystem of the encoder, and in the IDCT (DCT^{-1}) subsystem of the decoder. When the DCT is implemented in separable form, as is almost always the case, this is called *transpose* memory.

Level-shifting

The DCT formulation in JPEG is intended for signed sample values. In ordinary hardware or firmware, the DCT is implemented in fixed-point, two's complement arithmetic. Standard video interfaces use offset binary representation, so each luma or color difference sample is *level shifted* prior to DCT by subtracting 2^{k-1}, where k is the number of bits in use.

Discrete cosine transform (DCT)

The 8×8 forward DCT (FDCT) takes an 8×8 array of 64 sample values (denoted $\boldsymbol{f}$, whose elements are $f_{i,j}$), and produces an 8×8 array of 64 transform coefficients (denoted $\boldsymbol{F}$, whose elements are $F_{u,v}$). The FDCT is expressed by this equation:

Eq 38.1

$$F_{u,v} = \frac{1}{4} C(u) C(v) \sum_{i=0}^{7} \sum_{j=0}^{7} f_{i,j} \cos\left[\frac{(2i+1)u\pi}{16}\right] \cos\left[\frac{(2j+1)v\pi}{16}\right];$$

$$C(w) = \begin{cases} \frac{1}{\sqrt{2}}; & w = 0 \\ 1; & w = 1, 2, \ldots, 7 \end{cases}$$

The cosine terms need not be computed on-the-fly; they can be precomputed and stored in tables.

The inverse transform – the IDCT, or DCT^{-1} – is this:

Eq 38.2

$$f_{i,j} = \frac{1}{4} \sum_{u=0}^{7} \sum_{v=0}^{7} C(u) C(v) F_{u,v} \cos\left[\frac{(2i+1)u\pi}{16}\right] \cos\left[\frac{(2j+1)v\pi}{16}\right]$$

The forward and inverse transforms involve nearly identical arithmetic: The complexity of encoding and decoding is very similar. The DCT is its own inverse (within a scale factor), so performing the DCT on the transform coefficients would perfectly reconstruct the original samples, subject only to the roundoff error in the DCT and IDCT.

If implemented directly according to these equations, an 8×8 DCT requires 64 multiply operations (and 49 additions) for each of the 64 result coefficients, for a total of 4096 multiplies, an average of 8 multiplication operations per pixel. However, the DCT is *separable:* an 8×8 DCT can be computed as eight 8×1 horizontal transforms followed by eight 1×8 vertical transforms. This optimization, combined with other optimizations comparable to those of the fast Fourier transform (FFT), greatly reduces computational complexity: A fully optimized 8×8 DCT requires as few as 11 multiplies for each 8 samples (or in an IDCT, transform coefficients).

JPEG encoding example

I will illustrate JPEG encoding by walking through a numerical example. Figure 38.4 represents an 8×8 array of luma samples from an image, prior to level shifting:

Figure 38.4 **An 8×8 array of luma samples** from an image is shown. This 8×8 array is known in JPEG terminology as a *block*.

$$f = \begin{bmatrix} 139 & 144 & 149 & 153 & 155 & 155 & 155 & 155 \\ 144 & 151 & 153 & 156 & 159 & 156 & 156 & 156 \\ 150 & 155 & 160 & 163 & 158 & 156 & 156 & 156 \\ 159 & 161 & 162 & 160 & 160 & 159 & 159 & 159 \\ 159 & 160 & 161 & 162 & 162 & 155 & 155 & 155 \\ 161 & 161 & 161 & 161 & 160 & 157 & 157 & 157 \\ 162 & 162 & 161 & 163 & 162 & 157 & 157 & 157 \\ 162 & 162 & 161 & 161 & 163 & 158 & 158 & 158 \end{bmatrix}$$

The result of computing the DCT, rounded to integers, is shown in Figure 38.5:

Figure 38.5 **DCT tends to concentrate** the power of the image block into low-frequency DCT coefficients (those coefficients in the upper left-hand corner of the matrix). No information is lost at this stage. The DCT is its own inverse, so performing the DCT on these transform coefficients would reconstruct the original samples (subject only to roundoff error).

$$F = \begin{bmatrix} 1260 & -1 & -12 & -5 & 2 & -2 & -3 & 1 \\ -23 & -17 & -6 & -3 & -3 & 0 & 0 & 1 \\ -11 & -9 & -2 & 2 & 0 & -1 & -1 & 0 \\ -7 & -2 & 0 & 1 & 1 & 0 & 0 & 0 \\ -1 & -1 & 1 & 2 & 0 & -1 & 1 & 1 \\ 2 & 0 & 2 & 0 & -1 & 1 & 1 & -1 \\ -1 & 0 & 0 & -1 & 0 & 2 & 1 & -1 \\ -3 & 2 & -4 & -2 & 2 & 1 & -1 & 0 \end{bmatrix}$$

This example shows that image power is concentrated into low-frequency transform coefficients – that is, those coefficients in the upper left-hand corner of the DCT matrix. No information is lost at this stage. The DCT is its own inverse, so performing the DCT a second time would perfectly reconstruct the original samples, subject only to the roundoff error in the DCT and IDCT.

In MPEG-2, DC terms can be coded with 8, 9, or 10 bits – or, in 4:2:2 profile, 11 bits – of precision.

As expressed in Equation 38.1, the arithmetic of an 8×8 DCT effectively causes the coefficient values to be multiplied by a factor of 8 relative to the original sample values. The value 1260 in the [0, 0] entry – the *DC* coefficient, or term – is ⅛ of the sum of the original sample values. (All of the other coefficients are referred to as *AC*.)

The human visual system is not very sensitive to information at high spatial frequencies. Information at high spatial frequencies can be discarded, to some degree, without introducing noticeable impairments. JPEG uses a *quantizer matrix* (***Q***), which codes a step size for each of the 64 spatial frequencies. In the quantization step of compression, each transform coefficient is divided by the corresponding quantizer value (step size) entry in the ***Q*** matrix. The remainder (fraction) after division is discarded.

It is not the DCT itself, but the discarding of the fraction after quantization of the transform coefficients, that makes JPEG lossy!

In MPEG, default quantizer matrices are standardized, but they can be overridden by matrices conveyed in the bitstream.

JPEG has no standard or default quantizer matrix; however, sample matrices given in a nonnormative appendix are often used. Typically, there are two matrices, one for luma and one for color differences.

An example ***Q*** matrix is shown in Figure 38.6 overleaf. Its entries form a radially symmetric version of Figure 19.5, on page 201. The [0, 0] entry in the quantizer matrix is relatively small (here, 16), so the DC term is finely quantized. Further from [0, 0], the entries get larger, and the quantization becomes more coarse. Owing to the large step sizes associated with the high-order coefficients, they can be represented fewer bits.

$$
Q = \begin{bmatrix}
16 & 11 & 10 & 16 & 24 & 40 & 51 & 61 \\
12 & 12 & 14 & 19 & 26 & 58 & 60 & 55 \\
14 & 13 & 16 & 24 & 40 & 57 & 69 & 56 \\
14 & 17 & 22 & 29 & 51 & 87 & 80 & 62 \\
18 & 22 & 37 & 56 & 68 & 109 & 103 & 77 \\
24 & 35 & 55 & 64 & 81 & 104 & 113 & 92 \\
49 & 64 & 78 & 87 & 103 & 121 & 120 & 101 \\
72 & 92 & 95 & 98 & 112 & 100 & 103 & 99
\end{bmatrix}
$$

Figure 38.6 **Typical JPEG quantizer matrix** reflects the visual system's poor sensitivity to high spatial frequencies. Transform coefficients can be approximated, to some degree, without introducing noticeable impairments. The quantizer matrix codes a step size for each spatial frequency. Each transform coefficient is divided by the corresponding quantizer value; the remainder (or fraction) is discarded. Discarding the fraction is what makes JPEG lossy.

In the JPEG and MPEG standards, and in most JPEG-like schemes, each entry in the quantizer matrix takes a value between 1 and 255.

At first glance, the large step size associated with the DC coefficient (here, $Q_{0,0} = 16$) looks worrisome: With 8-bit data ranging from –127 to +128, owing to the divisor of 16, you might expect this quantized coefficient to be be represented with just 4 bits. However, as I mentioned earlier, the arithmetic of Equation 38.1 scales the coefficients by 8 with respect to the sample values, so a quantizer value of 16 corresponds to 7 bits of precision when referenced to the sample values.

DCT coefficients after quantization, and after discarding the quotient fractions, are shown in Figure 38.7:

Figure 38.7 **DCT coefficients after quantization** are shown. Most of the high-frequency information in this block – DCT entries at the right and the bottom of the matrix – are quantized to zero. The nonzero coefficients have small magnitudes.

$$
F^* = \begin{bmatrix}
79 & 0 & -1 & 0 & 0 & 0 & 0 & 0 \\
-2 & -1 & 0 & 0 & 0 & 0 & 0 & 0 \\
-1 & -1 & 0 & 0 & 0 & 0 & 0 & 0 \\
0 & 0 & 0 & 0 & 0 & 0 & 0 & 0 \\
0 & 0 & 0 & 0 & 0 & 0 & 0 & 0 \\
0 & 0 & 0 & 0 & 0 & 0 & 0 & 0 \\
0 & 0 & 0 & 0 & 0 & 0 & 0 & 0 \\
0 & 0 & 0 & 0 & 0 & 0 & 0 & 0
\end{bmatrix}
$$

Most of the high-frequency information in this block – the DCT entries at the right and the bottom of the matrix – are quantized to zero. Apart from the DC term, the nonzero coefficients have small magnitudes.

Following quantization, the quantized coefficients are rearranged according to the likely distribution of image power in the block. This is accomplished by *zigzag scanning*, sketched in Figure 38.8:

Figure 38.8 **Zigzag scanning** is used to rearrange quantized coefficients according to the likely distribution of image power in the block.

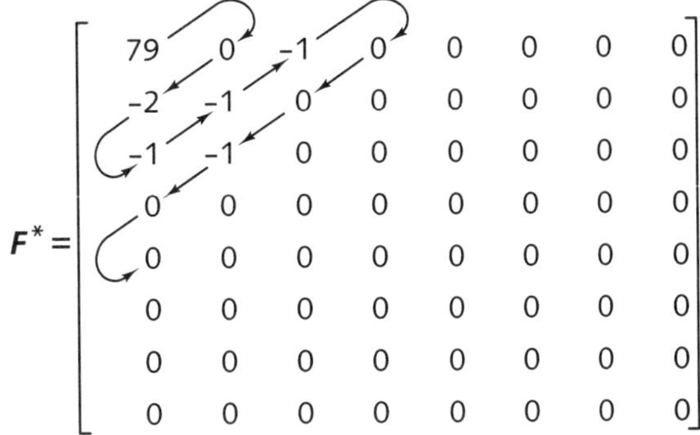

Once rearranged, the quantized coefficients are represented in a one-dimensional string; an *end of block* (EOB) code marks the location in the string where all succeeding coefficients are zero, as sketched in Figure 38.9:

79	0	–2	–1	–1	–1	0	0	–1	EOB

Figure 38.9 **Zigzag-scanned coefficient string**

In the usual case that just a few high-order quantized coefficients are nonzero, zigzag reordering tends to produce strings of repeating zeros. Additional compression can be accomplished by using *variable-length encoding* (VLE, also known as *Huffman* coding). Variable-length encoding is a lossless process that takes advantage of the statistics of the "run length" (the count of zero codes) and the "level" (absolute value, or magnitude) of the following transform coefficient.

In JPEG and MPEG terminology, the magnitude (absolute value) of a coefficient is called its *level*.

The DC term is treated specially: It is differentially coded. The first DC term is coded directly (using a DC VLE table), but successive DC terms are coded as differences from that. In essence, the previous DC term is used as a predictor for the current term. Separate predictors are maintained for Y', C_B, and C_R.

Zero AC coefficients are collapsed, and the string is represented in {run length, level} pairs, as shown in Figure 38.10:

{1: –2}, {0: –1}, {0: –1}, {0: –1}, {2: –1}, EOB

Figure 38.10 **VLE {run length, level} pairs**

MPEG's VLE tables are standardized; they do not need to be transmitted with each sequence or each picture.

A JPEG encoder has one or more VLE tables that map the set of {run length, level} pairs to variable-length bitstrings; pairs with high probability are assigned short bitstrings. JPEG has no standard VLE tables; however, sample tables given in a nonnormative appendix are often used. Typically, there are two tables, one for luma and one for color differences. The tables used for an image are included at the head of the JPEG bitstream, and thereby conveyed to the decoder.

JPEG decoding

Decompression is achieved by performing the inverse of the encoder operations, in reverse order. Figure 38.11 shows the matrix of differences between original sample values and reconstructed sample values for this example – the reconstruction error. As is typical of JPEG, the original sample values are not perfectly reconstructed. However, discarding information according to the spatial frequency response of human vision ensures that the errors introduced during compression will not be too perceptible.

$$\varepsilon = \begin{bmatrix} -5 & -2 & 0 & 1 & 1 & -1 & -1 & -1 \\ -4 & 1 & 1 & 2 & 3 & 0 & 0 & 0 \\ -5 & -1 & 3 & 5 & 0 & -1 & 0 & 1 \\ -1 & 0 & 1 & -2 & -1 & 0 & 2 & 4 \\ -4 & -3 & -3 & -1 & 0 & -5 & -3 & -1 \\ -2 & -2 & -3 & -3 & -2 & -3 & -1 & 0 \\ 2 & 1 & -1 & 1 & 0 & -4 & -2 & -1 \\ 4 & 3 & 0 & 0 & 1 & -3 & -1 & 0 \end{bmatrix}$$

Figure 38.11 **Reconstruction error** is shown in this matrix of differences between original sample values and reconstructed sample values. Original sample values are not perfectly reconstructed, but discarding information according to the spatial frequency response of human vision ensures that the errors will not be too perceptible.

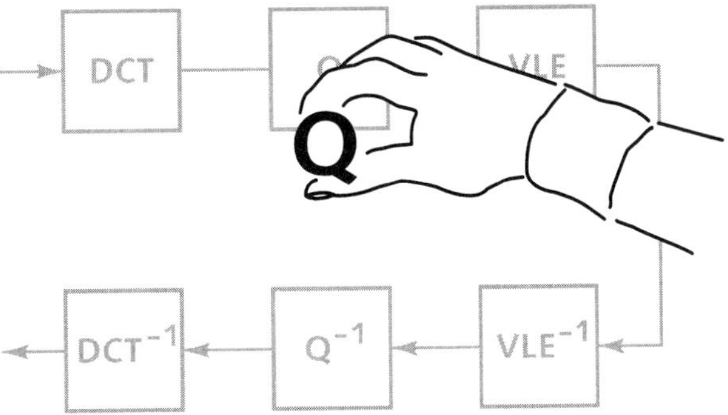

Figure 38.12 **Compression ratio control in JPEG** is effected by altering the quantizer matrix: The larger the entries in the quantizer matrix, the higher the compression ratio. The higher the compression ratio, the higher the reconstruction error. At some point, compression artifacts will become visible.

JPEG performance is loosely characterized by the error between the original image data and the reconstructed data. Metric such as mean-squared error (MSE) are used to objectify this measure; however, MSE (and other engineering and mathematical measures) don't necessarily correlate well with subjective performance. In practice, we take care to choose quantizer matrices according to the properties of perception. Imperfect recovery of the original image data after JPEG decompression effectively adds noise to the image. Imperfect reconstruction of the DC term can lead to JPEG's 8×8 blocks becoming visible – the JPEG *blocking artifact.*

The lossiness of JPEG, and its compression, come almost entirely from the quantizer step. The DCT itself may introduce a small amount of roundoff error; the inverse DCT may also introduce a slight roundoff error. The variable-length encoding and decoding processes are perfectly lossless.

Compression ratio control

The larger the entries in the quantizer matrix, the higher the compression ratio. Compression ratio control in JPEG can be achieved by altering the quantizer matrix, as suggested by the manual control sketched in Figure 38.12. Larger step sizes give higher compression ratios, but image quality is liable to suffer if the step sizes get too big. Smaller step sizes give better quality, at the expense of poorer compression ratio. There is no easy way to predict, in advance of actually performing the compression, how many bytes of compressed data will result from a particular image.

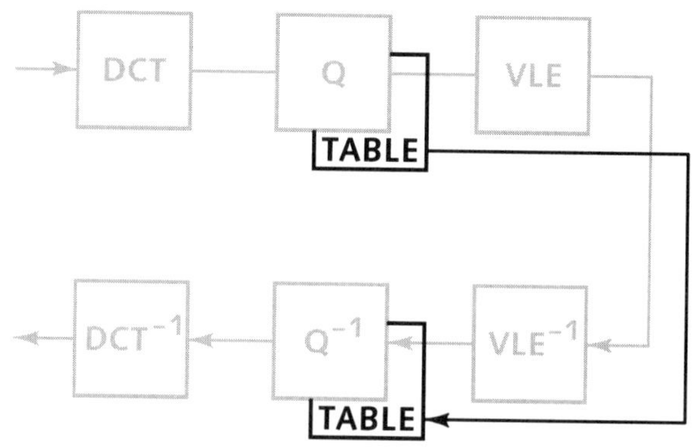

Figure 38.13 **Because the quantizer is adjustable,** the quantizer matrix must be conveyed through a side channel to the decoder. In color images, separate quantizer are used for the luma and chroma components.

In ISO JPEG, the quantizer matrix is directly conveyed in the bitstream. In the DV adaptation of JPEG, several quantizer matrices are defined in the standard; the bitstream indicates which one to use.

The quantizer matrix could, in principle, be chosen adaptively to maximize the performance for a particular image. However, this isn't practical. JPEG encoders for still images generally offer a choice of several compression settings, each associated with a fixed quantizer that is chosen by the system designer.

Because different quantizer matrices may be associated with different images, the quantizer matrix must be conveyed to the decoder, as sketched in Figure 38.13, either as part of the file, or through a side channel. In color images, separate quantizers are typically used for the luma and chroma components. In stillframe applications, the overhead of this operation is small. In a realtime system, the overhead of conveying quantizer matrices with every frame, or even within a frame, is a burden.

The notation *mquant* is found in the ITU-T H.261 standard for teleconferencing; *mquant* (or *MQUANT*) is not found in JPEG or MPEG documents, but is used informally.

A modified approach to compression ratio control is adopted in many forms of M-JPEG (and also, as you will see in the next chapter, in MPEG): Reference luma and chroma quantizer matrices are established, and all of their entries are scaled up and down by a single numerical parameter, the *quantizer scale factor* (QSF, sometimes denoted *Mquant*). The QSF is varied to accomplish rate control.

As I mentioned, JPEG ordinarily uses luma/chroma coding, and 4:2:0 chroma subsampling. But the JPEG standard accommodates *R'G'B'* image data without subsampling, and also accommodates four-channel image data (such as CMYK, used in print) without subsampling. These schemes are inapplicable to video.

JPEG/JFIF

The ISO/IEC standard for JPEG defines a bitstream, consistent with the original expectation that JPEG would be used across communication links. To apply the JPEG technique to computer files, a small amount of additional information was required; in addition, it is necessary to encode the ISO/IEC *bit*stream into a *byte*stream. The de facto standard for single-image JPEG files is the *JPEG file interchange format* (JFIF), adopted by an industry group led by C-Cube. A JFIF file encapsulates a JPEG bitstream, along with a small amount of supplementary data. If you are presented with an image data file described as JPEG, it is almost certainly an ISO/IEC JPEG bitstream in a JFIF wrapper. (On a Macintosh, it could be in a PICT wrapper.)

Hamilton, Eric, *JPEG File Interchange Format*, Version 1.02 (Milpitas, Calif.: C-Cube Microsystems, 1992).

The ITU community has responded to the deployment of industry-standard JFIF with SPIFF, which is forward compatible with JFIF. SPIFF is not yet widely deployed; it remains to be seen whether it will ever be.

ITU-T T.84, *Digital compression and coding of continuous-tone still images: Extensions.*

The JPEG standard itself implies that JPEG could be applied to linear-light *RGB* data. However, JPEG has poor visual performance unless applied to perceptually coded image data, that is, to gamma-corrected *R'G'B'*.

The ISO/IEC JPEG standard itself seems to suggest that the technique can be applied to arbitrary *RGB* data. The standard itself fails to mention primary chromaticities, white point, transfer function, or gamma correction. If accurate color is to be achieved, then means outside the standard must be employed to convey these parameters. In practice, there are two classes of JPEG/JFIF files, PC and Macintosh. Files that were created on a PC generally conform to sRGB coding. Files that were created on a Macintosh generally conform to the default Macintosh coding, where *R'G'B'* codes are expected to be raised to the 1.72 power and displayed in a relatively light environment. There is no reliable way to distinguish the two classes of files.

Motion-JPEG (M-JPEG)

Motion-JPEG (M-JPEG) refers to the use of a JPEG-like algorithm to compress every picture in a sequence of video fields or frames. I say "JPEG-like": The algorithms used have all of the general features of the algorithm standardized by JPEG, including DCT, quantization, zig-zag scanning, and variable-length encoding. However, ISO JPEG bitstreams are not typically produced, and some systems add algorithmic features outside of the JPEG standard. Various M-JPEG systems are widely used in desktop video editing; however, there are no well established standards, and compressed video files typically cannot be interchanged between M-JPEG systems.

In studio applications, file interchange is a practical necessity, and two approaches have emerged. Both are functionally equivalent to M-JPEG, but have firm standards.

The first approach is DV compression, developed for consumer digital recording on videotape, but now quite widely used in desktop video editing. DV compression is described in the following chapter.

The second approach is MPEG-2 video compression, described in the succeeding chapter (starting on page 473). MPEG-2 was developed to exploit inter-frame coherence to achieve much higher compression ratios than M-JPEG, and is intended mainly for video distribution. However, the I-picture-only variant of MPEG-2 (sometimes called *I-frame-only*) is functionally equivalent to M-JPEG, and is being used for studio editing.

A few studio DVTR formats, such as Digital Betacam and HD-D5, use M-JPEG-style compression, but are not intimately related to any of JPEG, DV or MPEG.

Further reading

Rabbani, Majid, and Paul W. Jones, *Digital Image Compression Techniques* (Bellingham, Wash.: SPIE, 1991).

Rabbani and Jones have written an excellent introduction to the mathematics of still image compression.

DV compression 39

DV denotes the compression and data packing scheme used in consumer *digital video cassette* (DVC) recorders and their professional derivatives. DV compression uses discrete cosine transform (DCT), quantization, and variable-length encoding (VLE) comparable to JPEG; however, DV does not *conform* to the JPEG standard: Optimizations have been made to accommodate interlaced scanning, constant bit-rate (CBR) operation, and other features related to videotape recording. Interlace is handled by allowing the encoder to dynamically choose between frame and field modes. Constant bit-rate is achieved by dynamically altering the quantization matrices to avoid exceeding the available capacity.

Concerning DVC recording, see page 422. D-7 is the SMPTE standard corresponding to DVCPRO and DVCPRO 50; D-9 corresponds to Digital-S.

Consumer DVC has a data rate of 25 Mb/s. I call this *DV25*. DV25 coding was adopted for studio use in D-7 (DVCPRO) and DVCAM; it was extended to 50 Mb/s (*DV50*), used in the DVCPRO50 and D-9 systems, and then to 100 Mb/s (*DV100*), used in D-11 (DVCPRO HD).

DV records either 480*i*29.97 or 576*i*25, according to the sampling parameters of Rec. 601. Chroma subsampling in DV is a smorgasbord; see Table 39.1.

	480*i*	576*i*
DV25 (consumer, DVCAM)	4:1:1	4:2:0
DV25 (D-7)	4:1:1	4:1:1
DV50 (DVCPRO50, D-9)	4:2:2	4:2:2

Table 39.1 **DV chroma subsampling**

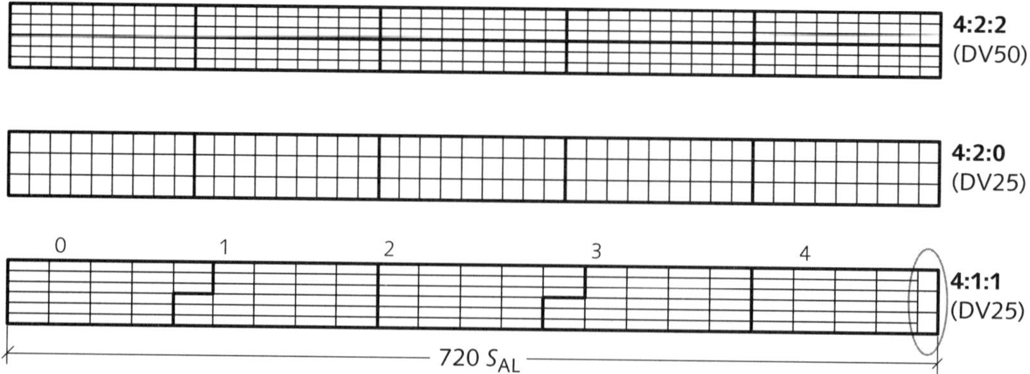

Figure 39.1 **DV superblocks** are shown for three chroma subsampling schemes – 4:2:2 (top), 4:2:0 (middle), and 4:1:1 (bottom). Thin lines enclose *macroblocks.* Each macroblock contains an 8×8 block of C_B, an 8×8 block of C_R, and two or more 8×8 blocks of luma. Thick lines enclose *superblocks;* each superblock comprises 27 macroblocks. A 4:1:1 macroblock is about four times wider than it is tall.

DV chroma subsampling

On page 468, I will discuss DV's SDL and HD modes, which use 3:1:0 and 3:1:1 subsampling, respectively.

Different versions of DV use different subsampling schemes: 4:2:2, 4:1:1, 4:2:0, and even 3:1:1 and 3:1:0! In DV, a macroblock comprises an 8×8 block of C_B samples, an 8×8 block of C_R samples, and the requisite number and arrangement of 8×8 blocks of luma samples.

SMPTE 314M defines DV25 and DV50 for studio use. The Blue Book, and IEC standards, use the word *decimated* instead of *discarded.*

SMPTE 314M declares that in subsampling 4:2:2 to 4:1:1, "every other pixel is discarded." Obviously, high image quality requires that proper filtering be performed before discarding samples. But even if proper filtering is performed, C_R samples in DV are not centered at the same locations as C_B samples. In DV's 4:1:1 subsampling, a C_R sample is centered two image columns to the right of the associated C_B sample. In DV's 4:2:0 subsampling, a C_R sample is centered two image rows below the associated C_B sample (with respect to the frame).

The DV format originated for consumer applications. Consumer DV25 aggregates 27 macroblocks into a *superblock* (SB), covering 48 image rows, whose arrangement is depicted in Figure 39.1 above. In 480*i*29.97 DV25, there are 50 superblocks per frame; in 576*i*25 DV25, there are 60 superblocks per frame.

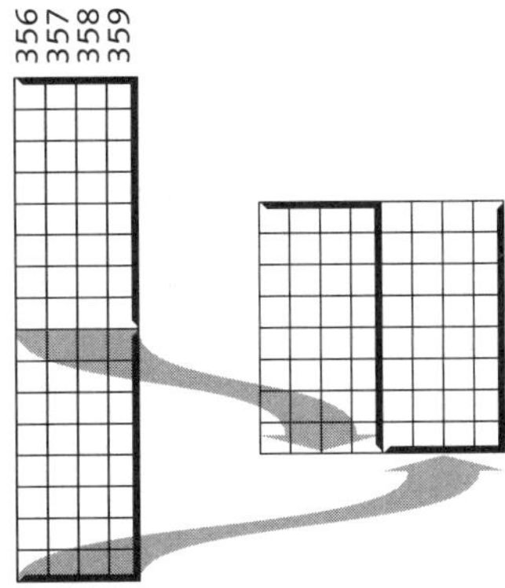

Figure 39.2 **Chroma samples in 4:1:1 DV** require special treatment at the right-hand edge of the picture. Here I show chroma as if square-sampled; actually, each 4:1:1 chroma sample is about four times wider than tall.

For consumer 576*i*25 DV25, and the 576*i*25 variant of DVCAM, 4:2:0 chroma subsampling was chosen, allegedly to offer some compatibility with DVB. The 4:2:0 superblock structure is shown in the middle sketch of Figure 39.1; in 4:2:0, each superblock comprises a regular array of 9×3 macroblocks.

For consumer 480*i*29.97 DV25, 4:1:1 subsampling was chosen. This was sufficient to achieve NTSC chroma bandwidth, and avoided conflict between subsampling and interlace. Rec. 601 video adapted to 4:1:1 subsampling has 180 active chroma samples per line; however, 180 isn't divisible by 8, so a regular superblock structure wasn't possible. To form 8×8 chroma blocks, C_B and C_R samples at the right-hand edge of the image are treated strangely, as detailed in Figure 39.2 in the margin: Pairs of vertically adjacent 4×8 arrays of chroma samples from the right end of each line are abutted horizontally to form 8×8 blocks.

The studio version of DV25 (used in D-7) uses 4:1:1 chroma subsampling in both 480*i*29.97 and 576*i*25; the strange 4:1:1 superblock structure is used.

DV50 has twice the data rate of DV25. DV50 uses 4:2:2 chroma subsampling for both 480*i*29.97 and 576*i*25. Owing to 4:2:2 subsampling, each macroblock has four blocks (instead of the six blocks of either 4:1:1 or 4:2:0); a frame has twice as many macroblocks as DV25, and twice as many superblocks. The 4:2:2 superblock structure is depicted in the top sketch of Figure 39.1. Today's DV50 recorders are implemented using two DV25 encoders, processing alternate 24-row bands of the image; they record the resulting two channels to parallel tracks.

DV frame/field modes

ISO JPEG assumes a progressive source image: All image rows are processed in spatial order. In video, the two fields of an interlaced frame can be woven together and processed as if progressive, where every 8×8 block has alternate rows taken from opposite fields. Providing interfield motion is limited, this scheme works well. In the presence of interfield motion, though, the high vertical frequency AC coefficients produced by the DCT will have high magnitude. This produces low quality for a given data rate. Higher quality can be obtained if the fields are coded separately. DV dynamically adapts to the degree of interfield motion by allowing the compressor to choose, on a block-by-block basis, whether to use *8-8-DCT mode* or *2-4-8-DCT mode*.

See *weave*, on page 438.

In 8-8-DCT ("frame") mode, opposite fields are woven together and subject to a single DCT as an 8×8 block.

This scheme involves two 8×4 DCTs; it should be called *2-8-4-DCT!* MPEG-2 has a similar scheme: An encoder can choose *frame DCT coding* or *field DCT coding* for each macroblock in an interlaced MPEG-2 sequence.

In 2-4-8-DCT ("field") mode, two 8×4 arrays of samples from like fields are formed. The element-by-element sums of the two 8×4 arrays, and their element-by-element differences, are subject to separate DCTs. The sum matrix is associated with a DC term; the difference array has only AC terms. Each of the sum and difference DCT arrays is zigzag scanned, and the coefficients are alternated for joint VLE encoding.

DV standards do not dictate how an encoder is to choose between 8-8-DCT and 2-4-8-DCT modes. Typically, luma differences are analyzed in the spatial domain to detect interfield motion, and 2-4-8-DCT mode is chosen if interfield motion is significant.

Picture-in-shuttle in DV

I described sync blocks on page 417.

It is a practical necessity that a VCR recover a usable picture in fast forward and rewind ("shuttle"). When a digital VCR is operating in shuttle mode, isolated sync blocks are read from the tape. In DV, recovering a usable picture in shuttle mode is made possible by having each sync block correspond to one *coded macroblock* (CM); an entire macroblock can thereby be reconstructed individually from an isolated sync block. This scheme precludes predictive coding of the DCT's DC terms: DC terms are represented directly in each CM.

The correspondence of sync blocks with coded macroblocks seems to require that *every* macroblock be coded into a fixed number of bits. In the DV system, every macroblock is associated with a 77-byte coded macroblock, and a sync block contains one CM. Each CM contains the DC term, and several AC terms, of each block's DCT. However, that's not the whole story.

DV overflow scheme

When a portion of an image is devoid of detail, a few low-frequency AC coefficients of its DCT may have significant magnitude, but nearly all high-frequency AC terms will have very small magnitude. When a portion of an image has a lot of fine detail, many high-frequency AC terms will have large magnitude. To reproduce the image accurately requires that these terms be recorded. Generally, increasing amounts of detail require increased data capacity.

It is unusual for an image to contain detail everywhere; typically, complexity is spatially concentrated in an image. A compression algorithm should adapt to the spatial distribution of image detail, by allocating bits where they are needed. If fine detail is distributed throughout an image – in a full-frame image of the leaves of a tree, perhaps – then even quite large reconstruction errors are likely to be imperceptible.

The requirement for picture-in-shuttle seems to preclude allocation of data capacity to the regions where more bits are required. However, DV implements an overflow scheme whereby the bits resulting from compression of a handful of macroblocks are shared among a handful of CMs. Should the VLE-coded AC coefficients for a complex block (augmented by a 4-bit EOB) require more bits than the fixed capacity assigned to that block in the CM, the overflow bits "spill" into other blocks whose capacity was not filled. Overflow data first spills into space that might remain in other blocks of the same CM; any remaining bits spill into available space in any of four other CMs associated with diverse regions of the image. The set of five coded macroblocks that share overflow space is called a *segment;* a segment has a fixed capacity of 385 bytes. The macroblocks of a segment are spatially distributed throughout the frame: No two macroblocks are taken from the same row or the same column of superblocks. This distribution exploits the statistical likelihood that only one or two of the macroblocks will be complex.

CMs in a segment are denoted *a* through *e*.

When a DV VCR is in shuttle mode, it is quite likely that a single CM will be recovered individually, without any of the other four CMs of its segment. Overflow data for the macroblock is quite likely to be missing. However, overflow data is limited to high-frequency AC coefficients. In shuttle playback, missing overflow coefficients are replaced by zero. This causes loss of picture detail in the reconstructed picture; however, the absence of these coefficients does not seriously degrade picture quality, and in any event users do not expect the same picture quality in shuttle mode as in normal playback.

DV quantization

The main challenge of DV encoding is to determine suitable quantization matrices for a segment's AC coefficients, such that when all of the quantized coefficients are subject to variable-length encoding, the VLE-coded coefficients just neatly fit in the available space. The goal is to quantize the AC terms as finely as possible, without exceeding the capacity of a segment. In essence, this is a form of rate control. Quantization of a segment takes place after the DCT, using this algorithm:

- First, each block in the segment is assigned to a *class* from 0 (fine) to 3 (coarse), representing the block's spatial complexity. DV standards provide a table that suggests how an encoder can assign a class number according to the magnitude of the largest AC term of a block; however, use of that algorithm is not mandatory.

- Then, up to 15 trial quantization passes are made, to determine a *quantization number* (QNO) from 0 (coarse) to 15 (fine). Class number and quantization number are combined to determine a quantization matrix according to tables in the standard. For each trial QNO, DCT coefficients are quantized and zigzag scanned. Nonzero AC coefficient are identified; {run length, level} pairs are computed for each nonzero coefficient; and the required number of variable-length-encoded bits is accumulated. Quantization is eased by the fact that the entries in the quantization matrices are all powers of two (1, 2, 4, 8, 16); each coefficient quantization opera-

What DV standards call *level* is the magnitude (i.e., absolute value) of the AC coefficient. Sign is coded separately.

tion is merely a binary shift. The lookup and assembly of VLE-coded bitstream need not be performed at this stage; it suffices for now to accumulate the bit count.

For a more elaborate description, and the quantization tables, see Symes, cited on page 496.

The final QNO for the segment is the one that produces the largest number of bits not exceeding the capacity of the segment – for DV25, 500 bits for luma AC coefficients (including four 4-bit EOBs), and 340 bits for chroma AC coefficients (including two 4-bit EOBs).

Once the segment's QNO is determined, VLE coding takes place, and the CMs of the segment are assembled. Each CM starts with one byte containing its QNO and error concealment *status* (STA) bits. Each block includes its DC coefficient, its mode (8-8-DCT or 2-4-8-DCT), and its class. Finally, the VLE-coded AC coefficients are distributed in a deterministic three-pass algorithm – first to the associated block, then to unused space in other blocks of the same CM (if space is available), and finally to unused space in other CMs of the segment. QNO has been chosen such that sufficient space for all coefficients is guaranteed to be available: Every bit of every coefficient will be stored somewhere within the segment.

This scheme is described as *three-pass;* however, the first pass is trivial.

Each CM comprises 77 bytes, including by a 1-byte header. In DV25, a CM includes four coded luma blocks and two coded chroma blocks:

- A coded luma block totals 14 bytes, and includes a 9-bit DC term, one mode bit, and a 2-bit class number. One hundred bits are available for AC coefficients.

- A coded chroma block totals 10 bytes, and includes a 9-bit DC term, one mode bit, and a 2-bit class number. Sixty-eight bits are available for AC coefficients.

For 4:2:2 subsampling in DV50, a CM has four blocks, not six; space that in 4:1:1 or 4:2:0 would be allocated to luma blocks is available for overflow data. For 3:1:0 subsampling (used in SDL, to be described in a moment), a CM has eight blocks, not six: Each luma block has 10 bytes; each chroma block has 8 bytes.

Consumer DV variants – SD, LP, SDL, HD

For consumer applications, a DV25 bitstream can be recorded in one of two modes, *SD* (standard definition) or *long play* (LP). Two additional modes, SDL and HD, are used for different bit rates. The four systems are summarized in Table 39.2 below, which includes digital interface parameters to be described in a moment.

DV SD

SD refers to *standard definition* mode.

DV LP

LP refers to *long play* mode, sometimes referred to as *LP mode, narrow track pitch*. This is identical to SD mode, except for track pitch, as described on page 424.

DV SDL

SDL stands for *standard definition, long play* mode (or *SD high compression*). In SDL, luma is downsampled to 540 S_{AL}. In addition, chroma is subsampled vertically, yielding a 3:1:0 subsampling structure with respect to downsampled luma. Audio is limited to two channels, sampled at 32 kHz. These factors combine to allow data rate – and consequently, tape speed – to be reduced to half that of SD mode. (I call this *DV12½*.) This yields twice the recording time as SD for a given tape length.

	SDL		*LP*		*SD*		*HD*	
Blue Book part	Part 5		Part 1 Annex A		Part 2		Part 3	
L_T	525	625	525	625	525	625	1125	1250
L_A	480	576	480	576	480	576	1024	1152
S_{AL}	540		720		720		1008	
Chroma format	3:1:0	3:1:0	4:1:1	4:2:0	4:1:1	4:2:0	3:1:1	3:1:1
Bit rate (approx.), Mb/s	12.5		25		25		50	
Tape speed, mm/s	$\frac{9.424}{1.001}$	9.424	$\frac{12.568}{1.001}$	12.568	$\frac{18.831}{1.001}$	18.831	37.594	37.594
Track pitch, μm	10		6.67		10		10	
Tracks/frame	5	6	10	12	10	12	20	24
DIF blocks/source packet	3		6		6		12	
Bytes/source packet	240		480		480		960	
Packets/DIF sequence	50		25		25		25	
DIF sequences/s	$5/1.001$	6	$10/1.001$	12	$10/1.001$	12	10	12

Table 39.2 **Consumer DV variants** are summarized.

DV HD

HD stands for *high definition.* The "Blue Book" and the IEC standards define an adaptation of DV coding at 50 Mb/s for consumer HDTV. At 30 Hz frame rate, the system could be denoted 1024*i*30.00, or at 25 Hz frame rate, 1152*i*25. The image arrays are, respectively, 1008×1024 and 1008×1152. Chroma is subsampled 3:1:1. This format has double the bit rate of SD, double the tape speed, and consequently half the program duration for tape of a given length. There is no strong engineering argument that 1024*i*30 offers superior performance to 720*p*60; however, the scheme was developed during a time when Japanese manufacturers denied the superiority of progressive scanning. DV HD is unlikely to be commercialized: It is likely to be rendered obsolete by direct recording of DTV MPEG-2 transport bitstreams as I outlined on page 427.

Professional DV variants

In *Studio adaptation of DV technology,* on page 425, I outlined adaptations of the DV system for studio use.

DV25 is used for studio SDTV in D-7 (DVCPRO) and DVCAM equipment.

DV50 has twice the data rate, twice as many macroblocks per second (or per frame), and twice as many superblocks per second (or per frame) as DV25. DV50 uses 4:2:2 subsampling; a CM contains just two luma blocks instead of four. Space that in DV25 would have been allocated to AC terms of the other two luma blocks is available for overflow AC terms. The corresponding DC terms, mode bits, and class bits are reserved; the first four bits of DV25's AC coefficient spaces are filled with EOB symbols. The D-9 (Digital-S) format records DV50 SDTV bitstreams onto ½-inch tape in VHS-style cassettes. The DVCPRO50 format, standardized in SMPTE's D-7 series, records DV50 SDTV bitstreams onto 6 mm tape in DVC-style cassettes.

DVCPRO P, sometimes denoted DVCPRO50 P, records 480*p*59.94 or 576*p*50, 4:2:0 video at 50 Mb/s, using an adaptation of the DV50 system.

The downsampling inherent in D-12 compression of 1080*i* means that luma sample aspect ratio is effectively $^3/_2$ (and chroma subsampling is equivalent to 3:1:1) relative to the original 1920×1080 image array.

The D-12 format, introduced by Panasonic as DVCPRO HD, adapts DV technology to 100 Mb/s (DV100), to compress and record 720*p* or 1080*i* HDTV. The D-12 compression system is based upon 1280×1080 image format and 4:2:2 chroma subsampling for 1080*i* or 1080*p*, or 960×720 image format and 4:2:2 chroma subsampling for 720*p*. Video interfaces in D-12 equipment are typically either 1080*i*30, or 720*p* at any of several different frame rates.

DV digital interface (DIF)

The superblocks that I have mentioned form the basis for digital interface of DV bitstreams. A 3-byte ID is prepended to each 77-byte coded macroblock to form an 80-byte *digital interface* (DIF) *block*.

A coded DV25 superblock is represented by 135 video DIF blocks. That is augmented with several nonvideo DIF blocks to form a *DIF sequence* of 150 DIF blocks:

- 1 header DIF block
- 2 subcode DIF blocks
- 3 VAUX DIF blocks
- 9 audio DIF blocks
- 135 video DIF blocks

Realtime DV25 video requires 10 or 12 DIF sequences – that is, about 1500 or 1800 DIF blocks – per second. DV12½ (SDL), DV HD, DV50, and DV100 systems have comparable structures, but different data rates. The major parameters for consumer systems are summarized in Table 39.2, on page 468.

Once packaged in DIF sequences, DV bitstreams can be conveyed across the IEEE 1394 interface, also known as *FireWire* and *i.LINK*, that I described on page 133. This interface is widely used in desktop video, and is suitable for consumer use. Studio video distribution equipment has been introduced using this interface.

For professional applications, DIF sequence bitstreams can be transported across the SDTI interface that I introduced on page 132. (The 3-byte ID is unused in DV-over-SDTI.)

Sony Digital Betacam compression

IEC 61904, *Video recording – Helical-scan digital component video cassette recording format using 12,65 mm magnetic tape and incorporating data compression (Format digital-L).*

Sony's Digital Betacam system records 480*i*29.97 or 576*i*25 video with 4:2:2 chroma subsampling, compressed to about 89.5 Mb/s using an M-JPEG-style technique similar, but not identical, to that of DV. Details are in IEC 61904.

Sony Betacam SX compression

Sony's Betacam SX system records 480*i*29.97 or 576*i*25 video with 4:2:2 chroma subsampling, compressed to about 18.7 Mb/s using MPEG-2 MP@ML with I-frame/B-frame GOP structure. No Betacam SX equipment provides a compressed interface, so the format is effectively proprietary.

D-5 HD compression

Panasonic's D-5 HD system, denoted HD-D5 by SMPTE, records 720*p* or 1080*i* video at either 59.94 Hz or 60.00 Hz, with 4:2:2 chroma subsampling. D-5 HD does not use DV directly, but uses M-JPEG-style coding quite similar to that of DV.

Malvar, H.S., *Signal Processing with Lapped Transforms* (Norwood, Mass.: Artech House, 1992).

One difference from DV is that D-5 HD compression uses a lapped (overlapped) transform, where the rightmost column of samples in an 8×8 block overlaps the leftmost column of the next block to the right. Upon decoding, the redundantly coded columns are reconstructed by averaging appropriate samples from two neighboring blocks. This scheme reduces blocking artifacts compared to the nonlapped transform used in DV.

D-11 (HDCAM) compression

The downsampling inherent in D-11 compression of 1080*i* or 1080*p* means that luma sample aspect ratio is effectively 4⁄3 (and chroma subsampling is equivalent to 4:1:1) relative to the original 1920×1080 image array.

The D-11 format was originated by Sony as HDCAM. This format uses M-JPEG-style coding quite similar to that of DV. The D-11 compression system is based upon a 1440×1080 image format and 3:1:1 chroma subsampling. Video interfaces in D-11 equipment are typically 1080*i* or 1080*p* at any of several different frame rates; downsampling is required upon compression, and upsampling is required upon decompression. Like D-5 HD, D-11 compression uses a lapped (overlapped) transform.

MPEG-2 video compression 40

I assume that you are familiar with *Introduction to video compression*, on page 117, and with JPEG, M-JPEG, and DV, described in the preceding two chapters.

The DCT-based intrafield or intraframe compression at the heart of M-JPEG is suitable for video production; however, for distribution, dramatically higher compression ratios can be obtained by using interframe coding. MPEG-2 video compression exploits temporal coherence – the statistical likelihood that successive pictures in a video sequence are very similar. MPEG-2's intended application ranges from below SDTV to beyond HDTV; the intended bit rate ranges from about 1.5 Mb/s to more than 20 Mb/s. MPEG-2 also defines audio compression, and provides for the transport of video with associated audio.

ISO/IEC 13818-1, *Generic coding of moving pictures and associated audio information: Systems* [MPEG-2], also published as ITU-T H.220.0.

ISO/IEC 13818-2, *Generic coding of moving pictures and associated audio information: Video* [MPEG-2], also published as ITU-T H.262.

MPEG-2 refers to a suite of standards, promulgated jointly by ISO, IEC, and ITU-T. The suite starts with Part 1: *Systems* and Part 2: *Video,* cited in the margin, which are jointly published by ISO, IEC, and ITU-T. Six other parts are jointly published by ISO and IEC – Part 3: *Audio;* Part 4: *Conformance testing;* Part 5: *Software simulation;* Part 6: *Extensions for DSM-CC;* Part 7: *Advanced Audio Coding (AAC*); Part 9: *Extension for real time interface for systems decoders;* and Part 10: *Conformance extensions for Digital Storage Media Command and Control (DSM-CC*). The projected Part 8, for 10-bit video, was discontinued. MPEG-2 standards were first issued in 1996; subsequently, two corrigenda and six amendments have been issued.

MPEG-2 specifies exactly what constitutes a legal bitstream: A legal ("conformant") encoder generates only legal bitstreams; a legal decoder correctly decodes any legal bitstream. MPEG-2 does *not* standardize how an encoder accomplishes compression!

The MPEG-2 standard implicitly defines how a decoder reconstructs pictures data from a coded bitstream, without dictating the implementation of the decoder. MPEG-2 explicitly avoids specifying what it calls the "display process" – how reconstructed pictures are displayed. Most MPEG-2 decoder implementations have flexible output formats; however, MPEG-2 decoder equipment is ordinarily designed to output a specific raster standard.

An MPEG-2 bitstream may represent interlaced or progressive pictures, but typical decoder equipment outputs either interlace or progressive without the capability to switch between the two. Because interlaced scanning remains dominant in consumer electronics – both in SDTV and in HDTV – a decoder system must be capable of producing an interlaced signal from a progressive sequence. Also, it is a practical necessity for an MPEG-2 decoder to have spatial resampling capability: If an HDTV MPEG-2 decoder is presented with an SDTV sequence, consumers would complain if reconstructed pictures were not upconverted for display in an HDTV raster.

MPEG-2 profiles and levels

MPEG-2 specifies several algorithmic features – such as arbitrary frame rate, and 4:4:4 chroma subsampling – that are not permitted in any standard profile. As such, these features are unlikely to see wide deployment.

An MPEG-2 bitstream can potentially invoke many algorithmic features at a decoder, and can reflect many possible parameter values. The MPEG-2 standard classifies bitstreams and decoders in a matrix of *profiles* and *levels*. A profile constrains the algorithmic features potentially used by an encoder, present in a bitstream, or implemented in a decoder. The higher the profile, the more complexity is required of the decoder. MPEG-2 defines six profiles: *Simple* (SP), *Main* (MP), *4:2:2* (422P), *SNR*, *Spatial* (Spt), *High* (HP), and *Multiview* (MVP). Levels place restrictions on the parameters of an encoder or decoder. The higher the level, the more memory or data throughput is required of a decoder. MPEG-2 defines four levels: *Low* (LL), *Main* (ML), *High-1440* (H14), and *High* (HL).

Profile @Level	MPEG-1 CPB	Simple (no B pictures)	Main (MP)	4:2:2 (422P)
High (HL)			1920×1088 60 Hz 80 Mb/s	1920×1088 60 Hz 300 Mb/s
High-1440 (H14)			1440×1088 60 Hz 47 Mb/s	
Main (ML)		720×576 30 Hz 15 Mb/s	720×576 30 Hz 15 Mb/s	720×608 30 Hz 50 Mb/s
Low (LL)			352×288 30 Hz 4 Mb/s	
MPEG-1 CPB †*max 99 Kpx*	768×576† 30 Hz 1.856 Mb/s			

Table 40.1 **MPEG-2 profiles,** here arranged in columns, specify algorithmic features. (I exclude SNR, Spt, HP, and MVP.) **MPEG-2 levels,** here arranged in rows, constrain parameter values. Each entry gives maximum picture size, frame rate, and bit rate. The two shaded entries are commercially dominant: Main profile at main level (MP@ML) is used for SDTV distribution; main profile at high level (MP@HL) is used for HDTV distribution. SMPTE 308M places constraints on GOP structure for 422@HL. Any compliant MPEG-2 decoder must decode an MPEG-1 *constrained-parameters bitstream* (CPB); I include MPEG-1 CPB here as if it were a profile and *a* level.

A combination is indicated by profile and level separated by an at sign, for example, MP@ML or MP@HL. The SNR, Spatial, High, and Multiview profiles have no relevance to video production or distribution, and they are unlikely to see significant commercial deployment. I won't discuss them further.

The profile and level combinations defined by MPEG-2 – excluding SNR, Spt, HP, and MVP – are summarized in Table 40.1 above. Excepting 422P, the combinations have a hierarchical relationship:
A decoder claiming conformance to any profile must be capable of decoding all profiles to its left in Table 40.1; also, a decoder claiming conformance to any level must be capable of decoding all lower levels. Exceptionally, a simple profile at main level (SP@ML) decoder must be capable of decoding main profile at low level (MP@LL).

Every compliant MPEG-2 decoder must be capable of decoding an MPEG-1 *constrained-parameters bitstream* (CPB). I include MPEG-1 CPB at the lower left of Table 40.1, as if it were both a profile and a level, to emphasize this MPEG-2 conformance requirement.

The simple profile has no B-pictures. Prohibition of B-pictures minimizes encoding latency, and minimizes buffer storage at the decoder. However, the simple profile lacks the compression efficiency of B-pictures.

Of the eight combinations in Table 40.1, only two are important to television. MP@ML is used for SDTV distribution, and for DVD, at rates from about 2 Mb/s to about 6 Mb/s. MP@HL is used for HDTV distribution, usually at about 20 Mb/s.

422P@ML allows 608 lines at 25 Hz frame rate, but is limited to 512 lines at 29.97 and 30 Hz frame rates.

The 4:2:2 profile allows 4:2:2 chroma subsampling; it is intended for use in television production. The major reason for a separate 4:2:2 profile is that main profile *disallows* 4:2:2 chroma subsampling. MPEG-2's high profile allows 4:2:2 subsampling, but to require high-profile conformance obliges a decoder to handle SNR and spatial scalability. Two combinations in Table 40.1 are relevant to television production: 422P@ML is expected to see some application in the studio, at about 50 Mb/s; 422P@HL may be used in HDTV production. Some numerical parameter limits of main and 4:2:2 profiles are presented in Table 40.2 opposite.

SMPTE 308M, *Television – MPEG-2 4:2:2 Profile at High Level.*

4:2:2 profile at high level (422P@HL) is defined in MPEG-2. In addition to MPEG-2's requirements for 422P@HL, SMPTE 308 imposes these restrictions on GOP structures permitted at high data rates, as shown in Table 40.3:

Bit rate	*Interlace?*	*GOP structure allowed*
0 to 175	any	any
175 to 230	any	I-only, IP, or IB
230 to 300	interlaced	I-only
	progressive	I-only, IP, or IB

Table 40.3 **GOP restrictions in SMPTE 308M**

Profile@Level	Samples/ line (S_{AL})	Lines/ frame (L_A)	Frame rate, Hz	Luma rate, samples/s	Bitrate, Mb/s	VBV size, bits
422P@HL	1920	1088	60	62 668 800	300	47 185 920
MP@HL	1920	1088	60	62 668 800	80	9 781 248
MP@H-14	1440	1088	60	47 001 600	60	7 340 032
422P@ML	720	608	60	11 059 200	50	9 437 184
MP@ML	720	576	30	10 368 000	15	1 835 008
MP@LL	352	288	30	3 041 280	4	475 136

Table 40.2 **MPEG-2 main and 4:2:2 profiles** are summarized. MP@ML and MP@HL are shaded to emphasize their commercial significance. The DVD-video specification requires MP@ML compliance, and imposes additional constraints. ATSC standards for 720*p*, 1080*p*, and 1080*i* HDTV require MP@HL compliance, and impose additional constraints.

Picture structure

Concerning the distinction between luminance and luma, see Appendix A, on page 595.

Each frame in MPEG-2 is coded with a fixed number of columns (S_{AL}, called *horizontal size* in MPEG) and rows (L_A, called *vertical size*) of luma samples. Here I use the term *luma;* MPEG documents use *luminance,* but that term is technically incorrect in MPEG's context.

Code	Value
0000	Forbidden
0001	Square sampling
0010	4:3
0011	16:9
0100	2.21:1
0101 … 1111	Reserved

Table 40.4 **MPEG-2 *aspect ratio information***

A frame in MPEG-2 has either square sampling, or 4:3, 16:9, or 2.21:1 picture aspect ratio. (Strangely, MPEG writes aspect ratio as height:width.) Table 40.4 presents MPEG-2's *aspect ratio information* field. The 2.21:1 value is not permitted in any defined profile.

MPEG-2 accommodates both progressive and interlaced material. An image having S_{AL} columns and L_A rows of luma samples can be coded directly as a *frame-structured picture*, as depicted at the left of Figure 40.1 overleaf. In a frame-structured picture, all of the luma and chroma samples of a frame are taken to originate at the same time, and are intended for display at the same time. A flag *progressive sequence* asserts that a sequence contains only frame-structured pictures.

Alternatively, a video frame (typically originated from an interlaced source) may be coded as a pair of *field-structured* pictures – a *top-field* picture and a *bottom-field* picture – each having S_{AL} columns and $L_A/2$ rows as

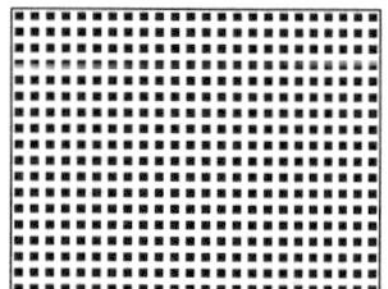

Figure 40.1 **MPEG-2 frame picture** contains an array of luma samples S_{AL} columns by L_A rows. It is implicit that an MPEG-2 frame picture occupies the entire frame time.

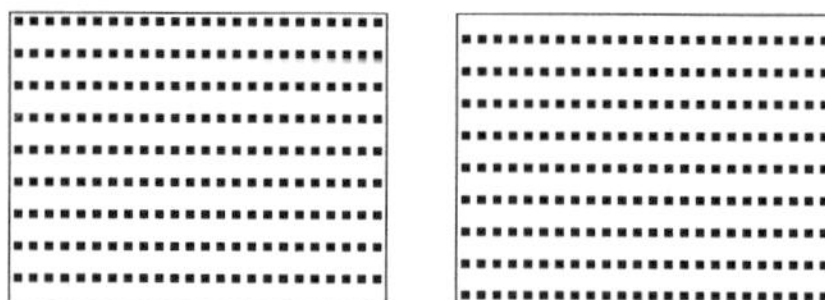

Figure 40.2 **MPEG-2 field picture pair** contains *a top field* picture and *a bottom field* picture, each S_{AL} columns by $L_A/2$ rows. The samples are vertically offset. Here I show a pair ordered {top, bottom}; alternatively, it could be {bottom, top}. Concerning the relation between top and bottom fields and video standards, see *Interlacing in MPEG-2,* on page 98.

depicted by Figure 40.2. The two fields are time-offset by half the frame time, and are intended for interlaced display. Field pictures always come in pairs having opposite parity (top/bottom). Both pictures in a field pair must have the same *picture coding type* (I, P, or B), except that an I-field may be followed by a P-field (in which case the pair functions as an I-frame, and may be termed an *IP-frame*).

I, P, and B picture coding types were introduced on page 121.

Frame rate and 2-3 pulldown in MPEG

Code	*Value*
0000	Forbidden
0001	$^{24}/_{1.001}$
0010	24
0011	25
0100	$^{30}/_{1.001}$
0101	30
0110	50
0111	$^{60}/_{1.001}$
1000	60
1001 … 1111	Reserved

Table 40.5 **MPEG-2 *frame rate code***

The defined profiles of MPEG-2 provide for the display frame rates shown in Table 40.5 in the margin. Frame rate is constant within a video *sequence* (to be defined on page 494). It is unspecified how long a decoder may take to adapt to a change in frame rate.

In a sequence of frame-structured pictures, provisions are made to include, in the MPEG-2 bitstream, information to enable the display process to impose 2-3 pulldown upon interlaced display. Frames in such a sequence are coded as frame-structured pictures; in each frame, both fields are associated with the same instant in time. The flag *repeat first field* may accompany a picture; if that flag is set, then interlaced display is expected to display the first field, the second field, and then the first field again – that is, to impose 2-3 pulldown. The frame rate in the bitstream specifies the display rate, after 2-3 processing. I sketched a 2-3 sequence of four film frames in Figure 36.1, on page 429; that sequence could be coded as the set of four progressive MPEG-2 frames flagged as indicated in Table 40.6 at the top of the facing page.

A frame-coded picture can code a top/bottom pair or a bottom/top pair – that is, a frame picture may correspond to a video frame, or may straddle two video frames. The latter case accommodates M-frames in 2-3 pulldown.

Film frame	*Top first field*	*Repeat first field*
A	0	0
B	0	1
C	1	0
D	1	1

Table 40.6 **2-3 pulldown sequence in MPEG-2**

Luma and chroma sampling structures

MPEG-2 accommodates 4:2:2 chroma subsampling, suitable for studio applications, and 4:2:0 chroma subsampling, suitable for video distribution. Unlike DV, C_B and C_R sample pairs are spatially coincident. The MPEG-2 standard includes 4:4:4 chroma format, but it isn't permitted in any defined profile, and so is unlikely to be deployed.

There is no vertical subsampling in 4:2:2 – in this case, subsampling and interlace do not interact. 4:2:2 chroma for both frame-structured and field-structured pictures is depicted in the third (Rec. 601) column of Figure 10.1, on page 90.

4:2:0 chroma subsampling in a frame-structured picture is depicted in the rightmost column of Figure 10.1; C_B and C_R samples are centered vertically midway between luma samples in the frame, and are cosited horizontally.

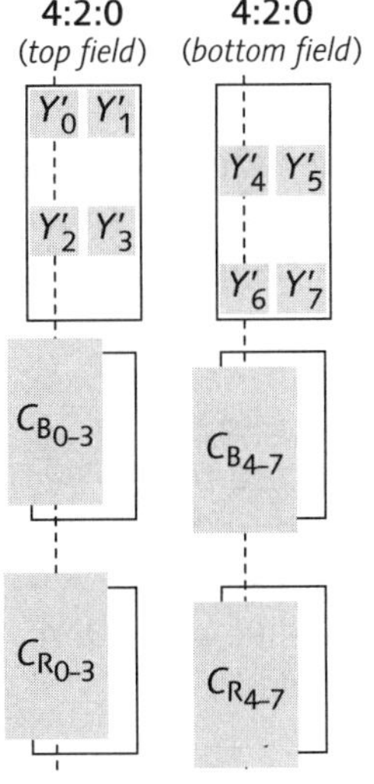

Figure 40.3 **Chroma subsampling in field-structured pictures**

4:2:0 chroma subsampling in a field-structured picture is depicted in Figure 40.3 in the margin. In the top field, chroma samples are centered 1⁄4 of the way vertically between a luma sample in the field and the luma sample immediately below in the same field. (In this example, $C_{B_{0-3}}$ is centered 1⁄4 of the way down from Y'_0 to Y'_2.) In the bottom field, chroma samples are centered 3⁄4 of the way vertically between a luma sample in the field and the luma sample immediately below in the same field. (In this example, $C_{B_{4-7}}$ is centered 3⁄4 of the way down from Y'_4 to Y'_6.) This scheme centers chroma samples at the same locations that they would take in a frame-structured picture; however, alternate rows of chroma samples in the frame are time-offset by half the frame time.

Macroblocks

If *horizontal size* or *vertical size* is not divisible by 16, then the encoder pads the image with a suitable number of black "overhang" samples at the right edge or bottom edge. These samples are discarded upon decoding. For example, when coding HDTV at 1920×1080, an encoder appends 8 rows of black pixels to the image array, to make the row count 1088.

At the core of MPEG compression is the DCT coding of 8×8 blocks of sample values (as in JPEG), or 8×8 blocks of prediction errors. To simplify the implementation of subsampled chroma, the same DCT and block coding scheme is used for both luma and chroma. When combined with 4:2:0 chroma subsampling, an 8×8 block of C_B or C_R is associated with a 16×16 block of luma. This leads to the tiling of a field or frame into units of 16×16 luma samples. Each such unit is a *macroblock* (MB). Macroblocks lie a on 16×16 grid aligned with the upper-left luma sample of the image.

Each macroblock comprises four 8×8 luma blocks, accompanied by the requisite number and arrangement of 8×8 C_B blocks and 8×8 C_R blocks, depending upon *chroma format*. In the usual 4:2:0 chroma format, a macroblock comprises six blocks: four luma blocks, a C_B block, and a C_R block. In the 4:2:2 chroma format, a macroblock comprises eight blocks: four luma blocks, two blocks of C_B, and two blocks of C_R.

Picture coding types – I, P, B

MPEG-2 uses the term *reference picture*. Because *reference* qualifies so many other terms in video, I find it more clear to say *anchor*.

I-pictures, P-pictures, and B-pictures were introduced on page 120. Coded I-picture and P-picture data are used to reconstruct *anchor pictures* – fields or frames that can be used for prediction. An MPEG decoder maintains two anchor framestores, one past and one future. An encoder also maintains two anchor framestores, reconstructed as if by a decoder; these track the contents of the decoder's anchor framestores. The simple profile has no B-pictures; a single anchor framestore suffices.

Each I-picture is coded independently of any other picture. When an I-picture is reconstructed by a decoder, it is displayed. Additionally, it is stored as an anchor frame so as to be available as a predictor. I-pictures are compressed using a JPEG-like algorithm, using perceptually based quantization matrices.

Each P-picture is coded using the past anchor picture as a predictor. Prediction errors are compressed using the same JPEG-like algorithm that is used for I-pictures, but typically with quite different quantization matrices. When a decoder reconstructs a P-picture, it is displayed; additionally, the picture is written into an anchor frame so as to be available for subsequent predictions.

Each B-picture contains elements that are predicted from one or both anchor frames. The encoder computes, compresses, and transmits prediction errors. A decoder reconstructs a B-picture, displays it, then discards it: No B-picture is used for prediction.

Each anchor picture is associated with a full frame of storage. When a decoder reconstructs an anchor *field* (an I-field or a P-field), half the lines of the anchor framestore are written; the other half retains the contents of the previous anchor field. After the first field of a field pair has been reconstructed, it is available as a predictor for the second field. (The first field of the previous anchor frame is no longer available.)

Prediction

In Figure 14.1, on page 121, I sketched a naive interpicture coding scheme. For any scene element that moves more than a pixel or two from one picture to the next, the naive scheme is liable to fail to produce small interpicture difference values. Motion can be more effectively coded by having the encoder form motion-compensated predictions. The encoder produces motion vectors; these are used to displace a region of a neighboring anchor picture to improve the prediction of the current picture relative to an undisplaced prediction. The prediction errors ("residuals") are then compressed using DCT, quantized, and VLE-encoded.

At a decoder, predictions are formed from the anchor picture(s), based upon the transmitted motion vectors and prediction modes. Prediction errors are recovered from the bitstream by VLE decoding, inverse quantization, and inverse DCT. Finally, the prediction error is added to the prediction to form the reconstructed picture. If the decoder is reconstructing an I-picture or a P-picture, the reconstructed picture is written to the appropriate portion (or the entirety) of an anchor frame.

Inverse quantization is sometimes denoted *IQ*, not to be confused with *IQ* color difference components.

The obvious way for an encoder to form forward inter picture differences is to subtract the current source picture from the previous source picture. (The previous source picture would have been subject to motion-compensated interpolation, according to the encoder's motion estimate.) Starting from an intracoded picture, the decoder would then accumulate interpicture differences. However, MPEG involves lossy compression: Both the I-picture starting point of a GOP and each set of decoded interpicture differences are subject to reconstruction errors. With the naive scheme of computing interpicture differences, reconstruction errors would accumulate at the decoder. To alleviate this source of decoder error, the encoder incorporates a decoder. The interpicture difference is formed by subtracting the current source picture from the previous anchor picture as a decoder will reconstruct it. Reconstruction errors are thereby brought "inside the loop," and are prevented from accumulating.

A prediction region in an anchor frame is not generally aligned to a 16-luma-sample macroblock grid; it is not properly referred to as a *macroblock*. Some authors fail to make the distinction between macroblocks and prediction regions; other authors use the term *prediction macroblocks* for prediction regions.

The prediction model used by MPEG-2 is blockwise translation of 16×16 blocks of luma samples (along with the associated chroma samples): A macroblock of the current picture is predicted from a like-sized region of a reconstructed anchor picture. The choice of 16×16 region size was a compromise between the desire for a large region (to effectively exploit spatial coherence, and to amortize motion vector overhead across a fairly large number of samples), and a small region (to efficiently code small scene elements in motion).

In a *closed GOP*, no B-picture is permitted to use forward prediction to the I-frame that starts the next GOP. See the caption to Figure 14.5, on page 123.

Macroblocks in a P-picture are typically forward-predicted. However, an encoder can decide that a particular macroblock is best intracoded (that is, not predicted at all). Macroblocks in a B-picture are typically predicted as averages of motion-compensated past and future anchor pictures – that is, they are ordinarily bidirectionally predicted. However, an encoder can decide that a particular macroblock in a B-picture is best intracoded, or unidirectionally predicted using forward or backward prediction. Table 40.7 overleaf indicates the four macroblock types. The macroblock types allowed in any picture are restricted by the declared picture type, as indicated in Table 40.8.

Table 40.7 **MPEG macroblock types**		*Prediction*	*Typ. quantizer matrix*
Intra		None – the macroblock is self-contained	Perceptual
Nonintra	Backward predictive-coded	Predicts from a future anchor picture	Flat
	Forward predictive-coded	Predicts from a past anchor picture	Flat
	Bidirectionally predictive-coded	Averages predictions from past and future anchor pictures	Flat

Table 40.8 **MPEG picture coding types**	*Binary code*	*Anchor picture?*	*Permitted macroblock types*
I-picture	001	Yes	Intra
P-picture	010	Yes	Intra Forward predictive-coded
B-picture	011	No	Intra Forward predictive-coded Backward predictive-coded Bidirectionally predictive-coded

Table 40.9 **MPEG-2 prediction modes**	*for*	*Description*	*Max. MVs* back.	*Max. MVs* fwd.
Frame prediction	(P, B)-frames	Predictions are made for the frame, using data from one or two previously reconstructed frames.	1	1
Field prediction	(P, B)-frames, (P, B)-fields	Predictions are made independently for each field, using data from one or two previously reconstructed fields.	1	1
16×8 motion compensation (16×8 MC)	(P, B)-fields	The upper 16×8 and lower 16×8 regions of the macroblock are predicted separately. (This is completely unrelated to top and bottom fields.)	2	2
Dual prime	P-fields with no intervening B-pictures	Two motion vectors are derived from the transmitted vector and a small *differential motion vector* (DMV, –1, 0, or +1); these are used to form predictions from two anchor fields (one top, one bottom), which are averaged to form the predictor.	1	1
Dual prime	P-frames with no intervening B-pictures	As in dual prime for P-fields (above), but repeated for 2 fields; 4 predictions are made and averaged.	1	1

Each nonintra macroblock in an interlaced sequence can be predicted either by frame prediction (typically chosen by the encoder when there is little motion between the fields), or by field prediction (typically chosen by the encoder when there is significant interfield motion). This is comparable to field/frame coding in DV, which I described on page 463. Predictors for a field picture must be field predictors. However, predictors for a frame picture may be chosen on a macroblock-by-macroblock basis to be either field predictors or frame predictors. MPEG-2 defines several additional prediction modes, which can be selected on a macroblock-by-macroblock basis. MPEG-2's prediction modes are summarized in Table 40.9 overleaf.

Motion vectors (MVs)

A *motion vector* identifies a region of 16×16 luma samples that are to be used for prediction. A motion vector refers to a prediction region that is potentially quite distant (spatially) from the region being coded – that is, the motion vector range can be quite large. Even in field pictures, motion vectors are specified in units of frame luma samples. A motion vector can be specified to half-sample precision: If the fractional bit of a motion vector is set, then the prediction is formed by averaging sample values at the neighboring integer coordinates – that is, by linear interpolation. Transmitted motion vector values are halved for use with subsampled chroma. All defined profiles require that no motion vector refers to any sample outside the bounds of the anchor frame.

Each macroblock's header contains a count of motion vectors. Motion vectors are themselves predicted! An initial MV is established at the start of a *slice* (see page 494); the motion vector for each successive nonintra macroblock is differentially coded with respect to the previous macroblock in raster-scan order.

Motion vectors are variable-length encoded (VLE), so that short vectors – the most likely ones in large areas of translational motion or no motion – are coded compactly. Zero-valued motion vectors are quite likely, so provision is made for compact coding of them.

Intra macroblocks are not predicted, so motion vectors are not necessary for them. However, in certain circumstances *concealment motion vectors* (CMVs) are allowed: If a macroblock is lost owing to transmission error, CMVs allow a decoder to use its prediction facilities to synthesize picture information to conceal the erred macroblock. A CMV would be useless if it were contained in its own macroblock! So, a CMV is associated with the macroblock immediately below.

Coding of a block

Each macroblock is accompanied by a small amount of prediction mode information; zero, one, or more *motion vectors* (MVs); and DCT-coded information.

A perverse encoder could use an intra quantizer matrix that isn't perceptually coded.

Each block of an intra macroblock is coded similarly to a block in JPEG. Transform coefficients are quantized with a quantizer matrix that is (ordinarily) perceptually weighted. Provision is made for 8-, 9-, and 10-bit DC coefficients. (In 422 profile, 11-bit DC coefficients are permitted.) DC coefficients are differentially coded within a slice (to be described on page 494).

In an I-picture, DC terms of the DCT are differentially coded: The DC term for each luma block is used as a predictor for the corresponding DC term of the following macroblock. DC terms for C_B and C_R blocks are similarly predicted.

A perverse encoder could use a nonintra quantizer matrix that isn't flat. Separate nonintra quantizer matrices can be provided for luma and chroma.

In principle, prediction errors in a nonintra macroblock could be encoded directly. In MPEG, they are coded using DCT, for two reasons. First, DCT coding exploits any spatial coherence that may be present in the prediction error. Second, DCT coding allows use of the same rate control (based upon quantization) and VLE encoding that are already in place for intra macroblocks. When the prediction error information in a nonintra block is dequantized, the prediction errors are added to the motion-compensated values from the anchor frame. Because the dequantized transform coefficients are not directly viewed, it is not appropriate to use a perceptually weighted quantizer matrix. By default, the quantizer matrix for nonintra blocks is *flat* – that is, it contains the same value in all entries.

Figure 40.4 **Frame DCT type** involves straightforward partitioning of luma samples of each 16×16 macroblock into four 8×8 blocks. This is most efficient for macroblocks of field pictures, native progressive frame pictures, and frame-structured pictures having little interfield motion.

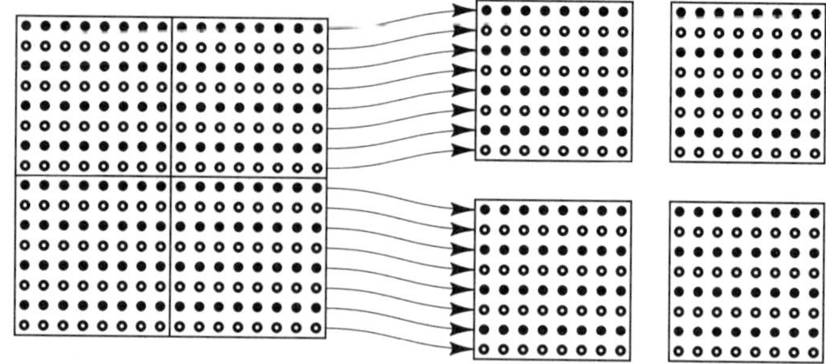

Frame and field DCT types

Luma in a macroblock is partitioned into four blocks according to one of two schemes, *frame DCT coding* or *field DCT coding*. I will describe three cases where frame DCT coding is appropriate, and then introduce field DCT coding.

- In a frame-structured picture that originated from a native-progressive source, every macroblock is best predicted by a spatially contiguous 16×16 region of an anchor frame. This is *frame DCT coding:* Luma samples of a macroblock are partitioned into 8×8 luma blocks as depicted in Figure 40.4 above.

At first glance it is a paradox that *field*-structured pictures must use *frame* DCT coding!

- In a field-structured picture, alternate image rows of each source frame have been unwoven by the encoder into two fields, each of which is free from interlace effects. Every macroblock in such a picture is best predicted from a spatially contiguous 16×16 region of an anchor field (or, if you prefer to think of it this way, from alternate lines of a 16×32 region of an anchor frame). This is also frame DCT coding.

- In a frame-structured picture from an interlaced source, a macroblock that contains no scene element in motion is ordinarily best predicted by frame DCT coding.

An alternate approach is necessary in a frame-structured picture from an interlaced source where a macroblock contains a scene element in motion. Such a scene element will take different positions in the first and second fields: A spatially contiguous 16×16 region of an anchor picture will form a poor predictor. MPEG-2

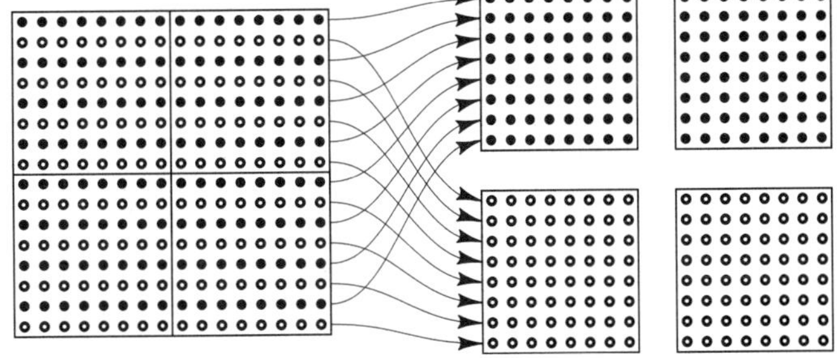

Figure 40.5 **Field DCT type** creates four 8×8 luma blocks by collecting alternate image rows. This allows efficient coding of a frame-structured picture from an interlaced source, where there is significant interfield motion. (Comparable unweaving is already implicit in field-structured pictures.)

provides a way to efficiently code such a macroblock. The scheme involves an alternate partitioning of luma into 8×8 blocks: Luma blocks are formed by collecting alternate rows of the anchor frame. The scheme is called *field DCT coding;* it is depicted in Figure 40.5 above.

You might think it a good idea to handle chroma samples in interlaced frame-pictures the same way that luma is handled. However, with 4:2:0 subsampling, that would force having either 8×4 chroma blocks or 16×32 macroblocks. Neither of these options is desirable; so, in a frame-structured picture with interfield motion, chroma blocks are generally poorly predicted. Owing to the absence of vertical subsampling in the 4:2:2 chroma format, 4:2:2 sequences are inherently free from such poor chroma prediction.

Zigzag and VLE

Once DCT coefficients are quantized, an encoder scans them in zigzag order. I sketched zigzag scanning in JPEG in Figure 38.8, on page 455. This scan order, depicted in Figure 40.6 overleaf, is also used in MPEG-1.

In addition to the JPEG/MPEG-1 scan order, MPEG-2 provides an alternate scan order optimized for frame-structured pictures from interlaced sources. The alternate scan, sketched in Figure 40.7; can be chosen by an encoder on a picture-by-picture basis.

In MPEG terminology, the absolute value of an AC coefficient is its *level*. I prefer to call it *amplitude.* Sign is coded separately.

After zigzag scanning, zero-valued AC coefficients are identified, then {run-length, level} pairs are formed and variable-length encoded (VLE). For intra macroblocks,

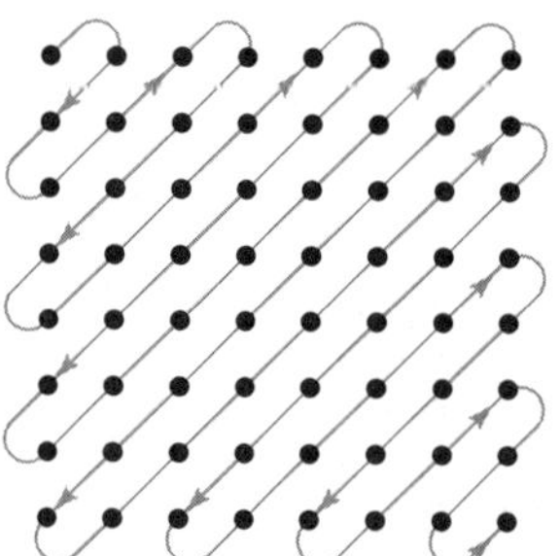

Figure 40.6 **Zigzag *scan*[0]** denotes the scan order used in JPEG and MPEG-1, and available in MPEG-2.

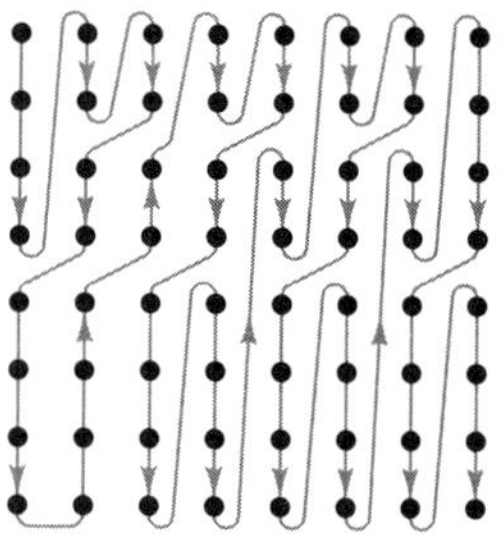

Figure 40.7 **Zigzag *scan*[1]** may be chosen by an MPEG-2 encoder on a picture-by-picture basis.

MPEG-2 allows an encoder to choose between two VLE schemes: the scheme first standardized in MPEG-1, and an alternate scheme more suitable for frame-structured pictures with interfield motion.

Block diagrams of an MPEG-2 encoder and decoder system are sketched in Figure 40.8 opposite.

Refresh

Occasional insertion of I-macroblocks is necessary for three main reasons: to establish an anchor picture upon channel acquisition; to limit the duration of artifacts introduced by uncorrectable transmission errors; and to limit the divergence of encoder and decoder predictors due to mistracking between the encoder's IDCT and the decoder's IDCT. MPEG-2 mandates that every macroblock in the frame be refreshed by an intra macroblock before the 132nd P-macroblock. Encoders usually meet this requirement by periodically or intermittently inserting I-pictures. However, I-pictures are not a strict requirement of MPEG-2, and *distributed refresh* – where I-macroblocks are used for refresh, instead of I-pictures – is occasionally used, especially for DBS.

Distributed refresh does not guarantee a deterministic time to complete refresh. See Lookabaugh, cited at the end of this chapter.

A sophisticated encoder examines the source video to detect scene cuts, and adapts its sequence of picture types according to picture content.

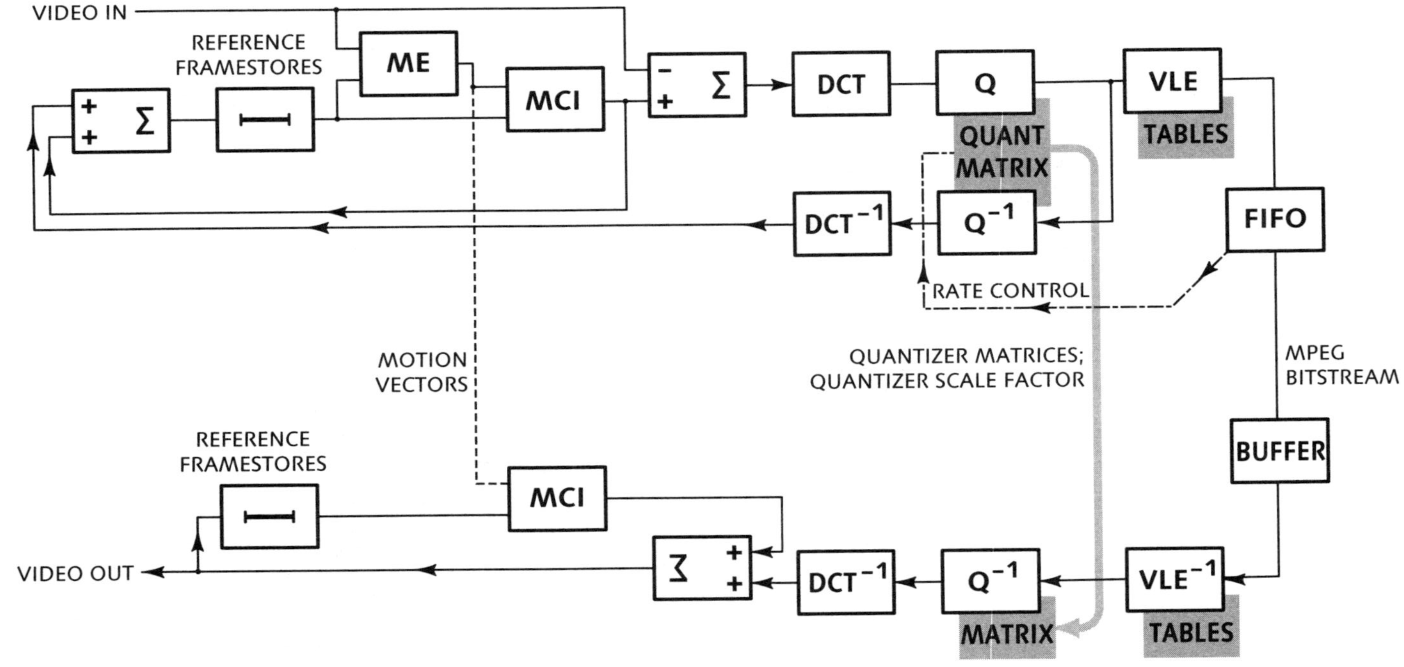

Figure 40.8 **MPEG encoder and decoder** block diagrams are sketched here. The encoder includes a motion estimator (ME); this involves huge computational complexity. Motion vectors (MVs) are incorporated into the bitstream and thereby conveyed to the decoder; the decoder does not need to estimate motion. The encoder effectively contains a copy of the decoder; the encoder's picture difference calculations are based upon reconstructed picture information that will be available at the decoder.

Motion estimation

A motion vector must do more than cover motion from one frame to the next: With B-frames, a motion vector must describe motion from one *anchor* frame to the next – that is, from an I-frame or P-frame to the picture immediately before the following I-frame or P-frame. As page 123's *m* value increases, motion vector range must increase. The cost and complexity of motion estimation increases dramatically as search range increases.

Whether an encoder actually searches this extent is not standardized!

The burden of *motion estimation* (ME) falls on the encoder. Motion estimation is very complex and computationally intensive. MPEG-2 allows a huge motion vector range: For MP@ML frame-structured pictures, the 16×16 prediction region can potentially lie anywhere within [–1024…+1023½] luma samples horizontally and [–128…+127½] luma samples vertically from the macroblock being decoded. Elements in the picture header (*f code*) specify the motion vector range used in each picture; this limits the number of bits that need to be allocated to motion vectors for that picture.

The purpose of the motion estimation in MPEG is not exactly to estimate motion in regions of the picture – rather, it is to access a prediction region that minimizes the amount of prediction error information that needs to be coded. Usually this goal will be achieved by using the best estimate of average motion in the 16×16 macroblock, but not always. I make this distinction because some video processing algorithms need accurate motion vectors, where the estimated motion is a good match to motion as perceived by a human observer. In many video processing algorithms, such as in temporal resampling used in standards converters, or in deinterlacing, a motion vector is needed for every luma sample, or every few samples. In MPEG, only one or two vectors are needed to predict a macroblock from a 16×16 region in an anchor picture.

If the fraction bit of a motion vector is set, then predictions are formed by averaging sample values from neighboring pixels (at integer coordinates). This is straightforward for a decoder. However, for an encoder to *produce* $\frac{1}{2}$-luma-sample motion vectors in both horizontal and vertical axes requires quadruple the computational effort of producing full-sample vectors.

There are three major methods of motion estimation:

- *Block matching,* also called *full search,* involves an exhaustive search for the best match of the target macroblock through some two-dimensional extent of the anchor frame. For the large ranges of MPEG-2, full block matching is impractical.

- *Pixel-recursive* (or *pel-recursive*) methods start with a small number of initial guesses at motion, based upon motion estimates from previous frames. The corresponding coordinates in the anchor frame are searched, and each guess is refined. The best guess is taken as the final motion vector.

This method is sometimes called "logarithmic," which I consider to be a very poor term in this context.

- *Pyramidal* methods form spatial lowpass-filtered versions of the target macroblock, and of the anchor frames; block matches are performed at low resolution. Surrounding the coordinates of the most promising candidates at one resolution level, less severely filtered versions of the anchor picture regions are formed, and block-matches are performed on those. Successive refinement produces the final motion vector. This technique tends to produce smooth motion-vector fields.

Rate control and buffer management

A typical video sequence, encoded by a typical MPEG-2 encoder, produces I-, P-, and B-pictures that consume bits roughly in the ratio 60:30:10. An I-picture requires perhaps six times the number of bits as a B-picture.

Many applications of MPEG-2, such as DTV, involve a transmission channel with a fixed data rate. This calls for *constant bit-rate* (CBR) operation. Other applications of MPEG-2, such as DVD, involve a recording channel with variable (but limited) data rate. This calls for *variable bit-rate* (VBR) operation, where the instantaneous bit-rate is varied to achieve the desired picture quality for each frame, maximizing storage utilization.

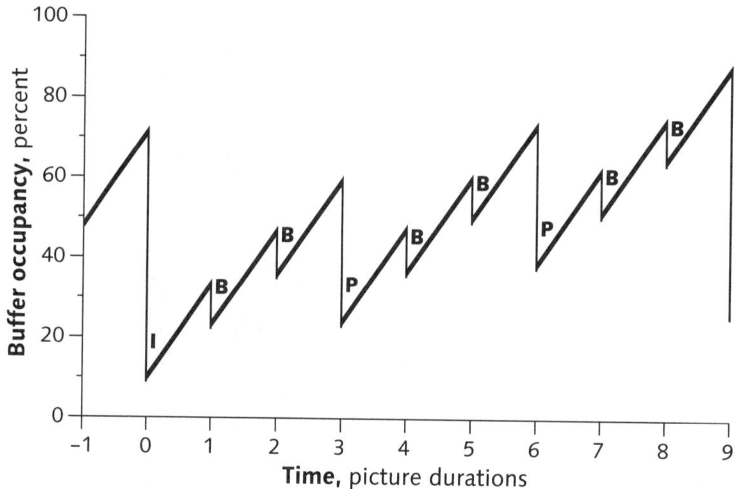

Figure 40.9 **Buffer occupancy** in MPEG-2 is managed through an idealized *video buffering verifier* (VBV) that analyzes the output bitstream produced by any encoder. This graph shows buffer occupancy for a typical GOP.

The larger the decoder's buffer size, the more flexibility is available to the encoder to allocate bits among pictures. However, a large buffer is expensive. Each profile/level combination dictates the minimum buffer size that a decoder must implement.

An encoder effects *rate control* by altering the quantization matrices – the perceptually weighted matrix used for intra macroblocks, and the flat matrix used for nonintra macroblocks. MPEG-2 allows quantizer matrices to be included in the bitstream. Additionally, and more importantly, a *quantizer scale code* is transmitted at the slice level, and may be updated at the macroblock level. This code determines an overall scale factor that is applied to the quantizer matrices. The encoder quantizes more or less severely to achieve the required bit rate; the quantizer scale code is conveyed to the decoder so that it dequantizes accordingly.

Video display requires a constant number of frames per second. Because an I-frame has a relatively large number of bits, during decoding and display of an I-frame in all but degenerate cases, the decoder's net buffer occupancy decreases. During decoding and display of a B-frame, net buffer occupancy increases. Figure 40.9 shows typical buffer occupancy at the start of a sequence, for a duration of about one GOP.

An MPEG bitstream must be constructed such that the decoder's buffer doesn't overflow: If it did, bits would be lost. The bitstream must also be constructed so that the buffer doesn't underflow: If it did, a picture to be displayed would not be available at the required time.

Buffer management in MPEG-2 is based upon an idealized model of the decoder's buffer: All of the bits associated with each picture are deemed to be extracted from the decoder's buffer at a certain precisely defined instant in time with respect to the bitstream. Every encoder implements a *video buffering verifier* (VBV) that tracks the state of this idealized buffer. Each picture header contains a *VBV delay* field that declares the fullness of the buffer at the start of that picture. After channel acquisition, a decoder waits for the specified amount of time before starting decoding. (If the decoder did not wait, buffer underflow could result.)

Bitstream syntax

The end product of MPEG-2 video compression is a bitstream partitioned into what MPEG calls a *syntactic hierarchy* having six layers: *sequence, GOP, picture, slice, macroblock,* and *block*. Except for the video sequence layer, which has a *sequence end* element, each syntactic element has a header and no trailer. The sequence, GOP, picture, and slice elements each begin with a 24-bit *start code prefix* of 23 zero-bits followed by a one-bit. A start code establishes byte alignment, and may be preceded by an arbitrary number of zero-stuffing bits. All other datastream elements are constructed so as to avoid the possibility of 23 or more consecutive zero bits.

Video sequence layer

The top layer of the MPEG syntax is the *video sequence*. The sequence header specifies high-level parameters such as bit rate, picture rate, picture size, picture aspect ratio, profile, level, progressive/interlace, and chroma format. The *VBV buffer size* parameter declares the maximum buffer size required within the sequence. The sequence header may specify quantizer matrices. At the encoder's discretion, the sequence header may be retransmitted intermittently or periodically throughout the sequence, to enable rapid channel acquisition by decoders.

The start of each interlaced video sequence establishes an immutable sequence of field pairs, ordered either {top, bottom, ...}, typical of 480*i*, or {bottom, top, ...}, typical of 576*i* and 1080*i*. Within a sequence, any individual field may be field-coded, and any two adjacent fields may be frame-coded; however, field parity must alternate in strict sequence.

Group of pictures (GOP header)

The GOP is MPEG's unit of random access. The GOP layer is optional in MPEG-2; however, it is a practical necessity for most applications. A GOP starts with an I-frame. (Additional I-frames are allowed.) The GOP header contains SMPTE timecode, and *closed GOP* and *broken link* flags.

A GOP header contains 23 bits of coded SMPTE timecode. If present, this applies to the first frame of the GOP (in display order). It is unused within MPEG.

If a GOP is *closed,* no coded B-frame in the GOP may reference the first I-frame of the following GOP. This is inefficient, because the following I-frame ordinarily contains useful prediction information. If a GOP is *open*, or the GOP header is absent, then B-pictures in the GOP may reference the first I-frame of the following GOP. To allow editing of an MPEG bitstream, GOPs must be closed.

A device that splices bitstreams at GOP boundaries can set *broken link;* this signals a decoder to invalidate B-frames immediately following the GOP's first I-frame.

Picture layer

The picture header specifies picture structure (frame, top field, or bottom field), and picture coding type (I, P, or B). The picture header can specify quantizer matrices and *quantizer scale type*. The *VBV delay* parameter is used for buffer management.

Slice layer

A slice aggregates macroblocks as you would read, left to right and top to bottom. No slice crosses the edge of the picture. All defined profiles have "restricted slice structure," where slices cover the picture with no gaps or overlaps. The slice header contains the *quantizer scale code*. The slice serves several purposes. First, the slice is the smallest unit of resynchronization in case of uncorrected data transmission error. Second, the slice is the unit of differential coding of intra-macroblock DC terms. Third, the slice is the unit for differential coding of nonintra motion vectors: The first macroblock of a slice has motion vectors coded absolutely, and motion vectors for subsequent macroblocks are coded in terms of successive differences from that.

Macroblock layer

The macroblock is MPEG's unit of motion prediction. A macroblock contains an indication of the macroblock type (intra, forward predicted, backward-predicted, or bidirectionally predicted); a *quantizer scale code*; 0, 1, or 2 forward motion vectors; and 0, 1, or 2 backward motion vectors. The *coded block pattern* flags provide a compact way to represent blocks that are not coded (owing to being adequately predicted without the need for prediction error).

Block layer

Each block is represented in the bitstream by VLE-coded DCT coefficients – a differentially encoded DC coefficient, and some number of AC coefficients. Each coded block's data is terminated by a 4-bit *end of block* (EOB).

Transport

The syntax elements of an MPEG video or audio bitstream are serialized to form an *elementary stream* (ES). MPEG-2 defines a mechanism to divide an ES into packets, forming a *packetized elementary stream* (PES). Each PES pack header contains system-level clock information, packet priority, packet sequence numbering, and (optionally) encryption information.

An MPEG-2 *program stream* (PS) is intended for storage of a single program on relatively error-free media, such as DVD. PS packets are variable-length; each packet can be as long as 64 KB, though packets of 1 KB or 2 KB are typical. Synchronization is achieved through a *system clock reference* (SCR).

An MPEG-2 *transport stream* (TS) is intended for transmission of multiple programs on relatively error-prone media. (For terrestrial or cable television, TS packets are expected to be suitably protected.) A *transport stream packet* (TSP) comprises 188 bytes – a 4-byte header (whose first byte has the value 47_h), and 184 bytes of payload. Packet size was designed with ATM in mind: One TS packet fits into four ATM cells. Synchronization is achieved through multiple independent *program clock references* (PCRs). Because there is a lack of external interfaces for program streams, a *single program transport stream* (SPTS) may be used to carry one program.

Further reading

On page 126, I cited the introduction to compression by Peter Symes.

Gibson, Jerry D., Toby Berger, Tom Lookabaugh, David Lindbergh, and Richard L. Baker, *Digital Compression for Multimedia* (San Francisco: Morgan Kaufmann, 1998).

Lookabaugh's chapter in *Digital Compression for Multimedia* provides an excellent 55-page description of MPEG-2. His chapter also covers MPEG audio.

Watkinson, John, *MPEG-2* (Oxford: Focal Press, 1999).

Watkinson introduces MPEG-2 video and audio.

Mitchell, Joan L., and William B. Pennebaker, Chad E. Fogg, and Didier J. LeGall, *MPEG Video Compression Standard* (New York: Chapman & Hall, 1997). [This book concentrates on MPEG-1. Egregiously incorrect information appears concerning chroma subsampling.]

Haskell, Barry G., Atul Puri, and Arun N. Netravali, *Digital Video: An Introduction to MPEG-2* (New York: Chapman & Hall, 1997). [This book fails to distinguish luminance and luma; both are called *luminance* and given the symbol *Y*. See Appendix A, *YUV and luminance considered harmful*, on page 595.]

The book by Mitchell and her colleagues contains detailed coverage of MPEG-1; the book by Haskell and his colleagues provides detailed treatment of MPEG-2. I'm sorry to say that both of these books contain errors. Few books are free from errors! However, neither of these has published errata, and for that reason, they are best used as guides to the standard itself rather than as definitive references.

Part 4

Studio standards

480*i* component video 41

This chapter details the scanning, timing, sync structure, and picture structure of 480*i*29.97 (525/59.94/2:1) video. The scanning and timing information in this chapter applies to all variants of 480*i* video, both analog and digital. The sync information relates to component analog, composite analog, and composite digital systems.

Frame rate

$$f_{FR} = \frac{30}{1.001} \approx 29.97\ \text{Hz}$$

480*i* video represents stationary or moving two-dimensional images sampled temporally at a constant rate of $^{30}/_{1.001}$ frames per second. For studio video, the tolerance on frame rate is normally ±10 ppm. In practice the tolerance applies to a master clock at a high frequency, but for purposes of computation and standards writing, it is convenient to reference the tolerance to the frame rate.

Interlace

$$f_{H} = \frac{9}{0.572} \approx 15.734\ \text{kHz}$$

It is confusing to refer to fields as *odd* and *even*. Use *first field* and *second field* instead.

A frame comprises a total of 525 horizontal raster lines of equal duration, uniformly scanned top to bottom and left to right. Scanning has 2:1 interlace to form a *first* field and a *second* field; scan lines in the second field are displaced vertically by half the vertical sampling pitch, and delayed temporally by half the frame time, from scanning lines in the first field. In MPEG-2 terms, the first field is the bottom field.

Lines are numbered consecutively throughout the frame, starting at 1.

Table 41.1 **480*i* line assignment**

EQ Equalization pulse

BR Broad pulse

CC Closed caption

[*n*] Line number relative to start of second field (deprecated)

§ $V=0$ in RP 125-1992, and in the 480*i* version of Rec. 601-4 (1994); in later standards, $V=1$ for these lines.

◊ The thick vertical bar at the right indicates lines carried in 480*i or* 480*p* MPEG-2 according to SMPTE RP 202. (The vertical center of the picture is located midway between lines 404 and 142.) Unfortunately, 480*i* DV systems digitize a range one image row up from this.

‡ In analog terminology, lines 1 through 3 are considered part of the first field; lines 264 and 265 are considered part of the second field.

Line number, First field ($F=0$)	*Line number, Second field* ($F=1$)	*V*	*Contents, Left half*	*Contents, Right half*
	266 [3]		EQ	BR
4			BR	BR
	267 [4]		BR	BR
5			BR	BR
	268 [5]		BR	BR
6			BR	BR
	269 [6]		BR	EQ
7			EQ	EQ
	270 [7]		EQ	EQ
8			EQ	EQ
	271 [8]		EQ	EQ
9			EQ	EQ
	272 [9]		EQ	none
10–19		$V=0$§	Vertical interval video (10 lines)	
	273–282 [10–19]	$V=0$§	Vertical interval video (10 lines)	
20		$V=0$ (487 lines)	Vertical interval video	
	283 [20]	$V=0$ (487 lines)	Vertical interval video	
21		$V=0$ (487 lines)	CC	
	284 [21]	$V=0$ (487 lines)	CC	
22		$V=0$ (487 lines)	Picture	
	285 [22]	$V=0$ (487 lines)	Picture	
23–261		$V=0$ (487 lines)	Picture (239 lines)	◊
	286–524 [23–261]	$V=0$ (487 lines)	Picture (239 lines)	
262		$V=0$ (487 lines)	Picture	
	525 [262]	$V=0$ (487 lines)	Picture	
263		$V=0$ (487 lines)	Picture	EQ
	‡1		EQ	EQ
‡264 [1]			EQ	EQ
	‡2		EQ	EQ
‡265 [2]			EQ	EQ
	‡3		EQ	EQ

Table 41.1 opposite shows the vertical structure of a frame in 480*i* video, and indicates the assignment of line numbers and their content.

Concerning closed captions, see ANSI/EIA/CEA-608-B, *Line 21 Data Services*.

In legacy equipment, the picture may start as early as line 20 or line 283. However, video on lines 21 and 284 is liable to be replaced by line 21 closed caption data upon NTSC transmission, so it is pointless to provide more than 483 picture lines in the studio. With the wide use of 480*i* DV and MPEG-2 systems, I argue that it is pointless to provide more than 480 lines; however, 483 lines are broadcast in analog NTSC.

For details concerning VITC line assignment, see SMPTE RP 164, *Location of Vertical Interval Timecode.*

Lines 10 through 21 and 273 through 284 may carry ancillary ("vertical interval") signals either related or unrelated to the picture. If *vertical interval timecode* (VITC) is used, it should be located on line 14 (277); a second, redundant copy can be placed on line 16 (279). Failing line 14, line 18 (281) is suggested. See *Vertical interval timecode (VITC),* on page 385.

Line sync

Horizontal events are referenced to an instant in time denoted 0_H. In the analog domain, 0_H is defined by the 50%-point of the leading (negative-going) edge of each line sync pulse. In a component digital interface, the correspondence between sync and the digital information is determined by a *timing reference signal* (TRS) conveyed across the interface. (See *Digital sync, TRS, ancillary data, and interface,* on page 389.)

In an analog interface, every line commences at 0_H with the negative-going edge of a sync pulse. With the exception of vertical sync lines, which I will describe in a moment, each line commences with a *normal* sync pulse, to be described. Each line that commences with normal sync may contain video information. In composite video, each line that commences with normal sync must contain *burst*, to be described on page 512. Component video has no burst. Every line that commences with a sync pulse other than normal sync maintains blanking level, except for the intervals occupied by sync pulses.

Field/frame sync

To define vertical sync, the frame is divided into intervals of halfline duration. Each halfline either contains no sync information or commences with the assertion of a sync pulse having one of three durations, each having a tolerance of ±0.100 μs:

EIA and FCC standards in the United States rounded the equalization pulse duration to two digits, to 2.3 μs, slightly less than the theoretical value of 2.35 μs. Equipment is usually designed to the letter of the regulation, rather than its intent.

- A *normal* sync pulse having a duration of 4.7 μs
- An *equalization* pulse having half the duration of a normal sync pulse
- A *broad* pulse, having a duration of half the line time less the duration of a normal sync pulse

Each set of 525 halflines in the field commences with a vertical sync sequence as follows:

Line 263 commences with a normal sync pulse and has an equalization pulse halfway through the line. Line 272 commences with an equalization pulse and remains at blanking with no sync pulse halfway through the line.

- Six preequalization pulses
- Six broad pulses
- Six postequalization pulses

Vertical events are referenced to an instant in time denoted 0_V; see Figure 34.2, on page 402). 0_V is defined by the first equalization pulse coincident with 0_H. Line number 1 is signalled by 0_V; lines count in interlaced time order (not spatial order) throughout the frame. 480*i* systems are exceptional in identifying 0_V and line 1 at the first equalization pulse: In 576*i*, and in HDTV, 0_V and line 1 are marked at the first broad pulse.

Historically, in the analog domain, 0_V was defined for each field by the 50%-point of the first equalization pulse; lines were numbered from 1 to 263 in the first field and from 1 to 262 in the second field. In the digital domain, the first field contains 262 lines and the second field contains 263 lines.

Figure 41.1 opposite shows details of the sync structure; this waveform diagram is the analog of Table 41.1, *480i line assignment*, on page 500.

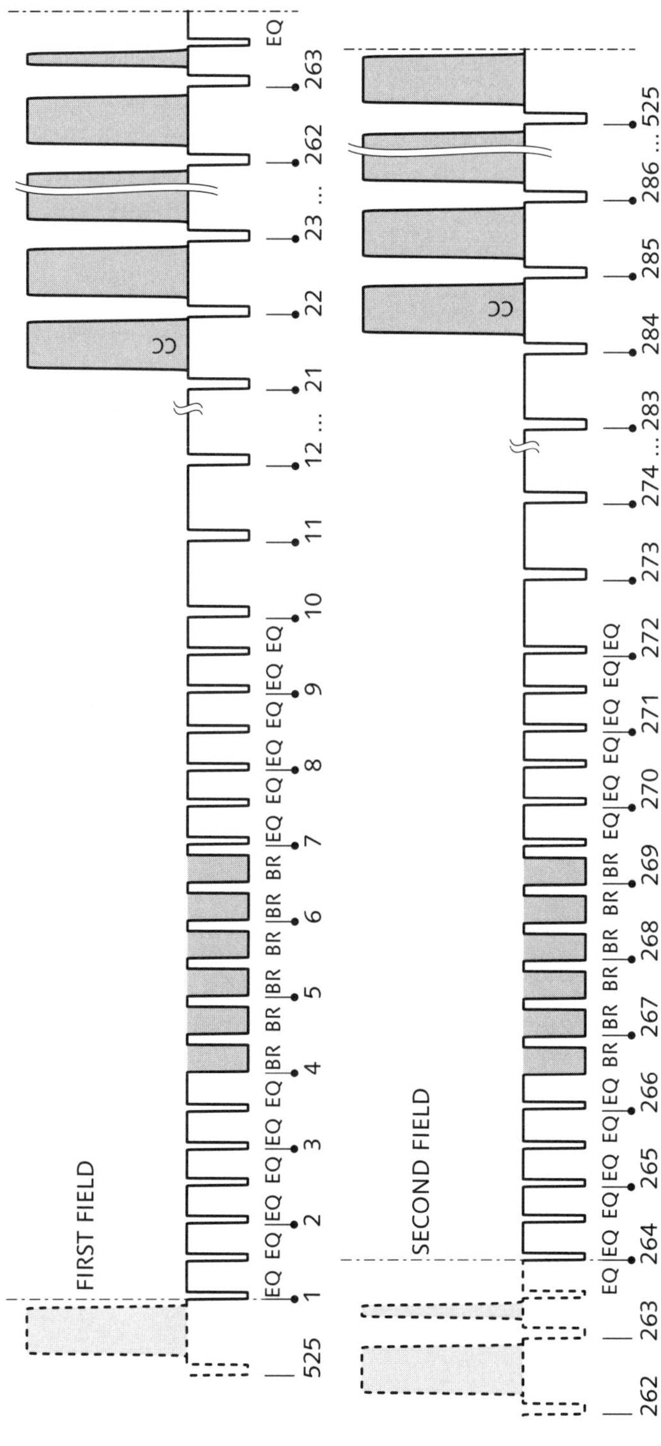

Figure 41.1 **480*i* raster, vertical.** This drawing shows waveforms of first and second fields, detailing the vertical sync intervals. CC indicates a line that may contain EIA 608 ("line 21") closed caption data.

When sync is represented in analog or digitized $4f_{SC}$ form, a raised-cosine transition having a risetime (from 10% to 90%) of 140±20 ns is imposed; the midpoint of the transition is coincident with the idealized sync.

SMPTE RP 168, *Definition of Vertical Interval Switching Point for Synchronous Video Switching*.

Switching between video sources is performed in the vertical interval, to avoid disruption of sync or picture. Switching occurs 30±5 µs after 0_H of the first normal line of each field. In 480*i* systems, switching occurs midway through line 10. (If field 2 were dominant, switching would occur midway through line 273.)

RGB primary components

Picture information originates with linear-light primary red, green, and blue (*RGB*) tristimulus components, represented in abstract terms in the range 0 (reference black) to +1 (reference white). In modern standards for 480*i*, the colorimetric properties of the primary components conform to *SMPTE RP 145 primaries*, described on page 239.

Nonlinear transfer function

From *RGB* tristimulus values, three nonlinear primary components are computed according to the optoelectronic transfer function of *Rec. 709 transfer function*, described on page 263. In Equation 41.1, *L* denotes a tristimulus component, and V'_{709} denotes a nonlinear primary component (one of *R'*, *G'*, or *B'*):

$$V'_{709} = \begin{cases} 4.5L; & 0 \le L < 0.018 \\ 1.099L^{0.45} - 0.099; & 0.018 \le L \le 1 \end{cases} \qquad \text{Eq 41.1}$$

This process is loosely called *gamma correction*.

The *R'*, *G'*, and *B'* components should maintain time-coincidence with each other, and with sync, within ±25 ns.

Luma (*Y'*)

Luma in 480*i* systems is computed as a weighted sum of nonlinear *R'*, *G'*, and *B'* primary components, according to the luma coefficients of Rec. 601, as detailed in *Rec. 601 luma*, on page 291:

$$^{601}Y' = 0.299\,R' + 0.587\,G' + 0.114\,B' \qquad \text{Eq 41.2}$$

The luma component Y', being a weighted sum of nonlinear $R'G'B'$ components, has no simple relationship with CIE luminance (denoted Y) or relative luminance used in color science. Video encoding specifications typically place no upper bound on luma bandwidth (though transmission standards may).

Picture center, aspect ratio, and blanking

SMPTE RP 187, *Center, Aspect Ratio and Blanking of Video Images.*

The center of the picture is located midway between the central two of the 720 active samples of Rec. 601, at the fraction $^{321}/_{572}$ between 0_H instants. Concerning the vertical center, see Table 41.1, on page 500.

$$\frac{S_{TL} - S_{EAV-0_H} + 0.5\left(S_{AL} - 1\right)}{S_{TL}} = \frac{858 - 736 + 0.5\left(720 - 1\right)}{858} = \frac{321}{572}$$

In 4:3 systems, aspect ratio is defined to be 4:3 with respect to a *clean aperture* pixel array, 708 samples wide at sampling rate of 13.5 MHz, and 480 lines high.

In widescreen 480*i* with luma sampled at 13.5 MHz, the clean aperture defines 16:9 aspect ratio. In widescreen 480*i* with luma sampled at 18 MHz, aspect ratio is defined to be 16:9 with respect to a clean aperture pixel array, 944 samples wide.

In *Transition samples,* on page 323, I mentioned that it is necessary to avoid, at the start of a line, an instantaneous transition from blanking to picture information. SMPTE standards call for picture information to have a risetime of 140±20 ns. For 480*i* or 576*i* video, a blanking transition is best implemented as a three-sample sequence where the video signal is limited in turn to 10%, 50%, and 90% of its full excursion.

No studio standard addresses square sampling of 480*i* video. I recommend using a sample rate of $780f_H$, that is, 12 $^{3}/_{11}$ MHz (i.e., $12.272\overline{727}$ MHz). I recommend using 648 samples – or, failing that, 644 or 640 – centered as mentioned above.

SMPTE RP 202, *Video Alignment for MPEG-2 Coding.*

When MPEG-2 with 480 or 512 image rows is used in the studio, the bottom image row corresponds to line 525 (as indicated in Table 41.1). The bottom left-hand halfline (on line 263) is not among the coded image rows. Unfortunately, 480*i* DV systems digitize a range one image row up from this.

Halfline blanking

Most component video equipment treats the top and bottom lines of both fields as integral lines; blanking of halflines is assumed to be imposed at the time of conversion to analog. In composite equipment and analog equipment, halfline blanking must be imposed.

$$30.593 \approx \frac{63.55\overline{5}}{2} - \frac{732-716}{13.5}$$

In the composite and analog domains, video information at the bottom of the picture, on the left half of line 263, should terminate 30.593 µs after 0_H. This timing is comparable to blanking at end of a full line, but preceding the midpoint between 0_H instants instead of preceding the 0_H instant itself.

$$41.259 \approx \frac{63.55\overline{5}}{2} - \frac{858-732-2}{13.5}$$

Historically, in the composite and analog domains, a right halfline at the top of the picture – such as picture on line 284 – commenced about 41 µs after 0_H. This timing is comparable to blanking at start of a full line, but following the midpoint between 0_H instants instead of following the 0_H instant itself. However, in NTSC broadcast, line 284 must remain available for closed captioning (along with line 21). So, it is now pointless for studio equipment to carry the traditional right-hand halfline of picture on line 284: Picture should be considered to comprise 482 full lines, plus a left-hand halfline on line 263.

Halfline blanking has been abolished from progressive scan video, and from JPEG, MPEG, and HDTV.

Component digital 4:2:2 interface

SDI was introduced on page 130. Mechanical and electrical details were presented on page 396.

The C_B and C_R color difference components of digital video are formed by scaling *B'-Y'* and *R'-Y'* components, as described in *C_BC_R components for SDTV* on page 305. $Y'C_BC_R$ signals are usually conveyed through the *serial digital interface* (SDI), which I introduced on page 130. *R'G'B'* 4:4:4 (or *R'G'B'A* 4:4:4:4) components can be conveyed across a dual-link interface using two SDI channels; alternatively, the single-link 540 Mb/s SDI interface of SMPTE 344M can be used.

8:8:8 refers to sampling of 480*i* (or 576*i*) at 27 MHz. Usually, subsampling notation starts with the digit 3 or 4.

In 13.5 MHz sampling of 480*i*, the sample located 16 sample clock intervals after EAV corresponds to the

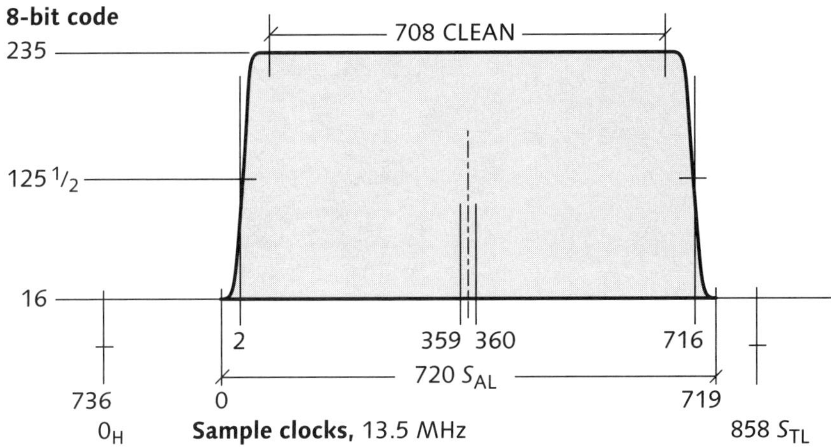

Figure 41.2 **480*i* component digital 4:2:2 luma waveform**

line sync datum (0_H): If digitized, that sample would take the 50% value of analog sync.

Figure 41.2 above shows a waveform drawing of luma in a 480*i* component digital 4:2:2 system.

Component analog *R'G'B'* interface

A component 480*i* *R'G'B'* interface is based on nonlinear *R'*, *G'*, and *B'* signals, conveyed according to *Analog electrical interface* and *Analog mechanical interface,* on page 408.

SMPTE 253M, *Three-Channel RGB Analog Video Interface.*

In studio systems, analog component *R'G'B'* signals usually have zero setup, so zero in Equation 41.1 corresponds to 0 V_{DC}. According to SMPTE 253M, unity corresponds to 700 mV. Sync is added to the green component according to Equation 41.3, where *sync* and *active* are taken to be unity when asserted and zero otherwise:

$$G'_{sync} = \frac{7}{10}\left(active \cdot G'\right) + \frac{3}{10}\left(-sync\right) \qquad \text{Eq 41.3}$$

Sadly, the SMPTE *R'G'B'* analog interface is unpopular, and "NTSC-related" levels are usually used, either with or without setup.

Some systems, such as 480*i* studio video in Japan, use a picture-to-sync ratio of 10:4 and zero setup. In this case, unity in Equation 41.1 corresponds to 5⁄7 V, about 714 mV:

$$V'_{\text{sync}} = \frac{5}{7}\left(active \cdot V'\right) + \frac{2}{7}\left(-sync\right) \qquad \text{Eq 41.4}$$

Many systems – such as computer framebuffers using the levels of the archaic EIA RS-343-A standard – code component video similarly to composite video, with 10:4 picture-to-sync ratio and 7.5% setup:

$$V'_{\text{sync}} = \frac{3}{56} active + \frac{37}{56}\left(active \cdot V'\right) + \frac{2}{7}\left(-sync\right) \qquad \text{Eq 41.5}$$

For details, see *Setup* on page 514.

Use of sync-on-green (RG_SB) in computer monitor interfaces was once common, but separate sync (RGBS) is now common.

The P_B and P_R scale factors are appropriate only for component analog interfaces. Consult *C_BC_R components for SDTV*, on page 305, for details concerning scale factors for component digital systems; consult *UV components*, on page 336, for details concerning scale factors for composite analog or digital NTSC or PAL.

Component analog $Y'P_BP_R$ interface, EBU N10

The P_B and P_R color difference components of analog video are formed by scaling $B'-Y'$ and $R'-Y'$ components, as described in *P_BP_R components for SDTV* on page 303. Wideband P_B and P_R components are theoretically possible but very rarely used; normally, they are lowpass filtered to half the bandwidth of luma.

Y', P_B, and P_R signals are conveyed electrically according to *Analog electrical interface* and *Analog mechanical interface*, on page 408.

Component $Y'P_BP_R$ signals in 480*i* are sometimes interfaced with zero setup, with levels according to the EBU Tech. N10 standard. Zero (reference blanking level) for Y', P_B, and P_R corresponds to a level of 0 V_{DC}, and unity corresponds to 700 mV. Sync is added to the luma component; *sync* is taken to be unity when asserted and zero otherwise:

$$Y'_{\text{sync}} = \frac{7}{10} Y' + \frac{3}{10}\left(-sync\right) \qquad \text{Eq 41.6}$$

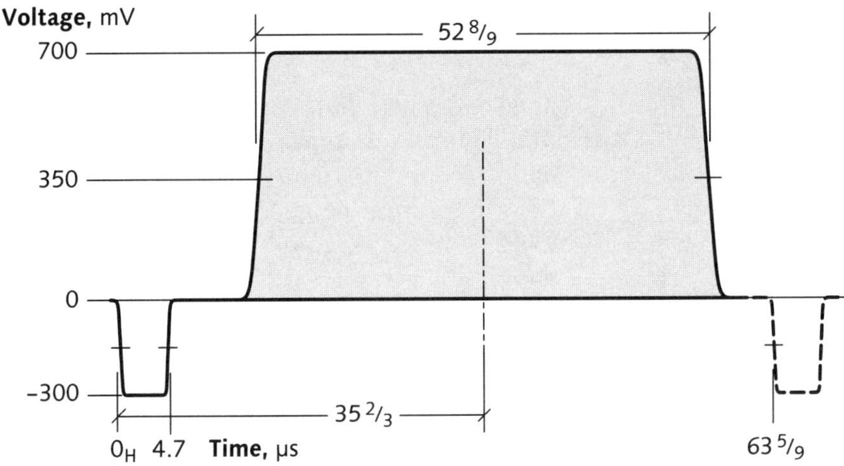

Figure 41.3 **480*i* component analog luma waveform** with SMPTE levels and zero setup.

Figure 41.3 shows a waveform drawing of luma in a 480*i* component analog interface according to the EBU Tech. N10 standard. In North America, the levels of EBU N10 mysteriously became known as "SMPTE levels," or "SMPTE/EBU N10 interface," even though N10 is solely an EBU standard, and though SMPTE has never standardized a component analog luma/color difference interface.

EIA/CEA-770.2, Standard Definition TV Analog Component Video Interface.

EIA/CEA has standardized the 700 mV, zero-setup levels for use by consumer electronics devices such as DVD players and set-top boxes, for 480*i* and 480*p* formats at 4:3 and 16:9 aspect ratios.

Component analog $Y'P_BP_R$ interface, industry standard

Unfortunately, equipment from two manufacturers was deployed before SMPTE reached agreement on a standard component video analog interface for studio equipment. Although it is sometimes available as an option, the SMPTE standard is rarely used in 480*i*. Instead, two "industry" standards are in use: Sony and Panasonic. Ideally the $Y'P_BP_R$ nomenclature would signify that luma has zero setup, and that color difference components have the same excursion (from black to white) as luma. However, both of the industry standards use setup, and neither gives the color difference components the same excursion as luma.

Sony equipment utilizes 10:4 picture-to-sync ratio (roughly 714 mV luma, 286 mV sync) with 7.5% setup on luma (giving a picture excursion of 660$\frac{5}{7}$ mV). Color differences range $\frac{4}{3}$ times ±350 mV, that is, ±466$\frac{2}{3}$ mV. (75% colorbars have a $P_B P_R$ excursion of ±350 mV.)

Panasonic equipment utilizes 7:3 picture-to-sync ratio (exactly 700 mV luma, 300 mV sync) with 7.5% setup on luma (giving a picture excursion of 647.5 mV). Color differences are scaled by the $\frac{37}{40}$ setup fraction, for an excursion of ±323.75 mV.

480*i* NTSC composite video 42

Although this book is mainly concerned with *digital* video, the installed base of hundreds of millions of units of analog video equipment cannot be ignored. Furthermore, composite $4f_{SC}$ digital video – including video recorded in the D-2 and D-3 formats – is essentially just digitized analog video. To understand $4f_{SC}$ equipment, you must understand conventional analog NTSC video.

This chapter details the technical parameters of composite 480*i* video. I discuss subcarrier, composite chroma, composite analog NTSC, and the S-video-525 interface. I assume that you have read the *Introduction to composite NTSC and PAL,* on page 103; additionally, I assume you are familiar with the sync structure and *R'G'B'* coding described in *480i component video,* on page 499. Before explaining the signal flow, I will introduce subcarrier and burst.

Subcarrier

Synchronous with the scanning raster is a pair of continuous-wave subcarriers having 227½ cycles per total raster line: a sine wave (referred to as *subcarrier*) whose zero-crossing is coincident ±10° with 0_H, and a cosine wave in quadrature (equivalent to a sine wave at a phase advance of 90°). Delay of the subcarrier's zero-crossing with respect to the 0_H datum, measured in degrees of subcarrier, is known as *subcarrier to horizontal* (SCH) *phase*, or if greater than 10°, *SCH error.* Derived color subcarrier frequency is $^{315}/_{88}$ MHz ±10 ppm, or about 3.58 MHz. Subcarrier drift should not exceed ±1⁄10 Hz per second. Subcarrier jitter should not exceed ±0.5 ns over one line time.

$$\frac{455}{2} \times 525 = 119437.5$$

NTSC two-frame sequence

Because the total number of subcarrier cycles per line is an odd multiple of one-half, and there is an odd number of lines per frame, subcarrier can fall in one of two relationships with the start of a frame. *Colorframes* denoted *A* and *B* are distinguished by the phase of subcarrier at 0_H at the start of the frame: colorframe *A* at 0°, and colorframe *B* at 180°. This relationship is also referred to as a four-field sequence of *colorfields* 1, 2, 3, and 4 (or I, II, III, and IV), corresponding to A_{FIRST}, A_{SECOND}, B_{FIRST}, B_{SECOND}.

Colorframe *A* relates to NTSC subcarrier phase. It is distinguished from *A-Frame*, which relates to 2-3 pulldown; see *2-3 pulldown*, on page 429.

NTSC burst

Burst is formed by multiplying the inverted sine subcarrier by a *burst gate* that is asserted 19 subcarrier cycles after 0_H, within a tolerance of $^{+200}_{-100}$ ns, on every line that commences with a normal sync pulse. Burst gate has a duration of 9±1 subcarrier cycles. Burst gate has raised-cosine transitions whose 50%-points are coincident with the time intervals specified above, and whose risetimes are 300^{+200}_{-100} ns.

The inversion of burst from subcarrier puts burst at 180° on a vectorscope display.

It is unfortunate that video standards specify cumulative ("stacked") tolerances at the end of the burst envelope.

Figure 42.1 below sketches the relationship of subcarrier, sync, and burst. Subcarrier may be in the phase indicated, or inverted, depending on colorframe.

Today, even monochrome (black-and-white) video signals have burst. A decoder should accept, as monochrome, any signal without burst.

Figure 42.1 **Subcarrier to horizontal (SCH) relationship**

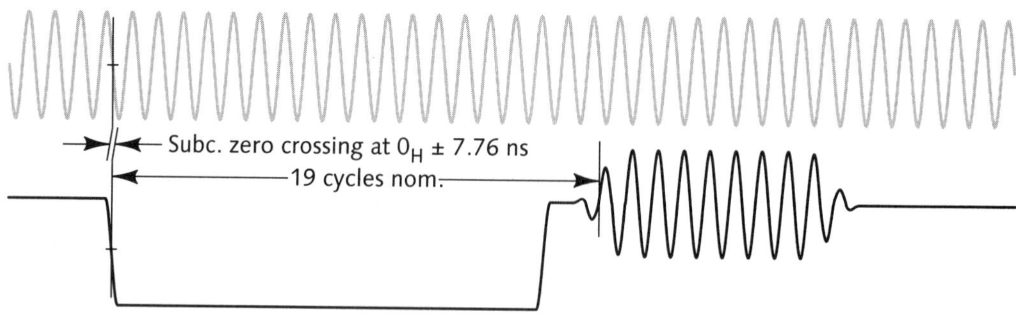

Color differences (U, V)

Color differences for S-video-525 and NTSC are computed by scaling $B'-Y'$ and $R'-Y'$ components to form U and V, as I described in *UV components*, on page 336. This scaling limits the maximum value of the composite signal, to be defined in *Composite NTSC encoding*, on page 515, to the range $-1/3$ to $+4/3$. The scale factors would cause 100% colorbars to have an excursion from $-33\frac{1}{3}$ IRE to $+133\frac{1}{3}$ IRE, were it not for the scaling by $37/40$ (i.e., 0.925) that occurs when setup is introduced. (Setup will be detailed on page 514.)

The $+4/3$ limit applies to composite studio equipment; a limit of +1.2 applies to terrestrial (VHF/UHF) broadcast.

Color difference filtering

The U and V color difference components are subject to lowpass filtering with the following attenuation:

- Less than 2 dB at frequencies less than 1.3 MHz
- At least 20 dB at frequencies greater than 3.6 MHz

In the studio, where 4.9 MHz or more of composite bandwidth is maintained, 1.3 MHz of chroma bandwidth is available. However, terrestrial VHF/UHF transmission of NTSC limits composite bandwidth to 4.2 MHz. Even if 1.3 MHz of chroma is encoded, upon filtering to 4.2 MHz, [U, V] chroma crosstalk is introduced: Only 600 kHz of crosstalk-free chroma is transmitted. These issues were detailed in *NTSC Y'IQ system*, on page 365.

Chroma (C)

As I explained in *NTSC chroma modulation*, on page 338, in NTSC, U and V color difference components are combined into a single *chroma* signal:

$$C = U \sin \omega t + V \cos \omega t; \qquad \omega = 2\pi f_{SC} \qquad \text{Eq 42.1}$$

Concerning the association of U with sin and V with cos, see the marginal note on page 339.

sin ωt and cos ωt represent the 3.58 MHz color subcarrier defined in *Subcarrier*, on page 511.

In the past, to be compliant with FCC regulations for broadcast, an NTSC modulator was supposed to operate on *I* and *Q* components, where the *Q* component was bandwidth limited more severely than the *I* component:

$$C = Q\sin\left(\omega t + 33°\right) + I\cos\left(\omega t + 33°\right);\ \omega = 2\pi f_{SC} \qquad \text{Eq 42.2}$$

The bandwidth limitation of *Q*, to about 600 kHz, was specified in the original design of NTSC to permit accurate recovery of the 1.3 MHz wideband *I* component from a signal transmitted through a 4.2 MHz channel. *Y'IQ* was important in the early days of NTSC, but contemporary NTSC equipment modulates equiband *U* and *V*, where only 600 kHz of bandwidth can be recovered from each color difference signal. This practice has been enshrined in SMPTE 170M. See *Y'IQ encoding*, on page 368.

The *Y'* and *C* components should be time-coincident within ±25 ns. Error in chroma timing is known as *chroma-luma delay*.

Setup

Certain elements of the vertical interval in NTSC – particularly VITC and closed caption data – are mandated to have zero setup. These elements can't be carried through component equipment, because Rec. 601's footroom does not extend to 0 IRE.

480*i* composite video usually has *7.5% setup*, which I introduced in *Setup (pedestal)*, on page 327: Luma is scaled and offset so that reference white remains at unity, but reference black is raised by the fraction 7.5% of full scale. The luma signal remains at zero – *reference blanking level* – during intervals when no picture is being conveyed.

When setup is used, the same scale factor that is applied to luma must also be applied to chroma, to ensure that the peak excursion (luma plus modulated chroma) remains at +4⁄3 of reference white, or, in other words, to ensure that the peaks of 75% colorbars exactly match reference white at 100% (100 IRE):

$$\begin{aligned} {}^{601}_{\text{setup}}Y' &= \frac{3}{40} + \frac{37}{40}\,{}^{601}Y' \\ {}_{\text{setup}}C &= \frac{37}{40}C \end{aligned} \qquad \text{Eq 42.3}$$

Setup originated in the vacuum tube era to prevent retrace lines from becoming visible due to unstable black levels. It now serves no useful purpose but is retained for compatibility reasons. Japan has abolished setup ("NTSC-J").

S-video-525 ($Y'/C3.58$)

IEC 60933-5 (1992-11) *Interconnections and matching values – Part 5: Y/C connector for video systems – Electrical matching values and description of the connector.*

As I introduced in *S-video interface*, on page 107, an S-video interface conveys luma and chroma separately in order to avoid the cross-luma and cross-color artifacts that would result if they were summed to form a single composite signal. S-video has three versions: *S-video-525* and *S-video-525-J* (to be described here), and *S-video-625* (to be described on page 531). Thankfully, there's no S-video-PAL-M, S-video-PAL-N, S-video-525-4.43, or S-video-SECAM! The S-video connector is shown in Figure 34.10, on page 409.

S-video-525, sometimes called *Y'/C3.58*, has 480*i* scanning, 3.58 MHz color subcarrier, NTSC color coding, and 7.5% setup. The Y' and C signals at an S-video-525 interface have structure and levels identical to the constituent parts of analog NTSC. If Y' and C are summed, a legal NTSC signal results:

$$\begin{aligned} Y'_{\text{S-video-525}} &= \frac{5}{7} \cdot {}^{601}_{\text{setup}}Y' &&+ \frac{2}{7}\left(-sync\right) \\ C_{\text{S-video-525}} &= \frac{5}{7} \cdot {}_{\text{setup}}C &&+ \frac{2}{7}\left(\frac{burst}{2}\right) \end{aligned} \qquad \text{Eq 42.4}$$

The zero-setup version of NTSC used in Japan ("NTSC-J") has led to a version of S-video that I denote *S-video-525-J*. It has 480*i* scanning, 3.58 MHz color subcarrier, and zero setup:

$$\begin{aligned} Y'_{\text{S-video-525-J}} &= \frac{5}{7} \cdot {}^{601}Y' &&+ \frac{2}{7}\left(-sync\right) \\ C_{\text{S-video-525-J}} &= \frac{5}{7} \cdot C &&+ \frac{2}{7}\left(\frac{burst}{2}\right) \end{aligned} \qquad \text{Eq 42.5}$$

Unfortunately, no signal element is present that enables a decoder to distinguish whether an S-video-525 signal has 7.5% setup or zero setup.

Composite NTSC encoding

A composite NTSC signal is formed by summing luma (Y') and modulated chroma (C) signals, along with sync and burst. In the following expressions, *sync* is taken to be unity when asserted and zero otherwise; *burst* is in the range ±1.

In composite 480*i* with setup, the expressions are these:

Eq 42.6

$$NTSC_{\text{setup}} = \frac{5}{7}\left({}^{601}_{\text{setup}}Y' + {}_{\text{setup}}C \right) \qquad + \frac{2}{7}\left(\frac{burst}{2} - sync \right)$$

The excursion of 480*i* luma, from synctip to reference white, ranges from -40 IRE to +100 IRE. When maximum chroma is added, the composite signal reaches a minimum of -23⅓ IRE (on 100% saturated blue and red colors), and a maximum of 130⅚ IRE (on 100% saturated cyan and yellow colors).

In the zero-setup NTSC system used in Japan, luma and modulated chroma are summed as follows:

Eq 42.7

$$NTSC_{J} = \frac{5}{7}\left({}^{601}Y' + C \right) \qquad + \frac{2}{7}\left(\frac{burst}{2} - sync \right)$$

The composite NTSC-J signal reaches a minimum of -33⅓ IRE and a maximum of 133⅓ IRE.

Composite digital NTSC interface ($4f_{SC}$)

SMPTE 259M, *10-Bit 4:2:2 Component and $4f_{SC}$ Composite Digital Signals – Serial Digital Interface.*

Digital composite NTSC – also known as the 480*i* version of $4f_{SC}$ – is formed by scaling and offsetting Equation 42.6 so that in an 8-bit system blanking (zero in the equation) is at codeword 60 and reference white is at codeword 200. With zero setup, as in NTSC-J, the luma excursion is 140 codes. With 7.5% setup, the luma excursion is 129½ codes – inconveniently, not an integer number of 8-bit codes.

In a 10-bit system, the reference codes are multiplied by four: The reference codes remain the same except for having two low-order zero bits appended. Codewords having the 8 most-significant bits all-one or all-zero are prohibited from video data. Figure 42.2 above shows a waveform drawing of luma in a $4f_{SC}$ NTSC composite digital interface, with 7.5% setup.

Composite $4f_{SC}$ NTSC is sampled on the *I* and *Q* axes. The 0_H datum does not coincide with a sample instant – 0_H is, in effect, located at sample number

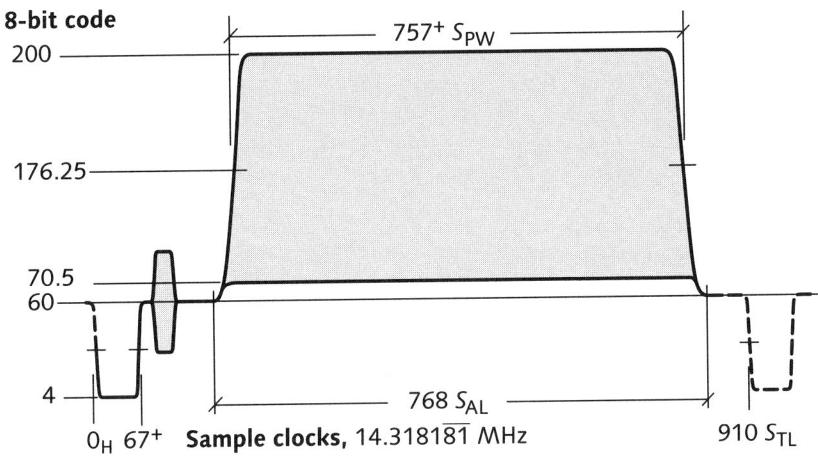

Figure 42.2 **$4f_{SC}$ NTSC digital waveform** with setup. The excursion indicated reflects the range of the luma component; the chroma component will cause excursions outside this range. It was a problem in 8-bit $4f_{SC}$ systems that the setup level had an inexact representation.

784 $^{33}/_{90}$. Burst samples lie at the -33°, 57°, 123°, and 213° phases of burst, and take 8-bit values {46, 83, 74, 37}. Although $4f_{SC}$ NTSC is sampled on the *IQ* axes, narrowband *Q* filtering is not necessarily applied.

Each line has 910 S_{TL} and 768 S_{AL}. Samples are numbered from 0 relative to the leftmost active sample.

The 50%-point of analog sync falls $^{57}/_{90}$ of the way between two samples. With conventional sample numbering, where sample 0 is the leftmost active sample in a line, 0_H falls between samples 784 and 785. The first word of TRS-ID is at sample 790.

The electrical and mechanical interface for $4f_{SC}$ is derived from the Rec. 656 parallel and serial interfaces; see *SDI coding,* on page 396.

Composite analog NTSC interface

SMPTE 170M, *Composite Analog Video Signal – NTSC for Studio Applications.*

Figure 42.3 above shows a waveform drawing of luma at a 480*i* composite analog interface, with 7.5% setup; the levels are detailed in *Composite analog levels,* on page 407. The excursion of 480*i* luma – from synctip to reference white – is normally 1 V_{PP}. Including

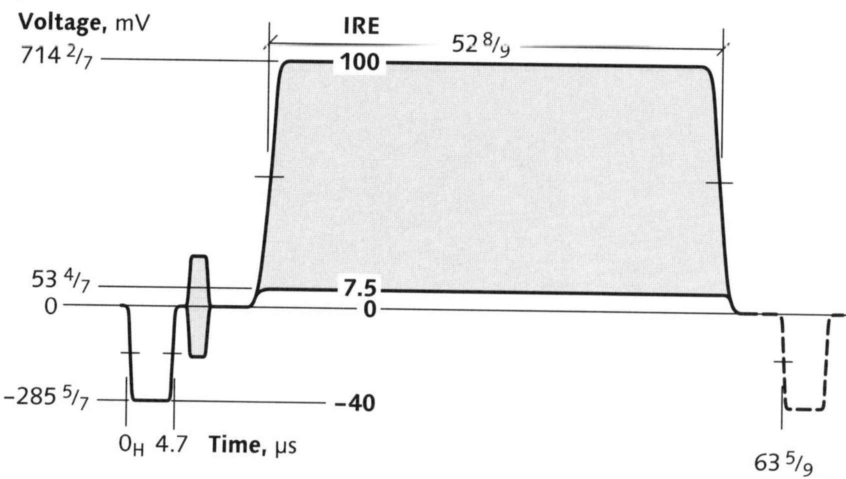

Figure 42.3 **480*i* composite NTSC analog waveform** showing the luma component, with setup.

maximum chroma excursion to about 131 IRE, the maximum excursion of the composite NTSC signal is about 1.22 V_{PP}.

EIA, *Industrial Electronics Tentative Standard No. 1* (IETNTS1), published on November 8, 1977.

The composite NTSC analog interface is sometimes called *RS-170*. EIA Recommended Standard 170 was adopted in 1957; it defined the signal format for 525/60.00 interlaced monochrome television at a field rate of exactly 60.00 Hz. This standard has been obsolete for nearly forty years. Revision A was proposed, but never adopted; had the revision been adopted, the standard would now properly be denoted *EIA-170-A.* The notation *RS-170-A* is technically erroneous, but it is widely used to refer to the timing diagram associated with 480*i* NTSC, as documented in the archaic EIA publication cited in the margin. SMPTE 170M, adopted in 1994, supersedes all of these.

576*i* component video 43

This chapter details the scanning, timing, sync structure, and picture structure of 576*i*25 (625/50/2:1) video. The scanning and timing information here applies to all variants of 576*i*25 video, both analog and digital. The sync information relates to component analog, composite analog, and composite digital systems. I assume that you are familiar with 480*i* component video, described on page 499.

Frame rate

576*i* video represents stationary or moving two-dimensional images sampled temporally at a constant rate of 25 frames per second. For studio video, the tolerance on frame rate is normally ±4 ppm. In practice the tolerance applies to a master clock at a high frequency, but for purposes of computation and standards writing it is convenient to reference the tolerance to the frame rate.

Interlace

Derived line rate is 15.625 kHz.

It is dangerous to refer to fields in 576*i* as *odd* and *even*. Use *first field* and *second field* instead.

A frame comprises a total of 625 horizontal raster lines of equal duration, uniformly scanned top to bottom and left to right, with 2:1 interlace to form a *first* field and a *second* field. Scanning lines in the second field are displaced vertically by half the vertical sampling pitch, and delayed temporally by half the frame time, from scanning lines in the first field. In MPEG-2 terms, the first field is the top field.

Lines are numbered consecutively throughout the frame, starting at 1.

Table 43.1 **576*i* line assignment**

EQ Equalization pulse

BR Broad pulse

‡ Burst suppressed if –135° phase

§ Burst suppressed unconditionally

¶ In $4f_{SC}$ PAL, line recommended for 1137 S_{TL} ("reset")

† VANC is permitted only on lines 20 through 22 and 333 through 335.

◊ The thick vertical bar at the right indicates lines carried in 576*i* or 576*p* MPEG-2 according to SMPTE RP 202. (The vertical center of the picture is located midway between lines 479 and 167.) Unfortunately, 576*i* DV systems digitize a range one image row up from this.

Line number, first field (F = 0)	*Line number, second field (F = 1)*	*V*	*Contents, Left half*	*Contents, Right half*
	¶313		EQ	BR
1			BR	BR
	314		BR	BR
2			BR	BR
	315		BR	BR
3			BR	EQ
	316		EQ	EQ
4			EQ	EQ
	317		EQ	EQ
5			EQ	EQ
	318		EQ	none
‡6			Vertical interval video	
	‡319		Vertical interval video	
7–18			Vertical interval video	
	320–331		Vertical interval video	
19			VITC	
	332		VITC	
†20			Vertical interval video	
	†333		Vertical interval video	
†21			VITC (ITS radiated)	
	†334		VITC (ITS radiated)	
†22			Quiet	
	†335		Quiet	
23		V = 0 (576 lines)	WSS	Picture ◊
	336–622		Picture (287 lines)	
24–‡310			Picture (287 lines)	
	§623		Picture	EQ
311			EQ	EQ
	624		EQ	EQ
312			EQ	EQ
	¶625		EQ	EQ

Table 43.1 opposite shows the vertical structure of a frame in 576*i* video, and indicates the assignment of line numbers and their content.

For details concerning VITC in 576*i*, see EBU Technical Standard N12, *Time-and-control codes for television recording*.

Lines 6 through 21 and 319 through 334 may carry ancillary ("vertical interval") signals either related or unrelated to the picture. If *vertical interval timecode* (VITC) is used, redundant copies should be placed on lines 19 (332) and 21 (334); see *Vertical interval timecode (VITC)*, on page 385.

Line sync

Horizontal events are referenced to an instant in time denoted 0_H. In the analog domain, 0_H is defined by the 50%-point of the leading (negative-going) edge of each line sync pulse. In a component digital interface, the correspondence between sync and the digital information is determined by a *timing reference signal* (TRS) conveyed across the interface. (See *Digital sync, TRS, ancillary data, and interface*, on page 389.)

In an analog interface, every line commences at 0_H with the negative-going edge of a sync pulse. With the exception of the vertical sync lines of each field, each line commences with the assertion of a *normal* sync pulse, to be described. Each line that commences with normal sync may contain video information. In composite video, each line that commences with normal sync must contain *burst*, to be described on page 530. Every line that commences with a sync pulse *other* than normal sync maintains blanking level, here denoted zero, except for the interval(s) occupied by sync pulses.

Analog field/frame sync

To define vertical sync, the frame is divided into intervals of halfline duration. Each halfline either contains no sync information, or commences with the assertion of a sync pulse having one of three durations, each having a tolerance of ±0.100 µs:

- A *normal* sync pulse having a duration of 4.7 µs

- An *equalization* pulse having half the duration of a normal sync pulse

- A *broad* pulse having a duration of half the line time less the duration of a normal sync pulse

Each set of 625 halflines in the frame is associated with a vertical sync sequence, as follows:

Line 623 commences with a normal sync pulse and has an equalization pulse halfway through the line. Line 318 commences with an equalization pulse and remains at blanking with no sync pulse halfway through the line.

- Five preequalization pulses

- Five broad pulses

- Five postequalization pulses

Line 1 and 0_V are defined by the first broad pulse coincident with 0_H; see Figure 34.3, on page 403. (This differs from the 480*i* convention.)

Figure 43.1 opposite shows the vertical sync structure of 576*i* analog video. This waveform diagram is the analog of Table 43.1, *576i line assignment,* on page 520.

See Table 11.1, on page 98, and Figures 34.2 and 34.3 on page 402.

Sync in 576*i* systems has several differences from 480*i* sync. There are five preequalization, broad, and postequalization pulses per field (instead of six of each). The frame is defined to start with the field containing the top line of the picture, actually a right-hand halfline. (In 480*i* scanning, the first picture line of a frame is a full line, and the right-hand halfline at the top of the picture is in the second field.)

In 576*i* systems, lines are numbered starting with the first broad sync pulse: preequalization pulses are counted at the end of one field instead of the beginning of the next. This could be considered to be solely a nomenclature issue, but because line numbers are encoded in digital video interfaces, the issue is substantive. In 576*i* systems, lines are always numbered throughout the frame.

When sync is represented in analog or digitized form, a raised-cosine transition having a risetime (from 10%

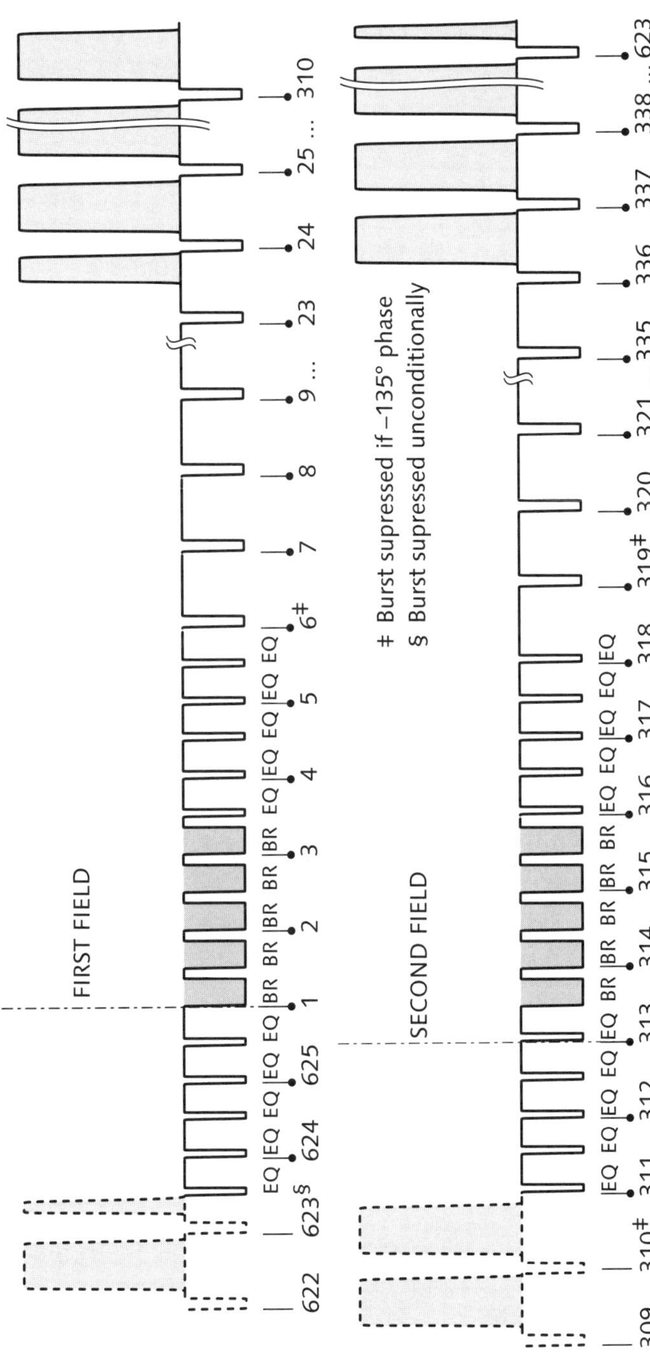

Figure 43.1 **576*i* raster, vertical.** This drawing shows waveforms of first and second fields, detailing vertical sync intervals. The first field comprises 312 lines, and the second field comprises 313 lines.

to 90%) of 200±20 ns is imposed, where the midpoint of the transition is coincident with the idealized sync.

SMPTE RP 168, *Definition of Vertical Interval Switching Point for Synchronous Video Switching*.

Switching between video sources is performed in the vertical interval, to avoid disruption of sync or picture. Switching occurs 30±5 μs after 0_H of the first normal line of each field. In 576*i* systems, switching occurs midway through line 6. (If field 2 were dominant, switching would occur midway through line 319.)

RGB primary components

Picture information originates with linear-light primary red, green, and blue (*RGB*) tristimulus components, represented in abstract terms in the range 0 (reference black) to +1 (reference white). In modern standards for 576*i*, the colorimetric properties of the primary components conform to *EBU Tech. 3213 primaries* on page 238.

Nonlinear transfer function

576*i* standards documents indicate a precorrection of $^1/_{2.8}$, approximately 0.36, but the Rec. 709 transfer function is usually used. See *Gamma in video* on page 261.

From *RGB* tristimulus values, three nonlinear primary components are computed according to the optoelectronic transfer function of *Rec. 709 transfer function*, described on page 263. In Equation 43.1, L denotes a tristimulus component, and V'_{709} denotes a nonlinear primary component (one of R', G', or B'):

$$V'_{709} = \begin{cases} 4.5L; & 0 \le L < 0.018 \\ 1.099\,L^{0.45} - 0.099; & 0.018 \le L \le 1 \end{cases} \qquad \text{Eq 43.1}$$

This process is loosely called *gamma correction*.

The R', G', and B' components should maintain time-coincidence with each other, and with sync, within ±25 ns.

Luma (Y')

Luma in 576*i* systems is computed as a weighted sum of nonlinear R', G', and B' primary components according to the luma coefficients of Rec. 601:

$$^{601}Y' = 0.299\,R' + 0.587\,G' + 0.114\,B' \qquad \text{Eq 43.2}$$

The luma component Y', being a weighted sum of nonlinear $R'G'B'$ components, has no simple relationship with the CIE luminance, denoted Y, or relative luminance, used in color science. Video encoding specifications typically place no upper bound on luma bandwidth (though transmission standards may).

Picture center, aspect ratio, and blanking

SMPTE RP 187, *Center, Aspect Ratio and Blanking of Video Images.*

The center of the picture is located midway between the central pair of the 720 active samples of Rec. 601, at the fraction $^{983}/_{1728}$ between 0_H instants. Concerning the vertical center, see Table 43.1, on page 520.

$$\frac{S_{TL} - S_{EAV-0_H} + 0.5(S_{AL} - 1)}{S_{TL}} = \frac{864 - 732 + 0.5(720 - 1)}{864} = \frac{983}{1728}$$

Aspect ratio is defined as 4:3 with respect to a *clean aperture* pixel array, 690 samples wide at sampling rate of 13.5 MHz, and 566 lines high. Blanking transitions should not intrude into the clean aperture.

In widescreen 576*i* with luma sampled at 18 MHz, aspect ratio is defined to be 16:9 with respect to a clean aperture pixel array, 920 samples wide.

In the composite and analog domains, video information on the left-hand halfline of line 623 terminates 30.350±0.1 µs after 0_H. Video information on the right-hand halfline of line 23 commences 42.500±0.1 µs after 0_H.

No studio standard addresses square sampling of 576*i* video. I recommend using a sample rate of $944 f_H$, that is, 14.75 MHz. I recommend using 768 active samples, centered as mentioned above.

SMPTE RP 202, *Video Alignment for MPEG-2 Coding.*

When MPEG-2 with 576 or 608 image rows is used in the studio, the bottom image row corresponds to line 623 (as indicated in Table 43.1). The bottom left-hand halfline (on line 623) is among the coded image rows. The right-hand half of this line will be blank when presented to the MPEG encoder; upon decoding, it may contain artifacts. Unfortunately, 576*i* DV systems digitize a range one image row up from this.

Component digital 4:2:2 interface

The C_B and C_R color difference components of digital video are formed by scaling *B'-Y'* and *R'-Y'* components, as described in *C_BC_R components for SDTV* on page 305. $Y'C_BC_R$ signals were once conveyed through the parallel digital interface specified in Rec. 656 and EBU Tech. 3246; nowadays, the *serial digital interface* (SDI) is used. (SDI was introduced on page 130. Mechanical and electrical details were presented on page 396.)

8:8:8 denoted sampling of 576*i* (or 480*i*) $R'G'B'$ or $Y'C_BC_R$ at 27 MHz. This is an exception to the convention that subsampling notation starts with the digit 3 or 4.

In 13.5 MHz sampling of 576*i*, sample 732 corresponds to the line sync datum, 0_H. If digitized, that sample would take the 50% value of analog sync. SMPTE RP 187 specifies that samples 8 and 710 correspond to the 50%-points of picture width. For flat-panel displays, EBU suggests that the central 702 samples contain active video.

The choice of 720 active samples for Rec. 601 accommodates the blanking requirements of both 480*i* and 576*i* analog video: 720 samples are sufficient to accommodate the necessary transition samples for either system. See page 323.

Unfortunately, the blanking tolerances between 480*i* and 576*i* do not permit a *single* choice of blanking transition samples: The narrowest possible picture width in 480*i* is several samples too wide to meet 576*i* tolerances.

Figure 43.2 at the top of the facing page shows a waveform drawing of luma in a 576*i* component digital 4:2:2 system.

Component analog *R'G'B'* interface

EBU Technical Standard N20, *Parallel interface for analogue component video signals in GRB form.*

The interface for analog R', G', and B' signals is described in *Analog electrical interface* and *Analog mechanical interface*, on page 408. Zero (reference blanking level) in the R', G', and B' expressions corresponds to a level of 0 V_{DC}, and unity corresponds to 700 mV.

Sync is added to the green component according to:

$$G'_{sync} = \frac{7}{10}\left(active \cdot G'\right) + \frac{3}{10}\left(-sync\right) \qquad \text{Eq 43.3}$$

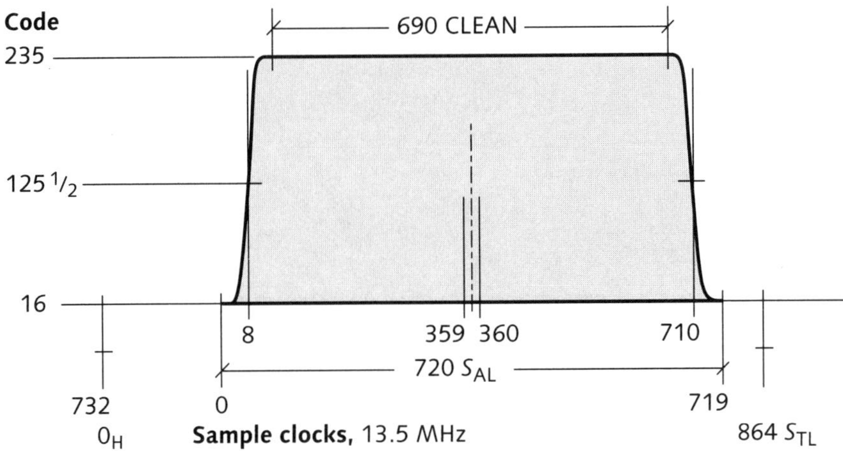

Figure 43.2 ***576i* component digital 4:2:2 luma waveform**

In component analog video, the excursion of the *G'* signal from synctip to reference white is 1 V_{PP}. Levels in 576*i* systems are usually specified in millivolts, not the IRE units common in 480*i* systems.

Component analog $Y'P_BP_R$ interface

The P_B and P_R color difference components of analog video are formed by scaling *B'-Y'* and *R'-Y'* components. Although it is possible in theory to have wideband P_B and P_R components, in practice they are lowpass filtered to about half the bandwidth of luma.

EBU Technical Standard N10, *Parallel interface for analogue component video signals.*

The interface for analog *Y'*, P_B, and P_R signals is described in *Analog electrical interface* and *Analog mechanical interface*, on page 408. Component 576*i* $Y'P_BP_R$ signals have zero setup. Sync is added to the luma component:

$$Y'_{sync} = \frac{7}{10}Y' + \frac{3}{10}\left(-sync\right) \qquad \text{Eq 43.4}$$

In analog 576*i* component interfaces, this excursion is conveyed as 1 V_{PP}, with reference blanking at 0 V_{DC}. The picture excursion of the *Y'* signal is 700 mV. Figure 43.3 overleaf shows a waveform drawing of luma in a 576*i* component analog interface.

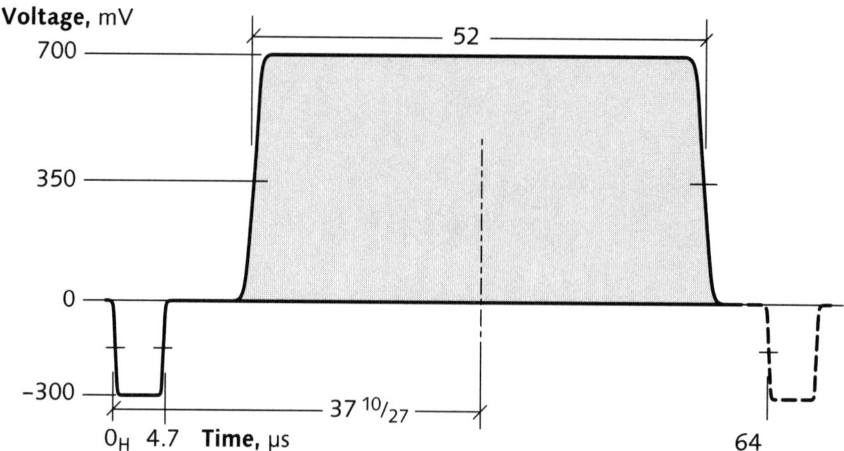

Figure 43.3 **576*i* component analog luma waveform**

576*i* PAL composite video 44

This chapter details the formation of 576*i* PAL-B/G/H/I composite video, and S-video-625. I assume that you are familiar with *576i component video* on page 519. I describe 576*i* PAL by explaining its differences from 480*i* NTSC, so I assume that you are quite familiar with NTSC composite video, described on page 511.

Subcarrier

$$\frac{1135}{4} + \frac{1}{625} = \frac{709379}{2500}$$

$$= 283.7516$$

There are 709379 samples in a composite $4f_{SC}$ PAL frame.

Synchronous with the 576*i* raster is a pair of continuous-wave subcarriers having exactly 283.7516 cycles per total raster line: a sine-wave (hereafter referred to as *subcarrier*) whose zero-crossing is coincident ±20° with 0_V, and a cosine-wave in quadrature (at 90°). Derived color subcarrier frequency is 4.43361875 MHz ±4 ppm. Subcarrier drift should not exceed ±$\frac{1}{10}$ Hz per second. Subcarrier jitter should not exceed ±0.5 ns over one line time.

PAL four-frame sequence

In PAL, the total number of subcarrier cycles per frame is an odd multiple of one-quarter. This causes subcarrier to fall in one of four relationships with the start of a frame. Where necessary, *colorframes I, II, III,* and *IV* are distinguished by the phase of subcarrier at 0_V at the start of the frame. The four-frame sequence is due to the $^{1135}/_4$ fraction, which relates subcarrier to line rate; the fraction $^1/_{625}$ contributes precisely one cycle per frame, so it has no effect on the four-frame sequence. (Some people call this an 8-field sequence.) Starting with $^{1135}/_4 f_H$ (i.e., $283\,^3/_4 f_H$), the $^1/_{625} f_H$ term is equivalent to a +25 Hz frequency offset; see page 355.

PAL burst

Burst – or *colorburst* – is formed by multiplying a phase-shifted version of subcarrier by a *burst gate* that has a duration of 10±1 cycles of subcarrier, and is asserted to unity, 5.6±0.1 μs after 0_H on every line that commences with a normal sync pulse (except lines 6, 310, 320, and 622, which are subject to *burst meander*, to be described in a moment). Burst gate has raised-cosine transitions whose 50%-points are coincident with the time intervals specified above, and whose rise-times are 300^{+200}_{-100}ns.

PAL +135° burst lies on the *U*–*V* axis; –135° burst lies on the *U*+*V* axis. The choice of addition or subtraction depends on the polarity of the *V*-switch.

In NTSC, burst is based on the inverted sine subcarrier. PAL uses what is known as *swinging* burst or *Brüch burst:* On one line, burst is advanced 135° from the sine subcarrier; on the next line, it is delayed 135° from the sine subcarrier. PAL burst is located at ±135°, or +135°/+225°, on a vectorscope display (compared to 180° for NTSC). The subcarrier regenerator of a typical PAL decoder does not process swinging burst explicitly, but relies on the loop filter to average the swinging burst to 180° phase.

Pronounced *mee-AND-er*.

A PAL decoder should recover *V*-switch polarity through burst averaging or burst phase detection, not by detecting burst meander.

PAL systems have a burst-blanking *meander* scheme (also known as *Brüch blanking*): Burst is suppressed from the first and last full lines of a field if it would take –135° phase. Burst is always suppressed from line 623. The suppression of burst ensures that the closest burst immediately preceding and following the vertical interval has +135° phase.

Color difference components (*U*, *V*)

Color differences for S-video-625 and PAL are computed by scaling *B'*–*Y'* and *R'*–*Y'* components to form *U* and *V* components, as described on page 336. The scaling limits the maximum value of the composite signal, to be defined in *Composite PAL encoding*, on page 532, to the range –⅓ to +4⁄3. The scale factors cause 100% colorbars to have an excursion from –33⅓% to +133⅓% of the picture excursion. The VHF/UHF PAL transmitter places no limit on composite picture excursion in this range.

This is unlike NTSC, where the transmitter imposes a limit of 120 IRE.

Color difference filtering

The *U* and *V* color difference components are subject to lowpass filtering with the following attenuation:

- Less than 3 dB at frequencies less than 1.3 MHz
- At least 20 dB at frequencies greater than 4 MHz

See *NTSC Y'IQ system*, on page 365.

PAL was standardized with a higher bandwidth than NTSC, so there was no need to severely bandlimit one of the color difference components: PAL always uses equiband 1.3 MHz *U* and *V* color differences in the studio. In PAL-G/H/I transmission, RF bandwidth of 5.5 MHz is available; in these systems, 1.1 MHz of chroma bandwidth can be broadcast. In PAL-B transmission, RF bandwidth is limited to 5 MHz; in this system, chroma bandwidth for broadcast is limited to 600 kHz. (See Table 48.1, on page 571.)

Chroma (*C*)

In PAL, the *U* and *V* color difference components are combined to form *chroma* signal as follows:

$$C = U \sin \omega t \pm V \cos \omega t; \qquad \omega = 2\pi f_{SC} \qquad \text{Eq 44.1}$$

Concerning the association of *U* with sin and *V* with cos, see the marginal note on page 339.

sin ωt and cos ωt represent the 4.43 MHz color subcarrier defined in *Subcarrier*, on page 529. The process is described in *PAL chroma modulation*, on page 341. The *V* component switches *Phase* (±1) on *Alternate Lines*; this is the origin of the acronym *PAL*. (If you prefer, you can think of the phase of the modulated *V* component altering ±90° line-by-line.)

The *Y'* and *C* components should be time-coincident with each other, and with sync, within ±25 ns.

S-video-625 (*Y'/C*4.43)

S-video is introduced on page 107; S-video-525 is described on page 515. The S-video connector is shown in Figure 34.10, on page 409.

S-video-625, sometimes called *Y'/C4.43*, has 576*i* scanning, 4.43 MHz color subcarrier, and zero setup. The IEC standard pertaining to S-video is cited in a marginal note on page 515. The *Y'* and *C* signals at the interface have structure and levels identical to the constituent parts of PAL; if the two signals are summed, a legal PAL signal results:

$$\begin{aligned} Y'_{\text{S-video-625}} &= \frac{7}{10}\,{}^{601}Y' &&+ \frac{3}{10}\left(-sync\right) \\ C_{\text{S-video-625}} &= \frac{7}{10}C &&+ \frac{3}{10}\left(\frac{burst}{2}\right) \end{aligned} \qquad \text{Eq 44.2}$$

Composite PAL encoding

A composite PAL signal is formed by summing luma (Y') and modulated chroma (C) signals, along with sync and colorburst.

The picture-to-sync ratio for PAL is 7:3, leading to a composite signal formed as follows, where *sync* is taken to be unity when asserted and zero otherwise, and *burst* is in the range ±1:

$$PAL = \frac{7}{10}\left({}^{601}Y' + C\right) \qquad + \frac{3}{10}\left(\frac{burst}{2} - sync\right) \qquad \text{Eq 44.3}$$

Composite digital PAL interface ($4f_{SC}$)

Coding extends to 1.3 times the picture excursion; it does not extend to 4⁄3. Apparently the choice of axes for modulated chroma prevents excursion beyond 1.3; however, I cannot find any authoritative technical reference to this.

Digital composite PAL – also known as the 576*i* version of $4f_{SC}$ – is formed by scaling and offsetting Equation 44.3 so that blanking in an 8-bit system (zero in the equation) is at codeword 64 and reference white is at codeword 211. Luma excursion is 147 codes. In a 10-bit system, these levels are multiplied by four: The reference levels have two low-order zero bits appended. Codewords having the 8 most-significant bits all-one or all-zero are prohibited from video data. Figure 44.1 opposite shows a waveform drawing of luma in a 576*i* composite digital interface.

Each line has 948 S_{AL}, of which the central 922 or so encompass the picture width.

Composite digital $4f_{SC}$ PAL systems sample on the [*U*+*V*, *U*–*V*] axes – that is, sampling is coincident with the 45°, 135°, 225°, and 315° phases of subcarrier. Burst samples lie at the 0°, 90°, 180°, and 270° phases of burst, and take 8-bit values {95.5, 64, 32.5, 64}.

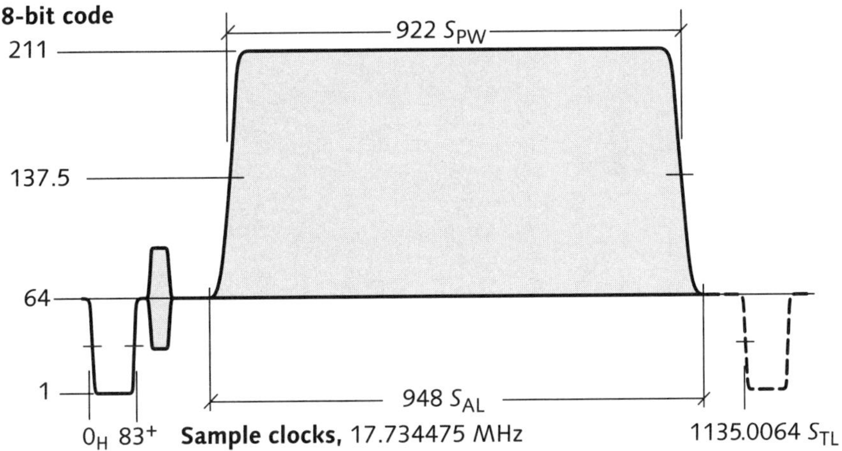

Figure 44.1 **576*i*, 4f_{SC} PAL digital waveform,** showing the range of the luma component. The chroma component will contribute to excursions outside this range.

EBU Tech. 3280, *Specification of interfaces for 625-line digital PAL signals.*

Owing to the complex relationship in "mathematical PAL" between subcarrier frequency and line rate, sampling in 4f_{SC} PAL is not line-locked: There is a non-integer number (1135 4⁄625) of sample periods per total line. (If analog sync were digitized, it would take different sets of values on different lines.) At a digital interface, we would prefer to have the same integer of sample periods per line in *every* line. 4f_{SC} PAL standards approximate this situation: TRS sequences define lines at the interface having the same number of sample periods per line (1135) in all but two lines in each field. Two lines per frame contain 1137 samples each – one line among {625, 1, 2, 3, 4}, ideally line 625, and one line among {313, 314, 315, 316, 317}, ideally line 313. The two extra samples take blanking value; they are inserted immediately prior to the first active sample of the associated line. SMPTE 259M allows some flexibility on the location of the extra pairs; however, EBU Tech. 3280 mandates that the extra pairs are on lines 625 and 313. Be liberal on what you accept and conservative on what you produce.

With conventional sample numbering, where sample 0 is the leftmost active sample in a line, 0_H falls between samples 957 and 958. The first word of TRS-ID is at sample 967.

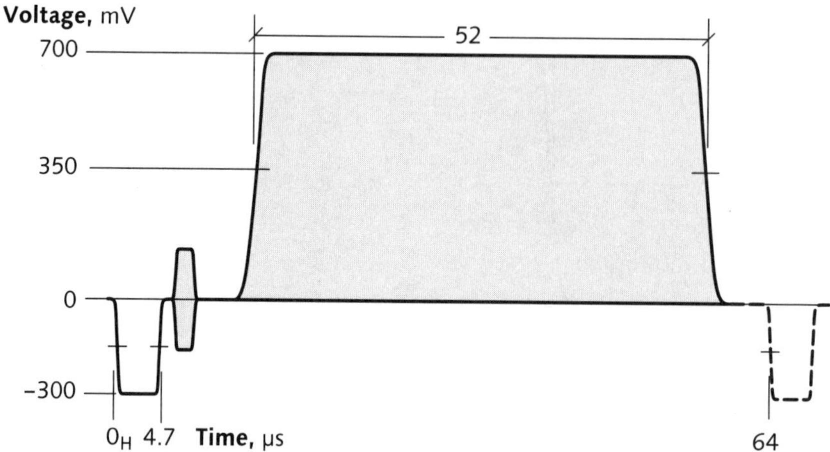

Figure 44.2 **576*i* PAL composite analog waveform**

The electrical and mechanical interfaces for $4f_{SC}$ PAL are derived from the Rec. 656 parallel and serial interfaces; see *SDI coding,* on page 396.

Composite analog PAL interface

Figure 44.2 overleaf shows a waveform drawing of luma in a 576*i* composite analog interface. The interface is detailed in *Analog electrical interface* and *Analog mechanical interface,* on page 408. The excursion of an analog composite 576*i* PAL signal with zero chroma, from synctip to reference white, is 1 V_{PP}, comprising 700 mV of picture and 300 mV of sync.

BBC/ITA, *Specification of television standards for 625-line system-I transmissions*, published jointly by the BBC and the Independent Television Authority (now Independent Television Commission, ITC), Jan. 1971.

The definitive reference to the 576*i*25 PAL composite analog signal is cited in the margin.

SDTV test signals 45

This chapter summarizes the principal test signals used for testing 480*i* and 576*i* video systems.

Colorbars

ANSI/EIA-189-A, *Encoded Color Bar Signal* (formerly denoted EIA RS-189-A).

SMPTE EG 1, *Alignment Color Bar Test Signal for Television Picture Monitors.*

Figure 45.1 below is a sketch of the image produced by the classic SMPTE colorbar test pattern. The upper 2⁄3 of the image contains a 100% white bar followed by primary and secondary colors of 75% saturation. The narrow, central region contains "reverse bars" interleaved with black; this section is used to set decoder HUE and SATURATION. The bottom 1⁄4 of the image contains subcarrier frequency at $-I$ phase, a white bar, subcarrier frequency at $+Q$ phase, and (at the right) the PLUGE element, which I will describe in a moment.

Pronounced *ploodge.*

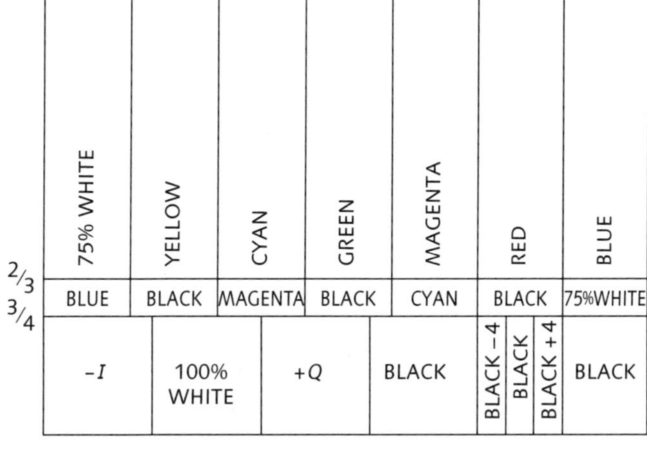

Figure 45.1 **SMPTE EG 1 colorbar test signal** is represented here as an image; however, it is standardized as a signal in the $R'G'B'$ domain. Its color interpretation depends upon the primary chromaticities in use; the corresponding $Y'C_BC_R$ or $Y'P_BP_R$ waveforms depend upon luma coefficients and scaling.

Figure 45.2 **Colorbar *R'G'B'* primary components** in SMPTE colorbars have amplitude of 75 IRE, denoted 75/0/75/0. A variation denoted 100/0/75/0, whose *R'*, *G'*, and *B'* waveforms are sketched here, places the white bar at 100 IRE. Other variations have different amplitudes for the uncolored and colored bars. The notation is described on page 539.

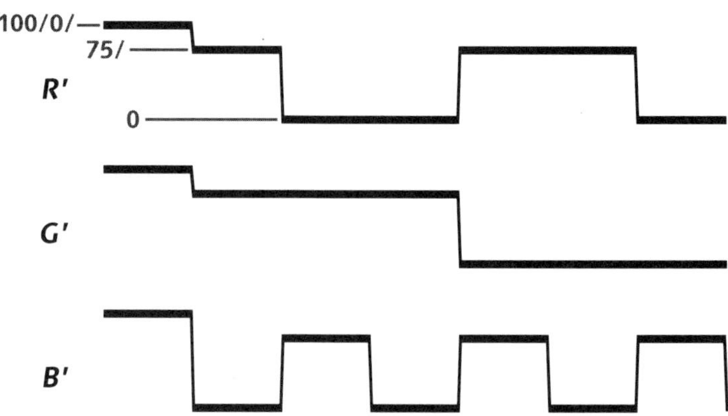

Figure 45.2 above shows the *R'G'B'* components that produce the upper ⅔ of the frame of SMPTE colorbars. Each scan line is based upon a binary sequence of red, green, and blue values either zero or unity. The components are arranged in order of their contributions to luma, so that the eventual luma component decreases from left to right. (The narrow, central region of SMPTE bars has the count sequence reversed, and the green component is forced to zero.)

In studio equipment, in component video, and in PAL broadcast, the processing, recording, and transmission channels can accommodate all encoded signals that can be produced from mixtures of *R'G'B'* where each component is in the range 0 to 1. The *100%* colorbar signal exercises eight points at these limits.

Figure 28.1, on page 336, sketches a vectorscope display of the *U* and *V* chroma components of colorbars in NTSC; a comparable diagram for PAL is shown in Figure 28.8, on page 344. Vectorscope diagrams of chroma in component systems are shown in *Component video color coding for SDTV*, on page 301, and *Component video color coding for HDTV*, on page 313.

Fully saturated yellow and fully saturated cyan cause a composite PAL signal to reach a peak value 133⅓% of reference white. However, as detailed on page 337, an NTSC transmitter's composite signal amplitude is limited to 120% of reference white. If 100% bars were presented to an NTSC transmitter, clipping would result. To avoid clipping, *75%* bars are ordinarily used to test NTSC transmission. The white bar comprises primaries at 100%, but the other bars have their primary components reduced to 75% so as to limit their composite NTSC peak to the level of reference white.

Figure 45.3 shows the NTSC composite waveform of a scan line in the upper region of 75% colorbar.

Figure 45.3 **NTSC-Encoded 100/0/75/0 colorbar waveform**

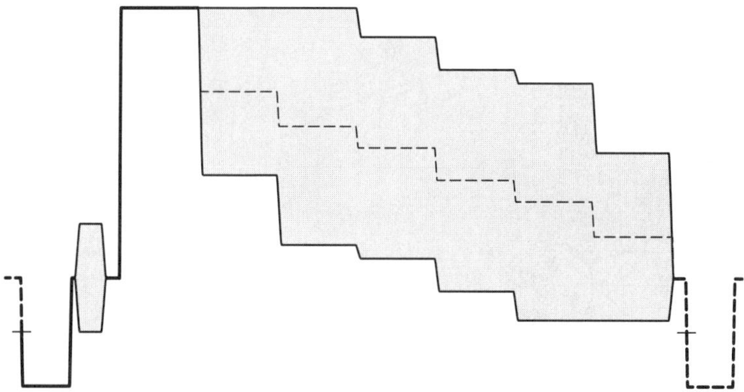

The -*I* and +Q elements correspond to *R'G'B'* values of [-0.3824, 0.1088, 0.4427] and [0.2483, -0.2589, 0.6817], respectively; and to $^{601}Y'C_BC_R$ values [0, 56.96, -61.10] and [0, 86.17, 39.68]. To produce *RGB*-legal codes having the same hue and saturation as -*I* and +Q, and having minimum luma, use *R'G'B'* values [0, 0.2456, 0.4125] and [0.2536, 0, 0.4703], respectively.

The lower-left quadrant of SMPTE colorbar contains subcarrier frequency components at –*I* and +*Q* phase. These elements were designed to exercise the encoding and decoding axes of the original NTSC chroma modulation method. Encoding and decoding on *I* and *Q* axes has fallen into disuse, being replaced by encoding and decoding on the *B'–Y'* and *R'–Y'* axes, so the utility of this portion of the signal is now lost. The –*I* and +*Q* elements contain high-magnitude chroma resting upon black (at 0 IRE). These combinations correspond to illegal mixtures of *R'G'B'*, where one or two components are negative; so the –*I* and +*Q* elements are not representable in the positive *R'G'B'* domain.

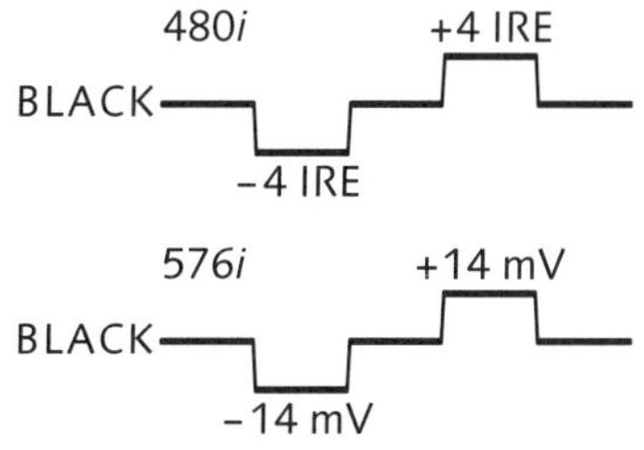

Figure 45.4 **PLUGE element** of the colorbar signal enables accurate setting of black level. The acronym originates with the "generating equipment," but nowadays PLUGE signifies the signal element.

The lower-right quadrant of colorbar contains elements produced by *picture line-up generating equipment* (PLUGE); see Figure 45.4 in the margin. Superimposed on black are two narrow bars, one slightly more negative than black, the other slightly more positive. If a monitor's black level is properly adjusted, the first of the bars will vanish and the second will be barely visible. The negative-going element of PLUGE cannot be represented in positive *R'G'B'*.

The -*I* element, the +*Q* element, and the negative-going element of PLUGE are generated synthetically. None of these elements represents picture information; none is useful in evaluating pictures; and none can be generated in, or survives transit through, the positive *R'G'B'* domain between 0 and 1 (or 0 and 255).

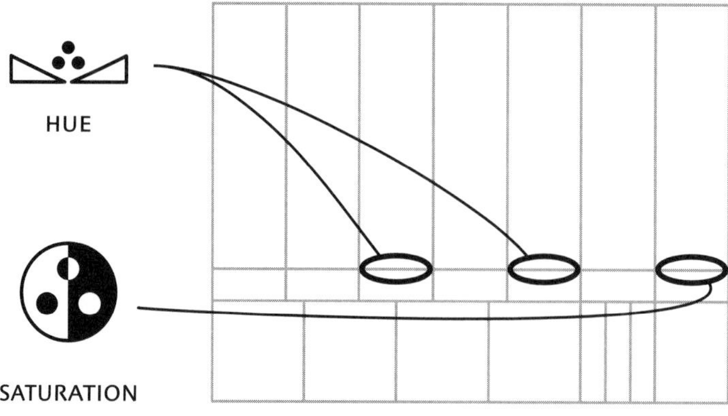

Figure 45.5 **HUE and SATURATION are adjusted** using the colorbar test image until the indicated vertical transitions disappear.

In fact, it is not just the *-I, +Q, and PLUGE* elements of colorbars that are synthetic: The entire signal is generated synthetically! The colorbar signal represents values of *R'G'B'* as if they came from a gamma-corrected camera and were inserted prior to an encoder. *R'G'B'* values of colorbars are implicitly gamma-corrected.

Alternatively, the red and green guns at the CRT can be turned off. If none of these options are available, the same effect can be accomplished by viewing the CRT through a blue gel filter.

When composite NTSC or PAL colorbars are decoded, the amount of blue decoded from the white, cyan, magenta, and blue bars should ideally be identical. Any chroma gain (saturation) error will affect the signal decoded from blue, but not the blue decoded from white. Chroma phase (hue) error will cause errors of opposite direction in the blue decoded from cyan and the blue decoded from magenta. A quick way to adjust a decoder's HUE and SATURATION controls involves displaying composite SMPTE colorbars, and disabling the red and green components at the decoder output. The amount of blue decoded from cyan and magenta is equalized by adjusting the decoder's HUE control. The amount of blue decoded from gray and blue is equalized by adjusting SATURATION. The comparison is facilitated by the reversed bar portion of SMPTE colorbars. Figure 45.5 above shows a representation of the colorbar image, showing the bars that are visually compared while adjusting HUE and SATURATION.

Fully saturated $R'G'B'$ components of colorbars take $R'G'B'$ (or RGB) values of zero or unity, independent of the chromaticity of the primaries: Owing to differences in primary chromaticities, the exact colors of the bars are not identical among SMPTE, EBU, and HDTV standards.

Colorbar notation

ITU-R Rec. BT.471, *Nomenclature and description of colour bar signals.*

I have referred to 100% and 75% colorbars. Several additional variations of colorbars are in use, so many that an international standard is required to denote them. A colorbar signal is denoted by four numbers, separated by slashes. The first pair of numbers gives the maximum and minimum values (respectively) of the primary components in uncolored bars – that is, the black or white bars. The second pair gives the maximum and minimum primary values (respectively) in the six colored bars.

The 100% bars, described earlier, are denoted 100/0/100/0. That variation is useful in the studio, in all forms of component video, and in PAL transmission. In 480*i* systems where 7.5% setup is used, *100% bars* refers to 100/7.5/100/7.5. That variation is useful in the studio. However, as I explained on page 536, terrestrial NTSC transmission cannot handle 100% bars. NTSC transmitters are tested using 75% bars with setup, denoted 100/7.5/75/7.5. Japan uses 480*i* video with zero setup; there, 75% bars, denoted 100/0/75/0, are used.

Frequency response

Magnitude frequency response of a video system can be tested using a frequency sweep signal comparable to the one sketched in Figure 7.1 on page 66. Usually, a *multiburst* signal having several discrete frequencies is used instead; see Figure 45.13, on page 545.

Differential gain (DG)

I introduced *Linearity* on page 21. A system is linear iff this condition is satisfied:

$$g(a \cdot x + b \cdot y) \equiv a \cdot g(x) + b \cdot g(y) \quad \text{[for scalar } a, b\text{]} \qquad \text{Eq 45.1}$$

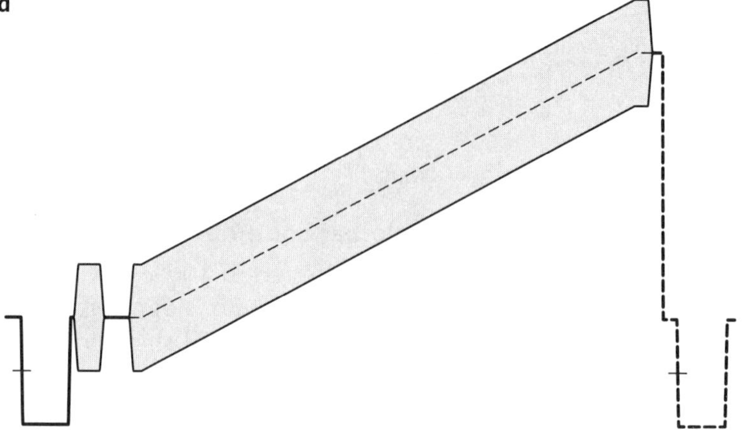

Figure 45.6 **Modulated ramp waveform**

A system or subsystem with linear amplitude response has a transfer function whose output plots as a straight-line function of its input; departure from this condition is differential gain error. Amplitude nonlinearity could be characterized directly by the departure of the transfer function from a straight line; ADC and DAC components and subsystems are specified this way. However, in video, amplitude nonlinearity is usually characterized by a parameter *differential gain* (DG) that is easier to measure.

To measure DG, you present to a system the sum of a high-frequency signal and a low-frequency signal – consider these as x and y in Equation 45.1 above. It is standard to use a sine wave at subcarrier frequency as the high-frequency signal. The low-frequency signal is either a ramp or a staircase. Figure 45.6 shows the preferred modulated ramp signal. The alternative modulated stair is shown in Figure 45.7 opposite.

Ideally, when measuring DG, the high-frequency sine wave component should emerge at the output of the system having its amplitude independent of the low-frequency component upon which it is superimposed. The DG measuring instrument has a filter that rejects (discards) the low-frequency component; DG is then determined from the amplitude of the remaining high-frequency (subcarrier-based) component. Nonlinear

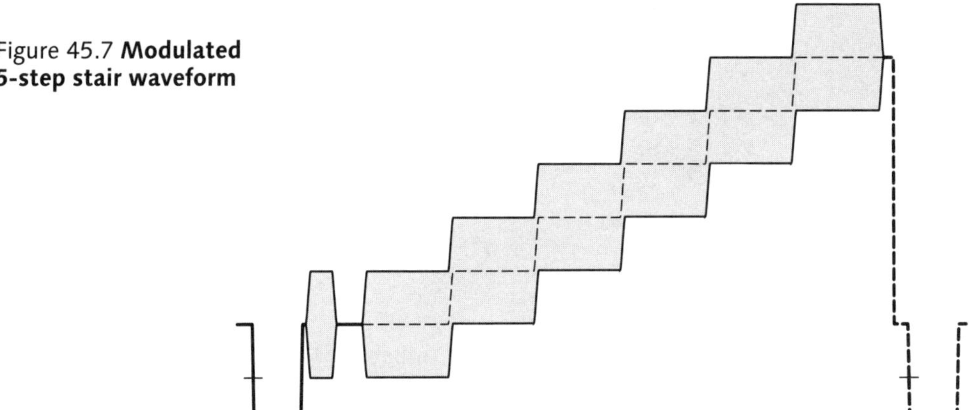

Figure 45.7 **Modulated 5-step stair waveform**

amplitude response is revealed if the amplitude of the sine wave varies across the line.

DG measurement directly applies the linearity principle in Equation 45.1. The system's input is the sum of two signals, $x+y$, where x is the high-frequency signal and y is the ramp or staircase. The system's output is $g(x+y)$; we compare this to the ideal $g(x)+g(y)$.

Differential phase (DP)

A potential defect of analog video recording or transmission is that phase may change as a function of DC (or low-frequency) amplitude. This error is known as *differential phase* (DP). Although in principle DP could be a problem at any frequency, in practice it is measured only at the subcarrier frequency. DP can be measured using the same test signal used to measure DG: a constant-amplitude sine wave at subcarrier frequency, superimposed on a ramp or staircase.

At the output of the system, low-frequency information is filtered out as in DG measurement, but this time the subcarrier-frequency signal is demodulated by a circuit identical to an NTSC chroma demodulator. The demodulated components can be displayed in vectorscope presentation, or the component at sine phase can be displayed in a waveform presentation.

Pulse signals

Pulse waveforms in video, such as sync, have waveforms chosen so as to be contained within the video bandwidth. If a pulse with a rapid transition is used, its high-frequency energy will not traverse the video system and is likely to produce ringing or distortion.

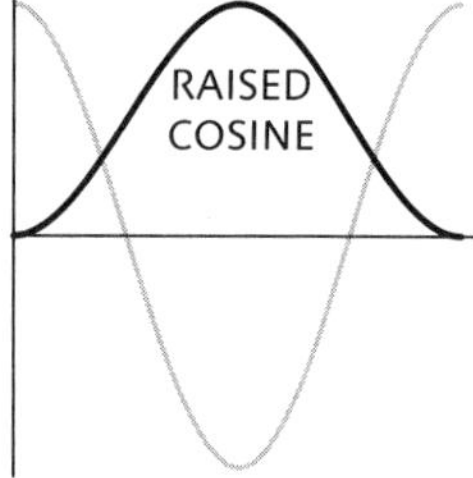

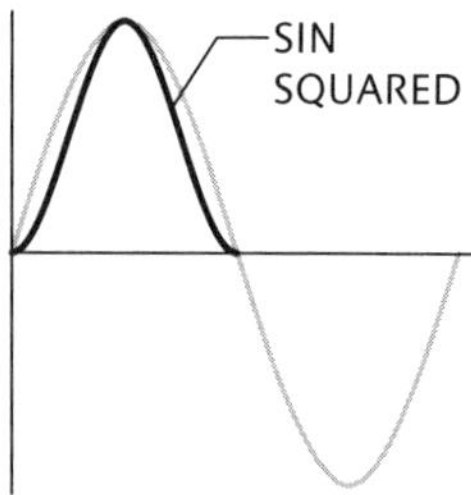

Figure 45.8 **Raised cosine and sine squared pulses**

The most common pulse shape used is the *raised cosine*. This signal comprises a single (360°) cycle of a cosine wave that has been scaled by -0.5 and "raised" +0.5 units: It is a single pulse with a cosine shape. It is also known as *sine squared* ($\sin^2$), because the pulse can be expressed as the square of a sine signal: A 180° segment of a sine wave, squared, forms a single pulse. (See Figure 45.8) In the analog domain, a raised cosine pulse can be obtained by passing a very short impulse through a suitable filter. A raised cosine step, for high-quality sync, can be obtained by passing a step waveform through a similar filter.

K rating is unrelated to Kell's *k factor;* see page 67.

A raised cosine pulse is often used for testing in video, because a single pulse can exercise a wide range of frequencies. Nonuniform frequency response is revealed by ringing in the system's response. Nonlinear phase response is revealed by a lack of symmetry. The amplitude of and phase of ringing is often characterized using a somewhat arbitrary measure called the *K rating* (or less desirably, *K factor*) whose definition is related to the subjective effect of the ringing. A system's K rating is related to the uniformity of its frequency response.

Craig, Margaret, *Television Measurements: NTSC Systems* (Beaverton, Or.: Tektronix, 1989).

The duration of a raised cosine pulse, or any similar pulse with a single major lobe in its waveform, is measured in terms of its *half-amplitude duration* (HAD). The HAD of a raised cosine pulse used in testing is denoted by a parameter *T*. In 480*i* video, *T* is given the value 125 ns – a *T* pulse occupies a bandwidth of about 8 MHz. This is well beyond the bandwidth limit of legal 480*i* studio video, but the pulse is useful for stress testing. A 2*T* pulse having HAD of 250 ns exercises a bandwidth of 4 MHz, just within the edge of legal NTSC broadcast video, so a 2*T* pulse should traverse a properly functioning video system.

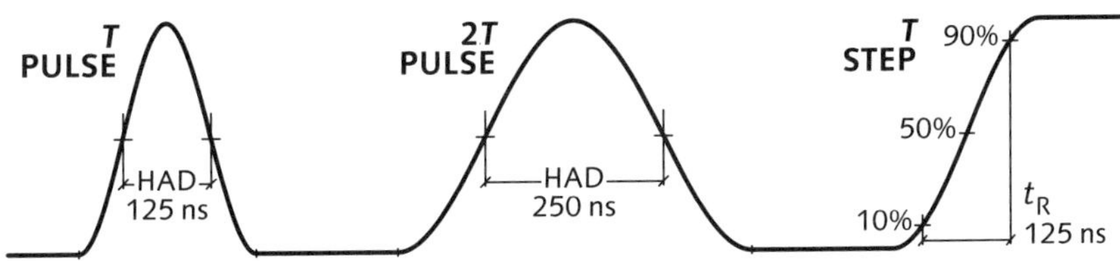

Figure 45.9 ***T* pulse, 2*T* pulse, and *T* step waveforms** are shown for 480*i* systems, where *T* has the value 125 ns. In 576*i* systems, bandwidths are generally higher, and *T* has the value 100 ns.

The risetime, from 10% to 90%, of a *T* step is about 1.18 times the risetime of a *T* pulse:

$$t_r = \frac{4\sin^{-1}\left(0.9 - 0.1\right)}{\pi} t_{HAD}$$
$$\approx 1.18 t_{HAD}$$

Although the term *raised cosine* or *sine squared* properly applies to a complete pulse, from baseline to maximum and returning to baseline, it is loosely applied to a transition from one level to another. For example, the leading edge of analog sync ideally has a raised cosine shape. When applied to a step, the parameter *T* denotes the usual risetime from 10% to 90% as in electrical engineering. Figure 45.9 above shows the waveforms of a *T* pulse, a 2*T* pulse, and a *T* step. Figure 45.10 below shows the frequency spectra of a *T* pulse and a 2*T* pulse, along with the spectrum of a triangle-shaped pulse having the same risetime.

A good approximation of a raised-cosine step waveform between zero and one, like that of the step at the right in Figure 45.9, can be obtained without trigonometry by evaluating this cubic polynomial for values of time (t) between zero and one:

$$3t^3 - 2t^2 \qquad \text{Eq 45.2}$$

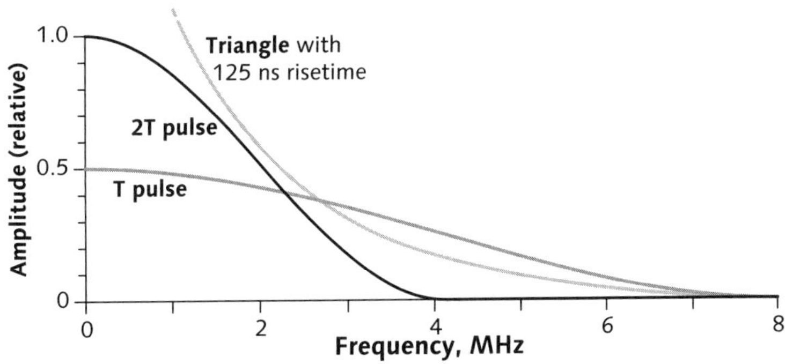

Figure 45.10
***T* pulse spectra**

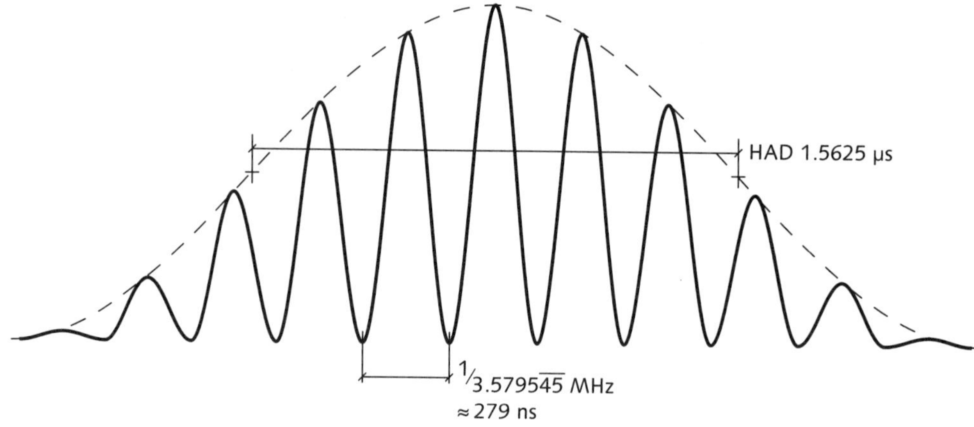

Figure 45.11 **Modulated 12.5*T* pulse waveform** for 480*i* systems

Modulated 12.5*T*, 20*T* pulses

In *Phase response (group delay)*, on page 159, I explained that the time delay through a filter can change as a function of frequency. This phenomenon can be a problem in a video system, which can be considered to be a long cascade of filters. This condition is tested through use of a signal having two widely spaced frequency components.

The modulated 12.5*T* pulse used to test group delay is shown in Figure 45.11 above. The signal comprises a low-frequency raised cosine of half amplitude duration 12.5*T* (1.5625 μs), upon which is superimposed a subcarrier-frequency cosine wave that has been amplitude modulated by the low-frequency raised cosine. In an ideal system the resulting signal has an envelope that matches the raised cosine above and sits precisely at the baseline. Should the subcarrier frequency suffer delay, the envelope exhibits distortion; this is particularly evident along the baseline. Sometimes a 20*T* pulse is used instead of 12.5*T*. Note that *T* denotes the HAD of the *envelope*, not of the high-frequency waves.

Figures 45.12 through 45.15 overleaf show several standard test signals that combine various elements discussed in this chapter. These signals may be broadcast as vertical interval test signals (VITS).

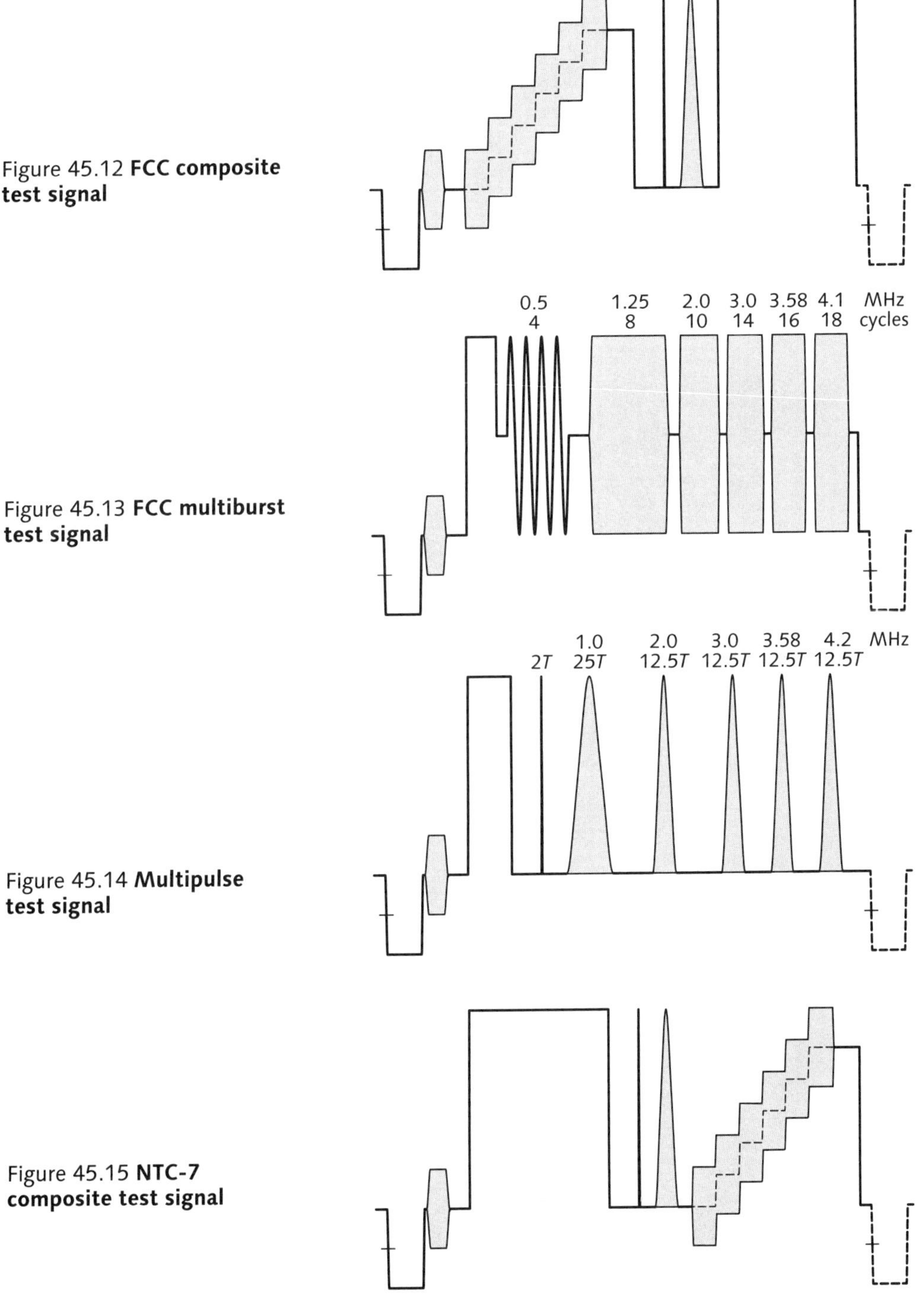

Figure 45.12 **FCC composite test signal**

Figure 45.13 **FCC multiburst test signal**

Figure 45.14 **Multipulse test signal**

Figure 45.15 **NTC-7 composite test signal**

1280×720 HDTV 46

SMPTE 296M, *1280×720 Progressive Image Sample Structure – Analog and Digital Representation and Analog Interface.*

This chapter details the scanning, timing, and sync structure of 1280×720 video, also called 720*p*. The scanning and timing information in this chapter applies to all variants of 720*p* video, both analog and digital.

Scanning

$$\frac{24}{1.001} \approx 23.976$$

$$\frac{30}{1.001} \approx 29.97$$

$$\frac{60}{1.001} \approx 59.94$$

720*p* video represents stationary or moving two-dimensional images sampled temporally at a constant rate of $^{24}/_{1.001}$, 24, 25, $^{30}/_{1.001}$, 30, 50, $^{60}/_{1.001}$, or 60 frames per second. The sampling rate is 74.25 MHz (modified by the ratio $^{1000}/_{1001}$ in 720*p*59.94, 720*p*29.97, and 720*p*23.976). All of these systems have 750 total lines (L_T). The number of samples per total line (S_{TL}) is adapted to achieve the desired frame rate.

Table 46.1 below summarizes the scanning parameters.

System	f_S *(MHz)*	S_{TL}
720*p*60	74.25	1650
720*p*59.94	$^{74.25}/_{1.001}$	1650
720*p*50	74.25	1980
720*p*30	74.25	3300
720*p*29.97	$^{74.25}/_{1.001}$	3300
720*p*25	74.25	3960
720*p*24	74.25	4125
720*p*23.976	$^{74.25}/_{1.001}$	4125

Table 46.1 **720*p* scanning parameters** are summarized.

tri Trilevel pulse

BR Broad pulse

The vertical center of the picture is located midway between lines 385 and 386.

Line number	*Contents*
1–5	tri/BR (5 lines)
6	Blanking
7–25 (19 lines)	Blanking/Ancillary
26–745 (720 lines)	Picture [Clean aperture 702 lines]
746–750 (5 lines)	Blanking

Table 46.2 **1280×720 line assignment**

A frame comprises a total of 750 horizontal raster lines of equal duration, uniformly progressively scanned top to bottom and left to right, numbered consecutively starting at 1. Of the 750 total lines, 720 contain picture. Table 46.2 above shows the assignment of line numbers and their content.

For studio video, the tolerance on frame rate is normally ±10 ppm. In practice the tolerance applies to a master clock at a high frequency, but for purposes of computation and standards writing it is convenient to reference the tolerance to the frame rate.

At a digital interface, video information is identified by a *timing reference signal* (TRS) conveyed across the interface. (See *Digital sync, TRS, ancillary data, and interface,* on page 389.) The last active line of a frame is terminated by EAV where the *V*-bit becomes asserted. That EAV marks the start of line 746; line 1 of the next frame starts on the fifth following EAV.

Analog interfaces are discouraged for all but the three highest-rate systems (720*p*60, 720*p*59.94, and 720*p*50). Analog signal timing is defined by the digital standard; the digital sampling frequency defines reference time intervals used to define analog timing.

0_H precedes the first word of SAV by 256 clocks.

0_H follows the first word of EAV by S_{TL} - 1280 - 260 clocks.

Analog sync

Horizontal events are referenced to 0_H, defined by the zero-crossing of trilevel sync. Digital samples and analog timing are related such that the first (zeroth) sample of active video follows the 0_H instant by 260 reference clock intervals.

At an analog interface, each line commences with a trilevel sync pulse. Trilevel sync comprises a negative portion asserted to -300±6 mV during the 40 reference clock intervals preceding 0_H, and a positive portion asserted to +300±6 mV during the 40 reference clock intervals after 0_H. The risetime of each transition is 4±1.5 reference clock intervals.

Vertical sync is signaled by *broad pulses*, one each on lines 1 through 5. Each broad pulse is asserted to -300±6 mV, with timing identical to active video – that is, to the production aperture's picture width. The risetime of each transition is 4±1.5 reference clock intervals. Line 1 can be detected as the first broad pulse of a frame – that is, by a line without a broad pulse followed by a line with one.

Lines 7 through 25 do not convey picture information. They may convey ancillary or other signals either related or unrelated to the picture.

Figure 46.1 overleaf shows details of the sync structure; this waveform diagram is the analog of Table 46.2.

Picture center, aspect ratio, and blanking

The center of the picture is located midway between the central two of the 1280 active samples (between samples 639 and 640), and midway between the central two 720 picture lines (between lines 385 and 386).

Aspect ratio is defined to be 16:9 with respect to the production aperture of 1280×720.

In *Transition samples,* on page 323, I mentioned that it is necessary to avoid, at the start of a line, an instantaneous transition from blanking to picture information. A *clean aperture* pixel array 1248 samples wide and

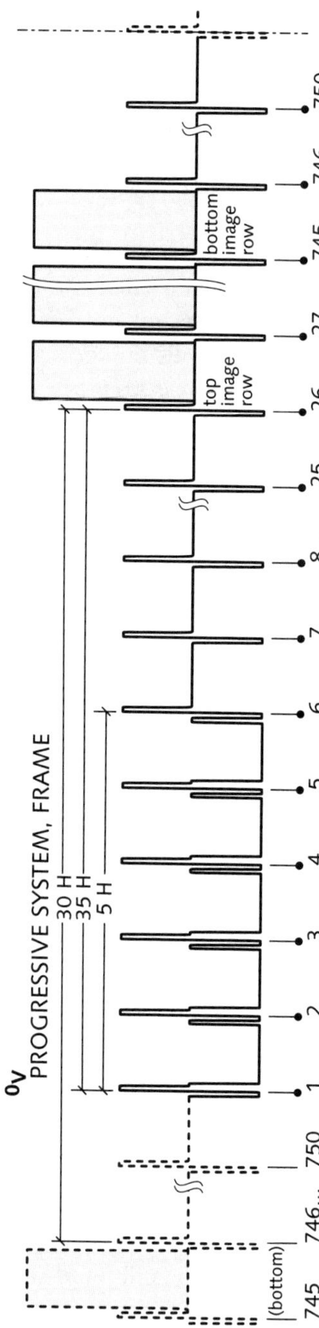

Figure 46.1 **720*p* raster, vertical**

702 lines high, centered on the production aperture, should remain subjectively uncontaminated by edge transients.

RGB primary components

Picture information originates with linear-light primary red, green, and blue (*RGB*) tristimulus components, represented in abstract terms in the range 0 (reference black) to +1 (reference white). In modern standards, the colorimetric properties of the primary components conform to *Rec. 709/sRGB primaries* described on page 239.

Nonlinear transfer function

From *RGB* tristimulus values, three nonlinear primary components are computed according to the optoelectronic transfer function of *Rec. 709 transfer function*, described on page 263. In this equation, L denotes a tristimulus component (R, G, or B), and V'_{709} denotes a nonlinear primary component (R', G', or B'):

$$V'_{709} = \begin{cases} 4.5L; & 0 \le L < 0.018 \\ 1.099L^{0.45} - 0.099; & 0.018 \le L \le 1 \end{cases} \qquad \text{Eq 46.1}$$

This process is loosely called *gamma correction.*

SMPTE standards do not specify tolerances on time-coincidence of R', G', and B' components. I recommend that the components be time-coincident with each other, and with sync, within ¼ of a sample clock – for 720*p*60, time-coincident within ±3.4 ns.

Luma (*Y'*)

Luma is computed as a weighted sum of nonlinear R', G', and B' components according to the luma coefficients of Rec. 709:

$$^{709}Y' = 0.2126\,R' + 0.7152\,G' + 0.0722\,B' \qquad \text{Eq 46.2}$$

The luma component Y', being a weighted sum of nonlinear $R'G'B'$ components, has no simple relationship with the CIE luminance, denoted Y, or relative luminance, used in color science. Video encoding specifications typically place no upper bound on luma bandwidth (though transmission standards may).

Component digital 4:2:2 interface

$Y'C_BC_R$ components are formed by scaling Y', $B'-Y'$ and $R'-Y'$ components, as described in *C_BC_R components for Rec. 709 HDTV* on page 316. TRS is inserted as described in *TRS in HD-SDI* on page 392. The HD-SDI interface is described *HD-SDI coding*, on page 398. It is standard to subsample according to the 4:2:2 scheme (sketched in the third column of Figure 10.1, on page 90). Image quality wouldn't suffer if subsampling were 4:2:0 – that is, if color differences were subsampled vertically as well as horizontally – but this would be inconvenient for hardware design and interface.

Component analog *R'G'B'* interface

The interface for analog R', G', and B' signals is described in *Analog electrical interface* and *Analog mechanical interface*, on page 408. Zero (reference blanking level) in the R', G', and B' expressions corresponds to a level of 0 V_{DC}, and unity corresponds to 700 mV.

Sync is added to the green component according to:

$$G'_{sync} = \frac{7}{10}\left(active \cdot G'\right) + \frac{3}{10}\left(-sync\right) \qquad \text{Eq 46.3}$$

Component analog $Y'P_BP_R$ interface

The P_B and P_R color difference components of analog HDTV are formed by scaling $B'-Y'$ and $R'-Y'$ components as described in *P_BP_R components for Rec. 709 HDTV* on page 314. Although it is possible in theory to have wideband P_B and P_R components, in practice they are lowpass filtered to about half the bandwidth of luma.

The interface for analog Y', P_B, and P_R signals is described in *Analog electrical interface* and *Analog mechanical interface*, on page 408. HDTV $Y'P_BP_R$ signals have zero setup. Sync is added to the luma component:

$$Y'_{sync} = \frac{7}{10}Y' + \frac{3}{10}\left(-sync\right) \qquad \text{Eq 46.4}$$

This excursion is conveyed as 1 V_{PP}, with reference blanking at 0 V_{DC}. The picture excursion of the Y'

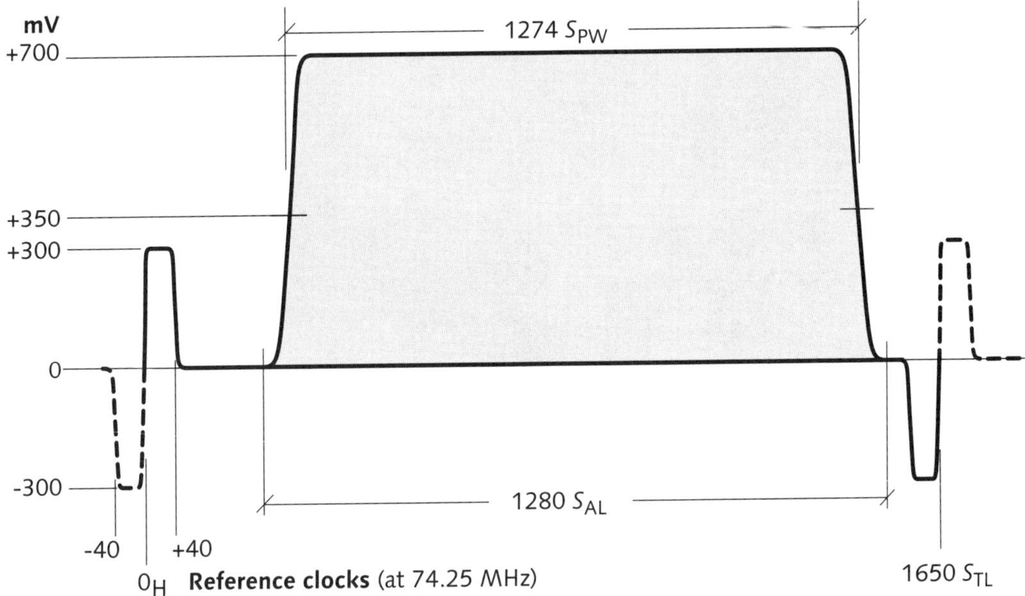

Figure 46.2 **720*p*60 component analog luma waveform**

signal is 700 mV. Figure 46.2 above shows a waveform drawing of luma in a 720*p*60 component analog interface.

EIA/CEA-770.3, High Definition TV Analog Component Video Interface.

EIA/CEA has standardized the 720*p*60 system as described here, including these $Y'P_BP_R$ levels, for use in consumer HDTV electronics devices.

Pre- and postfiltering characteristics

Component Y', R', G' or B' signals in 720*p*59.94 or 720*p*60 have a nominal passband of 30 MHz; color difference components have a nominal passband of 15 MHz.

Figure 46.3 overleaf, *Filter template for Y' and R'G'B' components*, depicts filter characteristics for pre- and postfiltering of R', G', B' and Y' component signals. Analog P_B and P_R color difference component signals are pre- and postfiltered using the same template scaled by a factor of two on the frequency axis. The characteristics are frequency-scaled from the template included in Rec. 601, with a few modifications.

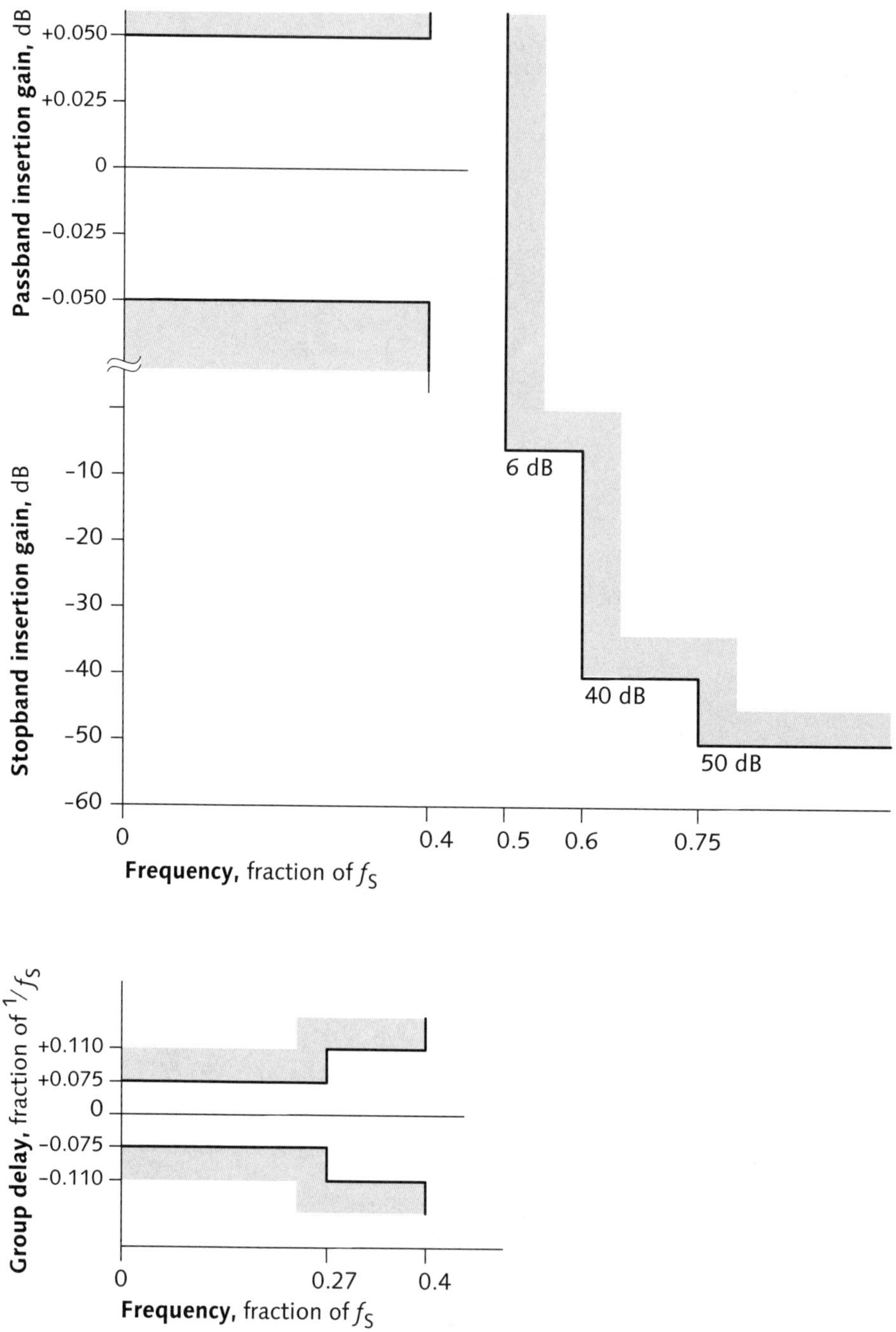

Passband insertion gain, dB
+0.050
+0.025
0
−0.025
−0.050

Stopband insertion gain, dB
-10
-20
-30
-40
-50
-60
6 dB
40 dB
50 dB
0
0.4
0.5
0.6
0.75
Frequency, fraction of f_S

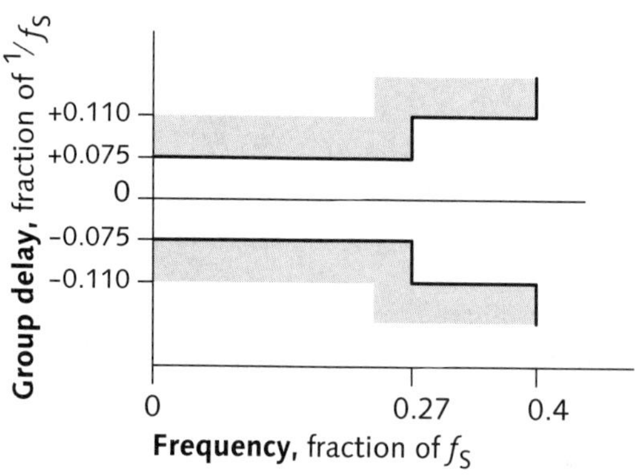

Figure 46.3 **Filter template for *Y'* and *R'G'B'* components**

Amplitude ripple tolerance in the passband is ±0.0.05 dB with respect to insertion loss at 100 kHz. Insertion loss is 6 dB or more at half the sampling rate of the Y', R', G' and B' components.

SMPTE 274M includes luma and color difference templates in "Annex B (Informative)." In standards lingo, the word *informative* signals that the information is distributed with the standard, but compliance with the annex is not required to claim conformance with the standard.

1920×1080 HDTV 47

SMPTE 274M, *1920×1080 Scanning and Analog and Parallel Digital Interfaces for Multiple Picture Rates.*

This chapter details a family of high-definition television systems standardized in SMPTE 274M. The systems have image format of 1920×1080, an aspect ratio of 16:9, and square sampling.

HDTV equipment based on 1125/60 scanning and 1920×1035 image format, with nonsquare sampling, has been deployed for several years and is standardized in SMPTE 240M. This system can now be considered an obsolete variant of 1080*i*30 or 1080*i*29.94 having 1035 picture lines instead of 1080, nonsquare sampling, and slightly different colorimetry.

SMPTE 274M represents agreement on colorimetry according to the international standard Rec. 709. Previous revisions of SMPTE 274M allowed use of 240M color and luma parameters on an "interim" basis. It will take some time for manufacturers and users to complete the transition to the new standard.

SMPTE 295M, *1920×1080 50 Hz Scanning and Interface.* (Despite having "50 Hz" in its title, this standard includes 25 Hz progressive scanning.)

Experimental HDTV systems in Europe used 1250 lines (twice 625), often with 1920×1152 image structure. The commercial success of 1920×1080 image structure led to the development of SMPTE 295M, which defines interlaced or progressive systems for 1920×1080 image data in a 1250-line raster. 1250-line scanning has, not surprisingly, failed to see commercial deployment. Since SMPTE 274M includes the 25 Hz frame rate (as well as 23.976, 24, 29.97, 30, 50, 59.94, and 60), I urge you to avoid SMPTE 295M, and to use the 1125-line scanning of SMPTE 274M instead.

System	f_S *(MHz)*	S_{TL}
1080*p*60¶	148	2200
1080*p*59.94¶	$^{148}/_{1.001}$	2200
1080*p*50¶	148	2640
1080*i*30	74.25	2200
1080*i*29.97	$^{74.25}/_{1.001}$	2200
1080*i*25	74.25	2640
1080*p*30	74.25	2200
1080*p*29.97	$^{74.25}/_{1.001}$	2200
1080*p*25	74.25	2640
1080*p*24	74.25	2750
1080*p*23.976	$^{74.25}/_{1.001}$	2750

Table 47.1 **1920×1080 scanning parameters** are summarized. Systems marked ¶ are beyond the limits of today's technology.

Scanning

$$\frac{24}{1.001} \approx 23.976$$

$$\frac{30}{1.001} \approx 29.97$$

$$\frac{60}{1.001} \approx 59.94$$

1920×1080 video represents stationary or moving two-dimensional images sampled temporally at a constant rate of $^{24}/_{1.001}$, 24, 25, $^{30}/_{1.001}$, 30, 50, $^{60}/_{1.001}$, or 60 frames per second. The base sampling rate is 74.25 MHz; this rate is modified by the ratio $^{1000}/_{1001}$ for systems having noninteger frame rate, and doubled to 148.5 MHz (possibly times $^{1000}/_{1001}$) for progressive systems at frame rates higher than 30 Hz. All of these systems have 1125 total lines (L_T); the number of samples per total line (S_{TL}) is adapted to achieve the desired frame rate. Table 47.1 above summarizes the scanning parameters.

For studio video, the tolerance on frame rate is normally ±10 ppm. In practice the tolerance applies to a master clock at a high frequency, but for purposes of computation and standards writing it is convenient to reference the tolerance to the frame rate.

A frame comprises a total of 1125 horizontal raster lines of equal duration, uniformly scanned top to bottom and left to right, numbered consecutively starting at 1. Of the 1125 total lines, 1080 contain picture. Table 47.2 opposite indicates the assignment of line numbers and their content.

tri Trilevel pulse

BR Broad pulse

Line number, progressive	Line number, first field (F = 0)	Line number, second field (F = 1)	V	Contents, left half	Contents, right half
		563		tri/none	tri/BR
1	1			tri/BR	tri/BR
		564		tri/BR	tri/BR
2	2			tri/BR	tri/BR
		565		tri/BR	tri/BR
3	3			tri/BR	tri/BR
		566		tri/BR	tri/BR
4	4			tri/BR	tri/BR
		567		tri/BR	tri/BR
5	5			tri/BR	tri/BR
		568		tri/BR	tri/none
6	6			tri/none	tri/none
7–41 (35 lines)	7–20 (14 lines)			vertical interval video	
		569–583 (15 lines)		vertical interval video	
42–1121 (1080 lines)	21–560 (540 lines)		V = 0 (1080 lines)	picture[a,b]	
		584–1123 (540 lines)		picture	
1122–1125 (4 lines)	561–562 (2 lines)	1124–1125 (2 lines)		tri/none	tri/none

a In 1035*i* systems, picture occupies 517 lines (41 through 557) in the first field, and 518 lines (603 through 1120) in the second field. Other lines are blank, with V = 1. Picture is centered vertically on line 258 of the first field.

b In the 1024*i*30.00 variant of DV HD, described on page 469, lines 44 through 555 of the first (top) field and lines 606 through 1117 of the second (bottom) field are carried.

Table 47.2 **1080*i* and 1080*p* line assignment**

A progressive system conveys 1080 active picture lines per frame in order top-to-bottom.

An interlaced system scans a frame as a *first* field then a *second* field. The scan lines of each field have half the vertical spatial sampling density of the frame. Scanning lines in the second field are displaced vertically by the vertical sampling pitch, and delayed temporally by half the frame time, from scanning lines in the first field. The first field conveys 540 active picture lines, starting with the top picture line of the frame. The second field conveys 540 active picture lines, ending with the bottom picture line of the frame.

At a digital interface, video information is identified by a *timing reference signal* (TRS) conveyed across the interface. (See *Digital sync, TRS, ancillary data, and interface,* on page 389.) In progressive systems, the last active line of a frame is terminated by EAV where the *V*-bit becomes asserted. That EAV marks the start of line 1122; line 1 of the next frame starts on the fourth following EAV. In interlaced systems, the last active line of a field is terminated by EAV where the *V*-bit becomes asserted. In the first field, that EAV marks the start of line 561. In the second field, that EAV marks the start of line 1124; line 1 of the next frame starts on the second following EAV.

Analog interfaces are discouraged for all but the highest-rate systems (1080*p*60, 1080*p*59.94, 1080*p*50, 1080*i*60, 1080*i*59.94, and 1080*i*50). Analog signal timing is defined by the digital standard; the digital sampling frequency defines reference time intervals used to define analog timing.

Analog sync

0_H precedes the first word of SAV by 192 clocks.

0_H follows the first word of EAV by S_{TL} - 1920 -192 clocks.

At an analog interface, each line commences with a trilevel sync pulse. The zero-crossing of trilevel sync defines the line sync datum 0_H, to which horizontal events are referenced. Digital samples and analog timing are related such that the first (zeroth) sample of active video follows the 0_H instant by 192 reference clock intervals.

Trilevel sync comprises a negative portion asserted to −300±6 mV during the 44 reference clock intervals preceding 0_H, and a positive portion asserted to +300±6 mV during the 44 reference clock intervals after 0_H. The risetime of each transition is 4±1.5 reference clock intervals.

Details of horizontal timing are shown in Figure 47.1 overleaf.

Vertical sync is signaled by *broad pulses*, whose structure differs between progressive and interlaced systems.

A progressive system has five broad pulses per frame, one each on lines 1 through 5. Each broad pulse is asserted to −300±6 mV, 132 reference clock intervals after 0_H, and deasserted 2112 reference clock intervals after 0_H. (Deassertion coincides with the end of active video – that is, with the right-hand edge of the production aperture.) The risetime of each transition is 4±1.5 reference clock intervals. Line 1 is defined by the first broad pulse of a frame – that is, by a line with a broad pulse preceded by a line without one. Line 6 has a second trilevel pulse whose zerocrossing is $S_{TL}/2$ reference clock intervals after 0_H. This pulse is reminiscent of an equalization pulse in analog SDTV.

In an interlaced system, several lines in the vertical interval have a second trilevel sync pulse whose zerocrossing is at $S_{TL}/2$ reference clock intervals after 0_H. An interlaced system has ten broad pulses per field, in the arrangement indicated in Table 47.2. Each broad pulse is asserted to −300±6 mV, 132 reference clock intervals after the zerocrossing of the immediately preceding trilevel sync, and is deasserted 880 reference clock intervals later. The risetime at each transition is 4±1.5 reference clock intervals. Line 1 can be decoded as the first broad pulse in a left-hand halfline – that is, by detecting a normal line (with no broad pulse and no mid-line trilevel sync) followed by a broad pulse immediately after 0_H. Each broad pulse is preceded by a trilevel pulse whose zerocrossing is either at 0_H or delayed $S_{TL}/2$ reference clock intervals from 0_H.

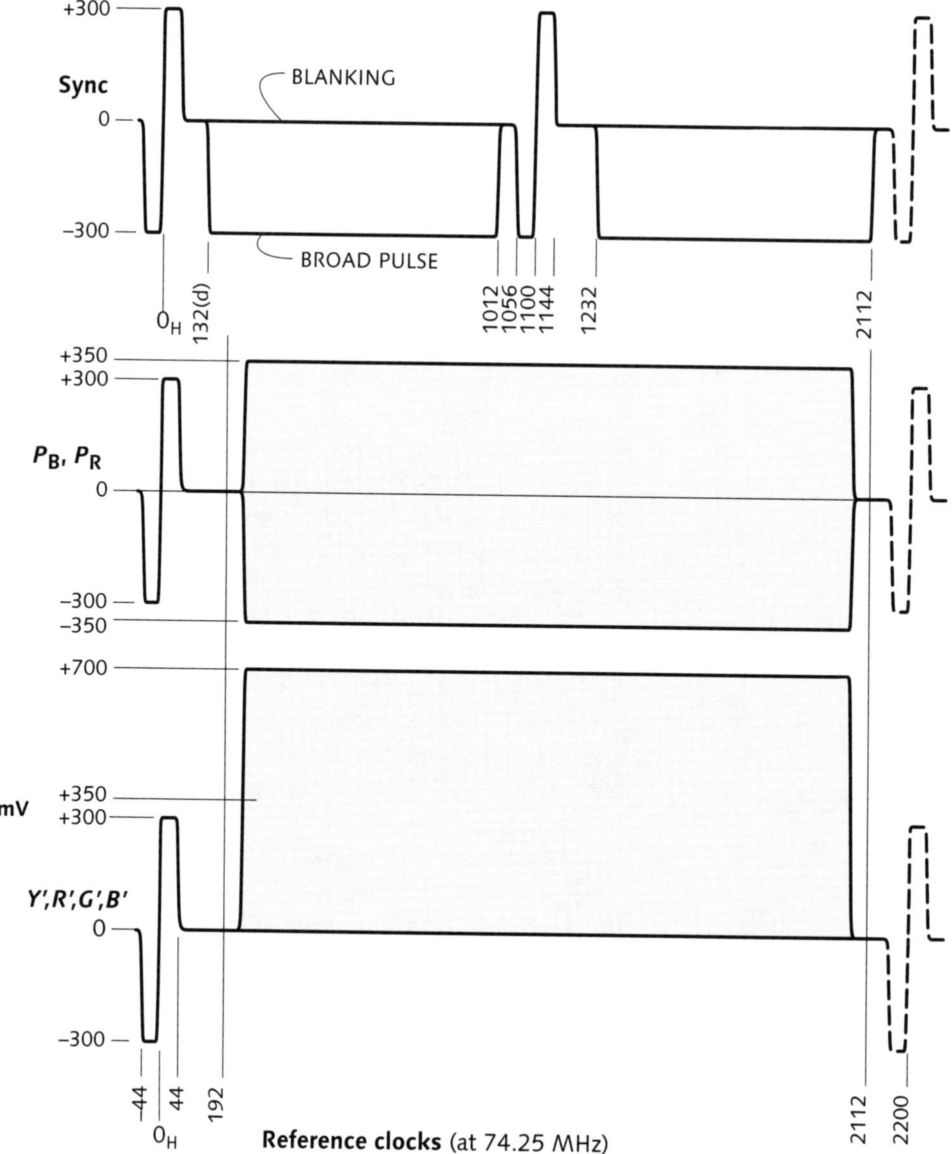

Figure 47.1 **1080*i*30 analog line details.** Time intervals are shown as intervals of a reference clock at 74.25 MHz, with reference clock zero defined at 0_H. To obtain sample numbers relative to the zeroth sample of active video, add $S_{AL} + 88$ (modulo S_{TL}) to these counts.

Vertical interval video lines do not convey picture information. They may convey ancillary or other signals either related or unrelated to the picture.

Figure 47.2 overleaf shows details of the vertical sync structure; this waveform diagram is the analog of Table 47.2, on page 559.

Picture center, aspect ratio, and blanking

The center of the picture is located midway between the central two of the 1920 active samples (between samples 959 and 960), and midway between the central two 1080 picture lines (between lines 581 and 582 in a progressive system, and between lines 290 and 853 in an interlaced system).

Aspect ratio is defined to be 16:9 with respect to the production aperture of 1920×1080.

In *Transition samples,* on page 323, I mentioned that it is necessary to avoid, at the start of a line, an instantaneous transition from blanking to picture information. A *clean aperture* pixel array 1888 samples wide and 1062 lines high, centered on the production aperture, should remain subjectively uncontaminated by edge transients.

Relationship to SMPTE 240M (1035*i*) scanning

SMPTE 240M defines the now-obsolete 1035*i*30 and 1035*i*29.97 systems, having 1035 picture lines. The first field has 517 picture lines starting at line 41. The second field has 518 picture lines starting with the top line of the picture at line 603 and including the bottom line of the frame at line 1120.

Aspect ratio is defined to be 16:9 with respect to the production aperture of 1920×1035. The clean aperture pixel array is 1888 samples wide and 1017 lines high, centered on the production aperture.

At a digital interface, 1035*i* signals are distinguished by the onset of picture as indicated by the *V*-bit; see Table 47.2, on page 559.

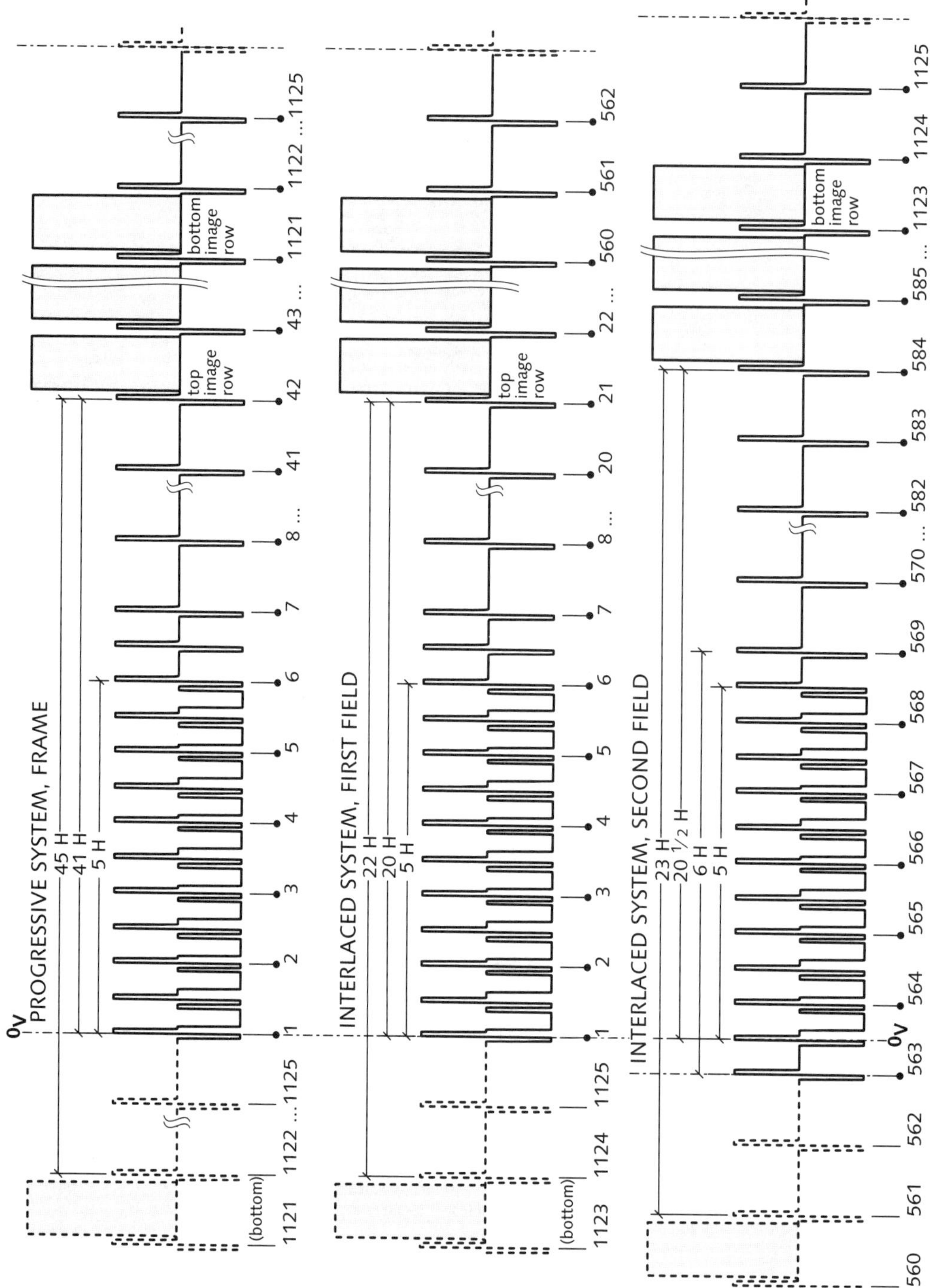

Figure 47.2 **1080*i* and 1080*p* vertical blanking interval**

RGB primary components

Picture information originates with linear-light primary red, green, and blue (*RGB*) tristimulus components, represented in abstract terms in the range 0 (reference black) to +1 (reference white). In modern standards, the colorimetric properties of the primary components conform to *Rec. 709/sRGB primaries* described on page 239.

Nonlinear transfer function

From *RGB* tristimulus values, three nonlinear primary components are computed according to the optoelectronic transfer function of *Rec. 709 transfer function*, described on page 263. In Equation 47.1, L denotes a tristimulus component, and V'_{709} denotes a nonlinear primary component (one of R', G', or B'):

$$V'_{709} = \begin{cases} 4.5L; & 0 \le L < 0.018 \\ 1.099L^{0.45} - 0.099; & 0.018 \le L \le 1 \end{cases} \qquad \text{Eq 47.1}$$

This process is loosely called *gamma correction.*

SMPTE standards do not specify tolerances on time-coincidence of R', G', and B' components. I recommend that the components be time-coincident with each other, and with sync, within ¼ of a sample clock – for 1080*i*30, time-coincident within ±3.4 ns.

Luma (Y')

Luma is computed as a weighted sum of nonlinear R', G', and B' primary components according to the luma coefficients of Rec. 709, introduced in *Rec. 709 luma,* on page 292:

$$^{709}Y' = 0.2126\,R' + 0.7152\,G' + 0.0722\,B' \qquad \text{Eq 47.2}$$

The luma component Y', being a weighted sum of nonlinear $R'G'B'$ components, has no simple relationship with the CIE luminance, denoted Y, or relative luminance, used in color science. The formulation of luma in HDTV differs from that of SDTV; see *SDTV and HDTV luma chaos,* on page 296. Video encoding specifications typically place no upper bound on luma bandwidth (though transmission standards may).

Component digital 4:2:2 interface

$Y'C_BC_R$ components are formed by scaling $B'-Y'$ and $R'-Y'$ components, as described in *C_BC_R components for Rec. 709 HDTV* on page 316. TRS is inserted as described in *TRS in HD-SDI* on page 392. The HD-SDI interface is described *HD-SDI coding,* on page 398.

Component analog *R'G'B'* interface

The interface for analog R', G', and B' signals is described in *Analog electrical interface* and *Analog mechanical interface,* on page 408. Zero (reference blanking level) in the R', G', and B' expressions corresponds to a level of 0 V_{DC}, and unity corresponds to 700 mV.

Sync is added to the green component according to:

$$G'_{sync} = \frac{7}{10}\left(active \cdot G'\right) + \frac{3}{10}\left(-sync\right) \qquad \text{Eq 47.3}$$

Component analog $Y'P_BP_R$ interface

The P_B and P_R color difference components of analog HDTV are formed by scaling $B'-Y'$ and $R'-Y'$ components as described in *P_BP_R components for Rec. 709 HDTV* on page 314. Although it is possible in theory to have wideband P_B and P_R components – that is, P_B and P_R components each having bandwidth similar to luma – in practice they are lowpass filtered to about half the bandwidth of luma.

The interface for analog Y', P_B, and P_R signals is described in *Analog electrical interface* and *Analog mechanical interface,* on page 408. HDTV $Y'P_BP_R$ signals have zero setup. Sync is added to the luma component:

$$Y'_{sync} = \frac{7}{10}Y' + \frac{3}{10}\left(-sync\right) \qquad \text{Eq 47.4}$$

This excursion is conveyed as 1 V_{PP}, with reference blanking at 0 V_{DC}. The picture excursion of the Y' signal is 700 mV. Figure 47.3 opposite shows a waveform drawing of luma in a 1080*i*30 component analog interface.

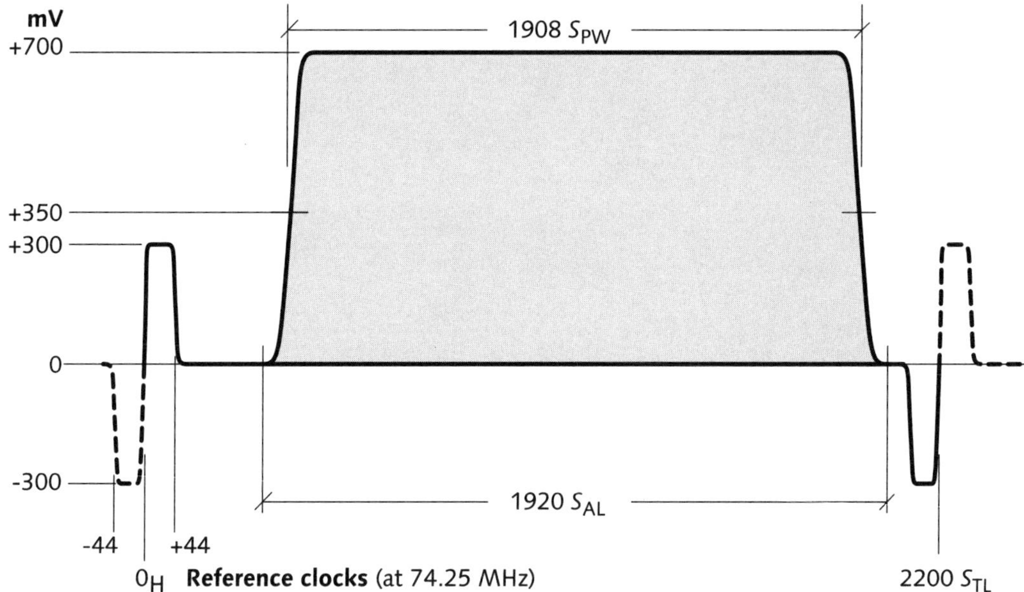

Figure 47.3 **1080*i*30 line showing analog luma levels.** Time intervals are shown as intervals of a reference clock at 74.25 MHz.

EIA/CEA-770.3, High Definition TV Analog Component Video Interface.

EIA/CEA has standardized the 1080*i*30 system as described here, including these $Y'P_BP_R$ levels, for use in consumer HDTV electronics devices.

Pre- and postfiltering characteristics

In systems with 30 Hz or 29.97 Hz frame rate, component Y', R', G' or B' signals have a nominal passband of 30 MHz; color difference components have a nominal passband of 15 MHz.

In *Pre- and postfiltering characteristics,* on page 553, I described filter templates applicable to the 720*p* system. The same templates apply to 1080*i* and 1080*p* systems, scaled to the sampling rate. SMPTE standards publish the templates in informative annexes; compliance with the annexes is not required to claim SMPTE standards conformance.

Part 5

Broadcast and consumer standards

Analog NTSC and PAL broadcast standards 48

ITU-R Rec. BT.470, *Conventional television systems.*

Table 48.1 below summarizes the six major standards used for conventional analog broadcast television. This chapter gives details of each system. ITU-R Rec. 470 contains a compilation of technical information from various national bodies regarding broadcast standards.

This chapter discusses basic parameter values, but not tolerances. Numeric values in this chapter are exact reference values unless otherwise indicated.

Chapter 50, *Digital television broadcast standards,* on page 587, introduces digital television broadcasting.

Table 48.1 **Summary of broadcast standards** This table summarizes the scanning system, video bandwidth, color encoding technique, and subcarrier frequency of standard television broadcast systems. The predominant systems, 480*i* NTSC and 576*i* PAL, are emphasized by shading.

Video bandwidth, MHz	4.2	4.2	5.0	5.5	6.0
480*i*29.97 (525/59.94) scanning:					
ITU-R System	**M/NTSC**	**M/PAL**			
Colloquial	NTSC	PAL-M, PAL-525			
f_{SC}	$3.5795454\overline{54}$	$3.5756118\overline{8}$			
Where used	N.A., Japan	Brazil			
576*i*25 (625/50) scanning:					
ITU-R System		**CN/PAL**	**B,G,H/PAL**	**I/PAL**	**L,D,K/SECAM**
Colloquial		PAL-N, PAL-3.58	PAL-B/G/H	PAL-I	SECAM
f_{SC}		3.58205625	4.433618750	4.433618750	
Where used		Argentina, Paraguay, Uruguay	Europe, Australia	U.K.	France, Russia

ITU-R (former CCIR)

In 1993, the International Radio Consultative Committee (CCIR) was renamed ITU-R. 576*i* (or 625/50) scanning is sometimes misleadingly and incorrectly referred to as *CCIR*.

International agreement is necessary to avoid contention in the use of the electromagnetic (radio frequency, RF) spectrum. The *International Telecommunications Union* (ITU) is the body that achieves international agreement on matters concerning RF spectrum. Its ITU-R branch is responsible for setting television broadcast standards. ITU-R agreements often result in *de jure* (regulatory) standards in its member states; those standards effectively have the force of law.

The ITU-R jurisdiction over radio transmission has, over the years, extended into the domain of international program exchange on videotape. Historically, videotape recording standards have been intimately related to studio signals; consequently, ITU-R is involved in studio video standards. Its agreements in that domain are called *Recommendations* in international standards lingo; they amount to voluntary standards, comparable to those of ISO or IEC.

The ITU-R also collects information from member states about technical aspects of broadcasting. The ITU-R publishes this information in *Reports*. ITU-R Reports are not standards, although they are important guides to implementors and users.

ITU-R scanning nomenclature

ITU-R notation for television transmission combines scanning lines per frame and field rate with various baseband video and RF transmission parameters, into a *system* designated by a single letter such as B, G, H, or M. ITU-R designations apply to the radiated signal; there is no standard system of nomenclature for signals at baseband, or signals on videotape or videodisc.

The ITU-R denotes a transmitted analog video signal by its scanning system and bandwidth, denoted by a letter, followed by a slash and its color-encoding method (NTSC, PAL, or SECAM). Full specification of a color video signal also requires the subcarrier frequency, though this is usually implicit because only certain combinations are in use. Informally, a color video signal is denoted by the color-encoding method, followed by

PAL-D is ambiguous, referring either to "deluxe" PAL (see the marginal note on page 342), or PAL System D (used for broadcasting in China).

a hyphen and the letter indicating the scanning system and bandwidth: What ITU-R denotes *B/PAL* is informally denoted *PAL-B*. The headings in the sections and tables of this chapter show the ITU-R nomenclature along with the informal nomenclature.

M/NTSC (NTSC)

System M refers to 480*i*29.97 (525/59.94) scanning, a video bandwidth of 4.2 MHz, and a channel spacing of 6 MHz. North America and Japan use system M/NTSC, with a subcarrier frequency of about 3.58 MHz. Japan uses zero setup; this is informally denoted NTSC-J.

In the 1970s and 1980s, NTSC broadcasts in North America included, on line 19, a *vertical interval reference signal* (VIRS, or VIR) standardized by EIA. VIRS enabled consumer receivers to automatically correct certain transmission impairments. VIRS is now obsolete.

ATSC A/49, *Ghost Canceling Reference Signal For NTSC*.

In 1992, a *ghost cancelling reference* (GCR) signal was introduced to NTSC in the United States. The GCR signal is transmitted on line 18. It comprises a swept-frequency sinewave designed to contain uniform spectral content between DC and 4.1 MHz and negligible content above 4.3 MHz. The polarity of the signal reverses in a four-frame sequence.

Audio in NTSC

NTSC television uses frequency-modulated (FM) sound, with ±25 kHz deviation around a 4.5 MHz carrier. (Broadcast FM radio uses a deviation of ±25 kHz.)

Electronics Industries Association of Japan (EIAJ) developed a stereo audio system using an FM subcarrier, carrying either the *L–R* signal (for stereo), or a second (mono) channel, but not both. The system was introduced to broadcasting in Japan in 1978.

EIA TV Systems Bulletin No. 5 (TVSB5), *Multichannel Television Sound BTSC System Recommended Practices* (Washington, D.C.: EIA, 1985).

In the early 1980s, the Multichannel Television Sound (MTS) initiative was established with the goal of adding stereo audio and second-language capability to NTSC broadcast television. In 1984, the resulting BTSC system was adopted in the United States; it has subsequently been adopted in Canada. Stereo audio is transmitted like FM radio: A suppressed-carrier AM subcarrier carries the *L–R* difference component (precoded with dbx-TV noise reduction, which involves proprietary frequency-selective compression). A *secondary audio program* (SAP) channel is typically used for a second language; this is also subject to dbx compression. A low-bandwidth "professional" channel is also provided, to allow voice or data communication for engineering and operational purposes. The signal composition is summarized in Table 48.2 below.

		Frequency range	Audio processing or preemphasis	Subcarrier frequency	Subcarrier type	Subcarrier deviation (kHz)
Main audio program, (monophonic)	*L+R*	50 Hz ... 15 kHz	75 μs			25[a]
Pilot				f_H		5
Stereo subchannel	*L–R*	50 Hz ... 15 kHz	dbx-TV compression	$2f_H$	AM DSB- SC	25[a]
Secondary audio program (SAP)		50 Hz ... 10 kHz	dbx-TV compression	$5f_H$	FM	15
Professional channel (not for consumer use)[b]	*voice*	50 Hz ... 3.5 kHz	150 μs	$6.5f_H$	FM	3
	data	50 Hz ... 1.5 kHz	none	$6.5f_H$	FSK	3
					Total	73

a Deviation of sum not to exceed 50 kHz.

b Professional channel can be used for either voice or data.

Table 48.2 **BTSC audio subchannel summary**

B,G,H,I/PAL (PAL)

A diverse collection of RF parameters are used for 576*i* broadcast, denoted by systems B, G, H, I (and others). The notation 576*i* should be used unless bandwidth and RF properties are being discussed.

Systems B, G, H, and I PAL all have 576*i* scanning and a video bandwidth ranging to 6 MHz. Australia and Europe (excluding France) use B,G,H/PAL; the U.K. uses I/PAL. The systems differ in their video bandwidths, channel spacing, and sound subcarrier frequencies; a summary is provided in Table 48.4, on page 578.

Audio in PAL

Historically, PAL television has used frequency-modulated sound, with ±50 kHz deviation, with sound carrier frequency dependent upon the broadcasting standard.

A system called Zweiton has been used to broadcast stereo audio in Germany since 1981.

Bower, A.J., *NICAM 728 – Digital Two-Channel Sound for Terrestrial Television*, BBC Research Dept. Report, 8/89. (Kingswood Warren, U.K.: BBC, 1989).

ETSI ETS 300163 V1.2.1, *NICAM 728: Transmission of two-channel digital sound with terrestrial television systems B, G, H, I, K1 and L.*

Many television broadcasters in Europe provide stereo sound using a system called NICAM (also known as NICAM 728). NICAM stands for *Near Instantaneous Companded Audio Multiplex*. "Near instantaneous companding" refers to a dynamic amplitude compression system that operates on a short time period (1 ms), whereby 14-bit original samples, taken at 32 kHz, are companded digitally to 10 bits. A high-frequency subcarrier – 5.85 MHz in System B/G, or 6.552 MHz in System I – is digitally modulated with a 728 kb/s datastream that comprises 728-bit NICAM packets, transmitted continuously, one packet every millisecond. "Multiplex" refers to several potential sources of audio data. The standard provides for several modes, but only two modes are widely deployed: NICAM typically transmits either one digital stereo sound channel, or two completely separate mono sound channels.

ETSI ETS 300732, *Enhanced 625-line PAL/SECAM television; Ghost cancellation reference (GCR) signals.*

In 1997, a *ghost cancellation reference* (GCR) signal virtually identical to the ghost canceling reference signal of NTSC was introduced to PAL and SECAM in Europe. It is transmitted on line 318. It has uniform spectral content between DC and 5.0 MHz and negligible content above 5.2 MHz.

PAL-M, PAL-N

In South America, PAL variants PAL-M and PAL-N are used, as introduced on page 96. The gratuitous parameter differences introduced by these systems have no technical merit; they have deterred image exchange and equipment commonality, and they have given many headaches to system designers. Today there is no production equipment for these standards: Production is accomplished using 480*i* or 576*i* equipment operating in the appropriate raster standard; the signal is transcoded to PAL-M or PAL-N prior to transmission.

Brazil uses PAL-M (formally M/PAL, sometimes denoted PAL-525), which has 480*i* scanning and PAL color encoding with a subcarrier close to 3.58 MHz (but not exactly that of NTSC).

Argentina, Paraguay, and Uruguay use system PAL-N (formally N/PAL or CN/PAL, also known as PAL-3.58). System N refers to 576*i* scanning with a bandwidth of about 4.2 MHz. N/PAL has a color subcarrier frequency close to 3.58 MHz (but not exactly the same as NTSC). Historically, monochrome System N had 7.5% setup and a picture-to-sync ratio of 10:4, but when color broadcasting was introduced, setup was eliminated and picture-to-sync ratio was altered to conform to PAL conventions. Use of 7:3 picture-to-sync ratio is denoted by *C* (for *combination*) preceding *N-PAL*.

Only CN/PAL is deployed today – in other words, all N/PAL systems in use are actually CN/PAL.

SECAM

SECAM is an acronym for *séquentiel couleur à mémoire*. This system is used with 576*i* scanning for terrestrial VHF and UHF broadcasting in France, Russia, and a few other countries. SECAM uses neither quadrature modulation nor frequency interleaving. Line-alternate color difference components are scaled (see Equation 48.1) to form D_B and D_R, equalized (preemphasized), then frequency-modulated (FM) onto a subcarrier. The resulting deviation ranges from about 3.9 MHz to 4.75 MHz, roughly the frequency range of PAL or NTSC modulated chroma. This FM chroma signal is then summed with luma, which has been notch-filtered in the region of the chroma subcarrier. Since the color difference components are transmitted line-sequentially, a SECAM receiver requires a one-line (1*H*) delay to recover chroma. SECAM has no coherent subcarrier *per se*, but has a pair of reference *rest* frequencies that are related to the line rate. Each video line includes a burst, alternating between D_B and D_R rest frequencies.

Eq 48.1

$$D_B = 1.505\left(B' - {}^{601}Y'\right)$$

$$D_R = -1.902\left(R' - {}^{601}Y'\right)$$

Systems D, K, and L use 576*i* scanning. D/SECAM and K/SECAM are used in the nations of the former USSR; System L/SECAM is used in France. The systems differ in their video and audio modulation. MESECAM is a VHS videotape format used in the Middle East. It is not a broadcast standard. (See page 584.)

SECAM had an advantage during the 1960s and 1970s: Because color difference signals in SECAM are frequency modulated (FM), instead of quadrature modulated (as thay are in NTSC and PAL), the color information of a SECAM signal with timebase error could be recovered without a timebase corrector. However, for decades now, SECAM has suffered two very serious drawbacks:

- FM chroma encoding is nonlinear: a SECAM signal cannot be processed in composite form, even for an operation as simple as fading between two signals. Decoding, processing, and reencoding are necessary.

- SECAM's use of FM for chroma abandons the frequency-interleaving principle. A so-called notch filter – actually, a lowpass filter – is necessary for luma/chroma separation. Poor luma/chroma separation, and relatively poor luma bandwidth, are inevitable.

Owing to SECAM's deficiencies as a production standard, no contemporary production equipment uses SECAM: Production in SECAM countries is accomplished using 576*i* component equipment, or composite PAL equipment; the signal is transcoded to SECAM immediately prior to transmission.

SECAM remains in use today only as a transmission standard, and in the consumer domain. Contrary to the remarkable stability of the NTSC and PAL broadcasting standards, SECAM has required many incremental improvements. Because SECAM broadcasting is obsolescent, and because SECAM has no application in the studio, I will not discuss it further.

Multiplexed analog components (MAC)

The *multiplexed analog components* (MAC) system was proposed in Europe for direct broadcast from satellite (DBS) of 576*i* material. In MAC, the color difference components were not combined with each other or with luma, but were time-compressed and transmitted serially. MAC was a commercial failure.

ITU-R system	*Colloquial*	*Scanning*	f_{SC}/f_H *ratio*		f_{SC} *(MHz)*	
M/NTSC	NTSC	480*i*29.97 (525/59.94)	$\frac{455}{2}$ =	227.5	3.579 545 $\overline{45}$	
M/PAL (Brazil)	PAL-M (PAL-525)	480*i*29.97 (525/59.94)	$\frac{909}{4}$ =	227.25	3.575 611 88$\overline{8}$	
CN/PAL (Argentina)	PAL-N (PAL-3.58)	576*i*25 (625/50)	$\frac{917}{4}+\frac{1}{625}$ =	229.2516	3.582 056 250	(exact)
B,G,H,I/PAL D/PAL	PAL	576*i*25 (625/50)	$\frac{1135}{4}+\frac{1}{625}$ =	283.7516	4.433 618 750	(exact)
D,K,L/SECAM	SECAM	576*i*25 (625/50)	272	(D_B rest freq.)	4.250 000 000	(exact)
			282	(D_R rest freq.)	4.406 250 000	(exact)

Table 48.3 **Color subcarrier characteristics of broadcast standards**

Summary of parameters

Table 48.3 above summarizes the color encoding parameters of broadcast video standards. There is a wide diversity of associated audio standards used worldwide; Table 48.4 below summarizes RF and audio characteristics of the major systems.

ITU-R system	*Colloquial*	*Video bandwidth (MHz)*	*Sound carrier (MHz)*	*Channel spacing (MHz)*	*Sound modulation*	*Where used*
M/NTSC	NTSC	4.2	4.5	6	FM, ±25 kHz	North America, Japan
M/PAL	PAL-M (PAL-525)	4.2	4.5	6	FM, ±25 kHz	Brazil
CN/PAL	PAL-N (PAL-3.58)	4.2	4.5	6	FM, ±25 kHz	Argentina
B/PAL	PAL	5	5.5	7	FM, ±50 kHz	Australia
G,H/PAL	PAL	5	5.5	8	FM, ±50 kHz	Europe
I/PAL	PAL	5.5	6	8	FM, ±50 kHz	U.K.
L/SECAM	SECAM	6 (+*ve video*)	6.5	8	AM	France
D,K/SECAM	SECAM	6	6.5	8	FM, ±50 kHz	Russia
D/PAL	PAL-D	6	6.5	8	FM, ±50 kHz	China

Table 48.4 **RF and audio characteristics of broadcast standards**

Consumer analog NTSC and PAL 49

Consumer electronics manufacturers have taken great liberties with video standards to achieve low-cost consumer devices. In this chapter, I describe the NTSC-4.43, PAL 60, and NTSC 50 schemes by which foreign videotapes can be viewed. I describe degenerate NTSC and PAL signals that are obtained when the color subcarrier is incoherent with scanning. I introduce the SCART connector common in Europe. Finally, I comment on the *heterodyne* (or *color-under*) technique used in consumer videotape recording.

Multistandard consumer equipment

The diversity of worldwide video broadcasting and recording standards is a big nuisance to consumers. Consumer electronics manufacturers have devised schemes whereby 480*i* NTSC tapes can be played on 576*i* PAL equipment, and 576*i* PAL tapes can be played on 480*i* NTSC equipment. These schemes can be considered to be degenerate NTSC and degenerate PAL. The schemes are features of VCRs, monitors, and receivers: They are not tape formats, and they are never broadcast.

I will briefly describe three schemes. The NTSC-4.43 and PAL 60 schemes are widely implemented in consumer equipment in Europe and Asia; they allow consumers in PAL regions to play NTSC tapes. The NTSC 50 scheme is much less common; it allows consumers in NTSC regions to play PAL tapes.

NTSC-4.43

The NTSC-4.43 scheme, sometimes called *pseudo-NTSC* or *hybrid-NTSC*, enables playback of 480*i* NTSC material on a monitor optimized for 576*i* PAL. The playback signal uses 480*i* scanning. Chroma is modulated using the NTSC method, but onto the 4.43 MHz color subcarrier frequency of PAL. (There is no PAL *V*-axis switch.) A monitor capable of NTSC-4.43 operation requires a vertical lock range sufficient to accommodate the 59.94 Hz field rate. The monitor's 4.43 MHz color subcarrier crystal is used to demodulate chroma; a 3.58 MHz crystal is unnecessary.

PAL 60

PAL 60, sometimes called *quasi-PAL, hybrid-PAL,* or *pseudo-PAL*, enables playback of 480*i* NTSC material on a monitor optimized for 576*i* PAL. As in NTSC-4.43, video is played back with 480*i* scanning. Chroma is modulated using the PAL method onto the 4.43 MHz subcarrier frequency of PAL. A monitor capable of PAL 60 requires a vertical lock range sufficient to accommodate the 59.94 Hz field rate. The monitor's 4.43 MHz color subcarrier crystal is used to demodulate chroma; a 3.58 MHz crystal is unnecessary. PAL 60 is comparable to PAL-M, except that PAL-M's precise ratio of f_{SC} to f_H is not maintained.

NTSC 50

This scheme enables playback of 576*i* PAL material on a monitor optimized for 480*i* NTSC. Video is played back with 576*i* scanning. Chroma is modulated using the NTSC method onto the 3.58 MHz subcarrier frequency of NTSC. An NTSC 50-capable monitor requires a vertical lock range sufficient to accommodate the 50 Hz field rate. The monitor's 3.58 MHz color subcarrier crystal is used to demodulate chroma; a 4.43 MHz crystal is unnecessary. NTSC 50 is comparable to PAL-N; however, chroma is modulated using the NTSC method, not PAL, and PAL-N's precise ratio of f_{SC} to f_H is not maintained.

A consumer-grade digital decoder can easily handle all of these schemes, by separating scanning from chroma demodulation, so as to mimic the processing done by a consumer television receiver.

Degenerate analog NTSC and PAL

In addition to studio-standard NTSC and PAL signals that I detailed in Chapters 28 and 29, there are three degenerate forms of composite analog NTSC and PAL video. The three degenerate modes are classified, along with studio-standard video, in Table 49.1:

	Stable timebase	*Unstable timebase*
Coherent subcarrier	Studio standard	Direct color (e.g., Type C)
Incoherent subcarrier	Industrial, Low-end consumer	Color-under (e.g., VHS)

Table 49.1 **Composite analog NTSC/PAL degenerate modes**

- Video played back from obsolete analog equipment, such as "direct color" Type-C analog VTRs or consumer laserdisc players, has an unstable timebase and coherent subcarrier. Such a signal must be processed through a *timebase corrector* (TBC) prior to processing or even monitoring.

- Upon playback from a VTR that uses the *color-under* recording scheme, not only is the timebase unstable, but color subcarrier is incoherent with sync.

- Consumer devices such as video games, and substandard industrial equipment, develop signals having stable timebase but incoherent subcarrier.

Coherent subcarrier

Macrovision is a proprietary, patented scheme to introduce electrical disturbances into the sync and burst elements of composite analog video so as to defeat subsequent VHS recording, without causing too much disruption to receivers and video monitors. In a sense, it is a degenerate form of NTSC or PAL.

In studio-quality NTSC video, the color subcarrier has a frequency of exactly 227.5 times the line rate. Although its phase may be subject to some uncertainty, its frequency is *coherent* with line rate, as introduced in *Frequency interleaving*, on page 107.

When NTSC subcarrier and sync are generated in a single circuit, it is simple to arrange for coherence of the subcarrier and the line rate: The two need simply be divided from the same master oscillator. In 576*i* PAL, subcarrier is considered coherent if there are either 283.75 or 283.7516 subcarrier cycles per line. Coherence is somewhat difficult to achieve in PAL owing to the +25 Hz offset.

Incoherent subcarrier

Many consumer and computer systems have no provision to generate coherent subcarrier, and in any case the tolerance on line rate would be an order of magnitude worse than that required for broadcast. Consumer VCRs employ the *heterodyne* (or *color-under)* technique to record chroma. In this technique, which I will describe in a moment, coherence is destroyed.

The frequency-interleaving principle rests upon coherence of luma and chroma, and thereby, upon the coherence of sync and subcarrier. In addition, comb filtering depends upon stable timebase. A comb filter should be used only with a signal having both stable timebase and coherence of subcarrier and sync.

If a luma/chroma separator is presented with an incoherent input signal, frequency interleaving should be abandoned: None of the three types of degenerate signals should undergo comb filtering; chroma and luma should instead be separated by lowpass and bandpass ("notch") filters. In this case, the decoder might as well limit luma bandwidth to about 3 MHz, and chroma bandwidth to about 600 kHz: In the absence of frequency interleaving, components outside this range are likely to suffer serious artifacts.

If equipment is to handle signals with incoherent subcarrier, sync should be used to establish the timing of the burst, but aside from that, subcarrier regeneration should be accomplished independently of sync.

Nonstandard scanning

Video outputs from low-cost consumer equipment such as video games produce progressive-scanned variants of 525-line and 625-line video. These signals amount to additional degenerate modes. If you need to generate a progressive signal, I recommend that you drop one scan line from the frame, while maintaining line rate: The progressive variant of 525-line video then has 262*p*60.05 scanning, and the progressive variant of 625-line video has 312*p*50.08 scanning.

When a consumer VCR is placed into a "trick" mode (such as pause, slow play, or fast forward), a nonstandard progressive-scanned signal is produced. In these modes, the VCR inserts synthetic sync into the vertical interval. In pause, video information comes from just one field, making it difficult or impossible to determine the parity of the field being played back.

SCART interface

CENELEC EN 50049-1:1989

IEC 60933-1, *Interconnections and matching values – Part 1: 21-pin connector for video systems – Application No. 1.*

IEC/TR 60933-2, *Interconnections and matching values – Part 2: 21-pin connector for video systems – Application No. 2.*

In about 1980, a French company, Péritel, devised an interface between a television set and a VCR. The interface was proposed to the *Syndicat des Constructeurs d'Appareils Radioélectriques et de Télévision*, where it became known as SCART. It was standardized by CENELEC, and then later by IEC (in two "applications" or versions). The interface is ubiquitous television receivers, VCRs, and other consumer video equipment in Europe.

Equipment has one or more 21-pin sockets. A cable with a (male) plug at each end connects equipment. Stereo audio, composite video, and control signals are conveyed in both directions. *R'G'B'* video signals are input-only.

Heterodyne (color-under) recording

Heterodyne (or *color-under*) video recording is ubiquitous in low-cost videocassette recorders, including ¾-inch (U-matic), ½-inch Betamax, VHS, S-VHS, Video-8 (8 mm), and Hi8. The luma and modulated chroma components of the NTSC or PAL input signal are separated prior to recording. In most color-under VCRs, luma bandwidth is less than 2.5 MHz, and chroma bandwidth is about 300 kHz. Luma is recorded by FM in a manner similar to direct recording. Chroma is mixed down to a low-frequency subcarrier between 600 kHz and 700 kHz, and recorded directly on tape, with the luma FM carrier acting as a bias signal.

Upon playback, the recorded color-under chroma is mixed onto a crystal-stable 3.58 MHz subcarrier. This locally generated subcarrier free-runs with respect to the original video, so this mixing destroys the coherence of subcarrier and line rate. Chroma, now on a 3.58 MHz subcarrier, is summed with luma to produce the composite playback output.

Although playback chroma from a color-under VCR is remodulated onto a crystal-stable subcarrier, the luma and chroma signals – and the sync component of both – contain timebase errors. However, the horizontal scanning of a television receiver has sufficient range to track the timebase error in sync, and a crystal oscillator can lock to the subcarrier. So a TBC is not necessary upon playback to a monitor or television receiver. Some residual timebase jitter will be visible if a TBC is not used; the residual jitter limits effective resolution.

Color-under recording was introduced in U-matic VCRs, using a low-frequency subcarrier of approximately 688 kHz. A *dub connector* carried separate luma and chroma components; this interface was known as *Y'/C688*. The original VHS VCRs used a low-frequency subcarrier at about 629 kHz, and some industrial equipment implements the corresponding *Y'/C629* interface. (Chroma carrier frequency in Hi8 VCRs is approximately 743 kHz.)

After color-under recording, the frequency interleaving that may have once been present in the signal is lost from the composite interface. There is no point in attempting to extract more than about 3 MHz of luma bandwidth. However, if an S-video interface is implemented in a color-under VCR, luma and chroma can be recorded without first having to be separated, and luma and chroma can be played without being combined. Much better performance can be obtained from the S-video interface than from the composite interface.

SECAM cannot use the same heterodyne technique as NTSC and PAL. Two different schemes have been adopted to record SECAM on VHS VCRs.

- In SECAM VHS machines in France and Russia, luma and SECAM frequency-modulated chroma are separated; the chroma component is then subject to frequency division by a factor of 4. The frequency-divided chroma is recorded using the color-under method. Upon playback, the chroma is frequency-multiplied by 4.

- In the MESECAM VHS videotape format used in the Middle East, SECAM (FM) chroma is downconverted similarly to color-under PAL or NTSC. MESECAM refers only to a VHS format; it is not a broadcast standard.

VHS trick mode playback

A VHS VCR has two heads with 59 μm track width; these are used for playback of tape recorded in *standard play* (SP) mode.

Trick playback (or *trick mode*) refers to playback of still fields when the tape is stationary, or playback when the tape is moving more slowly than normal play speed. In a 4-head VHS VCR, a pair of heads with a track width of 19 μm are fitted in addition to the standard pair of heads. In trick modes, the 19 μm heads are used to play 59 μm tracks. This produces a high-quality signal for a much wider angle of headwheel rotation than would a 59 μm head: Playback in trick modes is greatly improved. The pair of 19 μm heads is also used to record and play back the narrow tracks of *extended play* (EP) mode, providing an increase in recording capacity from 2 hours to 6. EP mode has disadvantages: Playback has higher noise, and trick mode playback in EP mode necessarily has low picture quality.

Timebase correction (TBC)

In normal VHS playback, timebase error can cause successive lines to be reproduced with durations differing by up to perhaps ±500 ns; over an entire field time, an advance or delay of several tens of microseconds can accumulate. The horizontal scanning circuits of consumer television receivers are sufficiently loose to track timebase error, and the color-under method enables simple subcarrier locking even in the presence of timebase error. However, for many applications timebase error must be removed prior to the processing of a signal. Timebase error can be removed by a subsystem or piece of equipment called a *timebase corrector*, which functions as an analog FIFO buffer. A TBC recovers timing information – a *jittered clock* – from the sync of the off-tape signal. The TBC writes the unstable signal into a buffer memory using the jittered clock, and reads it out several line times later based on a crystal-stable clock. TBCs were once standalone units; they are now internal to studio analog VTRs and to some high-end consumer VCRs. In digital VTRs, TBC capability is inherent in the FIFO buffers used in the data path.

Digital television broadcast standards 50

In this chapter I will briefly summarize the standards for digital television broadcasting. All digital broadcast systems that have been standardized are based upon MPEG-2 compression, described in *MPEG-2 video compression* on page 473.

HDTV transmission systems were conceived to deliver images of about twice the vertical and twice the horizontal resolution of SDTV – that is, about 2 megapixels – in a 6 MHz analog channel. MPEG-2 can compress 2 megapixel images at 30 frames per second to about 20 Mb/s. Modern digital modulation schemes suitable for terrestrial RF transmission have a payload of about 3.5 bits per hertz of channel bandwidth. Combining these numbers, you can see that one HDTV signal occupies one 6 MHz channel.

The basic parameters of the 525-line, 60-field-per-second interlaced transmission scheme have been frozen since the introduction of black-and-white television in 1941! The modulation scheme requires that potential channels at many locations remain unused, owing to potential interference into other channels. The unused channels are now called *taboo.* Digital television transmission takes advantage of half a century of technological improvements in modulation systems. The modulation system chosen allows very low power. This low power has two major consequences: It minimizes interference from digital transmitters into NTSC or PAL, and it allows use, for digital television transmission, of the channels that were formerly taboo. Digital television service is thus overlaid on top of analog service. (In early deployment of HDTV, the program material is simulcast on a conventional analog transmitter.)

Japan

NHK Science and Technical Research Laboratories, *High Definition Television: Hi-Vision Technology* (New York: Van Nostrand Reinhold, 1993).

HDTV broadcasting based on 1035*i*30.00 scanning and MUSE compression has been deployed in Japan since the early 1990s; this is called *Hi-Vision*. MUSE is a hybrid analog/digital system, optimized for direct broadcast from satellite (DBS); it is documented in the book from NHK Labs. MUSE predates the MPEG standards; nowadays, it is generally agreed that Japan adopted HDTV transmission standards prematurely.

United States

HDTV developers in the United States assumed that broadcasters would gradually replace SDTV transmission with HDTV transmission. Part way through the development of HDTV, it became clear that the same compression and transmission technology that would allow one HDTV channel to be coded and transmitted at about 20 Mb/s would be equally suited to allow five SDTV channels to be coded, multiplexed, and transmitted at 4 Mb/s each! Broadcasters apparently have more interest in broadcasting five SDTV channels than one HDTV channel. What began as high-definition television evolved – for good or for bad – into digital television (DTV), which subsumes SDTV and HDTV.

ATSC A/53, *Digital Television Standard.*

DTV standards in the United States were developed by the Advanced Television Systems Committee (ATSC). Those standards were adopted by the Federal Communications Commission (FCC), with one significant change: The FCC rejected the set of 18 formats documented in Table 3 of ATSC Standard A/53 (presented as my Table 13.1, on page 114). Bowing to pressure from the computer industry, the FCC deleted that table, but left the rest of the ATSC standards intact.

The FCC's deletion of Table 3 supposedly left the choice of raster standards to the marketplace: In principle, any format compliant with MPEG-2 MP@HL could be used. In practice, no U.S. broadcaster has chosen, and no consumer equipment is guaranteed to implement, any format outside ATSC's Table 3. In practice, DTV decoders conform to MPEG standards, and additionally conform to the restrictions imposed by the ATSC standards. The supposed flexibility in the FCC regulations has forced the consumer electronics industry to institute a branding program that places "DTV-ready" stickers on consumer equipment. The sticker supposedly indicates compliance with ATSC Table 3 and certain other provisions.

MPEG-2 specifies upper bounds for picture size at various levels. Surprisingly, ATSC A/53 specifies exact values. For example, MPEG-2 MP@ML allows 704 S_{AL}, but ATSC A/53 does not.

Some consumer HDTV displays use 1080*i* scanning, but on a 4:3 display surface ("4:3 glass"). To use such a display for standard 16:9 aspect ratio HDTV requires vertical downsampling by a ratio of 4:3. This yields 810 picture lines, rather than 1080; the display format is denoted 810*i*.

In the United States, DTV audio is standardized with Dolby Digital (AC-3) audio coding; this is outside the MPEG-2 standard. Dolby Digital is capable of "5.1" channels: left and right (stereo) channels, a front center channel, left and right surround channels, and a low-frequency effects (LFE) channel (the ".1" in the notation) intended for connection to a "subwoofer." ATSC audio consumes a maximum of 512 kb/s.

EIA-708-B, *Digital Television (DTV) Closed Captioning.*

EIA-708-B is the standard for conveying closed caption data in a digital television signal (DTVCC).

One or more MPEG-2 program streams, the associated audio streams, ancillary data, and other data is multiplexed into a transport stream with a bit rate of about 19.28 Mb/s. That stream is presented to the modulator.

ATSC modulation

$$4.5\frac{684}{286} \approx 10.762$$

The ATSC standardized 8-level digital vestigial sideband (8-VSB) modulation, transmitting about 10.762 million 3-bit symbols per second. To enable the receiver to overcome errors introduced in transmission, two forward error-correction (FEC) schemes are concatenated: The outer code is Reed-Solomon (R-S), and the inner code is a simple $^{3}/_{2}$ trellis code. Between the R-S and trellis coding stages, data is interleaved. Synchronization information comprising segment and field syncs is added after interleaving and coding. A low-level pilot carrier is inserted 310 kHz above the lower band edge to aid in carrier recovery. Analog techniques are used to upconvert to the UHF broadcast channel.

I and *Q* refer to *in-phase* and *quadrature;* these are the same concepts as in NTSC chroma modulation, but applied to completely different ends.

At a receiver, analog techniques downconvert the UHF broadcast to intermediate frequency (IF), typically 44 MHz. Demodulation is then accomplished digitally. Typically, an analog frequency and phase-locked loop (FPLL) recovers the carrier frequency based upon the pilot carrier. A quadrature demodulator then recovers *I* and *Q* components. The *I* component is converted from analog to digital at 10.76 MHz to recover the bitstream; the *Q* component is processed to effect phase control. The bitstream is then subject to trellis decoding, deinterleaving, R-S decoding, and MPEG-2 demultiplexing.

It is a challenge to design a demodulator that is immune to transmission impairments such as multipath distortion and co-channel interference from NTSC transmitters. An interference rejection filter – a variation of a comb filter – is built into the demodulator; it attenuates the video, chroma, and audio carriers of a potentially interfering NTSC signal. An adaptive equalizer built into the demodulator alleviates the effects of multipath distortion; the field sync component of the signal serves as its reference signal. An adaptive equalizer is typically implemented as an FIR filter whose coefficients are updated dynamically as a function of estimated channel parameters.

ATSC defines a cable mode using 16-VSB without trellis coding, but this mode hasn't been deployed.

Digital cable television is detailed in Ciciora, Walter, and James Farmer and David Large, *Modern Cable Television Technology* (San Francisco: Morgan Kaufmann, 1999).

Cable television has very different channel characteristics than terrestrial broadcast. DTV over cable typically does not use 8-VSB modulation: Quadrature amplitude modulation (QAM) is used instead, with either 64 or 256 levels (64-QAM or 256-QAM).

For direct broadcast from satellite (DBS), quadrature phase-shift keying (QPSK) is generally used.

Consumer receivers in the United States must accept the diversity of frame rates and raster standards in

ATSC's Table 3 (my Table 13.1 on page 114). Although multiscan monitors are ubiquitous in computing, both price and performance suffer when a monitor has to accommodate multiple rates. Most consumer HDTV receivers are designed with displays that operate over a limited range of scanning standards; the wide range of ATSC Table 3 is accommodated by digital resampling. Today, most consumer HDTV receivers are 1080*i*-native, and convert other formats to 1080*i*.

Europe

In Europe, huge efforts were made in the 1980s and 1990s to develop an HDTV broadcasting system using 1250/50 scanning and a transmission system built upon the MAC transmission technology originally designed for 576*i*. MAC failed in the marketplace. HD-MAC failed also; this was partially a consequence of the commercial failure of MAC, partially because of technical weaknesses of HD-MAC, and partially because HD-MAC did not address worldwide markets.

DVB standards are promulgated by ETSI [www.etsi.org].

See also Dambacher, Paul, *Digital Terrestrial Television Broadcasting* (Berlin: Springer, 1998).

HDTV broadcasting in Europe is dead, but digital broadcasting of SDTV is being deployed based upon MPEG-2 MP@ML, with 720×576 image structure. The Digital Video Broadcasting (DVB) organization has created a comprehensive set of standards for cable (DVB-C), satellite (DVB-S), and terrestrial (DVB-T) broadcasting. DVB audio conforms to MPEG-2 audio.

The RF modulation system chosen for DVB-T is coded orthogonal frequency division multiplexing (COFDM). COFDM uses a large number of subcarriers to spread the information content of a signal evenly across a channel. The subcarriers of COFDM are individually modulated, typically using QPSK or QAM. COFDM exhibits greatly improved immunity to multipath distortion compared to 8-VSB. Also, COFDM accommodates transmission using single-frequency networks (SFNs) where the same bitstream is transmitted from multiple transmitters at different locations but operating on the same frequency.

Further reading

Weiss, S. Merrill, *Issues in Advanced Television Technology* (Boston: Focal Press, 1997).

Between 1992 and 1995, when U.S. HDTV transmission standards were being developed, Merrill Weiss wrote a series of columns in *TV Technology* magazine. These columns have now been published; their focus is on systems issues, multiplexing, and transmission.

Appendices

YUV and *luminance* considered harmful — A

This is a plea for precise terminology. The notation *YUV*, and the term *luminance*, are widespread in digital video. In truth, digital video almost never uses *Y'UV* color difference components, and never directly represents the *luminance* of color science. The common terms are almost always wrong. This note explains why. I urge video engineers and computer graphics specialists to use the correct terms, almost always $Y'C_BC_R$ and *luma*.

Cement *vs.* concrete

I'll demonstrate by analogy why it is important to use correct terms. Next time you're waiting in line for a bus, ask the person next to you in line what building material is used to construct a sidewalk. Chances are that person will answer, "cement."

The correct answer is *concrete*. Cement is calcined lime and clay, in the form of a fine, gray powder. Cement is one ingredient of concrete; the other ingredients are sand, gravel, and water.

In an everyday situation, you need not be precise about which of these terms are used: If you refer to a sidewalk as being constructed of "cement," people will know what you mean. Lay people are not confused by the term *cement.* Interestingly, experts are not confused either. If a construction superintendent yells out to his foreman, "Get me 500 pounds of cement!" the foreman understands immediately from context whether the superintendent actually wants concrete. However, if you place an order with a building material supplier for 500 pounds of cement, you will certainly not receive 500 pounds of concrete! Lay people have no trouble with the loose nomenclature, and the experts have little trouble. It is the people in the middle who are liable to become confused. Worse still, they are liable to use a term without realizing that it is ambiguous or wrong!

True CIE luminance

The principles of color science dictate that true CIE luminance – denoted Y – is formed as a weighted sum of linear (tristimulus) *RGB* components. If CIE luminance were transmitted in a video system, the system would conform to the *Principle of Constant Luminance*. But in video we implement an engineering approximation that departs from this principle. It was standardized for NTSC in 1953, and remains standard for all contemporary video systems, to form *luma*, denoted Y', as a weighted sum of *nonlinear* (gamma-corrected) $R'G'B'$ components:

$$^{601}Y' = 0.299\,R' + 0.587\,G' + 0.114\,B' \qquad \text{Eq A.1}$$

The nonlinear transfer function is roughly comparable to a square root. We use the theoretical coefficients of color science, but we use them in a block diagram different from the one prescribed by color science: Gamma correction is applied *before* forming the weighted sum, not after. The "order of operations" is reversed from what you might expect from color science.

The misinterpretation of luminance

Video engineers in the 1950s recognized that the video quantity Y' was very different from CIE luminance, and that it needed to be distinguished from luminance. They described it by the phrase *the quantity representative of luminance*. They used the symbol Y, but augmented it with a prime to denote the nonlinearity: Y'. Obviously the qualifier "quantity representative of" was cumbersome, and over the decades, it was elided. And over time, the prime symbol was elided as well.

Unfortunately, no new word was invented to supplement *luminance*, to reinforce the distinction between the color science quantity and the video quantity. Most video engineers nowadays are unfamiliar with color science, and most do not understand the distinction. Engineers today often carelessly use the word *luminance*, and the symbol *Y*, to refer to the weighted sum of nonlinear (gamma-corrected) *R'G'B'* components.

Pritchard, D.H., "U.S. Color Television Fundamentals – A Review," in *SMPTE Journal*, 86 (11): 819–828 (Nov. 1977).

Smith, A.R., "Color Gamut Transform Pairs," in *Computer Graphics* 12 (2): 12–19 (Aug. 1978, Proc. SIGGRAPH 78).

Foley, James D., and Andries van Dam, *Fundamentals of Interactive Computer Graphics* (Reading, Mass.: Addison-Wesley, 1984).

Foley, James D., Andries van Dam, Steven Feiner, and John Hughes, *Computer Graphics: Principles and Practice*, Second Edition (Reading, Mass.: Addison-Wesley, 1990). 589 (Section 13.3.3).

The sloppy nomenclature made its way into ostensibly authoritative video references, such as Pritchard's SMPTE paper published in 1977.

The computer graphics pioneer Alvy Ray Smith encountered the word *luminance* in his quest to adapt video principles to computer graphics. Smith apparently correlated the use of the term *luminance* with his knowledge of color science, and understandably – though wrongly – concluded that video "luminance" and color science luminance were identical. Consequently, video *Y'IQ* was introduced to computer graphics, having its *Y* component alleged to be identical to CIE luminance.

That incorrect interpretation propagated into authoritative computer graphics textbooks. *Computer Graphics: Principles and Practice*, Second Edition, in the section entitled *The YIQ Color Model*, includes this sentence:

> The *Y* component of YIQ is not yellow but luminance, and is defined to be the same as the CIE **Y** primary.

The emphasis is in the original. "Yellow" refers to *CMY;* printing inks were mentioned in the immediately preceding section. "CIE **Y** primary" would be more accurately denoted "CIE *Y* component."

Widespread use of incorrect terminology is not a new phenomenon. The indigenous people of North America were, for many centuries, referred to as "Indians." Why? After his long voyage across what we now call the Atlantic Ocean, when Christopher Columbus finally saw land, he thought it was India.

Contrary to the quoted paragraph, the so-called *Y* component of video – more properly designated with a prime symbol, *Y'* – is *not* the same as CIE luminance. Video *Y'* cannot even be computed from CIE *Y*, unless two other color components are also available. The quoted passage is quite wrong. About 300,000 copies of various editions and adaptations of *CG:PP* have been printed. Confusion is rampant.

Pratt, William K., *Digital Image Processing*, Second Edition (New York: Wiley, 1991), 64.

The error propagated into the digital image-processing community. Pratt's textbook states:

> N.T.S.C. formulated a color coordinate system for transmission composed of three tristimulus values *YIQ*. The *Y* tristimulus value is the luminance of a color.

The video quantities are certainly *not* tristimulus values, which are, by CIE's definition, proportional to intensity.

Loose nomenclature on the part of video engineers has misled a generation of digital image processing, computer software, and computer hardware engineers.

The enshrining of luma

The term *luma* was used in video for a long time, without having had a precise interpretation.
I campaigned among video engineers, and among computer graphics experts, for adoption of the term *luma* to designate the nonlinear video quantity. The term offers no impediment to video engineers – in fact, it slides off the tongue more easily than *luminance*. By virtue of its being a different word from *luminance*, the word *luma* invites readers from other domains to investigate fully before drawing conclusions about its relationship with luminance.

SMPTE EG 28, *Annotated Glossary of Essential Terms for Electronic Production*.

With the help of Fred Kolb, my campaign succeeded: In 1993, SMPTE adopted Engineering Guideline EG 28, *Annotated Glossary of Essential Terms for Electronic Production*. EG 28 defines the term *luma*, and clarifies the two conflicting interpretations of the term *luminance*. While a SMPTE EG is not quite a SMPTE "Standard," at long last the term has received official recognition. There's no longer any excuse for sloppy use of the term *luminance* by the authors of video engineering papers and books. Had the term *luma* been widespread 20 years ago when A. R. Smith was writing about *YIQ*, or when Foley and van Dam were preparing *Computer Graphics: Principles and Practice*, this whole mess would have been avoided. But EG 28 was unavailable at the time.

It is a shame that today's SMPTE, ISO/IEC, ITU-R, and ITU-T standards persist in using the incorrect word *luminance*, without ever mentioning the ambiguity – even conflict – with the CIE standards of color science.

Color difference scale factors

To represent color, luma is accompanied by two *color difference* – or *chroma* – components, universally based on *blue minus luma* and *red minus luma*, where blue, red, and luma have all been subject to gamma correction: $B'-Y'$ and $R'-Y'$. Different scale factors are applied to the basic $B'-Y'$ and $R'-Y'$ components for different applications. $Y'P_BP_R$ scale factors are optimized for component analog video. $Y'C_BC_R$ scale factors are optimized for component digital video, such as 4:2:2 studio video, JPEG, and MPEG. Correct use of the $Y'UV$ and $Y'IQ$ scale factors is limited to the formation of composite NTSC and PAL video.

When I say *NTSC* and *PAL*, I refer to color encoding, not scanning. I do not mean 480*i* and 576*i*, or 525/59.94 and 625/50!

$Y'C_BC_R$ scaling as defined by Rec. 601 is appropriate for component digital video. $Y'C_BC_R$ chroma is almost always subsampled using one of three schemes: 4:2:2, or 4:2:0, or 4:1:1.

ITU-R Rec. BT.601-5, *Studio encoding parameters of digital television for standard 4:3 and widescreen 16:9 aspect ratios.*

$Y'UV$ scaling is properly used only as an intermediate step in the formation of composite NTSC or PAL video signals. $Y'UV$ scaling is not appropriate when the components are kept separate. However, the $Y'UV$ nomenclature is now used rather loosely, and sometimes – particularly in computing – it denotes *any* scaling of $B'-Y'$ and $R'-Y'$.

Digital disk recorders (DDRs) are generally able to transfer files across Ethernet. Abekas introduced the convention of using an extension ".yuv" for these files. But the scale factors – in Abekas equipment, at least – actually correspond to $Y'C_BC_R$. Use of the ".yuv" extension reinforces the misleading *YUV* nomenclature.

Subsampling is a digital technique, properly performed only on component digital video – that is, on $Y'C_BC_R$. Subsampling is inappropriate for $Y'UV$ in all but very specialized applications (namely, digital encoding of $4f_{SC}$ NTSC or PAL composite video). If you see a system

Chroma components are properly ordered $B'-Y'$ then $R'-Y'$, or C_B then C_R. Blue associates with *U*, and red with *V*; *U* and *V* are in alphabetic order.

described as *Y'UV 4:2:2*, you have a dilemma. Perhaps the person who wrote the description is unfamiliar with the principles of component video, and the scale factors actually implemented in the equipment (or the software) are correct. But you must allow for the possibility that the engineers who designed or implemented the system used the wrong scale factors! If the wrong equations were used, then color accuracy will suffer; however, this can be difficult to diagnose.

Hamilton, Eric, *JPEG File Interchange Format*, Version 1.02 (Milpitas, Calif.: C-Cube Microsystems, 1992).

Proper $Y'C_BC_R$ scaling is usual in Motion-JPEG, and in MPEG. However, the $Y'C_BC_R$ scaling used in stillframe JPEG/JFIF in computer applications usually uses full-range luma and chroma excursions, without any headroom or footroom. The chroma excursion is $^{256}/_{255}$ of the luma excursion. The scaling is almost exactly that of $Y'P_BP_R$, but is unfortunately described as $Y'C_BC_R$: Now even $Y'C_BC_R$ is ambiguous! I am hopeful that proper $Y'C_BC_R$ scaling will be incorporated into the next revision of JFIF, so that compressed stillframe and motion imagery in computing can be combined without suffering a conversion process.

Except for very limited use in the encoding, interface, and decoding of composite $4f_{SC}$ (or loosely, "D-2") studio video, *Y'IQ* coding is obsolete.

Conclusion: A plea

Using the term *luminance* for video *Y'* is tantamount to using the word *cement* instead of *concrete* to describe the main construction material of a sidewalk. Lay people don't care, and experts can live with it, but people in the middle – in this case, the programmers and engineers who are reimplementing video technology in the computer domain – are liable to draw the wrong conclusions from careless use of terms. Users suffer from this, because the exchange of images is compromised.

I urge video engineers and computer graphics specialists to avoid the terms *YUV, Y'UV, YIQ, Y'IQ*, and *luminance,* except in the highly specialized situations where those terms are technically correct. The appropriate terms are almost always $Y'C_BC_R$ and *luma*.

Introduction to radiometry and photometry B

The domain of *radiometry* involves optical power and its spatial and angular distributions. *Photometry* is, in essence, radiometry weighted by the spectral response of vision. These fields involve several subtle concepts, masked by a bewildering array of symbols and units. I strive to sort out some of the confusion, and make some suggestions concerning units and nomenclature.

ANSI/IESNA RP-16, *Nomenclature and Definitions for Illuminating Engineering*.

CIE Nº 17 (E-1.1), *International Lighting Vocabulary* (Vienna, Austria: Commission Internationale de L'Éclairage).

Table B.1 below summarizes radiometric quantities, symbols, and units (in the left columns) and the corresponding photometric quantities, symbols, and units (to the right). The symbol for a photometric quantity is just the symbol for the corresponding radiometric quantity, with the addition of the subscript v (for *visual*). Some people add the subscript e to the radiometric symbols.

Differentiate flux with respect to	*Radiometric (Radiant)*		*Photometric (Luminous)*	
	Quantity (Symbol)	*Unit*	*Quantity (Symbol)*	*Unit*
–	**radiant flux, power** (Φ, F, P)	watt, W	**luminous flux** (Φ_v, F_v, P_v)	lumen, lm
area	**irradiance** (E), **radiant exitance** (M)	$\mathrm{W \cdot m^{-2}}$	**illuminance** (E_v) **luminous exitance** (M_v)	$\mathrm{lm \cdot m^{-2}}$ = lux, lx
solid angle	**radiant intensity** (I)	$\mathrm{W \cdot sr^{-1}}$	**luminous intensity** (I_v)	$\mathrm{lm \cdot sr^{-1}}$ = candela, cd
area *and* solid angle	**radiance** (L)	$\mathrm{W \cdot m^{-2} \cdot sr^{-1}}$	**luminance** (L_v, Y)	$\mathrm{cd \cdot m^{-2}}$ = nit

Table B.1 **Quantities, symbols, and units of radiometry and photometry,** In radiometry, the symbol L_v is used for luminance; however, luminance is denoted Y in color science and in video.

Radiometry and photometry involve light, in space. No surface is necessary! Light properties may be described *at* a real or imaginary surface; however, they are not properties *of* a surface. Absorptance (α), reflectance (ρ), and transmittance (τ) are intrinsic properties of surfaces, not properties of light.

In what follows, I use the usual physics convention of writing letter symbols in italics and units in Roman type.

Radiometry

Radiometry starts with energy (symbol Q) at wavelengths between 100 nm and 1 mm. Energy is expressed in units of joules, J. A photon's energy (Q_{p}) is related to its wavelength (λ):

Eq B.1

$$Q_{\mathrm{p}} = \mathrm{h}\frac{\mathrm{c}}{\lambda}; \qquad \begin{array}{l} \mathrm{h} \approx 6.6260755 \cdot 10^{-34}\ \mathrm{J \cdot s}\ \text{(Planck's constant)} \\ \mathrm{c} \equiv 299972458\ \mathrm{m \cdot s^{-1}}\ \text{(speed of light)} \end{array}$$

The rate of flow – or formally, the time-derivative – of radiant energy is power (P), also known as radiant flux (F, or preferably, Φ), expressed in units of watts, W.

Radiant exitance sums emitted and reflected light. The former term *emittance* excludes reflected light.

Some thermal engineers use the term *radiosity* for radiant exitance. In computer graphics, *radiosity* refers to a specialized technique to compute illumination; it does not refer to any particular quantity.

Radiant flux per unit area – that is, flux density – arriving at a real or imaginary surface, throughout all directions in a hemisphere, is *irradiance* (E). Irradiance is expressed in units of watts per meter squared, $\mathrm{W \cdot m^{-2}}$ (or $\mathrm{W/m^2}$). Solar irradiance (*insolation*) at noon is about $1\ \mathrm{kW \cdot m^{-2}}$.

Radiant flux per unit area leaving a surface, in all directions, is *radiant exitance* (M). Formally, this is the derivative of radiant flux with respect to area. Radiant exitance is expressed in units of watts per meter squared, $\mathrm{W \cdot m^{-2}}$. Radiant exitance from a nonemissive surface is simply its irradiance times its reflectance.

In photography, the symbol I is often used for irradiance or illuminance, instead of intensity.

Radiant flux in a specified direction – or formally, radiant flux per unit solid angle – is *radiant intensity* (symbol I). The unit for intensity is watts per steradian, $\mathrm{W \cdot sr^{-1}}$ (or W/sr). Intensity must be specified in a particular direction; it is independent of the observer's location.

Palmer, James M., "Getting Intense on Intensity," in *Metrologia* 30 (4): 371–372 (1993).

James M. Palmer points out that the term *intensity* is widely misused, for no good reason, because it is one of the seven base units of the SI system! Beware so-called intensity expressed in units other than watts per steradian, $W \cdot sr^{-1}$. Some authors in thermal engineering, and some authors in the computer graphics field of radiosity, use the term *radiant intensity* for what I call *radiance*, which I will now describe.

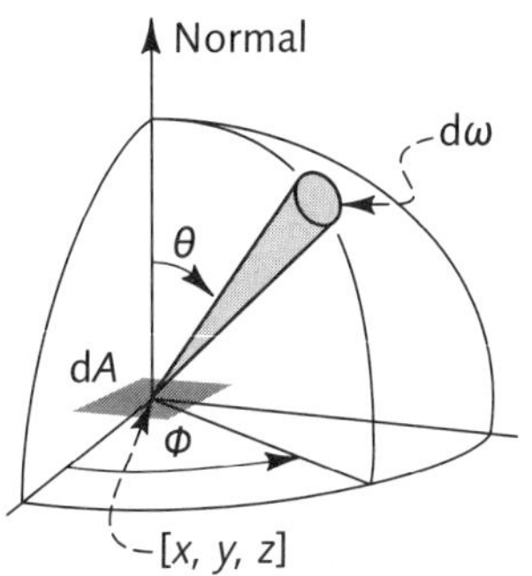

Figure B.1 **Geometry associated with the definition of radiance.** The quantity d*A* represents unit area; the quantity d*ω* represents unit solid angle. Projected area falls off as cos *θ*.

Radiant flux density in a specified direction is *radiance* (symbol *L*). Formally, radiance is radiant flux differentiated with respect to both solid angle and projected area; the geometry of this definition is depicted in Figure B.1. Radiance is expressed in units of watts per steradian per meter squared, $W \cdot sr^{-1} \cdot m^{-2}$ (or $W/sr/m^2$). For a large, non-point source, radiance is independent of distance.

Radiance can be considered to be the fundamental quantity of radiometry: All other radiometric quantities can be computed from it. You might find it intuitive to start with radiance, and then consider the following:

- Radiant intensity is radiance integrated across an area.
- Irradiance is radiance integrated through solid angle, that is, integrated across all directions in a hemisphere.
- Flux is irradiance integrated across area, or equivalently, radiant intensity integrated through solid angle.

All of these radiometric terms relate to a broad spectrum of wavelengths. Any of these terms may be limited to a narrow spectrum by prepending *spectral* to the term, subscripting the letter symbol with λ, and appending *per nanometer* ($\cdot nm^{-1}$) to the units.

Photometry

So far, I have discussed the physical quantities of radiometry. Photometry is entirely analogous, except that the spectral composition of each quantity is weighted by the spectral sensitivity of human vision, standardized as the luminous efficiency of the CIE Standard Observer (graphed in Figure 20.1 on page 205).

A lumen is produced by about 1.5 mW of monochromatic power at 555.5 nm. That wavelength, a frequency of 540 THz, corresponds to the peak luminous efficiency of vision.

Radiometry and photometry are linked by the definition of the candela: One candela (cd) is the luminous intensity of a monochromatic 540 THz source having a radiant intensity of $1/683$ W·sr^{-1}. Once this definition is established, the remaining photometric quantities and units parallel those of radiometry. The relationships are sketched in Figure B.2 opposite.

The photometric analog of radiant flux is luminous flux (Φ_V). To paraphrase James M. Palmer, luminous flux is what you want when you buy a light bulb. The measure of its brightness is lumens (lm), the photometric analog of watts; its efficacy is measured in lumens per watt. One lumen appears equally bright regardless of its spectral composition.

The quantity *illuminance* was formerly called *illumination*. However, use of *illumination* for this specific quantity is deprecated, owing to the more general meaning of the word as the act of illuminating, or the state of being illuminated.

The old *footcandle* and *metercandle* units for luminous exitance were misleading, because the old *candle* was a unit of intensity, not flux.

Luminous flux per unit area – that is, luminous flux density – arriving at a real or imaginary surface is *illuminance* (E_V), expressed in units of lux (lx), where 1 lux is defined as 1 lm·m^{-2}. Illuminance is the photometric analog of irradiance; it is the quantity measured by a light meter. Luminous flux per unit area leaving a surface is *luminous exitance* (M_V). Despite 1 lux being equal to 1 lm·m^{-2}, luminous exitance is conventionally given in units of lm·m^{-2}: the *lux* unit implies illuminance. Luminous exitance from a nonemissive surface is its illuminance times its reflectance.

Luminous flux in a particular, specified direction is *luminous intensity* (I_V), expressed in units of lm·sr^{-1}, or candela (cd). The candela is the modern equivalent of the old *candle* (colloquially, candlepower). Intensity is independent of distance: A candle has a luminous intensity of about 1 cd, at any viewing distance.

Luminous flux density in a particular direction is *luminance* (L_V, or Y). Formally, luminance is luminous flux differentiated with respect to both solid angle and projected area. Luminance is the photometric analog of radiance; it is expressed in units of cd·m^{-2}, or *nit*. Luminance is an important and useful measure, because it is invariant under transformation by a lens.

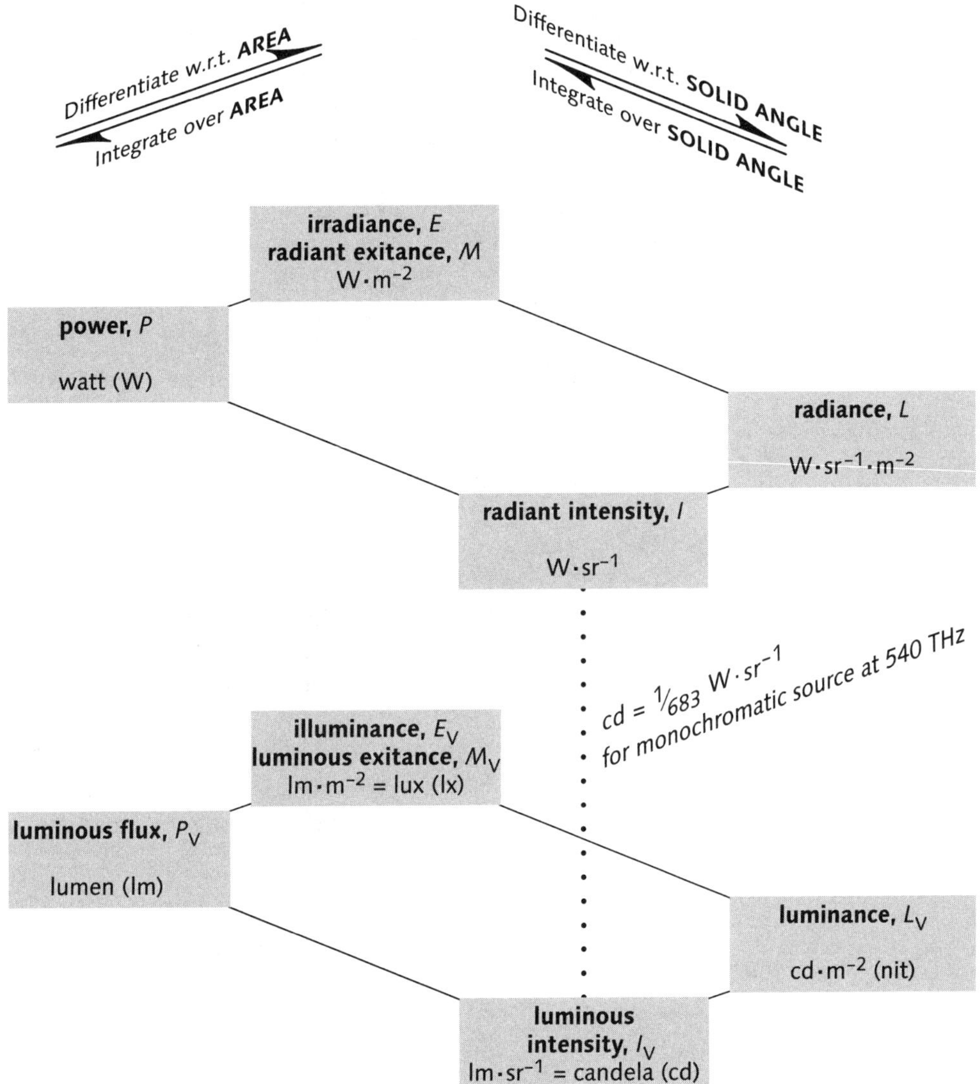

Figure B.2 **Radiometric and photometric quantities** and units are related in this diagram. The top quad shows radiometric quantities – radiant flux, irradiance, radiant intensity, and radiance. At the bottom are photometric quantities – luminous flux, illuminance, luminous intensity, and luminance. The systems are linked by the definition of the candela in terms of radiant intensity.

Image science

In image science, luminance is usually normalized to a range of 1 (or occasionally 100) with respect to a specified or implied white reference, and expressed without units. The term *luminance* is often used as shorthand to refer to this unitless quantity; however, it is properly called *relative luminance*. The term *luminance factor* should be avoided for this quantity, since that term refers to a property of a surface or material: *Luminance factor* is the ratio of luminance of a surface, under specified conditions of light source, incidence, and observation, to the luminance of a perfectly diffusing ("Lambertian") surface, under the same conditions.

In color science, luminance (Y) is one of three distinguished *tristimulus values* standardized by the CIE; the other two distinguished tristimulus values are X and Z. Other tristimulus values such as $[R, G, B]$ are related to CIE $[X, Y, Z]$ values by a 3×3 linear matrix product. As I mentioned above, absolute luminance has units of $\mathrm{cd \cdot m^{-2}}$, or nits. Relative luminance, and other tristimulus values such as X, Z, R, G, or B, are pure numbers.

Michael Brill and Bob Hunt agree that R, G, and B tristimulus values have no units. See Hunt, R.W.G., "The Heights of the CIE Colour-Matching Functions," in *Color Research and Application*, 22 (5): 337 (Oct. 1997).

Units

Many bizarre units have been used for illuminance and luminance. I urge you to abandon these, and to adopt the standard SI units.

To convert illuminance into lux (lx), use Table B.2:

$$\frac{10^6}{25.4^2 \cdot 12^2} \approx 10.764 \ \frac{\mathrm{ft}^2}{\mathrm{m}^2}$$

To obtain $\mathrm{lm \cdot m^{-2}}$ (lx), *multiply*	*by*	*numerically*
$\mathrm{lm \cdot cm^{-2}}$, phot, ph	10^4	10000
$\mathrm{lm \cdot ft^{-2}}$, footcandle, fc	10.764	10.764
metercandle	1	1

Table B.2 **Conversion of illuminance into lux**

To convert luminance into candelas per meter squared ($cd \cdot m^{-2}$, colloquially known as *nit*), use Table B.3:

To obtain $cd \cdot m^{-2}$ (nit), *multiply*	*by*	*numerically*
$cd \cdot cm^{-2}$, stilb, sb	10^4	10000
lambert, L	$10^4/\pi$	3183.1
$cd \cdot ft^{-2}$	10.764	10.764
footlambert, fL	$10.764/\pi$	3.4263
meterlambert, apostilb, asb	$1/\pi$	0.31831
skot, milliblondel	$10^{-3}/\pi$	0.0003183

Table B.3 **Conversion of luminance into $cd \cdot m^{-2}$**

Further reading

Ashdown, Ian, *Radiosity: A Programmer's Perspective* (New York: Wiley, 1994).

Chapter 1 of Ian Ashdown's book presents a very approachable introduction to measuring light. (The remainder of the book details the computer graphics technique called *radiosity*.)

Roberts, D. Allan, "A Guide to Speaking the Language of Radiometry and Photometry," in *Photonics Design and Applications Handbook*, 1994 edition, vol. 3, pages H-70 to H-73 (Pittsfield, Mass.: Laurin Publications).

D. Allan Roberts offers a terse summary of the basic quantities of radiometry and photometry, and describes the confusing units.

Glossary of video signal terms

This glossary is provided as a supplement to *Digital Video and HDTV Algorithms and Interfaces.* The Glossary is self-contained: It contains no references to the main text, and it is not indexed. For more detail concerning any term herein, consult the index.

0_H datum

The reference point of horizontal (line) sync. In bilevel sync, the 50%-point of the leading edge of the transition to synctip level. In trilevel sync, the zero-crossing between the negative and positive pulses.

0_V datum

The reference point of vertical sync; the start of line 1. In progressive systems, the start of the first broad pulse of a frame. In interlaced systems, the start of the first broad pulse of a field (except in 480*i*, where 0_V is the start of the first equalization pulse of the field).

1080*i*

An interlaced scanning standard for HDTV, having an image structure of 1920×1080, and a frame rate (written after the *i*) of either 29.97 Hz or 30.00 Hz.

1080*p*

A progressive scanning standard for HDTV, having an image structure of 1920×1080, and any of several frame rates (written after the *p*) including 23.976, 24, 29.97, or 30.00 Hz, and potentially 59.94 or 60.00 Hz.

1125/59.94/2:1

An interlaced scanning standard for HDTV, having a field rate of 59.94 Hz, and 1125 total lines per frame (of which formerly 1035, and now 1080, contain picture). The standard system with 1080 lines is now denoted 1080*i*29.97.

1125/60/2:1

An interlaced scanning standard for HDTV, having a field rate of 60 Hz, and 1125 total lines per frame (of which formerly 1035, and now 1080, contain picture). The standard system with 1080 lines is now denoted 1080*i*30.

2-2 pulldown

A process whereby motion picture film, running at 25 frames per second – that is, 4% faster than 24 – is transferred to video at a field (or, in progressive scanning, frame) rate of

50 Hz. Each film frame is scanned twice; once to produce the first field (or frame), and once again to produce the second field (or frame). See also *2-3 pulldown*, below.

2-3 pulldown

A process by which motion picture film is transferred to video at a field (or, in progressive scanning, frame) rate of 59.94 Hz or 60 Hz. Alternate film frames are scanned first two then three times to form successive video pictures. For transfer to 59.94 Hz, the film is run 0.1% slower than 24 frames per second.

2:1 interlace

See *Interlace*, on page 632.

24PsF

24 frames per second, progressive segmented-frame. Image format is typically 1920×1080. See *PsF*, on page 642.

+25 Hz offset

In studio or broadcast PAL with 576*i* scanning, subcarrier frequency is nominally an odd multiple of one-quarter the line rate (e.g., $^{1135}/_{4}\, f_H$), plus 25 Hz.

3:1:1

Component digital video wherein each C_B and C_R component is horizontally subsampled by a factor of 3 with respect to luma, and not subsampled vertically.

3-2 pulldown

See *2-3 pulldown*, above. The notation *3-2 pulldown* is misleading because SMPTE standards denote as the *A-frame* the first film frame in the four-frame sequence; that frame is associated with the first and second fields of one picture, and is scanned twice (not three times).

3.58 MHz

More precisely, 3.579545 MHz, or exactly, $5 \times {}^{63}/_{88}$ MHz: The color subcarrier frequency of 480*i* NTSC video.

$4f_{SC}$

Composite digital video using a sampling frequency of 4 times the color subcarrier frequency. There are 480*i* and 576*i* versions of $4f_{SC}$. The corresponding 19 mm videotape format is denoted *D-2*.

4:1:1

Chroma subsampling wherein C_B and C_R components are horizontally subsampled by a factor of 4 with respect to luma, and not subsampled vertically.

4:2:0

This confusing notation denotes chroma subsampling wherein C_B and C_R chroma components are subsampled both vertically and horizontally by a factor of 2, with respect to luma. There are two variants of 4:2:0 chroma: *interstitial* 4:2:0, used in JPEG/JFIF, H.261, and MPEG-1; and *cosited* 4:2:0, used in MPEG-2.

4:2:0*p*

A 483*p*59.94, 4:2:0 progressive-scan system specified in SMPTE 294M, using a variant of 4:2:0 chroma subsampling, typically conveyed on a single SDI link operating at 360 Mb/s.

4:2:2

1. Chroma subsampling wherein each C_B and C_R component is horizontally subsampled by a factor of 2 with respect to luma, and not subsampled vertically.

2. An SDTV component digital video coding or interface standard, based upon Rec. 601, using 4:2:2 chroma subsampling, having versions for both 480*i* or 576*i* scanning. The corresponding 19 mm videotape format is denoted D-1.

422P — The 4:2:2 profile of MPEG-2. (The colons are omitted; the P is written in Roman uppercase.)

4:2:2*p* — A 483*p*59.94, 4:2:2 progressive-scan system specified in SMPTE 294M, typically transmitted on dual SDI links each operating at 270 Mb/s.

4:2:2:4 — A 4:2:2 system, as in 4:2:2 above (2), augmented by a transparency or *alpha* channel sampled at the same rate as the luma component. See *Alpha, α*, on page 613.

4:4:4 — Component digital video, typically SDTV, where $R'G'B'$ or $Y'C_BC_R$ components are conveyed with equal data rate.

4:4:4:4 — A 4:4:4 system, as above, augmented by a transparency or *alpha* channel sampled at the same rate as the luma component. See *Alpha, α*, on page 613.

4.43 MHz — Expressed exactly, 4.433618750 MHz: The color subcarrier frequency of 576*i* PAL-B/G/H/I video.

480*i*, 480*i*29.97 — An interlaced scanning standard used primarily in North America and the Far East, having 525 total lines per frame, approximately 480 picture lines (usually in an image structure of 720×480), and 29.97 frames per second. A raster notation such as 480*i*29.97 does not specify color coding; color in 480*i*29.97 systems is conveyed in the studio using $R'G'B'$, $Y'C_BC_R$, or $Y'P_BP_R$ components, and encoded for transmission using composite NTSC (or in Brazil, composite PAL-M). Also denoted 525/59.94 (see below), or *ITU-R System M*. Often loosely referred to as *525/60*. Often incorrectly called *NTSC*, which properly refers to a color-encoding standard, not a scanning standard.

525/59.94 — 480*i*29.97; see above. Sometimes written 525/60. Sometimes written with "/2:1" appended to emphasize interlace.

525-line — 480*i*29.97; see above.

576*i*, 576*i*25 — An interlaced scanning standard used primarily in Europe, Australia, and Asia, having 625 total lines per frame, 576 picture lines (usually in an image structure of 720×576), and 25 frames per second. A raster notation such as 576*i*25 does not specify color coding; color in 576*i*25 systems is commonly conveyed in the studio using $R'G'B'$, $Y'C_BC_R$, or $Y'P_BP_R$ components, and distributed by terrestrial VHF/UHF television using composite PAL (although France, Russia, and certain other countries use SECAM). Commonly denoted 625/50. Often incorrectly called *PAL*, which properly refers to a color-encoding standard, not a scanning standard. Sometimes incorrectly called *CCIR*.

601 — See *Rec. 601,* on page 643.

625/50 — 576*i*25; see above. Sometimes written with "/2:1" appended to emphasize interlace.

625-line — 576*i*25; see above.

656 — See *Rec. 656,* on page 643.

7.5% setup — See *Setup,* on page 647.

709 — See *Rec. 709,* on page 643.

720*p* — A progressive scanning standard for HDTV, having an image structure of 1280×720, and any of several frame rates including 23.976, 24, 29.97, 30, 59.94, or 60 Hz.

8 mm — A consumer analog videocassette system using 8 mm tape; also known as *Video-8*. Its successor is *Hi8*.

8-VSB — See *VSB,* on page 651.

9300 K — In computer graphics, a white reference whose correlated color temperature is 9300 K.

AC — **1.** Alternating current: Historically, an electrical current or voltage that reverses in polarity periodically – that is, whose sign alternates periodically between positive and negative.

2. In modern usage, a signal whose value varies periodically between positive and negative. Distinguished from *DC, direct current;* see page 624.

3. In JPEG and MPEG, any or all DCT coefficients in an 8¥8 block apart from the DC coefficient.

Active — A signal element (sample, or line) defined by a scanning standard to contain part of the picture or its associated blanking transition. (Exceptionally, in 480*i*29.97, closed caption data on line 21 is considered to be active, despite its not containing picture.)

A-frame — In 2-3 pulldown, the first film frame in a sequence of four frames A, B, C, and D, or the corresponding video frame. The A-frame is scanned twice, to produce a first field then a second field comprising a single picture. If nondropframe timecode HH:MM:SS:F*u* is coherent with film scanning, the A-frame produces first and second fields where u=0; the B-frame produces first and second fields where u=1, then a first field where u=2; the C-frame produces a second field with u=2 and a first field with u=3; finally, the D-frame produces first and second fields where u=4. The sequence continues with A (5), B (6, 7), C (7, 8), then D (9).

a — In optics, absorptance: The fraction of light absorbed – that is, neither reflected nor transmitted.

Alpha, α
In computer graphics, a component of a pixel indicating transparency – conventionally between zero (opaque) and unity (fully transparent) – of the pixel's color components. Color component values ($R'G'B'$, $Y'P_BP_R$, or $Y'C_BC_R$) may have been premultiplied by the value of a corresponding alpha value; this is sometimes called *shaped video*. Color component values that have not been so premultiplied are *unassociated* (or *unshaped*). See also *Key,* on page 634.

Anamorphic
A subsidiary format, or its associated lens, in which the horizontal dimension of a widescreen image is squeezed by some factor with respect to the horizontal dimension of a base format having narrower aspect ratio. In film, the widescreen (anamorphic) image conventionally has 2.4:1 aspect ratio and the squeeze is by a factor of 2. In video, the widescreen (anamorphic) image has 16:9 aspect ratio, and the squeeze is typically by a factor $4/3$.

Anchor picture
In MPEG, a picture, or coded picture information, that is an I-picture or P-picture. An anchor picture may be used as the basis for prediction of a subsequent P-picture, or a previous or subsequent B-picture. (It is misleading to refer to an anchor *frame*, because when MPEG-2 is used with interlaced video, a picture may comprise a single field.)

APL, average picture level
1. In studio video, the average of luma throughout the entire active (picture) interval of a field or a frame.

2. In some other applications, the average of (linear-light) luminance throughout an entire image or scene.

ASI
Asynchronous serial interface: An industry standard electrical interface, standardized by DVB, used to convey an MPEG-2 transport stream.

Aspect ratio
The ratio of the width of an image to its height. (Some authors, such as MPEG, write this improperly as height:width.)

Aspect ratio, pixel (or sample)
The ratio of horizontal distance between samples to vertical distance between samples.

ATSC
Advanced Television Systems Committee: A U.S.-based organization that standardizes and promotes digital SDTV and HDTV broadcasting. ATSC advocates MPEG-2 video compression and Dolby Digital (AC-3) audio compression, supplemented by ATSC terrestrial broadcasting transmission standards.

B-field
In MPEG, a field-coded B-picture. B-fields come in pairs (either top then bottom, or bottom then top). See *B-picture,* below.

B-frame
In MPEG, either a frame-coded B-picture, or a pair of B-fields (one top field and one bottom field, in either order). See *B-picture,* below.

B/PAL
See *PAL-B/G/H,* on page 640.

B-picture

In MPEG, a bidirectionally predictive-coded picture: A picture, or coded picture information, in which one or more macroblocks involve prediction from a preceding or a following anchor picture. B-pictures exploit temporal coherence. They are computed and displayed, but do not form the basis for any subsequent predictions.

B'–Y', R'–Y'

A pair of color difference components, *B'* minus luma and *R'* minus luma. The red, green, and blue components are gamma-corrected prior to the formation of *Y'*, *B'–Y'* and *R'–Y'*. These color differences may subsequently be scaled to form C_B and C_R for component digital systems, scaled to form P_B and P_R for component analog systems, or scaled to form *U* and *V* (or in specialized forms of NTSC, *I* and *Q*) for composite encoding.

Back porch

The time interval between the trailing edge of a normal line sync pulse and the left-hand edge of active video on the associated video line. This interval is often used as a clamp reference.

Bandwidth

The frequency or frequency range where an analog or digital signal's magnitude has fallen 3 dB – that is, to 0.707 – from its value at a reference frequency (usually zero frequency, *DC*). Distinguished from *data rate;* see page 624.

BER

Bit error rate: The probability that recording or transmission in an error-prone medium corrupts any single bit transmitted or recorded.

Betacam

Sony's trademarked term for a professional component analog videotape format for 480*i* or 576*i*, using CTDM on ½-inch tape. The successor system, with higher bandwidth, is denoted Betacam SP. See also *Digital Betacam, Digital-β,* on page 625.

Bilevel sync

Sync information conveyed through a single pulse having a transition from blanking level to a level more negative than blanking (synctip level), then a transition back to blanking level. In analog systems, synctip level is either -285 5⁄7 mV or -300 mV. Bilevel sync is used in SDTV; distinguished from trilevel sync, used in HDTV.

Bit error rate

See *BER*, above.

BITC

Burnt-in timecode: Timecode keyed into picture content.

Black level

1. The level representing black: nominally 7.5 IRE for System M and the archaic RS-343-A, and zero in other systems. See also *Pedestal*, on page 641.

2. User-accessible means to adjust BLACK LEVEL (1). This term is preferred to BRIGHTNESS. (See *Brightness.*)

Black-to-white excursion

The excursion from reference black to reference white. Conventionally 92.5 IRE (37⁄56 V, approximately 660 mV) for System M and the archaic RS-343-A, 100 IRE (5⁄7 V, approximately 714 mV) in NTSC-J, 700 mV in other analog systems, and codes 16 through

235 at an 8-bit component (Rec. 601 or Rec. 709) digital interface.

Blanking (*n.*)
The time interval – in the vertical domain, the horizontal domain, or both – during which a video signal is defined by a scanning standard not to contain picture. Ancillary signals such as VITS and VITC may be conveyed during vertical blanking – they are not blanked during transmission, but are blanked at the display. (Exceptionally, closed caption signals in analog 480*i* NTSC are considered to be part of the active picture.)

Blanking (*v.*)
The process of turning off the beam in a CRT, such as a display tube, so that the tube can accomplish beam retrace without disturbing the picture.

Blanking level
Zero level; 0 IRE by definition.

Block
In JPEG, M-JPEG, and MPEG, an 8×8 array of samples, or coded information representing them.

BNC
Bayonet Neill-Concelman (contrary to the entry in the *IEEE Standard Dictionary of Electrical and Electronics Terms*): A coaxial connector, now standardized in IEC 169-8, used in video. Paul Neill, working at Bell Telephone Laboratories, developed a threaded connector adopted by the U.S. Navy and named the N connector, after him. Carl Concelman, working at Amphenol, came up with a bayonet version (slide on and twist), called the C connector. The two collaborated on a miniature version, which became the BNC. A screw-on relative, the threaded Neill-Concelman connector, is the TNC. [Mark Schubin/*Videography*]

BOB
Break-out box: A panel of connectors remote from the associated equipment.

Bob
In PC graphics, a deinterlacing technique that averages vertically adjacent samples in one field to create a synthetic intermediate image row.

Bottom field
In MPEG, the field that contains the bottom coded image row. Typically the first field in 480*i* and the second field in 576*i*.

Brightness
1. *The attribute of a visual sensation according to which an area appears to emit more or less light* [CIE]. Brightness is, by definition, subjective. Related objective quantities are *lightness*, *luma*, and *luminance*.

2. User-accessible means to adjust Black level; preferably called BLACK LEVEL.

Broad pulse
A pulse, part of the vertical sync sequence, that remains at sync level for substantially longer than normal line sync and indicates vertical sync. In bilevel sync, it is standard for a broad pulse to have a duration of half a line time less the duration of normal line sync.

BT.601, BT.709 — See *Rec. 601* and *Rec. 709*, respectively, on page 643.

Burst — A brief sample of eight to ten cycles of unmodulated color subcarrier inserted by an NTSC or PAL encoder onto the back porch of a composite video signal. An encoder inserts burst to enable a decoder to regenerate the continuous-wave color subcarrier.

Burst meander — In 576*i* PAL, selectively suppressing burst on lines adjacent to vertical sync if burst would take –135° phase.

Cadence — In a motion image sequence having 2-3 pulldown, the property of having strictly periodic A-frames. Careful editing preserves continuous cadence; careless editing disrupts it.

CAV — **1.** Component analog video; see below.

2. Constant angular velocity: A method of recording on optical disc where the media rotates at a constant rate. Contrasted with CLV (constant linear velocity).

C_B, C_R — **1.** Versions of color difference components B'–Y' and R'–Y', scaled and offset for digital component transmission. At an 8-bit interface, C_B and C_R have excursion 16 through 240. See also [B'–Y', R'–Y']; [P_B, P_R]; [U, V], and [I, Q]. In systems using Rec. 601 luma, such as 480*i* and 576*i*, it is standard to apply these scale factors (and interface offsets, shown below in gray) to B'–Y' and R'–Y':

$$C_B = 128 + 112\frac{1}{0.886}(B' - Y'); \quad C_R = 128 + 112\frac{1}{0.701}(R' - Y')$$

In HDTV systems using Rec. 709 luma, such as 1280×720 and 1920×1080, it is standard to apply these scale factors (and offsets) to B'–Y' and R'–Y':

$$C_B = 128 + 112\frac{1}{0.9278}(B' - Y'); \quad C_R = 128 + 112\frac{1}{0.7874}(R' - Y')$$

2. Versions of color difference components B'–Y' and R'–Y', scaled to "full-range" (±128, with code +128 clipped) for use in still-frame JPEG/JFIF. It is usual to apply these scale factors (and offsets) to B'–Y' and R'–Y':

$$C_B = 128 + 128\frac{1}{0.886}(B' - Y'); \quad C_R = 128 + 128\frac{1}{0.701}(R' - Y')$$

CC — Closed caption; see page 621.

CCIR — **1.** *Comité Consultatif Internationale des Radiocommunications* (International Radio Consultative Committee): A treaty organization, as of 1993 renamed ITU-R.

2. Sometimes incorrectly used to denote 576*i* scanning.

CCIR Rec. 601, Rec. 709 — Obsolete designations, now properly referred to as ITU-R Rec. BT.601 (colloquially, Rec. 601), or ITU-R Rec. BT.709 (colloquially, Rec. 709). See *Rec. 601* and *Rec. 709*, on page 643.

CCIR System

1. Former designation, now properly denoted *ITU-R System:* A set of parameters describing a video system, including scanning, bandwidth, and RF channel spacing, as described in ITU-R Report 624.

2. Sometimes incorrectly used to denote 576*i* scanning.

CCIR System M

Former designation, now properly denoted *ITU-R System M* or just *System M*. See *System M*, on page 648.

CDR

Common data rate: A single (common) worldwide standard sampling rate for digital video; the approach taken in Rec. 601, where a sampling rate of 13.5 MHz is standardized for both 480*i* and 576*i*. Contrasted with *CIF, common image format*, on page 618.

CGI

Computer-generated imagery: Synthetic image data, generated by computation (as opposed to being acquired from a physical scene).

Chroma

1. Generally, a component or set of components that conveys color independent of luma or luminance.

2. In component video, color independent of (or accompanied by) luma, conveyed as a pair of color difference signals such as $[C_B, C_R]$, or $[P_B, P_R]$.

3. In composite video, color subcarrier modulated using the NTSC or PAL technique by two color difference components $[U, V]$ or $[I, Q]$, to form *a modulated chroma* signal, C.

4. User-accessible means to adjust Saturation (2) [chroma gain]; preferably, SATURATION.

Chromaticity

1. Specification of color (in the absence of luminance), in terms of CIE $[x, y]$ or $[u', v']$ coordinates.

2. Loosely, the chromaticity (1) of the red, green, and blue primaries, and the chromaticity of the white reference, of a video system.

Chrominance

1. Formally, the color of a scene or scene element independent of its luminance; usually, expressed in the form of CIE $[x, y]$ chromaticity.

2. Loosely, *chroma;* see above.

CIE

Commission Internationale de L'Éclairage (International Commission on Illumination): The international standards organization that sets colorimetry standards.

CIE D_{65}

The standard spectral radiance (SPD) or chromaticity of white, representative of northern daylight and having a color temperature of approximately 6504 K. See *Reference white*, on page 643.

CIE luminance, CIE *Y* — See *Luminance*. The qualifier *CIE* is sometimes used to emphasize that the associated quantity is representative of tristimulus (linear-light) value proportional to intensity, as opposed to a nonlinear, gamma-corrected quantity.

CIF, common image format — **1.** The elusive goal of a single (common) worldwide standard pixel array for digital video, perhaps at different frame rates. Distinguished from *CDR*. Confusingly, the acronym collides with *CIF, common intermediate format* (see below).

2. In MPEG-2 or other video compression systems excepting those for videoconferencing, an image format of either 720×480 or 720×576. The term is an oxymoron, since there is not a single ("common") format, but two different formats. (In the deliberations that led to digital SDTV studio standards, agreement upon a common image format was not reached!)

CIF, common intermediate format — In ITU-T Rec. H.261, a progressive 352×288 image format with 4:2:0 chroma subsampling and a frame rate of 29.97 Hz. CIF image data is ordinarily subsampled from SDTV. The format is a compromise derived from the image structure of 576*i*25 and the frame rate of 480*i*29.97. Distinguished from *CIF, common image format*, above. See also *QCIF*, on page 642.

Clamp (*v.*) — **1.** Imposition of a DC offset onto a signal, so as to place a certain waveform feature (such as back porch) at a specific level (such as blanking level).

2. Loosely, *Clip;* see below.

Clean aperture — The specified or standardized rectangular portion of the pixel array that remains subjectively free from intrusion of artifacts resulting from filtering of the picture edges.

Clip (*v.*) — Forcing a signal to a certain maximum (or minimum) level, so as to avoid excursion above (or below) that level.

Closed caption (CC) — Digital data conveying textual information that can be decoded and displayed for the benefit of hearing-impaired viewers. In 480*i* NTSC analog video, closed caption data is inserted into line 21. (Unlike other vertical interval signals, NTSC line 21 is classified as active picture video.)

CLV — Constant linear velocity: A method of recording on optical disc where rotational speed is varied as a function of head actuator position so as to keep media speed constant with respect to the head. Contrasted with CAV (constant angular velocity).

CM — In DV compression, a coded (compressed) macroblock.

CN/PAL — "Combination" N/PAL, used in Argentina, Paraguay, and Uruguay. ITU-R defines System N as having 10:4 picture:sync ratio and 7.5% setup. However, these countries broadcast 7:3 picture:sync ratio and zero setup, so their system is described by ITU-R as a "combination" (of the RF parameters of NTSC and the levels of PAL). See *PAL-N, PAL-3.58,* on page 640.

Codec

1. Coder/decoder: Circuitry, software, or equipment to encode or decode data between two formats (perhaps between analog and digital).

2. In video, compressor/decompressor: Circuitry, software, or equipment to compress or decompress video signals.

Coherence, frequency

The property whereby two or more periodic signals are phase-locked to a common reference frequency. The unmodulated color subcarrier of a studio-quality NTSC or PAL composite video signal is coherent with its sync.

Coherence, spatial

In a single image, the property whereby adjacent samples have values that are correlated.

Coherence, temporal

In a motion image sequence, the property whereby corresponding samples in successive images, perhaps subject to spatial displacement, are correlated.

COFDM

Coded orthogonal frequency-division multiplexing: An RF modulation system using a large number of subcarriers to spread the information content of a signal evenly across a channel. The subcarriers of COFDM are individually modulated, typically using QPSK or QAM. COFDM is used in DVB-T.

COLOR

User-accessible means to adjust Hue (3); preferably, HUE.

Colorburst

See *Burst,* on page 616.

Colorframe

In NTSC, *colorframes* denoted *A* and *B* are distinguished by the phase of subcarrier at 0_H at the start of the frame: *Colorframe A* has subcarrier at 0°, and *colorframe B* has subcarrier at 180°. Distinguished from *A-frame*, which relates to 2-3 pulldown (see page 629).

Colorimetry

1. Formally, the science of measuring color, especially as standardized by the CIE.

2. In video, *Colorimetry* (1) as above, augmented by two concerns outside the domain of classical colorimetry: the parameters of the nonlinear transfer function applied to the linear-light (tristimulus) *RGB* components of classical colorimetry to form *R'G'B'*; and the parameters of the 3×3 matrix transform applied to *R'G'B'* to form luma and two color difference components.

Color difference

1. A numerical measure of the perceptual distance between two colors; for example, CIE ΔE^*_{uv} ("delta-*E*").

2. A signal that vanishes – that is, becomes identically zero – for pure luma without color. A video system conveys a color image using a set of three signals: a luma signal (*Y'*) and a pair of color difference signals. Spatial filtering may be applied to reduce the information rate of the color difference components without perceptible degradation. Usual color-difference pairs are [$B'-Y'$, $R'-Y'$], [C_B, C_R], [P_B, P_R], [I, Q], and [U, V].

Color standard

The parameters associated with encoding of color information – for example, $R'G'B'$, $Y'C_BC_R$, or MAC *component* video standards, or NTSC, PAL, or SECAM *composite* video standards. Distinguished from *scanning standard* (see page 646).

Color subcarrier

1. A continuous sine wave signal at about 3.58 MHz or 4.43 MHz used as the basis for quadrature modulation or demodulation of Chroma (3) in an NTSC or PAL composite video system. See also *Burst*, on page 616.

2. Color subcarrier (1), onto which two color difference signals have been imposed by quadrature modulation. Properly, modulated chroma.

Color temperature

Characterization of an illuminant or a white reference in terms of the absolute temperature (in units of kelvin) of a black body radiator having the same chromaticity.

Color-under

A degenerate form of composite analog NTSC or PAL video recording wherein modulated chroma is *heterodyned* onto a subcarrier whose frequency – roughly $1/6$ of the NTSC or PAL color subcarrier frequency – is crystal-stable but not coherent with line rate. The heterodyning process destroys the phase relationship of color subcarrier to sync, and severely limits chroma bandwidth. The technique is used in U-matic ($3/4$-inch), VHS, S-VHS, 8 mm (Video-8), and Hi8 videocassette recorders.

Comb filter

1. Generally, a filter having magnitude frequency response with periodic equal-magnitude maxima and minima.

2. In video, a comb filter (1) incorporating delay elements with line, field, or frame time duration.

3. In a composite NTSC video decoder, circuitry incorporating one or more line delay elements (linestores) to exploit the frequency interleaving of modulated chroma (1) to separate chroma from luma. A comb filter provides better separation than a notch filter, owing to its suppression of *cross-color* and *cross-luma* artifacts.

4. In a composite PAL video decoder, circuitry incorporating a line delay element (linestore) to separate the modulated U chroma component from the modulated V chroma component.

Combination N/PAL

See *CN/PAL*, on page 618.

Common data rate

See *CDR*, on page 617.

Common image format

See *CIF, common image format*, on page 618.

Component (*adj.*)

In video, a system that conveys three color values or signals independently, free from mutual interference. Examples are $R'G'B'$,

$Y'C_BC_R$, and MAC. Distinguished from *Composite video (adj.)*, below.

Component (*n.*)

1. One value or signal from the set of three necessary to completely specify a color.

2. A value, channel, or signal, such as transparency or depth, that is spatially associated with image data, or temporally associated with an image in a sequence, that does not contribute to the specification of color.

Component analog

An analog video system (as opposed to digital), using $R'G'B'$ or $Y'P_BP_R$ component color coding (as opposed to using composite color coding such as NTSC or PAL).

Component digital

A digital video system (as opposed to analog), using $R'G'B'$ or $Y'C_BC_R$ component color coding (as opposed to using composite color coding such as NTSC or PAL). Component digital SDTV systems are sometimes called "4:2:2," though the latter notation strictly refers to just the color subsampling, not any of the other encoding parameters.

Composite (*adj.*)

Combined, as in combined vertical and horizontal sync elements [see *Composite sync*, below]; combined luma and chroma [see *Composite video* (1), below]; or combined video and sync [see *Composite video* (2), below].

Composite (*v.*)

To combine images by layering, keying, or matting.

Composite digital

A digital video system (as opposed to analog), using composite color coding such as NTSC or PAL (as opposed to using component color coding such as $Y'C_BC_R$). Because all standard composite systems sample at four times the color subcarrier frequency, also known as $4f_{SC}$.

Composite sync

A deprecated term meaning *sync*. The word *sync* alone implies both horizontal and vertical elements, so *composite* is redundant. The adjective *composite* more meaningfully applies to *video* or *color*, so its use with *sync* is confusing.

Composite video

1. A video system in which three color components are simultaneously present in a single signal. Examples are NTSC and PAL, which use the *frequency-interleaving* principle to encode (combine) luma and chroma. SECAM is another form of composite video. Distinguished from *Component (adj.)*, above.

2. A composite video (1) signal, including luma, sync, chroma, and burst components; called *CVBS* in Europe.

Concatenated

In compression, two or more compression systems in series. Also known as *tandem codecs.*

Constant luminance

In a color video system that dedicates one component to lightness-related information, the property that true (CIE) relative luminance reproduced at the display is unaffected by the values of the other two components. All standard video systems, including NTSC, PAL, $Y'C_BC_R$, and HDTV, approximate constant luminance operation. However, because luma is computed as a weighted sum of gamma-corrected primary components, a certain amount of true luminance "leaks" into the color difference components and induces second-order artifacts.

Contrast

1. *Contrast ratio;* see below.

2. The luminance of subjectively correct midscale image information, compared to its reproduced luminance.

3. User-accessible means to adjust video gain. Preferably called VIDEO GAIN; sometimes called PICTURE.

Contrast ratio

The ratio between specified light and dark luminances.

Corner frequency

The frequency at which the output power of a lowpass or highpass filter or subsystem has fallen to half its value at a reference frequency, typically DC. (For a digital or constant-impedance system, this is equivalent to the frequency at which the output magnitude has been attenuated 3 dB.)

Cosited

Chroma subsampling in which each subsampled chroma sample is located at the same horizontal position as a luma sample. Rec. 601, Rec. 709, and MPEG-2 standards specify cosited chroma subsampling. (MPEG-2, 4:2:0 chroma subsampling places chroma samples interstitially in the vertical domain.)

CRC

Cyclic redundancy check (code). Information inserted prior to recording or transmission that allows playback or receiver equipment to determine whether errors were introduced. A CRC with a small number of bits provides error-detection capability; a CRC with a large number of bits provides error-correction capability. CRC codes involve multiplying and dividing polynomials whose coefficients are restricted to the set {0, 1}. Similar capability can be achieved using codes based upon mathematical principles other than CRC; see ECC.

Cross-color

An artifact of composite video encoding and/or decoding that involves the erroneous interpretation of luma information as color. The cross-color artifact appears frequently when luma information having a frequency near that of the color subcarrier appears as a swirling color rainbow pattern.

Cross-luma

An artifact of composite video encoding and/or decoding that involves the erroneous interpretation of color information as luma. Cross-luma frequently appears as *dot crawl* or *hanging dots*.

CTDM

Chroma time-division multiplexed: A system of recording component video, used in Betacam, whereby P_B, and P_R components are each time-compressed then combined in one recording channel.

Cutoff frequency

See *Corner frequency,* on page 622.

CVBS — Composite video with burst and syncs: A European term for *Composite video* (2).

D-1 — **1.** A SMPTE-standard component SDTV digital videotape format utilizing 19 mm tape cassettes to record component digital Rec. 601, 8-bit $Y'C_BC_R$ video signals having either 480*i* or 576*i* scanning.

2. Often improperly used to denote Rec. 601 $Y'C_BC_R$ SDI interface for component digital 480*i* or 576*i*.

D-2 — **1.** A SMPTE-standard composite digital SDTV videotape format utilizing 19 mm tape cassettes and recording either 480*i* NTSC video or 576*i* PAL video, sampled at $4f_{SC}$. D-2 recording is unrelated to the D2-MAC transmission system.

2. Often improperly used to refer to $4f_{SC}$ SDI interface for composite digital 480*i* NTSC or 576*i* PAL.

D2-MAC — An obsolete MAC system, based on 576*i* scanning, used in Europe for satellite broadcasting. Unrelated to D-2 video recording.

D-3 — A SMPTE-standard composite SDTV digital videotape format utilizing ½-inch tape cassettes and recording either 480*i* NTSC video or 576*i* PAL video, sampled at $4f_{SC}$.

D-5 — A SMPTE-standard component SDTV digital videotape format utilizing ½-inch tape cassettes and recording uncompressed Rec. 601 $Y'C_BC_R$ signals, having either 480*i* or 576*i* scanning.

D-5 HD — A component HDTV digital videotape format utilizing ½-inch tape cassettes and recording Rec. 709 $Y'C_BC_R$ signals, based upon either 720*p*60 or 1080*i*30, mildly compressed to about 270 Mb/s using motion-JPEG. Also known as *HD-D5*.

D-6 — A SMPTE-standard component HDTV digital videotape format utilizing ½-inch tape cassettes and recording uncompressed Rec. 709 $Y'C_BC_R$ signals, subsampled 4:2:2, at about 1.5 Gb/s.

D-7 — A SMPTE-standard component SDTV digital videotape format for professional use, utilizing 6.35 mm tape encased in a cassette of one of three sizes (small, medium, or large), recording Rec. 601 $Y'C_BC_R$ signals, based upon either 480*i* or 576*i* scanning, compressed using the DV motion-JPEG technique to about 25 Mb/s (DV25) or to about 50 Mb/s (DV50). Panasonic refers to D-7 by their trademarked term *DVCPRO* (at 25 Mb/s) or *DVCPRO50* (at 50 Mb/s).

D-9 — A SMPTE-standard component SDTV digital videotape format for professional use, utilizing ½-inch tape in VHS-type cassettes and recording Rec. 601 $Y'C_BC_R$ signals based upon either 480*i* or 576*i* scanning, mildly compressed to about 50 Mb/s using the DV motion-JPEG technique (DV50). Also known by JVC's trademarked term *Digital-S*.

D-10 — A SMPTE-standard component SDTV digital videotape format for professional use, utilizing ½-inch tape in Beta-type cassettes and recording Rec. 601 $Y'C_BC_R$, 4:2:2 signals based upon either 480*i* or 576*i* scanning, mildly compressed to about 50 Mb/s using a motion-JPEG technique. Also known by Sony's trademarked term *MPEG IMX*.

D-11 — A SMPTE-standard component HDTV digital videotape format for professional use, utilizing ½-inch tape in Beta-type cassettes and recording $Y'C_BC_R$ signals based upon 1440¥1080 image, scanned progressive or interlaced at any of several frame rates, chroma subsampled 3:1:1, and mildly compressed to about 50 Mb/s using a motion-JPEG technique. Also known by Sony's trademarked term *HDCAM*.

D-12 — A SMPTE-standard component HDTV digital videotape format for professional use, utilizing 6.35 mm tape encased in a cassette of one of three sizes (small, medium, or large), recording 720*p*, 1080*i*, or 1080*p*, 4:2:2 signals, compressed to about 100 Mb/s using the DV motion-JPEG technique (DV100). Also known by Panasonic's trademarked term *DVCPRO HD*.

D16 — Quantel's proprietary format for nonrealtime recording of digital film frames, each 2880×2048, on 576*i* D-1 videotape. Each film frame comprises sixteen 720×512 subimages; each is stored as one video frame.

D_{65} — See *Reference white*, on page 643; and *CIE* D_{65}, on page 617.

Data rate — Information rate of digital transmission, in bits per second (b/s) or bytes per second (B/s). Not to be confused with bandwidth.

Datum — See 0_H *datum* and 0_V *datum*, on page 609.

DC, direct current — **1.** Historically, an electrical current or voltage having no periodic reversal in polarity.

2. In modern usage, having zero frequency.

3. In video, a signal having frequency substantially lower than the frame rate.

4. In JPEG and MPEG, that spatial frequency component having uniform response over an 8×8 block. Distinguished from AC (3), on page 612.

DC restoration — Clamp (1) at blanking level (or in low-quality systems, at synctip level).

DCT — **1.** Discrete cosine transform: In video, the mathematics at the heart of the JPEG and MPEG algorithms.

2. An obsolete digital videotape format from Ampex; in this context, DCT is a registered trademark of Ampex.

Decimation — Resampling producing fewer output samples than original samples. Synonymous with *downsampling*.

Decoding — **1.** Generally, converting one or more coded signals into uncompressed form, reversing a previous encoding operation that was applied to reduce data rate for transmission or recording.

2. In traditional video usage, taking composite video, such as NTSC or PAL, performing luma/chroma separation and chroma demodulation, and producing component video output such as $Y'C_BC_R$ or $R'G'B'$.

3. In modern video usage, taking coded picture information (such as a JPEG, M-JPEG, or MPEG compressed bitstream) and recovering uncompressed picture data.

DIF — Digital interface standardized for DV bitstreams.

Digital8 — Sony's trademarked term for a component SDTV digital videotape format for consumer use, utilizing 8 mm tape cassettes and recording Rec. 601 $Y'C_BC_R$ signals, based upon either 480*i* or 576*i* scanning, compressed using the DV motion-JPEG technique.

Digital Betacam, Digital-β — Sony's trademarked term for a component SDTV digital videotape format for professional use, utilizing ½-inch tape and recording Rec. 601 $Y'C_BC_R$ signals, based upon either 480*i* or 576*i* scanning, mildly compressed using M-JPEG to about 90 Mb/s.

Digital-S — JVC's trademarked term for the digital videotape format now standardized as SMPTE D-9.

Direct color — **1.** In video, an analog VTR recording technique that records the composite signal directly, without separately processing luma and chroma.

2. In computer graphics, particularly the *X*-window system, a graphics system in which lookup tables (LUTs) can be altered under control of the application program. (In *X* terminology, *truecolor* refers to a graphics system that has no LUTs, or LUTs that cannot be altered under program control.)

Dominant field — See *Field dominance,* on page 629.

Dot crawl — A cross-luma artifact that results from a notch filter decoder, appearing as fine luma detail crawling up a vertical edge in a picture that contains a saturated color transition.

Downconversion — In video, conversion to a scanning standard, usually at the same frame rate, having substantially lower pixel count (e.g., HDTV to SDTV).

Downsampling — Resampling that produces fewer output samples than the number of input samples provided.

Drive (*n.*) — A periodic pulse signal that conveys synchronization information. See *Vertical drive (VD)*, on page 650; and *Horizontal drive (HD)*, on page 631.

Dropframe — A timecode stream associated with scanning at a field or frame rate of 59.94 Hz, wherein timecodes of the form *HH*:*Tu*:00:00 and *HH*:*Tu*:00:01 are omitted from the count sequence whenever *u* (the units digit of minutes) is nonzero, so that counting frames obtains a very close approximation to clock time. This adjustment almost exactly compensates for the field or frame rate being a factor of exactly $^{1000}/_{1001}$ slower than 60 Hz.

DTV — Digital television: A generic term including digital SDTV and digital HDTV. Generally, broadcast is implied.

DV — **1.** Generally, digital video.

2. A specific motion-JPEG compression technique, videotape recording format, and/or digital interface (DIF) bitstream, for $Y'C_BC_R$ digital video. See *DV25*, *DV50*, and *DV100*, below.

DV25 — DV (see above), coded at 25 Mb/s. DV25 is widely implemented in consumer DVC and Digital8 equipment, and in professional D-7 (DVCPRO) and DVCAM equipment.

DV50 — DV (see above), coded at 50 Mb/s. DV50 is used in professional D-7 (DVCPRO50), D-9 (Digital-S), DVCAM, and DVCPRO P equipment.

DV100 — DV (see above), coded at 100 Mb/s. DV100 is used in DVCPRO HD equipment.

DVB — Digital Video Broadcasting: An organization of the EBU that standardizes and promotes DTV broadcasting. DVB advocates MPEG-2 video and audio compression, supplemented by DVB transmission standards for cable (DVB-C), satellite (DVB-S), and terrestrial (DVB-T) broadcasting (for which DVB-T specifies COFDM transmission).

DVC — Digital video cassette: A component SDTV digital videotape format for consumer use, taking Rec. 601 $Y'C_BC_R$ video having either 480*i* or 576*i* scanning, compressing to about 25 Mb/s using the DV motion-JPEG technique (DV25), and recording on 6.35 mm tape encased in a cassette of one of two sizes – small ("MiniDV") or large.

DVCAM — Sony's trademarked term for a component SDTV digital videotape format for professional use, utilizing 6.35 mm tape cassettes and recording Rec. 601 $Y'C_BC_R$ video having either 480*i* or 576*i* scanning, compressed to about 25 Mb/s using the DV motion-JPEG technique.

DVCPRO — Digital video cassette, professional version: Panasonic's trademarked term for the digital videotape format now standardized as SMPTE D-7; see *D-7*, on page 623.

DVCPRO50 — Digital video cassette, professional version, 50 megabits per second: Panasonic's trademarked term for a digital videotape format for professional use subsequently incorporated by SMPTE into the D-7 series of standards; see *D-7*, on page 623.

DVCPRO HD — Digital video cassette, professional version, high-definition: Panasonic's trademarked term for the digital videotape format now standardized as SMPTE D-12. See *D-12*, on page 624.

DVCPRO P (DVCPRO50 P) — Digital video cassette, professional version, progressive: Panasonic's trademarked term for a component SDTV digital videotape format for professional use, utilizing 6.35 mm tape cassettes and recording Rec. 601 $Y'C_BC_R$ signals based upon either 480*p*59.94 or 480*p*60 scanning, mildly compressed to about 50 Mb/s using the DV motion-JPEG technique. Sometimes denoted *DVCPRO50 P*.

DVTR — Digital videotape recorder. See *VTR*, on page 651.

EAV — End of active video: A sequence of four words inserted into a 4:2:2 component digital video data stream, marking the end of active samples on a line. See also *SAV*, on page 646, and *TRS*, on page 649.

EBU — European Broadcasting Union: An organization of European state broadcasters and others.

ECC — Error checking and correction: A method of inserting redundant information prior to digital storage, recording or transmission, and processing that information upon subsequent playback or reception, so that recording or transmission errors can be detected (and in some cases, perfectly corrected). ECC systems can perfectly correct errors having certain statistical properties. Synonymous with EDC.

EDC — Error detection and correction: A synonym for ECC; see above.

EDH — Error detection and handling: A system standardized by SMPTE for encoding transmission error status into data conveyed across a series of SDI interfaces.

EIA — The U.S. Electronic Industries Association.

EIA No. 1 — EIA Industrial Electronics Tentative Standard No. 1. This document, dated November 7, 1977, served to define the 480*i*29.97 (525/59.94) NTSC system until the adoption of SMPTE 170M in 1994. See also *RS-170-A*, on page 645.

EIA RS-170, RS-170-A — See *RS-170* and *RS-170-A*, on page 645.

EIA RS-343-A — See *RS-343-A*, on page 645.

Encoding — **1.** Generally, the process of converting one or more signals into a more complex representation, with the goal of reducing data rate for transmission or recording.

2. In traditional video usage, the process of taking component video input (e.g., $Y'C_BC_R$ or $R'G'B'$), performing chroma modulation and luma/chroma summation, and producing composite video (e.g., NTSC or PAL).

3. In modern video usage, the processing of uncompressed image data to produce a compressed bitstream (such as in JPEG, M-JPEG, or MPEG compression).

Equalization

1. The correction of undesired frequency or phase response. Coaxial cable introduces a high-frequency rolloff that is dependent upon cable length and proportional to $1/\sqrt{f}$ (pronounced *one over root f*); this is corrected by a subsystem called an *equalizer.* A naively designed analog lowpass filter, or a simple digital IIR filter, has poor phase response; this can be corrected by an *equalizer* filter section.

2. Equalization pulse; see below.

Equalization pulse

A sync pulse, part of vertical sync, that is approximately half the duration of a normal sync and occurs at 0_H or halfway between two 0_H data. The original purpose of equalization pulses was to eliminate the line pairing that would otherwise occur with cheap, passive sync separator circuits. Equalization pulses are unnecessary today, except for reverse compatibility.

Error concealment

Masking, by playback or receiver circuits, of errors introduced in recording or transmission. Concealment is enabled by the playback or receiver circuits' detection of errors by using ECC codes. Concealment is accomplished by replacing errored samples by interpolated (estimated) signal information.

Error correction

Perfect correction, by playback or receiver circuits, of errors introduced in recording or transmission. Correction is effected by the decoder's using the redundant ECC information inserted by the recorder or transmitter to perfectly reconstruct the errored bits.

Even field

Historically, in 480*i* (interlaced) scanning, the field whose first broad pulse starts halfway between two line syncs. Compare *Odd field,* on page 639. The terms *odd* and *even* should be avoided, and *first* and *second* used instead.

Excursion

The amplitude difference between two levels. Unless otherwise noted, reference excursion.

Exponential function

A function of the form $y = a^x$, where a is constant. Exponential functions are rarely used in video. Gamma correction is a modified power function, and not an exponential function as is sometimes claimed.

FEC

Forward error-correction: A synonym for ECC (see page 627), particularly when used in transmission or video recording systems.

Field

In interlaced scanning, the smallest time interval that contains a set of scanning lines covering the height of the entire picture, along with all associated preceding sync elements. Fields were once denoted *odd* and *even;* these terms should be avoided, and *first* and *second* (or in MPEG-2, *top* and *bottom*) used instead.

Field dominance

In an interlaced motion image sequence, the field parity (first or second) where temporal coherence is susceptible to interruption due to editing. In principle, video edits can be made at any field, but good practice calls for edits at the beginning of the first field (i.e., first field dominant).

Field sync

In interlaced scanning, the analog sync pulse pattern that defines the start of a field. Field sync contains the 0_V *datum*. In 480*i* and 576*i* systems, field sync is a sequence comprising preequalization pulses, broad pulses, and postequalization pulses. In 480*i* systems there are six of each; in 576*i* systems there are five.

First field

In interlaced scanning, the first field of the pair of fields comprising a frame. In analog 480*i*, the field whose first equalization pulse starts coincident with 0_H. In analog 576*i*, the field whose first broad pulse starts coincident with 0_H. (See also *Field dominance*, above, and *Second field*, on page 647.)

Footprint, NTSC;
Footprint, PAL

The first time that the luma and modulated chroma components of an image are added together into a single composite signal, cross-luma and cross-color artifacts become permanently embedded: Subsequent decoding and reencoding cannot remove them. The permanence of these artifacts is referred to as the *NTSC footprint* or the *PAL footprint*.

Format conversion

An ambiguous term. See *Transcoding*, on page 649, *Scan conversion*, on page 646, *Downconversion*, on page 625, *Upconversion*, on page 650, and *Standards conversion*, on page 648.

Frame

The time interval of a video signal that contains all of the elements of one picture, complete with all of the associated preceding sync elements. In analog, measured between 0_V instants; in digital, measured between the EAVs preceding line 1. In an interlaced system, a frame comprises two fields, *first* and *second*, which normally exhibit temporal coherence; each field contains half the scanning lines and half the picture lines of the frame.

Frame A

Deprecated. See *A-frame*, on page 612.

Frequency interleaving

Modulation of chroma, and summation with luma, such that the modulated chroma signal occupies frequencies disjoint from the integer multiples of the line rate at and near which the luma signal is concentrated.

Front porch

The time interval between the right-hand edge of active video on a line and the 50%-point of the leading edge of the immediately following sync pulse.

G'B'R'

Green, blue, and red. An alternate notation for *R'G'B'*, with the components reordered to associate with [Y', C_B, C_R], respectively (or with [Y', P_B, P_R], respectively). G' associates with Y' because green dominates luma. Properly written with primes, but sometimes sloppily written *GBR*.

G/PAL

See *PAL-B/G/H,* on page 640.

Gamma, decoding (γ_D)

The numerical value (greater than unity) of the exponent to which a video component *R′, G′, or B′* is raised, by a power function of the form $(V')^{\gamma_D}$, to obtain a linear-light (luminance or tristimulus) value. A $^5/_2$-power function is inherent in the electron gun of a CRT display, so decoding gamma typically has the numerical value 2.5; this value characterizes a display system. The value is important throughout a video system because the approximate inverse power function is applied at the camera; R', G', and B' signals, and the derivative luma signal Y', are conveyed in gamma-corrected form throughout the system.

Gamma, encoding (γ_E)

The numerical value (smaller than unity) of the exponent to which a linear-light (luminance or tristimulus) signal is raised, by a power function of the form L^{γ_E}, to obtain a video signal R', G', or B'. (Subsequently, luma, Y', is computed.) Encoding gamma today typically has a value close to 0.5, though the 1953 NTSC and FCC standards mention $^1/_{2.2}$, and 576*i* standards mention $^1/_{2.8}$. For television, encoding gamma is typically about 1.25 times the reciprocal of the display gamma; see *Rendering intent,* on page 644. Encoding gamma properly has a value less than unity, though sometimes its reciprocal is quoted.

Gamma, system

The product of all of the power function exponents to which image data is subjected as it traverses a set of subsystems, starting from linear-light components captured from a scene by a camera (or from linear-light components captured from a previously reproduced image by a scanner), and ending with linear-light components reproduced at an image display. The term is best avoided owing to the difficulty of identifying exactly what constitutes the "system," and because it is used so widely without any consideration of rendering intent.

Gamma

See *Gamma, decoding (γ_D),* and *Gamma, encoding (γ_E),* above.

Gamma-corrected

A signal to which gamma correction has been applied – that is, a linear-light signal, such as a tristimulus value, raised to a power in the range 0.4 to 0.5; see *Gamma, encoding (γ_E),* above. Because gamma correction produces a video signal that mimics the lightness sensitivity of human vision, a gamma-corrected signal exhibits good perceptual uniformity: Noise or quantization error introduced into the signal is approximately equally perceptible across the tone range of the system from black to white. (Gamma correction also compensates for the nonlinear voltage-to-luminance transfer function inherent in a CRT display.)

Gamma correction

The process by which a quantity proportional to intensity, such as CIE luminance or some other tristimulus signal, is transformed into a signal by a power function with an exponent in the range 0.4 to 0.5. See *Gamma, encoding (γ_E),* above. In video, gamma correction is usually performed at a video camera or its control unit.

GOP — Group of pictures: In MPEG, a set of consecutive pictures starting with a coded I-picture. A GOP typically extends to (but does not include) the following I-picture; however, a GOP may contain more than one I-picture.

H/PAL — See *PAL-B/G/H*, on page 640.

Hanging dots — A cross-luma artifact appearing as a fine alternating pattern of dark and light dots along a horizontal edge in a picture having a saturated vertical color transition, when decoded by a comb filter. Hanging dots are particularly evident when viewing the SMPTE colorbar test signal.

HD-D5 — See *D-5 HD*, on page 623.

HD-SDI — High-definition serial digital interface: A SMPTE-standard interface, having a data rate of about 1.485 Gb/s, for uncompressed studio-quality HDTV.

HDCAM — Sony's trademarked term for the digital videotape format now standardized as SMPTE D-11; see *D-11*, on page 624.

HDTV — High-definition television: A video system having aspect ratio 16:9 whose image comprises ¾-million pixels or more.

Hi8 — A consumer analog videocassette system using color-under recording onto 8 mm tape; the successor to Video-8. (See *Video-8*, on page 651.)

Horizontal blanking — The time interval – usually expressed in microseconds or sample counts, or sometimes as a fraction of line time – between the right edge of picture information on one line and the left edge of picture information on the following picture line.

Horizontal drive (HD) — A pulse containing horizontal synchronization information that begins at the right edge of picture on a line and ends at the trailing edge of normal sync.

Hue — **1.** *The attribute of a visual sensation according to which an area appears to be similar to one of the perceived colours, red, yellow, green and blue, or a combination of two of them* [CIE]. Roughly speaking, if the dominant wavelength of an SPD shifts, the hue of the associated color will shift.

2. In color science, h^*_{uv}, the polar-coordinate angle of a color difference value in CIE $L^*u^*v^*$ components.

3. In video, the polar-coordinate angle of a color difference value as displayed on a vectorscope, in C_B, C_R coordinates for component digital video, P_B, P_R coordinates for component analog video, or U, V coordinates for composite video.

4. User-accessible means to adjust Hue (3).

I-field
In MPEG, a field-coded I-picture. I-fields come in pairs, either top then bottom, or bottom then top. See *I-picture,* below.

I-frame
In MPEG, either (i) a frame-coded I-picture, or (ii) a field-coded I-picture [either top or bottom], followed by a field-coded I-picture or P-picture [of opposite parity]. In the second case, the two fields form what is sometimes called an *IP-frame;* the P-field may involve prediction from the I-field. See *I-picture,* below.

I/PAL
See *PAL-I,* on page 640.

I-picture
In MPEG, an intraframe picture (field, or frame): A picture, or coded picture information, that makes no reference to preceding or following pictures. An I-picture is coded independently; it makes no use of temporal coherence.

I, Q
In-phase and Quadrature color difference components of NTSC: *U* and *V* components rotated +33° and then axis-exchanged. NTSC-modulated chroma was originally based on *I* and *Q* color differences, where *I* had considerably more bandwidth than *Q*. Nowadays, NTSC color modulation is usually performed on equiband *U* and *V* components. Except perhaps for bandwidth difference, it is impossible to tell from a composite analog NTSC signal whether it was encoded along [*U, V*], [*I, Q*], or any other pair of axes.

Intensity
Intensity is a measure over some interval of the electromagnetic spectrum of power (usually radiated from, or incident on, a surface), in a specified direction. Intensity is a linear-light measure, expressed in physical units such as watts per steradian ($W \cdot sr^{-1}$). The intensity produced by a CRT monitor is *not* proportional to the applied voltage, but proportional to approximately the $5/2$-power of applied voltage. Image scientists and video engineers are usually interested in intensity per unit area, weighted by the visual response – that is, they are usually interested not in intensity per se but in luminance or tristimulus values.

Interlace
A scanning standard in which alternate raster lines of a frame are displaced vertically by half the scan-line pitch and displaced temporally by half the frame time to form a *first field* and a *second field*. Examples are 480*i*29.97 (525/59.94), 576*i*25 (625/50), and 1080*i*30 (1125/60). Systems with high-order interlace have been proposed but none has been deployed, so modern usage of the term *interlace* implies 2:1 interlace. See also *Field,* on page 628.

Interlace factor
The ratio between the number of picture lines in a reference progressive system and the number of picture lines necessary to defeat twitter in an interlaced system having equivalent spatial resolution. Distinguished from, but often mistakenly described as, *Kell factor, k*.

Interpolation
Resampling that produces more output samples than original samples (synonymous with *upsampling*), or that produces the same number of output samples as input samples (phase shifting).

Interstitial

1. Chroma subsampling wherein each subsampled chroma sample is effectively horizontally positioned halfway between adjacent luma samples. Interstitial 4:2:0 chroma subsampling is implicit in the JPEG/JFIF, H.261, and MPEG-1 standards.

2. In television programming, a short element such as a commercial inserted into or between programs.

IRD

Integrated receiver-decoder: A device that receives an RF signal carrying digital television, and produces an uncompressed video signal, typically in analog form. An IRD performs demodulation, demultiplexing, and MPEG-2 decoding. An IRD is typically a set-top device (*set top box*, STB).

IRE

Institute of Radio Engineers, the predecessor of the IEEE.

IRE unit

One-hundredth of the excursion from blanking level to reference white level. Originally standardized by the IRE. In systems having picture-to-sync ratio of 10:4 (such as ITU-R System M and the archaic EIA RS-343-A), one IRE unit corresponds to $7\frac{1}{7}$ mV. In systems having picture-to-sync ratio of 7:3, one IRE unit corresponds to exactly 7 mV. In 50 Hz systems, levels are usually expressed in millivolts and not IRE units.

ITU-R

International Telecommunications Union, Radiocommunications Sector; successor to the *Comité Consultatif Internationale des Radiocommunications* (International Radio Consultative Committee, CCIR): A treaty organization that obtains international agreement on standards for radio and television broadcasting. The ITU-R BT series of Recommendations and Reports deals with television. Although studio standards do not involve radio transmission in a strict sense, they are used in the international exchange of programs, so they are under the jurisdiction of ITU-R.

ITU-R Rec. BT. 601, 709

Colloquially, *Rec. 601* and *Rec. 709;* see *Rec. 601* and *Rec. 709,* on page 643.

JFIF

JPEG file interchange format. A file format, adopted by an industry group led by C-Cube, that encapsulates a JPEG image, along with a small amount of supplementary data. If you are presented with an image data file described as JPEG, in all likelihood it is JFIF.

JPEG

1. Joint Photographic Experts Group: A standards committee, constituted jointly by the ISO and IEC and formally denoted ISO/IEC JTC1.

2. A standard, formally denoted ISO/IEC 10918, adopted by JPEG (1), for the lossy compression of digital still images (either color or grayscale).

K

Unit of absolute temperature, kelvin. Properly written with no degree sign. In color science, commonly used to quantify color temperature.

K-factor, *K*-rating

A numerical characterization of pulse fidelity, obtained by measuring the tightest fit of a specific set of time-domain envelope to a raised cosine test pulse. Distinguished from Kell factor, *k* below.

Kell effect

In a video system – including sensor, signal processing, and display – *Kell effect* refers to the loss of resolution, compared to the Nyquist limit, caused by the spatial dispersion of light power. Some dispersion is necessary to avoid aliasing upon capture, and to avoid objectionable scan line (or pixel) structure at display.

Kell factor, *k*

Historically, the ratio between effective resolution and theoretically obtainable resolution for a given number of active scan lines. Generally between 0.7 and 0.9. Now deprecated. Distinguished from *interlace factor;* also distinguished from *K*-factor, *K*-rating.

Key

A component signal indicating transparency of the accompanying foreground image data, coded between zero (fully transparent) and unity (fully opaque). In computer graphics, called *alpha*, α (see page 613). The keying (or *compositing*) operation is performed as: $R = \alpha \cdot FG + (1-\alpha) \cdot BG$, where FG represents foreground (*fill*) video and BG represents background video. Foreground image data that has been premultiplied by the key is called *shaped* in video (or *associated* or *premultiplied* in computer graphics). Foreground image data that has not been premultiplied by the key is called *unshaped* in video (or *unassociated* or *nonpremultiplied* in computer graphics).

L_A, active lines

The count of scan lines containing the picture. L_A for a frame is equivalent to the number of rows of image samples. (Vertical interval lines are not considered active; however, closed caption lines in 480*i* *are* considered active.)

L_T, total lines

The count of total scan lines in a frame.

Legal

1. In component video signal coding, the condition where each signal of a component set lies within its reference range. In an *R'G'B'*-legal combination, all of *R'*, *G'*, and *B'* lie within their reference ranges. (See also *Valid,* on page 650.)

2. In NTSC and PAL coding and transmission, compliance with broadcast standards. (NTSC broadcast transmission has a 120 IRE amplitude limit that requires limiting the saturation of colors near pure yellow and pure cyan.)

3. In JPEG or MPEG, a bitstream that is compliant with standards, an encoder that produces only compliant bitstreams, or a decoder that correctly decodes any compliant bitstream.

Letterbox

A widescreen image (such as 16:9 aspect ratio) conveyed or presented in a format having a narrower aspect ratio (such as 4:3), using the full width of the narrower format but not using the full height.

Level

1. In video, generally, the amplitude of a video signal, or one of its components, expressed in volts, millivolts, IRE units, or digital code value.

2. In JPEG, MPEG, and DV compression, the magnitude (i.e., absolute value) of a DCT coefficient.

Lightness

CIE L^*: An objective quantity related to brightness; approximately equal to relative luminance raised to the 0.4-power.

Line, active;
Line, picture

A scanning line that is specified by a scanning standard to contain picture. (Exceptionally, in 480*i* systems, closed caption lines are considered to be "active.")

Line frequency

1. In video, the frequency of horizontal scanning; about 15.7 kHz for SDTV, and 33.7 KHz or higher for HDTV.

2. AC power line (mains) frequency, typically 50 Hz or 60 Hz, usually similar to the vertical scan frequency.

Line frequency should be used with care in video because it may refer to the frequency of *horizontal* scanning, or to AC power (mains) frequency, which is usually similar or identical to the frequency of *vertical* scanning.

Line-locked

1. In digital video, having an integer number of samples per total line: If 0_H were digitized, it would take the same value every line. A line-locked system has coherent sampling and line frequencies, as in Rec. 601 or $4f_{SC}$ NTSC. Owing to the +25 Hz offset of the PAL subcarrier in PAL-B/G/H/I and PAL-N, PAL sampled at $4f_{SC}$ is not line-locked.

2. In industrial or security video, having vertical scan frequency locked to the AC power line (mains) frequency.

Line sync

The sync signal pulse that defines the start of a scan line. In 480*i* and 576*i* systems, line sync may be the start of a normal sync or the start of certain equalization or broad pulses. See also *0_H datum,* on page 609.

Line time

The time interval from the 0_H datum of one line to the 0_H datum of the next. In a digital system, from EAV to EAV.

Linear-light (*adj.*)

Proportional to intensity. Video signals are ordinarily not conveyed in linear-light form; instead, they are gamma-corrected.

Lines

1. Total number of lines per frame, L_T.

2. Active lines, L_A.

3. A unit of resolution; properly, *TV lines per picture height, TVL/PH* (see page 649).

Luma

A video signal representative of the monochrome – or roughly, lightness – component of a scene. For SDTV, Rec. 601 standardizes these coefficients:

$$ {}^{601}Y' = 0.299\,R' + 0.587\,G' + 0.114\,B' $$

For HDTV, Rec. 709 standardizes these coefficients:

$$ {}^{709}Y' = 0.2126\,R' + 0.7152\,G' + 0.0722\,B' $$

Luma coefficients

The coefficients of nonlinear (gamma-corrected) $R'G'B'$ in the weighted sum that forms luma.

Luminance

1. Luminous flux density in a particular direction: The spectral radiance of a scene, weighted by the luminous efficiency function $Y(\lambda)$ of the CIE Standard Observer. Denoted L_V or Y (CIE Y tristimulus value); properly expressed in units of $cd \cdot m^{-2}$, or colloquially, *nit*. Luminance is the photometric analog of radiance. Luminance is related to the brightness sensation of human vision.

2. Luminance (1), normalized to an excursion of 1 or 100 with respect to a reference white luminance. Properly called *relative luminance* (see below).

3. The term *luminance* is often carelessly used in video engineering to refer to *luma*. (See *Luma,* on page 636).

Much confusion surrounds the term *luminance*. In color science and physics, *luminance* is proportional to intensity (linear-light), and has the symbol Y; it can be computed as a properly weighted sum of RGB tristimulus values. In video, *luma* is computed as a weighted sum of nonlinear (gamma-corrected) $R'G'B'$ components, and is properly denoted Y'; often, the luminance coefficients are used. The term *luma*, and the prime, denote the nonlinear quantity in a manner that avoids ambiguity. However, the term *luminance* is often sloppily used for this quantity, and the prime on the symbol is often omitted. Sloppy use of the word *luminance* and omission of the prime renders both the term *luminance* and the symbol Y ambiguous: Whether the associated quantity is CIE luminance (linear) or video luma (nonlinear) must then be determined from context.

Luminance, relative

Luminance (1), as above, normalized to an excursion of 1 or 100 with respect to a reference white luminance. In video, absolute reproduction of luminance is unnecessary; video normally involves relative luminance.

Luminance coefficients

The coefficients of linear-light (tristimulus) RGB in the weighted sum that forms luminance.

M-frame

In 2-3 pulldown to 29.97Hz interlaced video, the video frame, unique in the 5-frame video sequence, comprising a first field from one film frame (conventionally film frame B) and a second field from another film frame (conventionally film frame C). A film edit could be present between these fields. See *2-3 pulldown,* on page 610, and *A-frame,* on page 612.

M-JPEG — A technique or file format using JPEG (2), or a JPEG-like algorithm, to individually compress each field or frame in a motion image sequence, without exploiting interfield or interframe coherence. M-JPEG is not standardized.

M/NTSC — See *NTSC* (3), on page 639.

M/PAL — See *PAL-M, PAL-525,* on page 640.

MAC — **1.** Multiplexed analog component: An obsolete component video encoding standard, used mainly with 576*i* scanning, encoding $Y'P_BP_R$ color components in time-compressed serial analog form. P_B and P_R are compressed by a factor of two with respect to Y'.

2. Multiplier-accumulator. An arithmetic device comprising a multiplier followed by an accumulator that is arranged to sum consecutive products.

Macroblock — **1.** In MPEG, image data comprising, or coded picture information representing, one of the 16×16 arrays of luma samples that tile the image, accompanied by the requisite number and arrangement of associated blocks of C_B and C_R. In the common MPEG-2 case of 4:2:0 chroma subsampling, four 8×8 luma blocks are accompanied by an 8×8 block of C_B and 8×8 block of C_R; in this case, a macroblock comprises six blocks.

2. In DV, image data comprising – or coded picture information representing – an 8×8 block of C_B, an 8×8 block of C_R, and the associated two (4:2:2), three (3:1:1), four (4:1:1 or 4:2:0), or six (3:1:0) 8×8 blocks of luma.

3. In JPEG, an MCU (minimum coded unit; see page 637).

Mathematical PAL — See *PAL, mathematical,* on page 640.

MB — Megabyte: 2^{20} (or 1048576) bytes, or in disk storage, $2^{10} \cdot 10^3$ (or 1024000) bytes.

MB — See *Macroblock*, above.

MCU, minimum coded unit — In JPEG without subsampling, image data comprising, or coded picture information representing, a set of 8×8 blocks of image data, one per component. In $Y'C_BC_R$ JPEG, with 4:2:0 subsampling, image data comprising, or coded picture information representing, an 8×8 block of C_B, the corresponding 8×8 block of C_R, and the four associated 8×8 luma blocks.

Meander, burst — See *Burst meander,* on page 616.

Metamerism — **1.** In color science, the condition that two different spectral power distributions, when weighted according to the three spectral response curves of the CIE Standard Observer, produce identical tristimulus values – that is, appear to be the same color to a color-normal observer. Metamerism frequently holds for spectra that are markedly different.

2. In a camera or scanner, the condition that two objects that are metameric with respect to the CIE Standard Observer produce different sets of *RGB* components, owing to the spectral response of the device departing from the CIE curves. A camera or scanner has metamerism errors when it "sees" color differently from a color-normal human observer.

Midframe — In 2-3 pulldown, M-frame; see page 636.

MiniDV — The small cassette size variant of DVC. (See page 626.)

Modulated chroma — **1.** In NTSC and PAL, a color subcarrier (1), onto which two color difference signals (typically *U* and *V*) have been imposed by quadrature modulation.

2. In SECAM, a frequency modulated signal conveying line-alternate color difference components.

Monochrome — **1.** In color science, shades of a single hue.

2. In video, the black and white (grayscale, or lightness) component of image data.

3. In computing, bilevel image data.

Motion-JPEG — See *M-JPEG,* on page 637.

MP3 or mp3 — Formally, MPEG Audio Layer III: An audio compression standard, defined in MPEG-1 and MPEG-2, that is widely used for distributing music on the Internet. Sometimes incorrectly called MPEG-3.

MPEG — Moving (not Motion!) Picture Experts Group: A standards committee, jointly constituted by ISO and IEC, that has developed standards for the lossy compression of digital motion images. The MPEG algorithms exploit the temporal coherence found in motion image sequences. The MPEG-2 standard (see below) is of interest to digital video and HDTV. Its predecessor, now denoted MPEG-1, offers VHS-quality. Other emergent MPEG standards, such as MPEG-4, MPEG-7, and MPEG-21, are for applications other than broadcast television.

MPEG-1 — A standard, adopted by MPEG (see above), formally denoted ISO/IEC 11172, optimized for data rates of about 1.5 Mb/s and having approximately VHS quality.

MPEG-2 — A standard, formally denoted ISO/IEC 13818, adopted by MPEG (see above), optimized for data rates of 4 Mb/s and higher, of interest to digital video and HDTV.

MPEG IMX — See *D-10,* on page 624.

N/PAL — See *PAL-N, PAL-3.58,* on page 640.

Nit — Candela per meter squared, cd·m^{-2} (colloquial). Derived from the Latin *nitere,* to shine.

Normal line sync — In analog SDTV, a line sync pulse that remains at sync level for about 4.7 μs. In interlaced systems, the leading edge of equalization and broad pulses are utilized as line syncs.

Notch filter — In a composite video decoder, circuitry that separates chroma from a composite signal using a simple bandpass filter centered at the color subcarrier frequency. A notch filter introduces dot crawl artifacts into any picture that has luma detail at frequencies near the color subcarrier.

NTSC, National Television System Committee — **1.** The group, now referred to as *NTSC-I*, that in 1941 standardized 525-line, 60.00 Hz field rate, interlaced monochrome television in the United States.

2. The group, formally referred to as *NTSC-II*, that in 1953 standardized 525-line, 59.94 Hz field rate, interlaced color television in the United States. NTSC-II introduced the composite video technique.

3. A method of composite video encoding based on quadrature modulation of *I* and *Q* (or *U* and *V*) color difference components onto a color subcarrier, then summing the resulting chroma signal with luma. Used only with 480*i* scanning, with a subcarrier frequency nominally $^{455}/_{2}$ times the horizontal line rate (i.e., a subcarrier frequency of about 3.579545 MHz).

4. Often incorrectly used to denote 480*i*29.97 (525/59.94) scanning.

NTSC-4.43 — A degenerate version of NTSC (3), having 480*i* scanning and NTSC chroma, but with chroma modulated onto a 4.43 MHz color subcarrier instead of 3.58 MHz. NTSC-4.43 is utilized by some European consumer equipment to play NTSC tapes. Provided the scanning range encompasses 15.734 kHz horizontal and 59.94 Hz vertical rates, the use of a 4.43 MHz color subcarrier eliminates the 3.58 MHz crystal that would otherwise be required.

NTSC-J — NTSC as used in Japan: NTSC (3) with zero setup (and luma and chroma levels modified accordingly).

NTSC-legal — The condition where an NTSC signal is *R'G'B'*-legal and additionally has no chroma content that would cause the composite signal to exceed +120 IRE units.

Odd field — In 480*i* (interlaced) scanning, the field whose first broad pulse is coincident with line sync. Compare *Even field,* on page 628. The terms *odd* and *even* should be avoided, and *first* and *second* used instead.

OFDM — Orthogonal frequency-division multiplexing. In video transmission, OFDM is always applied to digital data, and referred to as *coded;* see *COFDM* on page 619.

Offset sampling	Obsolete scanning technique in which the samples of one line are offset horizontally by one-half the sample pitch from samples of the previous line of the field (or frame). Also known as *quincunx sampling*. Contrasted with *orthogonal sampling*, which is now ubiquitous.
Orthogonal sampling	A digital video system in which the samples of a frame are arranged spatially in a rectangular array. (Distinguished from *offset sampling;* see above.)
P-field	In MPEG, a field-coded P-picture. P-fields come in pairs (either top then bottom, or bottom then top). See *P-picture,* below.
P-frame	In MPEG, either a frame-coded P-picture, or a pair of P-fields (one top field and one bottom field, in either order). See *P-picture,* below.
P-picture	In MPEG, a predictive-coded picture: A picture, or coded picture information, in which one or more macroblocks are predicted from a preceding anchor picture, and which may itself be used as the basis of subsequent predictions. P-pictures exploit temporal coherence.
PAL, phase alternate line (or phase alternation line)	**1.** A composite video standard similar to NTSC, except that the modulated *V* color difference component inverts phase on alternate scan lines, and burst meander is applied. Usually used in 576*i* systems with a subcarrier frequency of 4.433618750 MHz, but also used with subcarriers of about 3.58 MHz in the PAL-N and PAL-M systems. **2.** Often incorrectly used to denote 576*i* (625/50) scanning.
PAL-B/G/H	Versions of 576*i* PAL having 5.0 MHz video bandwidth, but differing RF parameters. According to ITU-R notation, B/PAL, G/PAL, and H/PAL, respectively.
PAL-I	Version of 576*i* PAL having 5.5 MHz video bandwidth. Formally, I/PAL.
PAL-M, PAL-525	A composite video standard used in Brazil, having 4.2 MHz video bandwidth, 480*i* scanning, and PAL color encoding using a subcarrier frequency of about 3.575612 MHz. In ITU-R notation, M/PAL.
PAL, mathematical	A PAL (1) system, with 576*i* scanning, wherein the unmodulated color subcarrier frequency is offset +25 Hz from an odd multiple of $\frac{1}{4}$ the line rate.
PAL-N, PAL-3.58	A composite video standard used in Argentina, Paraguay, and Uruguay, having 4.2 MHz video bandwidth, 576*i* scanning, and PAL color encoding using a subcarrier frequency of about 3.582056250 MHz. In ITU-R notation, Combination N/PAL (or CN/PAL).

PAL, nonmathematical

A PAL (1) system, with 576*i* scanning, wherein the unmodulated color subcarrier is incoherent with sync or the +25 Hz offset is absent. See *PAL, mathematical*, above.

P_B, P_R

Scaled color difference components, blue and red, used in component analog video: Versions of *B'* minus luma (*B'–Y'*) and *R'* minus luma (*R'–Y'*) scaled for excursion nominally identical to luma for component analog transmission. P_B and P_R according to the EBU N10 standard are equivalent to C_B and C_R scaled by the factor $^{219}/_{224}$; however, various different industry standards are in wide use for 480*i*. See also C_B, C_R, on page 616, and *U*, *V*, on page 649.

Peak white

The most positive excursion of a luma, *R'*, *G'*, or *B'* component. Distinguished from *reference white:* Reference white is usually not "peak," because studio video systems typically allow signals to excurse to a peak somewhat above the reference white level.

Pedestal

Black level (see page 614) expressed as an offset in voltage or IRE units relative to blanking level. Conventionally about 54 mV (7.5 IRE) in ITU-R System M, SMPTE 170M, and the archaic EIA RS-343-A; conventionally zero in all other systems, where blanking level and black level are identical. Pedestal is properly a voltage offset or a level; it is incorrect to express pedestal as a percentage. See also *Setup*, on page 647.

Picture

In MPEG-2, one of (i) a top field, (ii) a bottom field, or (iii) a progressive frame.

Picture excursion

The excursion from blanking to reference white. In 480*i*, 100 IRE by definition. In analog System M and the archaic EIA RS-343-A, $^5/_7$ V (about 714 mV); in other systems, particularly 576*i* and HDTV, 700 mV.

Picture:sync ratio

The ratio between picture excursion (from blanking to reference white) and sync excursion (from synctip to blanking). Conventionally 10:4 for System M and the archaic EIA RS-343-A, and 7:3 in other systems.

Pillarbox format

An image (such as 4:3 aspect ratio) conveyed or presented in a format having a wider aspect ratio (such as 16:9), using the full height of the widescreen format but not using the full width. The term echoes *letterbox;* it derives from the name for a tall postbox in the U.K.

Pixel

Picture element: The collection of quantized samples that are specific to a single spatial sampling site in an image; usually three color component samples, perhaps augmented by a transparency (*alpha* or *key*) component sample. The term is ambiguous when chroma subsampling is involved.

Power function

A function of the form $y = x^a$ (where *a* is constant). Distinguished from *exponential function*, which has the form $y = a^x$ (where *a* is constant). Gamma correction in video approximates a power function $V' = L^{\gamma_E}$, where γ_E (the *encoding gamma*) symbolizes a numerical parameter having a value of about 0.5 (or in some systems, about $1/_{2.2}$).

Production aperture In a video scanning standard, the active samples: The pixel array, comprising S_{AL} columns and L_A rows.

Progressive A scanning standard in which spatially adjacent picture lines are associated with consecutive periodic (or identical) instants in time. Examples are 1080*p*24 and 720*p*60. Distinguished from *Interlace*. See also *PsF*, below.

PsF Progressive segmented frame: An interface scheme for progressive scanned video whereby lines are rearranged to interlaced order for transmission or recording. Unlike true interlace, the first and second fields are sampled during the same time interval, and no vertical filtering is necessary. See also *24PsF,* on page 610.

PSF Point spread function.

QAM Quadrature amplitude modulation: A modulation system wherein two information signals independently modulate two subcarriers that are in *quadrature* (that is, offset in phase by 90°), which are then summed to form the modulated subcarrier. An analog version of QAM, usually called just *quadrature modulation*, combines two color difference components onto a color subcarrier in NTSC and PAL composite video. A digital version of QAM is used for RF modulation in some digital television transmission systems (e.g., 16-QAM, 64-QAM), particularly for cable television.

QCIF Quarter common intermediate format: In the ITU-T Rec. H.261 standard for videoconferencing, a progressively scanned raster with 4:2:0 chroma subsampling having 176×144 luma samples at 29.97 frames per second. QCIF image data is ordinarily subsampled from SDTV. See *CIF, common intermediate format,* on page 618.

QPSK Quadrature phase-shift keying: A modulation system wherein a signal alters the phase of a carrier (or subcarrier). In video, digital QPSK is used for RF modulation.

Quantization The process of assigning a discrete, numbered level to each of two or more intervals of amplitude of a sample. (In video or audio, there are typically hundreds or thousands of intervals.) In the usual *uniform quantization*, the *steps* between levels have equal amplitude.

Quasi-interlace Term in consumer electronics denoting progressive segmented frame; see *PsF,* on page 642.

Quincunx sampling A misleading term for *offset sampling;* see page 640. The term stems from the arrangement of club, diamond, heart, or spade symbols on a playing card of value five. The term is misleading because the sampling structure has nothing to do with the number 5.

R'–Y' — See *B'–Y', R'–Y'*, on page 614.

Radiance — Intensity per unit projected area.

Raster — The pattern of parallel horizontal scan lines that paints out a picture. The raster is the static spatial pattern that is refreshed with successive frames of video.

Rec. 601 — **1.** Formally, ITU-R Recommendation BT.601: The international standard for studio digital video sampling. Rec. 601 specifies a sampling frequency of 13.5 MHz, $Y'C_BC_R$ coding, and this luma equation:

$$^{601}Y' = 0.299\,R' + 0.587\,G' + 0.114\,B'$$

Rec. 601 is silent concerning *RGB* chromaticities. It is implicit that 480*i* systems use SMPTE RP 145 primaries, and that 576*i* systems use EBU Tech. 3213 primaries. Rec. 601 is also silent concerning encoding gamma.

2. Loosely, in computer graphics, a parallel interface for Rec. 601-style digital video, where synchronization is accomplished using separate HD and VD logic signals.

Rec. 656 — **1.** Formally, *ITU-R Recommendation BT.656*. The international standard for parallel or serial interface of Rec. 601 digital video signals.

2. Loosely, in computer graphics, a parallel interface for Rec. 601-style digital video, where synchronization is accomplished with embedded SAV and EAV sequences.

Rec. 709 — Formally, *ITU-R Recommendation BT.709:* The international standard for HDTV studio signals. Chromaticity and transfer function parameters of Rec. 709 have been introduced into modern studio standards for 480*i* and 576*i*. Rec. 709 specifies this luma equation (whose coefficients are unfortunately different from the Rec. 601 coefficients):

$$^{709}Y' = 0.2126\,R' + 0.7152\,G' + 0.0722\,B'$$

Reference black — The level corresponding to picture black. In systems having 7.5% setup, such as 480*i*, reference black is nominally at a level of 7.5 IRE units. In systems with zero setup, such as 576*i*, NTSC-J, and HDTV, reference black is nominally at zero level.

Reference picture — See *Anchor picture*, on page 613.

Reference white — The level corresponding to white, 100 IRE units by definition. In video, it is standard for reference white to correspond to light having the spectral and/or colorimetric properties of CIE Illuminant D_{65} (except in Japan, where the standard white reference is 9300 K).

Relative luminance — See *Luminance, relative*, on page 636.

Rendering intent

Encoding and subsequent decoding of relative luminance – or, in a color system, tristimulus values – incorporating correction for subjective effects at the display so that color appearance is correctly reproduced. In video, rendering intent is imposed by encoding approximately the 0.5-power of scene tristimulus values, and decoding with a 2.5-power; an end-to-end power function exponent of approximately 1.25 results.

Resampling

The process of estimating, from a given set of samples, the samples that would have been produced if sampling had taken place at different instants or at different positions.

Resolution (*n.*)

1. Generally, a measure of the ability to delineate picture detail.

2. In image science, horizontal resolution is the maximum number of cycles per picture width (C/PW) discriminated from a test chart containing a black and white square wave pattern; vertical resolution is the maximum number of cycles discriminated per picture height (C/PH).

3. In video, if unqualified by *horizontal* or *vertical*, horizontal resolution: twice the number of vertical black and white pairs (cycles) that can be discerned across a horizontal distance equal to the picture height, expressed in TVL/PH or colloquially, *"TV lines"* (see page 649). Horizontal resolution in video is sometimes expressed in units of megahertz. Also known as *limiting resolution;* see IEEE Std. 208.

4. In computing, the count of columns and rows of pixels in a device or in an image.

5. Often improperly used to refer to the number of quantization levels (or bits per sample).

RF modulation

In video, a composite video signal that has been modulated onto a *radio frequency* (VHF or UHF) carrier in the range 50 MHz to 1 GHz. RF-modulated video in electrical form is usually conveyed with coaxial cable using Type-F (cable TV) connectors. NTSC consumer video signals conveyed from a VCR to a receiver are often RF modulated onto VHF channel 3 or channel 4.

RGB

1. Strictly, red, green, and blue tristimulus components (linear-light). The precise color interpretation of *RGB* values depends on the *chromaticity coordinates* of the primaries and the chromaticity coordinates of reference white. The FCC 1953 NTSC standard (obsolete), SMPTE RP 145, EBU Tech. 3213, and Rec. 709 all specify different primary chromaticities.

2. Loosely, red, green, and blue nonlinear primary components, properly denoted *R'G'B'* (see below).

R'G'B'

Red, green, and blue nonlinear primary components. The prime symbol makes gamma correction explicit: *R'*, *G'*, and *B'* denote *RGB* tristimulus signals that have been subject to *gamma correc-*

tion. The precise color interpretation of *RGB* values depends on the characteristics of the *RGB* primaries; see *RGB*, above.

RS-170
: EIA Recommended Standard 170 defined the 525/60.00/2:1 (interlaced) scanning standard for monochrome television at a field rate of exactly 60 Hz. The standard is obsolete. See *RS-170-A*, below.

RS-170-A
: This notation refers to the proposed Revision A, which was never in fact adopted, to EIA Recommended Standard 170. The term is loosely used to refer to the timing diagram associated with 480*i*29.97 (525/59.94) NTSC, as documented in *EIA Industrial Electronics Tentative Standard No. 1* published on November 8, 1977. Had revision A to RS-170 been adopted, the standard would now properly be referred to as *EIA 170-A*. SMPTE 170M, adopted in 1994, supersedes all of these.

RS-343-A
: This notation refers to the archaic EIA Recommended Standard 343, Revision A, adopted in 1969. It applied to industrial monochrome television systems with interlace, 60.00 Hz field rate, a horizontal blanking time of 7 µs, 7.5% setup, and from 675 to 1023 total lines. Although RS-343-A was withdrawn long ago, and most of its parameters have been abandoned, its level parameters – particularly 7.5% setup – have unfortunately been inherited by computer equipment.

S-VHS
: Super-VHS: An analog videocassette system, derived from VHS, for recording 480*i* NTSC or 576*i* PAL, using color-under recording on ½-inch tape.

S-video
: An interface conveying luma (*Y'*) and quadrature-modulated chroma (*C*) separately on a specific four-pin mini-DIN connector. There are three types of S-video: *S-video-525*, *S-video-525-J* (used in Japan), and *S-video-625*. S-video uses quadrature modulation but typically does not use frequency interleaving – color subcarrier is ordinarily incoherent. S-video is not exactly component video, and not exactly composite. Most S-VHS and Hi8 VCRs implement the S-video interface.

S_{AL}, Samples per active line
: The count of luma samples in a scan line that are permitted by a scanning standard to convey picture (and the associated blanking transitions). Digital video systems typically store just active samples. S_{AL} is equivalent to the number of columns of image samples.

Sample
: **1.** The value of a bandlimited, continuous signal at an instant of time and/or space. Usually, but not necessarily, quantized.

: **2.** Component; see page 621.

: See also S_{PW}, *samples per picture width* and S_{TL}, *samples per total line*, on page 648.

Sampling, 1-D
: The process of forming, from a continuous bandlimited one-dimensional function of time, a series of discrete values, each of

which is a function of the distribution of intensity across a small time interval. *Uniform sampling*, where the time intervals are of equal duration, is nearly always used.

Sampling, 2-D

The process of assigning, to each element of a sampling grid (or lattice), a value that is a function of the distribution of intensity over the corresponding small area of the image plane. In digital video and in conventional image processing, the samples lie on a regular, rectangular grid.

Saturation

1. *The colourfulness of an area judged in proportion to its brightness* [CIE]. Saturation runs from neutral gray through pastel to saturated colors. Roughly speaking, the more an SPD is concentrated at one wavelength, the more saturated the associated color becomes. You can desaturate a color by adding light that contains power at all wavelengths. Subjective, by definition.

2. The radius, in polar coordinates, of a color difference value as displayed on a vectorscope, in C_B, C_R coordinates for component digital video, P_B, P_R coordinates for component analog video, or *U*, *V* coordinates associated with composite video.

3. User-accessible means to adjust Saturation (2).

SAV

Start of active video: A sequence of four words inserted into a 4:2:2 component digital video data stream, marking the start of active samples on a line. See also *EAV*, *TRS*.

Scan conversion

Conversion, without temporal filtering, among scanning standards having different spatial structures.

Scanning standard

The parameters of raster scanning of a pickup device or a display device, or of the associated signal. Historically, a scanning standard was denoted by its total line count and its field rate (in hertz), separated by a virgule (slash); for example, 525/59.94, 625/50, or 1125/60. Interlace was implicit. Modern notation gives the count of picture lines, *p* for progressive or *i* for interlace, and the frame rate; for example, 480*i*29.97, 576*i*25, 1080*i*30, or 720*p*60.

SCART

A specific connector and associated interface standard, widely implemented in consumer equipment in Europe, conveying baseband video, audio, and other signals.

SCH

The phase relationship of *subcarrier* to *horizontal* sync: The phase displacement measured in degrees of subcarrier between a reference point – usually the 0_H datum – and the closest subcarrier zero-crossing.

SDI

Serial digital interface: A SMPTE-standard studio video interface having data rate between 143 Mb/s and 360 Mb/s. Usually, uncompressed SDTV video is conveyed, though the SDTI variant may be used to encapsulate compressed data (such as from D-7).

SDTI — Serial data transmission interface: A SMPTE-standard variant of SDI used to convey arbitrary data instead of uncompressed digital video.

SDTV — Standard-definition television: A video system whose image comprises fewer than ¾-million pixels. The most widely deployed SDTV broadcasting systems are 480*i* (see page 611) and 576*i* (see page 611).

SECAM — *Séquential couleur avec mémoire:* A composite video (1) system based on line-alternate $B'-Y'$ and $R'-Y'$ color difference signals, frequency modulated onto a subcarrier, then summed with luma. Neither quadrature modulation nor frequency interleaving is used. SECAM is used for broadcast in certain countries with 576*i* scanning (e.g., France and Russia). SECAM production equipment has fallen into disuse: 576*i* component equipment or PAL composite equipment is used instead, and the signal is transcoded to SECAM prior to transmission.

Second field — In interlaced scanning, the second field of the pair of fields comprising a frame. In analog 480*i*, the field whose first equalization pulse starts midline. In analog 576*i*, the field whose first broad pulse starts at midline. (See also *Field dominance*, and *First field,* on page 629.)

Serration — In bilevel sync, the interval between the end of a broad pulse and the start of the following sync pulse. This term refers to the absence of a pulse rather than the presence of one, and is deprecated in favor of the terms *equalization, broad,* and *normal* sync pulses.

Setup — Black level expressed as a percentage of the blanking-to-reference-white excursion. Conventionally 7.5% in System M and the archaic EIA RS-343-A; and zero in all other systems, where blanking level and black level are identical. Setup is properly expressed as a percentage; it is incorrect to express setup in voltage, level, or IRE units. See also *Pedestal,* on page 641.

Sidebar format — Pillarbox format.

SIF, source input format — A term from MPEG-1 that denotes a progressively scanned raster with 4:2:0 chroma subsampling, having either 352×288 luma samples at 25 frames per second, or 352×240 luma samples at 29.97 frames per second. Video in this format is ordinarily subsampled from 576*i* or 480*i* SDTV, respectively.

SMPTE — Society of Motion Picture and Television Engineers: A professional society that is also an ANSI-accredited standards-writing organization.

SPD — Spectral power distribution: spectral radiance.

S_{PW}, samples per picture width — The number of samples in a scan line corresponding to the width of the picture, measured at the 50% points of a white flatfield.

Standards conversion — Conversion, involving temporal filtering, of a video input signal having one scanning standard into an output signal having a different scanning standard and a different frame rate. Historically, the output signal had similar pixel count to the input, for example, a 480*i*-to-576*i* standards converter (loosely known as an NTSC-to-PAL standards converter). Nowadays, standards conversion may incorporate upconversion or downconversion. See *Scanning standard*, on page 646. See also *Transcoding*, *Scan conversion*, *Downconversion*, and *Upconversion*.

STL — Studio-transmitter link: A communications circuit, often microwave, that connects the output of a television studio to the input of a remotely situated transmitter.

S_{TL}, samples per total line — The number of sample intervals between consecutive 0_H instants.

Sync (*n.*) — **1.** A signal comprising just the horizontal and vertical elements necessary to accomplish synchronization.

2. The component of a video signal that conveys horizontal and vertical synchronization information.

3. *Sync level;* see below.

4. *Sync pulse;* see below.

Sync (*v.*) — Synchronization, to a video source, of the scan timing of receiving, processing, or display equipment.

Sync level — The level of synctip. Conventionally -40 IRE (-285 $\frac{5}{7}$ mV) in analog System M and the archaic EIA RS-343-A, and -300 mV in other analog systems.

Sync pulse — A normal line sync pulse, equalization pulse, or broad pulse.

Synctip — The level or duration of the most extreme excursion of a sync pulse from blanking level.

System M — Formerly CCIR System M; now properly referred to as ITU-R System M: A television system having 480*i*29.97 scanning, interlace, 4.2 MHz video bandwidth, and 6 MHz channel spacing. The designation does not specify color encoding. Most 480*i* broadcasting uses System M/NTSC, although Brazil uses M/PAL.

Tandem — Two or more systems or subsystems cascaded in series.

Timecode — A number of the form *HH:MM:SS:FF* (hours, minutes, seconds, frames) that designates a single frame in a video or film motion image sequence.

TINT — User-accessible means to adjust Hue (3); preferably, HUE.

Top field — In MPEG, the field that contains the top coded image row.

Transcoding

1. Traditionally, converting a video signal having one color-encoding method into a signal having a different color-encoding method, without altering the scanning standard; for example, 576*i* PAL to 576*i* SECAM.

2. In compressed digital video distribution, various methods of recoding a compressed bitstream, or decompressing then recompressing.

Transition sample

An active sample near the left or right edge of the picture whose amplitude is reduced or forced to blanking level so as to limit the high-frequency content of the video signal at the picture edges.

Trichromaticity

The property of human vision whereby additive mixtures of exactly three properly chosen primary components are necessary and sufficient to match a wide range of colors. That this is possible is surprising, considering that physical spectra are infinitely variable; but not surprising, considering that the retina contains just three types of photoreceptor cone cells.

Trilevel sync

Sync information conveyed through an analog pulse having a transition from blanking level to +300 mV, then a transition from +300 mV to -300 mV, then a final transition back to blanking level. Standard for HDTV. Distinguished from *bilevel sync*, used in SDTV.

Tristimulus

A component value that represents spectral radiance weighted by a spectral sensitivity function having significance with respect to the trichromaticity of human vision (see *Trichromaticity*, above). In video, a tristimulus signal such as R, G, or B is proportional to intensity. RGB signals are subject to *gamma correction* as part of their conversion into video signals.

TRS

Timing reference signal: A sequence of four words that signals sync, inserted into 4:2:2 or $4f_{SC}$ data stream. See *EAV,* on page 627, and *SAV,* on page 646.

TV lines per picture height, TVL/PH

In video, a unit of horizontal resolution defined by the ratio of the distance between spatially adjacent scan lines in the frame (as numerator) and the picture height (as denominator). In an interlaced system, adjacent scan lines are in opposite fields. One TV line corresponds to a pixel, half a cycle, or half a line pair in film. See *Resolution (n.),* on page 644.

U, V

1. Color difference components, blue minus luma ($B'-Y'$) and red minus luma ($R'-Y'$), scaled prior to quadrature modulation by the factors 0.492111 and 0.877283, respectively, to contain the reference excursion of the composite video signal within the range $-33\frac{1}{3}$ IRE to $+133\frac{1}{3}$ IRE. See also [C_B, C_R]; [I, Q]; [P_B, P_R].

2. The symbols U and V are sometimes used loosely or incorrectly to refer to unscaled $B'-Y'$ and $R'-Y'$ components; to components C_B and C_R that are scaled for component digital transmission; to components P_B and P_R that are scaled for component analog transmission; or to color difference components having unspecified, nonstandard, or unknown scaling.

U-matic — An analog videocassette system for 480*i* NTSC or 576*i* PAL, using color-under recording on ¾-inch tape; its successor (with higher bandwidth) is denoted U-matic SP.

Uncompressed — In video, signal recording or transmission without using JPEG or MPEG techniques. (Chroma subsampling effects lossy compression with a ratio of about 1.5:1 or 2:1; however, the term *compression* in video is reserved for JPEG, M-JPEG, or MPEG techniques.)

Unit — See *IRE unit*, on page 633.

Upconversion — In video, conversion to a scanning standard, usually at the same frame rate, having substantially higher pixel count (e.g., SDTV to HDTV).

Upsampling — Resampling where more output samples are produced than the number of input samples provided.

V — See *U, V*, on page 649.

Valid — The condition where a combination of component signals represents a combination that is $R'G'B'$-legal, that is, where all of the corresponding R', G', and B' lie within their reference ranges.

Value — In color science, measures of lightness apart from CIE L^*.

VCR — Videocassette recorder. Implicitly, consumer-grade: In professional usage, VTR (with *T* for *tape*) is used even if the tape medium is encased in a cassette.

Vertical blanking interval (VBI) — Those scan lines of a field (or frame) that are precluded by a scanning standard from containing picture. The original FCC, NTSC, and EIA standards measured vertical blanking in microseconds; modern usage counts integral scan lines. The vertical interval may contain nonpicture video – uch as test signals (VITS), timecode (VITC), teletext, or other data – that is blanked by display equipment.

Vertical drive (VD) — A pulse that conveys vertical synchronization information. Nowadays this information is usually extracted from sync (3), rather than requiring a separate signal.

Vertical frequency — **1.** The vertical component of spatial frequency.

2. In interlaced scanning, field rate; in progressive scanning, frame rate.

Vertical interval — Vertical blanking interval (VBI); see above.

Vertical sync — Those nonpicture elements of a video signal that mark the boundary between fields (or frames).

VHS — Video Home System: A consumer analog videocassette system, invented by JVC, to record 480*i* or 576*i* using the color-under method on ½-inch tape.

VHS-C — VHS, Compact: A consumer analog videocassette system identical to VHS but with a smaller cassette.

Video-8 — A consumer analog videocassette system using 8 mm tape; also known as *8 mm*. Its successor is *Hi8*.

VITC — Vertical interval timecode: Timecode data encoded in an analog representation and conveyed in the VBI.

VITS — Vertical interval test signal. One or a few lines of analog test signals conveyed in the VBI.

VSB — Vestigial sideband: An RF modulation system. Analog VSB is used in the NTSC and PAL standards for terrestrial television. A form of digital VSB (8-VSB) is used in the ATSC standard for terrestrial digital television.

VTR — Videotape recorder. Implies professional: *T* for *tape* is used even if the tape medium is encased in a cassette.

Weave — **1.** In film, erratic side-to-side motion of the image owing to imperfect registration of the sprocket holes to the film gate.

2. In PC graphics, a deinterlacing technique that merges fields together irrespective of interfield motion.

White — See *Reference white,* on page 643.

Y — **1.** In physics and color science, and when used carefully in video and computer graphics, the symbol for (linear-light) luminance, the CIE *Y* tristimulus component. See *Luminance* (1) on page 636.

2. In video, in digital image processing, and in computer graphics, the symbol *Y* is often carelessly used to denote *luma* (properly *Y'*); see below.

Y' — In video, the symbol for luma: The sum of nonlinear (gamma-corrected) red, green, and blue primary components, each weighted by its luma coefficient. See *Luma,* on page 636. Distinguished from luminance, *Y*, which can be formed as a weighted sum of linear-light (tristimulus) red, green, and blue primary components. Historically, the *Y* symbol in video was *primed* (*Y'*), but the prime is often carelessly elided in modern times, leading to widespread confusion with luminance.

Y'/C, *Y'/C*3.58, *Y'/C*4.43 — Analog luma, *Y'* (not luminance), accompanied by a modulated chroma signal, *C*, quadrature modulated at approximately the subcarrier frequency indicated in megahertz. Preferably denoted S-video; S-video-525 (or in Japan, S-video-525-J); and S-video-625; respectively. May have stable or unstable timebase; may have coherent or incoherent color subcarrier.

$Y'/C629$, $Y'/C688$

Analog luma, Y' (not luminance), accompanied by a modulated chroma signal, C, quadrature modulated at approximately the subcarrier frequency indicated in kilohertz. Used as an interface standard for dubbing, editing, or timebase correction of certain color-under VCRs. Typically has unstable timebase and incoherent color subcarrier.

$Y'C_1C_2$

Luma, Y' (not luminance), accompanied by two color difference signals, where the components C_1 and C_2 are specified (or evident from context) and are not necessarily any of the common pairs [$B'-Y'$, $R'-Y'$], [P_B, P_R], [C_B, C_R], [U, V], or [I, Q].

$Y'C_BC_R$

1. In video, MPEG, and M-JPEG, luma, Y' (not luminance), accompanied by two color difference components scaled independently to have a peak-to-peak excursion $^{224}/_{219}$ that of the luma excursion. In an 8-bit Rec. 601 interface, C_B and C_R are scaled to a reference excursion of ±112; an offset of +128 is added. See *Luma*, on page 636; and C_B, C_R (1) on page 616.

2. In JPEG/JFIF as used in computing, luma, Y' (not luminance) having excursion 0 through 255, accompanied by two color difference components scaled independently to have a "full-range" (128±128) peak-to-peak excursion $^{256}/_{255}$ that of the luma excursion; pure blue and pure red are clipped. See *Luma*, on page 636; and C_B, C_R (2) on page 616.

$Y'IQ$

Luma, Y' (not luminance), accompanied by color difference components I (In-phase) and Q (Quadrature) derived from U and V by a +33° rotation and an exchange of axes. Historically, NTSC was formed from color difference components of unequal bandwidth, where Q was filtered more severely than I. Nowadays quadrature modulation based on equiband [U, V] color differences is almost universal and $Y'IQ$ is obsolete, except for $4f_{SC}$ NTSC composite digital interface and D-2 composite digital VTRs.

$Y'P_BP_R$

Luma, Y' (not luminance), accompanied by analog [P_B, P_R] color difference components. P historically stood for *parallel*. The EBU N10 standard specifies luma excursion of 700 mV and P_BP_R excursion of ±350 mV. This standard is used in 576*i* and in HDTV; however, different industry standards are usually used for 480*i*. See *Luma*, on page 636; and P_B, P_R, on page 641.

$Y'UV$

1. Properly, luma, Y' (not luminance), and two color difference components [U, V] scaled for subsequent encoding into a composite video signal, such as NTSC or PAL. For component analog video, [U, V] components are inappropriate, and [P_B, P_R] should be used. For component digital video, [U, V] components are inappropriate, and [C_B, C_R] should be used. See *Luma*, on page 636; and U, V, on page 649.

2. The notation $Y'UV$ – or, carelessly written, YUV – is often used to denote any component system employing luma, Y' (not luminance) accompanied by two scaled color difference components based upon $B'-Y'$ and $R'-Y'$, where scaling of $B'-Y'$ and $R'-Y'$ is unknown or implicit.

Index

A

C

D

E

F

G

I

M

N

O

P

Q

R

S

T

U

W

X

Y

Z

About the author

sketch by Kevin Melia

Charles Poynton is an independent contractor specializing in the physics, mathematics, and engineering of digital color imaging systems, including digital video, HDTV, and digital cinema (D-cinema).

In the early 1980s, Charles designed and built the digital video equipment used by NASA to convert video from the Space Shuttle into NTSC. In 1990, he initiated Sun Microsystems' HDTV research project, and introduced color management technology to Sun. He was responsible for Sun's founding membership in what later became the International Color Consortium (ICC).

Charles was a key contributor to current digital video and HDTV studio standards. A Fellow of the Society of Motion Picture and Television Engineers (SMPTE), he was awarded the Society's prestigious David Sarnoff Gold Medal for his work to integrate video technology with computing and communications.

Charles has taught many popular courses on video technology, HDTV, and color image coding, including many SIGGRAPH courses. He is the author of the widely respected book, *A Technical Introduction to Digital Video,* published in 1996.

Charles lives in Toronto with his partner Barbara and their two girls, Quinn and Georgia. It is over their strenuous objections that he spells *color* without the *u.* The sketch above was made prior to his granting Georgia's ninth-birthday wish to shave off his beard.

This book is set in the Syntax typeface. Syntax was designed by Hans Eduard Meier, and first issued by Stempel in 1969. Linotype issued a revision in 1999 that includes bold italics, small caps, and old-style figures. The body type is 10.2 points, leaded to 12.8 points, and set ragged right.

The mathematical work underlying this book was accomplished using *Mathematica,* from Wolfram Research. The illustrations were executed in Adobe *Illustrator;* for raster (bitmap) images, Adobe *Photoshop* was used. The equations were set using Design Science *MathType.* Text editing, layout, and typesetting were accomplished using Adobe *FrameMaker.* Adobe *Acrobat* was employed for electronic distribution.

The work was accomplished using Apple Macintosh computers. Proof printing was done on Apple Laser-Writer Pro 810 and Xerox DocuTech 6135 printers. The electronic master was produced using Adobe's *PostScript* language.